FOURTH EDITION

Marketing Foundations

William M. Pride
Texas A & M University

O. C. Ferrell
University of New Mexico

Australia • Brazil • Japan • Korea • Mexico • Singapore • Spain • United Kingdom • United States

Marketing Foundations, 4th Edition

William M. Pride and O. C. Ferrell

VP of Editorial Business: Jack W. Calhoun

Editor-in-Chief: Melissa Acuña

Acquisitions Editor: Mike Roche

Vice President of Marketing: Bill Hendee

Development Editor: Suzanna Bainbridge

Sr. Marketing Comm. Manager: Sarah Greber

Marketing Coordinator: Shanna Shelton

Content Project Manager: Scott Dillon

Managing Media Editor: Pamela Wallace

Media Editor: John Rich

Editorial Assistant: Kayti Purkiss

Manufacturing Coordinator: Miranda Klapper

Production House: S4Carlisle Publishing Services

Sr. Art Director: Stacy Jenkins Shirley

Photo Permissions Manager: Deanna Ettinger

Text Permissions Manager: Roberta Broyer

Cover Image: Shutterstock

B/W Image: Getty Images /Hissham Ibrahim

Printed in China by
China Translation & Printing Services Limited
1 2 3 4 5 6 7 13 12 11 10

Library of Congress Control Number: 2009939188
International Student Edition ISBN 13: 978-0-538-75637-2
International Student Edition ISBN 10: 0-538-75637-3

Cengage Learning International Offices

Asia
cengageasia.com
tel: (65) 6410 1200

Australia/New Zealand
cengage.com.au
tel: (61) 3 9685 4111

Brazil
cengage.com.br
tel: (011) 3665 9900

India
cengage.co.in
tel: (91) 11 30484837/38

Latin America
cengage.com.mx
tel: +52 (55) 1500 6000

UK/Europe/Middle East/Africa
cengage.co.uk
tel: (44) 207 067 2500

Represented in Canada by Nelson Education, Ltd.
nelson.com
tel: (416) 752 9100 / (800) 668 0671

For product information: **www.cengage.com/international**
Visit your local office: **www.cengage.com/global**
Visit our corporate website: **www.cengage.com**

BRIEF CONTENTS

CONTENTS

Strategic Marketing and Its Environment 1

CHAPTER 3 THE MARKETING ENVIRONMENT, SOCIAL RESPONSIBILITY, AND ETHICS 53

2 Marketing Research and Target Markets 82

CHAPTER 4 MARKETING RESEARCH AND INFORMATION SYSTEMS 83

CHAPTER 5 TARGET MARKETS: SEGMENTATION AND EVALUATION 110

3 Customer Behavior 136

4 Product Decisions 215

CHAPTER 9 PRODUCT, BRANDING, AND PACKAGING CONCEPTS 216

CHAPTER 10 DEVELOPING AND MANAGING GOODS AND SERVICES 249

6 Distribution Decisions 329

7 Promotion Decisions 395

PREFACE

Marketing in a Dynamic Environment

The need to adapt to the changing marketing environment has never been greater. *Marketing Foundations* leads the market with relevant concepts and best practices that relate to marketing's role in organizations and society. This new edition has undergone the most extensive revision ever, resulting in the most up-to-date text possible. In reflecting the need for efficiency and learning, we have paid careful attention to maintaining all key concepts with a reduced number of chapters and shorter page count. In making this book more compact, we have carefully analyzed and rebuilt the content to be current and reflect important changes in the marketing environment.

Marketing managers have faced the deepest recession in the last 80 years, with consumers facing high unemployment, personal financial losses, reduced credit, and lost confidence and trust in businesses. Transformations in the economy have strongly influenced marketing strategies and activities. Additions to this new edition reflect the need for marketing to change and adapt to existing and future developments of the business environment. The *Marketing in Transition* boxes reflect how marketing is changing and adapting to new technology, competitive forces, and to a global economy.

As business has begun to recognize the importance of sustainability initiatives, we have incorporated a green theme throughout the book. We view green marketing as a strategic process involving stakeholder assessment in order to create meaningful long-term relationships with customers while maintaining, supporting, and enhancing the natural environment. Green marketing has become important to business because of the many challenges we face in maintaining a habitable world for generations to come. With carbon emissions becoming a focal point of most reports on how to minimize global warming, the need to reduce, reuse, and recycle has become a source of green initiatives for most businesses. Each chapter has a *Sustainability Marketing* box that relates marketing activities to sustainability and the natural environment.

Consistent to the theme of change, the *Entrepreneurial Marketing* feature provides an opportunity to discuss the role of entrepreneurship and marketing and the need for creativity in developing successful marketing strategies in the changing environment.

Textbook Organization

Part 1: Strategic Marketing and Its Environment An overview of marketing; examines strategic market planning, marketing environment forces, and social responsibility and marketing ethics

Part 2: Marketing Research and Target Markets Considers marketing research and information systems; target market and segmentation evaluation

Part 3: Customer Behavior Consumer and business buying behavior; global markets and international marketing

Part 4: Product Decisions Developing and managing products; branding and packaging concepts

Part 5: Pricing Decisions Pricing fundamentals and the process marketers use to establish prices

Part 6: Distribution Decisions Marketing channels and supply-chain management, retailing, wholesaling, and direct marketing

Part 7: Promotion Decisions Integrated marketing communications and promotion methods, including advertising, personal selling, sales promotions, and public relations

Supplements

The authors have maintained a hands-on approach to teaching this material and revising the text and its ancillaries. This results in an integrated teaching package and approach that is accurate, sound, and successful in reaching students. The authors and publisher have worked together to provide a competent teaching package and ancillaries that are unsurpassed in the marketplace. The outcome of this involvement fosters trust and confidence in the teaching package and in student learning outcomes.

For Instructors

Instructor's Manual. The Instructor's Manual has been revamped to meet the needs of a engaging classroom environment. It has been updated with diverse and dynamic discussion starters, classroom activities, and group exercises. It also includes such tools as:

- Integrated Lecture Outline with features and multimedia callouts
- Chapter Quizzes
- Suggested Answers to end-of-chapter exercises and cases

PowerPoint® Slides. PowerPoint® continues to be a very popular teaching device, and a special effort has been made to upgrade the PowerPoint program to enhance classroom teaching. Premium lecture slides, containing such content as advertisements, video clips, Web links, and unique graphs and data, have been created to provide instructors with up-to-date unique content to increase student application and interest.

Test Bank. The test bank provides more than 4,000 test items including true/false, multiple-choice, and essay questions. Each objective test item is accompanied by the correct answer, appropriate learning objective, level of difficulty, main text page reference, and AACSB standard coding. Instructors are able to select, edit, and add questions, or generate randomly selected questions to produce a test master for easy duplication.

Marketing Video Case Series DVD. This series contains videos specifically tied to the video cases found in the book. The vast majority of our video cases are new to this edition and supported by current and engaging video clips of exciting companies such as Netflix, Harley-Davidson, Lonely Planet, Washburn Guitars, and Smart Car USA.

Instructor Companion Website (www.cengage.com/international). Password protected, the instructor website includes valuable tools to help design and teach the course. Content includes files from the Instructor's Manual, the Test Bank, premium PowerPoint® slides, access to the Interactive Marketing Plan, and more.

For Students

Companion Website (www.cengage.com/international). The companion website provides students with learning objectives, chapter summaries, glossary terms, and other text-specific tools.

Interactive Marketing Plan. The Marketing Plan Worksheets have been revamped and reproduced within an interactive and multimedia environment. A video program has been developed around the worksheets, allowing students to follow a company through the trials and tribulations of launching a new product. This video helps place the conceptual marketing plan in an applicable light and is supported by a summary of the specific stages of the marketing plan as well as a sample plan based on the events of the video. These elements act as the 1-2-3 punch supporting students while they complete their own plan, the last step of the Interactive Marketing Plan. The Plan is broken up into three functional sections that can either be completed in one simple project or carried over throughout the semester.

Thanks

Like most textbooks, this one reflects the ideas of many academicians and practitioners who have contributed to the development of the marketing discipline. We appreciate the opportunity to present their ideas in this book.

We would also like to thank the hundreds of reviewers who have provided invaluable feedback over the years as we have written and revised our introductory marketing title:

Zafar U. Ahmed
Minot State University

Thomas Ainscough
University of Massachusetts—Dartmouth

Sana Akili
Iowa State University

Katrece Albert
Southern University

Joe F. Alexander
University of Northern Colorado

Mark I. Alpert
University of Texas at Austin

David M. Ambrose
University of Nebraska

David Andrus
Kansas State University

Linda K. Anglin
Minnesota State University

George Avellano
Central State University

Emin Babakus
University of Memphis

Julie Baker
Texas Christian University

Siva Balasubramanian
Southern Illinois University

Joseph Ballenger
Stephen F. Austin State University

Guy Banville
Creighton University

Frank Barber
Cuyahoga Community College

Joseph Barr
Framingham State College

Thomas E. Barry
Southern Methodist University

Charles A. Bearchell
California State University—Northridge

Richard C. Becherer
University of Tennessee—Chattanooga

Walter H. Beck, Sr.
Reinhardt College

Russell Belk
University of Utah

John Bennett
University of Missouri—Columbia

W. R. Berdine
California State Polytechnic Institute

Karen Berger
Pace University

Bob Berl
University of Memphis

Stewart W. Bither
Pennsylvania State University

Roger Blackwell
Ohio State University

Peter Bloch
University of Missouri—Columbia

Wanda Blockhus
San Jose State University

Paul N. Bloom
University of North Carolina

Nancy Bloom
Nassau Community College

James P. Boespflug
Arapahoe Community College

Joseph G. Bonnice
Manhattan College

John Boos
Ohio Wesleyan University

Peter Bortolotti
Johnson & Wales University

Jenell Bramlage
University of Northwestern Ohio

James Brock
Susquehanna College

John R. Brooks, Jr.
Houston Baptist University

William G. Browne
Oregon State University

John Buckley
Orange County Community College

Gul T. Butaney
Bentley College

James Cagley
University of Tulsa

Pat J. Calabros
University of Texas—Arlington

Linda Calderone
State University of New York College of Technology at Farmingdale

Joseph Cangelosi
University of Central Arkansas

William J. Carner
University of Texas—Austin

James C. Carroll
University of Central Arkansas

Terry M. Chambers
Westminster College

Lawrence Chase
Tompkins Cortland Community College

Larry Chonko
Baylor University

Barbara Coe
University of North Texas

Ernest F. Cooke
Loyola College—Baltimore

Robert Copley
University of Louisville

John I. Coppett
University of Houston—Clear Lake

Robert Corey
West Virginia University

Deborah L. Cowles
Virginia Commonwealth University

Sandra Coyne
Springfield College

Melvin R. Crask
University of Georgia

William L. Cron
Texas Christian University

Gary Cutler
Dyersburg State Community College

Bernice N. Dandridge
Diablo Valley College

Tamara Davis
Davenport University

Lloyd M. DeBoer
George Mason University

Sally Dibb
University of Warwick

Ralph DiPietro
Montclair State University

Paul Dishman
Idaho State University

Suresh Divakar
State University of New York—Buffalo

Casey L. Donoho
Northern Arizona University

Todd Donovan
Colorado State University

Peter T. Doukas
Westchester Community College

Kent Drummond
University of Wyoming

Lee R. Duffus *Florida Gulf Coast University*

Robert F. Dwyer
University of Cincinnati

Roland Eyears
Central Ohio Technical College

Thomas Falcone
Indiana University of Pennsylvania

James Finch
University of Wisconsin—La Crosse

Letty C. Fisher
SUNY/Westchester Community College

Renée Florsheim
Loyola Marymount University

Charles W. Ford
Arkansas State University

John Fraedrich
Southern Illinois University, Carbondale

David J. Fritzsche
University of Washington

Donald A. Fuller
University of Central Florida

Terry Gable
Truman State University

Ralph Gaedeke
California State University, Sacramento

Robert Garrity
University of Hawaii

Cathy Goodwin
University of Manitoba

Geoffrey L. Gordon
Northern Illinois University

Robert Grafton-Small
University of Strathclyde

Harrison Grathwohl
California State University—Chico

Alan A. Greco
North Carolina A&T State University

Blaine S. Greenfield
Bucks County Community College

Thomas V. Greer
University of Maryland

Sharon F. Gregg
Middle Tennessee University

Jim L. Grimm
Illinois State University

Charles Gross
University of New Hampshire

Joseph Guiltinan
University of Notre Dame

John Hafer
University of Nebraska at Omaha

David Hansen
Texas Southern University

Richard C. Hansen
Ferris State University

Nancy Hanson-Rasmussen
University of Wisconsin—Eau Claire

Robert R. Harmon
Portland State University

Mary C. Harrison
Amber University

Lorraine Hartley
Franklin University

Michael Hartline
Florida State University

Timothy Hartman
Ohio University

Salah S. Hassan
George Washington University

Manoj Hastak
American University

Del I. Hawkins
University of Oregon

Dean Headley
Wichita State University

Esther Headley
Wichita State University

Debbora Heflin-Bullock
California State Polytechnic University—Pomona

Merlin Henry
Rancho Santiago College

Tony Henthorne
University of Southern Mississippi

Lois Herr
Elizabethtown College

Charles L. Hilton
Eastern Kentucky University

Elizabeth C. Hirschman
Rutgers, State University of New Jersey

George C. Hozier
University of New Mexico

John R. Huser
Illinois Central College

Joan M. Inzinga
Bay Path College

Deloris James
University of Maryland University College

Ron Johnson
Colorado Mountain College

Theodore F. Jula
Stonehill College

Peter F. Kaminski
Northern Illinois University

Yvonne Karsten
Minnesota State University

Jerome Katrichis
Temple University

Garland Keesling
Towson University

James Kellaris
University of Cincinnati

Alvin Kelly
Florida A&M University

Philip Kemp
DePaul University

Sylvia Keyes
Bridgewater State College

William M. Kincaid, Jr.
Oklahoma State University

Roy Klages
State University of New York at Albany

Hal Koenig
Oregon State University

Douglas Kornemann
Milwaukee Area Technical College

Kathleen Krentler
San Diego State University

John Krupa Jr.
Johnson & Wales University

Barbara Lafferty
University of South Florida

Patricia Laidler
Massasoit Community College

Bernard LaLond
Ohio State University

Richard A. Lancioni
Temple University

Irene Lange
California State University—Fullerton

Geoffrey P. Lantos
Stonehill College

Charles L. Lapp
University of Texas—Dallas

Virginia Larson
San Jose State University

John Lavin
Waukesha County Technical Institute

Marilyn Lavin
University of Wisconsin—Whitewater

Hugh E. Law
East Tennessee University

Monle Lee
Indiana University—South Bend

Ron Lennon
Barry University

Richard C. Leventhal
Metropolitan State College

Marilyn Liebrenz-Himes
George Washington University

Jay D. Lindquist
Western Michigan University

Terry Loe
Kennesaw State University

Mary Logan
Southwestern Assemblies of God College

Paul Londrigan
Mott Community College

Anthony Lucas
Community College of Allegheny County

George Lucas
U.S. Learning, Inc.

William Lundstrom
Cleveland State University

Rhonda Mack
College of Charleston

Stan Madden
Baylor University

Patricia M. Manninen
North Shore Community College

Gerald L. Manning
Des Moines Area Community College

Lalita A. Manrai
University of Delaware

Franklyn Manu
Morgan State University

Allen S. Marber
University of Bridgeport

Gayle J. Marco
Robert Morris College

Carolyn A. Massiah
University of Central Florida

James McAlexander
Oregon State University

Donald McCartney
University of Wisconsin—Green Bay

Anthony McGann
University of Wyoming

Jack McNiff
State University of New York College of Technology at Farmington

Lee Meadow
Eastern Illinois University

Carla Meeske
University of Oregon

Jeffrey A. Meier
Fox Valley Technical College

James Meszaros
County College of Morris

Brian Meyer
Minnesota State University

Martin Meyers
University of Wisconsin—Stevens Point

Stephen J. Miller
Oklahoma State University

William Moller
University of Michigan

Kent B. Monroe
University of Illinois

Carlos W. Moore
Baylor University

Carol Morris-Calder
Loyola Marymount University

David Murphy
Madisonville Community College

Keith Murray
Bryant College

Sue Ellen Neeley
University of Houston—Clear Lake

Carolyn Y. Nicholson
Stetson University

Francis L. Notturno, Sr.
Owens Community College

Terrence V. O'Brien
Northern Illinois University

James R. Ogden
Kutztown University of Pennsylvania

Lois Bitner Olson
San Diego State University

Mike O'Neill
California State University—Chico

Robert S. Owen
State University of New York—Oswego

Allan Palmer
University of North Carolina at Charlotte

David P. Paul, III
Monmouth University

Terry Paul
Ohio State University

Teresa Pavia
University of Utah

John Perrachione
Truman State University

Michael Peters
Boston College

Linda Pettijohn
Missouri State University

Lana Podolak
Community College of Beaver County

Raymond E. Polchow
Muskingum Area Technical College

Thomas Ponzurick
West Virginia University

William Presutti
Duquesne University

Kathy Pullins
Columbus State Community College

Edna J. Ragins
North Carolina A&T State University

Daniel Rajaratnam
Baylor University

Mohammed Rawwas
University of Northern Iowa

James D. Reed
Louisiana State University—Shreveport

William Rhey
University of Tampa

Glen Riecken
East Tennessee State University

Winston Ring
University of Wisconsin—Milwaukee

Ed Riordan
Wayne State University

Bruce Robertson
San Francisco State University

Robert A. Robicheaux
University of Alabama—Birmingham

Linda Rose
Westwood College Online

Bert Rosenbloom
Drexel University

Robert H. Ross
Wichita State University

Tom Rossi
Broome Community College

Vicki Rostedt
The University of Akron

Michael L. Rothschild
University of Wisconsin—Madison

Kenneth L. Rowe
Arizona State University

Don Roy
Middle Tennessee State University

Catherine Ruggieri
St. John's University

Elise Sautter
New Mexico State University

Ronald Schill
Brigham Young University

Bodo Schlegelmilch
Vienna University of Economics and Business Administration

Edward Schmitt
Villanova University

Thomas Schori
Illinois State University

Donald Sciglimpaglia
San Diego State University

Stanley Scott
University of Alaska—Anchorage

Harold S. Sekiguchi
University of Nevada—Reno

Gilbert Seligman
Dutchess Community College

Richard J. Semenik
University of Utah

Beheruz N. Sethna
Lamar University

Morris A. Shapero
Schiller International University

Terence A. Shimp
University of South Carolina

Mark Siders
Southern Oregon University

Carolyn F. Siegel
Eastern Kentucky University

Dean C. Siewers
Rochester Institute of Technology

Lyndon Simkin
University of Warwick

Roberta Slater
Cedar Crest College

Paul J. Solomon
University of South Florida

Sheldon Somerstein
City University of New York

Eric R. Spangenberg
University of Mississippi

Rosann L. Spiro
Indiana University

William Staples
University of Houston—Clear Lake

Bruce Stern
Portland State University

Claire F. Sullivan
Metropolitan State University

Carmen Sunda
University of New Orleans

Robert Swerdlow
Lamar University

Crina Tarasi
Central Michigan University

Steven A. Taylor
Illinois State University

Ruth Taylor
Texas State University

Hal Teer
James Madison University

Ira Teich
Long Island University—C.W. Post

Debbie Thorne
Texas State University

Dillard Tinsley
Stephen F. Austin State University

Sharynn Tomlin
Angelo State University

Hale Tongren
George Mason University

James Underwood
University of Southwest Louisiana—Lafayette

Barbara Unger
Western Washington University

Tinus Van Drunen
University Twente (Netherlands)

Dale Varble
Indiana State University

Bronis Verhage
Georgia State University

Charles Vitaska
Metropolitan State College

R. Vish Viswanathan
University of Northern Colorado

Kirk Wakefield
Baylor University

Harlan Wallingford
Pace University

Jacquelyn Warwick
Andrews University

James F. Wenthe
Georgia College

Sumner M. White
Massachusetts Bay Community College

Janice Williams
University of Central Oklahoma

Alan R. Wiman
Rider College

John Withey
Indiana University—South Bend

Ken Wright
West Australia College of Advanced Education—Churchland Campus

We'd like to thank Tomas Hult, Michigan State University, for his contribution to content in Part Six, "Distribution Decisions," as well as providing advice in integrating the global dimension throughout the text.

We're grateful to Phylis Mansfield for her work on the new feature, *Developing Your Marketing Plan,* and the test bank. In addition, we'd like to acknowledge Chuck Tomkovick for his expertise in updating the Instructor's Manual. And many thanks to Milton Pressley for his professional input and diligence in updating the PowerPoint® slides. Their work on our ancillary program met the demands and standards of this edition. We thank you.

Jennifer Jackson assisted in research, editing, content development, and writing for the text, supplements, and website. The authors deeply appreciate the assistance of Marian Wood for providing editorial suggestions, technical assistance, and support. For assistance in completing numerous tasks associated with the text and supplements, the authors express appreciation to Alexi Sherrill, Jennifer Sawayda, Courtney Bohannon, Saleha Amin, Clarissa Means, and Brenda Lake.

We express appreciation for the support and encouragement given to us by our colleagues at Texas A&M University and University of New Mexico. We are also grateful for the comments and suggestions we receive from our own students, student focus groups, and student correspondents who provide ongoing feedback.

A number of talented professionals at Cengage Learning have contributed to the development of this book. We are especially grateful to Mike Roche, Suzanna Bainbridge, Scott Dillon, Terri Miller, Deanna Ettinger, Stacy Shirley, Shanna Shelton, and Sarah Greber. Their inspiration, patience, support, and friendship are invaluable.

William M. Pride
O. C. Ferrell

To Nancy, Mike, and Allen Pride

To Linda Ferrell

FOURTH EDITION

Marketing Foundations

Strategic Marketing and Its Environment

Part 1 introduces the field of marketing and offers a broad perspective from which to explore and analyze various components of the marketing discipline. Chapter 1 defines *marketing* and explores some key concepts, including customers and target markets, the marketing mix, relationship marketing, the marketing concept, and value. Chapter 2 provides an overview of strategic marketing issues, such as the effect of organizational resources and opportunities on the planning process; the role of the mission statement; corporate, business-unit, and marketing strategies; and the creation of the marketing plan. These issues are profoundly affected by competitive, economic, political, legal and regulatory, technological, and sociocultural forces in the marketing environment. Chapter 3 deals with these environmental forces and with the role of social responsibility and ethics in marketing decisions.

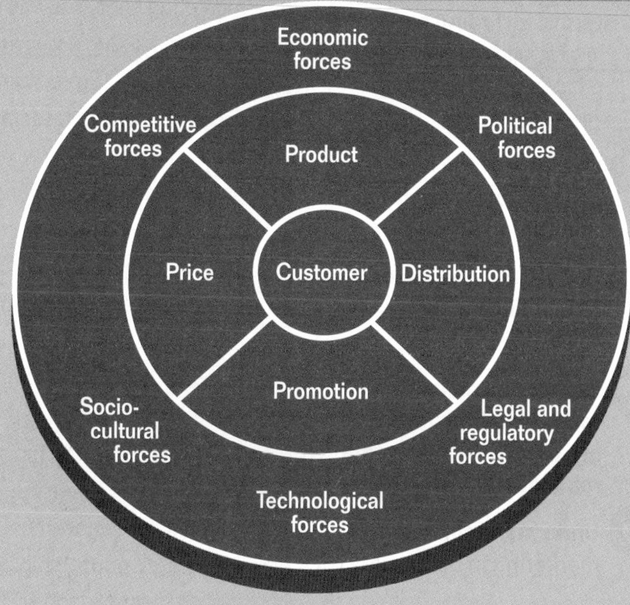

CHAPTER 1 Customer-Driven Strategic Marketing

© AL BELLO/GETTY IMAGES

OBJECTIVES:

1. Define marketing.
2. Understand several important marketing terms, including *target market, marketing mix, marketing exchanges*, and *marketing environment*.
3. Be aware of the marketing concept and marketing orientation.
4. Understand the importance of building customer relationships.
5. Explain the major marketing functions that are part of the marketing management process.
6. Understand the role of marketing in our society.

RED SOX MARKETERS DEVELOP ALLIANCE WITH PROFESSIONAL BULL RIDING CIRCUIT

What do the Red Sox and bull riding have in common? They are both connected through the marketing entity Fenway Sports Group (FSG). In an effort to promote corporate partnerships, FSG, a marketing organization created by Red Sox owners New England Sports Ventures, partnered with the Professional Bull Riders (PBR) in 2009. The partnership has made the FSG the exclusive sales representative of PBR. PBR demonstrates how a good but risky idea can pay off. It was started in 1992 when a group of 20 bull riders decided that bull riding, the most popular part of rodeos, could stand on its own. Each bull rider contributed $1,000 toward the venture. Since then PBR has become the top bull-riding circuit where 1,200 bull riders compete in over 300 competitions.

PBR is certainly different from other partnerships FSG has made over the years, which were more affiliated with East Coast organizations and baseball. A bull rider must stay on top of a bucking 2,000-pound angry bull for 8 seconds. The ordeal is dangerous, but the winning rider can earn $10 million in prize money. PBR is no stranger to marketing with other brands. Its $24 million sponsorship revenue comes from such corporate sponsors as Copenhagen, Wrangler, and Enterprise Rent-A-Car. "PBR has a talented team that has done a good job cultivating relationships with a few blue-chip companies, but they are underdeveloped from a corporate-sponsorship perspective," said FSG executive vice president Brian Corcoran, who looks forward to the additional corporate sponsorships their expertise can obtain.

The partnership between FSG and PBR comes at a time when other large companies are cutting their sports-related spending. However, FSG and PBR are hopeful that their strategic partnership will not only diversify the sports industry, but result in profitable relationships with other high-end brands and promote the sport of bull riding across the world.[1]

Like all organizations, Professional Bull Riding must figure out how to develop a product that customers want, communicate useful information about it through the use of different media outlets, price tickets appropriately, and make the product available where and when consumers want to buy it. Even if it does all these things well, uncontrollable factors like competition or an economic recession can affect the company's success.

This chapter introduces the strategic marketing concepts and decisions covered throughout the text. First, we develop a definition of *marketing* and explore each element of the definition in detail. Next, we introduce the marketing concept and consider several issues associated with implementing it. We also take a brief look at the management of customer relationships and then at the concept of value, which customers are demanding today more than ever before. We then explore the process of marketing management, which includes planning, organizing, implementing, and controlling marketing activities to encourage marketing exchanges. Finally, we examine the importance of marketing in our global society.

Marketing Defined

If you ask several people what *marketing* is, you are likely to hear a variety of descriptions. Although many people think marketing is advertising or selling, marketing actually encompasses many more activities than most people realize. In this book we define **marketing** as the process of creating, distributing, promoting, and pricing goods, services, and ideas to facilitate satisfying exchange relationships with customers and to develop and maintain favorable relationships with stakeholders in a dynamic environment. Our definition is consistent with that of the American Marketing Association (AMA), which defines *marketing* as "the activity, set of institutions, and processes for creating, communicating, delivering, and exchanging offerings that have value for customers, clients, partners, and society at large."[2] Our definition of *marketing* guides the organization of this first chapter.

marketing
The process of creating, distributing, promoting, and pricing goods, services, and ideas to facilitate satisfying exchange relationships with customers and to develop and maintain favorable relationships with stakeholders in a dynamic environment

CUSTOMERS ARE THE FOCUS

As the purchasers of the products that organizations develop, price, distribute, and promote, **customers** are the focal point of all marketing activities (see Figure 1.1). Organizations have to define their products not as what the companies make or produce but as what they do to satisfy customers. The Walt Disney Company is not in the business of establishing theme parks; it is in the business of making people happy. At Disney World, customers are guests, the crowd is an audience, and employees are cast members. Customer satisfaction and enjoyment can come from anything received when buying and using a product. For instance, Procter & Gamble's Fusion razors offer a very close shave, whereas its Swiffer dusters help clean house quickly and neatly.

customers
The purchasers of organizations' products; the focal point of all marketing activities

FIGURE 1.1 Components of Strategic Marketing

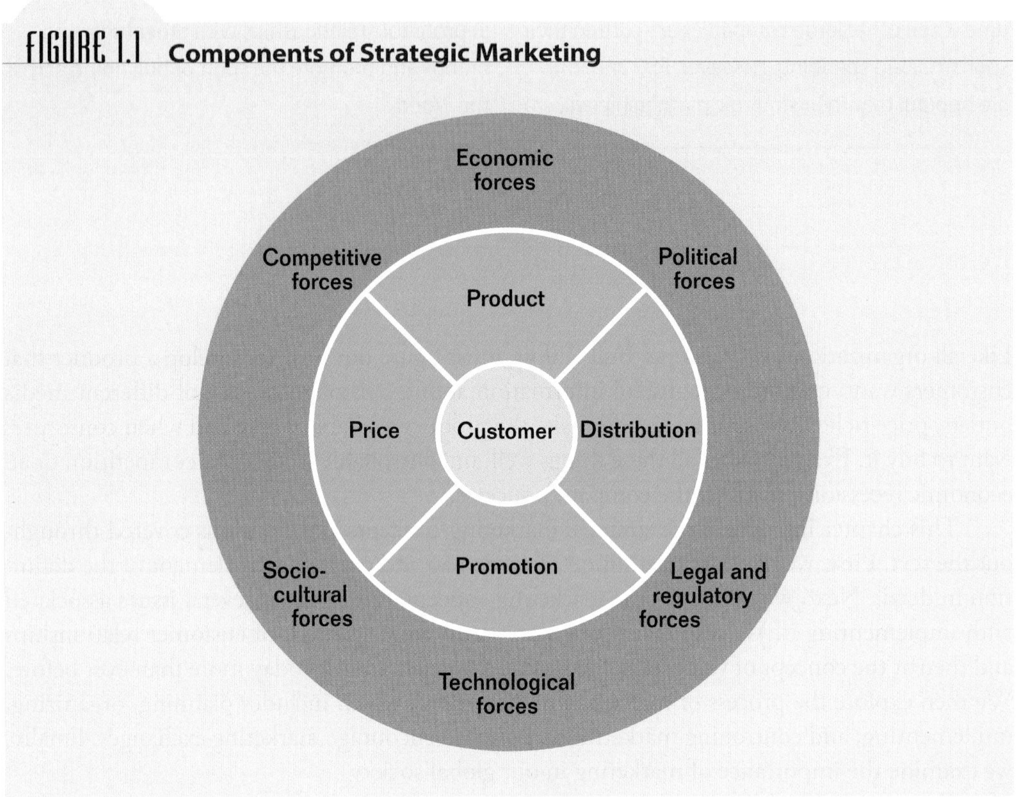

The essence of marketing is to develop satisfying exchanges from which both customers and marketers benefit. The customer expects to gain a reward or benefit in excess of the costs incurred in a marketing transaction. The marketer expects to gain something of value in return, generally the price charged for the product. Through buyer–seller interaction, a customer develops expectations about the seller's future behavior. To fulfill these expectations, the marketer must deliver on promises made. Over time, this interaction results in relationships between the two parties. Fast-food restaurants such as Wendy's and Burger King depend on repeat purchases from satisfied customers—many often live or work a few miles from these restaurants—whereas customer expectations revolve around tasty food, value, and dependable service.

Organizations generally focus their marketing efforts on a specific group of customers, called a **target market**. Marketing managers may define a target market as a vast number of people or a relatively small group. Firefly Mobile, for example, targets its FlyPhone cellular phone at 13–17-year-olds who want a phone with which they can take photos, play MP3 tunes, play games, and share photos with friends. Other companies target multiple markets with different products, promotions, prices, and distribution systems for each one. Nike uses this strategy, marketing different types of shoes and apparel to meet specific needs of cross-trainers, basketball players, aerobics enthusiasts, and other athletic-shoe buyers. Nike has even developed an athletic shoe for a single ethnicity—the Air Native N7 for American Indians.[3]

target market
A specific group of customers on whom an organization focuses its marketing efforts

MARKETING DEALS WITH PRODUCTS, PRICE, DISTRIBUTION, AND PROMOTION

Marketing is more than simply advertising or selling a product; it involves developing and managing a product that will satisfy customer needs. It focuses on making the product available in the right place and at a price acceptable to buyers. It also requires communicating information that helps customers determine if the product will satisfy their needs. These activities are planned, organized, implemented, and controlled to meet the needs of customers within the target market. Marketers refer to these activities—product, pricing, distribution, and promotion—as the **marketing mix** because they decide what type of each element to use and in what amounts. A primary goal of a marketing manager is to create and maintain the right mix of these elements to satisfy customers' needs for a general product type. Note in Figure 1.1 that the marketing mix is built around the customer.

Marketing managers strive to develop a marketing mix that matches the needs of customers in the target market. The marketing mix for the Nissan Rogue, for example, combines a crossover SUV with coordinated distribution, promotion, and price appropriate for the target market of primarily men and women in their 20s and early 30s. The marketing mix for the Rogue includes an economical engine, stylish design, and performance handling; a price around $20,000; as well as product placement and advertising during the hit show *Heroes* and a 5-car giveaway.[4]

Appealing to Target Markets
Special K targets health-conscious consumers.

Before marketers can develop a marketing mix, they must collect in-depth, up-to-date information about customer needs. Such information might include data about the age, income, ethnicity, gender, and educational level of people in the target market, their preferences for product features, their attitudes toward competitors' products, and the frequency with which they use the product. Research by Procter & Gamble, for example, introduced Old Spice High Endurance Hair & Body Wash, observing after hours of men's shower habits revealed that many men were already using body wash to shampoo their hair.[5] Armed with market information, marketing managers are better able to develop a marketing mix that satisfies a specific target market.

Let's look more closely at the decisions and activities related to each marketing mix variable.

Product Variable

Successful marketing efforts result in products that become part of everyday life. Consider the satisfaction customers have had over the years from Coca-Cola, Levi's jeans, Visa credit cards, Tylenol pain relievers, and 3M Post-it Notes. The product variable of the marketing mix deals with researching customers' needs and wants and designing a product that satisfies them. A **product** can be a good, a service, or an idea. A *good* is a physical entity you can touch. The Mini Cooper car, Apple iPhone, or a bar of Ivory soap are all examples of goods. A *service* is the application of human and mechanical efforts to people or objects to provide intangible benefits to customers. Air travel, dry cleaning, haircutting, banking, medical care, and day care are examples of services. *Ideas* include concepts, philosophies, images, and issues. For instance, a marriage counselor, for a fee, gives spouses ideas to help improve their relationship. Other marketers of ideas include political parties, churches, and schools.

The product variable also involves creating or modifying brand names and packaging and may include decisions regarding warranty and repair services. Even one of the world's best basketball players is a global brand. Yao Ming, the Houston Rockets' center, has endorsed products from McDonald's, PepsiCo, and Reebok, many of which are marketed in his Chinese homeland.[6]

Product variable decisions and related activities are important because they are directly involved with creating products that address customers' needs and wants. To maintain an

marketing mix
Four marketing activities—product, pricing, distribution, and promotion—that a firm can control to meet the needs of customers within its target market

product
A good, a service, or an idea

Marketing IN TRANSITION

Efficiency and Size Make Tiny Cars a Winning Segment

With environmental concerns increasing, the automobile market has seen a global decline in sales and people are looking for smarter solutions to transportation. One answer appears to be: go tiny. While global car sales have been declining precipitously, the Mini Cooper (made by BMW) and Smart cars (Smart is a member of Mercedes-Benz Cars) are two bright spots on the car industry horizon. The Smart car is like no other car on the American market; measuring in at around 106 inches long, it is three feet shorter than the Mini Cooper. Despite its small size, test drivers have found the interior to be roomier than expected. Over 770,000 of the original Smart Fortwo coupes have been sold in 36 countries since 2001 and the current Smart model is doing well in the United States—it is the first car that can be factory ordered over the Internet. Toyota's answer to the tiny car is called the iQ, which will first launch in small-car-friendly Japan and Europe, with sales expected to be 2,500 and 6,000 a month, respectively. Plans are to eventually sell the car in the United States as well.

© SION TOUHIG/GETTY IMAGES

Part of the success of smaller vehicles is that they appeal to the practical and emotional sides of consumers. Fuel efficiencies are higher. The Smart Fortwo coupe gets 40 mpg highway; the Mini Cooper gets 37 mpg; and the iQ is Toyota's most fuel-efficient vehicle at 54 mpg highway. The Fortwo has also earned the Ultra Low Emission designation from the Air Resources Board of California due to its low exhaust emissions. Increased parking options is another perk of the small car, especially in crowded cities where parking is a challenge. The cars also aim to be more affordable than their large counterparts with the Smart priced from $11,590 to $16,590; the iQ is set to sell for $13,720; and the Mini Cooper at the higher end at $18–$20,000. Buying tiny may very well display a high level of intelligence.[a]

assortment of products that helps an organization achieve its goals, marketers must develop new products, modify existing ones, and eliminate those that no longer satisfy enough buyers or that yield unacceptable profits. In the funeral home industry, for example, some companies have developed new products such as DVD memoirs, grave markers that display photos along with a soundtrack, and caskets with drawers to hold mementos from the bereaved. To appeal to the growing number of people who prefer to be cremated, other firms are offering more cremation and memorial services.[7] We consider such product issues and many more in Chapters 9 and 10.

Price Variable

The price variable relates to decisions and actions associated with establishing pricing objectives and policies and determining product prices. Price is a critical component of the marketing mix because customers are concerned about the value obtained in an exchange. Price is often used as a competitive tool, and intense price competition sometimes leads to price wars. High prices can be used competitively to establish a product's premium image. Waterman and Mont Blanc pens, for example, have an image of high quality and high price that has given them significant status. On the other hand, some luxury goods marketers are now offering lower-priced versions of their products to appeal to middle-class consumers who want to "trade up" to prestigious brand names. Handbag maker Coach, for example, markets fabric wristlets for as low as $48, with high-end leather handbags selling for as much as $6,000.[8] We explore pricing decisions in Chapters 11 and 12.

Distribution Variable

To satisfy customers, products must be available at the right time and in convenient locations. Subway, for example, locates not only in strip malls but also inside Walmarts, Home Depots, laundromats, churches, and hospitals, as well as inside a Goodwill store, a car dealership, and an appliance store. There are more than 30,000 Subways in 88 different countries, all of them franchises. Six thousand of these are placed in nontraditional locations, such as churches.[9] In dealing with the distribution variable, a marketing manager makes products available in the quantities desired to as many target-market customers as possible, keeping total inventory, transportation, and storage costs as low as possible. A marketing manager also may select and motivate intermediaries (wholesalers and retailers), establish and maintain inventory control procedures, and develop and manage transportation and storage systems. The advent of the Internet and electronic commerce also has dramatically influenced the distribution variable. Companies now can make their products available throughout the world without maintaining facilities in each country. Apple has benefitted from technological advances in distributing songs over the Internet via its iTunes store, rather than establishing brick and mortar venues to sell music. It has sold more than 6 billion songs since the iTunes Store was launched in 2003. Users of the Apple iPhone can even download songs from the iTunes Store via their cellular networks, rather than having to find a computer with Internet access.[10] We examine distribution issues in Chapters 13 and 14.

Product
Petzl's ad focuses on the quality, comfort, and reliability of its climbing helmet.

Promotion Variable

The promotion variable relates to activities used to inform individuals or groups about the organization and its products. Promotion can aim to increase public awareness of the organization and of new or existing products. Del Monte Foods, for example, used humorous television commercials, a traveling bus tour, and a website (SmoochablePooch.com) to advertise and promote its Kibbles 'n Bits Brushing Bites dog food.[11] Promotional activities also can educate customers about product features or urge people to take a particular stance on a political or social issue, such as smoking or drug abuse. For example, rising fuel prices prompted the U.S. Department of Energy to launch an advertising campaign featuring an Energy Hog mascot to urge the public to conserve energy, especially with regard to home heating. The campaign also used booklets, temporary tattoos for children, and two websites—one for children with games and one for adults with information about energy-saving tips and appliances.[12] Promotion can help to sustain interest in established products that have been available for decades, such as Arm & Hammer baking soda or Ivory soap. Many companies are using the Internet to communicate information about themselves and their products. Ragu's website, for example, offers Italian phrases, recipes, and a sweepstakes, whereas Southwest Airlines' website enables customers to make flight reservations. In Chapters 15 through 17 we take a detailed look at promotion activities.

The marketing-mix variables are often viewed as controllable because they can be modified. However, there are limits to how much marketing managers can alter them. Economic conditions, competitive structure, and government regulations may prevent a manager from adjusting prices frequently or significantly. Making changes in the size, shape, and design of most tangible goods is expensive; therefore, such product features cannot be altered very often. In addition, promotional campaigns and methods used to distribute products ordinarily cannot be rewritten or revamped overnight.

MARKETING BUILDS RELATIONSHIPS WITH CUSTOMERS AND OTHER STAKEHOLDERS

Individuals and organizations engage in marketing to facilitate **exchanges**, the provision or transfer of goods, services, or ideas in return for something of value. Any product (good, service, or even idea) may be involved in a marketing exchange. We assume only that individuals and organizations expect to gain a reward in excess of the costs incurred.

exchanges
The provision or transfer of goods, services, or ideas in return for something of value

FIGURE 1.2 Exchange Between Buyer and Seller

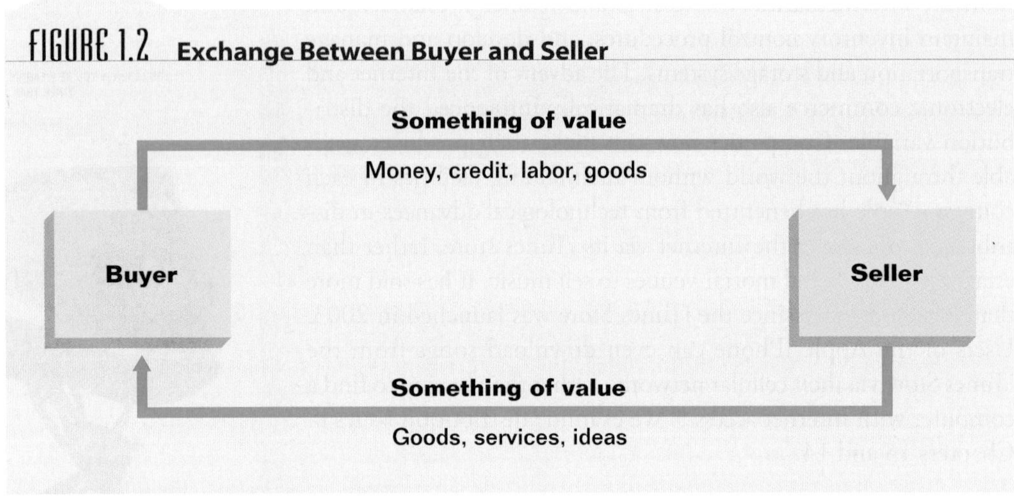

For an exchange to take place, four conditions must exist. First, two or more individuals, groups, or organizations must participate, and each must possess something of value that the other party desires. Second, the exchange should provide a benefit or satisfaction to both parties involved in the transaction. Third, each party must have confidence in the promise of the "something of value" held by the other. If you go to a Coldplay concert, for example, you go with the expectation of a great performance. Finally, to build trust, the parties to the exchange must meet expectations.

Figure 1.2 depicts the exchange process. The arrows indicate that the parties communicate that each has something of value available to exchange. An exchange will not necessarily take place just because these conditions exist; marketing activities can occur even without an actual transaction or sale. You may see an ad for a Sub-Zero refrigerator, for instance, but you might never buy the product. When an exchange occurs, products are traded for other products or for financial resources.

Marketing activities should attempt to create and maintain satisfying exchange relationships. To maintain an exchange relationship, buyers must be satisfied with the good, service, or idea obtained, and sellers must be satisfied with the financial reward or something else of value received. A dissatisfied customer who lacks trust in the relationship often searches for alternative organizations or products.

Marketers are concerned with building and maintaining relationships not only with customers but also with relevant stakeholders. **Stakeholders** include those constituents who have a "stake," or claim, in some aspect of a company's products, operations, markets, industry, and outcomes; these include customers, employees, investors and shareholders, suppliers, governments, communities, and many others. Developing and maintaining favorable relations with stakeholders is crucial to the long-term growth of an organization and its products.

stakeholders
Constituents who have a "stake," or claim, in some aspect of a company's products, operations, markets, industry, and outcomes

MARKETING OCCURS IN A DYNAMIC ENVIRONMENT

Marketing activities do not take place in a vacuum. The **marketing environment**, which includes competitive, economic, political, legal and regulatory, technological, and sociocultural forces, surrounds the customer and affects the marketing mix (see Figure 1.1). The effects of these forces on buyers and sellers can be dramatic and difficult to predict. They can create threats to marketers but also can generate opportunities for new products and new methods of reaching customers.

marketing environment
The competitive, economic, political, legal and regulatory, technological, and sociocultural forces that surround the customer and affect the marketing mix

The forces of the marketing environment affect a marketer's ability to facilitate exchanges in three general ways. First, they influence customers by affecting their lifestyles, standards of living, and preferences and needs for products. Because a marketing manager tries to develop and adjust the marketing mix to satisfy customers, effects of environmental forces on customers also have an indirect impact on marketing-mix components. Responding to health concerns from consumers, Burger King, for example, revamped its menu to include healthier Kids Meals with fewer than 560 calories, less than 30 percent of calories from fat, and no added trans fats. It also pledged to restrict advertising to children under age 12 using licensed characters only to promote products that meet health guidelines.[13] Likewise, Dunkin' Donuts eliminated trans fats from all items on its menu.[14] Second, marketing environment forces help to determine whether and how a marketing manager can perform certain marketing activities. Third, environmental forces may affect a marketing manager's decisions and actions by influencing buyers' reactions to the firm's marketing mix.

Marketing environment forces can fluctuate quickly and dramatically, which is one reason marketing is so interesting and challenging. Because these forces are closely interrelated, changes in one may cause changes in others. For example, evidence linking children's consumption of soft drinks and fast foods to health issues such as obesity, diabetes, and osteoporosis has exposed marketers of such products to negative publicity and generated calls for legislation regulating the sale of soft drinks in public schools. Some companies have responded to these concerns by voluntarily reformulating products to make them healthier or even introducing new products. Campbell's Soup responded to consumer concerns about their health by introducing a line of reduced sodium soups made with natural sea salt. The company also released a line of Campbell's V8 soups that contain a full serving of vegetables with no added preservatives. Campbell's also has responded to consumer concerns about wasteful packaging by advertising that its condensed soup cans are smaller, and therefore more eco-friendly, than soups that have the water already added.[15] Although changes in the marketing environment produce uncertainty for marketers and at times hurt marketing efforts, they also create opportunities. In the recent global recession, customers wanted more attention, better quality, and greater value for their money. In fact, during the recession, 90 percent of large companies trimmed cost in other areas of their business in order to avoid cuts in their marketing budget.[16] Marketers who are alert to changes in environmental forces not only can adjust to and influence these changes but also can capitalize on the opportunities such changes provide.

Marketing-mix variables—product, price distribution, and promotion—are factors over which an organization has control; the forces of the environment, however, are subject to far less control. Even though marketers know that they cannot predict changes in the marketing environment with certainty, however, they must nevertheless plan for them. Because these environmental forces have such a profound effect on marketing activities, we explore each of them in considerable depth in Chapter 3.

Understanding the Marketing Concept

Some firms have sought success by buying land, building a factory, equipping it with people and machines, and then making a product they believe buyers need. However, these firms frequently fail to attract customers with what they have to offer because they defined their business as "making a product" rather than as "helping potential customers satisfy their needs and wants." For example, when CDs became more popular than vinyl records, turntable manufacturers had an opportunity to develop new products to satisfy customers' needs for home entertainment. Companies that did not pursue this opportunity, such as Dual and Empire, are no longer in business. Such organizations have failed to implement the marketing concept.

The Marketing Concept
SSI understands the importance of a customer orientation by listening to customers and providing great service.

Likewise, the growing popularity of MP3 technology has enabled firms such as Apple Computer to develop products like the iPod to satisfy consumers' desire to store customized music libraries. Instead of buying CDs, a consumer can download a song for 99 cents from Apple's iTunes online music store.

According to the **marketing concept**, an organization should try to provide products that satisfy customers' needs through a coordinated set of activities that also allows the organization to achieve its goals. Customer satisfaction is the major focus of the marketing concept. To implement the marketing concept, an organization strives to determine what buyers want and uses this information to develop satisfying products. It focuses on customer analysis, competitor analysis, and integration of the firm's resources to provide customer value and satisfaction, as well as generate long-term profits.[17] The firm also must continue to alter, adapt, and develop products to keep pace with customers' changing desires and preferences. Ben & Jerry's Homemade Ice Cream, for example, constantly assesses customer demand for ice cream and sorbet. On its website it maintains a "flavor graveyard" listing combinations that were tried and ultimately failed. It also notes its top ten flavors each month. Pharmaceutical companies such as Merck and Pfizer continually strive to develop new products to fight infectious diseases, viruses, cancer, and other medical problems. Drugs that lower cholesterol, control diabetes, alleviate depression, or improve the quality of life in other ways also provide huge profits for the drug companies. When new products—such as Lyrica, a treatment for fibromyalgia pain—are developed, the companies must develop marketing activities to reach customers and communicate the products' benefits and side effects. Thus the marketing concept emphasizes that marketing begins and ends with customers. Research has found a positive association between customer satisfaction and shareholder value.[18]

The marketing concept is not a second definition of marketing. It is a management philosophy guiding an organization's overall activities. This philosophy affects all organizational activities, not just marketing. Production, finance, accounting, human resources, and marketing departments must work together.

The marketing concept is also not a philanthropic philosophy aimed at helping customers at the expense of the organization. A firm that adopts the marketing concept must satisfy not only its customers' objectives but also its own, or it will not stay in business long. The overall objectives of a business might relate to increasing profits, market share, sales, or a combination of all three. The marketing concept stresses that an organization can best achieve these objectives by being customer oriented. Thus, implementing the marketing concept should benefit the organization as well as its customers.

It is important for marketers to consider not only their current buyers' needs but also the long-term needs of society. Striving to satisfy customers' desires by sacrificing society's long-term welfare is unacceptable. For example, while many parents want disposable diapers that are comfortable, absorbent, and safe for their babies, society in general does not want nonbiodegradable disposable diapers that create tremendous landfill problems now and in the future. Marketers are expected to act in a socially responsible manner, an idea we discuss in more detail in Chapter 3.

marketing concept
A managerial philosophy that an organization should try to satisfy customers' needs through a coordinated set of activities that also allows the organization to achieve its goals

EVOLUTION OF THE MARKETING CONCEPT

The marketing concept may seem like an obvious approach to running a business. However, businesspeople have not always believed that the best way to make sales and profits is to satisfy customers (see Figure 1.3).

The Production Orientation

During the second half of the nineteenth century, the Industrial Revolution was in full swing in the United States. Electricity, rail transportation, division of labor, assembly lines, and mass production made it possible to produce goods more efficiently. With new technology and new ways of using labor, products poured into the marketplace, where demand for manufactured goods was strong.

The Sales Orientation

In the 1920s, strong demand for products subsided, and businesses realized that they would have to "sell" products to buyers. From the mid-1920s to the early 1950s, businesses viewed sales as the major means of increasing profits, and this period came to have a sales orientation. Businesspeople believed that the most important marketing activities were personal selling, advertising, and distribution. Today, some people incorrectly equate marketing with a sales orientation.

The Marketing Orientation

By the early 1950s, some businesspeople began to recognize that efficient production and extensive promotion did not guarantee that customers would buy products. These businesses, and many others since, found that they must first determine what customers want and then produce those products rather than making the products first and then trying to persuade customers that they need them. As more organizations realized the importance of satisfying customers' needs, U.S. businesses entered the marketing era, one of marketing orientation.

A **marketing orientation** requires the "organizationwide generation of market intelligence pertaining to current and future customer needs, dissemination of the intelligence across departments, and organizationwide responsiveness to it."[19] Marketing orientation is linked to new-product innovation by developing a strategic focus to explore and develop new products to serve target markets.[20] Ralph Lauren, well known throughout the world for designer clothing, introduced a line of moderately priced apparel and home furnishings for JCPenney to appeal to a broader target market. The new American Living line is not directly identified with the Ralph Lauren name, but word-of-mouth promotion was expected to create an awareness of the line's designer and attract new customers.[21] Top management, marketing managers, nonmarketing managers (those in production, finance, human resources, and so on), and customers are all important in developing and carrying out a marketing orientation. Trust, openness, honoring promises, respect, collaboration, and recognizing the market

Entrepreneurial Marketing

Leatherman's Marketing Appeals to Survivalists and More

Timothy S. Leatherman developed the idea for the Pocket Survival Tool when his car broke down on a driving tour of Europe with his wife. Leatherman's generic pocketknife lacked the tools he needed to repair the car. He wondered, why couldn't he just add pliers to a pocketknife? After he returned home, he worked on developing a prototype. When he took it to a Portland knife business, they looked at it and said, "This isn't a knife; it's a tool." Leatherman then decided to name his invention the Pocket Survival Tool to appeal to the outdoor survivalist market. Making his products available through mail order catalogs also helped him find the right market. It wasn't too long before Tim Leatherman and his partner were selling more than 1 million units a year. Leatherman succeeded in marketing by understanding his customers' needs and finding out how to reach them.[b]

marketing orientation An organizationwide commitment to researching and responding to customer needs

FIGURE 1.3 The Evolution of the Marketing Concept

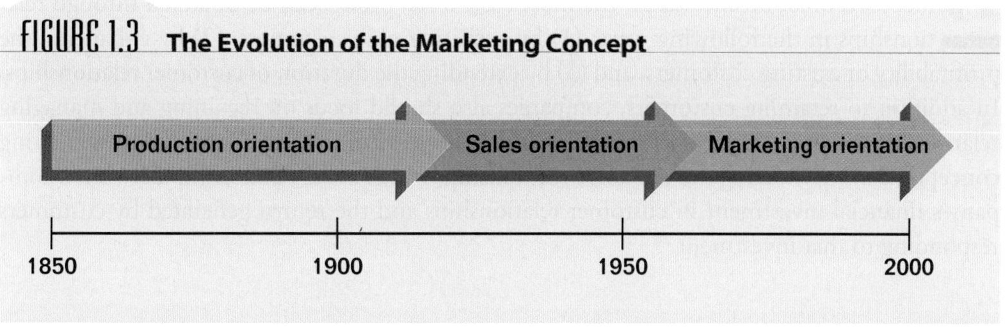

as the raison d'etre are six values required by organizations striving to become more marketing oriented.[22] Unless marketing managers provide continuous customer-focused leadership with minimal interdepartmental conflict, achieving a marketing orientation will be difficult. Nonmarketing managers must communicate with marketing managers to share information important to understanding the customer. Finally, a marketing orientation involves being responsive to ever-changing customer needs and wants. To accomplish this, Amazon.com, the online provider of books, CDs, DVDs, toys, and many other products, follows buyers' online purchases and recommends related topics. Trying to assess what customers want, which is difficult to begin with, is further complicated by the speed with which fashions and tastes can change. Today, businesses want to satisfy customers and build meaningful long-term buyer–seller relationships. Doing so helps a firm boost its own financial value.[23]

IMPLEMENTING THE MARKETING CONCEPT

A philosophy may sound reasonable and look good on paper, but this does not mean that it can be put into practice easily. To implement the marketing concept, a marketing-oriented organization must accept some general conditions and recognize and deal with several problems. Consequently, the marketing concept has yet to be fully accepted by all businesses.

Management must first establish an information system to discover customers' real needs and then use the information to create satisfying products. For example, research has shown that women want products that are customizable and relevant to their lives. Kimberly-Clark's Huggies brand, for example, has come out with a "Baby Countdown" widget for expectant mothers. All they do is type in their due date and the Countdown tells them what is happening in their bodies and what to expect.[24] As food prices increase, McDonald's has been engaged in large-scale tests to determine ways to cut costs on their $1 cheeseburgers. The company feels the pressure to keep prices low, while simultaneously satisfying customers.[25] An information system is usually expensive; management must commit money and time for its development and maintenance. Without an adequate information system, however, an organization cannot be marketing oriented.

To satisfy customers' objectives as well as its own, a company also must coordinate all its activities. To keep service quality high, cross training service employees to take on a variety of roles creates improved implementation of the marketing strategy.[26] This may require restructuring the internal operations and overall objectives of one or more departments. If the head of the marketing unit is not a member of the organization's top-level management, he or she should be. Some departments may have to be abolished and new ones created. Implementing the marketing concept demands the support not only of top management but also of managers and staff at all levels.

Managing Customer Relationships

Achieving the full profit potential of each customer relationship should be the fundamental goal of every marketing strategy. Marketing relationships with customers are the lifeblood of all businesses. At the most basic level, profits can be obtained through relationships in the following ways: (1) by acquiring new customers, (2) by enhancing the profitability of existing customers, and (3) by extending the duration of customer relationships. In addition to retaining customers, companies also should focus on regaining and managing relationships with customers who have abandoned the firm.[27] Implementing the marketing concept means optimizing the exchange relationship, which is the relationship between a company's financial investment in customer relationships and the return generated by customers responding to that investment.[28]

Maintaining positive relationships with customers is an important goal for marketers. The term **relationship marketing** refers to "long-term, mutually beneficial arrangements in which both the buyer and seller focus on value enhancement through the creation of more satisfying exchanges."[29] Relationship marketing continually deepens the buyer's trust in the company, and as the customer's confidence grows, this, in turn, increases the firm's understanding of the customer's needs. Successful marketers respond to customer needs and strive to increase value to buyers over time. Eventually this interaction becomes a solid relationship that allows for cooperation and mutual dependency.

To build these long-term customer relationships, marketers are increasingly turning to marketing research and information technology. **Customer relationship management (CRM)** focuses on using information about customers to create marketing strategies that develop and sustain desirable customer relationships. By increasing customer value over time, organizations try to retain and increase long-term profitability through customer loyalty.[30] For example, Best Buy has a reward zone program, wherein members collect a reward point for every $1 spent in the store, which can be redeemed for gift certificates. Every 250 points earns customers a $5 reward certificate.[31] Starbucks has also started a rewards program to lure its faithful customers to the chain more frequently. Loyalty cards and more frequent promotions are part of Starbucks' strategy to counter sagging sales.[32]

Managing customer relationships requires identifying patterns of buying behavior and using that information to focus on the most promising and profitable customers.[33] Companies must be sensitive to customers' requirements and desires and establish communication to build their trust and loyalty. Consider that the lifetime value of a Lexus customer is about 50 times that of a Taco Bell customer, but remember, there are many more Taco Bell customers. For either organization, a customer is important. A customer's lifetime value results from his or her frequency of purchases, average value of purchases, and brand-switching patterns.[34] In general, when marketers focus on customers chosen for their lifetime value, they earn higher profits in future periods than when they focus on customers selected for other reasons.[35] Because the loss of a loyal potential lifetime customer could result in lower profits, managing customer relationships has become a major focus of strategic marketing today. Firms need to understand the value of paying customers, but also the value of customers subsidized by other customers. Employment agencies, dating services, and even IT providers provide the word-of-mouth advertising and social networking value for so-called free customers. Customers attracting other customers can grow your business.[36]

Through the use of Internet-based marketing strategies (e-marketing), companies can personalize customer relationships on a nearly one-on-one basis. A wide range of products, such as computers, jeans, golf clubs, cosmetics, and greeting cards, can be tailored for specific customers. Customer relationship management provides a strategic bridge between information technology and marketing strategies aimed at long-term relationships. This involves finding and retaining customers using information to improve customer value and satisfaction. We take a closer look at some of these e-marketing strategies in Chapter 4.

relationship marketing
Establishing long-term, mutually satisfying buyer–seller relationships

customer relationship management (CRM)
Using information about customers to create marketing strategies that develop and sustain desirable customer relationships

Value-Driven Marketing

Value is an important element of managing long-term customer relationships and implementing the marketing concept. We view **value** as a customer's subjective assessment of benefits relative to costs in determining the worth of a product (customer value = customer benefits − customer costs).

value
A customer's subjective assessment of benefits relative to costs in determining the worth of a product

Customer benefits include anything a buyer receives in an exchange. Hotels and motels, for example, basically provide a room with a bed and bathroom, but each firm provides a different level of service, amenities, and atmosphere to satisfy its guests. Hampton Inns offers

© PRNEWSFOTO/MICHELIN/NEWSCOM

Value-Driven Marketing
To drive customer value, Michelin positions its tires as durable and efficient.

the minimum services necessary to maintain a quality, efficient, low-price overnight accommodation. In contrast, the Ritz-Carlton provides every imaginable service a guest might desire and strives to ensure that all service is of the highest quality. Customers judge which type of accommodation offers the best value according to the benefits they desire and their willingness and ability to pay for the costs associated with the benefits.

Customer costs include anything a buyer must give up to obtain the benefits the product provides. The most obvious cost is the monetary price of the product, but nonmonetary costs can be equally important in a customer's determination of value. Two nonmonetary costs are the time and effort customers expend to find and purchase desired products. To reduce time and effort, a company can increase product availability, thereby making it more convenient for buyers to purchase the firm's products. Another nonmonetary cost is risk, which can be reduced by offering good basic warranties or extended warranties for an additional charge.[37] Another risk-reduction strategy is the offer of a 100 percent satisfaction guarantee. This strategy is increasingly popular in today's catalog/telephone/Internet shopping environment. L.L. Bean, for example, uses such a guarantee to reduce the risk involved in ordering merchandise from its catalogs.

The process people use to determine the value of a product is not highly scientific. All of us tend to get a feel for the worth of products based on our own expectations and previous experience. We can, for example, compare the value of tires, batteries, and computers directly with the value of competing products. We evaluate movies, sporting events, and performances by entertainers on the more subjective basis of personal preferences and emotions. For most purchases, we do not consciously try to calculate the associated benefits and costs. It becomes an instinctive feeling that Kellogg's Corn Flakes are a good value or that McDonald's is a good place to take children for a quick lunch. The purchase of an automobile or a mountain bike may have emotional components, but more conscious decision making also may figure in the process of determining value.

In developing marketing activities, it is important to recognize that customers receive benefits based on their experiences. For example, many computer buyers consider services such as fast delivery, ease of installation, technical advice, and training assistance to be important elements of the product. Customers also derive benefits from the act of shopping and selecting products. These benefits can be affected by the atmosphere or environment of a store, such as Red Lobster's nautical/seafood theme. Even the ease of navigating a website can have a tremendous impact on perceived value. Direct marketing agency Epsilon discovered that permission-based e-mail mailings are a great way to generate loyal customers. A full 87 percent of respondents surveyed said that receiving permission-based e-mails is a good way to learn about new products. Sixty-three percent of respondents also said that they prefer it when content is customized. Therefore, companies such as Amazon that tailor their website and e-mails to individual companies have been found to be far more successful at maintaining customer loyalty and generating customer interest in their products.[38]

The marketing mix can be used to enhance perceptions of value. A product that demonstrates value usually has a feature or an enhancement that provides benefits. Promotional activities also can help to create an image and prestige characteristics that customers consider in their assessment of a product's value. In some cases value may be perceived simply as the lowest price. Many customers may not care about the quality of the paper towels they buy;

they simply want the cheapest ones for use in cleaning up spills because they plan to throw them in the trash anyway. On the other hand, more people are looking for the fastest, most convenient way to achieve a goal and therefore become insensitive to pricing. For example, many busy customers are buying more prepared meals in supermarkets to take home and serve quickly, even though these meals cost considerably more than meals prepared from scratch. In such cases the products with the greatest convenience may be perceived as having the greatest value. The availability or distribution of products also can enhance their value. Taco Bell wants to have its Mexican fast-food products available at any time and any place people are thinking about consuming food. It therefore has introduced Taco Bell products into supermarkets, vending machines, college campuses, and other convenient locations. Thus the development of an effective marketing strategy requires understanding the needs and desires of customers and designing a marketing mix to satisfy them and provide the value they want.

Marketing Management

Marketing management is the process of planning, organizing, implementing, and controlling marketing activities to facilitate exchanges effectively and efficiently. Effectiveness and efficiency are important dimensions of this definition. *Effectiveness* is the degree to which an exchange helps to achieve an organization's objectives. *Efficiency* refers to minimizing the resources an organization must spend to achieve a specific level of desired exchanges. Thus the overall goal of marketing management is to facilitate highly desirable exchanges and to minimize the costs of doing so. Consider that General Electric is significantly cutting back its 128-year-old incandescent light bulb business in favor of expanding its compact fluorescent and other energy-efficient lighting products. In recent years, the incandescent lighting business accounted for less than 2 percent of GE's revenues as consumers shifted to compact fluorescents under the perceptions that they have greater value and benefit for the natural environment.[39]

Planning is a systematic process of assessing opportunities and resources, determining marketing objectives, and developing a marketing strategy and plans for implementation and control. Planning determines when and how marketing activities are performed and who performs them. It forces marketing managers to think ahead, establish objectives, and consider future marketing activities and their impact on society. Effective planning also reduces or eliminates daily crises. We take a closer look at marketing strategies and plans in the next chapter.

Organizing marketing activities involves developing the internal structure of the marketing unit. The structure is the key to directing marketing activities. The marketing unit can be organized by functions, products, regions, types of customers, or a combination of all four.

Proper *implementation* of marketing plans hinges on coordination of marketing activities, motivation of marketing personnel, and effective communication within the unit. Marketing managers must motivate marketing personnel, coordinate their activities, and integrate their activities both with those in other areas of the company and with the marketing efforts of personnel in external organizations, such as advertising agencies and research firms. In order to sell more cars during the slow economy in 2009, Hyundai started a giveback program that allowed customers to break their contracts and return their cars if they lost their source of income. In order to make this offer, Hyundai had to ensure it had enough cars in stock to accommodate increased demand, as well as be prepared financially to handle a high volume of returned cars.[40] An organization's communication system must allow the marketing manager to stay in contact with high-level management, with managers of other functional areas within the firm, and with personnel involved in marketing activities both inside and outside the organization.

marketing management
The process of planning, organizing, implementing, and controlling marketing activities to facilitate exchanges effectively and efficiently

The marketing *control process* consists of establishing performance standards, comparing actual performance with established standards, and reducing the difference between desired and actual performance. An effective control process has four requirements. It should ensure a rate of information flow that allows the marketing manager to detect quickly any differences between actual and planned levels of performance. It must accurately monitor various activities and be flexible enough to accommodate changes. The costs of the control process must be low relative to costs that would arise without controls. Finally, the control process should be designed so that both managers and subordinates can understand it.

The Importance of Marketing in Our Global Economy

Our definition of marketing and discussion of marketing activities reveal some of the obvious reasons the study of marketing is relevant in today's world. In this section we look at how marketing affects us as individuals and at its role in our increasingly global society.

MARKETING COSTS CONSUME A SIZABLE PORTION OF BUYERS' DOLLARS

Studying marketing will make you aware that many marketing activities are necessary to provide satisfying goods and services. Obviously, these activities cost money. About one-half of a buyer's dollar goes for marketing costs. If you spend $16 on a new CD, 50 to 60 percent goes toward marketing expenses, including promotion and distribution, as well as profit margins. The production (pressing) of the CD represents about $1, or 6 percent of its price. A family with a monthly income of $3,000 that allocates $600 to taxes and savings spends about $2,400 for goods and services. Of this amount, $1,200 goes for marketing activities. If marketing expenses consume that much of your dollar, you should know how this money is used.

MARKETING IS USED IN NONPROFIT ORGANIZATIONS

Although the term *marketing* may bring to mind advertising for Burger King, Volkswagen, and Apple, marketing is also important in organizations working to achieve goals other than ordinary business objectives such as profit. Government agencies at the federal, state, and local levels engage in marketing activities to fulfill their mission and goals. The U.S. Army, for example, uses promotion, including television advertisements and event sponsorships, to communicate the benefits of enlisting to potential recruits. The U.S. Department of Agriculture launched a promotional website with games to help teach kids about eating right according to its revised Food Pyramid.[41] Universities and colleges engage in marketing activities to recruit new students, as well as to obtain donations from alumni and businesses.

In the private sector, nonprofit organizations also employ marketing activities to create, price, distribute, and promote programs that benefit particular segments of society. Habitat for Humanity, for example, must promote its philosophy of low-income housing to the public to raise funds and donations of supplies to build or renovate housing for low-income families who contribute "sweat equity" to the construction of their own homes. Such activities helped charitable organizations raise more than $300 billion a year in philanthropic contributions to assist them in fulfilling their missions.[42]

© UNITED NEGRO COLLEGE FUND/AD COUNCIL

© AP IMAGES/ PRNEWSFOTO/AIDS HEALTHCARE FOUNDATION

Nonprofit Organizations
The United Negro College Fund and the AIDS Healthcare Foundation use marketing to promote their causes.

MARKETING IS IMPORTANT TO BUSINESSES

Businesses must sell products to survive and grow, and marketing activities help to sell their products. Financial resources generated from sales can be used to develop innovative products. New products allow a firm to satisfy customers' changing needs, which, in turn, enables the firm to generate more profits. Even nonprofit businesses need to "sell" to survive.

Marketing activities help to produce the profits that are essential to the survival of individual businesses. Without profits, businesses would find it difficult, if not impossible, to buy more raw materials, hire more employees, attract more capital, and create additional products that, in turn, make more profits. Without profits, marketers cannot continue to provide jobs and contribute to social causes.

MARKETING FUELS OUR GLOBAL ECONOMY

Profits from marketing products contribute to the development of new products and technologies. Advances in technology, along with falling political and economic barriers and the universal desire for a higher standard of living, have made marketing across national borders commonplace while stimulating global economic growth. As a result of worldwide communications and increased international travel, many U.S. brands have achieved widespread acceptance around the world. At the same time, customers in the United States have greater choices among the products they buy because foreign brands such as Toyota (Japan), Bayer (Germany), and Nestlé (Switzerland) sell alongside U.S. brands such as General Motors, Tylenol, and Chevron. People around the world watch CNN and MTV on Toshiba and Sony televisions they purchased at WalMart. Electronic commerce via the Internet now enables businesses of all sizes to reach buyers around the world. We explore the international markets and opportunities for global marketing in Chapter 8.

Sustainable Marketing

Growing Eco-Responsible Buildings

Buildings in the United States account for 39 percent of the country's primary energy use, 70 percent of its resource consumption, 15 trillion gallons of water use, and 136 million tons of construction and demolition debris annually. Buildings are beginning to get more attention in the fight against global warming because carbon dioxide emissions could be cut by 6 million tons a year—the equivalent of taking 1 million cars off the road—if half the nation's new commercial buildings used 50 percent less energy. Consider that a ten-story office building in Los Angeles could save $141,000 annually on its electricity bill and extract 40 tons of carbon from the air if it were to have a green roof and four green walls.

© MARTINE HAMILTON KNIGHT/ARCAID/CORBIS

Marketing these new green building products requires educating customers about the new technologies available, as well as demonstrating that the technology works and provides benefits to both customers and society at large. Larger companies are joining the new green building revolution. Gap Inc. installed a 69,000-square-foot green roof on its headquarters in San Bruno, California, while the Ford Motor Company installed green roofs on its corporate headquarters.

Cities also encourage green building, such as the cities of Chicago and Portland, which have over 250 and 120 green roofs, respectively. As customers and society at large become more aware of the potential benefits and savings of these products, they are more likely to begin demanding them from contractors and builders. In this way, the welfare of customers and society will improve through value-driven marketing.[c]

MARKETING KNOWLEDGE ENHANCES CONSUMER AWARENESS

Besides contributing to the well-being of our economy, marketing activities help to improve the quality of our lives. Studying marketing allows us to assess a product's value and flaws more effectively. Consider that research suggests that low-fat nutrition claims for a food product can actually increase the intake of that product, thereby countering the desired effects of consuming low-fat snacks to lose weight.[43] We can determine which marketing efforts need improvement and how to attain that goal. For example, an unsatisfactory experience with a warranty may make you wish for stricter law enforcement so that sellers would fulfill their promises. You also may wish that you had more accurate information about a product before you purchased it. Understanding marketing enables us to evaluate corrective measures (such as laws, regulations, and industry guidelines) that could stop unfair, damaging, or unethical marketing practices. Thus, understanding how marketing activities work can help you to be a better consumer.

MARKETING CONNECTS PEOPLE THROUGH TECHNOLOGY

New technology, particularly technology related to computers and telecommunications, helps marketers to understand and satisfy more customers than ever before. Today, marketers must recognize the impact not only of websites but also of instant messaging, blogs, online forums, online games, mailing lists, and wikis, as well as text messaging via cell phones and podcasts via MP3 players. Increasingly, these tools are facilitating marketing exchanges. A consumer shopping for a new car, for example, can access automakers' Web pages, configure an ideal vehicle, and get instant feedback on its cost. Consumers can visit Autobytel, Edmund's, and other websites to find professional reviews and obtain comparative pricing information on both new and used cars to help them find the best value. They can then purchase a vehicle online or at a dealership. Technology lets Amazon serve customers without their ever talking to an employee. Amazon has a minimal sales staff, and orders ship with a few mouse clicks.[44]

© BILL ARON/PHOTOEDIT

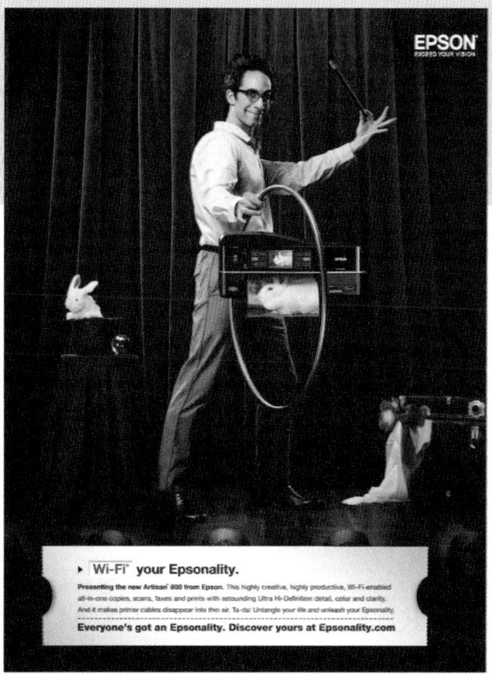

© AP IMAGES/GLOBE NEWSWIRE/EPSON AMERICA, INC.

Marketing and the Growth of Technology
Apple and Epson manage the development of technology to produce customer satisfaction and loyalty.

The Internet provides an opportunity for marketers of everything from computers to travel reservations to encourage exchanges. Southwest Airlines, for example, books more of its passenger revenue via its website—making it the number one airline for online revenue generation.[45] The Internet also has become a vital tool for marketing to other businesses. In fact, online sales now exceed $143 billion, accounting for about 6 percent of all retail sales.[46] Successful companies are using technology in their marketing strategies to develop profitable relationships with these customers.

SNAPSHOT

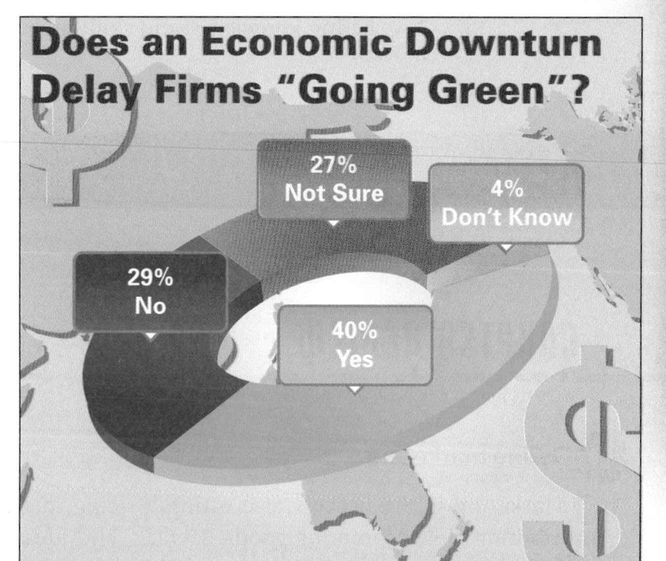

From a survey of CEOs indicating the likelihood that the most recent recession will delay plans to go green.
Source: Booz & Co. survey of 828 chief executive officers and managers. Printed in *USA Today*, February 19, 2009, p. A1.

SOCIALLY RESPONSIBLE MARKETING CAN PROMOTE THE WELFARE OF CUSTOMERS AND STAKEHOLDERS

The success of our economic system depends on marketers whose values promote trust and cooperative relationships in which customers and other stakeholders are treated with respect. The public is increasingly insisting that social responsibility and ethical concerns be considered in planning and implementing marketing activities. Although some marketers' irresponsible or unethical activities end up on the front pages of *USA Today* or *The Wall Street Journal,* more firms are working to develop a responsible approach to developing long-term relationships with customers *and* society. In the area of the natural environment, companies are increasingly embracing the notion of **green marketing**, which is a strategic process involving stakeholder assessment to create meaningful long-term relationships with customers, while maintaining, supporting, and enhancing the natural environment. The multinational enterprise Unilever, for example, not only produces and markets a variety of food and personal-care products around the world, but also operates a free community laundry in São Paulo, funds a hospital that provides free medical care in Bangladesh, provides financing and educational materials to help suppliers around the world convert to more environmentally friendly practices, and reports on its carbon dioxide and hazardous waste releases to interested stakeholders. Unilever's chief executive officer, Patrick Cescau, believes that such activities are necessary to remain competitive in future decades, declaring, "You can't ignore the impact your company has on the community and environment." Even Hollywood is "going green" with networks, television shows, and movies incorporating more green themes, like Homer and Marge Simpson tooling around in their biodiesel-fueled vehicle in *The Simpsons Movie* and *The Early Show*'s new "Going Green" segment.[47] By being concerned about the impact of marketing on society, a firm can protect the interests of the general public and the natural environment.

MARKETING OFFERS MANY EXCITING CAREER PROSPECTS

green marketing
A strategic process involving stakeholder assessment to create meaningful long-term relationships with customers while maintaining, supporting, and enhancing the natural environment

From 25 to 33 percent of all civilian workers in the United States perform marketing activities. The marketing field offers a variety of interesting and challenging career opportunities throughout the world, such as personal selling, advertising, packaging, transportation, storage, marketing research, product development, wholesaling, and retailing. In addition, many individuals working for nonbusiness organizations engage in marketing activities to promote political, educational, cultural, church, civic, and charitable activities. Whether a person earns a living through marketing activities or performs them voluntarily for a nonprofit group, marketing knowledge and skills are valuable personal and professional assets.

CHAPTER REVIEW

OBJECTIVES

1 Define marketing.

Marketing is the process of creating, pricing, distributing, and promoting goods, services, and ideas to facilitate satisfying exchange relationships with customers and to develop and maintain favorable relationships with stakeholders in a dynamic environment. The essence of marketing is to develop satisfying exchanges from which both customers and marketers benefit.

2 Understand several important marketing terms, including target market, marketing mix, marketing exchanges, and marketing environment.

A target market is the group of customers toward which a company directs a set of marketing efforts.

The variables—product, price, distribution, and promotion—are known as the marketing mix because marketing managers decide what type of each element to use and in what amounts. Marketing managers strive to develop a marketing mix that matches the needs of customers in the target market. Before marketers can develop a marketing mix, they must collect in-depth, up-to-date information about customer needs.

Individuals and organizations engage in marketing to facilitate exchanges—the provision or transfer of goods, services, and ideas in return for something of value. Four conditions must exist for an exchange to occur: (1) Two or more individuals, groups, or organizations must participate, and each must possess something of value that the other party desires; (2) the exchange should provide a benefit or satisfaction to both parties involved in the transaction; (3) each party must have confidence in the promise of the "something of value" held by the other; and (4) to build trust, the parties to the exchange must meet expectations. Marketing activities should attempt to create and maintain satisfying exchange relationships with all stakeholders—those constituents who have a "stake," or claim, in some aspect of a company's products, operations, markets, industry, and outcomes.

The marketing environment, which includes competitive, economic, political, legal and regulatory, technological, and sociocultural forces, surrounds the customer and the marketing mix. These forces can create threats to marketers, but they also generate opportunities for new products and new methods of reaching customers.

③ Be aware of the marketing concept and marketing orientation.

According to the marketing concept, an organization should try to provide products that satisfy customers' needs through a coordinated set of activities that also allows the organization to achieve its goals. Customer satisfaction is the marketing concept's major objective. The philosophy of the marketing concept emerged in the United States during the 1950s after the production and sales eras. Organizations that develop activities consistent with the marketing concept become marketing-oriented organizations.

④ Understand the importance of building customer relationships.

Relationship marketing involves establishing long-term, mutually satisfying buyer–seller relationships. Customer relationship management (CRM) focuses on using information about customers to create marketing strategies that develop and sustain desirable customer relationships. Managing customer relationships requires identifying patterns of buying behavior and using that information to focus on the most promising and profitable customers.

Value is a customer's subjective assessment of benefits relative to costs in determining the worth of a product. Benefits include anything a buyer receives in an exchange, whereas costs include anything a buyer must give up to obtain the benefits the product provides.

⑤ Explain the major marketing functions that are part of the marketing management process.

Marketing management is the process of planning, organizing, implementing, and controlling marketing activities to facilitate effective and efficient exchanges. Planning is a systematic process of assessing opportunities and resources, determining marketing objectives, developing a marketing strategy, and preparing for implementation and control. Organizing marketing activities involves developing the marketing unit's internal structure. Proper implementation of marketing plans depends on coordinating marketing activities, motivating marketing personnel, and communicating effectively within the unit. The marketing control process consists of establishing performance standards, comparing actual performance with established standards, and reducing the difference between desired and actual performance.

⑥ Understand the role of marketing in our society.

Marketing costs absorb about half of each buyer's dollar. Marketing activities are performed in both business and nonprofit organizations. Marketing activities help business organizations to generate profits, and they help fuel the increasingly global economy. Knowledge of marketing enhances consumer awareness. New technology improves marketers' abilities to connect with customers. Socially responsible marketing can promote the welfare of customers and society. Finally, marketing offers many exciting career opportunities.

Please visit the student website at www.cengage.com/international for quizzes and games that will help you prepare for exams and achieve the grade you want.

KEY CONCEPTS

marketing
customers
target market
marketing mix
product
exchanges
stakeholders
marketing environment
marketing concept
marketing orientation
relationship marketing
customer relationship management (CRM)
value
marketing management
green marketing

ISSUES FOR DISCUSSION AND REVIEW

1. What is marketing? How did you define the term before you read this chapter?
2. What is the focus of all marketing activities? Why?
3. What are the four variables of the marketing mix? Why are these elements known as variables?
4. What conditions must exist before a marketing exchange can occur? Describe a recent exchange in which you participated.
5. What are the forces in the marketing environment? How much control does a marketing manager have over these forces?
6. Discuss the basic elements of the marketing concept. Which businesses in your area use this philosophy? Explain why.
7. How can an organization implement the marketing concept?
8. What is customer relationship management? Why is it so important to "manage" this relationship?
9. What is value? How can marketers use the marketing mix to enhance the perception of value?
10. What types of activities are involved in the marketing management process?
11. Why is marketing important in our society? Why should you study marketing?

MARKETING APPLICATIONS

1. Identify several businesses in your area that have not adopted the marketing concept. What characteristics of these organizations indicate nonacceptance of the marketing concept?
2. Identify possible target markets for the following products:
   a. Kellogg's Corn Flakes
   b. Wilson tennis rackets
   c. Disney World
   d. Diet Pepsi
3. Discuss the variables of the marketing mix (product, price, promotion, and distribution) as they might relate to each of the following:
   a. A trucking company
   b. A men's clothing store
   c. A skating rink
   d. A campus bookstore

ONLINE EXERCISE

4. The American Marketing Association (AMA) is the marketing discipline's primary professional organization. In addition to sponsoring academic research, publishing marketing literature, and organizing meetings of local businesspeople with student members, it helps individual members to find employment in member firms. Visit the AMA website at http://www.marketingpower.com.
   a. What type of information is available on the AMA website to assist students in planning their careers and finding jobs?
   b. If you joined a student chapter of the AMA, what benefits would you receive?
   c. What marketing-mix variable does the AMA's Internet marketing effort exemplify?

DEVELOPING YOUR MARKETING PLAN

Successful companies develop strategies for marketing their products. The strategic plan guides the marketer in making many of the detailed decisions about the attributes of the product, its distribution, promotional activities, and pricing. A clear understanding of the foundations of marketing is essential in formulating a strategy and in the development of a specific marketing plan. To guide you in relating the information in this chapter to the development of your marketing plan, consider the following:

1. Discuss how the marketing concept contributes to a company's long-term success.
2. Describe the level of marketing orientation that currently exists in your company. How will a marketing orientation contribute to the success of your new product?
3. What benefits will your product provide to the customer? How will these benefits play a role in determining the customer value of your product?

The information obtained from these questions should assist you in developing various aspects of your marketing plan found in the *Interactive Marketing Plan* exercise.

VIDEO CASE 1

Method Cleans Up the Home Care Industry Using Green Marketing

"People against dirty" is the intriguing slogan of the San Francisco-based home and body care brand *Method*. The founders claim that they seek not only to clean our homes and bodies, but to remove harmful chemicals from our lives as well. All *Method* products are chemical-free and made with natural, safe ingredients. The company has embraced the marketing concepts, and its target market is receptive to a green marketing strategy. However, *Method* has not become one of the fastest-growing new brands in the United States (sold in more than 25,000 retail outlets) by focusing only on a green philosophy. The company has attracted customers through its cool brand with hip, eye-catching packaging, edgy marketing, and even a link to a blog about clean living on the company's website.

Method was founded in 2000 by former roommates and high school friends Adam Lowry, a chemical engineer who worked as a climatologist for the Carnegie Institute before becoming *Method's* "chief greens keeper," and Eric Ryan, a marketing expert with experience designing campaigns for Saturn and The Gap. Deciding to join forces to help wean people off of the harmful chemicals we use to clean our homes and bodies, Lowry and Ryan were able to combine their complementary skill sets to develop products that were not only effective and natural, but that looked great as well.

Method's concept is not new. Companies such as Seventh Generation and Ecover have been around for years, but they were never able to break into the mainstream. *Method*, however, looks like it will become a household name with annual revenues nearing $100 million. When choosing distribution channels, Lowry and Ryan decided to steer away from coops and health food stores and instead sought mass recognition and distribution at Target, Linens 'n Things, Amazon.com, and other large retailers. In order to make this possible, the founders knew that they could not charge the high prices established by other eco-friendly cleaner companies. They needed to compete head-on with the major cleaning brands. Although Lowry is dedicated to creating products that adhere to strict green standards, he and Ryan agreed from the beginning that taking the green slant would not be the best way to sell their products.

In order to literally stand out from the competition, they enlisted designer Karim Rashid (who also has designed for the likes of Prada and Dirt Devil) to design visually appealing packaging for their products. The result was affordable cleaning products contained in beautiful, standout bottles. In a highly competitive industry, the fight to get noticed on the shelf is fierce. Most large companies push the smaller brands out of the prime locations, but with *Method's* artistic packaging, people take notice even though it is a smaller company. Customers drawn to the product for its looks or the all-natural scents will be purchasing more non-polluting green products for their home without even knowing it. In the end, Lowry and Ryan hope that this approach does create a change in perspective among consumers previously uninterested in going green or unable to afford to do so.

As with any successful company, *Method* has had to be highly innovative. It has been ahead of the curve in developing new kinds of cleaning products. For example, *Method* was an industry leader when it created a triple-concentrated laundry detergent long before major companies began doing so. *Method* has also taken stock of competitive products on the market already, and continually works on making its own brand's versions more eco-friendly. Cases in point are dryer sheets and the Omop. Conventional dryer sheets are coated in beef fat in order to create soft clothing. Lowry found this disgusting and unacceptable. Looking for a vegetarian solution, the company developed dryer sheets coated with canola oil instead. The Omop, *Method's* answer to the Swiffer, is a stylish mop using cloths created from a corn-based plastic product. Unlike Swiffer's cloths, which are synthetic, the Omop's cloths are completely biodegradable.

Focusing on product quality, trends, price point, design, and accessibility have helped *Method* grow from a small, unknown company to one making a name for itself in mainstream media for its innovativeness and quality products. The company came in at number 16 on *Fast Company's* "World's Most Innovative Companies" 2008 list, and, through its high-profile distribution at major retail outlets, it is becoming increasingly popular among consumers.

Method may find that clever marketing and competitive pricing may, in the long run, be one of the best ways to help the environment. With these marketing techniques, they have given green products a competitive advantage in a large market segment . . . and they continue growing.

QUESTIONS FOR DISCUSSION

1. How has *Method* implemented the marketing concept?
2. Why is *Method* successful in a highly competitive industry?
3. Does the success of *Method* provide insights about the future of green marketing?

Method, http://methodhome.com (accessed October 27, 2009); "Fighting Dirty," *Grist*, March 14, 2008, http://www.grist.org/feature/2008/03/14/index.html?sources-rss (accessed Octboer 27, 2009).

CHAPTER 2 Planning Marketing Strategies

© AP IMAGES/WILFREDO LEE

OBJECTIVES:

1. Describe the strategic planning process.
2. Explain how organizational resources and opportunities affect the planning process.
3. Understand the role of the mission statement in strategic planning.
4. Examine corporate, business-unit, and marketing strategies.
5. Understand the process of creating the marketing plan.
6. Describe the marketing implementation process and the major approaches to marketing implementation.

LOWE'S VS. HOME DEPOT: LOCATION, LOCATION, LOCATION

Competition for consumer dollars is fierce between Lowe's and Home Depot. In a "Battle of the Brands" survey, 52 percent preferred Lowe's, with 48 percent preferring Home Depot. However, Home Depot nets much more revenue than Lowe's because of its numerous locations. Lowe's has 1,650 North American stores, while Home Depot boasts 2,234. Because the chains offer similar products, customers will often go to the nearest store. Home Depot primary customer groups include do-it-yourself, do-it-for-me, and professional contractors. The store offers a variety of installation services for products such as flooring, cabinets, and countertops. Lowe's has a similar customer profile, with both chains carrying up to 40,000 products. Lowe's generally appeals more to women because of its less warehouse-style atmosphere.

Because consumers patronize both chains, the companies must fight for sales and customer loyalty. The fight became even fiercer with the economic slowdown beginning in 2008 and declines in the home improvement industry. Both companies have been hard hit by the downturns in the housing market and the economy. As a result, both are cutting down on expansion and expenses. Home Depot, once famous for stellar customer service, is turning its focus back to the customer, making in-store service its number one priority. As part of this initiative, the company is working to improve its working environment and benefits—key motivators to retaining cheerful employees who will then offer quality customer service. Lowe's, for its part, appears to be staying true to its path of previous years by improving product options and creating a comfortable shopping environment. This being said, no one is more aware of what is on the line than these two companies. Each is trying to improve upon the other, which, one would think, can only lead to better shopping experiences for consumers all around.[1]

In the face of a dynamic environment, Home Depot and Lowe's are spending more time and resources on strategic planning, that is, on determining how to use their resources and abilities to achieve their objectives. Although most of this book deals with specific marketing decisions and strategies, this chapter focuses on the "big picture," on all the functional areas and activities—finance, production, human resources, and research and development, as well as marketing—that must be coordinated to reach organizational goals. Effectively implementing the marketing concept of satisfying customers and achieving organizational goals requires that all organizations engage in strategic planning.

We begin this chapter with an overview of the strategic planning process. Next, we examine how organizational resources and opportunities affect strategic planning and the role played by the organization's mission statement. After discussing the development of both corporate and business-unit strategy, we explore the nature of marketing strategy and creation of the marketing plan. These elements provide a framework for the development and implementation of marketing strategies, as we will see throughout the remainder of this book.

Understanding the Strategic Planning Process

Through the process of **strategic planning**, a firm establishes an organizational mission and formulates goals, corporate strategy, marketing objectives, marketing strategy, and finally, a marketing plan.[2] A marketing orientation should guide the process of strategic planning to ensure that a concern for customer satisfaction is an integral part of the process. A marketing orientation is also important for the successful implementation of marketing strategies.[3] Figure 2.1 shows the components of strategic planning.

The process begins with a detailed analysis of the organization's strengths and weaknesses and identification of opportunities and threats within the marketing environment. Based on this analysis, the firm can establish or revise its mission and goals and then develop corporate strategies to achieve those goals. Next, each functional area of the organization (marketing, production, finance, human resources, etc.) establishes its own objectives and develops strategies to achieve them.[4] The objectives and strategies of each functional area must support the organization's overall goals and mission. The strategies of each functional area also should be coordinated with a focus on marketing orientation.

Because our focus is marketing, we are most interested, of course, in the development of marketing objectives and strategies. Marketing objectives should be designed so that their achievement will contribute to the corporate strategy and can be accomplished through efficient use of the firm's resources. To achieve its marketing objectives, an organization must develop a **marketing strategy**, which includes identifying and analyzing a target market and developing a marketing mix to satisfy individuals in that market. Thus a marketing strategy includes a plan of action for developing, distributing, promoting, and pricing products that meet the needs of the target market. Marketing strategy is best formulated when it reflects

strategic planning
The process of establishing an organizational mission and formulating goals, corporate strategy, marketing objectives, marketing strategy, and a marketing plan

marketing strategy
A plan of action for identifying and analyzing a target market and developing a marketing mix to meet the needs of that market

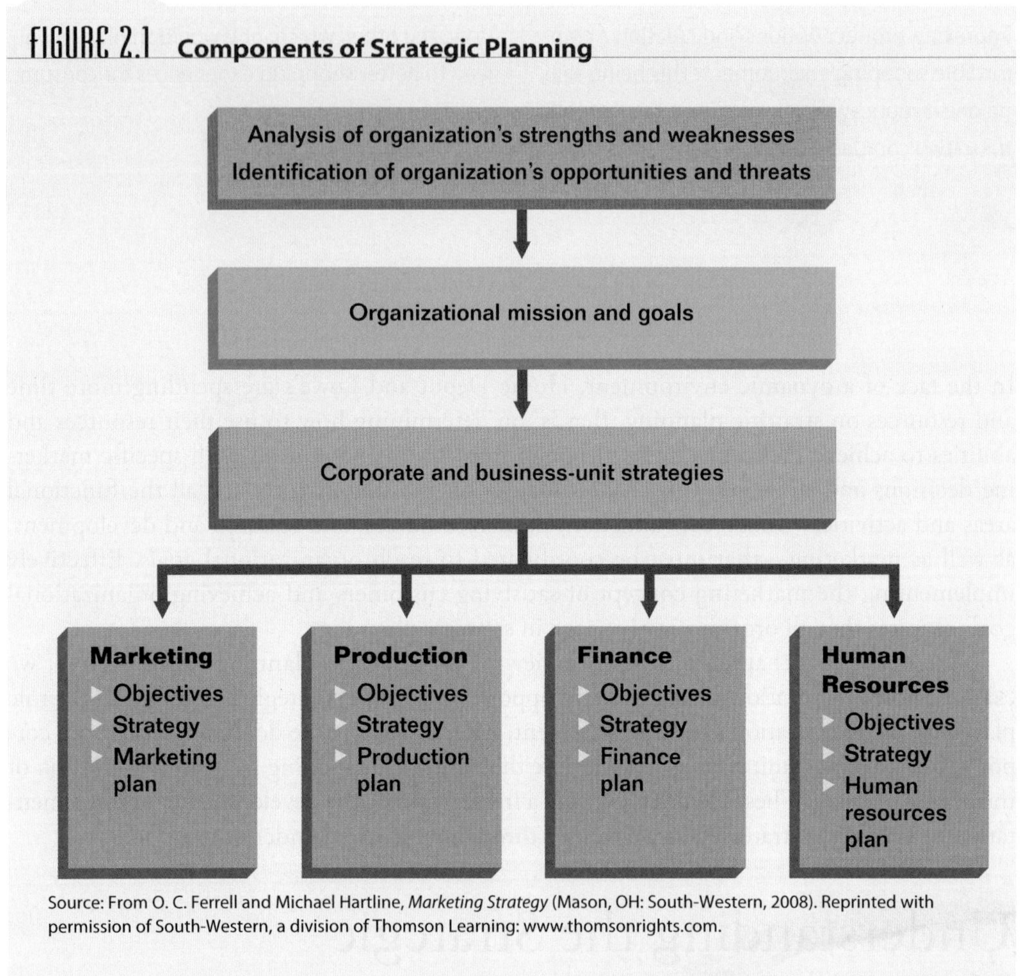

Source: From O. C. Ferrell and Michael Hartline, *Marketing Strategy* (Mason, OH: South-Western, 2008). Reprinted with permission of South-Western, a division of Thomson Learning: www.thomsonrights.com.

the overall direction of the organization and is coordinated with all the firm's functional areas. When properly implemented and controlled, a marketing strategy will contribute to the achievement not only of marketing objectives but also of the organization's overall goals. Consider that Apple's successful marketing strategy for its iPod line of music players helped to revitalize the computer firm's reputation for excellent design, which may transfer to other Apple products. The firm even designed its iMac G5 computer to mimic the look of an iPod with rounded corners and a translucent shell.[5]

The strategic planning process ultimately yields a marketing strategy that is the framework for a **marketing plan**, a written document that specifies the activities to be performed to implement and control the organization's marketing activities. In the remainder of this chapter we discuss the major components of the strategic planning process: organizational opportunities and resources, organizational mission and goals, corporate and business-unit strategy, marketing strategy, and the role of the marketing plan.

marketing plan A written document that specifies the activities to be performed to implement and control an organization's marketing activities

core competencies Things a firm does extremely well, which sometimes give it an advantage over its competition

Assessing Organizational Resources and Opportunities

The strategic planning process begins with an analysis of the marketing environment. As we shall see in Chapter 3, competitive, economic, political, legal and regulatory, technological, and sociocultural forces can threaten an organization and influence its overall goals; they also affect the amount and type of resources the firm can acquire.

However, these environmental forces can create favorable opportunities as well—opportunities that can be translated into overall organizational goals and marketing objectives.

Any strategic planning effort must assess the organization's available financial and human resources and capabilities, as well as how the level of these factors is likely to change in the future. Additional resources may be needed to achieve the organization's goals and mission.[6] Resources affect marketing and financial performance indirectly by helping to create customer satisfaction and loyalty.[7] They also can include goodwill, reputation, and brand names. The reputation and well-known brand names of Rolex watches and BMW automobiles, for example, are resources that give these firms an advantage over their competitors. Such strengths also include **core competencies**, things a firm does extremely well—sometimes so well that they give the company an advantage over its competition. Walmart's core competency, efficiency in supply chain management, has enabled the discount chain to build a strong reputation for low prices and even to expand the number of generic medications eligible for its pharmacies' $4 prescription plan.[8]

IMAGE COURTESY OF THE ADVERTISING ARCHIVES

Marketing Strategy
Wendy's targets the "late-night" market by keeping some of its locations open until midnight and beyond.

Analysis of the marketing environment involves not only an assessment of resources but also identification of opportunities in the marketplace. When the right combination of circumstances and timing permits an organization to take action to reach a particular target market, a **market opportunity** exists. For example, after consumers began to perceive bottled water products as having a negative impact on the natural environment because of their plastic containers, Sigg USA recognized a market opportunity for its reusable aluminum water bottles. The bottles can be refilled with tap water and easily carried, making them both an environmentally friendly and economical option.[9] Such opportunities are often called **strategic windows**, temporary periods of optimal fit between the key requirements of a market and the particular capabilities of a firm competing in that market.[10]

When a company matches a core competency to opportunities it has discovered in the marketplace, it is said to have a **competitive advantage**. In some cases a company may possess manufacturing, technical, or marketing skills that it can match to market opportunities to create a competitive advantage. For example, Tesco, a higher end grocer from the United Kingdom, entered the United States market in late 2007 with its Fresh & Easy stores. A year later, a recession hit that caused consumers to cut back on spending. The company reformulated its strategy and now seeks a competitive advantage by offering cheap options. Fresh & Easy offers packs of produce for under $1, as well as discount-priced cuts of meat—all of which average 10–25 percent lower than at competing grocery stores.[11]

market opportunity
A combination of circumstances and timing that permits an organization to take action to reach a target market

strategic windows
Temporary periods of optimal fit between the key requirements of a market and a firm's capabilities

competitive advantage
The result of a company's matching a core competency to opportunities in the marketplace

SWOT ANALYSIS

One tool that marketers use to assess an organization's strengths, weaknesses, opportunities, and threats is **SWOT analysis**. Strengths and weaknesses are internal factors that can influence an organization's ability to satisfy its target markets. *Strengths* refer to competitive advantages or core competencies that give the firm an advantage in meeting the needs of its target markets. John Deere, for example, promotes its service, experience, and reputation in the farm equipment business to emphasize the craftsmanship it uses in its lawn tractors and mowers for city dwellers. *Weaknesses* refer to any limitations that a company faces in developing or implementing a marketing strategy. For example, U.S. auto companies have

SWOT analysis
A tool that marketers use to assess an organization's strengths, weaknesses, opportunities, and threats

IMAGE COURTESY OF THE ADVERTISING ARCHIVES

Market Opportunity
Kettle Chips targets consumers concerned about artificial ingredients and preservatives in their snack food.

internal weaknesses, such as too much production capacity and higher wages, when compared to their foreign competition. Both strengths and weaknesses should be examined from a customer perspective because they are meaningful only when they help or hinder the firm in meeting customer needs. Only strengths that relate to satisfying customers should be considered true competitive advantages. Likewise, weaknesses that directly affect customer satisfaction should be considered competitive disadvantages. Alcoholic beverage company Constellation Brands, seeing a competitive disadvantage, sold a number of its low-priced spirits brands in order to focus on the most profitable brands. The company realized that it was focusing too much time and money on cheap brands, while the majority of growth in the alcoholic brands industry was from premium products.[12]

Opportunities and threats exist independently of the firm and therefore represent issues to be considered by all organizations, even those that do not compete with the firm. *Opportunities* refer to favorable conditions in the environment that could produce rewards for the organization if acted on properly. That is, opportunities are situations that exist but must be acted on if the firm is to benefit from them. *Threats,* on the other hand, refer to conditions or barriers that may prevent the firm from reaching its objectives. For example, Apple's top-selling iPod family of digital music players faces competition from cell phone makers and services that are incorporating MP3 technology into many new mobile phones. Indeed, Japanese consumers already download more songs onto their phones than onto their computers and digital players.[13] Threats must be acted on to prevent them from limiting the organization's capabilities. To counter the threat of increasing competition, Apple launched the iPhone, a cell phone with easy-to-use iTunes software, and iTunes' prices remain highly competitive.[14] Opportunities and

© AP IMAGES/ PRNEWSFOTO/STONYFIELD FARM

IMAGE COURTESY OF THE ADVERTISING ARCHIVES

Competitive Advantage
Organic ingredients have become widely used to create a competitive advantage for companies like Stoneyfield Farms and Philadelphia's Cream Cheese.

FIGURE 2.2 The Four-Cell SWOT Matrix

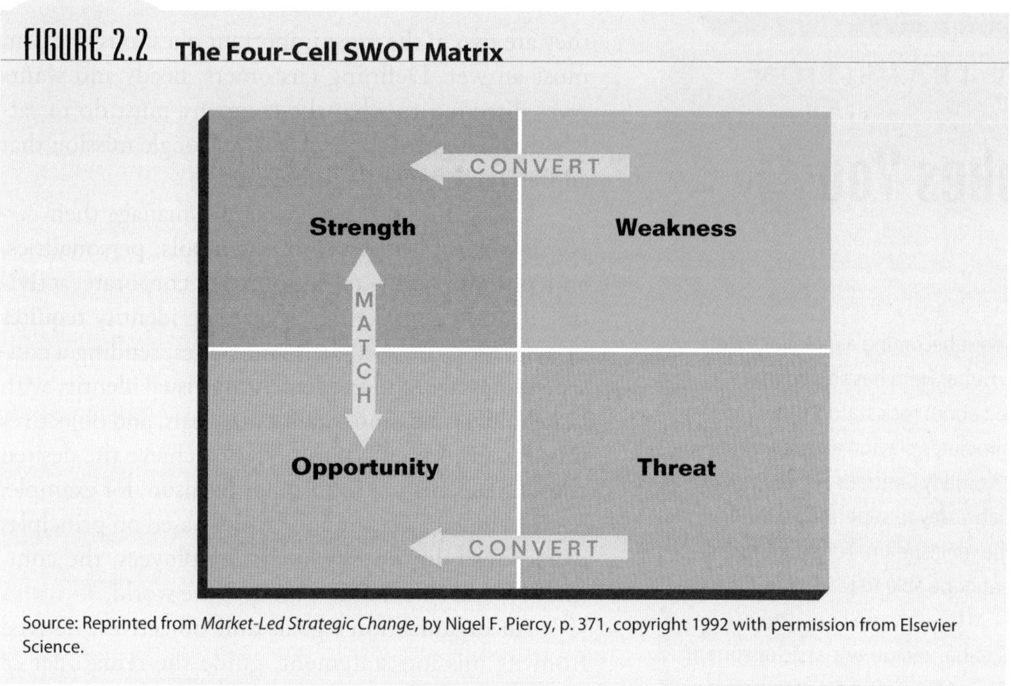

Source: Reprinted from *Market-Led Strategic Change*, by Nigel F. Piercy, p. 371, copyright 1992 with permission from Elsevier Science.

threats can stem from many sources within the environment. When a competitor's introduction of a new product threatens a firm, a defensive strategy may be required. If the firm can develop and launch a new product that meets or exceeds the competition's offering, it can transform the threat into an opportunity.[15]

Figure 2.2 depicts a four-cell SWOT matrix that can help managers in the planning process. When an organization matches internal strengths to external opportunities, it creates competitive advantages in meeting the needs of its customers. In addition, an organization should act to convert internal weaknesses into strengths and external threats into opportunities. Procter & Gamble, for instance, converted the weaknesses of not having competitive advantages in five areas that are essential to succeeding in consumer products—consumer understanding, brand building, innovation, go-to-market capability, and scale—into strengths by investing billions of dollars into areas such as marketing research and supply-chain management. Indeed, the company's research and development program has become a core competency that fosters significant innovation in areas such as enzymes, perfumes, flavors, polymers, substrates, and surfactants.[16] A firm that lacks adequate marketing skills can hire outside consultants to help convert a weakness into a strength.

Establishing an Organizational Mission and Goals

Once an organization has assessed its resources and opportunities, it can begin to establish goals and strategies to take advantage of those opportunities. The goals of any organization should derive from its **mission statement,** a long-term view, or vision, of what the organization wants to become. Herbal tea marketer Celestial Seasonings, for example, says that its mission is "To create and sell healthful, naturally oriented products that nurture people's bodies and uplift their spirits."[17]

mission statement
A long-term view of what the organization wants to become

When an organization decides on its mission, it really answers two questions: Who are our customers? What is our core competency? Although these questions seem very simple,

Marketing IN TRANSITION

Guitar Hero Makes You a Rock Star

Have you ever fantasized about becoming a rock star? With sales of six million copies, Guitar Hero has shown that millions have also dreamed about rock stardom. It supplies a plastic guitar-shaped device that simulates playing a guitar through the use of keys. Endorsements from Comedy Central's *South Park* to Fox's *American Idol* and singer Mariah Carey to supermodel Heidi Klum have branded Guitar Hero in the mainstream. To be successful, you do not need innate musical talent or be able to read music. If you can follow the simple tutorial guides, in less than an hour, you can be jamming to the tunes of Bon Jovi, Nirvana, and other classic or current rock groups. By competing against others for audiences with points and money, it is easy to become addicted.

© AP IMAGES/ACTIVISION

Robert Kotick, the creator of Guitar Hero, and his firm Activision are an amazing success story in the video game industry. He turned around a video game publisher $30 million in debt. Eighteen years later, Activision has $3 billion in revenue, $12.3 billion in net worth, and double the market value of the industry's top competitor, Electronic Arts. Kotick does not even like playing video games, yet he set up a franchising system that gave his designers creative autonomy and studio leaders some ownership by giving them a share of the profits or losses and input into the creation of the games. This is the company that created Tony Hawk's Pro Skater with earnings of $1.6 billion, Guitar Hero with profits of $2 billion, and Call of Duty with sales of $135 million.

The development of Guitar Hero recognized a target market that wanted an opportunity to simulate the feeling of being in a real band. The social networking opportunity to create a successful band including guitar, drums, and vocals provides an experience that creates identification with a successful rock star.[a]

they are two of the most important questions any firm must answer. Defining customers' needs and wants gives direction to what the company must do to satisfy them. Figure 2.3 displays the Google mission that addresses customer requirements.

Companies try to develop and manage their *corporate identity*—their unique symbols, personalities, and philosophies—to support all corporate activities, including marketing. Managing identity requires broadcasting mission goals and values, sending a consistent message, and implementing visual identity with stakeholders. Mission statements, goals, and objectives must be implemented properly to achieve the desired corporate identity.[18] Johnson & Johnson, for example, has developed a credo and identity based on principles of responsibility to customers, employees, the community, and shareholders around the world.[19]

An organization's goals and objectives, derived from its mission statement, guide the remainder of its planning efforts. Goals focus on the end results that the organization seeks. Johnson Controls, for example, has developed a new mission, "a more comfortable, safe and sustainable world" to highlight its focus on helping customers add value to their daily lives from its diverse product lines. The company also revamped its corporate logo and introduced a new slogan, "Ingenuity Welcome." In addition to a new advertising campaign, the firm added a new corporate logo to a number of the company's well-known brands including HomeLink (garage door openers), York (air conditioning and heating products), Optima (batteries), and Varta (auto batteries).[20]

A **marketing objective** states what is to be accomplished through marketing activities. A marketing objective of Ritz-Carlton hotels, for example, is to have more than 90 percent of its customers indicate that they had a memorable experience at the hotel. Marketing objectives should be based on a careful study of the SWOT analysis and should relate to matching strengths to opportunities and/or the conversion of weaknesses or threats. These objectives can be stated in terms of product introduction, product improvement or innovation, sales volume, profitability, market share, pricing, distribution, advertising, or employee training activities.

Marketing objectives should possess certain characteristics. First, a marketing objective should be expressed in clear, simple terms so that all marketing personnel understand exactly what they are trying to achieve. Second, an objective should be written so that it can be measured accurately. This allows the organization to determine if and when the objective has been achieved.

Google Corporate Information

Home

Corporate Info
Overview
Technology
Business
Culture
Management
Milestones
Initiatives

At a Glance
Quick Profile
Offices

Our Philosophy
Ten things
Software principles
Design principles
No pop-ups
Security

Find on this site:
Search

Our Philosophy

Ten things we know to be true

"The perfect search engine," says co-founder Larry Page, "would understand exactly what you mean and give back exactly what you want." When Google began, you would have been pleasantly surprised to enter a search query and immediately find the right answer. Google became successful precisely because we were better and faster at finding the right answer than other search engines at the time.

But technology has come a long way since then, and the face of the web has changed. Recognizing that search is a problem that will never be solved, we continue to push the limits of existing technology to provide a fast, accurate and easy-to-use service that anyone seeking information can access, whether they're at a desk in Boston or on a phone in Bangkok. We've also taken the lessons we've learned from search to tackle even more challenges.

As we keep looking towards the future, these core principles guide our actions.

1. Focus on the user and all else will follow.

Since the beginning, we've focused on providing the best user experience possible. Whether we're designing a new Internet browser or a new tweak to the look of the homepage, we take great care to ensure that they will ultimately serve **you**, rather than our own internal goal or bottom line. Our homepage interface is clear and simple, and pages load instantly. Placement in search results is never sold to anyone, and advertising is not only clearly marked as such, it offers relevant content and is not distracting. And when we build new tools and applications, we believe they should work so well you don't have to consider how they might have been designed differently.

2. It's best to do one thing really, really well.

We do search. With one of the world's largest research groups focused exclusively on solving search problems, we know what we do well, and how we could do it better. Through continued iteration on difficult problems, we've been able to solve complex issues and provide continuous improvements to a service that already makes finding information a fast and seamless experience for millions of people. Our dedication to improving search helps us apply what we've learned to new products, like Gmail and Google Maps. Our hope is to bring the power of search to previously unexplored areas, and to help people access and use even more of the ever-expanding information in their lives.

3. Fast is better than slow.

We know your time is valuable, so when you're seeking an answer on the web you want it right away – and we aim to please. We may be the only people in the world who can say our goal is to have people leave our homepage as quickly as possible. By shaving excess bits and bytes from our pages and increasing the efficiency of our serving environment, we've broken our own speed records many times over, so that the average response time on a search result is a fraction of a second. We keep speed in mind with each new product we release, whether it's a mobile application or Google Chrome, a browser designed to be fast enough for the modern web. And we continue to work on making it all go even faster.

4. Democracy on the web works.

Google search works because it relies on the millions of individuals posting links on websites to help determine which other sites offer content of value. We assess the importance of every web page using more than 200 signals and a variety of techniques, including our patented PageRank™ algorithm, which analyzes which sites have been "voted" to be the best sources of information by other pages across the web. As the web gets bigger, this approach actually improves, as each new site is another point of information and another vote to be counted. In the same vein, we are active in open source software development, where innovation takes place through the collective effort of many programmers.

FIGURE 2.3 Google Mission Statement

If an objective is to increase market share by 10 percent, the firm should be able to measure market share changes accurately. Third, a marketing objective should specify a time frame for its accomplishment. A firm that sets an objective of introducing a new product should state the time period in which to do this. Finally, a marketing objective should be consistent with both business-unit and corporate strategy. This ensures that the firm's mission is carried out at all levels of the organization. General Motors, for example, may have an overall marketing objective of maintaining a 25 percent share of the U.S. auto market. To achieve this objective, some GM divisions may have to increase market share while the shares of other divisions decline.

Developing Corporate, Business-Unit, and Marketing Strategies

In any organization, strategic planning begins at the corporate level and proceeds downward to the business-unit and marketing levels. Corporate strategy is the broadest of these three levels and should be developed with the organization's overall mission in mind. ■ Business-unit strategy should be consistent with the corporate strategy, and marketing strategy should be consistent with both the business-unit and corporate strategies. Figure 2.4 shows the relationships among these planning levels.

marketing objective
A statement of what is to be accomplished through marketing activities

CORPORATE STRATEGY

Corporate strategy determines the means for using resources in the functional areas of marketing, production, finance, research and development, and human resources to reach the organization's goals. A corporate strategy determines not only the scope of the business but

corporate strategy
A strategy that determines the means for using resources in the various functional areas to reach the organization's goals

also its resource deployment, competitive advantages, and overall coordination of functional areas. It addresses the two questions posed in the organization's mission statement: Who are our customers? What is our core competency? The term *corporate* in this context does not apply solely to corporations; corporate strategy is used by all organizations, from the smallest sole proprietorship to the largest multinational corporation.

Corporate strategy planners are concerned with broad issues such as corporate culture, competition, differentiation, diversification, interrelationships among business units, and environmental and social issues. They attempt to match the resources of the organization with the opportunities and threats in the environment. Google, for example, purchased

Corporate Strategy
Boeing continues to excel in producing innovative new jetliners such as the Dream Liner.

YouTube for $1.65 billion after recognizing that the video-sharing website's rapid growth reflected the growing popularity of viewing videos—professional and amateur—on every topic imaginable.[21] Corporate strategy planners are also concerned with defining the scope and role of the firm's business units so that they are coordinated to reach the ends desired. A firm's corporate strategy may affect its technological competence and ability to innovate.[22] Cellphone maker Nokia, for example, purchased Navteq, a producer of digital mapping and navigational software, for $8.1 billion after recognizing the opportunity to incorporate more satellite-based location services into its phones.[23]

BUSINESS-UNIT STRATEGY

After analyzing corporate operations and performance, the next step in strategic planning is to determine future business directions and develop strategies for individual business units. A **strategic business unit (SBU)** is a division, product line, or other profit center within the parent company. Borden's strategic business units, for example, consist of dairy products, snacks, pasta, niche grocery products such as ReaLemon juice and Cremora coffee creamer, and other units such as glue and paints. Each of these units sells a distinct set of products to an identifiable group of customers, and each competes with a well-defined set of competitors. The revenues, costs, investments, and strategic plans of each SBU can be separated from those of the parent company. SBUs operate in a variety of markets that have differing growth rates, opportunities, degrees of competition, and profit-making potential. Recognizing this fact in the 1990s, Procter & Gamble implemented business strategies intended to reduce its reliance on two SBUs that accounted for 85 percent of the value it created during the 1990s. Today, the multinational corporation's portfolio is spread across 22 categories to balance fast-growing, high-margin businesses, such as home care and beauty products, with foundation businesses including baby care and laundry products.[24]

Strategic planners should recognize the different performance capabilities of each SBU and carefully allocate scarce resources among those divisions. Several tools allow a firm's portfolio of SBUs, or even individual products, to be classified and visually displayed according to the attractiveness of various markets and the business's relative market share within those markets. A **market** is a group of individuals and/or organizations that have needs for products in a product class and have the ability, willingness, and authority to purchase those products. The percentage of a market that actually buys a specific product from a particular company is referred to as that product's (or business unit's) **market share**. Hershey Foods, for example, controls 43 percent of the market for chocolate candy in the United States, whereas its rivals, Masterfoods and Nestlé, command 23 and 8 percent, respectively.[25] Product quality, order of entry into the market, and market share have been associated with SBU success.[26]

One of the most helpful tools is the **market-growth/market-share matrix,** the Boston Consulting Group (BCG) approach, which is based on the philosophy that a product's market growth rate and its market share are important considerations in determining its marketing strategy. All the firm's SBUs and products should be integrated into a single, overall matrix and evaluated to determine appropriate strategies for individual products and overall portfolio strategies. Managers can use this model to determine and classify each product's expected future cash contributions and future cash requirements. Generally, managers who use this model should examine the competitive position of a product (or SBU) and the opportunities for improving that product's contribution to profitability and cash flow.[27] The BCG analytical approach is more of a diagnostic tool than a guide for making strategy prescriptions.

Figure 2.5, which is based on work by the BCG, enables the strategic planner to classify a firm's products into four basic types: stars, cash cows, dogs, and question marks.[28] *Stars* are products with a dominant share of the market and good prospects for growth. However, they use more cash than they generate to finance growth, add capacity, and increase market

strategic business unit (SBU)
A division, product line, or other profit center within a parent company

market
A group of individuals and/or organizations that have needs for products in a product class and have the ability, willingness, and authority to purchase those products

market share
The percentage of a market that actually buys a specific product from a particular company

market-growth/market-share matrix
A strategic planning tool based on the philosophy that a product's market growth rate and market share are important in determining marketing strategy

FIGURE 2.5 Growth-Share Matrix Developed by the Boston Consulting Group

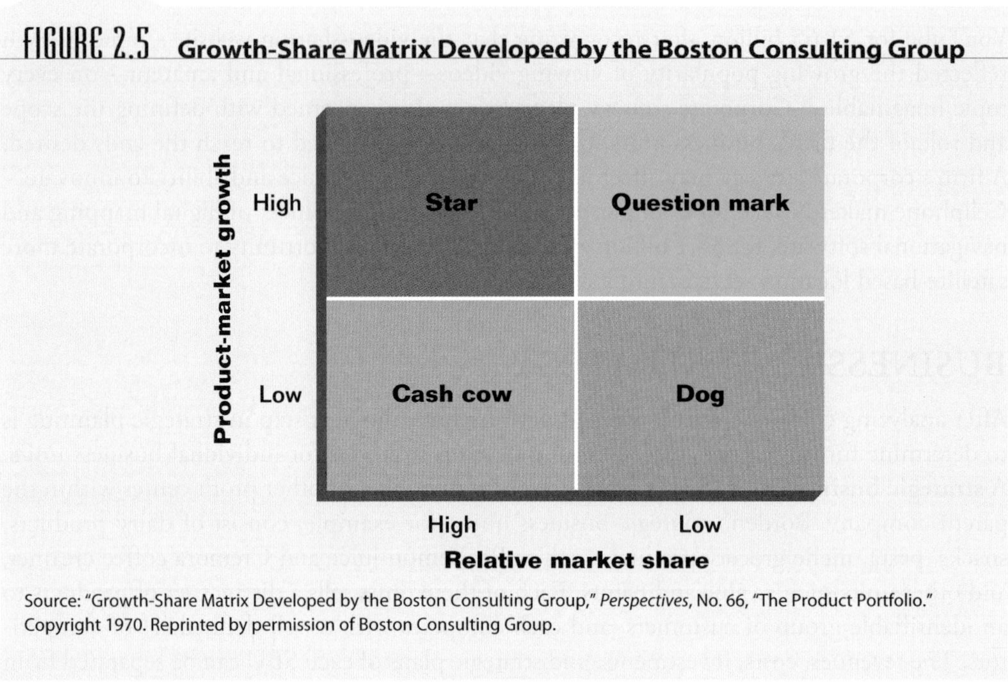

Source: "Growth-Share Matrix Developed by the Boston Consulting Group," *Perspectives*, No. 66, "The Product Portfolio." Copyright 1970. Reprinted by permission of Boston Consulting Group.

share. An example of a star might be Nintendo's Wii videogame system. *Cash cows* have a dominant share of the market but low prospects for growth; typically, they generate more cash than is required to maintain market share. Bounty, the best-selling paper towels in the United States, represents a cash cow for Procter & Gamble. *Dogs* have a subordinate share of the market and low prospects for growth; these products are often found in established markets. During the most recent recession, General Electric's business unit, GE Capital, became a dog with this financial arm of the company creating losses that lowered prices and stock prices.[29] *Question marks,* sometimes called "problem children," have a small share of a growing market and generally require a large amount of cash to build market share. XM Satellite Radio is a question mark because the company has experienced difficulties finding financing for the growing satellite radio infrastructure.

The long-term health of an organization depends on having some products that generate cash (and provide acceptable profits) and others that use cash to support growth. Among the indicators of overall health are the size and vulnerability of the cash cows; the prospects for the stars, if any; and the number of question marks and dogs. Particular attention should be paid to products with large cash appetites. Unless the company has an abundant cash flow, it cannot afford to sponsor many such products at one time. If resources, including debt capacity, are spread too thin, the company will end up with too many marginal products and will be unable to finance promising new-product entries or acquisitions in the future.

MARKETING STRATEGY

The next phase in strategic planning is the development of sound strategies for each functional area of the organization. Corporate strategy and marketing strategy must balance and synchronize the organization's mission and goals with stakeholder relationships. This means that marketing must deliver value and be responsible in facilitating effective relationships with all relevant stakeholders.[30] An effective marketing strategy must gain the support of key stakeholders, including employees, investors, and communities, as well as government regulators. When Bank of America (BofA) purchased Merrill Lynch for $50 billion, it obtained 16,700 investment brokers with more than 5 million clients. However, Merrill Lynch's management and corporate strategy was not compatible with BofA's. Losses in bad investments at Merrill Lynch hobbled BofA with bad loans and debt, requiring a large government bailout.[31] There is a need in marketing to develop more of a stakeholder orientation to go beyond markets, competitors, and channel members to understand and address all stakeholder concerns.[32]

Within the marketing area, a strategy is typically designed around two components: (1) the selection of a target market and (2) the creation of a marketing mix that will satisfy the needs of the chosen target market. A marketing strategy articulates the best use of the firm's resources and tactics to achieve its marketing objectives. It also should match customers' desire for value with the organization's distinctive capabilities. Internal capabilities should be used to maximize external opportunities. The planning process should be guided by a marketing-oriented culture and processes in the organization.[33] A comprehensive strategy involves a thorough search for information, the analysis of many potential courses of action, and the use of specific criteria for making decisions regarding strategy development and implementation.[34] When implemented properly, a good marketing strategy also enables a company to achieve its business-unit and corporate objectives. Although corporate, business-unit, and marketing strategies all overlap to some extent, the marketing strategy is the most detailed and specific of the three.

Target Market Selection

Selecting an appropriate target market may be the most important decision a company has to make in the planning process because the target market must be chosen before the organization can adapt its marketing mix to meet this market's needs and preferences. Defining the target market and developing an appropriate marketing mix are the keys to strategic success. Toyota, for example, targeted its Yaris sedan at 18- to 34-year-olds by striving to give the compact cars a mischievous personality to complement their quirky styling and promoting them wherever Generation Y consumers could be found: MySpace and Facebook, a user-generated-content website, and "mobisodes" (short mobile-phone episodes) of television shows.

Accurate target-market selection is crucial to productive marketing efforts. Products and even companies sometimes fail because marketers do not identify appropriate customer groups at whom to aim their efforts. If a company selects the wrong target market, all other marketing decisions will be a waste of time. Ford Motor, for example, experienced poor sales of its

COURTESY OF L.L. BEAN

Target Market Selection
L.L. Bean targets the outdoor enthusiast with many of its products.

Creating the Marketing Mix
Tropicana has designed a marketing mix (product, price, distribution, and promotion) to satisfy the needs of health-conscious customers.

reintroduced Thunderbird in part because its $35,000 to $40,000 price tag was too steep for the retro-styled convertible's target market of younger baby boomers and older Generation Xers. However, the Thunderbird could not compete with luxury high-performance vehicles such as the BMW Z4 and the Audi TT, which offer greater horsepower and more features.[35] Organizations that try to be all things to all people rarely satisfy the needs of any customer group very well. An organization's management therefore should designate which customer groups the firm is trying to serve and gather adequate information about those customers. Marketers of health-food supplements and diet programs, for example, would be very interested in knowing about consumer attitudes and behaviors related to diet and exercise. A study by ACNielsen identified seven distinct segments based on information from surveys on eating habits, participation in diet plans, exercise habits, and health conditions, as well as consumers' product purchasing history for items such as fruits and vegetables; low-carb, organic, and low-fat foods; and vitamins and supplements.[36] Identification and analysis of a target market provide a foundation on which the firm can develop a marketing mix.

When exploring possible target markets, marketing managers try to evaluate how entering them would affect the company's sales, costs, and profits. Marketing information should be organized to facilitate a focus on the chosen target customers. Accounting and information systems, for example, can be used to track revenues and costs by customer (or group of customers). In addition, managers and employees need to be rewarded for focusing on profitable customers. Teamwork skills can be developed with organizational structures that promote a customer orientation that allows quick responses to changes in the marketing environment.[37] Marketers also should assess whether the company has the resources to develop the right mix of product, price, promotion, and distribution to meet the needs of a particular target market. In addition, they determine if satisfying those needs is consistent with the firm's overall objectives and mission. When Amazon.com, the number one Internet bookseller, began selling electronics on its website, it made the decision that efforts to target this market would increase profits and be consistent with its objectives to be the largest online retailer. The size and number of competitors already marketing products in possible target markets are of concern as well.

Creating the Marketing Mix

The selection of a target market serves as the basis for creating a marketing mix to satisfy the needs of that market. The decisions made in creating a marketing mix are only as good as the organization's understanding of the target market. This understanding typically comes from careful, in-depth research into the characteristics of the target market. Thus, while demographic information is important, the organization also should analyze customer needs, preferences, and behavior with respect to product design, pricing, distribution, and promotion. For example, Kimberly-Clark's marketing researchers found that younger, design-conscious consumers are loath to place a run-of-the-mill box of Kleenex tissue even on top of the toilet. Kimberly-Clark therefore introduced Kleenex Oval Expressions, first as a holiday offering, in a contemporary oval package in bright colors and patterns that is stylish enough to place in more places around the house.[38]

sustainable competitive advantage
An advantage that the competition cannot copy

marketing planning
The process of assessing opportunities and resources, determining objectives, defining strategies, and establishing guidelines for implementation and control of the marketing program

Marketing-mix decisions should have two additional characteristics: consistency and flexibility. All marketing-mix decisions should be consistent with the business-unit and corporate strategies. Such consistency allows the organization to achieve its objectives on all three levels of planning. Flexibility, on the other hand, permits the organization to alter the marketing mix in response to changes in market conditions, competition, and customer needs. Marketing strategy flexibility has a positive influence on organizational performance. Marketing orientation and strategic flexibility complement each other to help the organization manage varying environmental conditions.[39]

The concept of the four marketing-mix variables has stood the test of time, providing marketers with a rich set of questions for the four most important decisions in strategic marketing. Consider the efforts of Harley-Davidson to improve its competitive position. The company worked to improve its product by eliminating oil leaks and other problems and set prices that customers considered fair. The firm used promotional tools to build a community of Harley riders renowned for their camaraderie. Harley-Davidson also fostered strong relationships with the dealers who distribute the company's motorcycles and related products and who reinforce the firm's promotional messages. Even the Internet has not altered the importance of finding the right marketing mix, although it has affected specific marketing-mix elements. Amazon.com, for example, has exploited information technology to facilitate sales promotion by offering product feedback from other customers to help shoppers make a purchase decision.[40]

At the marketing-mix level, a firm can detail how it will achieve a competitive advantage. To gain an advantage, the firm must do something better than its competition. In other words, its products must be of higher quality, its prices must be consistent with the level of quality (value), its distribution methods must be efficient and cost as little as possible, and its promotion must be more effective than the competition's. It is also important that the firm attempt to make these advantages sustainable. A **sustainable competitive advantage** is one that the competition cannot copy. Walmart, for example, maintains a sustainable competitive advantage in groceries over supermarkets because of its very efficient and low-cost distribution system. This allows Walmart to offer lower prices and helped it to gain the largest share of the supermarket business. Maintaining a sustainable competitive advantage requires flexibility in the marketing mix when facing uncertain competitive environments.[41]

Creating the Marketing Plan

A major concern in the strategic planning process is **marketing planning**, the systematic process of assessing marketing opportunities and resources, determining marketing objectives, defining marketing strategies, and establishing guidelines for implementation and control of the

Sustainable Marketing

Spudware... Not Just for Potato Heads

In the United States approximately 39 billion pieces of plastic cutlery are used every year. Many West Coast cities, however, are voting them out of existence because polystyrene containers and plastics are not recyclable or biodegradable. Dozens of cities in California have banned the products, and other cities are debating bans. This is great news for a company called Excellent Packaging & Supply (EPS), a wholesale distributor in bioplastics, biodegradable and compostable tableware derived from plants.

© JONELLE WEAVER/PHOTODISC/GETTY IMAGES

EPS offers restaurants a complete line of biodegradable or compostable items, not just one or two products. SpudWare®, cutlery made from 80 percent potato or corn starch and 20 percent soy or other vegetable oils, made its debut at ESPN's X Games, where thousands of attendees used SpudWare® cutlery along with its other plant-based product lines. All the products were gathered after use in compostable garbage can liners so that they could be composted locally after the event.

SpudWare® was a major breakthrough in the search for a functional and green alternative to plastic cutlery. It is manufactured in China by a number of vendors that market it under different names. The new move toward environmentally friendly products enables companies to thrive with new products that replace older, more harmful products, which is especially useful when legal and social changes create a new strategic window for this new marketing opportunity.[b]

marketing implementation The process of putting marketing strategies into action

intended strategy The strategy the company decides on during the planning phase

realized strategy The strategy that actually takes place

marketing program. The outcome of marketing planning is the development of a marketing plan. As noted earlier, a marketing plan is a written document that outlines and explains all the activities necessary to implement marketing strategies. It describes the firm's current position or situation, establishes marketing objectives for the product or product group, and specifies how the organization will attempt to achieve those objectives.

Developing a clear, well-written marketing plan, though time-consuming, is important. The plan is the basis for internal communication among employees. It covers the assignment of responsibilities and tasks, as well as schedules for implementation. It presents objectives and specifies how resources are to be allocated to achieve those objectives. Finally, it helps marketing managers monitor and evaluate the performance of a marketing strategy.

Marketing planning and implementation are inextricably linked in successful companies. The marketing plan provides a framework to stimulate thinking and provide strategic direction, whereas implementation occurs as an adaptive response to day-to-day issues, opportunities, and unanticipated situations—for example, increasing interest rates or an economic slowdown—that cannot be incorporated into the marketing plan. For example, the worth of an entire American household increased by almost 6 percent a year from 2004–2007, while the real net worth of American households fell by 13 percent in 2008.[42] Implementation-related adaptations directly affect an organization's marketing orientation, rate of growth, and strategic effectiveness.

Organizations use many different formats when devising marketing plans. Plans may be written for SBUs, product lines, individual products or brands, or specific markets. Most plans share some common ground, however, by including many of the same components. Table 2.1 describes the major parts of a typical marketing plan.

Implementing Marketing Strategies

Marketing implementation is the process of executing marketing strategies. Although implementation is often neglected in favor of strategic planning, the implementation process itself can determine whether a marketing strategy succeeds. It is also important to recognize that marketing strategies almost always turn out differently than expected. In essence, all organizations have two types of strategy: intended strategy and realized strategy.[43]

The **intended strategy** is the strategy the organization decided on during the planning phase and wants to use, whereas the **realized strategy** is the strategy that actually takes place. The difference between the two is often the result of how the intended strategy is implemented. When Japanese fast-food restaurants were first introduced in the United States, they were generally located in food courts. However, Japanese- and Asian-fare fast-food chains such as Yoshinoya and Hibachi-San Japanese Grill are growing at three times the rate of other fast-food restaurants in the United States. Yoshinoya is Japan's largest beef-bowl restaurant franchise and has benefitted from increasing numbers of global consumers seeking filling, tasty, budget-conscious meals.[44] The realized strategy may live up to planners' expectations or turn out differently than expected.

Entrepreneurial Marketing

Marketing Entrepreneurs

Have you ever wondered how Crocs became such a popular trend? Three friends from Boulder, Colorado got the idea from a Canadian company making boating shoes. They purchased the company, Foam Creations, that created the original clogs and began marketing and distributing the products in the United States under the Crocs brand. The shoes are made of Crosslite™, a proprietary closed-cell resin that makes them antimicrobial, lightweight, and odor-resistant while providing flexibility and support. Despite an initial lack of funding and the derision of many (not everyone thinks they are fashionable), the multicolored Crocs—with their vent holes and lightweight, skid-resistant, nonmarking soles—quickly became a global phenomenon.[c]

CUSTOMER RELATIONSHIP MANAGEMENT

Customer relationship management (CRM) focuses on using information about customers to create marketing

TABLE 2.1 **Components of the Marketing Plan**

Plan Component	Component Summary	Highlights
Executive summary	One- to two-stage synopsis of the entire marketing plan	
Environmental analysis	Information about the company's current situation with respect to the marketing environment	1. Assessment of marketing environment factors 2. Assessment of target market(s) 3. Assessment of current marketing objectives and performance
SWOT analysis	Assessment of the organization's strengths, weaknesses, opportunities, and threats	1. Strengths 2. Weaknesses 3. Opportunities 4. Threats
Marketing objectives	Specification of the firm's marketing objectives	Qualitative measures of what is to be accomplished
Marketing strategies	Outline of how the firm will achieve its objectives	1. Target market(s) 2. Marketing mix
Marketing implementation	Outline of how the firm will implement its marketing strategies	1. Marketing organization 2. Activities and responsibilities 3. Implementation timetable
Evaluation and control	Explanation of how the firm will measure and evaluate the results of the implemented plan	1. Performance standards 2. Financial controls 3. Monitoring procedures (audits)

Source: VALS/Mediamark Research, Inc., survey, SRI Consulting Business Intelligence, www.sric-bi.com/VALS. Reprinted with permission.

strategies that develop and sustain desirable long-term customer relationships. Relationship-building efforts have been shown to increase customer value.[45] CRM strives to build satisfying exchange relationships between buyers and sellers by gathering useful data at all customer-contact points—telephone, fax, Internet, and personal—and analyzing those data to better understand customers' needs, desires, and habits. It focuses on analyzing and using databases and leveraging technologies to identify strategies and methods that will maximize the lifetime value of each desirable customer to the firm.[46] It is imperative that marketers attempt to learn about their customers' expectations in order to satisfy them, for failure to do so can lead to customer dissatisfaction and defection.[47]

CRM technologies enable marketers to identify specific customers, establish interactive dialogues with them to learn about their needs, and combine this information with their purchase histories to customize products to meet those needs. Like many online retailers, Amazon.com stores and analyzes purchase data to understand each customer's interests. This information helps the retailer improve its ability to satisfy individual customers and thereby increase sales of books, music, movies, and other products to each customer. The ability to identify individual customers allows marketers to shift their focus from targeting groups of similar customers to increasing their share of an individual customer's purchases. Thus, the emphasis shifts from *share of market* to *share of customer*.

Focusing on share of customer requires recognizing that all customers have different needs and that all customers do not have equal value to a firm. CRM technologies help marketers analyze individual customers' purchases and identify the most profitable and loyal customers. The most basic application of this idea is the 80/20 rule: 80 percent of business profits come from 20 percent of customers. The goal is to assess the worth of individual customers and thus estimate their lifetime value to the firm. The concept of *customer lifetime value* (CLV) may include not only an individual's propensity to engage in purchases but also his or her strong word-of-mouth communication about the firm's products.[48] Some customers—those who require considerable hand-holding or who return products frequently—may simply be too expensive to retain given the low level of profits they generate. Companies can discourage these unprofitable customers by requiring them to pay higher fees for additional services.

CLV is a key measurement that forecasts a customer's lifetime economic contribution based on continued relationship marketing efforts. It can be calculated by taking the sum of the customer's present value contributions to profit margins over a specific timeframe. For example, the lifetime value of a Lexus customer could be predicted by how many new automobiles Lexus could sell the customer over a period of years and developing a summation of the contribution to margins across the time period. While this is not an exact science, knowing a customer's potential lifetime value can help marketers determine how best to allocate resources to marketing strategies to sustain that customer over a lifetime.

APPROACHES TO MARKETING IMPLEMENTATION

Just as organizations can achieve their goals by using different marketing strategies, they can implement their marketing strategies by using different approaches. In this section we discuss two general approaches to marketing implementation: internal marketing and total quality management. Both approaches represent mindsets that marketing managers may adopt when organizing and planning marketing activities. These approaches are not mutually exclusive; indeed, many companies adopt both when designing marketing activities.

Internal Marketing

External customers are the individuals who patronize a business—the familiar definition of customers—whereas **internal customers** are the company's employees. For implementation to succeed, the needs of both groups of customers must be addressed. If internal customers are not satisfied, it is likely that external customers will not be either. Thus, in addition to targeting marketing activities at external customers, a firm uses internal marketing to attract, motivate, and retain qualified internal customers by designing internal products (jobs) that satisfy their wants and needs. **Internal marketing** is a management philosophy that coordinates internal exchanges between the organization and its employees to achieve successful external exchanges between the organization and its customers. Internal marketing is a process through which leaders instill in employees a sense of oneness with the organization. Middle managers are especially important in creating the foundation for internal marketing.[49]

Generally speaking, internal marketing refers to the managerial actions necessary to make all members of the marketing organization understand and accept their respective roles in implementing the marketing strategy. Thus marketing managers need to focus internally on employees as well as externally on customers.[50] This means that all employees, from the president of the company down to the hourly workers on the shop floor, must understand the role they play in carrying out their jobs and implementing the marketing strategy. At Starbucks, all employees get training and support, including health care benefits, and this fosters an organizational culture founded on product quality and environmental concern. In short, anyone invested in the firm, both marketers and those who perform other functions, must recognize the tenet of customer orientation and service that underlies the marketing concept.

As with external marketing activities, internal marketing may involve market segmentation, product development, research, distribution, and even public relations and sales promotion.[51] For instance, an organization may sponsor sales contests to inspire sales personnel to boost their selling efforts. While it has been estimated that two-thirds of companies use sales

external customers
Individuals who patronize a business

internal customers
A company's employees

internal marketing
Coordinating internal exchanges between the firm and its employees to achieve successful external exchanges between the firm and its customers

contests, incentives can vary widely. Most contests offer financial rewards, although one IBM sales manager offered recognition with a free lunch as the reward.[52] Such efforts help employees (and ultimately the company) to understand customers' needs and problems, teach them valuable new skills, and heighten their enthusiasm for their regular jobs. In addition, many companies use planning sessions, websites, workshops, letters, formal reports, and personal conversations to ensure that employees comprehend the corporate mission, the organization's goals, and the marketing strategy. The ultimate results are more satisfied employees and improved customer relations.

IMAGE COURTESY OF THE ADVERTISING ARCHIVES

Total Quality Management
Sony utilizes total quality management in the production of its consumer electronics.

Total Quality Management

Quality has become a major concern in many organizations, particularly in light of intense foreign competition, more demanding customers, and poorer profit performance owing to reduced market share and higher costs. To regain a competitive edge, a number of firms have adopted a total quality management approach. **Total quality management (TQM)** is a philosophy that uniform commitment to quality in all areas of the organization will promote a culture that meets customers' perceptions of quality. Indeed, research has shown that both quality orientation and marketing orientation are sources of superior performance.[53] TQM involves coordinating efforts to improve customer satisfaction, increase employee participation and empowerment, form and strengthen supplier partnerships, and facilitate an organizational culture of continuous quality improvement. TQM requires continuous quality improvement and employee empowerment.

Continuous improvement of an organization's goods and services is built around the notion that quality is free; by contrast, *not* having high-quality goods and services can be very expensive, especially in terms of dissatisfied customers.[54] A primary tool of the continuous improvement process is **benchmarking**, the measuring and evaluating of the quality of the organization's goods, services, or processes as compared with the quality produced by the best-performing companies in the industry.[55] Benchmarking fosters organizational "learning" by helping firms to identify and enhance valuable marketing capabilities.[56] It also helps an organization to assess where it stands competitively in its industry, thus giving it a goal to aim for over time.

Ultimately, TQM succeeds or fails because of the efforts of the organization's employees. Thus employee recruitment, selection, and training are critical to the success of marketing implementation. **Empowerment** gives customer-contact employees the authority and responsibility to make marketing decisions without seeking the approval of their supervisors.[57] Although employees at any level in an organization can be empowered to make decisions, empowerment is used most often at the front line, where employees interact daily with customers.

One characteristic of empowerment is that employees can perform their jobs the way they see fit, as long as their methods and outcomes are consistent with the organization's mission. However, empowering employees is successful only if the organization is guided by an overall corporate vision, shared goals, and a culture that supports the TQM effort.[58] For example, Ritz-Carlton hotels give each customer-contact employee permission to take care of customer needs as he or she observes issues. A great deal of time, effort, and patience are needed to develop and sustain a quality-oriented culture in an organization.

total quality management (TQM) A philosophy that uniform commitment to quality in all areas of the organization will promote a culture that meets customers' perceptions of quality

benchmarking Comparing the quality of the firm's goods, services, or processes with that of the best-performing competitors

empowerment Giving customer-contact employees authority and responsibility to make marketing decisions on their own

ORGANIZING MARKETING ACTIVITIES

The structure and relationships of a marketing unit, including lines of authority and responsibility that connect and coordinate individuals, strongly affect marketing activities. Firms that truly adopt the marketing concept develop a distinct organizational culture: a culture based on a shared set of beliefs that makes the customer's needs the pivotal point of the firm's decisions about strategy and operations.[59] Instead of developing products in a vacuum and then trying to persuade customers to purchase them, companies using the marketing concept begin with an orientation toward their customers' needs and desires. Recreational Equipment, Inc. (REI), for example, gives customers a chance to try out sporting goods in conditions that approximate how the products actually will be used. Customers can try out hiking boots on a simulated hiking path with a variety of trail surfaces and inclines or test climbing gear on an indoor climbing wall. In addition, REI offers clinics to customers, such as "Rock Climbing Basics," "Basic Backpacking," and "REI's Outdoor School."[60]

If the marketing concept serves as a guiding philosophy, the marketing unit will be closely coordinated with other functional areas, such as production, finance, and human resources. Marketing must interact with other departments in a number of key areas. It needs to work with manufacturing in determining the volume and variety of the company's products. Those in charge of production rely on marketers for accurate sales forecasts. Research and development departments depend heavily on information gathered by marketers about product features and benefits consumers desire. Decisions made by the physical distribution department hinge on information about the urgency of delivery schedules and cost/service tradeoffs. Information technology is often a crucial ingredient in managing customer relationships effectively, but successful customer relationship management (CRM) programs must include every department involved in customer relations.[61]

How effectively a firm's marketing management can plan and implement marketing strategies also depends on how the marketing unit is organized. Organizing marketing activities in ways that mesh with a firm's strategic marketing approach enhances performance.[62] Effective organizational planning can give the firm a competitive advantage. The organizational structure of a marketing department establishes the authority relationships among marketing personnel and specifies who is responsible for making certain decisions and performing particular activities. This internal structure helps direct marketing activities. The marketing department's ability to develop connections with customers increases the marketing orientation of the firm and is positively correlated to the firm's performance.[63]

One crucial decision regarding structural authority is centralization versus decentralization. In a **centralized organization**, top-level managers delegate very little authority to lower levels. In a **decentralized organization**, decision-making authority is delegated as far down the chain of command as possible. The decision to centralize or decentralize the organization directly affects marketing. Most traditional organizations are highly centralized. In these organizations, most, if not all, marketing decisions are made at the top levels. However, as organizations become more marketing oriented, centralized decision-making proves somewhat ineffective. In these organizations, decentralized authority allows the company to respond to customer needs more quickly.

centralized organization
A structure in which top management delegates little authority to levels below it

decentralized organization
A structure in which decision-making authority is delegated as far down the chain of command as possible

No single approach to organizing a marketing unit works equally well in all businesses. The best approach or approaches depends on the number and diversity of the firm's products, the characteristics and needs of the people in the target market, and many other factors. A marketing unit can be organized according to (1) functions, (2) products, (3) regions, or (4) types of customers. Firms often use some combination of these organizational approaches. Product features may dictate that the marketing unit be structured by products, whereas customer characteristics may require that it be organized by geographic region or types of customers. By using more than one type of structure, a flexible marketing unit can develop and implement marketing plans to match customers' needs precisely.

Organizing by Functions

Some marketing departments are organized by general marketing functions, such as marketing research, product development, distribution, sales, advertising, and customer relations. The personnel who direct these functions report directly to the top-level marketing executive. This structure is fairly common because it works well for some businesses with centralized marketing operations, such as Ford and General Motors. In more decentralized firms, such as grocery store chains, functional organization can cause serious coordination problems. However, the functional approach may suit a large, centralized company whose products and customers are neither numerous nor diverse.

Organizing by Type of Customer
Marketing is often organized by type of customer, as seen in this SAS ad targeting a specific type of business customer.

Organizing by Products

An organization that produces and markets diverse products may find the functional approach inadequate. The decisions and problems related to a single marketing function for one product may be quite different from those related to the same marketing function for another product. As a result, businesses that produce diverse products sometimes organize their marketing units according to product groups. Organizing by product groups gives a firm the flexibility to develop special marketing mixes for different products. Procter & Gamble, like many firms in the consumer packaged goods industry, is organized by product group. Although organizing by products allows a company to remain flexible, this approach can be rather expensive unless efficient categories of products are grouped together to reduce duplication and improve coordination of product management.

Organizing by Regions

A large company that markets products nationally (or internationally) may organize its marketing activities by geographic regions. Managers of marketing functions for each region report to their regional marketing manager; all the regional marketing managers report directly to the executive marketing manager. Frito-Lay, for example, is organized into four regional divisions, allowing the company to get closer to its customers and respond more quickly and efficiently to regional competitors. This form of organization is especially effective for a firm whose customers' characteristics and needs vary greatly from one region to another. Firms that try to penetrate the national market intensively may divide regions into subregions.

Organizing by Types of Customers

Sometimes a company's marketing unit is organized according to types of customers. This form of internal organization works well for a firm that has several groups of customers whose needs and problems differ significantly. For example, Home Depot targets home builders and contractors as well as do-it-yourself customers and consumers who desire installation and service. Retailers may want more rapid delivery of small shipments and more personal selling by the producer than do either wholesalers or institutional buyers. Because the marketing decisions and activities required for these two groups of customers differ considerably, the company may find it efficient to organize its marketing unit by types of customers.

CONTROLLING MARKETING ACTIVITIES

To achieve both marketing and general organizational objectives, marketing managers must control marketing efforts effectively. The **marketing control process** consists of establishing performance standards, evaluating actual performance by comparing it with established standards, and reducing the differences between desired and actual performance.

marketing control process
Establishing performance standards and trying to match actual performance to those standards

Although the control function is a fundamental management activity, it has received little attention in marketing. Organizations have both formal and informal control systems. The formal marketing control process, as mentioned before, involves performance standards, evaluation of actual performance, and corrective action to remedy shortfalls (see Figure 2.6). The informal control process involves self-control, social or group control, and cultural control through acceptance of a firm's value system. Which type of control system dominates depends on the environmental context of the firm.[64] We now discuss these steps in the formal control process and consider the major problems they involve.

Establishing Performance Standards

Planning and controlling are closely linked because plans include statements about what is to be accomplished. For purposes of control, these statements function as performance standards. A **performance standard** is an expected level of performance against which actual performance can be compared. A performance standard might be a reduction of customers' complaints by 20 percent, a monthly sales quota of $150,000, or a 10 percent increase per month in new-customer accounts. Toyota, for example, had a global sales goal of selling 400,000 hybrid cars in 2010, with an objective of 180,000 Prius sales in the United States. If only 350,000 Prius units were sold globally in 2010, this means the company did not meet its sales objective.[65] As stated earlier, performance standards should be tied to organizational goals.

performance standard An expected level of performance

Evaluating Actual Performance

To compare actual performance with performance standards, marketing managers must know what employees within the company are doing and have information about the activities of external organizations that provide the firm with marketing assistance. For example, Porsche, like many automakers, evaluates its product and service levels by how well it ranks on the J.D. Power and Associates Customer Service Index. J.D. Power ranked Porsche as the highest rated automobile brand in overall quality in 2008. This rating could be used in advertising and sales activities.[66] Records of actual performance are compared with performance standards to determine whether and how much of a discrepancy exists. For example, if Toyota determines that only 162,000 Prius were sold in 2008, a discrepancy exists because its goal for the Prius was 175,000 vehicles sold annually.

FIGURE 2.6 The Marketing Control Process

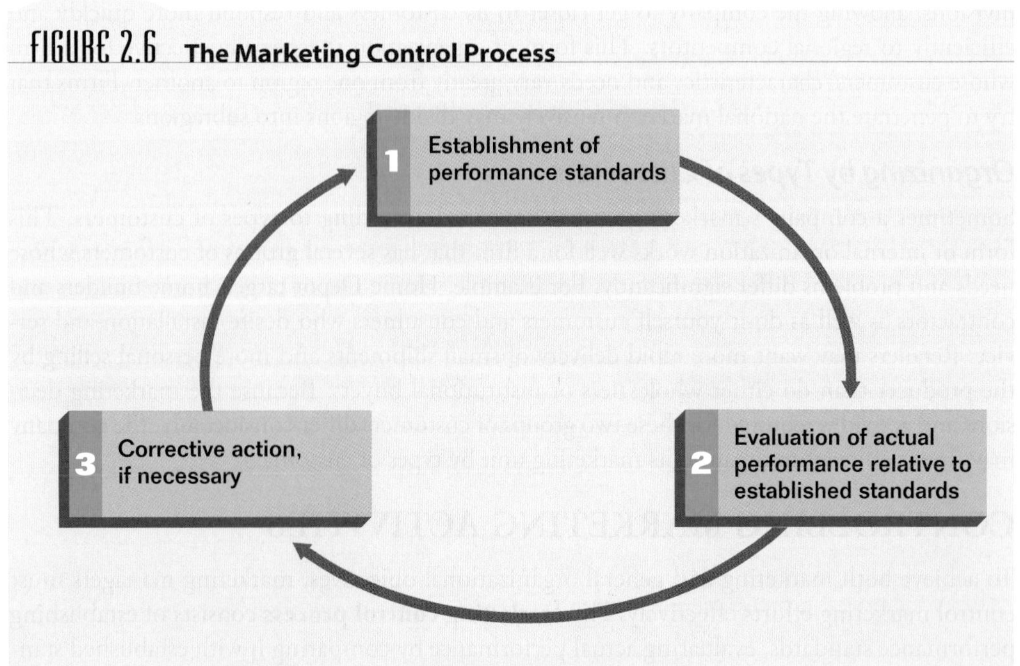

Taking Corrective Action

Marketing managers have several options for reducing a discrepancy between established performance standards and actual performance. They can take steps to improve actual performance, reduce or totally change the performance standard, or do both. When seeking to understand a reduction in the purchases of razor blades in the United States, Gillette found that reduced shaving frequency and better, more durable products were the cause. Gillette had to alter its sales objectives and used advertising public relations to try to increase sales.[67] To improve actual performance, the marketing manager may have to use better methods of motivating marketing personnel or find more effective techniques for coordinating marketing efforts.

SNAPSHOT

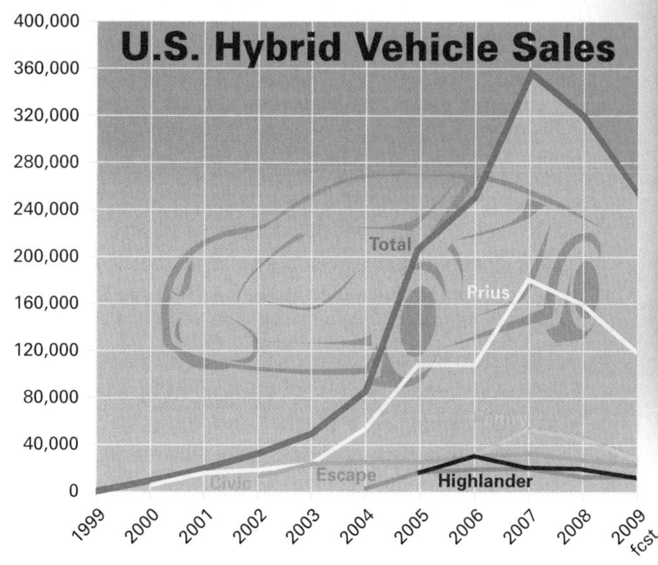

Fuel-efficient vehicles lose some appeal when gasoline prices are low

Source: Dashboard, Hybrid Pickups Arrive, www.hybridcars.com/hybrid-sales-dashboard/march-2009-dashboard-did-hybrid-sales-bottom-out-25712.html (accessed April 22, 2009).

Problems in Controlling Marketing Activities

In their efforts to control marketing activities, marketing managers frequently run into several problems. Often the information required to control marketing activities is unavailable or is available only at a high cost. Even though marketing controls should be flexible enough to allow for environmental changes, the frequency, intensity, and unpredictability of such changes may hamper control. In addition, the time lag between marketing activities and their results limits a marketing manager's ability to measure the effectiveness of specific marketing activities. This is especially true for all advertising activities.

Because marketing and other business activities overlap, marketing managers often cannot determine the precise costs of marketing activities. Without an accurate measure of marketing costs, it is difficult to know if the outcome of marketing activities is worth the expense. Finally, marketing control may be difficult because it is very hard to develop exact performance standards for marketing personnel.

CHAPTER REVIEW

OBJECTIVES

1 Describe the strategic planning process.

Through the process of strategic planning, a firm identifies or establishes its organizational mission and goals, corporate strategy, marketing goals and objectives, marketing strategy, and marketing plan. To achieve its marketing objectives, an organization must develop a marketing strategy, which includes identifying a target market and developing a plan of action for developing, distributing, promoting, and pricing products that meets the needs of customers in that target market. Customer relationship management (CRM) focuses on using information about customers to create marketing strategies that develop and sustain desirable customer relationships. By increasing customer value over time, organizations try to retain and increase long-term profitability through customer loyalty. The strategic planning process ultimately yields the framework for a marketing plan, which is a written document that specifies the activities to be performed for implementing and controlling an organization's marketing activities.

② Explain how organizational resources and opportunities affect the planning process.

The marketing environment, including competitive, economic, political, legal and regulatory, technological, and sociocultural forces, can affect the resources a firm can acquire and create favorable opportunities. Resources may include core competencies, which are things that a firm does extremely well, sometimes so well that it gives the company an advantage over its competition. When the right combination of circumstances and timing permits an organization to take action toward reaching a particular target market, a market opportunity exists. Strategic windows are temporary periods of optimal fit between the key requirements of a market and the particular capabilities of a firm competing in that market. When a company matches a core competency to opportunities it has discovered in the marketplace, it is said to have a competitive advantage.

③ Understand the role of the mission statement in strategic planning.

An organization's goals should be derived from its mission statement, which is a long-term view, or vision, of what the organization wants to become. A well-formulated mission statement helps to give an organization a clear purpose and direction, distinguish it from competitors, provide direction for strategic planning, and foster a focus on customers. An organization's goals and objectives, which focus on the end results sought, guide the remainder of its planning efforts.

④ Examine corporate, business-unit, and marketing strategies.

Corporate strategy determines the means for using resources in the areas of production, finance, research and development, human resources, and marketing to reach the organization's goals. Business-unit strategy focuses on strategic business units (SBUs)—divisions, product lines, or other profit centers within the parent company used to define areas for consideration in a specific strategic market plan. The Boston Consulting Group's market-growth/market-share matrix integrates a firm's products or SBUs into a single, overall matrix for evaluation to determine appropriate strategies for individual products and business units. Marketing strategies, the most detailed and specific of the three levels of strategy, are composed of two elements: selection of a target market and creation of a marketing mix that will satisfy the needs of the chosen target market. The selection of a target market serves as the basis for creation of the marketing mix to satisfy the needs of that market. Marketing-mix decisions also should be consistent with business-unit and corporate strategies and be flexible enough to respond to changes in market conditions, competition, and customer needs. Different elements of the marketing mix can be changed to accommodate different marketing strategies.

⑤ Understand the process of creating the marketing plan.

The outcome of marketing planning is the development of a marketing plan, which outlines all the activities necessary to implement marketing strategies. The plan fosters communication among employees, assigns responsibilities and schedules, specifies how resources are to be allocated to achieve objectives, and helps marketing managers monitor and evaluate the performance of a marketing strategy.

⑥ Describe the marketing implementation process and the major approaches to marketing implementation.

Marketing implementation is the process of executing marketing strategies. Marketing strategies do not always turn out as expected. Realized marketing strategies often differ from the intended strategies because of issues related to implementation. Proper implementation requires efficient organizational structures and effective control and evaluation.

One major approach to marketing implementation is internal marketing, a management philosophy that coordinates internal exchanges between the organization and its employees to achieve successful external exchanges between the organization and its customers. For strategy implementation to be successful, the needs of both internal and external customers must be met. Another approach is total quality management (TQM), which relies heavily on the talents of employees to improve continually the quality of the organization's goods and services.

Please visit the student website at www.cengage.com/international for quizzes and games that will help you prepare for exams and achieve the grade you want.

KEY CONCEPTS

strategic planning
marketing strategy
marketing plan
core competencies
market opportunity
strategic windows
competitive advantage
SWOT analysis
mission statement
marketing objective
corporate strategy
strategic business unit (SBU)
market
market share
market-growth/market-share matrix
sustainable competitive advantage
marketing planning
marketing implementation
intended strategy
realized strategy
external customers
internal customers
internal marketing
total quality management (TQM)
benchmarking
empowerment
centralized organization
decentralized organization
marketing control process
performance standard

ISSUES FOR DISCUSSION AND REVIEW

1. Identify the major components of strategic planning, and explain how they are interrelated.
2. What are the two major parts of a marketing strategy?
3. What are some issues to consider in analyzing a firm's resources and opportunities? How do these issues affect marketing objectives and marketing strategy?
4. How important is SWOT analysis to the marketing planning process?
5. How should organizations set marketing objectives?
6. Explain how an organization can create a competitive advantage at the corporate, business-unit, and marketing-strategy levels.
7. Refer to question 6. How can an organization make its competitive advantages sustainable over time? How difficult is it to create sustainable competitive advantages?
8. What benefits do marketing managers gain from planning? Is planning necessary for long-run survival? Why or why not?
9. Why does an organization's intended strategy often differ from its realized strategy?
10. Why might an organization use multiple bases for organizing its marketing unit?
11. What are the major steps of the marketing control process?

MARKETING APPLICATIONS

1. Contact three organizations that appear to be successful. Talk with one of the managers or executives in the company, and ask if he or she would share with you the company's mission statement or organizational goals. Obtain as much information as possible about the statement and the organizational goals. Discuss how the statement matches the criteria outlined in the text.
2. Assume that you own a new family-style restaurant that will open for business in the coming year. Formulate a long-term goal for the company, and then develop short-term goals that will assist you in achieving the long-term goal.

3. Amazon.com identified an opportunity to capitalize on a desire of many consumers to shop at home. This strategic window gave Amazon.com a very competitive position in a new market. Consider the opportunities that may be present in your city, region, or the United States as a whole. Identify a strategic window, and discuss how a company could take advantage of this opportunity. What kind of core competencies are necessary?

4. Marketing units may be organized according to functions, products, regions, or types of customers. Describe how you would organize the marketing units for the following:
   a. Toothpaste with whitener; toothpaste with extra-strong nicotine cleaners; toothpaste with bubble-gum flavor
   b. A national line offering all types of winter and summer sports clothing for men and women
   c. A life insurance company that provides life, health, and disability insurance

ONLINE EXERCISE

5. Internet analysts have praised Sony's website as one of the best organized and most informative on the Internet. See why by accessing http://www.sony.com.
   a. Based on the information provided at the website, describe Sony's strategic business units.
   b. Based on your existing knowledge of Sony as an innovative leader in the consumer electronics industry, describe the company's primary competitive advantage. How does Sony's website support this competitive advantage?
   c. Assess the quality and effectiveness of Sony's website. Specifically, perform a preliminary SWOT analysis comparing Sony's website with other high-quality websites you have visited.

DEVELOPING YOUR MARKETING PLAN

One of the foundations of a successful marketing strategy is a thorough analysis of your company. To make the best decisions about what products to offer, which markets to target, and how to reach them, you need to know more about your company's strengths and weaknesses. The information collected in this analysis should be referenced when making many of the decisions in your marketing plan. When thinking about writing the beginning of your plan, the information in this chapter can help you with the following issues:

1. Can you identify the core competencies of your company? Do they currently contribute to a competitive advantage? If not, what changes could your company make in order to establish a competitive advantage?

2. Conduct a SWOT analysis of your company in order to identify its strengths and weaknesses. Continue your analysis to include the business environment, discovering any opportunities that exist, or threats that may impact your company.

3. Using the information from your SWOT analysis, have you identified any opportunities that are a good match with your company's core competencies? Likewise, have you discovered any weaknesses that could be converted to strengths through careful marketing planning?

The information obtained from these questions should assist you in developing various aspects of your marketing plan found in the *Interactive Marketing Plan* exercise.

VIDEO CASE 2

Green Mountain Coffee Roasters Brews Up the Best Market Strategy

Green Mountain Coffee Roasters, Inc., is a leader in the specialty coffee industry. Founded in 1981 as a small café in Waitsfield, Vermont, Green Mountain quickly gained a reputation for its high quality, and demand for its freshly roasted coffee grew among local restaurants and inns. Incorporated in 1993, the firm today markets more than $342 million worth of coffee and related products through a coordinated multichannel distribution network with both wholesale and direct-to-consumer operations. This distribution network is designed to maximize brand recognition and product availability.

Green Mountain derives the majority of its revenue from more than 8,000 wholesale customer accounts located primarily in the eastern United States. The wholesale operation serves customers such as supermarkets, specialty food stores, convenience stores, food service companies, hotels, restaurants, universities, and office coffee services. Many of these wholesale customers then resell the coffee in whole bean or ground form for home consumption or brew and sell coffee beverages at their places of business.

Green Mountain Coffee roasts 100 varieties of high-quality Arabica coffee beans and offers more than 100 selections of coffee such as single-origin, estate, and certified organic coffee, as well as proprietary blends and flavored coffees sold under the Green Mountain Coffee Roasters and Newman's Own Organics brand names. It has made a point of marketing certified Fair Trade™ coffees that help struggling coffee farmers earn fair market value for their efforts. It carefully selects its coffee beans and then roasts them to maximize their taste and flavor differences. Green Mountain Coffee is delivered in a variety of packages, including whole bean, fractional packages, and premium one-cup coffee pods.

Green Mountain's objective is to be the leading specialty coffee company. It aims to achieve the highest market share in its target markets while maximizing company values. To meet these objectives, Green Mountain differentiates and reinforces the Green Mountain Coffee brand by distributing only the highest-quality products, providing superior customer service and distribution, stressing corporate governance and employee development, and implementing socially responsible business practices. Through these strategies, Green Mountain believes it engenders a high degree of customer loyalty.

The company employs 849 people but has a flat organizational structure, which makes all employees responsible for implementation. Although it has functional departments that vary across the company, there are typically about four layers of hierarchy in each department. There is openness in all aspects of communication that allows employees to have regular access to all levels of the organization, including CEO Bob Stiller. The company urges each employee to voice his or her opinions and ideas. This encourages passion and commitment so employees can get to the heart of issues and challenges instead of playing office politics. In this way, Green Mountain has fostered a culture that involves its workers in decision making and challenges them to find solutions to problems. Empowering employees to this degree means that the company may sometimes appear chaotic, but the communication across channels in what is sometimes termed a "constellation of communication" ensures the collaborative nature of getting things done.

In addition to growing sales and a reputation for quality, Green Mountain Coffee Roasters has been ranked among *Forbes* magazine's list of 200 Best Small Companies in America for seven out of eight years. The company's commitment to social responsibility—not only to secure fair trade prices for coffee growers but also its support of social and environmental programs in coffee-growing regions—earned it a first place on *Business Ethics* magazine's annual list of 100 Best Corporate Citizens in 2007 for the second year in a row.

QUESTIONS FOR DISCUSSION

1. Describe Green Mountain's marketing strategy.
2. How does Green Mountain use implementation to achieve success in a very competitive market?
3. How does empowerment work at Green Mountain?

"100 Best Corporate Citizens 2007," Business Ethics, www.business-ethics.com/node/75 (accessed Jan. 2, 2008); "200 Best Small Companies in America," Forbes, Oct. 11, 2007, www.forbes.com/2007/10/11/best-small-companies-biz-07200best-cz_jg_cs_1011bestsmall_land.html; Green Mountain Coffee, www.greenmountaincoffee.com (accessed Jan. 2, 2008); Green Mountain Coffee Annual Report 10-K; "Green Mountain Coffee Roasters," Hoover's Online, www.hoovers.com/green-mountain-coffee/—ID__45721—/free-co-factsheet.xhtml (accessed Jan. 2, 2008).

The Marketing Environment, Social Responsibility, and Ethics

CHAPTER 3

© AP IMAGES/CHARLIE RIEDEL

T. Boone Pickens Wants Wind to Replace Oil

The billionaire tycoon T. Boone Pickens is turning his back on the oil that made his fortune and is now focusing on wind power. The Pickens Plan is an example of an entrepreneur responding to a problem, in this case the country's oil dependence. He hopes to build a $10 billion Texas wind farm consisting of 2,700 wind turbines. It would pump renewable energy into the national grid to supply much of the country's energy.

Unfortunately for Pickens, the economic crisis has put some of his plans on delay. Oil prices have fluctuated from over $145 a barrel to as low as $35 a barrel, so demand for alternative means of energy has fallen. Although this is a setback, Pickens maintains that oil prices will rise in the future, once more generating support for his plan.

Despite his emphasis on renewable energy, Pickens doesn't fit the bill of an environmentalist. In fact, he emphasizes that it's all economical. "First thing, it's about the money. . . . I'm not going to do a 4,000-megawatt wind farm for the environment first and money second," Pickens says.

He's also embarking on a new venture, exchanging "black gold" for "blue gold" by attaining billions of dollars in water rights. Pickens is generating controversy by drilling for water in Texas' Ogallala aquifer. Pickens plans to ship 65 billion gallons of water through a 300-mile pipeline requiring about 650 tracts of private property. A recent bill makes it easier for Pickens to acquire the land under eminent domain, which is angering many ranchers whose land might be taken.

OBJECTIVES:

1. Recognize the importance of environmental scanning and analysis.
2. Explore the effects of competitive, economic, political, legal and regulatory, technological, and sociocultural factors on marketing strategies.
3. Understand the concept and dimensions of social responsibility.
4. Differentiate between ethics and social responsibility.

This has led some to question Pickens's motives. Pickens appears to be a die-hard businessman who only cares about the bottom line: money. Yet others believe Pickens holds the key to America's energy problem. Time will tell whether Pickens's plans will push the United States into being self-sufficient in terms of energy.[1]

To succeed in today's highly competitive marketplace, companies must respond to changes in the marketing environment, particularly changes in customer and public desires and competitors' actions. Increasingly, success also requires that marketers act responsibly and ethically. Because recognizing and responding to such changes in the marketing environment are crucial to marketing success, this chapter explores in some detail the forces that contribute to these changes.

The first half of this chapter explores the competitive, economic, political, legal and regulatory, technological, and sociocultural forces that make up the marketing environment. This discussion addresses the importance of scanning and analyzing the marketing environment, as well as how each of these forces influences marketing strategy decisions. The second half of the chapter considers the role of social responsibility and ethics. These increasingly important forces raise several issues that pose threats and opportunities to marketers, such as the natural environment and consumerism.

The Marketing Environment

The marketing environment consists of external forces that directly or indirectly influence an organization's acquisition of inputs (human, financial, natural resources and raw materials, and information) and creation of outputs (goods, services, or ideas). As indicated in Chapter 1, the marketing environment includes six such forces: competitive, economic, political, legal and regulatory, technological, and sociocultural.

Whether fluctuating rapidly or slowly, environmental forces are always dynamic. Changes in the marketing environment create uncertainty, threats, and opportunities for marketers. Consider how dramatic changes in oil prices can change consumer purchasing behavior. In 2008, oil spiked to $147 a barrel, only to drop to $35 a barrel in early 2009. After oil prices fell sharply, hybrid car sales dropped because the added cost of purchasing a hybrid could not be recovered as quickly through savings on gasoline. However, fears of future rising gas prices and incentives such as tax credits have helped hybrid car sales remain healthier than for larger vehicles like Hummers and trucks.[2] Marketing managers who fail to recognize changes in environmental forces leave their firms unprepared to capitalize on marketing opportunities or to cope with threats created by changes in the environment. Monitoring the environment therefore is crucial to an organization's survival and to the long-term achievement of its goals.

To monitor changes in the marketing environment effectively, marketers engage in environmental scanning and analysis. **Environmental scanning** is the process of collecting information about forces in the marketing environment. Scanning involves observation; secondary sources such as business, trade, government, and Internet sources; and marketing research. The Internet has become a popular scanning tool because it makes data more accessible and allows companies to gather needed information quickly.

environmental scanning
The process of collecting information about forces in the marketing environment

Environmental analysis is the process of assessing and interpreting the information gathered through environmental scanning. A manager evaluates the information for accuracy, tries to resolve inconsistencies in the data, and if warranted, assigns significance to the findings. By evaluating this information, the manager should be able to identify potential threats and opportunities linked to environmental changes.

Understanding the current state of the marketing environment and recognizing threats and opportunities arising from changes within it help companies with strategic planning. In particular, they can help marketing managers assess the performance of current marketing efforts and develop future marketing strategies.

IMAGE COURTESY OF THE ADVERTISING ARCHIVES

Responding to Environmental Forces
Ribena juice company demonstrates its commitment to environmental responsibility through its 100% recycled bottles.

RESPONDING TO THE MARKETING ENVIRONMENT

Marketing managers take two general approaches to environmental forces: accepting them as uncontrollable or attempting to influence and shape them.[3] An organization that views environmental forces as uncontrollable remains passive and reactive toward the environment. Instead of trying to influence forces in the environment, its marketing managers adjust current marketing strategies to environmental changes. They approach with caution market opportunities discovered through environmental scanning and analysis. On the other hand, marketing managers who believe that environmental forces can be shaped adopt a more proactive approach. For example, if a market is blocked by traditional environmental constraints, proactive marketing managers may apply economic, psychological, political, and promotional skills to gain access to and operate within it. Once they identify what is blocking a market opportunity, they assess the power of the various parties involved and develop strategies to overcome the obstructing environmental forces. Microsoft, Intel, and Google, for example, have responded to political, legal, and regulatory concerns about their power in the computer industry by communicating the value of their competitive approaches to various publics. The computer giants contend that their competitive success results in superior products for their customers.

A proactive approach can be constructive and bring desired results. To exert influence on environmental forces, marketing managers seek to identify market opportunities or to extract greater benefits relative to costs from existing market opportunities. Political action is another way to affect environmental forces. The pharmaceutical industry, for example, has lobbied very effectively for fewer restrictions on prescription drug marketing. However, managers must recognize that there are limits on how much environmental forces can be shaped. Microsoft, for example, can take a proactive approach because of its financial resources and the highly visible image of its founder, Bill Gates. Although an organization may be able to influence legislation through lobbying, it is unlikely that a single organization can significantly increase the national birthrate or move the economy from recession to prosperity.

COMPETITIVE FORCES

Few firms, if any, operate free of competition. In fact, for most products, customers have many alternatives from which to choose. For example, while the five best-selling soft drinks are Coke Classic, PepsiCola, Diet Coke, Mountain Dew, and Diet Pepsi, soft drink sales in general have flattened as consumers have turned to alternatives such as bottled water, flavored water, fruit

environmental analysis
The process of assessing and interpreting the information gathered through environmental scanning

IMAGE COURTESY OF THE ADVERTISING ARCHIVES

IMAGE COURTESY OF THE ADVERTISING ARCHIVES

Brand and Product Competition
AEG and Bosch compete in the home appliances market.

juice, and iced-tea products.[4] Thus, when marketing managers define the target market(s) their firm will serve, they simultaneously establish a set of competitors.[5] The number of firms that supply a product may affect the strength of competitors. When just one or a few firms control supply, competitive factors exert a different sort of influence on marketing activities than when many competitors exist.

competition
Other firms that market products that are similar to or can be substituted for a firm's products in the same geographic area

brand competitors
Firms that market products with similar features and benefits to the same customers at similar prices

product competitors
Firms that compete in the same product class but market products with different features, benefits, and prices

generic competitors
Firms that provide very different products that solve the same problem or satisfy the same basic customer need

total budget competitors
Firms that compete for the limited financial resources of the same customers

Broadly speaking, all firms compete with one another for customers' dollars. More practically, however, a marketer generally defines **competition** as other firms that market products that are similar to or can be substituted for its products in the same geographic area. These competitors can be classified into one of four types. **Brand competitors** market products with similar features and benefits to the same customers at similar prices. For example, a thirsty, calorie-conscious customer may choose a diet soda such as Diet Coke or Diet Pepsi from the soda machine. However, these sodas face competition from other types of beverages. **Product competitors** compete in the same product class but market products with different features, benefits, and prices. The thirsty dieter, for instance, might purchase iced tea, juice, mineral water, or bottled water instead of a soda. **Generic competitors** provide very different products that solve the same problem or satisfy the same basic customer need. Our dieter, for example, might simply have a glass of water from the kitchen tap to satisfy his or her thirst. **Total budget competitors** compete for the limited financial resources of the same customers.[6] Total budget competitors for Diet Coke, for example, might include gum, a newspaper, and bananas. Although all four types of competition can affect a firm's marketing performance, brand competitors are the most significant because buyers typically see the different products of these firms as direct substitutes for one another. Consequently, marketers tend to concentrate environmental analyses on brand competitors.

When just one or a few firms control supply, competitive factors exert a different form of influence on marketing activities than when many competitors exist. Table 3.1 presents four general types of competitive structures: monopoly, oligopoly, monopolistic competition, and pure competition. A **monopoly** exists when an organization offers a product that has no close substitutes, making that organization the sole source of supply. Because the organization has no competitors, it controls supply of the product completely and, as a single seller, can erect barriers to potential competitors. In reality, most monopolies surviving today are local utilities, which are heavily regulated by local, state, or federal agencies. An **oligopoly** exists when a few sellers control the supply of a large proportion of a product. In

TABLE 3.1 Selected Characteristics of Competitive Structures

Type of Structure	Number of Competitors	Ease of Entry into Market	Product	Example
Monopoly	One	Many barriers	Almost no substitutes	Water utilities
Oligopoly	Few	Some barriers	Homogeneous or differentiated (with real or perceived differences)	Toyota Motors (autos)
Monopolistic competition	Many	Few barriers	Product differentiation, with many substitutes	Wrangler, Levi Strauss (jeans)
Pure competition	Unlimited	No barriers	Homogeneous products	Vegetable farm (sweet corn)

this case each seller considers the reactions of other sellers to changes in marketing activities. Products facing oligopolistic competition may be homogeneous, such as aluminum, or differentiated, such as automobiles. **Monopolistic competition** exists when a firm with many potential competitors attempts to develop a marketing strategy to differentiate its product. For example, Levi Strauss and Wrangler have established an advantage for their blue jeans through well-known trademarks, design, advertising, and a reputation for quality. Wrangler is associated with a cowboy image and is the official jeans of NASCAR driver Dale Earnhardt, Jr. Although many competing brands of blue jeans are available, these firms have carved out market niches by emphasizing differences in their products, especially style and image. **Pure competition**, if it existed at all, would entail a large number of sellers, none of which could significantly influence price or supply. The closest thing to an example of pure competition is an unregulated farmers' market, where local growers gather to sell their produce. Pure competition is an ideal at one end of the continuum; monopoly is at the other end. Most marketers function in a competitive environment somewhere between these two extremes.

Marketers need to monitor the actions of major competitors to determine what specific strategies competitors are using and how those strategies affect their own. Price is one of the marketing strategy variables that most competitors monitor. When Frontier or Southwest Airlines lowers the fare on a route, most major airlines attempt to match the price. Monitoring guides marketers in developing competitive advantages and aids them in adjusting current marketing strategies and planning new ones.

In monitoring competition, it is not enough to analyze available information; the firm must develop a system for gathering ongoing information about competitors. Understanding the market and what customers want, as well as what the competition is providing, will assist in maintaining a marketing orientation.[7] Information about competitors allows marketing managers to assess the performance of their own marketing efforts and to recognize the strengths and weaknesses in their own marketing strategies. Data about market shares, product movement, sales volume, and expenditure levels can be useful. However, accurate information on these matters is often difficult to obtain. We explore how marketers collect and organize such data in Chapter 4.

ECONOMIC FORCES

Economic forces in the marketing environment influence both marketers' and customers' decisions and activities. In this section we examine the effects of buying power and willingness to spend, as well as general economic conditions.

monopoly
A competitive structure in which an organization offers a product that has no close substitutes, making that organization the sole source of supply

oligopoly
A competitive structure in which a few sellers control the supply of a large proportion of a product

monopolistic competition
A competitive structure in which a firm has many potential competitors and tries to develop a marketing strategy to differentiate its product

pure competition
A market structure characterized by an extremely large number of sellers, none strong enough to significantly influence price or supply

Buying Power and Willingness to Spend

The strength of a person's **buying power** depends on economic conditions and the size of the resources—money, goods, and services that can be traded in an exchange—that enable the individual to make purchases. The major financial sources of buying power are income, credit, and wealth.

For an individual, *income* is the amount of money received through wages, rents, investments, pensions, and subsidy payments for a given period, such as a month or a year. Normally, this money is allocated among taxes, spending for goods and services, and savings. Marketers are most interested in the amount of money left after payment of taxes because this **disposable income** is used for spending or saving. Because disposable income is a ready source of buying power, the total amount available in a nation is important to marketers. Several factors determine the size of total disposable income, including the total amount of income—which is affected by wage levels, the rate of unemployment, interest rates, and dividend rates—and the number and amount of taxes. Disposable income that is available for spending and saving after an individual has purchased the basic necessities of food, clothing, and shelter is called **discretionary income**. People use discretionary income to purchase entertainment, vacations, automobiles, education, pets, furniture, appliances, and so on. Changes in total discretionary income affect sales of these products, especially automobiles, furniture, large appliances, and other costly durable goods.

Credit is also important because it enables people to spend future income now or in the near future. However, credit increases current buying power at the expense of future buying power. Several factors determine whether people use or forgo credit. Interest rates affect buyers' decisions to use credit, especially for expensive purchases such as homes, appliances, and automobiles. When interest rates are low, the total cost of automobiles and houses becomes more affordable. In contrast, when interest rates are high, consumers are more likely to delay buying such expensive items. Use of credit is also affected by credit terms, such as size of the down payment and amount and number of monthly payments.

Wealth is the accumulation of past income, natural resources, and financial resources. It exists in many forms, including cash, securities, savings accounts, jewelry, and real estate. The significance of wealth to marketers is that as people become wealthier, they gain buying power in three ways: They can use their wealth to make current purchases, to generate income, and to acquire large amounts of credit.

People's **willingness to spend**—their inclination to buy because of expected satisfaction from a product—is related, to some degree, to their ability to buy. That is, people are sometimes more willing to buy if they have the buying power. However, several other elements also influence willingness to spend. Some elements affect specific products; others influence spending in general. A product's price and value influence almost all of us. Rolex watches, for example, appeal to customers who are willing to spend more for fine timepieces even when lower-priced watches are readily available. In the most recent recession, middle-class consumers were not willing to spend as much on luxury products because of economic uncertainty. Credit was not as available; for example, American Express slashed credit limits and offered $300 payments to select customers to close their troubled accounts.[8] The amount of satisfaction received from a product already owned also may influence customers' desire to buy other products. Satisfaction depends not only on the quality of the currently owned product but also on numerous psychological and social forces. The American Customer Satisfaction Index, computed by the National Quality Research Center at the University of Michigan (see Figure 3.1), offers an indicator of customer satisfaction with a wide variety of businesses. Among other things, the index suggests that if customers become more dissatisfied, they may curtail their overall spending, which could stifle economic growth.[9] Other factors that affect customers' general willingness to spend are expectations about future employment, income levels, prices, family size, and general economic conditions.

buying power
Resources, such as money, goods, and services, that can be traded in an exchange

disposable income
After-tax income

discretionary income
Disposable income available for spending and saving after an individual has purchased the basic necessities of food, clothing, and shelter

willingness to spend
An inclination to buy because of expected satisfaction from a product, influenced by the ability to buy and numerous psychological and social forces

FIGURE 3.1 American Customer Satisfaction Index

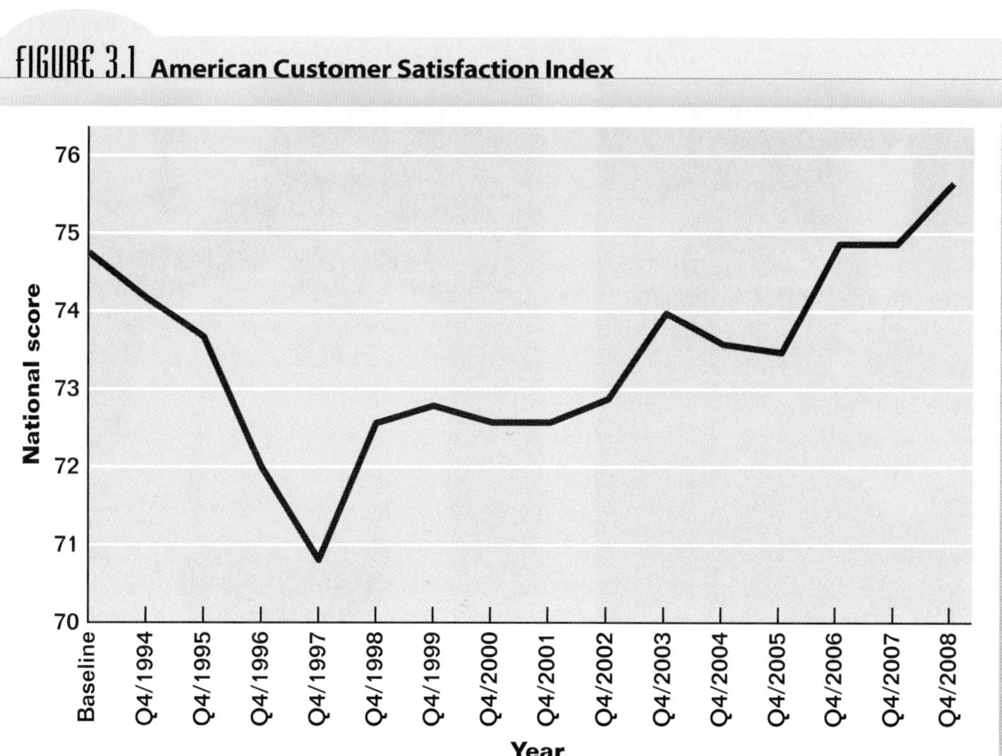

Source: "National Quarterly Scores," American Customer Satisfaction Index, http://www.theacsi.org/index.php?option=com_content&task=view&id=31&Itemid=35 (accessed April 22, 2009).

Economic Conditions

The overall state of the economy fluctuates in all countries. Changes in general economic conditions affect (and are affected by) supply and demand, buying power, willingness to spend, consumer expenditure levels, and the intensity of competitive behavior. Therefore, current economic conditions and changes in the economy have a broad impact on the success of organizations' marketing strategies.

Fluctuations in the economy follow a general pattern, often referred to as the **business cycle**. In the traditional view, the business cycle consists of four stages: prosperity, recession, depression, and recovery. During *prosperity,* unemployment is low, and total income is relatively high. Assuming a low inflation rate, this combination ensures high buying power. During a *recession,* however, unemployment rises, while total buying power declines. Pessimism accompanying a recession often stifles both consumer and business spending. A prolonged recession may become a *depression,* a period in which unemployment is extremely high, wages are very low, total disposable income is at a minimum, and consumers lack confidence in the economy. During *recovery,* the economy moves from depression or recession to prosperity. It is possible to have a recession without a full-blown depression. During this period, high unemployment begins to decline, total disposable income increases, and the economic gloom that reduced consumers' willingness to buy subsides. Both the ability and willingness to buy increase.

The business cycle can enhance the success of marketing strategies. In the prosperity stage, for example, marketers may expand their product offerings to take advantage of increased buying power. They may be able to capture a larger market share by intensifying distribution and promotion efforts. In times of recession or depression, when buying power decreases, many customers may become more price conscious and seek more basic, functional products. During economic downturns, a company should focus its efforts on determining precisely what functions buyers want and ensure that these functions are available in its product offerings. Promotional efforts should emphasize value and utility. Some firms make the mistake of

business cycle
A pattern of economic fluctuations that has four stages: prosperity, recession, depression, and recovery

IMAGE COURTESY OF THE ADVERTISING ARCHIVES

IMAGE COURTESY OF THE ADVERTISING ARCHIVES

Economic Forces
Tag Heuer and Omega rely on consumers with significant discretionary income to purchase their watches.

drastically reducing their marketing efforts during a recession, harming their ability to compete. The United States and most of the world experienced a period of prosperity from 2004–2007. During this time household net worth increased by almost 6 percent a year with rapidly increasing home values, low unemployment, low interest rates, and expanding credit availability. The decision by the government and financial institutions to grant subprime loans (higher interest loans to people with poor credit ratings) triggered the default of these loans and the deepest recession since the Great Depression of the 1930s. In 2008 investors lost $10.2 trillion in stock value and net household worth declined by 13 percent.[10] One out of nine homeowners were struggling to avoid foreclosure of the loans on their houses and over 4.4 million jobs were lost. More than 21 million Americans shifted in 2008–2009 from "thriving" to "struggling," according to a Gallup poll.[11] Americans' financial health declined during the recession with banks and lenders closing a record number of credit card accounts, lowering consumers' credit scores, and reducing credit lines.[12] The government provided trillions of dollars in financing to rescue financial institutions as well as stimulus spending to increase jobs. The result was that luxury retailers and even mid-priced department stores struggled to attract shoppers. On the other hand discounters such as Walmart Stores, Inc., BJ's Wholesale Club, Costco Wholesale Corporation, and fast-food restaurants such as McDonald's saw sales gains.[13] Because of fears of job loss, savings increased and consumers lowered their expectations and trusted that things would get better. Most experts believed that the recovery would be slow and that marketers would have to keep adjusting their strategies to appeal to consumers as recovery developed. The most recent recession illustrates the need to change marketing strategies during the business cycle. Marketers need to remain flexible and make needed adjustments as the various phases of the business cycle change.

POLITICAL FORCES

Political, legal, and regulatory forces of the marketing environment are closely interrelated. Legislation is enacted, legal decisions are interpreted by courts, and regulatory agencies are created and operated, for the most part, by elected or appointed officials. Legislation and regulations (or their lack) reflect the current political outlook. Consequently, the political forces of the marketing environment have the potential to influence marketing decisions and strategies.

Reactive marketers view political forces as beyond their control and simply adjust to conditions arising from those forces. Some firms are more proactive, however, and seek to influence the political process. In some cases organizations publicly protest the actions of legislative bodies. More often organizations help to elect to political offices individuals who regard them positively. Much of this help is in the form of campaign contributions—often in the form of "soft money," which refers to money that is donated to a political party with no specification on how the money will be spent. For example, Citigroup has made corporate donations amounting to tens of millions of dollars over the past 2 decades.[14] Marketers also can influence the political process through political action committees (PACs) that solicit donations from individuals and then contribute those funds to candidates running for political office.

Companies also can participate in the political process through lobbying to persuade public and/or government officials to favor a particular position in decision-making. Many companies concerned about the threat of legislation or regulation that may negatively affect their operations employ lobbyists to communicate their concerns to elected officials. Marketers of cigarettes, for example, spend millions on lobbyists to persuade state and local officials that their governments should not increase taxes on cigarettes, which effectively raises their price to consumers.[15]

Even court decisions can change, making decisions related to the marketing mix variable. For example, a Supreme Court ruling in 2008 allowed manufacturers broader powers to set minimum prices and restrict retailers from discounting—which amounted to price fixing—something that had previously been illegal. Lobbyists and the political activities of firms can influence these decisions.[16]

LEGAL AND REGULATORY FORCES

A number of federal laws influence marketing decisions and activities. Table 3.2 lists some of the most significant pieces of legislation. Regulatory agencies and self-regulatory forces also affect marketing efforts.

Regulatory Agencies

Federal regulatory agencies influence many marketing activities, including product development, pricing, packaging, advertising, personal selling, and distribution. Usually these bodies have the power to enforce specific laws, as well as some discretion in establishing operating rules and regulations to guide certain types of industry practices.

Of all the federal regulatory units, the **Federal Trade Commission (FTC)** influences marketing activities most. Although the FTC regulates a variety of business practices, it allocates considerable resources to curbing false advertising, misleading pricing, and deceptive packaging and labeling. When it receives a complaint or otherwise has reason to believe that a firm is violating a law, the commission issues a complaint stating that the business is in violation. For example, American Telecom Services once sold telephones and telephone services through retailers across the nation, including Office Depot and Staples, but was barred by the Federal Trade Commission (FTC) after failing to provide the rebates it had promised to tens of thousands of customers. The FTC charged the company with deceptive marketing by promising to provide the rebates within two months of customers' submitting the appropriate paperwork.[17] If a company continues the questionable practice, the FTC can issue a cease-and-desist order demanding that the business stop doing whatever caused the complaint. The firm can appeal to the federal courts to have the order rescinded. However, the FTC can seek civil penalties in court, up to a maximum penalty of $10,000 a day for each infraction if a cease-and-desist order is violated. The commission can require companies to run corrective advertising in response to previous ads considered misleading. The FTC also assists businesses in complying with laws, and it evaluates new marketing methods every year.

Federal Trade Commission (FTC)
An agency that regulates a variety of business practices and curbs false advertising, misleading pricing, and deceptive packaging and labeling

TABLE 3.2 Major Federal Laws Affecting Marketing Decisions

Act (Date Enacted)	Purpose
Procompetitive legislation	
Sherman Antitrust Act (1890)	Prohibits contracts, combinations, or conspiracies to restrain trade; calls monopolizing or attempting to monopolize a misdemeanor offense.
Clayton Act (1914)	Prohibits specific practices such as price discrimination, exclusive dealer arrangements, and stock acquisitions in which the effect may notably lessen competition or tend to create a monopoly.
Federal Trade Commission Act (1914)	Created the Federal Trade Commission; also gives the FTC investigatory powers to be used in preventing unfair methods of competition.
Robinson-Patman Act (1936)	Prohibits price discrimination that lessens competition among wholesalers or retailers; prohibits producers from giving disproportionate services of facilities to large buyers.
Wheeler-Lea Act (1938)	Prohibits unfair and deceptive acts and practices, regardless of whether competition is injured; places advertising of foods and drugs under the jurisdiction of the FTC.
Celler-Kefauver Act (1950)	Prohibits any corporation engaged in commerce from acquiring the whole or any part of the stock or other share of the capital assets of another corporation when the effect substantially lessens competition or tends to create a monopoly.
Consumer Goods Pricing Act (1975)	Prohibits the use of price-maintenance agreements among manufacturers and resellers in interstate commerce.
Antitrust Improvements Act (1976)	Requires large corporations to inform federal regulators of prospective mergers or acquisitions so that they can be studied for any possible violations of the law.
Consumer protection legislation	
Pure Food and Drug Act (1906)	Prohibits the adulteration and mislabeling of food and drug products; established the Food and Drug Administration.
Fair Packaging and Labeling Act (1966)	Makes illegal the unfair or deceptive packaging or labeling of consumer products.
Consumer Product Safety Act (1972)	Established the Consumer Product Safety Commission; protects the public against unreasonable risk of injury and death associated with products.
Magnuson-Moss Warranty (FTC) Act (1975)	Provides for minimum disclosure standards for written consumer product warranties; defines minimum consent standards for written warranties; allows the FTC to prescribe interpretive rules in policy statements regarding unfair or deceptive practices.
Nutrition Labeling and Education Act (1990)	Prohibits exaggerated health claims and requires all processed foods to contain labels showing nutritional information.

TABLE 3.2 Major Federal Laws Affecting Marketing Decisions (Continued)

Act (Date Enacted)	Purpose
Telephone Consumer Protection Act (1991)	Establishes procedures to avoid unwanted telephone solicitations; prohibits marketers from using an automated telephone dialing system or an artificial or prerecorded voice to certain telephone lines.
Children's Online Privacy Protection Act (2000)	Regulates the online collection of personally identifiable information (name, mailing address, e-mail address, hobbies, interests, or information collected through cookies) from children under age 13.
Do Not Call Implementation Act (2003)	Directs the Federal Communications Commission (FCC) and the FTC to coordinate so that their rules are consistent regarding telemarketing call practices, including the Do Not Call Registry and other lists, as well as call abandonment.
Trademark and copyright protection legislation	
Lanham Act (1946)	Provides protections and regulation of brand names, brand marks, trade names, and trademarks.
Trademark Law Revision Act (1988)	Amends the Lanham Act to allow brands not yet introduced to be protected through registration with the Patent and Trademark Office.
Federal Trademark Dilution Act (1995)	Gives trademark owners the right to protect trademarks and requires relinquishment of names that match or parallel existing trademarks.
Digital Millennium Copyright Act (1998)	Refines copyright laws to protect digital versions of copyrighted materials, including music and movies.

The FTC required Darden Restaurants, Inc., which owns the Olive Garden and Red Lobster restaurant chains, to restore fees deducted from consumer gift cards and to prominently disclose fees and expiration dates in all advertising for future gift card offers, after the company settled charges that it had engaged in deceptive practices associated with marketing its gift cards. The FTC works to make sure consumers have the facts they need to make smart decisions, no matter what they're buying.[18]

Unlike the FTC, other regulatory units are limited to dealing with specific products, services, or business activities. For example, the Food and Drug Administration (FDA) enforces regulations prohibiting the sale and distribution of adulterated, misbranded, or hazardous food and drug products. The Consumer Product Safety Commission (CPSC) ensures compliance with the Consumer Product Safety Act and protects the public from unreasonable risk of injury from any consumer product not covered by other regulatory agencies.

In addition, all states, as well as many cities and towns, have regulatory agencies that enforce laws and regulations regarding marketing practices within their states or municipalities. State and local regulatory agencies try not to establish regulations that conflict with those of federal regulatory agencies. They generally enforce laws dealing with the production and sale of particular goods and services. Utility, insurance, financial, and liquor industries are commonly regulated by state agencies. Among these agencies' targets are misleading advertising and pricing.

SNAPSHOT

Products That Receive the Most Complaints at the BBB

The Better Business Bureau settled three-fourths of 862,000 complaints in 2008.

Cellphone service/supplies	35,631
New car dealers	26,723
Banks	20,935
Internet retailers	19,186
Cable/satellite TV	18,020

Source: *USA TODAY*, Snapshots®, March 2, 2009.

Self-Regulation

In an attempt to be good corporate citizens and to prevent government intervention, some businesses try to regulate themselves. Kraft Foods, for example, stopped advertising sugary snacks and cereals to children under age 12 in response to growing concerns about childhood obesity and its effects on children's long-term health. While some competitors were astonished by the decision, Kraft executives recognized that if food product marketers did not begin to police themselves, the government could impose restrictions on advertising to children, and the industry could face potential lawsuits.[19] Several trade associations have developed self-regulatory programs. Although these programs are not a direct outgrowth of laws, many were established to stop or stall the development of laws and governmental regulatory groups that would regulate the associations' marketing practices.

Perhaps the best-known nongovernmental regulatory group is the **Better Business Bureau**, a local regulatory agency supported by local businesses. More than 140 bureaus help to settle problems between consumers and specific business firms. Each bureau also acts to preserve good business practices in a locality, although it usually lacks strong enforcement tools for dealing with firms that employ questionable practices. When a firm continues to violate what the Better Business Bureau believes to be good business practices, the bureau warns consumers through local newspapers or broadcast media. If the offending organization is a Better Business Bureau member, it may be expelled from the local bureau. For example, Cingular Wireless had its membership revoked by the Better Business Bureau of Upstate New York for having too many unresolved complaints on file.[20]

The National Advertising Division (NAD) of the Council of Better Business Bureaus operates a self-regulatory program that investigates claims regarding alleged deceptive advertising. For example, after NAD investigated a complaint from Procter & Gamble, it recommended that McNail–PPC modify the advertising for its Tylenol Cold Multi-Symptom Nighttime medicine to avoid misleading consumers about its effectiveness relative to Procter & Gamble's Nyquil Multi-Symptom Cold/Flu Relief medicine after both firms reformulated their products.[21]

Better Business Bureau
A local, nongovernmental regulatory agency, supported by local businesses, that helps settle problems between customers and specific business firms

National Advertising Review Board (NARB)
A self-regulatory unit that considers challenges to issues raised by the National Advertising Division (an arm of the Council of Better Business Bureaus) about an advertisement

Another self-regulatory entity, the **National Advertising Review Board (NARB)**, considers cases in which an advertiser challenges issues raised by the National Advertising Division about an advertisement. Cases are reviewed by panels drawn from NARB members representing advertisers, agencies, and the public. For example, General Mills appealed to NARB about a NAD order to abandon the claim "Betcha Can't Taste the Difference" between its Malt-O-Meal cereal and those of other manufacturers because NAD stated that the claim could not be substantiated. NARB concurred with NAD on the issue.[22] The NARB, sponsored by the Council of Better Business Bureaus and three advertising trade organizations, has no official enforcement powers. However, if a firm refuses to comply with its decision, the NARB may publicize the questionable practice and file a complaint with the FTC.

Self-regulatory programs have several advantages over governmental laws and regulatory agencies. Establishment and implementation are usually less expensive, and guidelines are generally more realistic and operational. In addition, effective self-regulatory programs reduce the need to expand government bureaucracy. However, these programs have several limitations. When a trade association creates a set of industry guidelines for its members, nonmember firms do not have to abide by them. Furthermore, many self-regulatory programs lack the tools or authority to enforce guidelines. Finally, guidelines in self-regulatory programs are often less strict than those established by government agencies.

technology
The application of knowledge and tools to solve problems and perform tasks more efficiently

TECHNOLOGICAL FORCES

The word *technology* brings to mind scientific advances such as computers, spacecraft, DVDs, cell phones, cloning, lifestyle drugs, the Internet, radio frequency identification tags, and more. Such developments make it possible for marketers to operate ever more efficiently and to provide an exciting array of products for consumers. However, even though these innovations are outgrowths of technology, none of them *is* technology. **Technology** is the application of knowledge and tools to solve problems and perform tasks more efficiently.

Technology determines how we, as members of society, satisfy our physiologic needs. In various ways and to varying degrees, eating and drinking habits, sleeping patterns, sexual activities, health care, and work performance are all influenced by both existing technology and advances in technology. Because of the technological revolution in communications, for example, marketers can now reach vast numbers of people more efficiently through a variety of media. Electronic mail, voice mail, cell phones, personal digital assistants (PDAs), and computers help marketers to interact with customers, make appointments, and handle last-minute orders or cancellations. Consider that a growing number of U.S. households have given up their "land lines" in favor of using cell phones as their primary phones, and that growth in wireless subscriptions is expected to continue at a compounded 2.9 percent through 2010.[23] The proliferation of cell phones, most with text-message capabilities, has led experts to project that 89 percent of brands will employ text and multimedia messaging on cell phones to reach their target markets. Restaurants, for example, can send their lunch specials to subscribers' cell phones.[24]

Personal computers are now in three-quarters of U.S. consumers' homes, and most of them include broadband or modems for accessing the Internet. The Internet has become a major tool in most households for communicating, researching, shopping, and entertaining. The use of video online, especially through websites such as YouTube, has exploded from 7 percent of all Internet traffic in 2005 to 17 percent in 2009, with 100 million users in the United States alone.[25] Although we enjoy the benefits of communicating through the Internet, we are increasingly concerned about protecting our privacy and intellectual property. Likewise, although health and medical research has created new drugs that save lives, cloning and genetically modified foods have become controversial issues to many segments of society. Home environments, health care, leisure, and work performance are all shaped profoundly by both current technology and advances in technology.[26]

COURTESY OF BASF CORPORATION AND ED JAMES

Impact of Technology
The use of corn ethanol is having an impact on many industries and companies such as BASF.

The effects of technology relate to such characteristics as dynamics, reach, and the self-sustaining nature of technological progress. The *dynamics* of technology involve the constant change that often challenges the structures of social institutions, including social relationships, the legal system, religion, education, business, and leisure. *Reach* refers to the broad nature of technology as it moves through society. Consider the impact of cellular and wireless

Marketing IN TRANSITION

New Technology Provides Opportunities for Social Network Marketing

In today's digital era, marketers are finding that their traditional marketing campaigns are losing their effectiveness. More people are spending their time online, where they are constantly inundated with advertisements. This change in behavior was driven by the advance of the Internet and new technology.

Consequently, marketers have begun using social networks like Facebook and MySpace as ways to advertise products. Additionally, new forums are now evolving that allow consumers to track ordinary aspects of their lives, from a person's daily calorie intake to infant feeding times, and share them with online communities. They are hoping to use these Internet data collections to improve their own lives, but some companies are using this information to improve sales. Netflix and Amazon, for example, use personal information to profile customers and recommend new products for them.

© JERRY ARCIERI/CORBIS

Unfortunately, with so many distractions and competing advertisements on the Web, marketers must adapt their traditional marketing methods to attract consumers. Online communities are becoming powerful tools for promoting products and gathering information. Some companies, like Johnson & Johnson, are even creating their own social networks for customers. One new tool marketers are using is rewards for consumers who pass company advertising messages on to other consumers in their online communities.

Of course, the amount of personal information consumers are providing online could have unintended negative consequences. For example, everything that you do online leaves a digital trail that can be traced, and some fear may come back to haunt people. Yet for marketers, it creates new opportunities to target customers and sell products.[a]

telephones. The ability to call from almost any location has many benefits but also has negative side effects, including increases in traffic accidents, increased noise pollution, and fears about potential health risks.[27] The *self-sustaining* nature of technology relates to the fact that technology acts as a catalyst to spur even faster development. As new innovations are introduced, they stimulate the need for more advancements to facilitate further development. For example, the Internet has created the need for ever-faster transmission of signals through broadband connections such as high-speed phone lines (DSL), satellite, and cable. Technology initiates a change process that creates new opportunities for new technologies in every industry segment or personal life experience that it touches. At some point there is even a multiplier effect that causes still greater demand for more change to improve performance.[28]

It is important for firms to determine when a technology is changing an industry and to define the strategic influence of the new technology. For example, wireless devices in use today include radios, cell phones, laptop computers, TVs, pagers, and car keys. To remain competitive, companies today must keep up with and adapt to these technological advances. Through a procedure known as *technology assessment,* managers try to foresee the effects of new products and processes on their firms' operation, on other business organizations, and on society in general. With information obtained through a technology assessment, management tries to estimate whether benefits of adopting a specific technology outweigh costs to the firm and to society at large. The degree to which a business is technologically based also influences its managers' response to technology.

SOCIOCULTURAL FORCES

Sociocultural forces are the influences in a society and its culture(s) that bring about changes in attitudes, beliefs, norms, customs, and lifestyles. Profoundly affecting how people live, these forces help to determine what, where, how, and when people buy products. Like the other environmental forces, sociocultural forces present marketers with both challenges and opportunities.

Changes in a population's demographic characteristics—age, gender, race, ethnicity, marital and parental status, income, and education—have a significant bearing on relationships and individual behavior. These shifts lead to changes in how people live and ultimately in their consumption of products such as food, clothing, housing, transportation, communication, recreation, education, and health services. We look at a few of the changes in demographics and diversity that are affecting marketing activities.

sociocultural forces The influences in a society and its culture(s) that change people's attitudes, beliefs, norms, customs, and lifestyles

One demographic change affecting the marketplace is the increasing proportion of older consumers. According to the U.S. Bureau of the Census, the number of people age 65 and older is expected to more than double by the year 2050, reaching 87 million.[29] Consequently, marketers can expect significant increases in the demand for health care services, recreation, tourism, retirement housing, and selected skin-care products.

The number of singles is also on the rise. Nearly 41 percent of U.S. adults are unmarried, and many plan to remain that way. Moreover, single men living alone comprise 11 percent of all households (up from 3.5 percent in 1970), and single women living alone make up nearly 15 percent (up from 7.3 percent in 1970).[30] Single people have quite different spending patterns than couples and families with children. They are less likely to own homes and thus buy less furniture and fewer appliances. They spend more heavily on convenience foods, restaurants, travel, entertainment, and recreation. In addition, they tend to prefer smaller packages, whereas families often buy bulk goods and products packaged in multiple servings.

The United States is entering another baby boom, with more than 81 million Americans age 19 or younger. The new baby boom represents 27.6 percent of the total population; the original baby boomers, born between 1946 and 1964, account for nearly 28 percent.[31] The children of the original baby boomers differ from one another radically in terms of race, living arrangements, and socioeconomic class. Thus the newest baby boom is much more diverse than previous generations.

Another noteworthy population trend is the increasingly multicultural nature of U.S. society. The number of immigrants into the United States has risen steadily during the last 40 years. By the turn of the twentieth century, the U.S. population had shifted from one dominated by whites to one consisting largely of three racial and ethnic groups: whites, blacks, and Hispanics. The U.S. government projects that by the year 2050, more than 102 million Hispanics, 61 million blacks, and 33 million Asians will call the United States home.[32] Figure 3.2 shows how experts believe the U.S. population will change over the next 50 years.

Marketers recognize that these profound changes in the U.S. population bring unique problems and opportunities. Hispanics, for example, wield about $862 billion in annual buying power, and experts project that figure will grow to $1.2 trillion by 2012.[33] But a diverse population means a more diverse customer base, and marketing practices must be modified—and diversified—to meet its changing needs. The California Milk Processor Board, for example, has been targeting Latinos with Spanish-language campaigns designed to resonate among the diverse Hispanic market, which includes Mexicans, Cubans, Puerto Ricans, Dominicans, Salvadorans, and more Hispanic subcultures. The industry group recently moved away from its long-running campaign, "Familia, Amor y Leche" ("Family, Love, and Milk") to the "Toma Leche" ("Drink Milk") campaign to promote the health benefits to younger Latinos.[34]

COURTESY OF ROCKY MOUNTAIN HEALTH PLANS

Sociocultural Forces
In our culture, there are changing values regarding the provision of health care.

Changes in social and cultural values have dramatically influenced people's needs and desires for products. Although these values do not shift overnight, they do change at varying speeds. Marketers try to monitor these changes because knowing this

FIGURE 3.2 **U.S. Population Projections by Race**

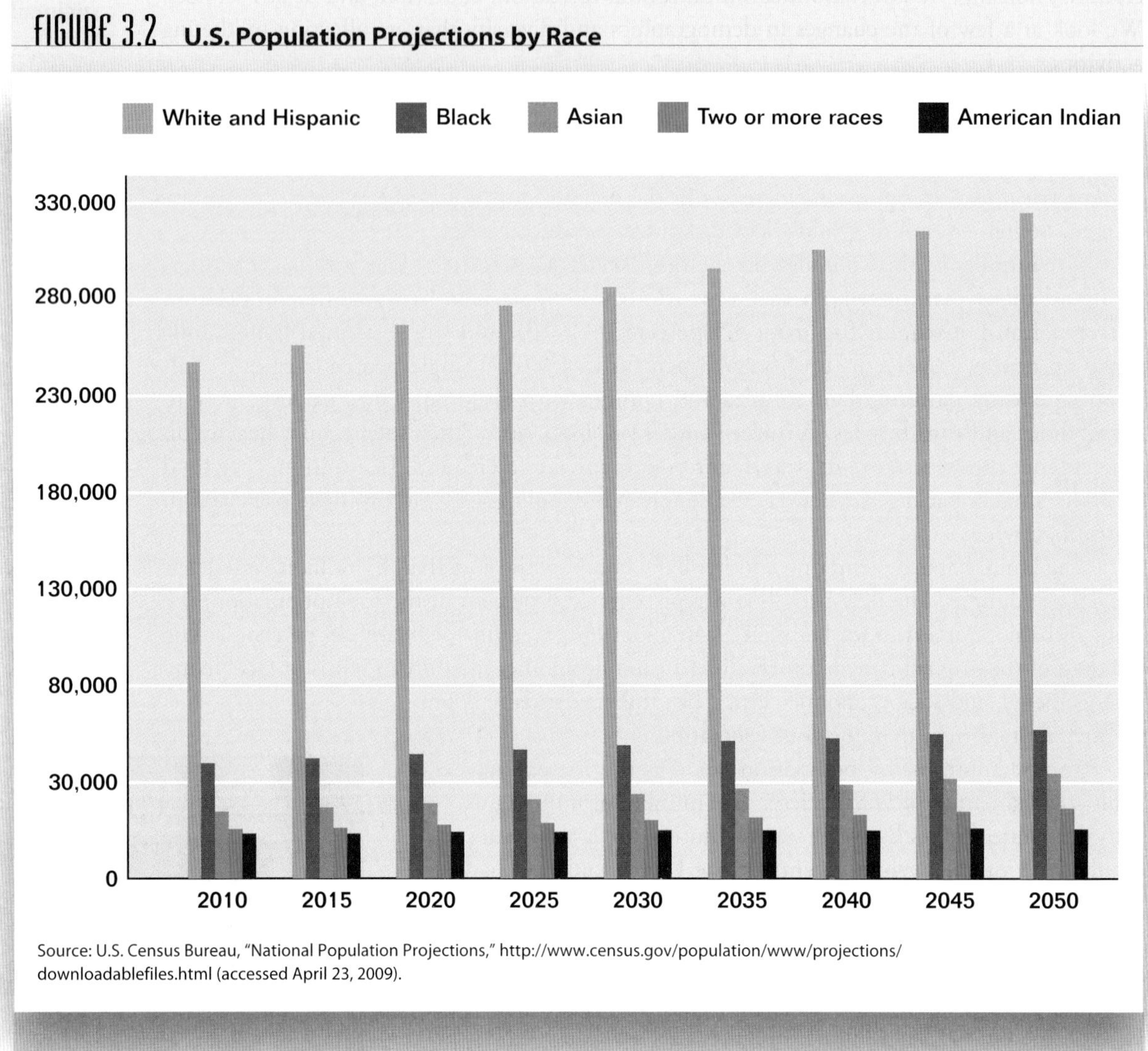

Source: U.S. Census Bureau, "National Population Projections," http://www.census.gov/population/www/projections/downloadablefiles.html (accessed April 23, 2009).

information can equip them to predict changes in consumers' needs for products, at least in the near future.

People today are more concerned about the foods they eat and thus are choosing more low-fat, organic, natural, and healthy products. Marketers have responded with a proliferation of foods, beverages, and exercise products that fit this new lifestyle. In addition to the proliferation of new organic brands, such as Earthbound Farm, Horizon Dairy, and Whole Foods' 365, many conventional marketers have introduced organic versions of their products, including Orville Redenbacher, Heinz, and even Walmart.

The major source of values is the family. Values about the permanence of marriage are changing, but children remain important. Marketers have responded with safer, upscale baby gear and supplies, children's electronics, and family entertainment products. Marketers are also aiming more marketing efforts directly at children because children often play pivotal roles in purchasing decisions. Children and family values are also a factor in the trend toward more eat-out and takeout meals. Busy families generally want to spend less time in the kitchen and more time together enjoying themselves. Beneficiaries of this trend primarily have been fast-food and casual restaurants like McDonald's, Taco Bell, Boston Market, and Applebee's, but most supermarkets have added more ready-to-cook or ready-to-serve meal components to meet the needs of busy customers. Some, like H-E-B.'s Central Market grocery stores, also offer eat-in gourmet cafes.

Social Responsibility and Ethics in Marketing

In marketing, **social responsibility** refers to an organization's obligation to maximize its positive impact and minimize its negative impact on society. Social responsibility thus deals with the total effect of all marketing decisions on society. In marketing, social responsibility includes the managerial processes needed to monitor, satisfy, and even exceed stakeholder expectations and needs.[35] Remember from Chapter 1 that stakeholders are groups that have a "stake," or claim, in some aspect of a company's products, operations, markets, industry, and outcomes. CEOs such as Indra Nooyi, chairman and CEO of PepsiCo, are increasingly recognizing that in the future companies will have to "do better by doing better." She says, in harmony with "employees, regulators, consumers, customers, communities, and many other stakeholders, it will leave no doubt that performance without purpose is not a long-term sustainable formula."[36]

social responsibility
An organization's obligation to maximize its positive impact and minimize its negative impact on society

marketing citizenship
The adoption of a strategic focus for fulfilling the economic, legal, ethical, and philanthropic social responsibilities expected by stakeholders

Ample evidence demonstrates that ignoring stakeholders' demands for responsible marketing can destroy customers' trust and even prompt government regulations. Irresponsible actions that anger customers, employees, or competitors not only may jeopardize a marketer's financial standing but also may have legal repercussions as well. For instance, after news reports that pharmaceutical giant Merck was aware that its arthritis-fighting drug Vioxx may cause heart problems, the firm's stock plummeted, and thousands of lawsuits were filed against the company. The company had already pulled the drug from the market.[37] In contrast, socially responsible activities can generate positive publicity and boost sales. The Breast Cancer Awareness Crusade sponsored by Avon Products, for example, has helped to raise $585 million in 50 countries to fund community-based breast cancer education and early-detection services. Hundreds of stories about Avon's efforts have appeared in major media, which contributed to an increase in company sales.[38]

Socially responsible efforts such as Avon's have a positive impact on local communities; at the same time, they indirectly help the sponsoring organization by attracting goodwill, publicity, and potential customers and employees. Thus, while social responsibility is certainly a positive concept in itself, most organizations embrace it in the expectation of indirect long-term benefits.

Socially responsible organizations strive for **marketing citizenship** by adopting a strategic focus for fulfilling the economic, legal, ethical, and philanthropic social responsibilities that their stakeholders expect of them. Companies that consider the diverse perspectives of stakeholders in their daily operations and strategic planning are said to have a *stakeholder orientation,* an important element of corporate citizenship.[39] A stakeholder orientation in marketing goes beyond customers, competitors, and regulators to include understanding and addressing the needs of all stakeholders, including communities and special-interest groups. As a result, organizations are now under pressure to undertake initiatives that demonstrate a balanced perspective on stakeholder interests.[40] Pfizer, for example, has secured stakeholder input on a number of issues, including rising health care costs and health care reform.[41] As Figure 3.3 shows, the economic, legal, ethical, and philanthropic dimensions of social responsibility can be viewed as a pyramid.[42] The economic and legal aspects have long been acknowledged, but ethical and philanthropic issues have gained recognition more recently.

© THE HOME DEPOT

The Nature of Social Responsibility
The Home Depot recognizes its social responsibility in hiring over 50,000 members of the military community over the past several years.

FIGURE 3.3 The Pyramid of Corporate Social Responsibility

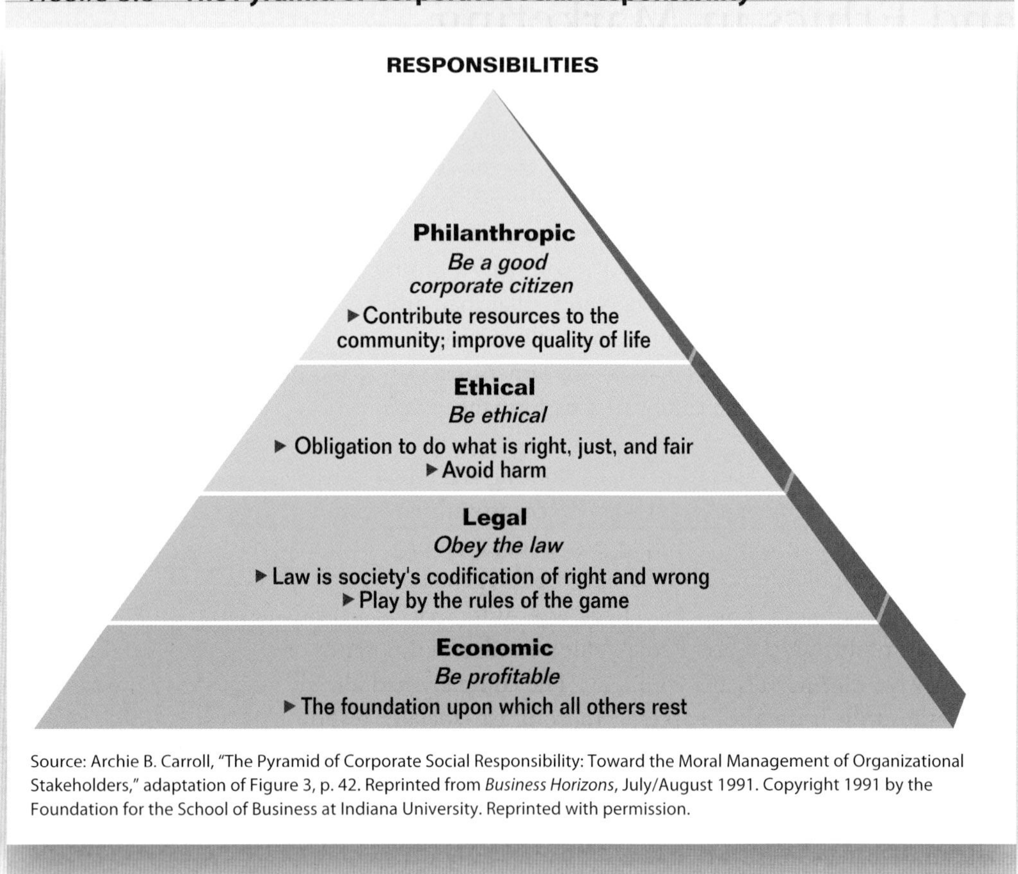

Source: Archie B. Carroll, "The Pyramid of Corporate Social Responsibility: Toward the Moral Management of Organizational Stakeholders," adaptation of Figure 3, p. 42. Reprinted from *Business Horizons*, July/August 1991. Copyright 1991 by the Foundation for the School of Business at Indiana University. Reprinted with permission.

ECONOMIC DIMENSION

At the most basic level, all companies have an economic responsibility to be profitable so that they can provide a return on investment to their owners and investors, create jobs for the community, and contribute goods and services to the economy. How organizations relate to stockholders, employees, competitors, customers, the community, and the natural environment affects the economy.

Marketers also have an economic responsibility to compete fairly. Size frequently gives companies an advantage over others. Large firms often can generate economies of scale that allow them to put smaller firms out of business. Consequently, small companies and even whole communities may resist the efforts of firms such as Walmart, Home Depot, and Best Buy to open stores in their vicinity. These firms can operate at such low costs that small, local firms often cannot compete. Such issues create concerns about social responsibility for organizations, communities, and consumers.

LEGAL DIMENSION

Marketers are also expected, of course, to obey laws and regulations. The efforts of elected representatives and special-interest groups to promote responsible corporate behavior have resulted in laws and regulations designed to keep U.S. companies' actions within the range of acceptable conduct. When marketers engage in deceptive practices to advance their own interests over those of others, charges of fraud may result. In general, fraud is any purposeful communication that deceives, manipulates, or conceals facts in order to create a false impression. It is considered a crime, and convictions may result in fines, imprisonment, or both. Fraud costs U.S. companies more than $600 billion a year; the average company loses about 6 percent of total revenues to fraud and abuses committed by its own employees.[43]

When customers, interest groups, or businesses become outraged over what they perceive as irresponsibility on the part of a marketing organization, they may urge their legislators to draft new legislation to regulate the behavior, or they may engage in litigation to force the organization to "play by the rules." Deceptive advertising in particular causes consumers to become defensive toward all promotional messages and become distrustful of all advertising; thus it harms not only consumers but also marketers themselves.[44]

ETHICAL DIMENSION

Economic and legal responsibilities are the most basic levels of social responsibility for a good reason: Failure to consider them may mean that a marketer is not around long enough to engage in ethical or philanthropic activities. Beyond these dimensions is **marketing ethics**, principles and standards that define acceptable conduct in marketing, as determined by various stakeholders, including the public, government regulators, private-interest groups, consumers, industry, and the organization itself. The most basic of these principles have been codified as laws and regulations to encourage marketers to conform to society's expectations of conduct. However, marketing ethics goes beyond legal issues. Ethical marketing decisions foster trust, which helps to build long-term marketing relationships.

Marketers should be aware of ethical standards for acceptable conduct from several viewpoints—company, industry, government, customers, special-interest groups, and society at large. When marketing activities deviate from accepted standards, the exchange process can break down, resulting in customer dissatisfaction, lack of trust, and lawsuits. In fact, 78 percent of consumers say that they avoid certain businesses or products because of negative perceptions about them.[45] Research has shown that one out of every five advertisements contains misleading information. For example, Burger King staged a taste test that the company claims showed that participants preferred its sandwiches over McDonald's. However, Burger King will not release any of the data to support its claim. Domino's Pizza claims that its sandwiches are preferred two-to-one over Subway's. The problem with claims like these is that they are highly subjective, yet advertisers attempt to make the numbers seem scientific. There is recourse for competitors insisting that their product tastes the best; however, federal agencies generally only step in when the product in question is making dangerous claims. To further avoid scrutiny, advertisers are taking their dubious claims to less regulated channels such as local television or the Internet. If it comes out that a company has been making hyped-up claims or lying in its advertisements, it could suffer negative consequences from consumers who do not want to patronize unethical or irresponsible businesses.[46] When managers engage in activities that deviate from accepted principles, continued marketing exchanges become difficult, if not impossible. The best time to deal with such problems is during the strategic planning process, not after major problems materialize.

An **ethical issue** is an identifiable problem, situation, or opportunity requiring an individual or organization to choose from among several actions that must be evaluated as right or wrong, ethical or unethical. Any time an activity causes marketing managers or customers in their target market to feel manipulated or cheated, a marketing ethical issue exists, regardless of the legality of that activity. For example, a Los Angeles consumer filed a lawsuit against Kraft Foods after recognizing from the label that her "guacamole" dip did not contain significant quantities of avocado. Although most consumers assume that Kraft's top-selling guacamole dip contains avocado, the product consists primarily of modified food starch, coconut and soybean oils, food coloring, and less than 2 percent avocado. Although Kraft quickly changed the labeling to "guacamole-flavored" dip, the California Avocado Commission expressed dismay at the dearth of avocado in the dip and asked its own lawyers to look at the suit.[47] Regardless of

marketing ethics
Principles and standards that define acceptable marketing conduct as determined by various stakeholders

ethical issue
An identifiable problem, situation, or opportunity requiring a choice among several actions that must be evaluated as right or wrong, ethical or unethical

Demonstrating Social Responsibility
Georgia Power recognizes its environmental and economic responsibilities by providing customers with home energy audits.

the reasons behind specific ethical issues, marketers must be able to identify these issues and decide how to resolve them. To do so requires familiarity with the many kinds of ethical issues that may arise in marketing. Research suggests that the greater the consequences associated with an issue, the more likely it will be recognized as an ethics issue, and the more important it will be to making an ethical decision.[48] Some examples of ethical issues related to product, promotion, price, and distribution (the marketing mix) appear in Table 3.3.

PHILANTHROPIC DIMENSION

At the top of the pyramid are philanthropic responsibilities. These responsibilities, which go beyond marketing ethics, are not required of a company, but they promote human welfare or goodwill, as do the economic, legal, and ethical dimensions of social responsibility. That many companies have demonstrated philanthropic responsibility is evidenced by the nearly $13.7 billion in annual corporate donations and contributions to environmental and social causes and relief efforts.[49] After Hurricane Katrina killed more than 1,000 people and devastated New Orleans and parts of the Gulf Coast, many corporations—including Anheuser-Busch, BP, Capital One, Cingular, DuPont, General Motors, Lowe's, Office Depot, Toyota, Walmart, and many more—donated millions of dollars in cash, supplies, equipment, food, and

TABLE 3.3 Ethical Issues in Marketing

Issue Category	Examples
Product	• Failing to disclose risks associated with a product • Failing to disclose information about a product's function, value, or use • Failing to disclose information about changes in the nature, quality, or size of a product
Distribution	• Failing to live up to the rights and responsibilities associated with specific intermediary roles • Manipulating product availability • Using coercion to force other intermediaries to behave in a certain way
Promotion	• False or misleading advertising • Using manipulative or deceptive sales promotions, tactics, and publicity • Offering or accepting bribes in personal selling situations
Pricing	• Price fixing • Predatory pricing • Failing to disclose the full price of a purchase

medicine to help victims. Other firms matched employee donations or provided mechanisms through which customers could donate funds and supplies to help with relief efforts.[50] Even small companies participate in philanthropy through donations and volunteer support of local causes and national charities, such as the Red Cross and the United Way. Boston-based Dancing Deer Baking, for example, uses environmentally friendly packaging for its scones, cookies, brownies, and cakes, and it donates 35 percent of the profits from its Sweet Home cakes to Boston nonprofits that help homeless people find jobs and housing.[51]

More companies than ever are adopting a strategic approach to corporate philanthropy. Many firms link their products to a particular social cause on an ongoing or short-term basis, a practice known as **cause-related marketing**. Target, for example, contributes significant resources to education through its Take Charge of Education program. Customers using a Target Red Card can designate a specific school to which Target donates 1 percent of their total purchase.[52] Research further indicates that such corporate support of causes generates trust in a company for 80 percent of those surveyed.[53] Some companies are beginning to extend the concept of corporate philanthropy beyond financial contributions by adopting a **strategic philanthropy** approach, the synergistic use of organizational core competencies and resources to address key stakeholders' interests and achieve both organizational and social benefits. Strategic philanthropy involves employees, organizational resources and expertise, and the ability to link these assets to the concerns of key stakeholders, including employees, customers, suppliers, and social needs. Strategic philanthropy involves both financial and nonfinancial contributions to stakeholders (employee time, goods and services, and company technology and equipment, as well as facilities), but it also benefits the company. Home Depot, for example, has been progressive in aligning its expertise and resources to address community needs. Its relationship with Habitat for Humanity gives employees a chance to improve their skills and bring direct knowledge back into the workplace to benefit customers. It also enhances Home Depot's image of expertise as the "do-it-yourself" center.[54]

Although social responsibility may seem to be an abstract ideal, managers make decisions related to social responsibility every day. To be successful, a business must determine what customers, government regulators, and competitors, as well as society in general, want or expect in terms of social responsibility. Two major categories of social responsibility issues are the natural environment and consumerism.

The Natural Environment

One of the more common ways marketers demonstrate social responsibility is through programs designed to protect and preserve the natural environment. Most *Fortune* 500 companies now engage in recycling activities and make significant efforts to reduce waste and conserve energy. Many companies are making contributions to environmental protection organizations, sponsoring and participating in cleanup events, promoting recycling, retooling manufacturing processes to minimize waste and pollution, employing more environmentally friendly energy sources, and generally reevaluating the effects of their products on the natural environment. The approach to environment is to reduce, reuse, and recycle. Americans generate 251 million tons of trash annually, with the average person generating about 4.6 pounds of trash a day.[55]

Green marketing is a strategic process involving stakeholder assessment to create meaningful long-term relationships with customers while maintaining, supporting, and enhancing the natural environment. For example, SC Johnson is using methane gas from a landfill near its Racine, Wisconsin, plant to generate half of the electricity and steam needed to run its largest plant where Windex is produced.[56] New Leaf Paper has taken a leadership role in the paper-production industry, producing paper made from 50 to 100 percent postconsumer waste instead of virgin tree pulp. The small firm's success has forced many larger competitors to introduce their own sustainable paper products. The growing trend of recycled

cause-related marketing
The practice of linking products to a particular social cause on an ongoing or short-term basis

strategic philanthropy
The synergistic use of organizational core competencies and resources to address key stakeholders' interests and achieve both organizational and social benefits

papers is saving trees and reducing the amount of solid waste going into landfills.[57] On the other hand, some stakeholders, including customers, try to dictate companies' use of responsible suppliers and sources of products.[58] Aveda, for example, requires magazines in which it places ads for its earth-friendly personal-care products to be printed on recycled paper. The requirement has already prompted *Natural Health* to switch to recycled paper.[59]

Entrepreneurial Marketing

Entrepreneurs Fight Hunger with Plumpy'nut

More than 850 million people live in a state of hunger today, killing more people annually than AIDS, malaria, and tuberculosis combined. Nutriset has been selling food products to combat hunger and malnutrition since 1986. The company launched "Plumpy'nut," a three-ounce peanut butter–based food packet with 500 calories that does not require clean water and can be consumed by a child without assistance from an adult, a true revolution in the management of severe malnutrition. A day's worth of product costs about $1 per child. Nutriset has partnered with entrepreneurs in Africa and the Caribbean to make the product locally, even using local ingredients when possible. The nonprofit organization Nutriset has found a way to combine entrepreneurship and social responsibility.[b]

Consumerism

Consumerism consists of organized efforts by individuals, groups, and organizations seeking to protect consumers' rights. The movement's major forces are individual consumer advocates, consumer organizations and other interest groups, consumer education, and consumer laws.

To achieve their objectives, consumers and their advocates write letters or send e-mails to companies, lobby government agencies, broadcast public-service announcements, and boycott companies whose activities they deem irresponsible. Some consumers choose to boycott firms and products out of a desire to support a cause and make a difference.[60] For example, several organizations evaluate children's products for safety, often announcing dangerous products before Christmas so that parents can avoid them. Other actions by the consumer movement have resulted in seat belts and air bags in automobiles, dolphin-safe tuna, the banning of unsafe three-wheel motorized vehicles, and numerous laws regulating product safety and information.

Also of great importance to the consumer movement are four basic rights spelled out in a "consumer bill of rights" drafted by President John F. Kennedy. These rights include the right to safety, the right to be informed, the right to choose, and the right to be heard. Ensuring consumers' *right to safety* means that marketers have an obligation not to market a product that they know could harm consumers. This right can be extended to imply that all products must be safe for their intended use, include thorough and explicit instructions for proper and safe use, and have been tested to ensure reliability and quality. Consumers' *right to be informed* means that consumers should have access to and the opportunity to review all relevant information about a product before buying it. Many laws require specific labeling on product packaging to satisfy this right. In addition, labels on alcoholic and tobacco products inform consumers that these products may cause illness and other problems. The Federal Trade Commission provides a wealth of consumer information at its website (http://www.ftc.gov/bcp/consumer.shtm) on a variety of topics ranging from automobiles and the Internet to diet, health, and fitness to identity theft. The *right to choose* means that consumers should have access to a variety of products and services at competitive prices. They also should be assured of satisfactory quality and service at a fair price. Activities that reduce competition among businesses in an industry might jeopardize this right. The *right to be heard* ensures that consumers' interests will receive full and sympathetic consideration in the formulation of government policy. The right to be heard also promises consumers fair treatment when they complain to marketers about products. This right benefits marketers too because when consumers complain about a product, the manufacturer can use this information to modify the product and make it more satisfying.

consumerism
Organized efforts by individuals, groups, and organizations to protect consumers' rights

codes of conduct
Formalized rules and standards that describe what the company expects of its employees

INCORPORATING SOCIAL RESPONSIBILITY AND ETHICS INTO STRATEGIC PLANNING

Although the concepts of marketing ethics and social responsibility are often used interchangeably, it is important to distinguish between them. *Ethics* relates to individual and group decisions—judgments about what is right or wrong in a particular decision-making situation—whereas *social responsibility* deals with the total effect of marketing decisions on society. The two concepts are interrelated because a company that supports socially responsible decisions and adheres to a code of conduct is likely to have a positive effect on society. Because ethics and social responsibility programs can be profitable as well, an increasing number of companies are incorporating them into their overall strategic market planning.

Without compliance programs and uniform standards and policies regarding conduct, it is hard for a company's employees to determine what conduct is acceptable within the company. In the absence of such programs and standards, employees generally will make decisions based on their observations of how their peers and superiors behave. To improve ethics, many organizations have developed **codes of conduct** (also called *codes of ethics*) consisting of formalized rules and standards that describe what the company expects of its employees. The New York Stock Exchange now requires every member corporation to have a formal code of conduct. Codes of conduct promote ethical behavior by reducing opportunities for unethical behavior; employees know both what is expected of them and what kind of punishment they face if they violate the rules. Codes help marketers deal with ethical issues or dilemmas that develop in daily operations by prescribing or limiting specific activities. Codes of conduct often include general ethical values such as honesty and integrity, general legal compliance, discreditable or harmful acts, and obligations related to social values, as well as more marketing-specific issues such as confidentiality, responsibilities to employers and clients, obligations to the profession, independence and objectivity, and marketing-specific legal and technical compliance issues.[61]

It is important that companies consistently enforce standards and impose penalties or punishment on those who violate codes of conduct. Clear Channel Communications, for example, fired two

Sustainable Marketing

Solar Helps Create a Renewable World

The multitude of incentives and renewable energy–related jobs that have increased over the last decade illustrate the sociocultural shift in attitudes about energy. It is common knowledge that finite resources have a relatively short life but renewable resources, such as the sun, can be utilized for long-term energy needs. Solar photovoltaic (PV) panels use the sun's energy to produce electricity while solar thermal panels use the sun's energy to produce hot water. Many organizations such as PepsiCo, General Electric, and Toyota are employing renewable energy in their production processes as part of a marketing strategy. For example, Frito-Lay added solar panels to the factory that produces SunChips, their green product line, to provide up to 75 percent of energy needs to produce the product.

International nonprofits such as Solar Electric Light Fund (SELF) provide solar electricity to underdeveloped nations. SELF partners with for-profit companies such as Sun Crystals®, a product line of McNeil Nutritionals, which donates 1 percent of its sales as part of a "do good" strategy. One of SELF's exciting projects in South Africa provided 2,000 students access to reliable lighting and the Internet. This particular project was made possible through donations from the Kellogg Foundation and JP Morgan Chase.

Through cultural and societal shifts, companies have an opportunity to demonstrate their contribution to environmental initiatives such as supporting solar as well as creating a positive company image by appreciating consumers' concern for the future of the world.[c]

Incorporating Social Responsibility

Toyota, as well as some other car manufacturers, provides products that are environment-friendly.

The EPA recognizes companies as "Climate Leaders" who reduce their carbon footprint and control greenhouse gas emissions.

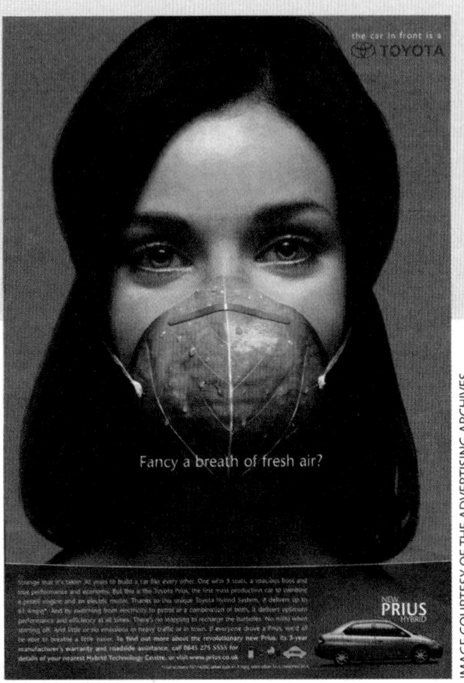

IMAGE COURTESY OF THE ADVERTISING ARCHIVES

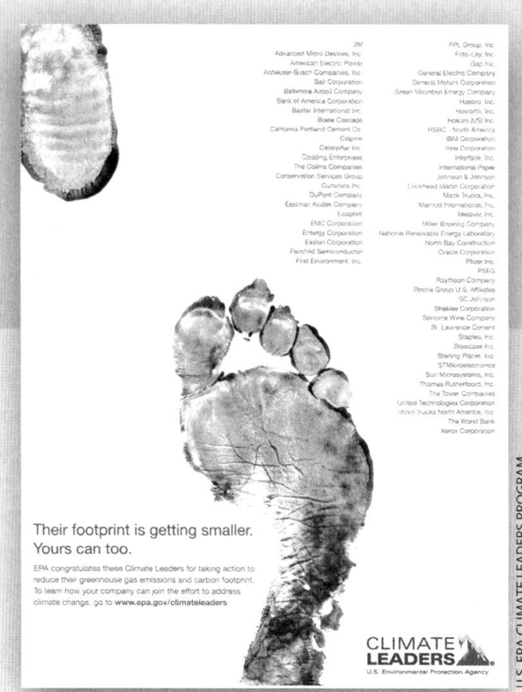

U.S. EPA CLIMATE LEADERS PROGRAM

executives and disciplined other employees for violating the firm's policies on "payola," the illegal practice of accepting payment for playing songs on the air without divulging such deals. The firm, which owns approximately 1,200 radio stations, also required station managers and programming personnel to undergo additional training on its policies.[62] In addition, a company must take reasonable steps in response to violations of standards and, as appropriate, revise the compliance program to diminish the likelihood of future misconduct. Table 3.4 lists some commonly observed types of misconduct as reported in the National Business Ethics Survey (NBES). To succeed, a compliance program must be viewed as part of the overall marketing strategy implementation. If ethics officers and other executives are not committed to the principles and initiatives of marketing ethics and social responsibility, the program's effectiveness will be in question.

Increasing evidence indicates that being ethical and socially responsible pays off. Research suggests that a relationship exists between a marketing orientation and an organizational climate that supports marketing ethics and social responsibility. This relationship implies that being ethically and socially concerned is consistent with meeting the demands of customers and other stakeholders. By encouraging their employees to understand their markets, companies can help them to respond to stakeholders' demands.[63]

There is a direct association between corporate social responsibility and customer satisfaction, profits, and market value.[64] In a survey of consumers, nearly 86 percent indicated that when quality and price are similar among competitors, they would be more likely to buy from the company associated with a particular cause. In addition, young adults aged 18 to 25 are especially likely to take a company's citizenship efforts into account when making not only purchasing but also employment and investment decisions.[65]

Thus recognition is growing that the long-term value of conducting business in a socially responsible manner far outweighs short-term costs.[66] Companies that fail to develop strategies and programs to incorporate ethics and social responsibility into their organizational culture may pay the price with poor marketing performance and the potential costs of legal violations, civil litigation, and damaging publicity when questionable activities are made public.

TABLE 3.4 Observed Misconduct

Type of Conduct Observed	Employees Observing It (%)
Putting own interests ahead of organization	22
Abusive behavior	21
Lying to employees	20
Misreporting hours worked	17
Internet abuse	16
Safety violations	15
Lying to stakeholders	14
Discrimination	13
Stealing	11
Sexual harassment	10
Provision of low-quality goods and services	10
Improper hiring practices	10
Environmental violations	7
Misuse of confidential organizational information	6
Alteration of documents	5
Alteration of financial records	5
Bribes	4
Using competitor's inside information	4

Source: From Ethics Resource Center, "The Ethics Resource Center's 2007 *National Business Ethics Survey: An Inside View of Private Sector Ethics*" (Washington, DC: Ethics Resource Center, 2007), p. 14. © Ethics Resource Center, Washington, DC.

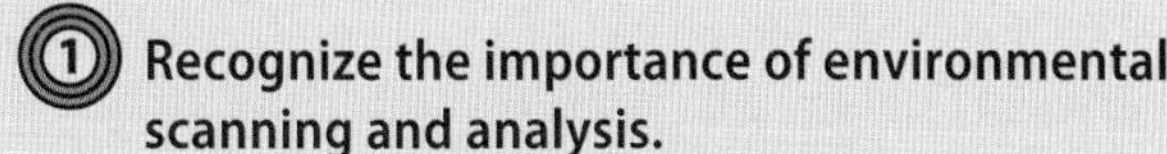

CHAPTER REVIEW

OBJECTIVES

① Recognize the importance of environmental scanning and analysis.

Environmental scanning is the process of collecting information about the forces in the marketing environment; environmental analysis is the process of assessing and interpreting the information gathered through environmental scanning. This information helps marketing managers to minimize uncertainty and threats and to capitalize on opportunities presented by environmental factors.

② Explore the effects of competitive, economic, political, legal and regulatory, technological, and sociocultural factors on marketing strategies.

Marketers need to monitor the actions of competitors to determine what strategies competitors are using and how those strategies affect their own. Economic conditions influence consumers' buying power and willingness to spend. Legislation is enacted, legal decisions are interpreted by courts, and regulatory agencies are created and operated by elected or appointed officials. Marketers also can choose to regulate themselves. Technology determines how members of society satisfy needs and wants and helps to improve the quality of life. Sociocultural forces are the influences in a society that bring about changes in attitudes, beliefs, norms, customs, and lifestyles. Changes in any of these forces can create opportunities and threats for marketers.

3 Understand the concept and dimensions of social responsibility.

Social responsibility refers to an organization's obligation to maximize its positive impact and minimize its negative impact on society. At the most basic level, companies have an economic responsibility to be profitable so that they can provide a return on investment to their stockholders, create jobs for the community, and contribute goods and services to the economy. Marketers are also expected to obey laws and regulations. Marketing ethics refers to principles and standards that define acceptable conduct in marketing as determined by various stakeholders. Philanthropic responsibilities go beyond marketing ethics; they are not required of a company but promote human welfare or goodwill.

4 Differentiate between ethics and social responsibility.

Whereas social responsibility is achieved by balancing the interests of all stakeholders in an organization, ethics relates to acceptable standards of conduct in making individual and group decisions.

Please visit the student website at www.cengage.com/international for quizzes and games that will help you prepare for exams and achieve the grade you want.

KEY CONCEPTS

environmental scanning
environmental analysis
competition
brand competitors
product competitors
generic competitors
total budget competitors
monopoly
oligopoly
monopolistic competition
pure competition
buying power
disposable income
discretionary income
willingness to spend
business cycle
Federal Trade Commission (FTC)
Better Business Bureau
National Advertising Review Board (NARB)
technology
sociocultural forces
social responsibility
marketing citizenship
marketing ethics
ethical issue
cause-related marketing
strategic philanthropy
consumerism
codes of conduct

ISSUES FOR DISCUSSION AND REVIEW

1. Why are environmental scanning and analysis important to marketers?
2. What are four types of competition? Which is most important to marketers?
3. Define *income, disposable income,* and *discretionary income.* How does each type of income affect consumer buying power?
4. What factors influence a buyer's willingness to spend?
5. What are the goals of the Federal Trade Commission? List the ways in which the FTC affects marketing activities. Do you think that a single regulatory agency should have such broad jurisdiction over so many marketing practices? Why or why not?
6. Name several nongovernmental regulatory forces. Do you believe that self-regulation is more or less effective than governmental regulatory agencies? Why?
7. Discuss the impact of technology on marketing activities.

8. In what ways are cultural values changing? How are marketers responding to these changes?
9. What is social responsibility, and why is it important?
10. What are four dimensions of social responsibility? What impact do they have on marketing decisions?
11. What are some major social responsibility issues? Give an example of each.
12. Describe consumerism. Analyze some active consumer forces in your area.
13. What is the difference between ethics and social responsibility?

MARKETING APPLICATIONS

1. Assume that you are opening *one* of the following retail businesses. Identify publications at the library or online that provide information about the environmental forces likely to affect the business. Briefly summarize the information each provides.
   a. Convenience store
   b. Women's clothing store
   c. Grocery store
   d. Fast-food restaurant
   e. Furniture store
2. Identify at least one technological advancement and one sociocultural change that have affected you as a consumer. Explain the impact of each on your needs as a customer.
3. Identify an organization in your community that has a reputation for being ethical and socially responsible. What activities account for this image? Is the company successful? Why or why not?

ONLINE EXERCISE

4. Business for Social Responsibility (BSR) is a nonprofit organization for companies desiring to operate responsibly and demonstrate respect for ethical values, people, communities, and the natural environment. Founded in 1992, BSR offers members practical information, research, educational programs, and technical assistance as well as the opportunity to network with peers on current social responsibility issues. Visit **http://www.bsr.org.**
   a. What types of businesses join BSR, and why?
   b. In the CSR Resources section, go to the CSR News Releases section and pick three recent articles that deal with social responsibility issues in marketing. For each article, explain how these issues relate to a concept covered in Chapter 3.
   c. In the CSR Resources section, go to the Issue Briefs section and find the white paper on ethics codes and ethics training. Using this report, list some examples of corporate codes of ethics, and describe the benefits of establishing a code of ethics.

DEVELOPING YOUR MARKETING PLAN

A marketing strategy is dynamic. Companies must continually monitor the marketing environment not only to create their marketing strategy, but also to revise it if necessary. Information about various forces in the marketplace is collected, analyzed, and used as a foundation for several marketing plan decisions. The following questions will help you to understand how the information in this chapter contributes to the development of your marketing plan:

1. Describe the current competitive market for your product. Can you identify the number of brands or market share that they hold? Expand your analysis to include other products that are similar or could be substituted for yours.
2. Using the business cycle pattern, in which of the four stages is the current state of the economy? Can you identify any changes in consumer buying power that would affect the sale and use of your product?
3. Referring to Tables 3.2 and 3.3, do you recognize any laws or regulatory agencies that would have jurisdiction over your type of product?
4. Conduct a brief technology assessment, determining the impact that technology has on your product, its sale, or use.
5. Discuss how your product could be affected by changes in social attitudes, demographic characteristics, or lifestyles.

The information obtained from these questions should assist you in developing various aspects of your marketing plan found in the *Interactive Marketing Plan* exercise.

VIDEO CASE 3

Organic Valley Responds to a Changing Environment

Founded in 1988, Organic Valley is one of the nation's largest organic dairy cooperatives with 1,266 farm families in 28 states. Organic Valley works with small, independent organic dairy farmers, ensuring a high standard of quality and a fair price for farmer output.

Paul Deutsch of Sweet Ridge Organic Dairy Farm is one of these farmers. After working for some time at a conventional commercial dairy farm, Deutsch became fed up over the miserable conditions of the animals, the drugs administered to animals, and the huge amount of pollution that the factory farms caused. And, ultimately, he determined that large conventional farms produced an inferior product with less taste and less nutritional value. Deutsch purchased his own land so he could work on his own terms—cultivating healthier land and happier, healthier, more productive cows. By the late 1990s he was certified organic and soon after became a member of the Organic Valley co-op. Deutsch now benefits from the good reputation and extensive distribution channels of Organic Valley as well as the large network of knowledge and support of fellow organic farmers.

While the life of an organic farmer is not an easy one—keeping plants and animals healthy without resorting to chemicals can be labor intensive and complicated—marketing and selling organic products is growing easier by the day. Changing consumer attitudes toward organic products profoundly affect how, when, where, and what people purchase. As more news comes out about salmonella-tainted vegetables, infected meat, and the harmful environmental effects of conventional farming, more and more people are going organic. The media coverage of the potential harm of conventionally grown foods has acted like an endorsement of organic products as the safer, more nutritious, and more environmentally friendly alternative. In fact, the entire organic industry has enjoyed 20 percent annual growth rates for over a decade, while organic dairy has exceeded that with 27 percent annual growth. Farmers' markets have never been so popular. Organic grocers, like Whole Foods, are as large as and more profitable than conventional supermarkets. Organic food brands, once available only in specialty shops and health food stores, are showing up in all supermarkets. Also, the farmers often benefit from higher profit margins and healthier, chemical-free work environments.

While organic has not caught on in all parts of the country, it is a growing trend that has afforded the likes of Paul Deutsch a means of doing what he loves while supplying the marketplace with nutritious, safe products. Consumer demand is driving the expansion of the organic industry and providing brands like Organic Valley with increased distribution opportunities. Because Organic Valley is a cooperative, as it expands and takes on new members, farmers like Deutsch can directly benefit from growth of Organic Valley as well as the industry at large. The cooperative model also encourages collaboration, not competition, between other members of the co-op. For example, to learn from each other, Deutsch and other farmers in the region get together periodically to share advice, knowledge, and methods so that they can all benefit from the best practices of their peers.

Organic Valley and other co-ops like it are concerned not only about the health of the cows and the environment but also with the well-being of small farmers and their communities. To meet these means, the Organic Valley cooperative has developed a profit-sharing model wherein farmers and employees each receive 45 percent of the profits and their communities receive the remaining 10 percent. This model not only builds loyal producers; it also encourages a growing base of loyal consumers as more people recognize the health benefits of organic and the good things the company does for small farming communities. These current sociocultural trends are providing opportunities for Organic Valley and all of its co-op members.

As more news emerges daily about food-related health scares, diminished nutritional value of conventionally produced foods, environmental damage wrought by pesticides, and other dire topics, Paul Deutsch and company are able to look forward to using organic dairy products as a competitive advantage.[42]

QUESTIONS FOR DISCUSSION

1. How has Organic Valley differentiated its product offerings from traditional dairies?
2. How has Organic Valley benefited from changing attitudes of the health-conscious consumer toward food products?
3. Why do you think a growing market segment of consumers is willing to pay more for organic foods?

CROPP Cooperative, http://www.farmers.coop; Organic Valley, www.organicvalley.coop.

2 Marketing Research and Target Markets

CORBIS ROYALTY-FREE

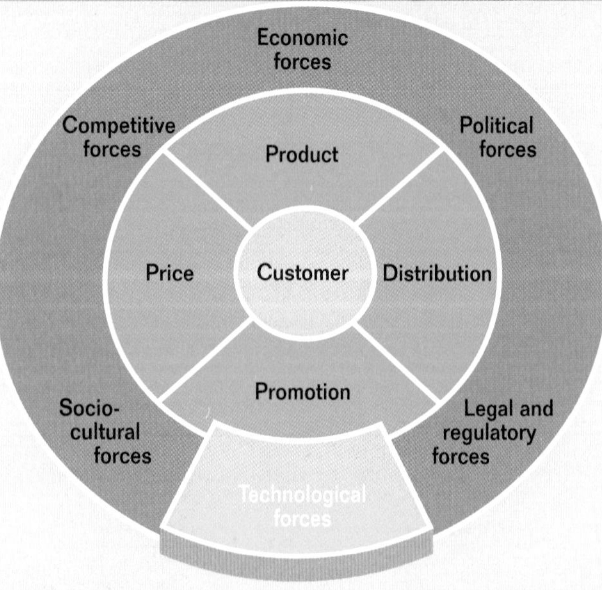

Part 2 examines how marketers use information and technology to better understand and reach customers. Chapter 4 provides a foundation for analyzing buyers through a discussion of marketing information systems and the basic steps in the marketing research process. Understanding elements that affect buying decisions enables marketers to better analyze customers' needs and to evaluate how specific marketing strategies can satisfy those needs. Chapter 5 deals with selecting and analyzing target markets, which is one of the major steps in marketing strategy development.

Marketing Research and Information Systems

CHAPTER 4

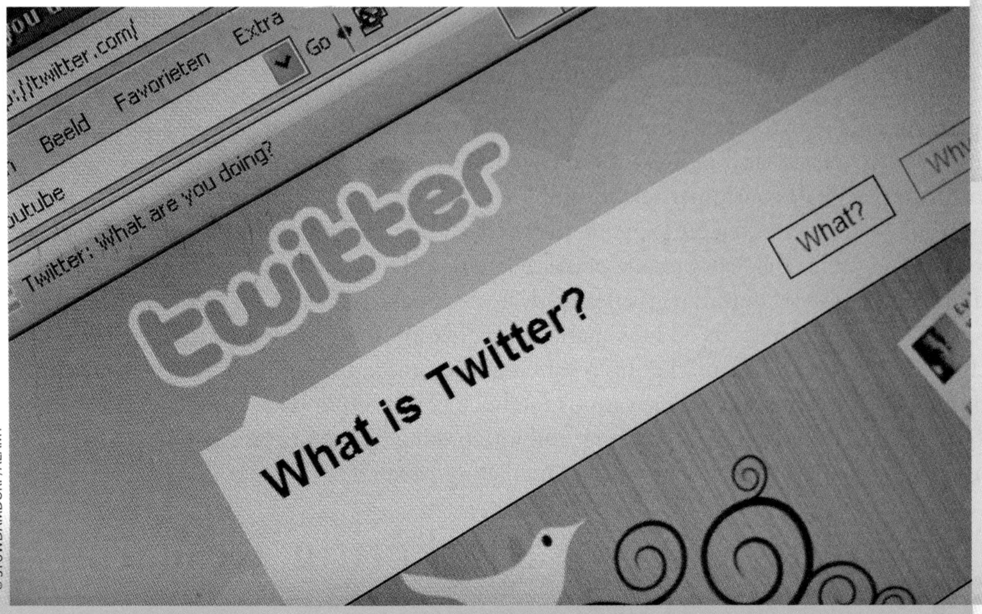

© STUWDAMDORP/ALAMY

ONLINE CUSTOMER FEEDBACK IS A GREAT SOURCE OF MARKETING INFORMATION

In today's high-tech world, Internet sites allow customers to share their opinions about products like never before. One would think companies would take advantage of this, yet this has not been the case. For example, surveys have shown that only 16 percent of businesses do a simple thing like regularly check their message board for customer complaints. This failure to address customer concerns means businesses are missing feedback that could help them improve marketing research and information systems. By communicating with customers online, businesses are essentially creating an internal source of information that marketers can analyze to help improve marketing decisions. An online forum also allows customers to communicate with one another, creating a social network of interactive resources.

This leads to another reason why companies should manage online customer feedback: 77 percent of online shoppers use customer reviews in their purchasing decisions. Businesses that know what consumers are saying have the chance to address complaints and positively influence customer satisfaction. As a result, some companies are beginning to take online feedback more seriously. Bank of America and Comcast are now using the social networking site Twitter as an opportunity to develop a database useful in marketing information systems. Twitter allows them to post short messages to their customers, address queries, and obtain customer feedback.

OBJECTIVES:

1. **Define *marketing research* and understand its importance.**
2. **Describe the basic steps in conducting marketing research.**
3. **Explore the fundamental methods of gathering data for marketing research.**
4. **Describe how tools such as databases, decision support systems, and the Internet facilitate marketing information systems and research.**
5. **Identify key ethical and international considerations in marketing research.**

For other companies that want to jump on the bandwagon, numerous sites can help them collect customer feedback. For instance, Yelp.com is one of many that collect customer reviews of local businesses. The Web offers a variety of ways for companies to gather customer feedback, and those that learn to use this feedback as a marketing information resource will gain an edge over their competition.[1]

Implementing the marketing concept requires that marketers obtain information about the characteristics, needs, and desires of target-market customers. When used effectively, such information facilitates customer relationship management by helping marketers to focus their efforts on meeting and even anticipating the needs of their customers. Marketing research and information systems that can provide practical and objective information to help firms develop and implement marketing strategies therefore are essential to effective marketing.

In this chapter we focus on how marketers gather information needed to make marketing decisions. First, we define marketing research and examine the individual steps of the marketing research process, including various methods of collecting data. Next, we look at how technology aids in collecting, organizing, and interpreting marketing research data. Finally, we consider ethical and international issues in marketing research.

The Importance of Marketing Research

marketing research
The systematic design, collection, interpretation, and reporting of information to help marketers solve specific marketing problems or take advantage of marketing opportunities

Marketing research is the systematic design, collection, interpretation, and reporting of information to help marketers solve specific marketing problems or take advantage of marketing opportunities. As the word *research* implies, it is a process for gathering information not currently available to decision makers. The purpose of marketing research is to inform an organization about customers' needs and desires, marketing opportunities

Importance of Marketing Research
Irwin provides services to help companies better understand their customers' needs.

COURTESY IRWIN RESEARCH

for particular goods and services, and changing attitudes and purchase patterns of customers. Market information increases marketers' ability to respond to customer needs, which leads to improved organizational performance.[2] Detecting shifts in buyers' behaviors and attitudes helps companies to stay in touch with the ever-changing marketplace. Coffee marketers, for example, would be very interested to know that demand for supermarket brands such as Folgers and Maxwell House is declining, while demand for on-the-go brands such as Starbucks, Dunkin' Donuts, and McDonald's has been growing at an annual rate of 15 percent. Moreover, just 37 percent of 18–24-year-olds drink coffee today, compared with 60 percent of those between 40 and 59 years of age.[3] Strategic planning requires marketing research to facilitate the process of assessing such opportunities or threats.

All sorts of organizations use marketing research to help them develop marketing mixes to match the needs of customers. Marketing research can help a firm better understand market opportunities, ascertain the potential for success of new products, and determine the feasibility of a particular marketing strategy. Unilever conducted research on the men's hair care market because it believed this was a good target market opportunity. Research indicated that 85 percent of men thought their hair looked "pretty good," but 50 percent of women did not agree. Therefore the Axe product line was designed to address the contrast between what men perceive about their own appearance and what women think about men's hair. With 41 percent of men thinking that "all grooming products work the same," Axe created a marketing strategy designed to distinguish itself from other grooming products.[4] A study by SPSS, Inc., found that the most common reasons for conducting marketing research surveys included determining satisfaction (43 percent), product development (29 percent), branding (23 percent), segmentation (18 percent), business markets (11 percent), and awareness, trend tracking, and concept testing (18 percent).[5]

The real value of marketing research is measured by improvements in a marketer's ability to make decisions. Marketing research conducted for OfficeMax, for example, highlighted problems with the store layout, which was confusing shoppers, and helped executives to make decisions to improve the layout. As a result, OfficeMax is replacing gridlike aisles with a less cluttered "racetrack" layout that gives shoppers a clear view all the way to the back wall and invites them to peruse expensive electronics showcased inside a main aisle that loops inside each store.[6] Marketers should treat information in the same manner as they use other resources, and they must weigh the costs of obtaining information against the benefits derived. Information should be judged worthwhile if it results in marketing activities that better satisfy the firm's target customers, leads to increased sales and profits, or helps the firm to achieve some other goal.

Entrepreneurial Marketing

iModerate Uses Text Messaging to Research Consumer Feelings

iModerate LLC, a marketing research company, is attempting to address a weakness in online surveys. They only provide one-way communication without offering any insight into feelings and attitudes beneath the surface of respondents. Carl Rosso co-founded the company with Joel Bensensen after working in polling for President Clinton's administration. He had observed that an important element was missing when conducting surveys on the Internet. Those surveys simply did not provide enough information on the thoughts and feelings of each respondent, so he created an interactive online questionnaire that helps to expose feelings, uncover connections, and enhance survey data. iModerate is an example of using evolving technology and the Internet to allow for considerable flexibility in designing online questionnaires.[a]

The Marketing Research Process

To maintain the control needed to obtain accurate information, marketers approach marketing research as a process with logical steps: (1) locating and defining issues or problems, (2) designing the research project, (3) collecting data, (4) interpreting research findings, and (5) reporting research findings (Figure 4.1). These steps should be viewed as an overall

FIGURE 4.1 The Five Steps of the Marketing Research Process

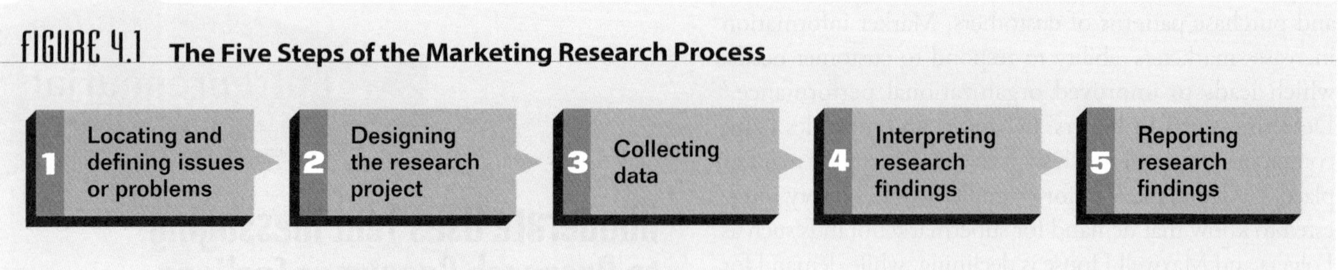

approach to conducting research rather than as a rigid set of rules to be followed in each project. In planning research projects, marketers must consider each step carefully and determine how they can best adapt them to resolve the particular issues at hand.

LOCATING AND DEFINING RESEARCH ISSUES OR PROBLEMS

The first step in launching a research study is issue or problem definition, which focuses on uncovering the nature and boundaries of a situation or question related to marketing strategy or implementation. The first sign of a problem is typically a departure from some normal function, such as failure to attain objectives. If a corporation's objective is a 12 percent sales increase and the current marketing strategy resulted in a 6 percent increase, this discrepancy should be analyzed to help guide future marketing strategies. Declining sales, increasing expenses, and decreasing profits also signal problems. Armed with this knowledge, a firm could define a problem as finding a way to adjust for biases stemming from existing customers when gathering data or to develop methods for gathering information to help find new customers. Conversely, when an organization experiences a dramatic rise in sales or some other positive event, it may conduct marketing research to discover the reasons and maximize the opportunities stemming from them.

Marketing research often focuses on identifying and defining market opportunities or changes in the environment. When a firm discovers a market opportunity, it may need to conduct research to understand the situation more precisely so that it can craft an appropriate marketing strategy. For example, Cisco saw an opportunity to appeal to a $34 billion market of businesses that wished to engage in collaborative projects. Cisco conducted marketing research to determine that it would take 3 to 5 years to build a good reputation among businesses that use the Internet and want to collaborate online. Cisco also discovered that it needed to customize software utilized by specific users and to avoid introducing products too similar to ones already sold by competitors.[7] The company can use this information to focus its efforts on specific target markets and to refine its marketing strategy appropriately.

To pin down the specific boundaries of a problem or an issue through research, marketers must define the nature and scope of the situation in a way that requires probing beneath the superficial symptoms. The interaction between the marketing manager and the marketing researcher should yield a clear definition of the research need. Researchers and decision makers should remain in the issue or problem definition stage until they have determined precisely what they want from marketing research and how they will use it. Deciding how to refine a broad, indefinite issue or problem into a precise, researchable statement is a prerequisite for the next step in the research process.

DESIGNING THE RESEARCH PROJECT

research design
An overall plan for obtaining the information needed to address a research problem or issue

Once the problem or issue has been defined, the next step is **research design**, an overall plan for obtaining the information needed to address it. This step requires formulating a hypothesis and determining what type of research is most appropriate for testing the hypothesis to ensure that the results are reliable and valid.

Developing a Hypothesis

The objective statement of a marketing research project should include hypotheses based on both previous research and expected research findings. A **hypothesis** is an informed guess or assumption about a certain problem or set of circumstances. It is based on all the insight and knowledge available about the problem or circumstances from previous research studies and other sources. As information is gathered, a researcher can test the hypothesis. For example, a food marketer such as H. J. Heinz might propose the hypothesis that children today have considerable influence on their families' buying decisions regarding ketchup and other grocery products. A marketing researcher then would gather data, perhaps through surveys of children and their parents, and draw conclusions about whether the hypothesis is correct. Sometimes several hypotheses are developed during an actual research project; the hypotheses that are accepted or rejected become the study's chief conclusions.

Types of Research

The nature and type of research varies based on the research design and the hypotheses under investigation. Marketers may elect to conduct either exploratory research or conclusive research. While each has distinct purposes, the major differences between them are formalization and flexibility rather than the specific research methods used. Table 4.1 summarizes the differences.

hypothesis
An informed guess or assumption about a certain problem or set of circumstances

EXPLORATORY RESEARCH. When marketers need more information about a problem or want to make a tentative hypothesis more specific, they may conduct **exploratory research**. The main purpose of exploratory research is to better understand a problem or situation and/or to help identify additional data needs or decision alternatives.[8] Consider that until recently there was no research available to help marketers understand how consumers perceive the term *clearance* versus the term *sale* in describing a discounted-price event. An exploratory study asked one group of 80 consumers to write down their thoughts about a store window sign that said "sale" and another group of 80 consumers about a store window sign that read "clearance." The results revealed

exploratory research
Research conducted to gather more information about a problem or to make a tentative hypothesis more specific

TABLE 4.1 Differences Between Exploratory and Conclusive Research

Research Project Components	Exploratory Research	Conclusive Research
Research purpose	General: to generate insights about a situation	Specific: to verify insights and aid in selecting a course of action
Data needs	Vague	Clear
Data sources	Ill-defined	Well-defined
Data collection form	Open-ended, rough	Usually structured
Sample	Relatively small; subjectively selected to maximize generalization of insights	Relatively large; objectively selected to permit generalization of findings
Data collection	Flexible; no set procedure	Rigid; well-laid-out procedure
Data analysis	Informal: typically nonquantitative	Formal; typically quantitative
Inferences/ recommendations	More tentative than final	More final than tentative

Source: A. Parasuraman, Dhruv Grewal, and R. Krishnan, *Marketing Research* (Boston: Houghton Mifflin, 2007).

that consumers expected deeper discounts when the term *clearance* was used, and they expected the quality of the clearance products to be lower than that of products on sale.[9] This exploratory research helped marketers to better understand how consumers view these terms and opened up the opportunity for additional research hypotheses about decision alternatives for retail pricing.

CONCLUSIVE RESEARCH. **Conclusive research** is designed to verify insights through an objective procedure to help marketers in making decisions. It is used when the marketer has in mind one or more alternatives and needs assistance in the final stages of decision-making.[10] For example, exploratory research revealed that *clearance* and *sale* terms send different signals to consumers, but in order to make a decision, a well-defined and -structured research project could be used to help marketers decide which approach is best for a specific set of products and target consumers. The study would be specific to selecting a course of action and typically quantitative, using methods that can be verified. Two types of conclusive research are descriptive and experimental research.

If marketers need to understand the characteristics of certain phenomena to solve a particular problem, **descriptive research** can aid them. Such studies may range from general surveys of customers' education, occupation, or age to specific surveys on how often teenagers eat at fast-food restaurants after school or how often customers buy new pairs of athletic shoes. For example, if Nike and Reebok want to target more young women, they might ask 15- to 35-year-old females how often they work out, how frequently they wear athletic shoes for casual use, and how many pairs of athletic shoes they buy in a year. Such descriptive research can be used to develop specific marketing strategies for the athletic shoe market. Descriptive studies generally demand much prior knowledge and assume that the issue or problem is clearly defined. Some descriptive studies require statistical analysis and predictive tools. The marketer's major task is to choose adequate methods for collecting and measuring data.

Descriptive research is limited in providing the evidence necessary to make causal inferences (i.e., that variable *x* causes a variable *y*). **Experimental research** allows marketers to make causal deductions about relationships.[11] Such experimentation requires that an independent variable (one not influenced by or dependent on other variables) be manipulated and the resulting changes in a dependent variable (one contingent on, or restricted to, one value or set of values assumed by the independent variable) be measured. For example, when Coca-Cola introduced Dasani flavored waters, managers needed to estimate sales at various potential price points. In some markets Dasani was introduced at $6.99 per six-pack. By holding variables such as advertising and shelf position constant, Coca-Cola could manipulate the price variable to study its effect on sales. If sales increased 40 percent when the price was reduced by $2, then managers could make an informed decision about the effect of price on sales. Coca-Cola also could use experimental research to manipulate other variables such as advertising or in-store shelf position to determine their effect on sales. Manipulation of the causal variable and control of other variables is what makes experimental research unique. As a result, it can provide much stronger evidence of cause and effect than data collected through descriptive research.

conclusive research
Research designed to verify insights through objective procedures and to help marketers in making decisions

descriptive research
Research conducted to clarify the characteristics of certain phenomena and thus solve a particular problem

experimental research
Research that allows marketers to make causal inferences about relationships

reliability
A condition existing when a research technique produces almost identical results in repeated trials

validity
A condition existing when a research method measures what it is supposed to measure

Research Reliability and Validity

In designing research, marketing researchers must ensure that research techniques are both reliable and valid. A research technique has **reliability** if it produces almost identical results in repeated trials. But a reliable technique is not necessarily valid. To have **validity,** the research method must measure what it is supposed to measure, not something else. For example, although a group of customers may express the same level of satisfaction based on a rating scale, the individuals may not exhibit the same repurchase behavior because of different personal characteristics. This result might cause the researcher to question the validity of the satisfaction scale if the purpose of rating satisfaction were to estimate potential repurchase behavior.[12] Kellogg's, for example, has found that much research focuses on the wrong measures. In doing research on packaging, Kellogg's discovered that side-by-side comparisons of different packages did not provide a measure of validity as good as shopping behavior in a virtual supermarket. Using an alternative research method, package alternatives were tested on potential shoppers using a virtual supermarket shelf.[13] Repeated trials generated similar results, which proved the reliability of this alternative measuring technique.

COURTESY M/A/R/C RESEARCH, CREATED BY AVREAFOSTER

Primary Data Collection
M/A/R/C works with multinational companies to collect primary data to maintain strong brand equity.

COLLECTING DATA

The next step in the marketing research process is collecting data to help prove (or disprove) the research hypothesis. The research design must specify what types of data to collect and how they will be collected.

Types of Data

Marketing researchers have two types of data at their disposal. **Primary data** are observed and recorded or collected directly from respondents. These data must be gathered by observing phenomena or surveying people of interest. **Secondary data** are compiled both inside and outside the organization for some purpose other than the current investigation. Secondary data include general reports supplied to an enterprise by various data services and internal and online databases. Such reports might concern market share, retail inventory levels, and customers' buying behavior. Secondary data are commonly available in private or public reports or have been collected and stored by the organization itself. Given the opportunity to obtain data via the Internet, more than half of all marketing research now comes from secondary sources.

Sources of Secondary Data

Marketers often begin the data-collection phase of the marketing research process by gathering secondary data. They may use available reports and other information from both internal and external sources to study a marketing problem.

Internal sources of secondary data can contribute tremendously to research. An organization's own database may contain information about past marketing activities, such as sales records and research reports, that can be used to test hypotheses and pinpoint problems. From sales reports, for example, a firm may be able to determine not only which product sold best at certain times of the year but also which colors and sizes customers preferred. BMW of North America maintains a corporate intranet system as part of its database collection and access strategy. This system allow field staff to routinely access retailer financials, check vehicle supply and delivery statuses, and view marketing information for such things as advertising and prospecting.[14] Such information may have been gathered using customer relationship management (CRM) tools for marketing, management, or financial purposes. Table 4.2 lists some commonly available internal company information that may be useful for marketing research purposes.

Accounting records are also an excellent source of data but, strangely enough, are often overlooked. The large volume of data an accounting department collects does not automatically flow to other departments. As a result, detailed information about costs, sales, customer accounts, or profits by product category may not be easily accessible to the marketing area. This condition develops particularly in organizations that do not store marketing information on a systematic basis.

primary data Data observed and recorded or collected directly from respondents

secondary data Data compiled both inside and outside the organization for some purpose other than the current investigation

TABLE 4.2 Internal Sources of Secondary Data

• Sales data, which may be broken down by geographic area, product type, or even type of customer
• Accounting information, such as costs, prices, and profits, by product category
• Competitive information gathered by the sales force

External sources of secondary data include periodicals, government publications, unpublished sources, and online databases. Periodicals such as *BusinessWeek, The Wall Street Journal, Sales & Marketing Management, Marketing Research,* and *Industrial Marketing* publish general information that can help marketers define problems and develop hypotheses. *Survey of Buying Power,* an annual supplement to *Sales & Marketing Management,* contains sales data for major industries on a county-by-county basis. Many marketers also consult federal government publications such as the *Statistical Abstract of the United States,* the *Census of Business,* the *Census of Agriculture,* and the *Census of Population;* most of these government publications are available online. Although the government still conducts its primary census every ten years, it now surveys 250,000 households every month, providing decision makers with a more up-to-date demographic picture of the nation's population every year. Such data help Target executives make merchandising and marketing decisions as well as identify promising locations for new Target stores.[15]

In addition, companies may subscribe to services such as ACNielsen or Information Resources, Inc. (IRI), which track retail sales and other information. IRI, for example, tracks consumer purchases using in-store, scanner-based technology. Marketers can purchase information from IRI about a product category, such as frozen orange juice, as secondary data.[16] Small businesses may be unable to afford such services, but they can still find a wealth of information through industry publications and trade associations.[17]

The Internet can be especially useful to marketing researchers. As we've already seen, search engines such as Google can help marketers locate many types of secondary data or research topics of interest. Of course, companies can mine their own websites for useful information using CRM tools. Amazon.com, for example, has built a relationship with its customers by tracking the types of books, music, and other products they purchase. Each time a customer logs on to the website, the company can offer recommendations based on the customer's previous purchases. Such a marketing system helps the company track the changing desires and buying habits of its most valued customers. And marketing researchers are increasingly monitoring blogs to discover what consumers are saying about their products—both positive and negative. Some, including yogurt maker Stonyfield Farms, have even established their own blogs in order to monitor

SNAPSHOT

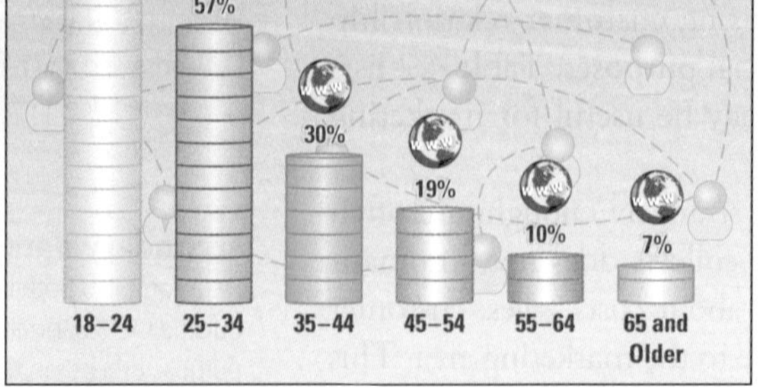

Percentage of Internet users who have an account on a social networking site, by age:

18–24	25–34	35–44	45–54	55–64	65 and Older
75%	57%	30%	19%	10%	7%

Source: Pew Internet & American Life Project telephone survey of 1,650 Internet users. The margin of error is plus or minus 3 percentage points. January 14, 2009

TABLE 4.3 External Sources of Secondary Data

Government sources	
Economic census	http://www.census.gov/econ/census02/index.html
Export.gov—country and industry market research	http://www.export.gov/mrktresearch/index.asp
National Technical Information Services	http://www.ntis.gov/
STAT-USA	http://www.stat-usa.gov/
Strategis—Canadian trade	http://strategis.ic.gc.ca/engdoc/main.html
Trade associations and shows	
American Society of Association Executives	http://www.asaecenter.org/peoplegroups/content.cfm?ItemNumber=16433&navItemNumber=14962
Directory of Associations	http://www.marketingsource.com/associations/
Trade Show News Network	http://www.tsnn.com/
Tradeshow Week	http://www.tradeshowweek.com/
Magazines, newspapers, video, audio news programming	
Blinkx	http://www.blinkx.com/home?safefilter=off
FindArticles.com	http://www.directcontactpr.com/jumpstation/
Google Video Search	http://video.google.com/
Media Jumpstation	http://www.directcontactpr.com/jumpstation/
News Directory	http://www.newsdirectory.com/magazine.php?cat=3&sub=&c=
Yahoo! Video Search	http://video.search.yahoo.com/
Corporate information	
Annual Report Service	http://www.annualreportservice.com/
Bitpipe	http://www.bitpipe.com/
Business Wire—press releases	http://home.businesswire.com/portal/site/home/index.jsp?front_door=true
Hoover's Online	http://www.hoovers.com/free/
Open Directory Project	http://dmoz.org/
PR Newswire—press releases	http://www.prnewswire.com/

Source: Adapted from "Tutorial: Finding Information for Market Research," KnowThis.com, http://www.knowthis.com/tutorials/principles-of-marketing/finding-secondary-research.htm (accessed March 23, 2009).

consumer dialog on issues of their choice. Social networking sites have become an important source of primary marketing research information, as shown in the Snapshot on the previous page. Table 4.3, on the other hand, summarizes sources of secondary data.

Methods of Collecting Primary Data

The collection of primary data is a more lengthy, expensive, and complex process than the collection of secondary data. To gather primary data, researchers use sampling procedures, survey methods, and observation. These efforts can be handled in-house by the firm's own research department or contracted to a private research firm such as ACNielsen, Information Resources, Inc., IMS International, and Quality Controlled Services.

SAMPLING. Because the time and resources available for research are limited, it is almost impossible to investigate all the members of a target market or other population. A **population**, or "universe," includes all the elements, units, or individuals of interest to researchers for a specific study. For a Gallup poll designed to predict the results of a presidential election, all registered voters in the United States would constitute the population. By systematically choosing a limited number of units—a **sample**—to represent the characteristics of a total population, researchers can project the reactions of a total market or market segment. **Sampling** in marketing research, therefore, is the process of selecting representative units from a total population. Sampling techniques allow marketers to predict buying behavior fairly accurately on the basis of the responses from a representative portion of the population of interest. Most types of marketing research employ sampling techniques.

There are two basic types of sampling: probability sampling and nonprobability sampling. With **probability sampling**, every element in the population being studied has a known chance of being selected for study. Random sampling is a kind of probability sampling. When marketers employ **random sampling**, all the units in a population have an equal chance of appearing in the sample. The various events that can occur have an equal or known chance of taking place. For example, a specific card in a regulation deck should have a 1/52 probability of being drawn at any one time. Sample units ordinarily are chosen by selecting from a table of random numbers statistically generated so that each digit, 0 through 9, will have an equal probability of occurring in each position in the sequence. The sequentially numbered elements of a population are sampled randomly by selecting the units whose numbers appear in the table of random numbers.

Another kind of probability sampling is **stratified sampling**, in which the population of interest is divided into groups according to a common attribute, and a random sample is then chosen within each group. The stratified sample may reduce some of the error that could occur in a simple random sample. By ensuring that each major group or segment of the population receives its proportionate share of sample units, investigators avoid including too many or too few sample units from each group. Samples are usually stratified when researchers believe that there may be variations among different types of respondents. For example, many political opinion surveys are stratified by gender, race, age, and/or geographic location.

The second type of sampling, **nonprobability sampling**, is more subjective than probability sampling because there is no way to calculate the likelihood that a specific element of the population being studied will be chosen. Quota sampling, for example, is highly judgmental because the final choice of participants is left to the researchers. In **quota sampling**, researchers divide the population into groups and then arbitrarily choose participants from each group. A study of people who wear eyeglasses, for example, may be conducted by interviewing equal numbers of men and women who wear eyeglasses. In quota sampling, there are some controls—usually limited to two or three variables, such as age, gender, or race—over the selection of participants. The controls attempt to ensure that representative categories of respondents are interviewed. Because quota samples are not probability samples, not everyone has an equal chance of being selected, and sampling error therefore cannot be measured statistically. Quota samples are used most often in exploratory studies, when hypotheses are being developed. Often a small quota sample will not be projected to the total population, although the findings may provide valuable insights into a problem. Quota samples are useful when people with some common characteristic are found and questioned about the topic of interest. A probability sample used to study people allergic to cats would be highly inefficient.

SURVEY METHODS. Marketing researchers often employ sampling to collect primary data through mail, telephone, online, or personal-interview surveys. The results of such surveys are used to describe and analyze buying behavior. Selection of a survey method depends on the nature of the problem or issue, the data needed to test the hypothesis, and the resources, such

population
All the elements, units, or individuals of interest to researchers for a specific study

sample
A limited number of units chosen to represent the characteristics of the population

sampling
The process of selecting representative units from a total population

probability sampling
A sampling technique in which every element in the population being studied has a known chance of being selected for study

random sampling
A type of probability sampling in which all units in a population have an equal chance of appearing in a sample

stratified sampling
A type of probability sampling in which the population is divided into groups according to a common attribute, and a random sample is then chosen within each group

nonprobability sampling
A sampling technique in which there is no way to calculate the likelihood that a specific element of the population being studied will be chosen

quota sampling
A nonprobability sampling technique in which researchers divide the population into groups and then arbitrarily choose participants from each group

as funding and personnel, available to the researcher. Marketers may employ more than one survey method depending on the goals of the research. The SPSS, Inc., survey of American Marketing Association members found that 43.8 percent use telephone surveys, 39.3 percent use Web-based surveys, 36.8 percent use focus groups, 19 percent use mail surveys, 11.8 percent use e-mail surveys, and 9.6 percent use in-person interviews.[18] Surveys can be quite expensive (Procter & Gamble spends about $200 million to have 600 organizations conduct surveys), but small businesses can turn to sites such as SurveyMonkey.com and zoomerang .com for inexpensive or even free online surveys.[19] Table 4.4 summarizes and compares the advantages of the various survey methods.

Gathering information through surveys is becoming increasingly difficult because fewer people are willing to participate.[20] Many people believe that responding to surveys takes up too much scarce personal time, especially as surveys become longer and more detailed. Others have concerns about how much information marketers are gathering and whether their privacy is being invaded. The unethical use of selling techniques disguised as marketing surveys also has led to decreased cooperation. These factors contribute to nonresponse rates for any type of survey. Most researchers consider nonresponse the greatest threat to valid survey research.[21]

mail survey A research method in which respondents answer a questionnaire sent through the mail

In a **mail survey**, questionnaires are sent to respondents, who are encouraged to complete and return them. Mail surveys are used most often when the individuals in the sample are spread over a wide area and funds for the survey are limited. A mail survey is potentially the least

TABLE 4.4 Comparison of the Four Basic Survey Methods

	Mail Surveys	Telephone Surveys	Online Surveys	Personal Interview Surveys
Economy	Potentially lower in cost per interview than telephone or personal surveys if there is an adequate response rate.	Avoids interviewers' travel expenses; less expensive than in-home interviews.	The least expensive method if there is an adequate response rate.	The most expensive survey method; shopping-mall and focus-group interviews have lower costs than in-home interviews.
Flexibility	Inflexible; questionnaire must be short and easy for respondents to complete.	Flexible because interviewers can ask probing questions, but observations are impossible.	Less flexible; survey must be easy for online users to receive and return; short, dichotomous, or multiple-choice questions work best.	Most flexible method; respondents can react to visual materials; demographic data are more accurate; in-depth probes are possible.
Interviewer bias	Interviewer bias is eliminated; questionnaires can be returned anonymously.	Some anonymity; may be hard to develop trust in respondents.	Interviewer bias is eliminated, but e-mail address on the return eliminates anonymity.	Interviewers' personal characteristics or inability to maintain objectivity may result in bias.
Sampling and respondents' cooperation	Obtaining a complete mailing list is difficult; nonresponse is a major disadvantage.	Sample limited to respondents with telephones; devices that screen calls, busy signals, and refusals are a problem.	Sample limited to respondents with computer access; the available e-mail address list may not be a representative sample for some purposes.	Not-at-homes are a problem, which may be overcome by focus-group and shopping-mall interviewing.

Collecting Data Through Surveys
Domino's Pizza collects information through online surveys.

expensive survey method as long as the response rate is high enough to produce reliable results. The main disadvantages of this method are the possibilities of a low response rate and of misleading results if respondents differ significantly from the population being sampled. Research has found that providing a monetary incentive to respond to a mail survey has a significant impact on response rates for both consumer and business samples. However, such incentives may reduce the cost-effectiveness of this survey method.[22] As a result of these issues, companies are increasingly moving to Internet surveys and automated telephone surveys, as discussed below.

In a **telephone survey**, an interviewer records respondents' answers to a questionnaire over a phone line. A telephone survey has some advantages over a mail survey. The rate of response is higher because it takes less effort to answer the telephone and talk than to fill out and return a questionnaire. If there are enough interviewers, a telephone survey can be conducted very quickly. Thus political candidates or organizations seeking an immediate reaction to an event may choose this method. In addition, a telephone survey permits interviewers to gain rapport with respondents and ask probing questions. *Automated telephone surveys,* also known as *interactive voice response surveys* or "robosurveys," rely on a recorded voice to ask questions while a computer program records respondents' answers. The primary benefit of automated surveys is the elimination of "bias" introduced by a live researcher.

telephone survey
A research method in which respondents' answers to a questionnaire are recorded by interviewers on the phone

However, only a small proportion of the population likes to participate in telephone surveys. Just one-third of Americans are willing to participate in telephone interviews, down from two-thirds 20 years ago.[23] This poor image can limit participation significantly and distort representation in a telephone survey. Moreover, telephone surveys are limited to oral communication; visual aids or observation cannot be included. Many households are excluded from telephone directories by choice (unlisted numbers) or because the residents moved after the directory was published. Potential respondents often use telephone answering machines, voice mail, or caller ID to screen or block calls; millions have signed up for "Do Not Call Lists." Moreover, an increasing number of younger Americans have given up their fixed phone lines in favor of wireless phones.[24] These issues have serious implications for the use of telephone samples in conducting surveys.

Online surveys are evolving as an alternative to mail and telephone surveys. In an **online survey**, questionnaires can be transmitted to respondents who have agreed to be contacted and have provided their e-mail addresses. More firms are using their websites to conduct surveys. Online surveys also can make use of online communities—such as chat rooms, Web-based forums, and newsgroups—to identify trends in interests and consumption patterns. Movies, consumer electronics, food, and computers are popular topics in many online communities.[25] Indeed, by "listening in" on these ongoing conversations, marketers may be able to identify new-product opportunities and consumer needs. Moreover, this type of online data can be gathered at little incremental cost compared with alternative data sources.[26] Evolving technology and the interactive nature of the Internet allow for considerable flexibility in designing questionnaires for online surveys.

COURTESY WESTERN WATS

Online Surveys
Western Wats provides its customers with research delivered by a readily available online survey panel.

Given the growing number of households that have computers with Internet access, marketing research is likely to rely heavily on online surveys in the future. Furthermore, as negative attitudes toward telephone surveys render that technique less representative and more expensive, the integration of e-mail, fax, and voice-mail functions into one computer-based system provides a promising alternative for survey research. E-mail surveys have especially strong potential within organizations whose employees are networked and for associations that publish members' e-mail addresses. College students in particular often are willing to provide their e-mail address and other personal information in exchange for incentives such as T-shirts and other giveaways.[27] However, there are some ethical issues to consider when using e-mail for marketing research, such as unsolicited e-mail, which could be viewed as "spam," and privacy, because some potential survey respondents fear that their personal information will be given or sold to third parties without their knowledge or permission.

Social networking sites are a new way for marketers to conduct research. Online social networks function similarly to traditional social networks in that they are often used to gather useful information in understanding consumer decisions. Twitter, Facebook, MySpace, and LinkedIn are some of the most popular social networking sites. They reduce the effort and cost of staying in touch with people. Research using online social networking sites can be a good substitute for focus groups. Once a person gathers his or her friends online, they can do the same things they have traditionally done around the neighborhood, socializing, or at a party. Friends online can share photos, videos, brands they like, even complete product satisfaction evaluations.

online survey
A research method in which respondents answer a questionnaire via e-mail or on a website

social networking sites
Used to gather useful information in understanding consumer decisions

Facebook now has around 200 million users and is continuing to grow rapidly. The goal of Facebook is to become a standard communication and marketing platform, similar to the telephone, but more interactive and multidimensional. The site can be used for asking information

Marketing IN TRANSITION

Social Networks and Online Communities as Marketing Research

In today's business world, social networks may be the new answer to conducting effective marketing research. Millions of people today are involved in social networking sites like MySpace and Twitter, and companies are hoping to cash in on this involvement. For example, Skittles has started featuring on its website user-generated content taken from Wikipedia and Twitter. The website takes Skittles-related comments from these sites and posts them for all to see. In addition to generating publicity, Skittles can then examine the posts to gauge market reaction to their products.

© GARY LUCKEN/ALAMY

Of course, posting consumer-generated comments is risky. Pranksters have already begun posting ridiculous comments about Skittles to make Skittles look bad. So why choose online communities over traditional, safer marketing research? The low cost is one advantage. One firm estimates that an online community of 300 can cost $130,000–$175,000 for six months, versus the $200,000–$300,000 it would cost with traditional research methods. Generating feedback online also lets companies get past barriers found in traditional research. By giving consumers the ability to express themselves freely, companies are turning them into fellow participants in the research process. This can serve to create stronger bonds between online consumers and companies.

Most importantly, online communities allow companies to quickly test new ideas before making large investments. This was useful for one publishing company contemplating whether to buy a manuscript. It tested a chapter on an online community. Responses to the chapter were negative, prompting it to reject the manuscript and save over $100,000. Therefore, though companies have some kinks to work out, corporate online communities offer a unique opportunity to perform market research quickly, less expensively, and, if worked right, efficiently.[b]

about or providing insights on desirable features of a new product. Facebook, MySpace, LinkedIn, and Twitter have all become important as a kind of interactive digital phone book, but also as place where market researchers can obtain useful information.

In a **personal-interview survey**, participants respond to questions face to face. Various audiovisual aids—pictures, products, diagrams, or prerecorded advertising copy—can be incorporated in a personal interview. Rapport gained through direct interaction usually permits more in-depth interviewing, including probes, follow-up questions, or psychological tests. In addition, because personal interviews can be longer, they may yield more information. Finally, respondents can be selected more carefully, and reasons for nonresponse can be explored.

One such research technique is the **in-home (door-to-door) interview**. The in-home interview offers a clear advantage when thoroughness of self-disclosure and elimination of group influence are important. In an in-depth interview of 45 to 90 minutes, respondents can be probed to reveal their real motivations, feelings, behaviors, and aspirations.

The object of a **focus-group interview** is to observe group interaction when members are exposed to an idea or a concept. Media companies, including Microsoft, Yahoo, and CBS, conduct joint focus groups to learn more about online video advertising. The focus groups are used to determine advertising formats, which are beta tested on media companies' websites. Companies such as Allstate and Capital One agreed to purchase the time on the media companies' sites, with the aim of airing the best online video ads.[28] Often these interviews are conducted informally, without a structured questionnaire, in small groups of 8 to 12 people. They allow customer attitudes, behaviors, lifestyles, needs, and desires to be explored in a flexible and creative manner. Questions are open-ended and stimulate respondents to answer in their own words. Researchers can ask probing questions to clarify something they do not fully understand or something unexpected and interesting that may help to explain ideas. Even the president of the United States uses focus groups to examine ideas. After a focus group is held, President Obama instructs his staff to develop a document that summarizes the key points learned from the focus groups so that he can use the information when making policy decisions.[29] It may be necessary to use separate focus groups for each major market segment studied—men, women, and age groups—and experts recommend the use of at least two focus groups per segment in case one group is unusually idiosyncratic.[30] Focus groups have been found to be especially useful to set new-product prices.[31] However, they generally provide only qualitative, not quantitative, data and thus are best used to uncover issues that can then be explored using quantifiable marketing research techniques. Some criticism of focus groups comes from their failures. After using focus groups to conduct research, Tropicana released a new orange juice package. The new design provoked much negative feedback from loyal consumers who complained via e-mails and phone calls. Some believe that utilizing social networking sites such as Twitter, which could have gotten the response of hundreds of people nearly instantly, would have been a better and more reliable source of information on the package redesign.[32]

More organizations are starting **customer advisory boards**, which are small groups of actual customers who serve as sounding boards for new-product ideas and offer insights into their feelings and attitudes toward a firm's products, promotion, pricing, and other elements of marketing strategy. While these advisory boards help companies maintain strong relationships with valuable customers, they also can provide great insight into marketing research questions.[33] Yum! Brands' KFC, for example, formed the KFC Moms Matter! Advisory Board to obtain insight and recommendations from mothers about its brand and products.[34]

Still another option is the **telephone depth interview**, which combines the traditional focus group's ability to probe with the confidentiality provided by telephone surveys. This type of interview is most appropriate for qualitative research projects among a small targeted group that is difficult to bring together for a traditional focus group because of members' profession, location, or lifestyle. Respondents can choose the time and day for the interview. Although this method is difficult to implement, it can yield revealing information from respondents who otherwise would be unwilling to participate in marketing research.[35] Similar efforts can be conducted online through WebEx meetings.

The nature of personal interviews has changed. In the past, most personal interviews, which were based on random sampling or prearranged appointments, were conducted in the respondent's home. Today, most personal interviews are conducted outside the home. **Shopping-mall intercept interviews** involve interviewing a percentage of individuals passing by certain "intercept" points in a mall. As with any face-to-face interviewing method, shopping-mall intercept interviewing has many advantages. The interviewer is in a position to recognize and react to respondents' nonverbal indications of confusion. Respondents can be shown product prototypes, videotapes of commercials, and the like and asked for their reactions. The mall environment lets the researcher deal with complex situations. For example, in taste tests, researchers know that all the respondents are reacting to the same product, which can be prepared and monitored from the mall test kitchen. In addition to the ability to conduct tests requiring bulky equipment, lower cost and greater control make shopping-mall intercept interviews popular.

personal-interview survey
A research method in which participants respond to survey questions face to face

in-home (door-to-door) interview
A personal interview that takes place in the respondent's home

focus-group interview
A research method involving observation of group interaction when members are exposed to an idea or a concept

customer advisory boards
Small groups of actual customers who serve as sounding boards for new-product ideas and offer insights into their feelings and attitudes toward a firm's products and other elements of marketing strategy

telephone depth interview
An interview that combines the traditional focus group's ability to probe with the confidentiality provided by telephone surveys

shopping-mall intercept interviews
A research method that involves interviewing a percentage of persons passing by "intercept" points in a mall

QUESTIONNAIRE CONSTRUCTION. A carefully constructed questionnaire is essential to the success of any survey. Questions must be clear, easy to understand, and directed toward a specific objective; that is, they must be designed to elicit information that meets the study's data requirements. Researchers need to define the objective before trying to develop a questionnaire because the objective determines the substance of the questions and the amount of detail. A common mistake in constructing questionnaires is to ask questions that interest the researchers but do not yield information useful in deciding whether to accept or reject a hypothesis. Finally, the most important rule in composing questions is to maintain impartiality.

The questions are usually of three kinds: open-ended, dichotomous, and multiple-choice.

Open-ended question

What is your general opinion about broadband Internet access?

____

Sustainable Marketing

Message in a Bottle: Secondary Data Provide Recycling Lessons

Many marketing problems can be analyzed through secondary data. An example of secondary data related to social responsibility and environmental challenges is the branded-water market. Leading companies such as Coca-Cola, Nestlé, and PepsiCo are gathering information on the current impact of discarded plastic bottles on the environment. The Beverage Container Recycling Report, compiled by As You Sow, provides current data on beverage companies' recycling efforts for consumers and other stakeholders. The report evaluated twelve beverage companies by using publicly available information from websites, annual reports, and survey responses.

© CHRIS SATTLBERGER/ GETTY IMAGES

Last year, over 5 billion pounds of polyethylene terephthalate (PET) was used in plastic containers; of that only about 1 billion pounds was recycled. With salvage prices as high as 25 cents per pound, the remaining 4 billion pounds represent the equivalent of sending one billion $1 bills to landfills. Although beverage makers have shrunk the weight of their PET bottles, recycling rates have slowed. Every day in the United States, more than 60 million plastic water bottles are thrown away, with most ending up in landfills or incinerators. However, millions litter America's streets, parks, and waterways as well.

Beverage companies must rethink and develop new strategies to deal with the problem that their products are creating. In this case, secondary data are providing information about the issues associated with plastic beverage bottles not only to beverage companies but also to consumer groups, regulatory officials, and other stakeholders concerned with ecology and the environment.[c]

Dichotomous question

Do you presently have broadband access at home, work, or school?

Yes ____________ No ____________

Multiple-choice question

What age group are you in?

Under 20 ____________

20–35 ____________

36 and over ____________

Researchers must be very careful about questions that a respondent might consider too personal or that might require an admission of activities that other people are likely to condemn. Questions of this type should be worded to make them less offensive.

OBSERVATION METHODS. In using observation methods, researchers record individuals' overt behavior, taking note of physical conditions and events. Direct contact with them is avoided; instead, their actions are examined and noted systematically. For instance, researchers might use observation methods to answer the question, "How long does the average McDonald's restaurant customer have to wait in line before being served?" Observation may include the use of ethnographic techniques, such as watching customers interact with a product in a real-world environment.

Microsoft employed ethnographic techniques when it sent researchers into 50 consumers' homes to observe and videotape how the entire family used the firm's Vista operating system software, which had not yet been released to the public. Based on the company's observations and interactions with the households, Microsoft made a number of changes to improve the system, including correcting about 1,000 problems identified by the participant households.[36]

Observation also may be combined with interviews. For example, during a personal interview, the condition of a respondent's home or other possessions may be observed and recorded. The interviewer also can observe directly and confirm demographic information such as race, approximate age, and sex.

Data gathered through observation sometimes can be biased if the person is aware of the observation process. However, an observer can be placed in a natural market environment, such as a grocery store, without biasing or influencing shoppers' actions. If the presence of a human observer is likely to bias the outcome, or

REPRINTED WITH PERMISSION OF BURKE, INC.

Interpreting Research
Companies like Burke can help interpret the data collected from market research and offer insights into the areas investigated.

if human sensory abilities are inadequate, mechanical means may be used to record behavior. Mechanical observation devices include cameras, recorders, counting machines, scanners, and equipment that records physiologic changes. The electronic scanners used in supermarkets are very useful in marketing research. They provide accurate data on sales and customers' purchase patterns, and marketing researchers may obtain such data from the supermarkets.

Observation is straightforward and avoids a central problem of survey methods: motivating respondents to state their true feelings or opinions. However, observation tends to be descriptive. When it is the only method of data collection, it may not provide insights into causal relationships. Another drawback is that analyses based on observation are subject to the biases of the observer or the limitations of the mechanical device.

INTERPRETING RESEARCH FINDINGS

After collecting data to test their hypotheses, marketers need to interpret the research findings. Interpretation of the data is easier if marketers carefully plan their data-analysis methods early in the research process. They also should allow for continual evaluation of the data during the entire collection period. They can then gain valuable insight into areas that should be probed during the formal interpretation.

The first step in drawing conclusions from most research is to display the data in table format. If marketers intend to apply the results to individual categories of the things or people being studied, cross-tabulation may be quite useful, especially in tabulating joint occurrences. For example, using the two variables gender and purchase rates of automobile tires, a cross-tabulation could show how men and women differ in purchasing automobile tires.

After the data are tabulated, they must be analyzed. **Statistical interpretation** focuses on what is typical or what deviates from the average. It indicates how widely responses vary and how they are distributed in relation to the variable being measured. When marketers interpret statistics, they must take into account estimates of expected error or deviation from the true values of the population. The analysis of data may lead researchers to accept or reject the hypothesis being studied.

statistical interpretation
Analysis of what is typical or what deviates from the average

REPORTING RESEARCH FINDINGS

The final step in the marketing research process is to report the research findings. Before preparing the report, the marketer must take a clear, objective look at the findings to see how well the gathered facts answer the research question or support or negate the initial hypotheses. In most cases it is extremely unlikely that the study can provide everything needed to answer the research question. Thus the researcher must point out the deficiencies, along with the reasons for them, in the report.

The report of research results is usually a formal, written document. Researchers must allow time for the writing task when they plan and schedule the project. Because the report is a means of communicating with the decision makers who will use the research findings, researchers need to determine beforehand how much detail and supporting data to include. They should keep in mind that corporate executives prefer reports that are short, clear, and simply expressed. Researchers often give their summary and recommendations first, especially if decision makers do not have time to study how the results were obtained. A technical report allows its users to analyze data and interpret recommendations because it describes the research methods and procedures and the most important data gathered. Thus researchers must recognize the needs and expectations of the report user and adapt to them.

Using Technology to Improve Marketing Information Gathering and Analysis

Technology is making information for marketing decisions increasingly accessible. The ability of marketers to track customer buying behavior and to discern what buyers want is changing the nature of marketing. Customer relationship management is being enhanced by integrating data from all customer contacts and combining that information to improve customer retention. Information technology permits internal research and

COURTESY OF REREZ

Using Technology
Re Rez uses some of the most advanced marketing research technology to assist clients.

quick information gathering to understand and satisfy customers. For example, company responses to e-mail complaints, as well as to communications through mail, telephone, and fax, can be used to improve customer satisfaction, retention, and value.[37] Armed with such information, marketers can fine-tune marketing mixes to satisfy the needs of their customers.

The integration of telecommunications and computer technologies is allowing marketers to access a growing array of valuable information sources related to industry forecasts, business trends, and customer buying behavior. Electronic communication tools can be used effectively to gain accurate information with minimal customer interaction. Most marketing researchers have e-mail, voice mail, teleconferencing, and fax machines at their disposal. In fact, many firms use marketing information systems and customer relationship management technologies to network all these technologies and organize all the marketing data available to them. In this section we look at marketing information systems and specific technologies that are helping marketing researchers obtain and manage marketing research data.

MARKETING INFORMATION SYSTEMS

A **marketing information system (MIS)** is a framework for the day-to-day management and structuring of information gathered regularly from sources both inside and outside an organization. An MIS provides a continuous flow of information about prices, advertising expenditures, sales, competition, and distribution expenses. Anheuser-Busch, for example, uses a system called BudNet that compiles information about past sales at individual stores, inventory, competitors' displays and prices, and a host of other information collected by distributors' sales representatives on handheld computers. BudNet allows managers to respond quickly to changes in social trends or competitors' strategies with an appropriate promotional message, package, display, or discount.[38]

The main focus of the MIS is on data storage and retrieval, as well as on computer capabilities and management's information requirements. Regular reports of sales by product or market categories, data on inventory levels, and records of salespeople's activities are examples of information that is useful in making decisions. In the MIS, the means of *gathering* data receive less attention than do the procedures for expediting the *flow* of information.

An effective MIS starts by determining the objective of the information, that is, by identifying decision needs that require certain information. The firm then can specify an information system for continuous monitoring to provide regular, pertinent information on both the external and internal environment. FedEx, for example, has developed interactive marketing systems to provide instantaneous communication between the company and its customers. Through use of the telephone and Internet, customers can track their packages and receive immediate feedback concerning delivery. The company's website provides valuable information about customer usage, and it allows customers to express directly what they think about company services. The evolving telecommunications and computer technology is allowing marketing information systems to cultivate one-to-one relationships with customers.

marketing information system (MIS)
A framework for the management and structuring of information gathered regularly from sources inside and outside an organization

DATABASES

Most marketing information systems include internal databases. They allow marketers to tap into an abundance of information useful in making marketing decisions: internal sales reports, newspaper articles, company news releases, government economic reports, bibliographies, and more, typically accessed through a computer system. Information technology has made it possible to develop databases to guide strategic planning and help improve customer services.

Customer relationship management (CRM) employs database marketing techniques to identify different types of customers and to develop specific strategies for interacting with each customer. CRM incorporates three elements:

1. Identifying and building a database of current and potential consumers, including a wide range of demographic, lifestyle, and purchase information
2. Delivering differential messages according to each consumer's preferences and characteristics through established and new media channels
3. Tracking customer relationships to monitor the costs of retaining individual customers and the lifetime value of their purchases[39]

It is important for marketers to distinguish between *active* customers—those likely to continue buying from the firm—and *inactive* customers—those who are likely to defect, or already have defected. This information should (1) identify profitable inactive customers who can be reactivated; (2) remove inactive, unprofitable customers from the customer database, and (3) identify active customers who should be targeted with regular marketing activities.[40]

When Pulte Homes, the nation's top homebuilder, analyzed information in its database, it realized that 80 percent of its home buyers were selecting the same countertops, carpet, fixtures, lighting, and so on. The company used this information to streamline its 2,000 floorplans and reduce the number of fixtures and other home features to better match customer desires and to improve overall efficiency and decision-making.[41] Many commercial websites require consumers to register and provide personal information to access the site or make a purchase. Ace Hardware has ten and a half million discount reward members. These customers can be analyzed by looking at rewards customer purchases as a percentage of total revenue, potential households in the United States per segment, and percentage composition of the rewards database. Nationally, marketers for Ace identify consumers and target them with direct mail that speaks to their particular needs and interests.[42] Grocery stores gain a significant amount of data through checkout scanners tied to store discount cards. According to ACNielsen, 78 percent of U.S. households now use at least one store discount card.[43] In fact, one of the best ways to predict market behavior is the use of database information gathered through loyalty programs or other transaction-based processes.[44]

Marketing researchers also can use commercial databases developed by information research firms such as LexisNexis to obtain useful information for marketing decisions. Many of these commercial databases are accessible online for a fee. They also can be obtained in printed form or on CD-ROMs. In most commercial databases, the user typically does a computer search by keyword, topic, or company, and the database service generates abstracts, articles, or reports that can be printed out. Accessing multiple reports or a complete article may cost extra.

Information provided by a single firm on household demographics, purchases, television viewing behavior, and responses to promotions such as coupons and free samples is called **single-source data.**[45] For example, Behavior Scan, offered by Information Resources, Inc., screens about 60,000 households in 26 U.S. markets. This single-source information service monitors consumer household televisions and records the programs and commercials watched. When buyers from these households shop in stores equipped with scanning registers, they present Hotline cards (similar to credit cards) to cashiers. This enables each customer's identification to be electronically coded so that the firm can track each product purchased and store the information in a database.

single-source data
Information provided by a single marketing research firm

MARKETING DECISION SUPPORT SYSTEMS

A **marketing decision support system (MDSS)** is customized computer software that aids marketing managers in decision-making by helping them anticipate the effects of certain decisions. Some MDSSs have a broader range and offer greater computational and modeling capabilities than spreadsheets; they let managers explore a greater number of alternatives. For example, an MDSS can determine how sales and profits might be affected by higher or lower interest rates or how sales forecasts, advertising expenditures, production levels, and the like might affect overall profits. For this reason, MDSS software often is a major component of a company's MIS. Customized decision support systems can support a customer orientation and customer satisfaction in business marketing.[46] Some MDSSs incorporate artificial intelligence and other advanced computer technologies.

Issues in Marketing Research

THE IMPORTANCE OF ETHICAL MARKETING RESEARCH

Marketing managers and other professionals are relying more and more on marketing research, marketing information systems, and new technologies to make better decisions. It is therefore essential that professional standards be established by which to judge the reliability of such research. Such standards are necessary because of the ethical and legal issues that develop in gathering marketing research data. In the area of online interaction, for example, consumers remain wary of how the personal information collected by marketers will be used, especially whether it will be sold to third parties. In addition, the relationships between research suppliers, such as marketing research agencies, and the marketing managers who make strategy decisions require ethical behavior. Organizations such as the Marketing Research Association have developed codes of conduct and guidelines to promote ethical marketing research. To be effective, such guidelines must instruct those who participate in marketing research on how to avoid misconduct. Table 4.5 recommends explicit steps interviewers should follow when introducing a questionnaire.

INTERNATIONAL ISSUES IN MARKETING RESEARCH

Sociocultural, economic, political, legal, and technological forces vary in different regions of the world, and these variations create challenges for organizations attempting to understand foreign customers through marketing research. The marketing research process we describe in this chapter is used globally, but to ensure that the research is valid and reliable, data-gathering methods may have to be modified to allow for regional differences. For example, experts have found that Latin Americans do not respond well to focus groups or in-depth interviews lasting more than 90 minutes. Researchers therefore need to adjust their tactics to generate information useful for marketing products in Latin America.[47] To ensure that global and regional differences are addressed satisfactorily, many companies retain a research firm with experience in the country of interest. Most of the largest marketing research firms derive a significant share of their revenues from research conducted outside the United States.

Experts recommend a two-pronged approach to international marketing research. The first phase involves a detailed search for and analysis of secondary data to gain greater

marketing decision support system (MDSS) Customized computer software that aids marketing managers in decision-making

TABLE 4.5 Guidelines for Questionnaire Introduction

Questionnaire introduction should
• Allow interviewers to introduce themselves by name.
• State the name of the research company.
• Indicate that this questionnaire is a marketing research project.
• Explain that no sales will be involved.
• Note the general topic of discussion (if this is a problem in a "blind" study, a statement such as "consumer opinion" is acceptable).
• State the likely duration of the interview.
• Ensure the anonymity of the respondent and the confidentiality of all answers.
• State the honorarium if applicable (for many business-to-business and medical studies, this is done up front for both qualitative and quantitative studies).
• Reassure the respondent with a statement such as, "There are no right or wrong answers, so please give thoughtful and honest answers to each question" (recommended by many clients).

Source: Reprinted with permission of The Marketing Research Association, P.O. Box 230, Rocky Hill, CT 06067-0230, (860) 257-4008.

understanding of a particular marketing environment and to pinpoint issues that must be taken into account in gathering primary research data. Secondary data can be particularly helpful in building a general understanding of the market, including economic, legal, cultural, and demographic issues, as well as in assessing the risks of doing business in that market and in forecasting demand.[48] Marketing researchers often begin by studying country trade reports from the U.S. Department of Commerce, as well as country-specific information from local sources, such as a country's website, and trade and general business publications such as *The Wall Street Journal.* These sources can offer insight into the marketing environment in a particular country and even can indicate untapped market opportunities abroad.

The second phase involves field research using many of the methods described earlier, including focus groups and telephone surveys, to refine a firm's understanding of specific customer needs and preferences. Specific differences among countries can have a profound influence on data gathering. For example, in-home (door-to-door) interviews are illegal in some countries. In China, few people have regular telephone lines, making telephone surveys both impractical and nonrepresentative of the total population. Primary data gathering may have a greater chance of success if the firm employs local researchers who better understand how to approach potential respondents and can do so in their own language.[49] Regardless of the specific methods used to gather primary data, whether in the United States or abroad, the goal is to understand the needs of specific target markets and thus craft the best marketing strategy to satisfy the needs of customers in each market, as we will see in the next chapter.

CHAPTER REVIEW

OBJECTIVES

1 Define *marketing research* and understand its importance.

Marketing research is the systematic design, collection, interpretation, and reporting of information to help marketers solve specific marketing problems or take advantage of marketing opportunities. Marketing research can help a firm to better understand market opportunities, ascertain the potential for success for new products, and determine the feasibility of a particular marketing strategy. The value of marketing research is measured by improvements in a marketer's ability to make decisions.

2 Describe the basic steps in conducting marketing research.

To maintain the control needed to obtain accurate information, marketers approach marketing research as a process with logical steps: (1) defining and locating issues or problems, (2) designing the research project, (3) collecting data, (4) interpreting research findings, and (5) reporting research findings. The first step, issue or problem definition, focuses on uncovering the nature and boundaries of a situation or question related to marketing strategy or implementation. The second step involves designing a research project to obtain needed information, formulating a hypothesis, and determining what type of research to employ that will test the hypothesis so that the results are reliable and valid. Marketers conduct exploratory research when they need more information about a problem or want to make a tentative hypothesis more specific; they use conclusive research to verify insights through an objective procedure. Research is considered reliable if it produces almost identical results in successive repeated trials; it is valid if it measures what it is supposed to measure and not something else. The third step is the data-gathering phase. To apply research data to decision-making, marketers must interpret and report their findings properly—the final two steps in the research process. Statistical interpretation focuses on what is typical or what deviates from the average. After interpreting the research findings, the researchers must prepare a report on the findings that the decision makers can understand and use.

3 Explore the fundamental methods of gathering data for marketing research.

For the third step in the marketing research process, two types of data are available. Primary data are observed and recorded or collected directly from subjects; secondary data are compiled inside or outside the organization for some purpose other than the current investigation. Secondary data may be collected from an organization's database and other internal sources or from periodicals, government publications, online, and unpublished sources. Methods for collecting primary data include sampling, surveys, observation, and experimentation. Sampling involves selecting representative units from a total population. In probability sampling, every element in the population being studied has a known chance of being selected for study. Nonprobability sampling is more subjective because there is no way to calculate the likelihood that a specific element of the population being studied will be chosen. Marketing researchers employ sampling to collect primary data through surveys by mail, telephone, or the Internet or through personal or group interviews. A carefully constructed questionnaire is essential to the success of any survey. In using observation methods, researchers record respondents' overt behavior and take note of physical conditions and events but avoid direct contact with respondents. In an experiment, marketing researchers attempt to maintain certain variables while measuring the effects of experimental variables.

4 Describe how tools such as databases, decision support systems, and the Internet facilitate marketing information systems and research.

Many firms use computer technology to create a marketing information system (MIS), which is a framework for gathering and managing information from sources both inside and outside the organization. A database is a collection of information arranged for easy access and retrieval. A marketing decision support system (MDSS) is customized computer software that aids marketing managers in decision-making by helping them anticipate what effect certain decisions will have. The World Wide Web also enables marketers to communicate with customers and obtain information.

5 Identify key ethical and international considerations in marketing research.

Eliminating unethical marketing research practices and establishing generally acceptable procedures for conducting research are important goals of marketing research. International marketing uses the same marketing research process, but data-gathering methods may require modification to address differences.

Please visit the student website at www.cengage.com/international for quizzes and games that will help you prepare for exams and achieve the grade you want.

KEY CONCEPTS

- marketing research
- research design
- hypothesis
- exploratory research
- conclusive research
- descriptive research
- experimental research
- reliability
- validity
- primary data
- secondary data
- population
- sample
- sampling
- probability sampling
- random sampling
- stratified sampling
- nonprobability sampling
- quota sampling
- mail survey
- telephone survey
- online survey
- social networking sites
- personal-interview survey
- in-home (door-to-door) interview
- focus-group interview
- customer advisory boards
- telephone depth interview
- shopping-mall intercept interview
- statistical interpretation
- marketing information system (MIS)
- single-source data
- marketing decision support system (MDSS)

ISSUES FOR DISCUSSION AND REVIEW

1. What is marketing research? Why is it important?
2. Describe the five steps in the marketing research process.
3. What is the difference between defining a research problem and developing a hypothesis?
4. Describe the different types of approaches to marketing research, and indicate when each should be used.
5. Where are data for marketing research obtained? Give examples of internal and external data.
6. What is the difference between probability sampling and nonprobability sampling? In what situation would it be best to use random sampling? Stratified sampling? Quota sampling?
7. Suggest some ways to encourage respondents to cooperate in mail surveys.
8. Describe some marketing problems that could be solved through information gained from observation.
9. What is a marketing information system, and what should it provide?
10. How does marketing research in other countries differ from marketing research in the United States?

MARKETING APPLICATIONS

1. After observing customers' traffic patterns, Bashas Markets repositioned the greeting card section in its stores, and card sales increased substantially. To increase sales for the following types of companies, what information might marketing researchers want to gather from customers?
   a. Furniture stores
   b. Gasoline outlets/service stations
   c. Investment companies
   d. Medical clinics
2. Choose a company in your city or town that you think might benefit from a research project. Develop a research question and outline a method to approach this question. Explain why you think the research question is relevant to the organization and why the particular methodology is suited to the question and the company.

3. Input for marketing information systems can come from internal or external sources. Indicate two firms or companies in your city or town that might benefit from internal sources and two that would benefit from external sources, and explain why they would benefit. Suggest the type of information each should gather.

4. Suppose that you were opening a health insurance brokerage firm and wanted to market your services to small businesses with fewer than 50 employees. Determine which database for marketing information you would use in your marketing efforts, and explain why you would use it.

ONLINE EXERCISE

5. The World Association of Opinion and Marketing Research Professionals [founded as the European Society for Opinion and Marketing Research (ESOMAR) in 1948] is a nonprofit association for marketing research professionals. The European organization promotes the use of opinion and marketing research to improve marketing decisions in companies worldwide and works to protect personal privacy in the research process. Visit the association's website at http://www.esomar.org/.

   a. How can ESOMAR help marketing professionals conduct research to guide marketing strategy?
   b. How can ESOMAR help marketers protect the privacy of research subjects when conducting marketing research in other countries?
   c. ESOMAR introduced the first professional code of conduct for marketing research professionals in 1948. The association continues to update the document to address new technology and other changes in the marketing environment. According to ESOMAR's code, what are the specific professional responsibilities of marketing researchers?

For a marketing research company, an important element in gathering data for a market is the level of information technology infrastructure that exists. NationMaster.com's website offers a subcategory of personal computers that can provide insight on the level of personal computer usage in a country. Use the search term "compare various statistics" at http://globaledge.msu.edu/ibrd (and check the box "Resource Desk only") to reach NationMaster.com, and then select the "Media" category and then the subcategory of "Personal Computers (PCs)." Give a summary of the top 15 countries as ranked by the number of PCs used. From this specified list of markets, include an assessment of the three countries with the most and least access to PCs. What conclusions can you draw?

DEVELOPING YOUR MARKETING PLAN

Decisions about which market opportunities to pursue, what customer needs to satisfy, and how to reach potential customers are not made in a vacuum. The information provided by marketing research activities is essential in developing both the strategic plan and the specific marketing mix. Focus on the following issues as you relate the concepts in this chapter to the development of your marketing plan.

1. Define the nature and scope of the questions you must answer with regard to your market. Identify the types of information you will need about the market to answer those questions. For example, do you need to know about the buying habits, household income levels, or attitudes of potential customers?
2. Determine whether or not this information can be obtained from secondary sources. Visit the websites provided in Table 4.3 as possible resources for the secondary data.
3. Using Table 4.4, choose the appropriate survey method(s) you would use to collect primary data for one of your information needs. What sampling method would you use?

The information obtained from these questions should assist you in developing various aspects of your marketing plan found in the *Interactive Marketing* Plan exercise.

VIDEO CASE 4

Getting to the Heart of the Matter: Research Design at LSPMA

Lake Research Partners, previously known as Lake, Snell, Perry, Mermin & Associates, Inc. (LSPMA), is a national public opinion and political strategy research firm. Its expertise lies in conducting objective opinion polls to assess the attitudes and behaviors of important target groups that concern its clients. The Washington, D.C.-based firm is nationally recognized for its knowledge of women's issues, children's and youth's concerns, and environmental political issues. Among the company's clients are the Democratic National Committee, the Democratic Governor's Association, Sierra Club, Planned Parenthood, Human Rights Campaign, Emily's List, and the Kaiser Foundation. LSPMA also conducts regular polls for *U.S. News & World Report,* and with the Terrance Group it conducts the Battleground Poll, which surveys the year's political landscape and draws attention to critical issues that Washington insiders can't afford to ignore. In 2005 LPSMA acquired the Washington- and San Diego-based polling firm Decision Research, giving it even greater capacity to conduct research for both business and political clients.

LSPMA's primary goal is to discover what the public thinks for people who want to know. Its staff serves among the Democratic Party's leading strategists, acting as tacticians and senior advisers to dozens of political incumbents and challengers at all levels of the electoral process, as well as to a wide range of advocacy organizations, nonprofit organizations, and foundations. Its client base is split evenly among three groups: political candidates such as senators and governors; progressive issue organizations that want research on social issues such as poverty, education, health care, and teen pregnancy; and foundations or major institutions such as the American Cancer Society.

Through research techniques, including reconnaissance and espionage, LSPMA gathers and presents hard data regarding what specific segments of the public think about certain issues or candidates. LSPMA's work helps clients identify potential problems or opportunities and determine what strategies and messages would best help them achieve their goals and reach their target audiences. It is important to know what different segments of the population think, feel, and need so that advertising can then be targeted at the people who organizations want to reach. LSPMA uses a variety of methods, including telephone interviews, online polls, and focus groups, to create portraits of groups of people, such as "soccer moms," "waitress moms," or "NASCAR dads," so its clients can understand these segments and recognize important trends.

Research allows LSPMA's clients to know what Americans are thinking and helps them determine how to target those segments of the population who are likely to think their firm has the right product or the right candidate. It allows clients to understand where they are most vulnerable and where they have the greatest opportunities to gain more support. By knowing which people feel strongly, which are sitting on the fence, and which are capable of changing their opinions, it is possible to segment people according to what they think and how they act and behave. Once organizations know whom to target and which issues are most important to those they wish to target, they can narrow their approaches to accomplish their goals in the most cost-efficient way.

There are many reasons to segment the public. Since people are different, segmentation enables marketers and pollsters to cluster together like-minded people to better understand who they are. It is then possible to craft a message that precisely targets a particular audience. Markets can be segmented by age, gender, education, geographic region, income, or race to create new ways of looking at a group that tends to behave similarly.

There are pitfalls to segmentation, however. It can sometimes make people seem more diverse than they actually are. For example, women hold similar views on 80 percent of political issues. Segmentation can help an individual or organization only so much; the rest depends on the hottest new trends. Few groups are static or truly homogeneous, which means that continuous research is necessary to remain up to date with changes in attitudes and behaviors and to ensure that messages still reach their target audiences.

Like all marketing research firms, LSPMA plans its marketing research strategy well in advance, including such details as deciding what questions to ask, which audience to target, in what setting to target them, what time frame to use, and how to manage costs. It enables the firm to know what it has to do and how to do it. All research firms, regardless of their clients, create information for more informed understanding and decisions.

Getting to the Heart of the Matter: Research Design at LSPMA—(continued)

QUESTIONS FOR DISCUSSION

1. Why do political organizations need marketing research conducted by LSPMA?
2. What is the relationship between marketing research conducted by LSPMA and identifying the needs and wants of specific market segments?
3. Why would a business rely on a marketing research firm that is heavily into political polling?

Steve Bassill, "How to Implement a Winning Segment Strategy," Marketing Profs.com, Feb. 21, 2006, www.marketingprofs.com/6/bassill1.asp; Lake Snell Perry Mermin & Associates, www.lakesnellperry.com (accessed Jan. 9, 2008); "Leading Democratic Polling Firm Celebrates 10th Anniversary with New Partner," Lake Snell Perry Mermin & Associates, press release, Mar. 11, 2005, www.lakesnellperry.com/new/Mermin0311.htm.

CHAPTER 5 Target Markets: Segmentation and Evaluation

OBJECTIVES:

1. Learn what a market is.
2. Understand the differences among general targeting strategies.
3. Become familiar with the major segmentation variables.
4. Know what segment profiles are and how they are used.
5. Understand how to evaluate market segments.
6. Identify the factors that influence the selection of specific market segments for use as target markets.
7. Become familiar with sales forecasting methods.

HIGH SCHOOL MUSICAL: THE HIT

From Memphis to Moscow, Budapest to Bangalore, teen, tween, and unknown numbers of adult fans in 100 countries have made Disney's *High School Musical* a mega-hit. The Disney Channel became the leading basic-cable channel in prime time among preteens and young teens after a record 17 million viewers tuned in to the premiere of *HSM2*. Prior to the October 2008 release of Disney's *HSM3* (which had the biggest opening ever for a movie musical), an estimated 455 million viewers had already seen the first two *HSMs*—which translates to a mind-boggling one-fifteenth of the globe.

The original Disney Channel cable TV movie cost just $4.2 million to produce. According to one analyst, *HSM* has generated $1B, as in billion, in operating revenue for Disney. Millions bought the DVD and/or the CD so they and their friends could sing and dance along with Troy, Gabriella, Sharpay, and Ryan, their aspirational reference group. The movie quickly became a marketing springboard for Disney to launch a successful concert tour, a stage musical, and sales of branded items like dolls, novels, and stationery.

Disney partnered with ABC to develop an *American Idol*–style *HSM* TV show. The winner appeared in an *HSM3* music video (which rolled during the closing credits of the movie). To keep the excitement going, the movie's website posts behind-the-scenes interviews, quizzes, downloadable posters, party-planning ideas, and more.

Disney has licensed the movie brand to appear on cosmetics, clothing, iPod accessories, and even an ice-skating show, while marketing partners like Dannon, Honda, and Walmart created tie-in promotions for kids and their parents. Disney has earned hundreds of millions in profits from the *High School Musical* brand by understanding the behavior of its audience.[1]

To compete effectively against other entertainment providers, Disney has singled out specific customer groups toward which it directs its marketing efforts. Any organization that wants to succeed must identify its customers and develop and maintain marketing mixes that satisfy the needs of those customers.

In this chapter we explore markets and market segmentation. Initially we define the term *market* and discuss the major requirements of a market. Then we examine the steps in the target-market selection process, including identifying the appropriate targeting strategy, determining which variables to use for segmenting consumer and business markets, developing market segment profiles, evaluating relevant market segments, and selecting target markets. Finally, we discuss various methods for developing sales forecasts.

What Is a Market?

In Chapter 2, we defined a *market* as a group of people who, as individuals or as organizations, have needs for products in a product class and have the ability, willingness, and authority to purchase such products. Students, for example, are part of the market for textbooks; they are also part of the markets for computers, clothes, food, music, and other products. Individuals can have the desire, the buying power, and the willingness to purchase certain products but may not have the authority to do so. For example, teenagers may have the desire, the money, and the willingness to buy liquor, but a liquor producer does not consider them a market because teenagers are prohibited by law from buying alcoholic beverages. A group of people that lacks any one of the four requirements thus does not constitute a market.

Markets fall into one of two categories: consumer markets and business markets. These categories are based on the characteristics of the individuals and groups that make up a specific market and the purposes for which they buy products. A **consumer market** consists of purchasers and household members who intend to consume or benefit from the purchased products and do not buy products for the main purpose of making a profit. Consumer markets are sometimes also referred to as *business-to-consumer* (B2C) *markets.* Each of us belongs to numerous consumer markets. The millions of individuals with the ability, willingness, and authority to buy make up a multitude of consumer markets for products such as housing, food, clothing, vehicles, personal services, appliances, furniture, recreational equipment, and so on, as we shall see in Chapter 6.

A **business market** consists of individuals or groups that purchase a specific kind of product for one of three purposes: resale, direct use in producing other products, or use in general daily operations. For example, a lamp producer that buys electrical wire to use in the production of lamps is part of a business market for electrical wire. This same firm purchases dust mops to clean its office areas. Although the mops are not used in the direct production of lamps, they are used in the operations of the firm; thus this manufacturer is part of a business market for dust mops. Business markets also may be called *business-to-business* (B2B), *industrial,* or *organizational markets.* They also can be classified into producer, reseller, government, and institutional markets.

consumer market
Purchasers and household members who intend to consume or benefit from the purchased products and do not buy products to make profits

business market
Individuals or groups that purchase a specific kind of product for resale, direct use in producing other products, or use in general daily operations

Target-Market Selection Process

In Chapter 2, we indicated that the first of two major components for developing a marketing strategy is to select a target market. Although marketers may employ several methods for target-market selection, generally they use a five-step process. This process is shown in Figure 5.1, and we discuss it in the following sections.

FIGURE 5.1 Target-Market Selection Process

1 Identify the appropriate targeting strategy → 2 Determine which segmentation variables to use → 3 Develop market segment profiles → 4 Evaluate relevant market segments → 5 Select specific target markets

Step 1: Identify the Appropriate Targeting Strategy

A target market is a group of people or organizations for which a business creates and maintains a marketing mix specifically designed to satisfy the needs of group members. The strategy used to select a target market is affected by target-market needs and characteristics, product attributes, and the organization's objectives and resources. Figure 5.2 illustrates the three basic targeting strategies: undifferentiated, concentrated, and differentiated.

The letters in each target market represent potential customers. Customers with the same letters have similar characteristics and similar product needs.

undifferentiated targeting strategy A strategy in which an organization designs a single marketing mix and directs it at the entire market for a particular product

UNDIFFERENTIATED TARGETING STRATEGY

An organization sometimes defines an entire market for a particular product as its target market. When a company designs a single marketing mix and directs it at the entire market for a particular product, it is using an **undifferentiated targeting strategy**. As Figure 5.2 shows, the strategy assumes that all customers in the target market for a specific kind of product have similar needs, so the organization can satisfy most customers with a single marketing mix. This

IMAGE COURTESY OF THE ADVERTISING ARCHIVES

COURTESY OF INTEL CORPORATION

Types of Markets
The producer of Altoids mints aims its advertisements at consumer markets. The Intel ad is aimed at business markets.

FIGURE 5.2 **Targeting Strategies**

The letters in each target market represent potential customers. Customers with the same letters have similar characteristics and similar product needs.

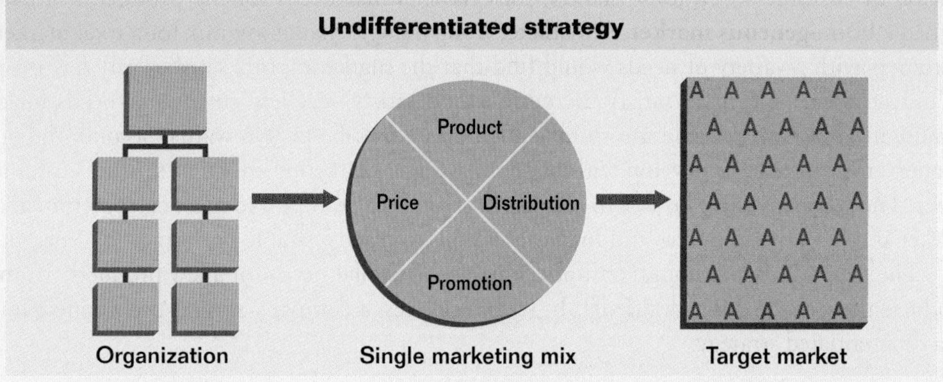

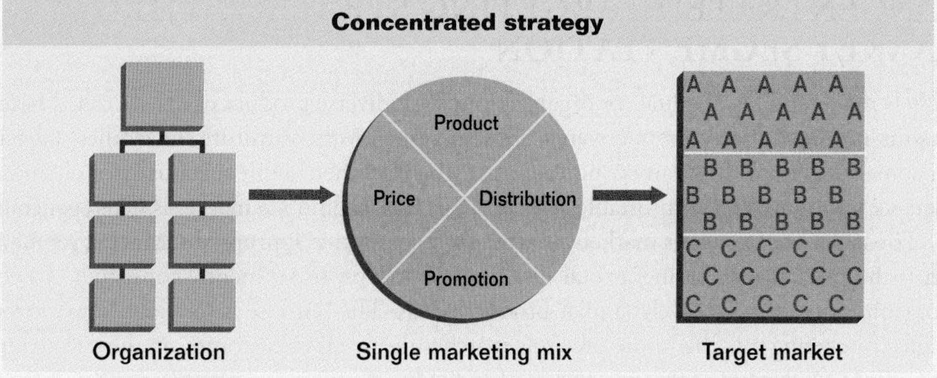

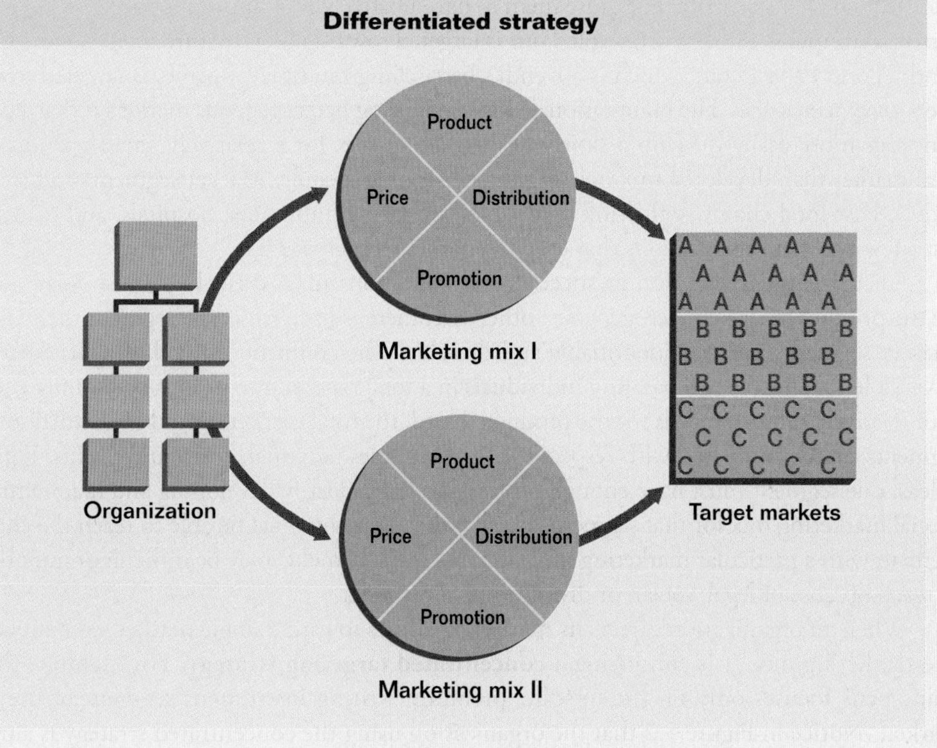

mix consists of one type of product with little or no variation, one price, one promotional program aimed at everybody, and one distribution system to reach most customers in the total market. Products marketed successfully through the undifferentiated strategy include commodities and staple food items, such as sugar and salt, and certain kinds of farm produce.

The undifferentiated targeting strategy is effective under two conditions. First, a large proportion of customers in a total market must have similar needs for the product, a situation termed a **homogeneous market**. A marketer using a single marketing mix for a total market of customers with a variety of needs would find that the marketing mix satisfies very few people. A "universal car" meant to satisfy everyone would satisfy very few customers' needs for cars because it would not provide the specific attributes a specific person wants. Second, the organization must be able to develop and maintain a single marketing mix that satisfies customers' needs. The company must be able to identify a set of needs common to most customers in a total market and have the resources and managerial skills to reach a sizable portion of that market.

The reality is that although customers may have similar needs for a few products, for most products their needs differ decidedly. In such instances, a company should use a concentrated or a differentiated strategy.

CONCENTRATED TARGETING STRATEGY THROUGH MARKET SEGMENTATION

Markets made up of individuals or organizations with diverse product needs are called **heterogeneous markets**. Not everyone wants the same type of car, furniture, or clothes. Consider that some individuals want an economical car, whereas others desire a status symbol, and still others seek a roomy and comfortable vehicle. Thus the automobile market is heterogeneous.

For such heterogeneous markets, market segmentation is appropriate. **Market segmentation** is the process of dividing a total market into groups, or segments, consisting of people or organizations with relatively similar product needs. The purpose is to enable a marketer to design a marketing mix that more precisely matches the needs of customers in the selected market segment. A **market segment** consists of individuals, groups, or organizations with one or more similar characteristics that cause them to have relatively similar product needs. The online personal computer game World Golf Tour is targeted toward older, mature men. On the other hand, World of Warcraft, which is Vivendi's best-selling multiplayer game, is targeted toward Web-savvy teenagers.[2] The main rationale for segmenting heterogeneous markets is that a company can more easily develop a satisfying marketing mix for a relatively small portion of a total market than develop a mix meeting the needs of all people. Market segmentation is used widely. Fast-food chains, soft-drink companies, magazine publishers, hospitals, and banks are just a few types of organizations that employ market segmentation.

For market segmentation to succeed, five conditions must exist. First, customers' needs for the product must be heterogeneous; otherwise, there is little reason to segment the market. Second, segments must be identifiable and divisible. The company must find a characteristic or variable for effectively separating individuals in a total market into groups containing people with relatively uniform needs for the product. Third, the total market should be divided so that segments can be compared with respect to estimated sales potential, costs, and profits. Fourth, at least one segment must have enough profit potential to justify developing and maintaining a special marketing mix for that segment. Finally, the company must be able to reach the chosen segment with a particular marketing mix. Some market segments may be difficult or impossible to reach because of legal, social, or distribution constraints.

When an organization directs its marketing efforts toward a single market segment using one marketing mix, it is employing a **concentrated targeting strategy**. For example, Mont Blanc pens focuses only on the upscale, premium writing instrument segment of the pen market.[3] Notice in Figure 5.2 that the organization using the concentrated strategy is aiming its marketing mix only at "B" customers.

homogeneous market
A market in which a large proportion of customers have similar needs for a product

heterogeneous markets
Markets made up of individuals or organizations with diverse needs for products in a specific product class

market segmentation
The process of dividing a total market into groups with relatively similar product needs to design a marketing mix that matches those needs

market segment
Individuals, groups, or organizations with one or more similar characteristics that cause them to have similar product needs

concentrated targeting strategy
A strategy in which an organization targets a single market segment using one marketing mix

differentiated targeting strategy
A strategy in which an organization targets two or more segments by developing a marketing mix for each

The chief advantage of the concentrated strategy is that it allows a firm to specialize. The firm analyzes characteristics and needs of a distinct customer group and then focuses all its energies on satisfying that group's needs. A firm may generate a large sales volume by reaching a single segment. Also, concentrating on a single segment permits a firm with limited resources to compete with larger organizations that may have overlooked smaller segments.

Specialization, however, means that a company puts all its eggs in one basket, which can be risky. If a company's sales depend on a single segment and the segment's demand for the product declines, the company's financial strength also declines. When a firm penetrates one segment and becomes well entrenched, its popularity may keep it from moving into other segments. For example, it is very unlikely that Bentley could or would want to compete with General Motors in the pickup truck and sport-utility vehicle market segment.

DIFFERENTIATED TARGETING STRATEGY THROUGH MARKET SEGMENTATION

With a **differentiated targeting strategy**, an organization directs its marketing efforts at two or more segments by developing a marketing mix for each (see Figure 5.2). After a firm uses a concentrated strategy successfully in one market segment, it sometimes expands its efforts to include additional segments. For example, Fruit of the Loom underwear traditionally has been aimed at one segment: men. However, the company now markets underwear for women and children as well. Marketing mixes for a differentiated strategy may vary according to product features, distribution methods, promotion methods, and prices.

A firm may increase sales in the aggregate market through a differentiated strategy because its marketing mixes are aimed at more people. For example, Neiman Marcus, which established its retail apparel reputation by targeting wealthy people in their fifties with luxurious environments, is now experimenting with several boutiques geared toward other age groups. One experimental concept is Cusp, a casual boutique chain that is targeted at young women. The stores, which do not reference Neiman Marcus in any way, carry designer jeans, T-shirts, short dresses, and other casual attire.[4] A company with excess production capacity may find a differentiated strategy advantageous because the sale of products to additional segments may absorb excess capacity. On the other hand, a differentiated strategy often demands more production processes, materials, and people. Thus production and costs may be higher than with a concentrated strategy.

Targeting Technology Goes Social

Targeting technology is going social. Today marketers have the tools to identify customer segments among the hundreds of millions of users of social networking sites such as MySpace and Facebook. With just a few clicks, marketers can examine different segments and determine which to select for marketing attention.

© AP IMAGES/MARK LENNIHAN

For example, MySpace analyzes and stores the personal details that its users post on their profiles. Then the site groups users into segments according to gender, age, geographic location, interests, and other variables. Marketers who use the MyAds program can see how many MySpace users are in each segment and learn more to rule out inappropriate segments and focus on those with the most potential. A MySpace executive explains that companies can apply multiple variables to identify extremely precise segments among its users. If a company wants to reach "25- to 40-year-old mom NASCAR fans who love romantic comedies and live in 12 specific zip codes, we can do that," he says.

Facebook offers similar tools for targeting segments within its user base. Marketers can identify small segments at specific colleges and universities or look for larger segments by targeting Facebook users who live in certain cities or countries. Among the psychographic variables that marketers can apply are hobbies and entertainment likes and dislikes. The CBS television network has used Facebook's targeting tools to identify consumers who play interactive games online, for example.

As these social networking sites continue expanding and their users update their profiles and interests, marketers will have even more opportunities for up-to-the-minute targeting in the future.[a]

COURTESY OF FRITO-LAY, INC. USED BY PERMISSION.

Differentiated Targeting Strategy
Many companies employ the differentiated targeting strategy by focusing on more than one market segment, using multiple marketing mixes. Snack food companies, like Frito-Lay, produce multiple marketing mixes and aim them at multiple market segments.

Step 2: Determine Which Segmentation Variables to Use

Segmentation variables are the characteristics of individuals, groups, or organizations used to divide a market into segments. For example, location, age, gender, and rate of product usage all can be bases for segmenting markets. Most marketers use several variables in combination. According to Solutions Research Group, the average iPhone customer is a 31-year-old (age) man (gender) with a college degree (education) and an income of $75,600 per year (income)—a salary 26 percent higher than the American average.[5]

To select a segmentation variable, several factors are considered. The segmentation variable should relate to customers' needs for, uses of, or behavior toward the product. Stereo marketers might segment the stereo market based on income and age but not based on religion because people's stereo needs do not differ due to religion. If individuals or organizations in a total market are to be classified accurately, the segmentation variable must be measurable. Age, location, and gender are measurable because such information can be obtained through observation or questioning. Segmenting a market on the basis of a variable such as intelligence, however, would be extremely difficult because this attribute is harder to measure accurately. Furthermore, a company's resources and capabilities affect the number and size of segment variables used. The type of product and degree of variation in customers' needs also dictate the number and size of segments targeted. In short, there is no best way to segment markets.

Marketers try to segment markets in ways that may help them to build and manage relationships with targeted customers. Marketing research is often necessary to acquire information about customers' preferences and interests; basic demographic information about target customers' age, income, employment status, household structure, and family roles also may be revealing. Marketers are increasingly using customer relationship management techniques to track their customers' purchases over time and to mine their databases to identify trends and develop more appropriate marketing mixes for repeat customers.

Choosing one or more segmentation variables is a critical step in targeting a market. Selecting inappropriate variables limits the chances of developing a successful marketing strategy. To help you better understand potential segmentation variables, we examine the major types of variables used to segment consumer markets and business markets.

VARIABLES FOR SEGMENTING CONSUMER MARKETS

A marketer using segmentation to reach a consumer market can choose one or several variables from an assortment of possibilities. As Figure 5.3 shows, segmentation variables can be grouped into four categories: demographic, geographic, psychographic, and behavioristic.

segmentation variables Characteristics of individuals, groups, or organizations used to divide a market into segments

Demographic Variables

Demographic characteristics that marketers commonly use in segmenting markets include age, gender, race, ethnicity, income, education, occupation, family size, family life cycle, religion, and social class. Marketers rely on these demographic characteristics because they are often closely linked to

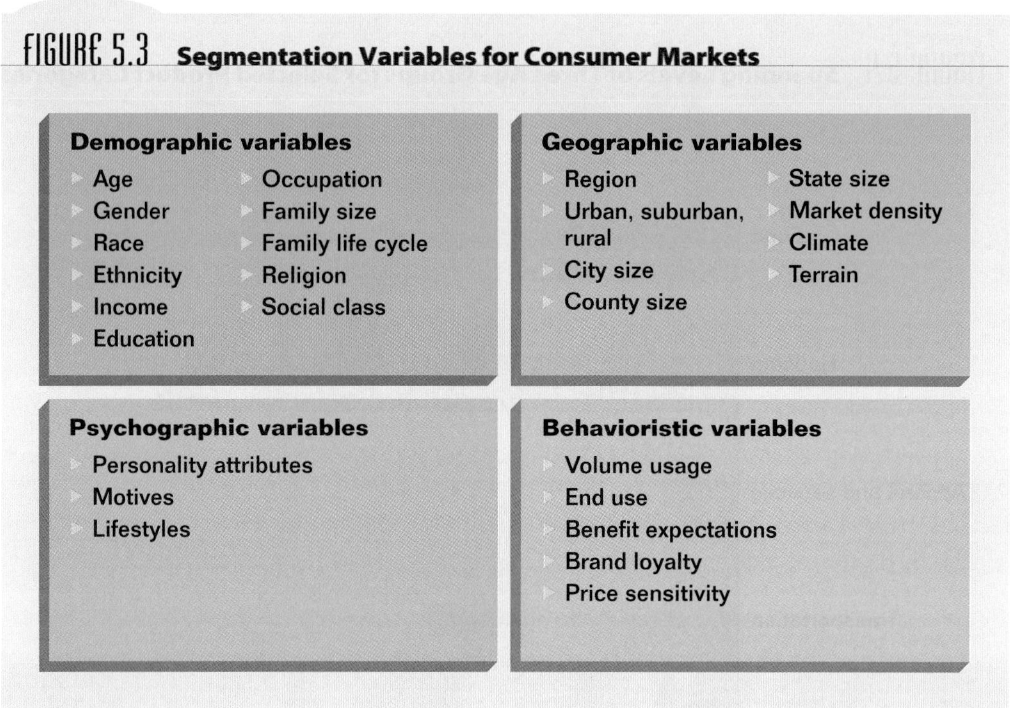

FIGURE 5.3 Segmentation Variables for Consumer Markets

customers' needs and purchasing behavior and can be readily measured. Like demographers, a few marketers even use mortality rates. Service Corporation International (SCI), the largest U.S. funeral services company, attempts to locate its facilities in higher-income suburban areas with high mortality rates. SCI operates more than 1,700 funeral service locations, cemeteries, and crematoriums.[6]

Age is a commonly used variable for segmentation purposes. Many products are aimed at teenagers. For example, "Teens Turning Green" is a company targeted toward teens. It encourages them to opt for safe and healthy alternatives in their day-to-day lives. It has come up with a new range of products called "Teens for safe cosmetics" that gives greener alternative choices for teenage girls who are looking for cosmetics and personal care products.[7] Marketers need to be aware of age distribution and how that distribution is changing. All age groups under 55 years are expected to decrease by the year 2025, and all age categories 55 years of age and older are expected to increase. In 1970, the average age of a U.S. citizen was 27.9 years; currently, it is about 36.2 years. As Figure 5.4 shows, Americans 65 years of age and older spend as much as or more on health care and entertainment than Americans in the two younger age groups.

Many marketers recognize the purchase influence of children and are targeting more marketing efforts at them. As a group, parents of children ages 4 to12 have annual incomes in excess of $40 billion. Numerous products are aimed specifically at children—toys, clothing, food and beverages, and entertainment such as movies and TV cable channels. In addition, children in this age group influence $500 billion of parental spending yearly.[8] In households

Entrepreneurial Marketing

Tasty Bite: Coming to America

Featuring authentic Indian recipes and all-natural ingredients, Tasty Bite meals, which were originally made in Pune, India, were introduced to the U.S. market when Ashok Vasudevan and his wife, Meera, bought the company. Now a $15 million business, Tasty Bite produces nonrefrigerated, heat-and-eat meals that combine quality food with convenience.

To appeal to American consumers, Vasudevan and Meera first renamed the dishes. For example, what was once "Palak Paneer" became "Kashmir Spinach." Then, they packaged the products in colorful boxes to attract attention.

By playing up Tasty Bite's natural ingredients, the new owners got placement in specialty stores like Whole Foods and Trader Joe's. To change the misperception that Indian food is overly spicy, they held hundreds of in-store taste demonstrations, with great results, which persuaded bigger supermarket chains to stock the product line. The company continues to expand into other ethnic specialties.[b]

FIGURE 5.4 Spending Levels of Three Age Groups for Selected Product Categories

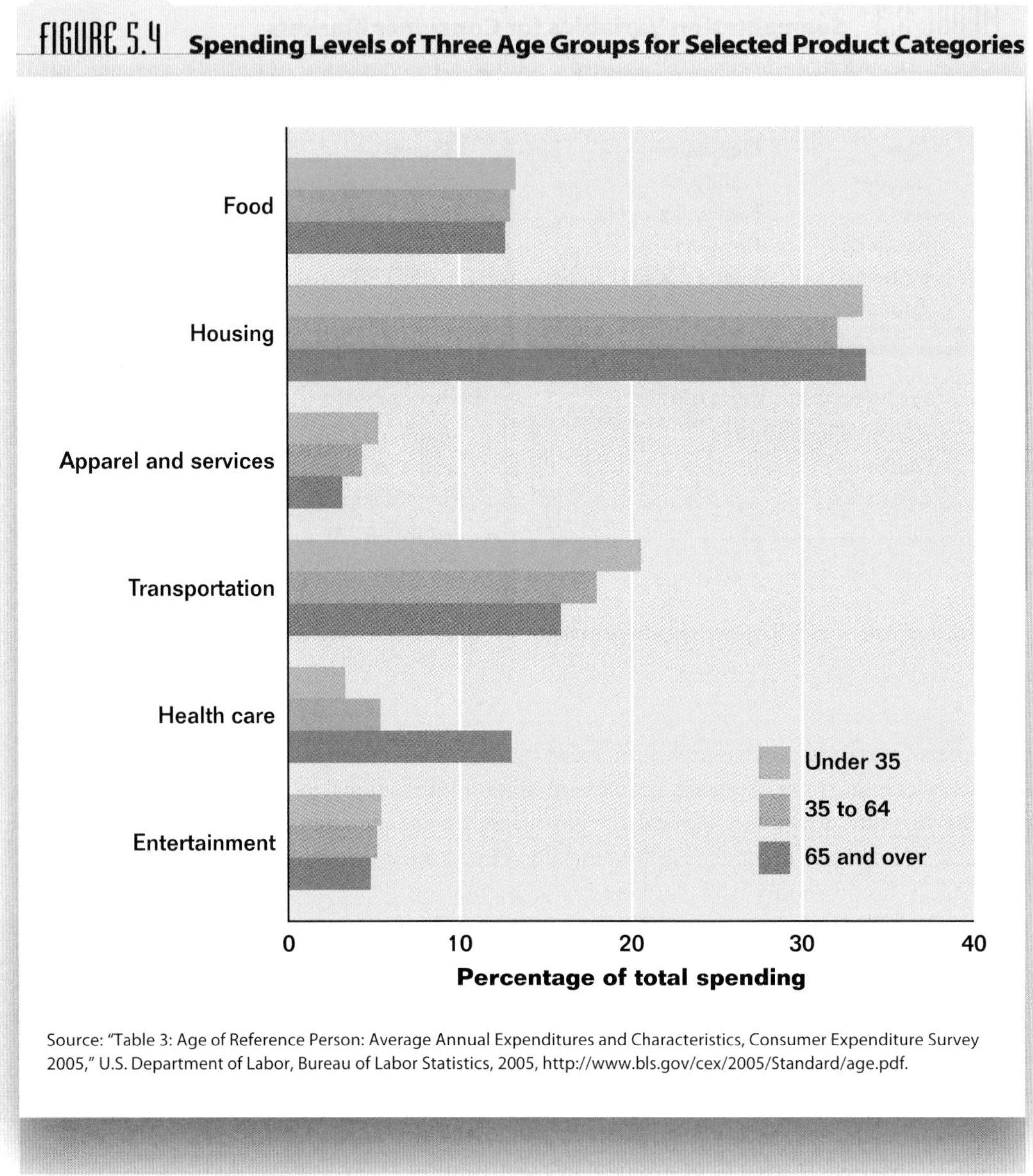

Source: "Table 3: Age of Reference Person: Average Annual Expenditures and Characteristics, Consumer Expenditure Survey 2005," U.S. Department of Labor, Bureau of Labor Statistics, 2005, http://www.bls.gov/cex/2005/Standard/age.pdf.

with only one parent or those in which both parents work, children often take on additional responsibilities such as cooking, cleaning, and grocery shopping, and thus influence the types of products and brands these households purchase.

Gender is another demographic variable commonly used to segment markets, including the markets for clothing, soft drinks, nonprescription medications, toiletries, magazines, and even cigarettes. The U.S. Census Bureau reports that girls and women account for 50.7 percent and boys and men for 49.3 percent of the total U.S. population.[9] Some deodorant marketers use gender segmentation: Secret and Lady Speedstick deodorants are marketed specifically to women, whereas Old Spice and Mitchum deodorants are directed toward men.

Marketers also use race and ethnicity as variables for segmenting markets for products such as food, music, clothing, and cosmetics and for services such as banking and insurance. The U.S. Hispanic population illustrates the importance of ethnicity as a segmentation variable. Made up of people of Mexican, Cuban, Puerto Rican, and Central and South American heritage, this ethnic group is growing five times faster than the general population. Asian

Americans are another important subculture for many companies. Kmart, for example, launched an initiative to stock more multicultural dolls in all of its 1,400 stores, not just those located in predominantly minority neighborhoods. Designed to appeal to Asian Americans, African Americans, and Hispanics, the four dozen types of dolls—including Dora the Explorer and Baby Abuelita—are supported with an advertising campaign in the stores' weekly circulars.[10]

Income often provides a way to divide markets because it strongly influences people's product needs. It affects their ability to buy and their desires for certain lifestyles. Product markets segmented by income include sporting goods, housing, furniture, cosmetics, clothing, jewelry, home appliances, automobiles, and electronics. While many retailers choose to target consumers with upscale incomes, some marketers are instead going after lower-income consumers with new products ranging from prepaid cell phones and debit cards to budget paper towels.

Among the factors influencing household income and product needs are marital status and the presence and ages of children. These characteristics, often combined and called the *family life cycle,* affect needs for housing, appliances, food and beverages, automobiles, and recreational equipment. Family life cycles can be broken down in a number of ways. Figure 5.5 shows a breakdown into nine categories. The composition of the U.S. household in relation to the family life cycle has changed significantly over the last several decades. Single-parent families are on the rise, meaning that the "typical" family no longer consists of a married couple with children. Since 1970, households headed by a single mother increased from 12 to 26 percent of total family households, and that number grew from 1 to 6 percent for families headed by a single father. Another factor influencing the family life cycle is the increase in median marrying age for both women and men. The median marrying age for women has

Age-Based Segmentation
Geico aims its services at a specific age group.

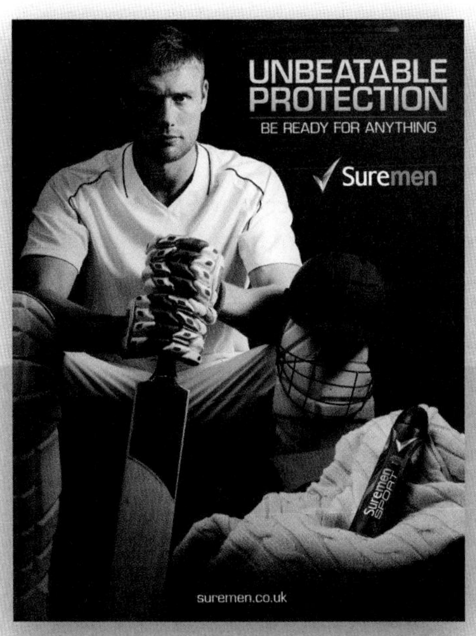

Gender-Based Segmentation
These companies use gender-based market segmentation. Suremen deodorant is aimed at men. In this ad, Adidas aims its products at women.

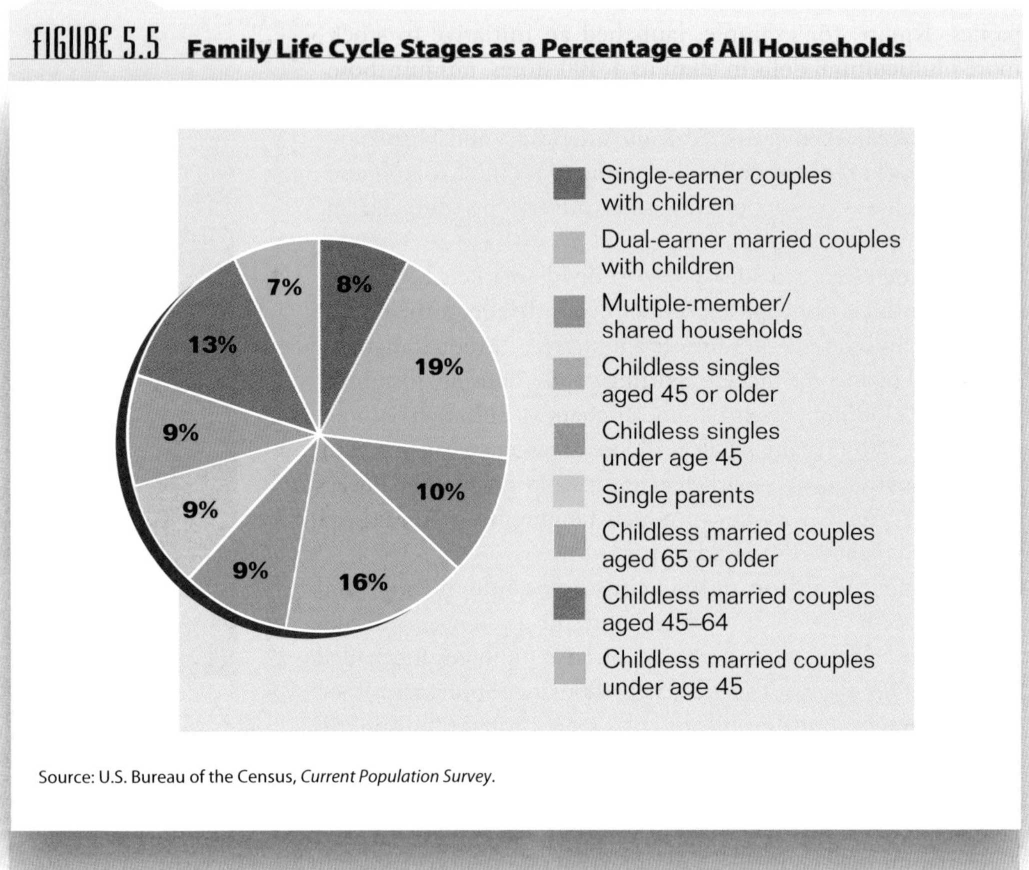

FIGURE 5.5 Family Life Cycle Stages as a Percentage of All Households

Source: U.S. Bureau of the Census, *Current Population Survey*.

increased from 20.8 to 25.3 years since 1970, whereas for men it increased to 27.1 from 23.2 years. More significantly, the proportion of women ages 20 to 24 years who have never been married has more than doubled over this time, and for women ages 30 to 34 years, this number has nearly tripled. Other important changes in the family life cycle include the rise in the number of people living alone and the number of unmarried couples living together.[11] Tracking these changes helps marketers to satisfy the needs of particular target markets through new marketing mixes. For example, MicroMarketing, Inc., helps companies target customers through what it calls "lifestage marketing." MicroMarketing can create a direct-mail campaign aimed at groups such as people who recently moved, soon-to-be newlyweds, recent high school and college graduates, and expectant parents. By focusing on such narrow target markets, MicroMarketing boasts a return on investments of up to 2,000 percent.[12]

Marketers also use many other demographic variables. For instance, dictionary publishing companies segment markets by education level. Some insurance companies segment markets using occupation, targeting health insurance at college students and at younger workers for small employers that do not provide health coverage.

Geographic Variables

Geographic variables—climate, terrain, city size, population density, and urban/rural areas—also influence customer product needs. Consumers in the South, for instance, rarely have need for snow tires. Markets may be divided into regions because one or more geographic variables can cause customers to differ from one region to another. A company selling products to a national market might divide the United States into the following regions: Pacific, Southwest, Central, Midwest, Southeast, Middle Atlantic, and New England. A firm operating in one or several states might regionalize its market by counties, cities, zip code areas, or other units.

City size can be an important segmentation variable. Some marketers focus efforts on cities of a certain size. For example, one franchised restaurant organization will not locate in cities of fewer than 200,000 people. It concluded that a smaller population base would result in inadequate profits. Other firms actively seek opportunities in smaller towns. A classic example is Walmart, which initially located only in small towns.

Market density refers to the number of potential customers within a unit of land area, such as a square mile. Although market density relates generally to population density, the correlation is not exact. For example, in two different geographic markets of approximately equal size and population, market density for office supplies would be much higher in one area if it contained a much greater proportion of business customers than the other area. Market density may be a useful segmentation variable because low-density markets often require different sales, advertising, and distribution activities than high-density markets.

Several marketers are using geodemographic segmentation. **Geodemographic segmentation** clusters people in zip code areas and even smaller neighborhood units based on lifestyle information and especially demographic data, such as income, education, occupation, type of housing, ethnicity, family life cycle, and level of urbanization. These small, precisely described population clusters help marketers to isolate demographic units as small as neighborhoods where the demand for specific products is strongest. Geodemographic segmentation allows marketers to engage in micromarketing. **Micromarketing** is the focusing of precise marketing efforts on very small geodemographic markets, such as community and even neighborhood markets. Providers of financial and health care services, retailers, and consumer products companies use micromarketing. Special advertising campaigns, promotions, retail site-location analyses, special pricing, and unique retail product offerings are a few examples of micromarketing facilitated through geodemographic segmentation. Many retailers use micromarketing to determine the merchandise mix for individual stores. Best Buy store number 952 in Baytown has noticed a different type of shopper: Eastern European workers from cargo ships or oil tankers, temporarily docked at Baytown's busy port, are spending their precious shore hours scouring the store's aisles. They take a 15-minute cab or shuttle ride to stock up on iPods and Apple laptops priced cheaper than back home. To speed their shopping, the Baytown Best Buy has moved the iPods from the back corner of the store to the front, paired them with overseas power converters, and simplified the signage. Since the changes were made over the Christmas holidays, cash register receipts for the boat workers ballooned by 67 percent.[13]

Climate is commonly used as a geographic segmentation variable because of its broad impact on people's behavior and product needs. Product markets affected by climate include air-conditioning and heating equipment, fireplace accessories, clothing, gardening equipment, recreational products, and building materials.

Psychographic Variables

Marketers sometimes use psychographic variables, such as personality characteristics, motives, and lifestyles, to segment markets. A psychographic dimension can be used by itself to segment a market or can be combined with other types of segmentation variables.

Personality characteristics can be useful for segmentation when a product resembles many competing products and consumers' needs are not significantly related to other segmentation variables. However, segmenting a market according to personality traits can be risky. Although marketing practitioners have long believed consumer choice and product use vary with personality, until recently, marketing research had indicated only weak relationships. It is hard to

market density
The number of potential customers within a unit of land area

geodemographic segmentation
Market segmentation that clusters people in zip code areas and smaller neighborhood units based on lifestyle and demographic information

micromarketing
An approach to market segmentation in which organizations focus precise marketing efforts on very small geodemographic markets

Sustainable Marketing

Who's Green?

Marketers who position their products as eco-friendly should look for three shades of green when they segment their markets. "True Green" consumers—12 percent of the U.S. population, according to one survey—buy green products regularly. "Light Green" consumers (68 percent of the population) sometimes buy green, particularly when the products are easily available. "Never Green" consumers, who make up 20 percent of the population, just don't buy green.

Fairmont Resort Hotels has been seeing shades of green since 1990, when it repositioned itself on the basis of commitment to environmental sustainability. "It really has become a point of differentiation for us," says Fairmont's director of environmental affairs. The company also positions its conference facilities as green by offering earth-friendly conference meals.

© AP IMAGES/PRNEWSFOTO/ZERO MOTORCYCLES

Zero Motorcycles is targeting true and light green segments with a new line of electric motorcycles. Instead of running on gasoline, these bikes have rechargeable lithium-ion batteries to drive electric motors that are clean, efficient, and powerful. In fact, green motorcycles for street and off-road use are becoming so popular that Zero is struggling to keep up with demand.

Packaging can support a product's green positioning. Unilever is a case in point. Now a 32-ounce container of its "Small & Mighty" concentrated All laundry detergent cleans the same amount of clothing as a 100-ounce container of the previous version. Yet the "Small & Mighty" container requires half as much plastic as the older container, which saves 150 million pounds of plastic and millions of gallons of oil each year—an important marketing issue for green consumers.[c]

measure personality traits accurately, especially since most personality tests were developed for clinical use, not for segmentation purposes.

When appealing to a personality characteristic, marketers almost always select one that many people view positively. Individuals with this characteristic, as well as those who would like to have it, may be influenced to buy that marketer's brand. Marketers taking this approach do not worry about measuring how many people have the positively valued characteristic; they assume that a sizable proportion of people in the target market either have or want to have it.

When motives are used to segment a market, the market is divided according to consumers' reasons for making a purchase. Personal appearance, affiliation, status, safety, and health are examples of motives affecting the types of products purchased and the choice of stores in which they are bought. Marketing efforts based on health and fitness motives can be a point of competitive advantage. For example, Taco Bell, Jack-in-the-Box, and Starbucks each introduced new "light" products at the beginning of the year to target consumers who overindulged during the holidays or set weight-loss resolutions. Jack-in-the-Box launched a 300-calorie chicken fajita pita and grilled chicken strips with a teriyaki dipping sauce. Taco Bell introduced a "Fresco menu" with nine items with 350 or fewer calories.[14]

Lifestyle segmentation groups individuals according to how they spend their time, the importance of things in their surroundings (homes or jobs, for example), beliefs about themselves and broad issues, and some demographic characteristics, such as income and education.[15] Lifestyle analysis provides a broad view of buyers because it encompasses numerous characteristics related to people's activities (work, hobbies, entertainment, and sports), interests (family, home, fashion, food, and technology), and opinions (politics, social issues, education, and the future).

One of the most popular consumer frameworks is VALS™ from SRI Consulting Business Intelligence. VALS classifies consumers based on psychological characteristics (personality characteristics) that are correlated with purchase behavior and key demographics. The VALS classification questionnaire, which is used to determine a consumers' VALS type, can be integrated into larger questionnaires to find out about consumers' lifestyle choices. Figure 5.6 is an example of VALS data that show the proportion of each VALS group that purchased a mountain bike, purchased golf clubs, owns a fishing rod, and goes

FIGURE 5.6 VALS Types and Sports Preferences

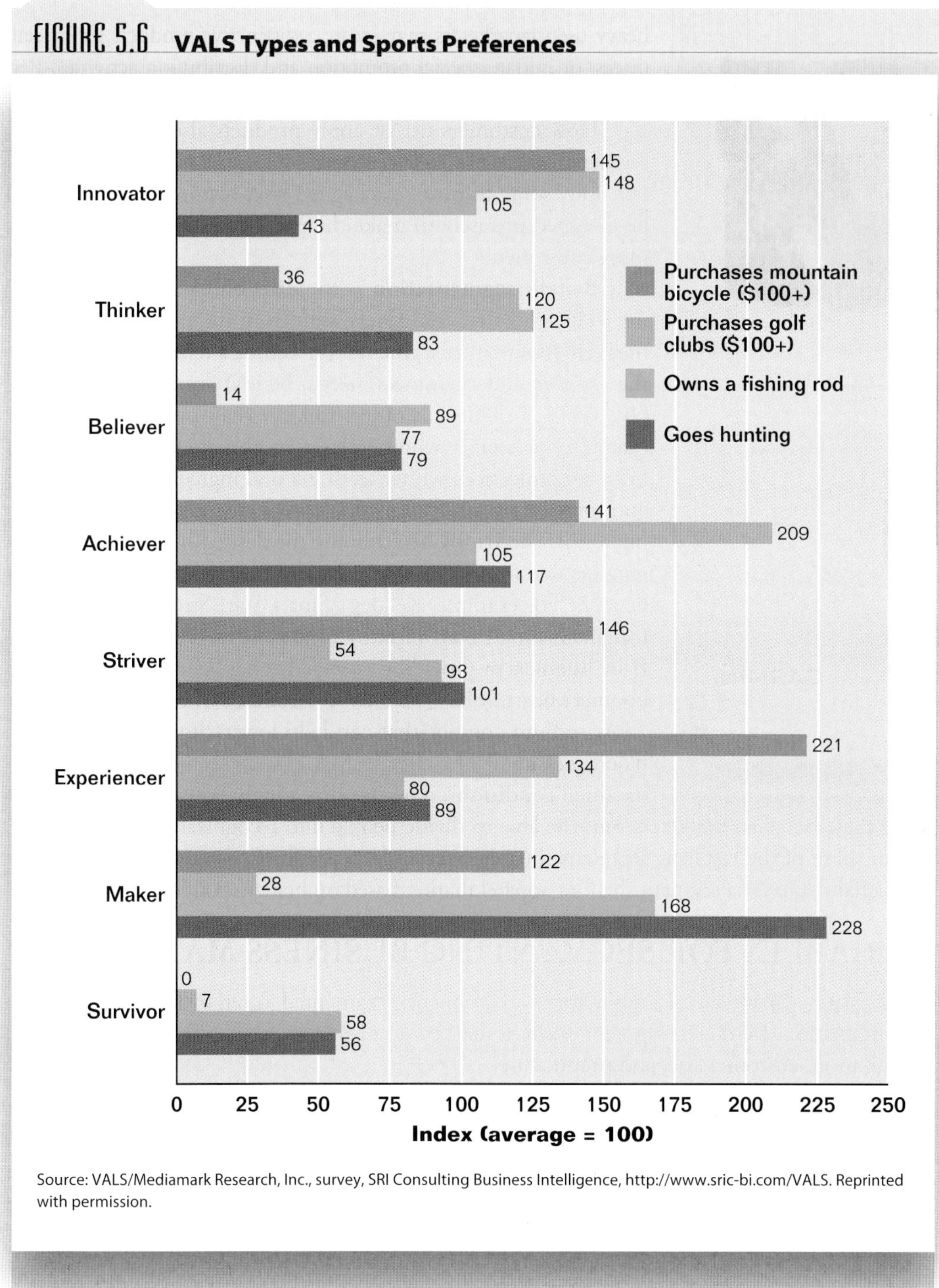

Source: VALS/Mediamark Research, Inc., survey, SRI Consulting Business Intelligence, http://www.sric-bi.com/VALS. Reprinted with permission.

hunting. VALS research is also used to create new products as well as to segment existing markets. VALS systems have been developed for the United States, Japan, and the United Kingdom.[16] Many other lifestyle classification systems exist. Several companies, such as Experian's Behavior Bank, collect lifestyle data on millions of consumers.

Behavioristic Variables

Firms can divide a market according to some feature of consumer behavior toward a product, commonly involving some aspect of product use. For example, a market may be separated into users—classified as heavy, moderate, or light—and nonusers. To satisfy a specific group, such as

© GARMIN

Lifestyle Segmentation
In this advertisement, Garmin GPS targets people who enjoy an outdoors lifestyle.

heavy users, marketers may create a distinctive product, set special prices, or initiate special promotion and distribution activities. Per capita consumption data help to identify different levels of usage.[17]

How customers use or apply products also may determine segmentation. To satisfy customers who use a product in a certain way, some feature—packaging, size, texture, or color—may be designed precisely to make the product easier to use, safer, or more convenient.

Benefit segmentation is the division of a market according to benefits that consumers want from the product. Although most types of market segmentation assume a relationship between the variable and customers' needs, benefit segmentation differs because the benefits customers seek *are* their product needs. For example, a customer who purchases toothpaste may be interested in cavity protection, whiter teeth, natural ingredients, or sensitive gum protection. Thus individuals are segmented directly according to their needs. By determining the desired benefits, marketers may be able to divide people into groups seeking certain sets of benefits. For example, Kellogg's Smart Start Strong Heart cereals (originally Smart Start Healthy Heart) are targeted toward female Baby Boomers by providing a cereal that has benefits for the female boomer's heart. It has vitamins A, C, and E, whole grain oats, and a low sodium content that can help lower cholesterol and high blood pressure.[18] The effectiveness of such segmentation depends on three conditions: The benefits sought must be identifiable; using these benefits, marketers must be able to divide people into recognizable segments; and one or more of the resulting segments must be accessible to the firm's marketing efforts. Both Timberland and Avia segment the foot apparel market based on benefits sought by purchasers.

VARIABLES FOR SEGMENTING BUSINESS MARKETS

Like consumer markets, business markets are frequently segmented, often by multiple variables in combination. Marketers segment business markets according to geographic location, type of organization, customer size, and product use.

Geographic Location

We noted earlier that the demand for some consumer products varies considerably among geographic areas because of differences in climate, terrain, customer preferences, and similar factors. Demand for business products also varies according to geographic location. For example, producers of certain types of lumber divide their markets geographically because their customers' needs vary from region to region. Geographic segmentation may be especially appropriate for reaching industries concentrated in certain locations. Furniture and textile producers, for example, are concentrated in the Southeast.

Type of Organization

A company sometimes segments a market by types of organizations within that market. Different types of organizations often require different product features, distribution systems, price structures, and selling strategies. Given these variations, a firm may either concentrate on a single segment with one marketing mix (concentration strategy) or focus on several groups with multiple mixes (a differentiated targeting strategy). A carpet producer, for example, could segment potential customers into several groups, such as automobile makers, commercial carpet contractors (firms that carpet large commercial buildings), apartment complex developers, carpet wholesalers, and large retail carpet outlets.

benefit segmentation
The division of a market according to benefits that customers want from the product

Customer Size

An organization's size may affect its purchasing procedures and the types and quantities of products it wants. Size thus can be an effective variable for segmenting a business market. To reach a segment of a particular size, marketers may have to adjust one or more marketing-mix components. For example, customers who buy in extremely large quantities are sometimes offered discounts. In addition, marketers often must expand personal selling efforts to serve large organizational buyers properly. Because the needs of large and small buyers tend to be quite distinct, marketers frequently use different marketing practices to reach various customer groups.

Product Use

Certain products, especially basic raw materials such as steel, petroleum, plastics, and lumber, are used in numerous ways. How a company uses products affects the types and amounts of products purchased, as well as the purchasing method. For example, computers are used for engineering purposes, basic scientific research, and business operations such as word processing, accounting, and telecommunications. A computer maker therefore may segment the computer market by types of use because organizations' needs for computer hardware and software depend on the purpose for which products are purchased.

Step 3: Develop Market Segment Profiles

A market segment profile describes the similarities among potential customers within a segment and explains the differences among people and organizations in different segments. A profile may cover aspects such as demographic characteristics, geographic factors, product benefits sought, lifestyles, brand preferences, and usage rates. Individuals and organizations within segments should be quite similar with respect to several characteristics and product needs and differ considerably from those within other market segments. Marketers use market segment profiles to assess the degree to which the organization's possible products can match or fit potential customers' product needs. Market segment profiles help marketers to understand how a business can use its capabilities to serve potential customer groups.

The use of market segment profiles benefits marketers in several ways. Such profiles help a marketer determine which segment or segments are most attractive to the organization relative to the firm's strengths, weaknesses, objectives, and resources. While marketers initially may believe that certain segments are quite attractive, development of market segment profiles may yield information that indicates the opposite. For the market segment or segments chosen by the organization, the information included in market segment profiles can be highly useful in making marketing decisions.

Step 4: Evaluate Relevant Market Segments

After analyzing the market segment profiles, a marketer is likely to identify several relevant market segments that require further analysis and to eliminate certain other segments from consideration. To assess relevant market segments further, several important factors, including sales estimates, competition, and estimated costs associated with each segment, should be analyzed.

SALES ESTIMATES

Potential sales for a segment can be measured along several dimensions, including product level, geographic area, time, and level of competition.[19] With respect to product level, potential sales can be estimated for a specific product item (for example, Diet Coke) or an entire product line (for example, Coca-Cola Classic, Caffeine-Free Coke, Diet Coke, Caffeine-Free Diet Coke, Cherry Coca-Cola, Diet Cherry Coca-Cola, Vanilla Coke, and Diet Vanilla Coke).

A marketer also must determine the geographic area to be included in the estimate. In relation to time, sales estimates can be short range (one year or less), medium range (one to five years), or long range (longer than five years). The competitive level specifies whether sales are being estimated for a single firm or for an entire industry.

Market potential is the total amount of a product, for all firms in an industry, that customers will purchase within a specified period at a specific level of industrywide marketing activity. Market potential can be stated in terms of dollars or units. A segment's market potential is affected by economic, sociocultural, and other environmental forces. Marketers must assume a certain general level of marketing effort in the industry when they estimate market potential. The specific level of marketing effort varies from one firm to another, but the sum of all firms' marketing activities equals industrywide marketing efforts. A marketing manager also must consider whether and to what extent industry marketing efforts will change.

Company sales potential is the maximum percentage of market potential that an individual firm within an industry can expect to obtain for a specific product. Several factors influence company sales potential for a market segment. First, the market potential places absolute limits on the size of the company's sales potential. Second, the magnitude of industrywide marketing activities has an indirect but definite impact on the company's sales potential. Those activities have a direct bearing on the size of the market potential. When Domino's Pizza advertises home-delivered pizza, for example, it indirectly promotes pizza in general; its commercials also may help to sell Pizza Hut's and other competitors' home-delivered pizza. Third, the intensity and effectiveness of a company's marketing activities relative to those of its competitors affect the size of the company's sales potential. If a company spends twice as much as any of its competitors on marketing efforts, and if each dollar spent is more effective in generating sales, the firm's sales potential will be quite high compared with its competitors'.

market potential
The total amount of a product that customers will purchase within a specified period at a specific level of industrywide marketing activity

company sales potential
The maximum percentage of market potential that an individual firm can expect to obtain for a specific product

breakdown approach
Measuring company sales potential based on a general economic forecast for a specific period and the market potential derived from it

buildup approach
Measuring company sales potential by estimating how much of a product a potential buyer in a specific geographic area will purchase in a given period, multiplying the estimate by the number of potential buyers, and adding the totals of all the geographic areas considered

There are two general approaches to measuring company sales potential: breakdown and buildup. In the **breakdown approach**, the marketing manager first develops a general economic forecast for a specific time period. Next, market potential is estimated on the basis of this economic forecast. The company's sales potential then is derived from the general economic forecast and estimate of market potential. In the **buildup approach**, the marketing manager begins by estimating how much of a product a potential buyer in a specific geographic area, such as a sales territory, will purchase in a given period. The manager then multiplies that amount by the total number of potential buyers in that area. The manager performs the same calculation for each geographic area in which the firm sells products and then adds the totals for each area to calculate market potential. To determine company sales potential, the manager must estimate, based on planned levels of company marketing activities, the proportion of the total market potential the company can obtain.

COMPETITIVE ASSESSMENT

Besides obtaining sales estimates, it is crucial to assess competitors already operating in the segments being considered. Without competitive information, sales estimates may be misleading. A market segment that seems attractive based on sales estimates may prove to be much less so following a competitive assessment. Such an assessment should ask several questions about competitors: How many exist? What are their strengths and weaknesses? Do several competitors have major market shares and together dominate the segment? Can our company create a marketing mix to compete effectively against competitors' marketing mixes? Is it likely that new competitors will enter this segment? If so, how will they affect our firm's ability to compete successfully? Answers to such questions are important for proper assessment of the competition in potential market segments.

COST ESTIMATES

To fulfill the needs of a target segment, an organization must develop and maintain a marketing mix that precisely meets the wants and needs of individuals and organizations in that segment. Developing and maintaining such a mix can be expensive. Distinctive product features, attractive package design, generous product warranties, extensive advertising, attractive promotional offers, competitive prices, and high-quality personal service consume considerable organizational resources. Indeed, to reach certain segments, the costs may be so high that a marketer may see the segment as inaccessible. Another cost consideration is whether the organization can reach a segment effectively at costs equal to or below competitors' costs. If the firm's costs are likely to be higher, it will be unable to compete in that segment in the long run.

Identifying and Analyzing Customers
Numerous companies and software solutions are used to find customers.

Step 5: Select Specific Target Markets

An important initial issue to consider in selecting a target market is whether customers' needs differ enough to warrant the use of market segmentation. If segmentation analysis shows customer needs to be fairly homogeneous, the firm's management may decide to use the undifferentiated approach, discussed earlier. However, if customer needs are heterogeneous, which is much more likely, one or more target markets must be selected. On the other hand, marketers may decide not to enter and compete in any of the segments.

Assuming that one or more segments offer significant opportunities for the organization to achieve its objectives, marketers must decide in which segments to participate. Ordinarily, information gathered in the previous step—information about sales estimates, competitors, and cost estimates—requires careful consideration in this final step to determine long-term profit opportunities. Also, the firm's management must investigate whether the organization has the financial resources, managerial skills, employee expertise, and facilities to enter and compete effectively in selected segments. Furthermore, the requirements of some market segments may be at odds with the firm's overall objectives, and the possibility of legal problems, conflicts with stakeholders, and technological advancements could make certain segments unattractive. In addition, when prospects for long-term growth are taken into account, some segments may appear very attractive and others less desirable.

Selecting appropriate target markets is important to an organization's adoption and use of the marketing concept philosophy. Identifying the right target market is the key to implementing a successful marketing strategy, whereas failure to do so can lead to low sales, high costs, and severe financial losses. A careful target-market analysis places an organization in a better position both to serve customers' needs and to achieve its objectives.

Developing Sales Forecasts

A **sales forecast** is the amount of a product a company actually expects to sell during a specific period at a specified level of marketing activities. The sales forecast differs from the company sales potential. It concentrates on what actual sales will be at a certain level of company marketing effort, whereas the company sales potential assesses what sales are possible at various levels of marketing activities, assuming that certain environmental conditions will exist. Businesses use the sales forecast for planning, organizing, implementing, and controlling their activities. The success of numerous activities depends on this forecast's accuracy.

sales forecast
The amount of a product a company expects to sell during a specific period at a specified level of marketing activities

Common problems in companies that fail are improper planning and lack of realistic sales forecasts. Overly optimistic sales forecasts can lead to overbuying, overinvestment, and higher costs.

To forecast sales, a marketer can choose from several forecasting methods, some arbitrary and others more scientific, complex, and time-consuming. A firm's choice of method or methods depends on the costs involved, type of product, market characteristics, time span of the forecast, purposes of the forecast, stability of the historical sales data, availability of required information, managerial preferences, and forecasters' expertise and experience.[20] Common forecasting techniques fall into five categories: executive judgment, surveys, time-series analysis, regression analysis, and market tests.

EXECUTIVE JUDGMENT

At times, a company forecasts sales chiefly on the basis of **executive judgment**, the intuition of one or more executives. This approach is unscientific but expedient and inexpensive. Executive judgment may work reasonably well when product demand is relatively stable, and the forecaster has years of market-related experience. However, because intuition is swayed most heavily by recent experience, the forecast may be overly optimistic or overly pessimistic. Another drawback to intuition is that the forecaster has only past experience as a guide for deciding where to go in the future.

SURVEYS

executive judgment
Sales forecasting based on the intuition of one or more executives

customer forecasting survey
A survey of customers regarding the types and quantities of products they intend to buy during a specific period

sales force forecasting survey
A survey of a firm's sales force regarding anticipated sales in their territories for a specified period

expert forecasting survey
Sales forecasts prepared by experts such as economists, management consultants, advertising executives, college professors, or other persons outside the firm

Delphi technique
A procedure in which experts create initial forecasts, submit them to the company for averaging, and then refine the forecasts

Another way to forecast sales is to question customers, sales personnel, or experts regarding their expectations about future purchases. In a **customer forecasting survey**, marketers ask customers what types and quantities of products they intend to buy during a specific period. This approach may be useful to a business with relatively few customers. For example, Intel, which markets to a limited number of companies (primarily computer manufacturers), could conduct customer forecasting surveys effectively. PepsiCo, in contrast, has millions of customers and could not feasibly use a customer survey to forecast future sales.

In a **sales force forecasting survey**, the firm's salespeople estimate anticipated sales in their territories for a specified period. The forecaster combines these territorial estimates to arrive at a tentative forecast. A marketer may survey the sales staff for several reasons. The most important is that the sales staff is closer to customers on a daily basis than other company personnel and therefore should know more about customers' future product needs. When sales representatives assist in developing the forecast, they are more likely to work toward its achievement. Another advantage of this method is that forecasts can be prepared for single territories, divisions consisting of several territories, regions made up of multiple divisions, and the total geographic market. Thus the method provides sales forecasts from the smallest geographic sales unit to the largest.

When a company wants an **expert forecasting survey**, it hires professionals to help prepare the sales forecast. These experts are usually economists, management consultants, advertising executives, college professors, or other persons outside the firm with solid experience in a specific market. Drawing on this experience and their analyses of available information about the company and the market, experts prepare and present forecasts or answer questions regarding a forecast. Using experts is expedient and relatively inexpensive. However, because they work outside the firm, these forecasters may be less motivated than company personnel to do an effective job.

A more complex form of the expert forecasting survey incorporates the Delphi technique. The **Delphi technique** is a procedure in which experts create initial forecasts, submit them to the company for averaging, and have the results returned to them so that they can make individual refined forecasts. The premise is that the experts will use the averaged results when making refined forecasts and that these forecasts will be in a narrower range. The procedure may be repeated several times until the experts, each working separately, reach a consensus on the forecasts. The ultimate goal in using the Delphi technique is to develop a highly accurate sales forecast.

TIME-SERIES ANALYSIS

With **time-series analysis**, the forecaster uses the firm's historical sales data to discover a pattern or patterns in the firm's sales over time. If a pattern is found, it can be used to forecast sales. This forecasting method assumes that past sales patterns will continue in the future. The accuracy, and thus usefulness, of time-series analysis hinges on the validity of this assumption.

In a time-series analysis, a forecaster usually performs four types of analyses: trend, cycle, seasonal, and random factor. **Trend analysis** focuses on aggregate sales data, such as the company's annual sales figures, covering a period of many years to determine whether annual sales are generally rising, falling, or staying about the same. Through **cycle analysis**, a forecaster analyzes sales figures (often monthly sales data) from a period of three to five years to ascertain whether sales fluctuate in a consistent, periodic manner. When performing **seasonal analysis**, the analyst studies daily, weekly, or monthly sales figures to evaluate the degree to which seasonal factors, such as climate and holiday activities, influence sales. In a **random factor analysis**, the forecaster attempts to attribute erratic sales variations to random, nonrecurrent events, such as a regional power failure, a natural disaster, or political unrest in a foreign market. After performing each of these analyses, the forecaster combines the results to develop the sales forecast. Time-series analysis is an effective forecasting method for products with reasonably stable demand, but not for products with highly erratic demand.

time-series analysis
A forecasting method that uses historical sales data to discover patterns in the firm's sales over time and generally involves trend, cycle, seasonal, and random factor analyses

trend analysis
An analysis that focuses on aggregate sales data over a period of many years to determine general trends in annual sales

cycle analysis
An analysis of sales figures for a period of three to five years to ascertain whether sales fluctuate in a consistent, periodic manner

seasonal analysis
An analysis of daily, weekly, or monthly sales figures to evaluate the degree to which seasonal factors influence sales

random factor analysis
An analysis attempting to attribute erratic sales variation to random, nonrecurrent events

REGRESSION ANALYSIS

Like time-series analysis, regression analysis requires the use of historical sales data. In **regression analysis**, the forecaster seeks to find a relationship between past sales (the dependent variable) and one or more independent variables, such as population, per capita income, or gross domestic product. Simple regression analysis uses one independent variable, whereas multiple regression analysis includes two or more independent variables. The objective of regression analysis is to develop a mathematical formula that accurately describes a relationship between the firm's sales and one or more variables; however, the formula indicates only an association, not a causal relationship. Once an accurate formula is established, the analyst plugs the necessary information into the formula to derive the sales forecast.

Regression analysis is useful when a precise association can be established. However, a forecaster seldom finds a perfect association. Furthermore, this method can be used only when available historical sales data are extensive. Thus regression analysis is futile for forecasting sales of new products.

regression analysis
A method of predicting sales based on finding a relationship between past sales and one or more variables, such as population or income

MARKET TESTS

A **market test** involves making a product available to buyers in one or more test areas and measuring purchases and consumer responses to distribution, promotion, and price. Test areas are often cities with populations of 200,000 to 500,000 but can be larger metropolitan areas or towns with populations of 50,000 to 200,000. For example, ACNielsen Market Decisions, a marketing research firm, conducts market tests for client firms in Boise, Tucson, Colorado Springs, Peoria, Evansville, Charleston, and Portland (Maine), in addition to custom test markets in cities chosen by clients.[21]

A market test provides information about consumers' actual, rather than intended, purchases. In addition, purchase volume can be evaluated in relation to the intensity of other marketing activities—advertising, in-store promotions, pricing, packaging, and distribution. For example, Procter & Gamble conducted market tests for new concentrated versions of its Tide, Gain, Dreft, Cheer, and Era laundry detergents in Cedar Rapids, Iowa. The company, which anticipated the new, more environmentally friendly products replacing current versions

market test
Making a product available to buyers in one or more test areas and measuring purchases and consumer responses

of the laundry detergent, needed to assess consumer reaction to the products, their price, and TV, instore, and online promotional efforts.[22] Forecasters base their sales estimates for larger geographic units on customer response in test areas.

Because it does not require historical sales data, a market test is effective for forecasting sales of new products or sales of existing products in new geographic areas. A market test also gives a marketer an opportunity to test various elements of the marketing mix. However, these tests are often time-consuming and expensive. In addition, a marketer cannot be certain that consumer response during a market test represents the total market response or that such a response will continue in the future.

MULTIPLE FORECASTING METHODS

Although some businesses depend on a single sales forecasting method, most firms use several techniques. Sometimes a company is forced to use several methods when marketing diverse product lines, but even for a single product line, several forecasts may be needed, especially when the product is sold to different market segments. Thus a producer of automobile tires may rely on one technique to forecast tire sales for new cars and on another to forecast sales of replacement tires. Variation in the length of needed forecasts may call for several forecasting methods. A firm that employs one method for a short-range forecast may find it inappropriate for long-range forecasting. Sometimes a marketer verifies results of one method by using one or more other methods and comparing outcomes.

CHAPTER REVIEW

OBJECTIVES

1 Learn what a market is.

A market is a group of people who, as individuals or as organizations, have needs for products in a product class and have the ability, willingness, and authority to purchase such products.

2 Understand the differences among general targeting strategies.

The undifferentiated targeting strategy involves designing a single marketing mix directed toward the entire market for a particular product. This strategy is effective in a homogeneous market, whereas a concentrated targeting strategy or differentiated targeting strategy is more appropriate for a heterogeneous market. The concentrated strategy and differentiated strategy both divide markets into segments consisting of individuals, groups, or organizations that have one or more similar characteristics and so can be linked to similar product needs. The concentrated strategy involves targeting a single market segment with one marketing mix. The differentiated targeting strategy targets two or more market segments with marketing mixes customized for each.

3 Become familiar with the major segmentation variables.

Segmentation variables are the characteristics of individuals, groups, or organizations used to segment a total market. The variable(s) used should relate to customers' needs for, uses of, or behavior toward the product. Segmentation variables for consumer markets can be grouped into four categories: demographic (age, gender, income, ethnicity, and family life cycle), geographic (population, market density, and climate), psychographic (personality traits, motives, and lifestyles), and behavioristic (volume usage, end use, expected benefits, brand loyalty, and price sensitivity). Variables for segmenting business markets include geographic location, type of organization, customer size, and product use.

4 Know what segment profiles are and how they are used.

Segment profiles describe the similarities among potential customers within a segment and explain the differences among people and organizations in different market segments. They are used to assess the degree to which the firm's products can match potential customers' product needs.

5 Understand how to evaluate market segments.

Marketers evaluate relevant market segments by analyzing several important factors associated with each segment, such as sales estimates (including market potential and company sales potential), competitive assessments, and cost estimates.

6 Identify the factors that influence the selection of specific market segments for use as target markets.

Actual selection of specific target-market segments requires an assessment of whether customers' needs differ enough to warrant segmentation and which segments to focus on. Sales estimates, competitive assessments, and cost estimates for each potential segment and the firm's financial resources, managerial skills, employee expertise, facilities, and objectives are important factors in this decision, as are legal issues, potential conflicts with stakeholders, technological advancements, and the long-term prospects for growth.

7 Become familiar with sales forecasting methods.

A sales forecast is the amount of a product a company expects to sell during a specific period at a specified level of marketing activities. To forecast sales, marketers can choose from several techniques, including executive judgment, surveys, time-series analysis, regression analysis, and market tests. Executive judgment is based on the intuition of one or more executives. Surveys include customer, sales force, and expert forecasting surveys. Time-series analysis uses the firm's historical sales data to discover patterns in the firm's sales over time and employs four major types of analyses: trend, cycle, seasonal, and random factor. With regression analysis, forecasters attempt to find a relationship between past sales and one or more independent variables. Market testing involves making a product available to buyers in one or more test areas and measuring purchases and consumer responses to distribution, promotion, and price. Many companies employ multiple forecasting methods.

Please visit the student website at www.cengage.com/international for quizzes and games that will help you prepare for exams and achieve the grade you want.

KEY CONCEPTS

consumer market
business market
undifferentiated targeting strategy
homogeneous market
heterogeneous markets
market segmentation
market segment
concentrated targeting strategy
differentiated targeting strategy
segmentation variables
market density
geodemographic segmentation
micromarketing
benefit segmentation
market potential
company sales potential
breakdown approach
buildup approach
sales forecast
executive judgment
customer forecasting survey
sales force forecasting survey
expert forecasting survey
Delphi technique
time-series analysis
trend analysis
cycle analysis
seasonal analysis
random factor analysis
regression analysis
market test

ISSUES FOR DISCUSSION AND REVIEW

1. In your local area, identify a group of people with unsatisfied product needs who represent a market. Could this market be reached by a business organization? Why or why not?
2. Outline the five major steps in the target-market selection process.
3. What is an undifferentiated strategy? Under what conditions is it most useful? Describe a present market situation in which a company is using an undifferentiated strategy. Is the business successful? Why or why not?
4. What is market segmentation? Describe the basic conditions required for effective segmentation. Identify several firms that use market segmentation.
5. List the differences between concentrated and differentiated strategies, and describe the advantages and disadvantages of each.
6. Identify and describe four major categories of variables that can be used to segment consumer markets. Give examples of product markets that are segmented by variables in each category.
7. What dimensions are used to segment business markets?
8. What is a market segment profile? Why is it an important step in the target-market selection process?
9. Describe the important factors that marketers should analyze to evaluate market segments.
10. Why is a marketer concerned about sales potential when trying to select a target market?
11. Why is selecting appropriate target markets important to an organization that wants to adopt the marketing concept philosophy?
12. What is a sales forecast? Why is it important?

MARKETING APPLICATIONS

1. MTV Latino targets the growing Hispanic market in the United States. Identify another product marketed to a distinct target market. Describe the target market, and explain how the marketing mix appeals specifically to that group.
2. Locate an article that describes the targeting strategy of a particular organization. Describe the target market, and explain the strategy being used to reach that market.
3. The stereo market may be segmented according to income and age. Name two ways the market for each of the following products might be segmented.
   a. Candy bars
   b. Travel agency services
   c. Bicycles
   d. Hair spray
4. If you were using a time-series analysis to forecast sales for your company for the next year, how would you use the following sets of sales figures?

a.

2000	$145,000	2005	$149,000
2001	$144,000	2006	$148,000
2002	$147,000	2007	$180,000
2003	$145,000	2008	$191,000
2004	$148,000	2009	$227,000

b.

	2007	2008	2009
Jan.	$12,000	$14,000	$16,000
Feb.	$13,000	$14,000	$15,500
Mar.	$12,000	$14,000	$17,000
Apr.	$13,000	$15,000	$17,000
May	$15,000	$17,000	$20,000
June	$18,000	$18,000	$21,000
July	$18,500	$18,000	$21,500
Aug.	$18,500	$19,000	$22,000
Sep.	$17,000	$18,000	$21,000
Oct.	$16,000	$15,000	$19,000
Nov.	$13,000	$14,000	$19,000
Dec.	$14,000	$15,000	$18,000

c. 2007 sales increased 21.2 percent (opened an additional store in 2007).
2008 sales increased 18.8 percent (opened another store in 2008).

ONLINE EXERCISE

5. iExplore is an Internet company that offers a variety of travel and adventure products. Visit its website at **http://www.iexplore.com.**
   a. Based on the information provided at the website, what are some of iExplore's basic products?
   b. What market segments does iExplore appear to be targeting with its website? What segmentation variables are being used to segment these markets?
   c. How does iExplore appeal to comparison shoppers?

DEVELOPING YOUR MARKETING PLAN

Identifying and analyzing a target market is a major component of formulating a marketing strategy. A clear understanding and explanation of a product's target market is crucial to developing a useful marketing plan. References to various dimensions of a target market are likely to appear in several locations in a marketing plan. To assist you in understanding how information in this chapter relates to the creation of your marketing plan, focus on the following considerations:

1. What type of targeting strategy is being used for your product and should a different targeting strategy be employed?
2. Select and justify the segmentation variables that are most appropriate for segmenting the market for your product. If your product is a consumer product, use Figure 5.3 for ideas regarding the most appropriate segmentation variables. If your marketing plan focuses on a business product, review the information in the section entitled "Variables for Segmenting Business Markets."

The information obtained from these questions should assist you in developing various aspects of your marketing plan found in the *Interactive Marketing Plan* exercise.

VIDEO CASE 5

Is There a Harley for Everyone?

More than a century after the first Harley-Davidson motorcycle hit the road, the company dominates the U.S. motorcycle market. The company teetered on the brink of bankruptcy in the 1980s and then roared back with a renewed focus on product quality. Now, with annual worldwide sales of nearly $6 billion, Harley-Davidson is building a solid foundation for future profits by focusing on younger customers and women.

According to the Motorcycle Industry Council, the average age of motorcyclists is 42. The average age of Harley-Davidson's customers is 48, but its customers are intensely loyal to the iconic brand. If the company can bring in younger customers, especially first-time buyers, it has a good chance of keeping them as they trade up to more powerful and expensive motorcycles in the coming years.

As a result, Harley-Davidson is putting special targeting emphasis on consumers in their 20s and on women. Its newer models marry the brand's image of freedom and individuality to motorcycles with styling, performance, and features that appeal to these two segments. To attract first-time buyers as well as experienced riders trading up to better bikes, Harley-Davidson prices its motorcycles starting at $6,695 and offers financing and insurance, as well.

Buyers can also order limited-edition motorcycles custom-built with distinctive paint designs and accessories, to express their personality. However, Harley-Davidson selects annually only a small number of orders for custom-built bikes. Not surprisingly, these custom products are in high demand in all targeted segments, despite their higher price tags.

To encourage new riders to learn to safely ride a motorcycle and then perhaps buy a Harley-Davidson bike, many of the company's dealers offer the Rider's Edge driving course. In the past decade, thousands of consumers have graduated and earned a motorcycle license through this course. The Rider's Edge also helps experienced riders to hone their riding skills and learn special techniques for riding in groups.

Although competitors, such as Yamaha and Suzuki, are targeting younger motorcyclists worldwide, Harley-Davidson sees its uniquely American brand and its reputation for quality as two major strengths. Knowing that members of its target market are passionate about motorcycles, the company offers tours of its factories in Wisconsin, Pennsylvania, and Missouri. It also set up the Harley-Davidson Museum in its headquarters city of Milwaukee, with 130,000 square feet of exhibits featuring Harley-Davidson products of the past, present, and future.

On the lifestyle side, the Harley Owners Group (HOG) fosters a sense of community among customers, both young and old, male and female. HOG's more than a million members enjoy benefits such as access to dozens of exclusive group rides, a special customer service hotline, and subscriptions to motorcycling magazines. In addition, members can use the Harley-Davidson website to plan travel, book hotels, rent bikes, or ship their bikes for their next riding adventures.

Like a number of companies, global economic woes have been a real challenge for Harley-Davidson. Sales of the most profitable models are declining, while sales of low-profit models are increasing. The company still builds and sells more than 300,000 motorcycles each year, but its ability to grow profitably depends, in large part, on the success of its targeting strategy.

QUESTIONS FOR DISCUSSION

1. What targeting strategy is Harley-Davidson using, and why is it appropriate?
2. Of the four categories of segmentation variables for consumer markets, which are being used by Harley-Davidson?
3. Why is it important for Harley-Davidson to monitor the marketing segmentation efforts of competitors like Yamaha and Suzuki?

Steven Gray, "Harley-Davidson Tries to Rejuvenate Its Business," *Time*, February 18, 2009, www.time.com; Rick Barrett, "Harley Says It Will Cut 1,100 Jobs, After Dismal Fourth Quarter," *Milwaukee Journal Sentinel*, January 24, 2009, www.jsonline.com; Susan Carpenter, "Women Drive Increase in Sales of Motorcycles, Survey Shows," *Los Angeles Times*, November 20, 2008, p. C3; Susan Carpenter, "Harley Is Thrown by Bumps in the Road," September 23, 2008, p. C1; Karl Greenberg, "Harley Targets Younger Consumer with Sub-Brand," *Marketing Daily MediaPost News*, May 1, 2008, www.mediapost.com.

3 Customer Behavior

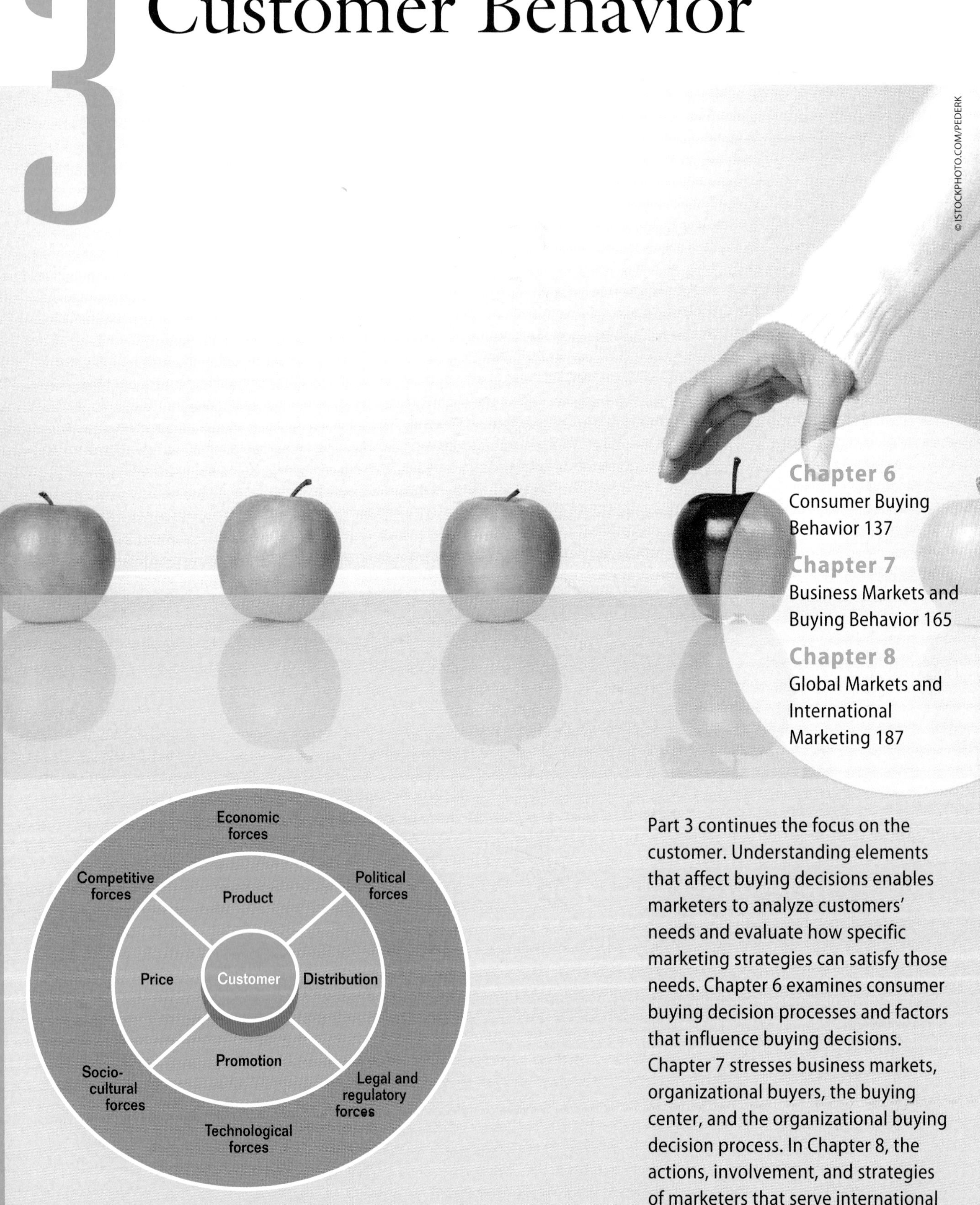

Part 3 continues the focus on the customer. Understanding elements that affect buying decisions enables marketers to analyze customers' needs and evaluate how specific marketing strategies can satisfy those needs. Chapter 6 examines consumer buying decision processes and factors that influence buying decisions. Chapter 7 stresses business markets, organizational buyers, the buying center, and the organizational buying decision process. In Chapter 8, the actions, involvement, and strategies of marketers that serve international customers are considered.

Consumer Buying Behavior

CHAPTER 6

UNDERSTANDING CUSTOMERS THROUGH HIGH SCHOOL AND COLLEGIATE ATHLETICS

In the stadium, on the track, at the gym, or wherever high school sports are played, companies are focusing on student athletes. For example, to understand teens and get them talking about its personal care products, Procter & Gamble (P&G) gives away samples of its Herbal Essences shampoo, CoverGirl makeup, and other items at cheerleader training camps. It's "a unique way to get involved with an influential set of our consumers," observes P&G Beauty's teen external relations manager.

Allstate Insurance, an active sponsor of NASCAR and other sports, is also jumping into high school sports with a program for local agents who want to support teams or athletic departments. "In many, many communities, high school athletics is one of the premier events," an Allstate executive explains. "Teenagers themselves are not big customers for insurance, but their parents are." And after students graduate and need car or home insurance, Allstate wants to be sure its brand is in the game.

Teens are a sizable customer group for PepsiCo's vitamin-fortified Propel fitness water. In the past few years, Pepsi has held workshops at hundreds of high school sports events and taught 500,000 students about nutrition and water. Because the workshops are educational, the teens "lose some of that wall they put up" against mainstream marketing, says the senior vice president of sports marketing for Propel.

OBJECTIVES:

1. Describe the level of involvement and types of consumer problem-solving processes.
2. Recognize the stages of the consumer buying decision process.
3. Explain how situational influences may affect the consumer buying decision process.
4. Understand the psychological influences that may affect the consumer buying decision process.
5. Be familiar with the social influences that affect the consumer buying decision process.

American Collegiate Intramural Sports, which arranges corporate sponsorships for college sports programs and fitness centers, has helped P&G, Nike, and other companies connect with student athletes across the country. For instance, it has helped Microsoft promote its Xbox game consoles during campus sports events. It has also set up temporary "pop-up" stores that feature branded workout fashions at dozens of campuses. Looking ahead, can more brands speed to the head of the pack by tapping into the interests of student athletes?[1]

Marketers at successful organizations such as Procter & Gamble, Allstate, and American Collegiate Intramural Sports go to great lengths to understand their customers' needs and gain a better grasp of customers' buying behavior. A firm's ability to establish and maintain satisfying customer relationships requires an understanding of **buying behavior**, which is the decision processes and acts of people involved in buying and using products. **Consumer buying behavior** refers to the buying behavior of ultimate consumers, those who purchase products for personal or household use and not for business purposes. Marketers strive to understand buying behavior for several reasons. First, buyers' reactions to a firm's marketing strategy have a great impact on the firm's success. Second, as indicated in Chapter 1, the marketing concept stresses that a firm should create a marketing mix that satisfies customers. To find out what satisfies buyers, marketers must examine the main influences on what, where, when, and how consumers buy. Third, by gaining a better understanding of the factors that affect buying behavior, marketers are in a better position to predict how consumers will respond to marketing strategies.

In this chapter, we first examine how the customer's level of involvement affects the type of problem solving employed and discuss the types of consumer problem-solving processes. Then we analyze the major stages of the consumer buying decision process, beginning with problem recognition, information search, and evaluation of alternatives and proceeding through purchase and postpurchase evaluation. Next, we examine situational influences that affect purchasing decisions: surroundings, time, purchase reason, and buyer's mood and condition. We go on to consider psychological influences on purchasing decisions: perception, motives, learning, attitudes, personality and self-concept, and lifestyles. We conclude with a discussion of social influences that affect buying behavior: roles, family, reference groups and opinion leaders, social classes, and culture and subcultures.

buying behavior
The decision processes and acts of people involved in buying and using products

consumer buying behavior
Buying behavior of people who purchase products for personal or household use and not for business purposes

level of involvement
An individual's degree of interest in a product and the importance of the product for that person

Level of Involvement and Consumer Problem-Solving Processes

In order to acquire and maintain products that satisfy their current and future needs, consumers engage in problem solving. People engage in different types of problem-solving processes depending on the nature of the products involved. The amount of effort, both mental and physical, that buyers expend in solving problems varies considerably. A major determinant of the type of problem-solving process employed depends on the customer's **level of involvement**, the degree of interest in a product and the importance the individual places on this product. High-involvement products tend to be those that are visible to others (such as clothing, furniture, or automobiles) and expensive. Expensive bicycles, for example, are usually

TABLE 6.1 Consumer Problem Solving

	Routinized Response	Limited	Extended
Product cost	Low	Low to moderate	High
Search effort	Little	Little to moderate	Extensive
Time spent	Short	Short to medium	Lengthy
Brand preference	More than one is acceptable, although one may be preferred	Several	Varies; usually many

Source: VALS/Mediamark Research, Inc., survey, SRI Consulting Business Intelligence, www.sric-bi.com/VALS. Reprinted with permission.

high-involvement products. High-importance issues, such as health care, are also associated with high levels of involvement. Low-involvement products tend to be those that are less expensive and have less associated social risk, such as many grocery items. A person's interest in a product or product category that is ongoing and long term is referred to as *enduring involvement.* In contrast, *situational involvement* is temporary and dynamic and results from a particular set of circumstances, such as the need to buy a new car after being involved in an accident. Consumer involvement may be attached to product categories (such as sports), loyalty to a specific brand, interest in a specific advertisement (e.g., a funny commercial) or a medium (such as a particular television show), or certain decisions and behaviors (e.g., a love of shopping). On the other hand, a consumer may find a particular commercial entertaining yet have little involvement with the brand advertised because of loyalty to another brand.[2] Involvement level, as well as other factors, affects a person's selection of one of three types of consumer problem solving: routinized response behavior, limited problem solving, or extended problem solving (Table 6.1).

A consumer uses **routinized response behavior** when buying frequently purchased, low-cost items requiring very little search and decision effort. When buying such items, a consumer may prefer a particular brand but is familiar with several brands in the product class and views more than one as being acceptable. Typically, low-involvement products are bought through routinized response behavior, that is, almost automatically. For example, most buyers spend little time or effort selecting a soft drink or a brand of cereal.

routinized response behavior
A type of consumer problem-solving process used when buying frequently purchased, low-cost items that require very little search and decision effort

Buyers engage in **limited problem solving** when buying products occasionally or when they need to obtain information about an unfamiliar brand in a familiar product category. This type of problem solving requires a moderate amount of time for information gathering and deliberation. For example, if Procter & Gamble introduces an improved Tide laundry detergent, interested buyers will seek additional information about the new product, perhaps by asking a friend who has used it, watching a commercial about it, or visiting the company's website, before making a trial purchase.

limited problem solving
A type of consumer problem-solving process that buyers use when purchasing products occasionally or when they need information about an unfamiliar brand in a familiar product category

The most complex type of problem solving, **extended problem solving**, occurs when purchasing unfamiliar, expensive, or infrequently bought products—for instance, a car, home, or a college education. The buyer uses many criteria to evaluate alternative brands or choices and spends much time seeking information and deciding on the purchase. Extended problem solving is frequently used for purchasing high-involvement products.

extended problem solving
A type of consumer problem-solving process employed when purchasing unfamiliar, expensive, or infrequently bought products

Purchase of a particular product does not always elicit the same type of problem-solving process. In some instances we engage in extended problem solving the first time we buy a certain product but find that limited problem solving suffices when we buy it again. If a routinely purchased, formerly satisfying brand no longer satisfies us, we may use limited or extended problem solving to switch to a new brand. Thus, if we notice that the brand of pain reliever we normally buy is no longer working, we may seek out a different brand through limited problem solving. Most consumers occasionally make purchases solely on impulse and not on the basis of any of these three problem-solving processes. **Impulse buying** involves no conscious planning but results from a powerful urge to buy something immediately.

Consumer Buying Decision Process

impulse buying
An unplanned buying behavior resulting from a powerful urge to buy something immediately

consumer buying decision process
A five-stage purchase decision process that includes problem recognition, information search, evaluation of alternatives, purchase, and postpurchase evaluation

The **consumer buying decision process** shown in Figure 6.1 includes five stages: problem recognition, information search, evaluation of alternatives, purchase, and postpurchase evaluation. Before we examine each stage, consider these important points. First, the act of purchasing is just one stage in the process and usually not the first stage. Second, even though we indicate that a purchase occurs, not all decision processes lead to a purchase. Individuals may end the process at any stage. Finally, not all consumer decisions include all five stages. People engaged in extended problem solving usually go through all stages of this decision process, whereas those engaged in limited problem solving and routinized response behavior may omit some stages.

PROBLEM RECOGNITION

Problem recognition occurs when a buyer becomes aware of a difference between a desired state and an actual condition. Consider a student who owns a nonprogrammable calculator and

FIGURE 6.1 Consumer Buying Decision Process and Possible Influences on the Process

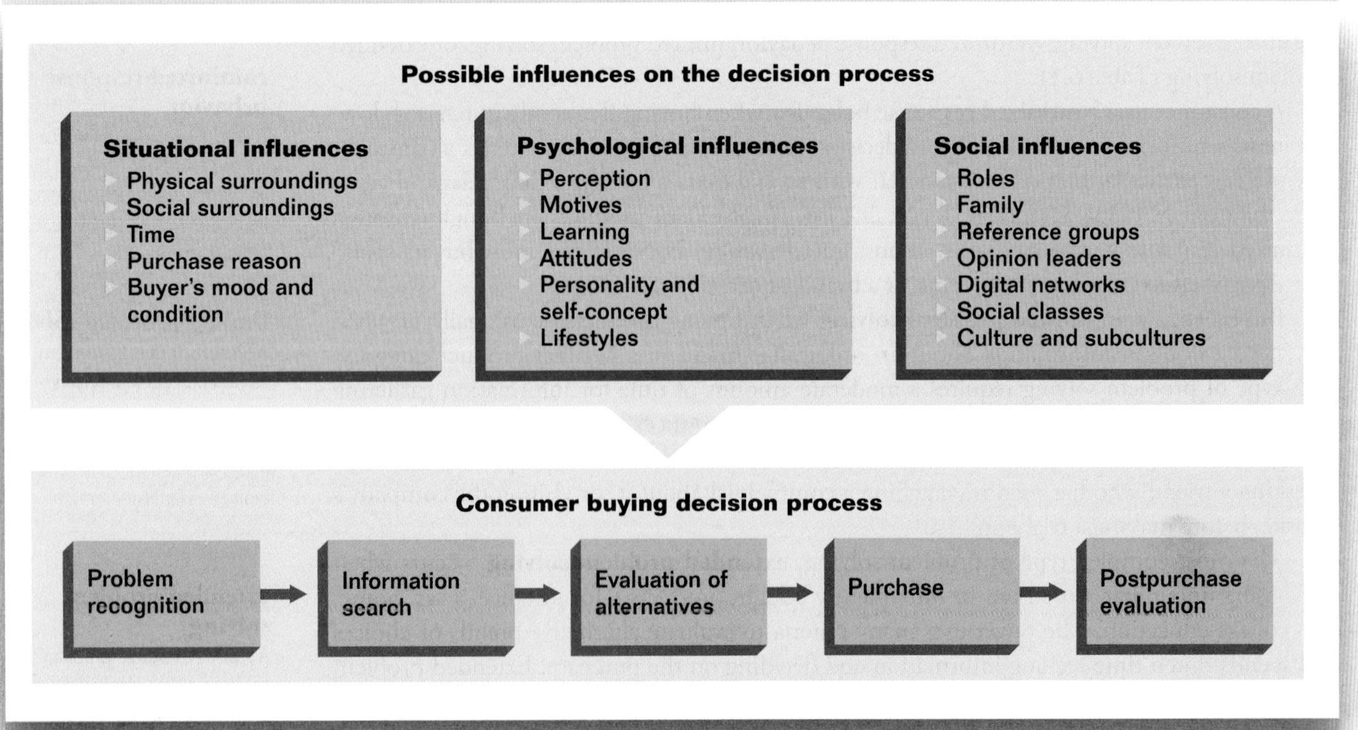

Possible influences on the decision process

Situational influences
- Physical surroundings
- Social surroundings
- Time
- Purchase reason
- Buyer's mood and condition

Psychological influences
- Perception
- Motives
- Learning
- Attitudes
- Personality and self-concept
- Lifestyles

Social influences
- Roles
- Family
- Reference groups
- Opinion leaders
- Digital networks
- Social classes
- Culture and subcultures

Consumer buying decision process

Problem recognition → Information search → Evaluation of alternatives → Purchase → Postpurchase evaluation

Problem Recognition
State Farm, in the first line of this advertisement, tells us, "Life doesn't always go as planned." This advertisement attempts to stimulate problem recognition regarding the purchase of life insurance.

learns that she needs a programmable one for her math course. She recognizes that a difference exists between the desired state—having a programmable calculator—and her actual condition. She therefore decides to buy a new calculator.

The speed of consumer problem recognition can be quite rapid or rather slow. Sometimes a person has a problem or need but is unaware of it. Marketers use sales personnel, advertising, and packaging to help trigger recognition of such needs or problems. For example, a university bookstore may advertise programmable calculators in the school newspaper at the beginning of the term. Students who see the advertisement may recognize that they need these calculators for their course work.

INFORMATION SEARCH

After recognizing the problem or need, a buyer (if continuing the decision process) searches for product information that will help resolve the problem or satisfy the need. For example, the above-mentioned student, after recognizing the need for a programmable calculator, may search for information about different types and brands of calculators. She acquires information over time from her surroundings. However, the information's impact depends on how she interprets it.

An information search has two aspects. In an **internal search**, buyers search their memories for information about products that might solve the problem. If they cannot retrieve enough information from memory to make a decision, they seek additional information from outside sources in an **external search**. The external search may focus on communication with friends or relatives, comparison of available brands and prices, marketer-dominated sources, and/or public sources. An individual's personal contacts—friends, relatives, and associates—often are influential sources of information because the person trusts and respects them. However, research suggests that consumers may overestimate friends' knowledge about products and their ability to evaluate them.[3] Using marketer-dominated sources of information, such as salespeople, advertising, websites, package labeling, and in-store demonstrations and displays, typically requires little effort on the consumer's part. Indeed, the Internet has become a major information source during the consumer buying decision process, especially for

internal search
An information search in which buyers search their memories for information about products that might solve their problem

external search
An information search in which buyers seek information from outside sources

SNAPSHOT

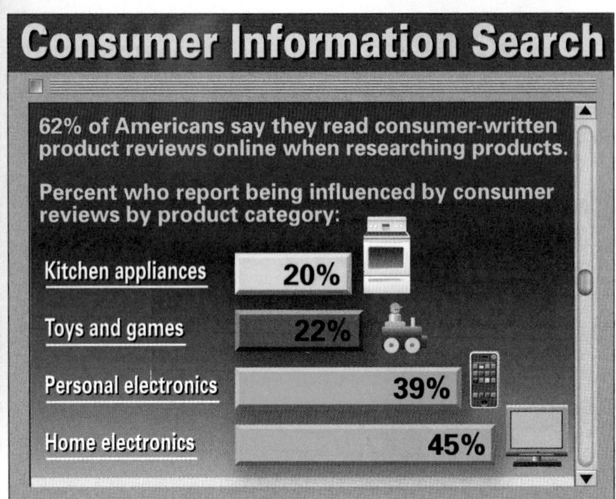

Source: Deloitte & Touche. Margin of error ±3%. As seen in *USA Today Snapshort* on Nov. 7, 2007, p. B1.

product and pricing information. Buyers also obtain information from independent sources—for instance, government reports, news presentations, publications such as *Consumer Reports,* and reports from product-testing organizations. Consumers frequently view information from these sources as highly credible because of their factual and unbiased nature. Repetition, a technique well known to advertisers, increases consumers' learning of information. When seeing or hearing an advertising message for the first time, recipients may not grasp all its important details, but they learn more details as the message is repeated.

EVALUATION OF ALTERNATIVES

A successful information search yields a group of brands that a buyer views as possible alternatives—a **consideration set** (also called an *evoked set*). For example, a consideration set of programmable calculators might include those made by Texas Instruments, Hewlett-Packard, Sharp, and Casio. Research suggests that consumers assign a greater value to a brand they have heard of than to one they have not—even when they do not know anything else about the brand. Thus, when attempting to choose between two airlines for an emergency trip, most consumers will choose the one they have heard of over an unfamiliar name.[4]

To assess the products in a consideration set, the buyer uses **evaluative criteria**, which are objective (such as an EPA mileage rating) and subjective (such as style) characteristics that are important to him or her. For example, one calculator buyer may want a rechargeable unit with a large display and large buttons, whereas another may have no size preferences but dislikes rechargeable calculators. The buyer also assigns a certain level of importance to each criterion; some features and characteristics carry more weight than others. Using the criteria, the buyer rates and eventually ranks brands in the consideration set. The evaluation stage may yield no brand the buyer is willing to purchase. In such a case, a further information search may be necessary.

Marketers may influence consumers' evaluations by *framing* the alternatives, that is, by describing the alternatives and their attributes in a certain manner. Framing can make a characteristic seem more important to a consumer and facilitate its recall from memory. For example, by stressing a car's superior comfort and safety features over those of a competitor's car, an automaker can direct consumers' attention toward those points of superiority. Framing probably influences the decision processes of inexperienced buyers more than those of experienced ones.

PURCHASE

In the purchase stage, the consumer chooses the product to be bought. Selection is based on the outcome of the evaluation stage and on other dimensions. Product availability may influence which brand is purchased. For example, if a consumer wants a black pair of Nikes and cannot find them in his size, he might buy a black pair of Reeboks.

During this stage, buyers also pick the seller from whom they will buy the product. The choice of seller may affect final product selection—and so may the terms of sale, which, if negotiable, are determined at this stage. Other issues, such as price, delivery, warranties, maintenance agreements, installation, and credit arrangements, are also settled. Finally, the actual purchase takes place during this stage, unless the consumer decides to terminate the buying decision process.

consideration set
A group of brands that a buyer views as alternatives for possible purchase

evaluative criteria
Objective and subjective characteristics that are important to a buyer

POSTPURCHASE EVALUATION

After the purchase, the buyer begins evaluating the product to ascertain if its actual performance meets expected levels. Many criteria used in evaluating alternatives are applied again during postpurchase evaluation. The outcome of this stage is either satisfaction or dissatisfaction, which influences whether the consumer complains, communicates with other possible buyers, and repurchases the product.

Shortly after purchase of an expensive product, evaluation may result in **cognitive dissonance**, doubts in the buyer's mind about whether purchasing the product was the right decision. For example, after buying a $199 iPod, a person may feel guilty about the purchase or wonder whether he or she purchased the right brand and quality. Cognitive dissonance is most likely to arise when a person has recently bought an expensive, high-involvement product that lacks some of the desirable features of competing brands. A buyer experiencing cognitive dissonance may attempt to return the product or seek positive information about it to justify choosing it. Marketers sometimes attempt to reduce cognitive dissonance by having salespeople contact recent purchasers to make sure that they are satisfied with their new purchases.

COURTESY OF COLGATE-PALMOLIVE COMPANY

Framing Product Attributes
The maker of Palmolive Pure + Clear frames product attributes that include no unnecessary chemicals, no heavy fragrances, non-irritating dyes, and no harmful residue left on dishes.

As Figure 6.1 shows, three major categories of influences are believed to affect the consumer buying decision process: situational, psychological, and social. In the remainder of this chapter we focus on these influences. Although we discuss each major influence separately, their effects on the consumer decision process are interrelated.

Situational Influences on the Buying Decision Process

Situational influences result from circumstances, time, and location that affect the consumer buying decision process. For example, buying an automobile tire after noticing while washing your car that a tire is badly worn is a different experience from buying a tire right after a blowout on the highway spoils your vacation. Situational factors can influence the buyer during any stage of the consumer buying decision process and may cause the individual to shorten, lengthen, or terminate the process. Situational factors can be classified into five categories: physical surroundings, social surroundings, time perspective, reason for purchase, and the buyer's momentary mood and condition.[5]

Physical surroundings include location, store atmosphere, aromas, sounds, lighting, weather, and other factors in the physical environment in which the decision process occurs. Research suggests that retail store chains should design their store environment to make browsing as easy as possible to increase shoppers' willingness to choose and eventually make purchases.[6] Numerous restaurant chains, such as Olive Garden and Chili's, invest heavily in facilities, often building from the ground up, to provide special surroundings that enhance customers' dining experiences. Clearly, in some settings, dimensions, such as weather, traffic sounds, and odors, are beyond the marketers' control. Yet they must try to make customers more comfortable. General climatic conditions, for example, may influence a customer's decision to buy a specific type of vehicle (such as a sports-utility vehicle) and certain accessories (such as four-wheel drive). Current weather conditions, depending on whether they are

cognitive dissonance
A buyer's doubts shortly after a purchase about whether the decision was the right one

situational influences
Influences resulting from circumstances, time, and location that affect the consumer buying decision process

favorable or unfavorable, may either encourage or discourage consumers to go shopping and to seek out specific products.

Social surroundings include characteristics and interactions of others, such as friends, relatives, salespeople, and other customers, who are present when a purchase decision is being made. Buyers may feel pressured to behave in a certain way because they are in public places such as restaurants, stores, or sports arenas. Thoughts about who will be around when the product is used or consumed are another dimension of the social setting. An overcrowded store or an argument between a customer and a salesperson may cause consumers to stop shopping or even leave the store.

The time dimension, such as the amount of time required to become knowledgeable about a product, to search for it, and to buy it, also influences the buying decision process in several ways. For instance, to make an informed decision at their own convenience, more men than ever are buying diamond engagement rings online. A high-end Internet jeweler such as Blue Nile features interactive tools on its website to help men educate themselves about diamonds and then select a unique combination from its large inventory of diamonds and settings.[7] Time plays a major role because the buyer considers the possible frequency of product use, the length of time required to use the product, and the length of the overall product life. Other time dimensions that influence purchases include time of day, day of the week or month, seasons, and holidays. The amount of time pressure a consumer is under affects how much time is devoted to purchase decisions. A customer under severe time constraints is likely either to make quick purchase decisions or to delay them.

The purchase reason raises the questions of what exactly the product purchase should accomplish and for whom. Generally, consumers purchase an item for their own use, for household use, or as a gift. For example, people who are buying a gift may buy a different product than if they were purchasing the product for themselves. If you own a Cross pen, for example, it is unlikely that you bought it for yourself.

The buyer's momentary moods (such as anger, anxiety, or contentment) or momentary conditions (such as fatigue, illness, or being flush with cash) may have a bearing on the consumer buying decision process. These moods or conditions immediately precede the current situation and are not chronic. Any of these moods or conditions can affect a person's ability and desire to search for information, receive information, or seek and evaluate alternatives. There is evidence to suggest that sad buyers are more inclined to take risks, whereas happy buyers are more likely to be risk-aversive in buying decisions.[8] Moods also can influence a consumer's postpurchase evaluation significantly.

Psychological Influences on the Buying Decision Process

Psychological influences partly determine people's general behavior and thus influence their behavior as consumers. Primary psychological influences on consumer behavior are perception, motives, learning, attitudes, personality and self-concept, and lifestyles. Even though these psychological factors operate internally, they are very much affected by social forces outside the individual.

PERCEPTION

Different people perceive the same thing at the same time in different ways. When you first look at Figure 6.2, do you see fish or birds? Similarly, an individual at different times may perceive the same item in a number of ways. **Perception** is the process of selecting, organizing, and interpreting information inputs to produce meaning. **Information inputs** are sensations

psychological influences
Factors that partly determine people's general behavior, thus influencing their behavior as consumers

perception
The process of selecting, organizing, and interpreting information inputs to produce meaning

information inputs
Sensations received through the sense organs

selective exposure
The process of selecting inputs to be exposed to our awareness while ignoring others

selective distortion
An individual's changing or twisting of information when it is inconsistent with personal feelings or beliefs

selective retention
Remembering information inputs that support personal feelings and beliefs and forgetting inputs that do not

received through sight, taste, hearing, smell, and touch. When we hear an advertisement, see a friend, smell food cooking at a nearby restaurant, or touch a product, we receive information inputs. Marketers are increasingly employing scent to help attract consumers who may be in the problem-recognition or information-search stages of the buying decision process. For example, some cleaning-product makers have found they can't let their goods smell too pleasant. Clorox bleach, available in fragrances such as fresh meadow, clean linen, and lavender, takes care to keep the original bleach scent faintly detectable. Instead of completely covering up the bleach scent, consumers preferred the product to keep its bleach smell, just not as strong as it was before.[9]

As the definition indicates, perception is a three-step process. Although we receive numerous pieces of information at once, only a few reach our awareness. We select some inputs and ignore others because we do not have the ability to be conscious of all inputs at one time. This phenomenon is sometimes called **selective exposure** because an individual selects which inputs will reach awareness. If you are concentrating on this paragraph, you probably are not aware that cars outside are making noise, that the room light is on, or that you are touching this page. Even though you receive these inputs, they do not reach your awareness until they are pointed out.

An individual's current set of needs affects selective exposure. Information inputs that relate to one's strongest needs at a given time are more likely to be selected to reach awareness. It is not by random chance that many fast-food commercials are aired near mealtimes. Customers are more likely to tune in to these advertisements at these times.

The selective nature of perception may result not only in selective exposure but also in two other conditions: selective distortion and selective retention. **Selective distortion** is changing or twisting currently received information; it occurs when a person receives information inconsistent with personal feelings or beliefs. For example, on seeing an advertisement promoting a disliked brand, a viewer may distort the information to make it more consistent with his or her own prior views. This distortion substantially lessens the effect of the advertisement on the individual. In **selective retention**, a person remembers information inputs that support personal feelings and beliefs and forgets inputs that do not. After hearing a sales presentation and leaving a store, a customer may forget many selling points if they contradict his or her personal beliefs.

The second step in the process of perception is perceptual organization. Information inputs that reach

Marketing IN TRANSITION

Brand Fans Say: Lights, Camera, Action

The homemade commercial is one of the newest trends in consumer behavior. Contests sponsored by PepsiCo's Frito-Lay division, H.J. Heinz, Best Western hotels, Klondike, and other companies have prompted thousands of consumers to write, film, edit, and submit their own commercials for a chance to win prizes and 30 seconds of fame on television, online, and beyond. Homemade commercials get consumers involved with their favorite brands, whether they submit entries or simply click to watch and vote for the ads they like.

When PepsiCo's Frito-Lay held a contest inviting consumers to make their own Doritos commercials to air during the Super Bowl in 2009, it received 1,900 entries. The company selected five finalists, invited the public to vote for their favorite online, and showed the two top vote-getters during the Super Bowl. When a *USA Today* consumer panel ranked the 2009 Super Bowl ads, one of the homemade Doritos commercials topped the list. The consumers behind the camera earned $1 million and Frito-Lay earned millions in free publicity.

H.J. Heinz has run two contests inviting consumers to submit homemade commercials, as a way to build extra buzz. In both, consumers were asked to upload their ketchup commercials to YouTube and then register on Heinz's http://www.TopThisTV.com site. Company marketers chose 10 semifinalists from more than 4,000 entries and asked YouTube visitors to vote for the winner. The top prize for the best commercial: $57,000, a spot on national television, and an everlasting presence on YouTube. The top prize for Heinz: Millions of dollars worth of free media attention and a starring role for its ketchup in thousands of consumer-generated commercials.[a]

FIGURE 6.2 Fish or Birds: Which Do You See?

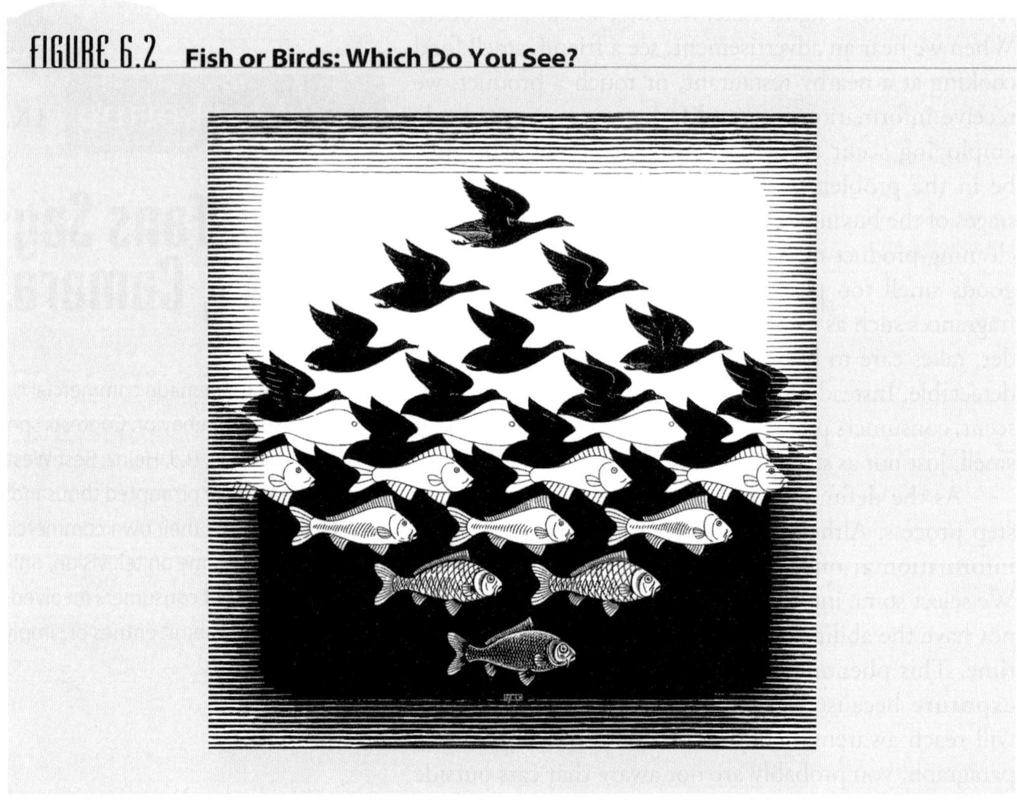

awareness are not received in an organized form. To produce meaning, an individual must mentally organize and integrate new information with what is already stored in memory. People use several methods to organize. One method, called *closure,* occurs when a person mentally fills in missing elements in a pattern or statement. In an attempt to draw attention to its brand, an advertiser will capitalize on closure by using incomplete images, sounds, or statements in its advertisements.

Interpretation, the third step in the perceptual process, is the assignment of meaning to what has been organized. A person bases interpretation on what he or she expects or what is familiar. For this reason, a manufacturer that changes a product or its package faces a major problem. When people are looking for the old, familiar product or package, they may not recognize the new one. Unless a product or package change is accompanied by a promotional program that makes people aware of the change, an organization may suffer a sales decline.

motive
An internal energizing force that directs a person's behavior toward satisfying needs or achieving goals

Maslow's hierarchy of needs
The five levels of needs that humans seek to satisfy, from most to least important

patronage motives
Motives that influence where a person purchases products on a regular basis

learning
Changes in an individual's thought processes and behavior caused by information and experience

MOTIVES

A **motive** is an internal energizing force that orients a person's activities toward satisfying needs or achieving goals. Buyers' actions are affected by a set of motives rather than by just one motive. At a single point in time, some of a person's motives are stronger than others. For example, a person's motives for having a cup of coffee are much stronger right after waking up than just before going to bed. Motives also affect the direction and intensity of behavior. Some motives may help an individual achieve his or her goals, whereas others create barriers to goal achievement.

Abraham Maslow, an American psychologist, conceived a theory of motivation based on a hierarchy of needs. According to Maslow, humans seek to satisfy five levels of needs, from most important to least important, as shown in Figure 6.3. This sequence is known as **Maslow's hierarchy of needs**. Once needs at one level are met, humans seek to fulfill needs at the next level up in the hierarchy. At the most basic level are *physiological needs,* requirements

FIGURE 6.3 **Maslow's Hierarchy of Needs**

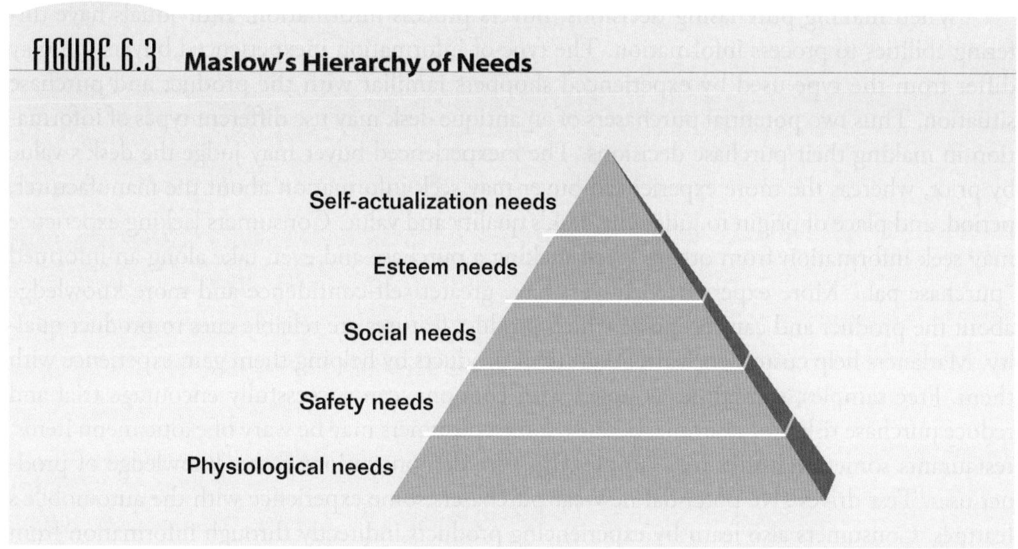

for survival such as food, water, sex, clothing, and shelter, which people try to satisfy first. Food and beverage marketers often appeal to physiological needs. At the next level are *safety needs,* which include security and freedom from physical and emotional pain and suffering. Marketers of alarm systems and insurance strive to play on people's safety needs in their promotions. Next are *social needs,* the human requirements for love and affection and a sense of belonging. Ads for cosmetics and other beauty products, jewelry, and even cars often suggest that purchasing these products will bring love. At the level of *esteem needs,* people require respect and recognition from others as well as self-esteem, a sense of their own worth. Owning a Lexus automobile, having a beauty makeover, or flying first class can satisfy esteem needs. At the top of the hierarchy are *self-actualization needs.* These refer to people's need to grow and develop and to become all they are capable of becoming. In its recruiting advertisements, the U.S. Army told potential enlistees to "Be all that you can be in the Army."

Motives that influence where a person purchases a product on a regular basis are called **patronage motives**. A buyer may shop at a specific store because of patronage motives such as price, service, location, product variety, or friendliness of the salespeople. To capitalize on patronage motives, marketers try to determine why regular customers patronize a particular store and to emphasize these characteristics in the store's marketing mix.

IMAGE COURTESY OF THE ADVERTISING ARCHIVES

Which Level of Maslow's Hierarchy of Needs?
People that use Nintendo's Wii products are likely striving to satisfy social needs.

LEARNING

Learning refers to changes in a person's thought processes and behavior caused by information and experience. Consequences of behavior strongly influence the learning process. Behaviors that result in satisfying consequences tend to be repeated. For example, a consumer who buys a Snickers candy bar and enjoys the taste is more likely to buy a Snickers again. In fact, the individual probably will continue to purchase that brand until it no longer provides satisfaction. When effects of the behavior are no longer satisfying, the person may switch brands or stop eating candy bars altogether.

When making purchasing decisions, buyers process information. Individuals have differing abilities to process information. The type of information inexperienced buyers use may differ from the type used by experienced shoppers familiar with the product and purchase situation. Thus two potential purchasers of an antique desk may use different types of information in making their purchase decisions. The inexperienced buyer may judge the desk's value by price, whereas the more experienced buyer may seek information about the manufacturer, period, and place of origin to judge the desk's quality and value. Consumers lacking experience may seek information from others when making a purchase and even take along an informed "purchase pal." More experienced buyers have greater self-confidence and more knowledge about the product and can recognize which product features are reliable cues to product quality. Marketers help customers learn about their products by helping them gain experience with them. Free samples, sometimes coupled with coupons, can successfully encourage trial and reduce purchase risk. For example, because some consumers may be wary of exotic menu items, restaurants sometimes offer free samples. In-store demonstrations foster knowledge of product uses. Test drives give potential new-car purchasers some experience with the automobile's features. Consumers also learn by experiencing products indirectly through information from salespeople, advertisements, friends, and relatives. Through sales personnel and advertisements, marketers offer information before (and sometimes after) purchases to influence what consumers learn and to create more favorable attitudes toward the product.

ATTITUDES

An **attitude** is an individual's enduring evaluation of, feelings about, and behavioral tendencies toward an object or idea. The objects toward which we have attitudes may be tangible or intangible, living or nonliving. For example, we have attitudes toward sex, religion, politics, and music, just as we do toward cars, football, and breakfast cereals. Although attitudes can change, they tend to remain stable and do not vary from moment to moment. However, all of a person's attitudes do not have equal impact at any one time; some are stronger than others. Individuals acquire attitudes through experience and interaction with other people.

An attitude consists of three major components: cognitive, affective, and behavioral. The cognitive component is the person's knowledge and information about the object or idea. The affective component consists of feelings and emotions toward the object or idea. The behavioral component manifests itself in the person's actions regarding the object or idea. Changes in one of these components may or may not alter the other components. Thus a consumer may become more knowledgeable about a specific brand without changing the affective or behavioral components of his or her attitude toward that brand.

Consumer attitudes toward a company and its products greatly influence success or failure of the firm's marketing strategy. When consumers have strong negative attitudes toward one or more aspects of a firm's marketing practices, they not only may stop using its products, but they also may urge relatives and friends to do likewise.

Because attitudes play such an important part in determining consumer behavior, marketers should measure consumer attitudes toward prices, package designs, brand names, advertisements, salespeople, repair services, store locations, features of existing or proposed products, and social responsibility efforts. Several methods help marketers gauge these attitudes. One of the simplest ways is to question people directly. Hampton Hotels, for example, asked travelers about their attitudes toward hotel cleaning smells. Most travelers (86 percent) reported that they found the smell of fresh air and linens most indicative of a clean hotel room, whereas only 14 percent said the smell of cleaning products indicate a clean room. The research helped the hotel chain refine its cleaning practices and use of cleaning products to leave rooms smelling of fresh air and linens—and nothing else.[10] Marketers also evaluate attitudes through attitude scales. An **attitude scale** usually consists of a series of adjectives, phrases, or sentences about an

attitude
An individual's enduring evaluation of, feelings about, and behavioral tendencies toward an object or idea

attitude scale
Means of measuring consumer attitudes by gauging the intensity of individuals' reactions to adjectives, phrases, or sentences about an object

object. Respondents indicate the intensity of their feelings toward the object by reacting to the adjectives, phrases, or sentences in a certain way. For example, a marketer measuring people's attitudes toward shopping might ask respondents to indicate the extent to which they agree or disagree with a number of statements such as, "Shopping is more fun than watching television."

When marketers determine that a significant number of consumers have negative attitudes toward an aspect of a marketing mix, they may try to change those attitudes to make them more favorable. This task is generally lengthy, expensive, and difficult, and may require extensive promotional efforts. For example, the California Prune Growers, an organization of prune producers, has tried to use advertising to change consumers' attitudes toward prunes by presenting them as a nutritious snack high in potassium and fiber. To alter consumers' responses so that more of them buy a given brand, a firm might launch an information-focused campaign to change the cognitive component of a consumer's attitude or a persuasive (emotional) campaign to influence the affective component. Distributing free samples might help change the behavioral component. Both business and nonbusiness organizations try to change people's attitudes about many issues, from health and safety to prices and product features.

© AP IMAGES/PRNEWSFOTO/TRAVEL INDUSTRY ASSOCIATION OF AMERICA

Attempting to Change Attitudes
SeeAmerica.org attempts to influence peoples' attitudes regarding preservation.

PERSONALITY AND SELF-CONCEPT

Personality is a set of internal traits and distinct behavioral tendencies that result in consistent patterns of behavior in certain situations. An individual's personality arises from hereditary characteristics and personal experiences that make the person unique. Personalities typically are described as having one or more characteristics such as compulsiveness, ambition, gregariousness, dogmatism, authoritarianism, introversion, extroversion, and competitiveness. Marketing researchers look for relationships between such characteristics and buying behavior. Even though a few links between several personality traits and buyer behavior have been determined, results of many studies have been inconclusive. The weak association between personality and buying behavior may be the result of unreliable measures rather than a lack of a relationship. Some marketers are convinced that consumers' personalities do influence types and brands of products purchased. For example, the type of clothing, jewelry, or automobile a person buys may reflect one or more personality characteristics.

At times, marketers aim advertising at certain types of personalities. For example, ads for certain cigarette brands are directed toward specific personality types. Marketers focus on positively valued personality characteristics, such as security consciousness, sociability, independence, or competitiveness, rather than on negatively valued ones such as insensitivity or timidity.

A person's self-concept is closely linked to personality. **Self-concept** (sometimes called *self-image*) is a person's view or perception of himself or herself. Individuals develop and alter their self-concepts based on an interaction of psychological and social dimensions. Research shows that a buyer purchases products that reflect and enhance the self-concept and that purchase decisions are important to the development and maintenance of a stable self-concept. Consumers' self-concepts may influence whether they buy a product in a specific product category and may affect brand selection as well as where they buy.

personality
A set of internal traits and distinct behavioral tendencies that result in consistent patterns of behavior

self-concept
Perception or view of oneself

LIFESTYLES

As we saw in Chapter 5, many marketers attempt to segment markets by lifestyle. A **lifestyle** is an individual's pattern of living expressed through activities, interests, and opinions. Lifestyle patterns include the ways people spend time, the extent of their interaction with others, and their general outlook on life and living. People partially determine their own lifestyles, but the pattern is also affected by personality, as well as by demographic factors such as age, education, income, and social class. Lifestyles are measured through a lengthy series of questions.

Lifestyles have a strong impact on many aspects of the consumer buying decision process, from problem recognition to postpurchase evaluation. Lifestyles influence consumers' product needs, brand preferences, types of media used, and how and where they shop.

lifestyle An individual's pattern of living expressed through activities, interests, and opinions

One of the most popular frameworks for exploring consumer lifestyles is a survey from SRI Consulting Business Intelligence. The company's VALS™ Program uses a short questionnaire to help classify consumers into eight basic groups: Innovators, Thinkers, Achievers, Experiencers, Believers, Strivers, Makers, and Survivors (see Figure 6.4). The segmentation

FIGURE 6.4 VALS™ Types

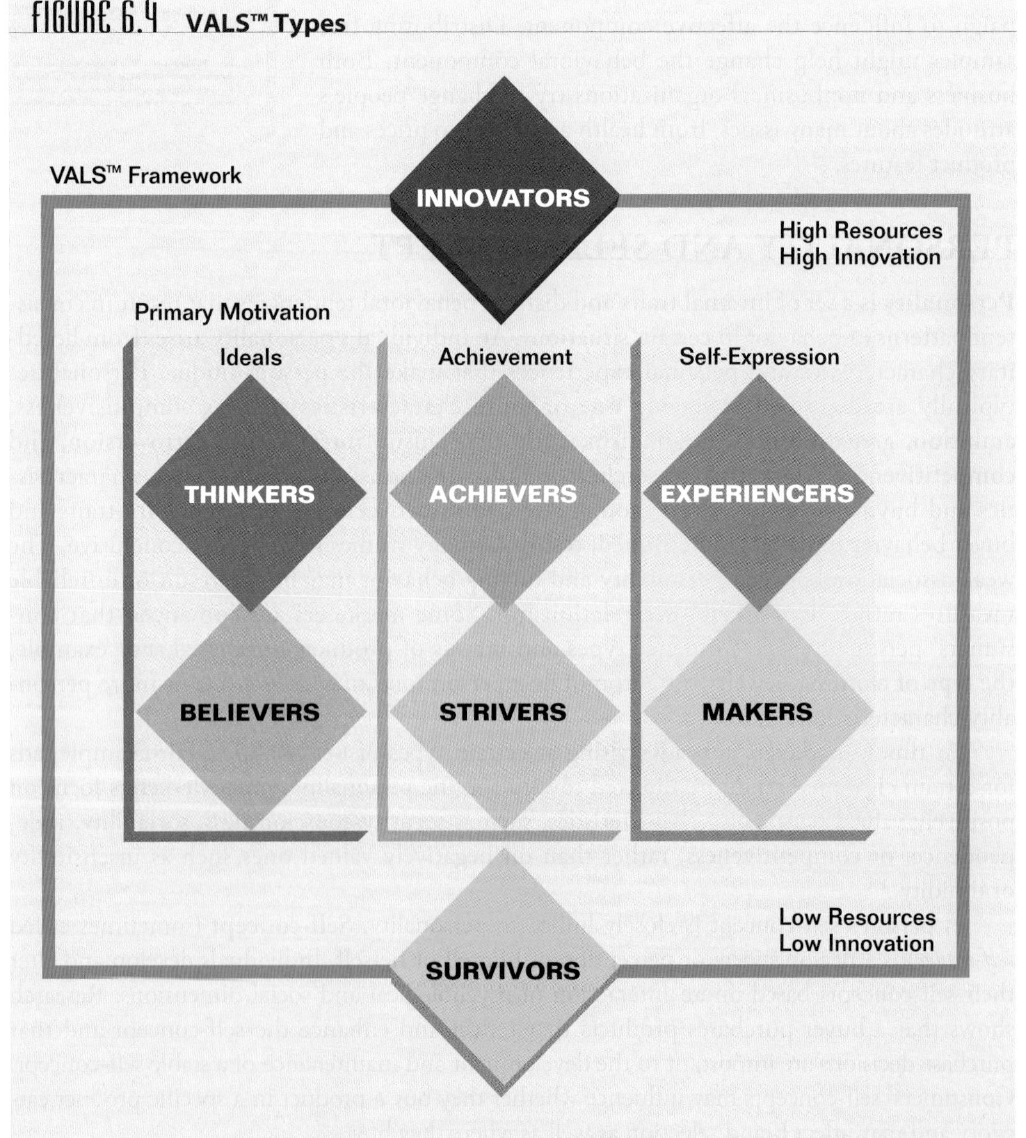

is based on psychological characteristics that are correlated with purchase behavior and four key demographics. This VALS™ questionnaire is then attached to larger surveys that focus on particular products, services, leisure activities, or media preferences to learn about the lifestyles of the eight groups.[11] VALS™ is a framework that links personality with consumers' lifestyles.

Lifestyle
KYMCO promotes specific types of lifestyles in its advertisements.

Social Influences on the Buying Decision Process

Forces that other people exert on buying behavior are called **social influences**. As Figure 6.1 shows, they are grouped into seven major areas: roles, family, reference groups, opinion leaders, digital networks, social classes, and culture and subcultures.

ROLES

All of us occupy positions within groups, organizations, and institutions. Associated with each position is a **role**, a set of actions and activities a person in a particular position is supposed to perform based on expectations of both the individual and surrounding persons. Because people occupy numerous positions, they have many roles. For example, a man may perform the roles of son, husband, father, employee or employer, church member, civic organization member, and student in an evening college class. Thus multiple sets of expectations are placed on each person's behavior.

An individual's roles influence both general behavior and buying behavior. The demands of a person's many roles may be diverse and even inconsistent. Consider the various types of clothes that you buy and wear depending on whether you are going to class, to work, to a party, to a place of worship, or to a yoga class. You and others involved in these settings have expectations about what is acceptable clothing for these events. Thus the expectations of those around us affect our purchases of clothing and many other products.

FAMILY INFLUENCES

Family influences have a very direct impact on the consumer buying decision process. Parents (and other household adults) teach children how to cope with various problems, including those dealing with purchase decisions. **Consumer socialization** is the process through which a person acquires the knowledge and skills to function as a consumer. Often children gain this knowledge and set of skills by observing parents and older siblings in purchase situations, as well as through their own purchase experiences. Children observe brand preferences and buying practices in their families and, as adults, maintain some of these brand preferences and buying practices as they establish households and raise their own families. Buying decisions made by a family are a combination of group and individual decision making.

The extent to which adult family members take part in family decision making varies among families and product categories. Traditionally, family decision-making processes have been grouped into four categories: autonomic, husband-dominant, wife-dominant, and syncratic, as shown in Table 6.2. Although female roles continue to change, women still make buying decisions related to many household items, including health care

social influences
The forces other people exert on one's buying behavior

role
Actions and activities that a person in a particular position is supposed to perform based on expectations of the individual and surrounding persons

consumer socialization
The process through which a person acquires the knowledge and skills to function as a consumer

TABLE 6.2 Types of Family Decision Making

Decision-Making Type	Decision Maker	Types of Products
Husband-dominant	Male head of household	Lawn mowers, hardware and tools, stereos, refrigerators, washer and dryer
Wife-dominant	Female head of household	Children's clothing, women's clothing, groceries, pots and pans, toiletries, home decoration
Autonomic	Equally likely to be made by the husband or wife but not by both	Men's clothing, luggage, toys and games, sporting equipment, cameras
Syncratic	Made jointly by husband and wife	Vacations, TVs, living-room furniture, carpets, financial planning services, family cars

products, laundry supplies, paper products, and foods. It is believed that women make over 80 percent of all household buying decisions. Spouses participate jointly in the purchase of several products, especially durable goods. Owing to changes in men's roles, a significant proportion of men now are the primary grocery shoppers. Children make many purchase decisions and influence numerous household purchase decisions. The type of family decision making employed depends on the composition of the family as well as on the values and attitudes of family members.

When two or more family members participate in a purchase, their roles may dictate that each is responsible for performing certain purchase-related tasks, such as initiating the idea, gathering information, determining if the product is affordable, deciding whether to buy the product, or selecting the specific brand. The specific purchase tasks performed depend on the types of products being considered, the kind of family purchase decision process typically employed, and the amount of influence children have in the decision process. Thus different family members may play different roles in the family buying process. To develop a marketing mix that meets the needs of target-market members precisely, marketers must know not only who does the actual buying but also which other family members perform purchase-related tasks.

The family life cycle stage affects individual and joint needs of family members. (Family life cycle stages are discussed in Chapter 5.) For example, consider how the car needs of recently married twenty-somethings differ from those of the same couple when they are forty-somethings with a 13-year-old daughter and a 17-year-old son. Family life cycle changes can affect which family members are involved in purchase decisions and the types of products purchased.

REFERENCE GROUPS

reference group Any group that positively or negatively affects a person's values, attitudes, or behavior

A **reference group** is any group that positively or negatively affects a person's values, attitudes, or behavior. Reference groups can be large or small. Most people have several reference groups, such as families, work-related groups, fraternities or sororities, civic clubs, professional organizations, or church-related groups.

In general, there are three major types of reference groups: membership, aspirational, and disassociative. A membership reference group is one to which an individual actually belongs; the individual identifies with group members strongly enough to take on the values, attitudes, and behaviors of people in that group. An aspirational reference group is a group to which one aspires to belong; one desires to be like those group members. A group that a person does not wish to be associated with is a disassociative reference group; the individual does not want to take on the values, attitudes, and behavior of group members.

A reference group may serve as an individual's point of comparison and source of information. A customer's behavior may change to be more in line with the actions and beliefs of group members. For example, a person might stop buying one brand of shirts and switch to another based on reference group members' advice. An individual also may seek information from the reference group about other factors regarding a prospective purchase, such as where to buy a certain product.

The extent to which a reference group affects a purchase decision depends on the product's conspicuousness and the individual's susceptibility to reference group influence. Generally, the more conspicuous a product, the more likely that the purchase decision will be influenced by reference groups. A product's conspicuousness is determined by whether others can see it and whether it can attract attention. Reference groups can affect whether a person does or does not buy a product at all, buys a type of product within a product category, or buys a specific brand. One way that reference groups may influence behavior is by ridiculing people who violate group norms; researchers have identified this practice among adolescents who admonish, haze, or even shun peers who deviate from group norms.[12] A marketer sometimes tries to use reference group influence in advertisements by suggesting that people in a specific group buy a product and are highly satisfied with it.

OPINION LEADERS

In most reference groups, one or more members stand out as opinion leaders. An **opinion leader** provides information about a specific sphere that interests reference group participants who seek information. Opinion leaders are viewed by other group members as being well informed about a particular area and as easily accessible. An opinion leader is not the foremost authority on all issues, but he or she is in a position or has knowledge or expertise that makes him or her a credible source of information on one or more topics (see Table 6.3).

opinion leader
A reference group member who provide information about a specific sphere that interests reference group participants

TABLE 6.3 Examples of Opinion Leaders and Topics

Opinion Leader	Possible Topics
Local religious leader	Charities to support, political ideas, lifestyle choices
Sorority president	Clothing and shoe purchases, hairstyles and stylists, nail and hair salons
"Movie buff" friend	Movies to see in theater or rent, DVDs to buy, television programs to watch
Family doctor	Prescription drugs, vitamins, health products
"Techie" acquaintance	Computer and other electronics purchases, software purchases, Internet service choices, video game purchases

Because such individuals know they are opinion leaders, they may feel a responsibility to remain informed about their sphere of interest and thus seek out advertisements, manufacturers' brochures, salespeople, and other sources of information. An opinion leader is likely to be most influential when consumers have high product involvement but low product knowledge, when they share the opinion leader's values and attitudes, and when the product details are numerous or complicated.

Sustainable Marketing

Toyota's Prius Steers in Green Direction

With one million Prius cars sold worldwide—more than 400,000 in the United States alone—Toyota is far and away the hybrid leader. Why? One big reason is fuel efficiency. On the highway, the Prius's hybrid gas-electric motor delivers nearly 50 miles per gallon. Another reason is that the Prius is considerably more eco-friendly than ordinary cars, leaving only a tiny trail of smog-forming emissions. But the main reason many owners buy a Prius, according to a recent study, is that it "makes a statement about me." In other words, they're proud to be driving an icon of green.

The Prius is hardly the only hybrid on the road. In fact, Toyota also makes a Camry Hybrid sedan and a Highlander Hybrid SUV. And rivals like Honda, Ford, and General Motors are driving deeper into hybrid territory. Still, the Prius is a very distinctive car, with a clean, spare silhouette that's unmistakable.

© AP/WIDE WORLD

And that's where "makes a statement about me" comes in: Onlookers who spot a Prius know immediately that the owner cares about environmental issues. In the words of Prius owner Dan Becker, who heads the Sierra Club's global warming program: "The Prius allowed you to make a green statement with a car for the first time ever." Prius owners are so satisfied, in fact, that 90 percent say they would buy another one next time they're shopping for a car—putting more green into the pockets of parent company Toyota.[b]

DIGITAL NETWORKS

Although consumers often rely on the recommendations and suggestions from friends and family when making purchasing decisions, they are increasingly turning to electronic network sources during the decision-making process for consumer products. Some websites, such as http://www.CNET.com and http://www.consumerreports.org, have established themselves as reliable sources of information for consumers because of their unbiased product comparisons and stringent testing procedures. However, many lesser-known consumer advocate sites and even many individuals are exerting a stronger influence on consumers who are turning to the Internet for product reviews.

Consumers' reliance on the Internet for assistance during the decision-making process can be seen in the proliferation of blogs, social networking sites, online forums, mailing lists, and wikis, as well as text messaging via cell phones and podcasts via MP3 players. **Blogs** (short for "web logs") are Web-based journals in which writers can editorialize and interact with other Internet users, and **wikis** are software that create an interface that enables users to add or edit the content of some types of websites (also called wikipages). One of the best-known wikis is http://www.Wikipedia.org, an online encyclopedia. **Social networks**, such as Facebook, MySpace, CarSpace, LiveJournal, or Slashdot, allow members to share personal profiles that include blogs, pictures, audios, and videos. For example, after Jeff Jarvis had an unhappy experience with Dell's ineffective attempts to resolve problems with his new laptop, he wrote about it on his blog. Within days, his blog became one of the most-visited websites, and it triggered a surge of Dell horror stories across the Web. Soon after, when people typed "Dell" into search engines, Jarvis's blog and websites with unflattering names would appear on the first listings page.[13]

Another way consumers share information is through video sites such as YouTube, where they can post videos they make, perhaps of themselves using a particular product. Companies can also post videos about their product, and their use, on their own websites, or on third-party video sites.

blogs
Web-based journals in which people can editorialize and interact with other Internet users

wikis
Software that creates an interface that enables users to add or edit the content of some types of websites (also called wikipages)

social networks
Web-based services that allow members to share personal profiles that include blogs, pictures, audios, and videos

social class
An open group of individuals with similar social rank

SOCIAL CLASSES

In all societies people rank others into higher or lower positions of respect. This ranking results in social classes. A **social class** is an open group of individuals with similar social rank. A class is referred to as *open* because people can move into and out of it. Criteria for grouping people into classes vary from one society to another. In the United States we take into account many factors, including occupation, education, income, wealth, race, ethnic group, and possessions. A person who is ranking someone does not necessarily apply all of a society's criteria. Sometimes, too, the role of income in social class determination tends to be overemphasized. Although income does help establish social class, the other factors also play a role. Within social classes, both incomes and spending habits differ significantly among members.

Analyses of social class in the United States commonly divide people into three to seven categories. Social scientist Richard P. Coleman suggests that, for purposes of consumer analysis, the population be divided into the three major status groups shown in Table 6.4. However, he cautions marketers that considerable diversity exists in people's life situations within each status group.

To some degree, individuals within social classes develop and assume common behavioral patterns. They may have similar attitudes, values, language patterns, and possessions. Social class influences many aspects of people's lives. For example, it affects their chances of having children and their children's chances of surviving infancy. It influences their childhood training, choice of religion, access to higher education, selection of occupation, and leisure time activities. Because social class has a bearing on so many aspects of a person's life, it also affects buying decisions.

Social class influences people's spending, saving, and credit practices. It determines to some extent the type, quality, and quantity of products a person buys and uses. For example, it affects purchases of clothing, foods, financial and health care services, travel, recreation, entertainment, and home furnishings. To some extent, members of lower classes attempt to emulate members of higher social classes, such as by purchasing expensive automobiles, homes, appliances, and other status symbols. Social class also affects an individual's shopping patterns and types of stores patronized. In some instances, marketers attempt to focus on certain social classes through store location and interior design, product design and features, pricing strategies, personal sales efforts, and advertising. Many companies focus on the middle and working classes because they account for such a large portion of the population. Outside the United States, the middle class is growing in India, China, Mexico, and other countries, making these consumers increasingly desirable to marketers as well. Some firms target different classes with different products. BMW, for example, introduced several models priced in the mid-$20,000 range to target middle-class consumers, although it usually targets upper-class customers with more expensive vehicles.

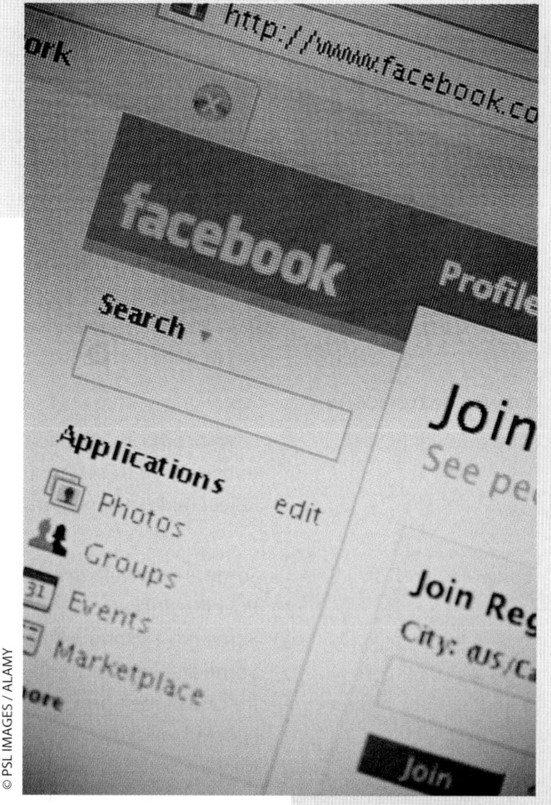

Social Networks
Facebook provides numerous online activities and opportunities for social and professional interaction.

TABLE 6.4 Social Class Behavioral Traits and Purchasing Characteristics

Class (% of population)	Behavioral Traits	Buying Characteristics
Upper Americans		
Upper-upper (0.5)	• Social elite • Aristocratic, prominent families • Inherited their position in society	• Children attend private preparatory schools and best colleges • Do not consume ostentatiously • Spend money on private clubs, various causes, and the arts
Lower-upper (3.8)	• Newer social elite • Successful professionals earning very high incomes • Earned their position in society	• Purchase material symbols of their status such as large, suburban houses and expensive automobiles • Provide a substantial market for luxury product offerings • Visit museums and attend live theater • Spend money on skiing, golf, swimming, and tennis
Upper-middle (13.8)	• Career-oriented, professional degree holders • Demand educational attainment of their children	• Provide a substantial market for quality product offerings • Family lifestyle characterized as gracious, yet careful • Spend money on movies, outdoor gardening, and photography
Middle Americans		
Middle class (32.8)	• "Typical" Americans • Work conscientiously and adhere to culturally defined standards • Average pay white-collar workers • Attend church and obey the law • Often very involved in children's school and sports activities	• Greatly value living in a respected neighborhood and keep their homes well furnished • Generally price-sensitive • Adopt conventional consumption tastes and consult category experts • Spend on family-oriented, physical activities such as fishing, camping, boating, and hunting
Working class (32.3)	• Average pay blue-collar workers • Live a routine life with unchanging day-to-day activities • Hold jobs that entail manual labor and moderate skills • Some are union members • Socially not involved in civic or church activities; limit social interaction to close neighbors and relatives	• Reside in small houses/apartments • Impulsive as consumers yet display high loyalty to national brands • Seek best bargains • Enjoy leisure activities like local travel and recreational parks
Lower Americans		
Upper-lower (9.5)	• Low-income individuals who generally fail to rise above this class • Reject middle-class morality	• Living standard is just above poverty • Seek pleasure whenever possible, especially through impulse purchases • Frequently purchase on credit
Lower-lower (7.3)	• Some are on welfare and may be homeless • Poverty-stricken • Some have strong religious beliefs • Some are unemployed • In spite of their problems, often good-hearted toward others • May be forced to live in less desirable neighborhoods	• Spend on products needed for survival • Able to convert discarded goods into usable items

Source: Roger D. Blackwell, Paul W. Miniard, and James F. Engel, *Consumer Behavior,* 10th ed. (Mason, OH: South-Western, 2005); "The Continuing Significance of Social Class Marketing," *Journal of Consumer Research,* 10 (December 1983): 265–280; Eugene Sivadas, George Mathew, and David J. Curry, "A Preliminary Examination of the Continued Significance of Social Class in Marketing," *Journal of Consumer Marketing,* 14 (Number 6, 1997): 463–469.

CULTURE AND SUBCULTURES

Culture is the accumulation of values, knowledge, beliefs, customs, objects, and concepts that a society uses to cope with its environment and passes on to future generations. Examples of objects are foods, furniture, buildings, clothing, and tools. Concepts include education, welfare, and laws. Culture also includes core values and the degree of acceptability of a wide range of behaviors in a specific society. For example, in our culture, customers as well as businesspeople are expected to behave ethically.

Culture influences buying behavior because it permeates our daily lives. Our culture determines what we wear and eat and where we reside and travel. Society's interest in the healthfulness of food affects food companies' approaches to developing and promoting their products. Culture also influences how we buy and use products and our satisfaction from them.

When U.S. marketers sell products in other countries, they realize the tremendous impact those cultures have on product purchases and use. Global marketers find that people in other regions of the world have different attitudes, values, and needs, which call for different methods of doing business as well as different types of marketing mixes. Some international marketers fail because they do not or cannot adjust to cultural differences.

Entrepreneurial Marketing

Some Can Face It, Some Can't

Are you one of the 40 million people who can't go a day—or an hour—without checking Facebook? Facebook was started just a few years ago as an online directory for Harvard students. Two weeks after the site went live over 4,000 members had posted their profiles. Within a few months, Facebook was a full-blown social phenomenon that connected young people all over the globe.

A recent study shows a staggering jump in the number of 35- to 54-year-old users—doubling roughly every two months. And the 55+ users are increasing almost as fast. The result? Teens are looking for new places to hang out where they won't be running into Granny and her "25 things about me."[c]

A culture consists of various subcultures. **Subcultures** are groups of individuals whose characteristic values and behavior patterns are similar to each other and differ from those of the surrounding culture. Subcultural boundaries are usually based on geographic designations and demographic characteristics such as age, religion, race, and ethnicity. Our culture is marked by many different subcultures, among them West Coast, gay, Asian American, and college students. Within subcultures, greater similarities exist in people's attitudes, values, and actions than within the broader culture. Relative to other subcultures, individuals in one subculture may have stronger preferences for specific types of clothing, furniture, or foods. Studies show that subcultures can play a significant role in how people respond to advertisements, particularly when pressured to make a snap judgment.[14] It is important to understand that a person can be a member of more than one subculture and that the behavioral patterns and values attributed to specific subcultures do not necessarily apply to all group members.

The percentage of the U.S. population comprising ethnic and racial subcultures is expected to grow. By 2050, about half the people of the United States will be members of racial and ethnic minorities. The Bureau of the Census reports that the three largest and fastest-growing ethnic U.S. subcultures are African Americans, Hispanics, and Asians. The population growth of these subcultures interests marketers. To target these groups more precisely, marketers are striving to become increasingly sensitive to and knowledgeable about their differences. Businesses recognize that to succeed, their marketing strategies will have to take into account the values, needs, interests, shopping patterns, and buying habits of various subcultures.

culture
The values, knowledge, beliefs, customs, objects, and concepts of a society

subcultures
Groups of individuals whose characteristic values and behavior patterns are similar to each other and differ from those of the surrounding culture

African American Subculture

In the United States, the African American subculture represents 13.1 percent of the population.[15] Like all subcultures, African American consumers possess distinct buying patterns. For example, African American consumers spend more money on utilities, footwear, women's and children's apparel, groceries, and housing than do Caucasian consumers. The combined buying power of African American consumers is projected to reach $1.2 trillion by the end of 2013.[16]

IMAGE COURTESY OF THE ADVERTISING ARCHIVES

Subculture
Subcultures can be based on geographic areas and demographic characteristics such as age, religion, race, and ethnicity.

Total spending on African American media for the first three quarters of last year was $1.8 billion. Procter & Gamble was the largest spender in this category.[17] By including African American actors in their ads, the companies believe that it can encourage a positive response to its products, increasing sales among African American consumers while still maintaining ties with Caucasian consumers.

Many other corporations are reaching out to the African American community with targeted efforts. Walmart, for example, has adjusted the merchandising of 1,500 stores located in areas with large African American populations to include more products favored by African American customers, such as ethnic hair-care products and a larger selection of more urban music offerings. The retailer also has included more African American actors in its advertising campaigns.[18] Another retailer, Target, launched a year-long campaign called "Dream in Color" to celebrate diversity. The campaign included numerous Martin Luther King Day events, guest appearances by poet Dr. Maya Angelou, free posters for schools, and a unique online curriculum to provide access to historical and contemporary African American poets.[19]

Hispanic Subculture

Hispanics represent 14.7 percent of the U.S. population, and their buying power is expected to reach $1.4 trillion by the end of 2013.[20] When considering the buying behavior of Hispanics, marketers must keep in mind that this subculture consists of nearly two dozen nationalities and ethnicities, including Cuban, Mexican, Puerto Rican, Spanish, and Dominican. Each has its own history and unique culture that affect consumer preferences and buying behavior. Marketers also should recognize that the terms *Hispanic* and *Latino* refer to an ethnic category rather than a racial distinction. Because of the group's growth and purchasing power, understanding the Hispanic subculture is critical to marketers. In general, Hispanics have strong family values, concern for product quality, and strong brand loyalty, and they will pay more for a well-known brand.[21] Like African American consumers, Hispanics spend more on housing, groceries, telephone services, clothing, footwear, and gas and motor oil. But they also spend more on men's apparel and appliances, whereas they spend less than average on health care, entertainment, and education.[22]

To attract this powerful subculture, marketers are taking Hispanic values and preferences into account when developing products and creating advertising and promotions. For example, a growing number of retailers, including Walmart, are promoting the Hispanic holiday of Three Kings Day on January 6 in markets with a significant concentration of Latino consumers.[23] American Airlines has launched a Spanish-language advertising campaign to encourage more Latinos to fly across the country during the holiday. The *destino* campaign, which includes ads on television, radio, online, and out-of-home, includes vignettes showing Latinos' lives to illustrate how the airline can help them fulfill their destinies.[24]

Asian American Subculture

The term *Asian American* includes people from more than 15 ethnic groups, including Filipinos, Chinese, Japanese, Asian Indians, Koreans, and Vietnamese, and they represent 4.9 percent of the U.S. population. The individual language, religion, and value system of each group influence its members' purchasing decisions. Some traits of this subculture, however, carry across ethnic divisions, including an emphasis on hard work, strong family ties, and a high value placed on education.[25] Asian Americans are the fastest-growing American subculture, and they are expected to wield $752 billion in buying power by 2013.[26]

Marketers are targeting the diverse Asian American market in many ways. Walmart stores have established a multicultural marketing department and new Asian American strategies, among other moves. Walmart launched a back-to-school micro-site in both English and Vietnamese. The site was positioned as a back-to-school resource for study and clothing tips, school supplies, and other suggestions.[27]

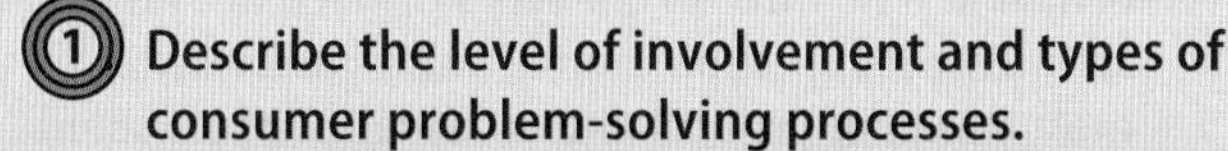

CHAPTER REVIEW

OBJECTIVES

1 Describe the level of involvement and types of consumer problem-solving processes.

An individual's level of involvement—the importance and intensity of his or her interest in a product in a particular situation—affects the type of problem-solving processes used. Enduring involvement is an ongoing interest in a product class because of personal relevance, whereas situational involvement is a temporary interest stemming from the particular circumstance or environment in which buyers find themselves. There are three kinds of consumer problem solving: routinized response behavior, limited problem solving, and extended problem solving. Consumers rely on routinized response behavior when buying frequently purchased low-cost items requiring little search and decision effort. Limited problem solving is used for products purchased occasionally or when buyers need to acquire information about an unfamiliar brand in a familiar product category. Consumers engage in extended problem solving when purchasing an unfamiliar, expensive, or infrequently bought product.

2 Recognize the stages of the consumer buying decision process.

The consumer buying decision process includes five stages: problem recognition, information search, evaluation of alternatives, purchase, and postpurchase evaluation. Not all decision processes culminate in a purchase, nor do all consumer decisions include all five stages. Problem recognition occurs when buyers become aware of a difference between a desired state and an actual condition. After recognizing the problem or need, buyers search for information about products to help resolve the problem or satisfy the need. A successful search yields a group of brands, called a *consideration set,* that a buyer views as possible alternatives. To evaluate the product in the consideration set, the buyer establishes certain criteria by which to compare, rate, and rank different products. Marketers can influence consumers' evaluation by framing alternatives. In the purchase stage, consumers select products or brands on the basis of results from the evaluation stage and other dimensions. Buyers also choose the seller from whom they will buy the product. After the purchase, buyers evaluate the product to determine if its actual performance meets expected levels.

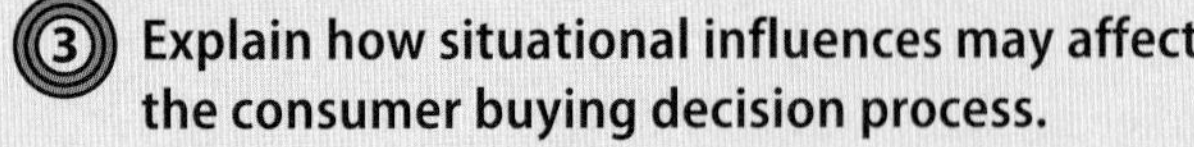

Explain how situational influences may affect the consumer buying decision process.

Situational influences are external circumstances or conditions existing when a consumer makes a purchase decision. Situational influences include surroundings, time, reason for purchase, and the buyer's mood and condition.

Understand the psychological influences that may affect the consumer buying decision process.

Psychological influences partly determine people's general behavior, thus influencing their behavior as consumers. The primary psychological influences on consumer behavior are perception, motives, learning, attitudes, personality and self-concept, and lifestyles. Perception is the process of selecting, organizing, and interpreting information inputs (sensations received through sight, taste, hearing, smell, and touch) to produce meaning. The three steps in the perceptual process are selection, organization, and interpretation. An individual has numerous perceptions of packages, products, brands, and organizations, all of which affect the buying decision process. A motive is an internal energizing force that orients a person's activities toward satisfying needs or achieving goals. Learning refers to changes in a person's thought processes and behavior caused by information and experience. Marketers try to shape what consumers learn to influence what they buy. An attitude is an individual's enduring evaluation, feelings, and behavioral tendencies toward an object or idea and consists of three major components: cognitive, affective, and behavioral. Personality is the set of traits and behaviors that make a person unique. Self-concept, closely linked to personality, is a person's view or perception of himself or herself. Research indicates that a buyer purchases products that reflect and enhance self-concept. Lifestyle is an individual's pattern of living expressed through activities, interests, and opinions.

Please visit the student website at www.cengage.com/international for quizzes and games that will help you prepare for exams and help achieve the grade you want.

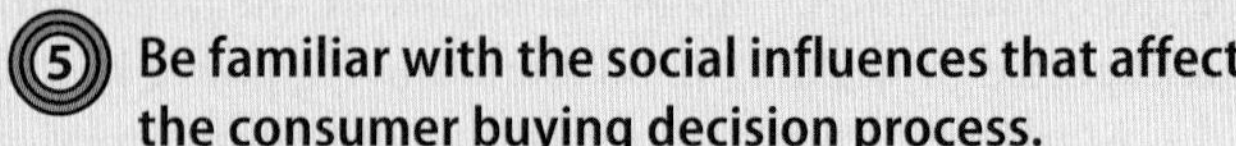

Be familiar with the social influences that affect the consumer buying decision process.

Social influences are forces that other people exert on buying behavior. They include roles, family, reference groups and opinion leaders, social class, and culture and subcultures. Everyone occupies positions within groups, organizations, and institutions, and each position has a role—a set of actions and activities that a person in a particular position is supposed to perform based on expectations of both the individual and surrounding persons. In a family, children learn from parents (and other household adults) and older siblings how to make decisions, such as purchase decisions. Consumer socialization is the process through which a person acquires the knowledge and skills to function as a consumer. The consumer socialization process is partially accomplished through family influences. A reference group is any group that positively or negatively affects a person's values, attitudes, or behavior. The three major types of reference groups are membership, aspirational, and disassociative. In most reference groups, one or more members stand out as opinion leaders by furnishing requested information to reference group participants. Consumers sometimes use Internet networks—especially blogs, wikis, and social networks—for information to aid them in buying decisions. A social class is an open group of individuals with similar social rank. Social class influences people's spending, saving, and credit practices. Culture is the accumulation of values, knowledge, beliefs, customs, objects, and concepts that a society uses to cope with its environment and passes on to future generations. A culture is made up of subcultures. A subculture is a group of individuals whose characteristics, values, and behavior patterns are similar to and differ from those of the surrounding culture. U.S. marketers focus on three major ethnic subcultures: African American, Hispanic, and Asian American.

KEY CONCEPTS

buying behavior
consumer buying behavior
level of involvement
routinized response behavior
limited problem solving
extended problem solving
impulse buying
consumer buying decision process
internal search
external search
consideration set
evaluative criteria
cognitive dissonance
situational influences
psychological influences
perception
information inputs
selective exposure
selective distortion
selective retention
motive
Maslow's hierarchy of needs
patronage motives
learning
attitude
attitude scale
personality
self-concept
lifestyle
social influences
role
consumer socialization
reference group
opinion leader
blog
wikis
social networks
social class
culture
subcultures

ISSUES FOR DISCUSSION AND REVIEW

1. How does a consumer's level of involvement affect his or her choice of problem-solving process?
2. Name the types of consumer problem-solving processes. List some products you have bought using each type. Have you ever bought a product on impulse? If so, describe the circumstances.
3. What are the major stages in the consumer buying decision process? Are all these stages used in all consumer purchase decisions? Why or why not?
4. What are the categories of situational factors that influence consumer buying behavior? Explain how each of these factors influences buyers' decisions.
5. What is selective exposure? Why do people engage in it?
6. How do marketers attempt to shape consumers' learning?
7. Why are marketers concerned about consumer attitudes?
8. In what ways do lifestyles affect the consumer buying decision process?
9. How do roles affect a person's buying behavior? Provide examples.
10. What are family influences, and how do they affect buying behavior?
11. What are reference groups? How do they influence buying behavior? Name some of your own reference groups.
12. How does an opinion leader influence the buying decision process of reference group members?
13. In what ways might consumer behavior be affected by digital networks?
14. In what ways does social class affect a person's purchase decisions?
15. What is culture? How does it affect a person's buying behavior?
16. Describe the subcultures to which you belong. Identify buying behavior that is unique to one of your subcultures.

MARKETING APPLICATIONS

1. Describe three buying experiences you have had—one for each type of problem solving—and identify which problem-solving process you used. Discuss why that particular process was appropriate.
2. Interview a classmate about the last purchase he or she made. Report the stages of the consumer buying process used and those skipped, if any.
3. Briefly describe how a beer company might alter the cognitive and affective components of consumer attitudes toward beer products and toward the company.
4. Identify two of your roles and give an example of how they have influenced your buying decisions.
5. Select five brands of toothpaste and explain how the appeals used in advertising these brands relate to Maslow's hierarchy of needs.

ONLINE EXERCISE

6. Some mass-market e-commerce sites, such as Amazon.com, have extended the concept of customization to their customer base. Amazon has created an affinity group by drawing on certain users' likes and dislikes to make product recommendations to other users. Check out this pioneering online retailer at http://www.amazon.com.
   a. What might motivate some consumers to read a "top selling" list?
   b. Is the consumer's level of involvement with online book purchase likely to be high or low?
   c. Discuss the consumer buying decision process as it relates to a decision to purchase from Amazon .com.

DEVELOPING YOUR MARKETING PLAN

Understanding the process an individual consumer goes through when purchasing a product is essential for developing marketing strategy. Knowledge about the potential customers' buying behavior will become the basis for many of the decisions in the specific marketing plan. Using the information from this chapter, you should be able to determine the following:

1. What type of problem solving are your customers likely to use when purchasing your product (see Table 6.1)?
2. Determine the evaluative criteria that your target market(s) would use when choosing between alternative brands.
3. Using Table 6.2, what types of family decision making, if any, would your target market(s) use?
4. Identify the reference groups or subcultures that may influence your target market's product selection.

The information obtained from these questions should assist you in developing various aspects of your marketing plan found in the *Interactive Marketing Plan* exercise.

VIDEO CASE 6

Travelocity Goes the Extra Mile for Travelers

When Travelocity began in 1996, it was one of the first Internet travel websites, offering airline and hotel reservations, cruises, vacation packages, and car rentals. Today, Travelocity offers consumers a choice of more than 70,000 hotels, 50 car rental companies, 6,000 travel packages, and flights on dozens of airlines worldwide.

Now that Travelocity faces intense competition from Expedia, Orbitz, and other travel websites, its marketers are making the company stand out by standing behind travelers every step of the way. The result is the unique four-point Travelocity Guarantee.

First, Travelocity guarantees its low price. If, within 24 hours, consumers find a lower price for travel they have booked through Travelocity, the company will refund the difference and add a credit toward future travel. Second, Travelocity allows customers to change passenger names, flight dates, and flight times without a fee if they make the change within 24 hours of booking their travel. Third, Travelocity will alert customers in advance to any issues that might negatively affect their travel arrangements and try to fix the problem by switching hotels or making other changes.

Fourth, if something goes wrong during a trip, Travelocity will work to put things right. For example, if a customer books a hotel with a swimming pool but finds that the swimming pool is closed on arrival, Travelocity will, at its own expense, move the customer to a comparable or better-quality hotel. Travelocity maintains a round-the-clock hotline to ensure that customers get what they want. The Travelocity Guarantee allays the concerns of customers who may be worried about booking online.

The company has promoted the guarantee with a "Roaming Gnome Enforcer of the Travelocity Guarantee" advertising campaign. The distinctive Roaming Gnome humanized the brand, embodied the joy of travel, and symbolized seeing the world with new eyes. The advertising campaign created a tremendous buzz about Travelocity and boosted revenues by 37 percent. Based on this customer reaction, Travelocity opened an online store to sell mugs, magnets, tote bags, and other items featuring the Roaming Gnome, who even has his own page on MySpace.com.

Over time, Travelocity has acquired a number of travel sites to broaden its offerings. When it purchased Site59, for example, Travelocity solidified its position as a major player in the last-minute travel business. Now customers who feel the urge to travel can get special deals by booking no more than 14 days before they want to leave. The savings are even bigger when customers book a vacation package just a few days in advance.

Travelocity has seven testers clicking all over its website to determine what customers might find confusing and how to make the site faster and more convenient. One lesson Travelocity learned was that customers don't always remember their passwords. To counteract this problem, Travelocity changed the system so that customers could reenter an address or e-mail address and use those details to access their personal profile rather than relying on a password. Thanks to this change, revenues quickly rose by 10 percent. Watch for more changes ahead as Travelocity finds new ways to satisfy its customers and new places for its Gnome to visit.

QUESTIONS FOR DISCUSSION

1. How does the Travelocity Guarantee give Travelocity a competitive advantage in various stages of the consumer buying decision process?
2. What is Travelocity doing to influence consumer perceptions of and attitudes toward its product offerings?
3. What are the major situational influences that affect Travelocity customers' buying decisions? Explain.

William Weir, "Tripping on the Web," *Hartford Courant,* March 1, 2009, http://www.courant.com/travel/hc-travelede0301 .artmar01,0,3887383.story; Wendy Pedrero, "Changing Travel One Step at a Time: Michelle Peluso: CEO, Travelocity," *Latino Leaders,* February–March 2008, pp. 14+; www.breakingtravelnews.com/article.php?story=20031222221110443&mode=print; Josh Roberts, "Travelocity, Expedia Aim to Prove Their Differences," *USA Today,* May 11, 2005, www.usatoday.com/travel/deals/inside/2005-05-11-column_x.htm; Travelocity, www.travelocity.com.

Business Markets and Buying Behavior

CHAPTER 7

© AFP PHOTO DDP/NIGEL TREBLIN GERMANY OUT/NEWSCOM

BUSINESS MARKETERS AND CUSTOMERS RELY ON VIRTUAL MARKETING

Many business customers try to find virtual product demonstrations or visit virtual trade shows as they search for goods and services to solve problems or satisfy business needs. Small wonder that virtual marketing is a key activity for many companies seeking to reach business buyers across the country or around the world.

IBM is using virtual marketing to sell sophisticated information technology systems. "As we looked at our market segmentation, we knew that 30 to 60 percent of the purchase decision is based on buzz," explains the company's vice president for Service Oriented Architecture and WebSphere Marketing. To create buzz, she used virtual marketing to help "reach an audience we hadn't reached before and help us reach it in a very effective way."

First, IBM posted a product demonstration on Yahoo! Video, which proved so popular that the team planned a 30-minute movie about Service Oriented Architecture, promoted by trailers uploaded to YouTube and Yahoo! Video. Next, the company invited prospects to screenings around the world and then posted the movie online for buyers to watch at their convenience. The result: tens of thousands of new sales leads for IBM.

All kinds of businesses are turning to virtual marketing. For example, one way Visa markets credit-card services to small businesses is by sponsoring online networking tools and pages on Facebook. In less than three months, Visa's Facebook community attracted 20,000 small

OBJECTIVES:

1. **Be able to distinguish among the various types of business markets.**
2. **Identify the major characteristics of business customers and transactions.**
3. **Understand several attributes of the demand for business products.**
4. **Become familiar with the major components of a buying center.**
5. **Understand the stages of the business buying decision process and the factors that affect this process.**
6. **Describe industrial classification systems and explain how they can be used to identify and analyze business markets.**

business members and is aiming to bring its services to thousands as the community expands. As another example, businesses that buy marble and other stone materials can visit "The Virtual Stone Show" and examine suppliers' wares both day and night. Thanks to virtual marketing, the search for suppliers and partners can click along quickly.[1]

Serving business markets effectively requires business marketers like IBM to understand business customers. Business marketers go to considerable lengths to understand and reach their customers so that they can provide better services and develop and maintain long-term customer relationships. Like consumer marketers, business marketers are concerned about satisfying their customers.

In this chapter we look at business markets and business buying decision processes. We first discuss various kinds of business markets and the types of buyers making up these markets. Next, we explore several dimensions of business buying, such as characteristics of transactions, attributes and concerns of buyers, methods of buying, and distinctive features of demand for products sold to business purchasers. We then examine how business buying decisions are made and who makes the purchases. Finally, we consider how business markets are analyzed.

Business Markets

As defined in Chapter 5, a business market (also called a *business-to-business*, or *B2B, market*) consists of individuals, organizations, or groups that purchase a specific kind of product for resale, direct use in producing other products, or use in general daily operations. Although B2B marketing employs the same concepts as marketing to ultimate consumers, such as defining target markets, understanding buying behavior, and developing effective marketing mixes, there are structural and behavioral differences in business markets. A company marketing to business customers must recognize how its product will influence other associated firms such as wholesalers, retailers, and even other manufacturers. Business products can be technically complex, and the market often consists of sophisticated buyers. Because the business market consists of relatively smaller customer populations, a segment of the market could be as small as a few customers. The market for railway equipment in the United States, for example, is limited to a few major carriers. On the other hand, a business product can be a commodity such as corn or a bolt or screw, but the quantity purchased and the buying methods differ significantly from the consumer market, as we shall see. Business marketing is often based on long-term mutually profitable relationships across members of the marketing channel. Networks of suppliers and customers recognize the importance of building strong alliances based on cooperation, trust, and collaboration. For example, the senior buyer for strategic procurement and planning at Alliant Energy Corp. in Cedar Rapids, Iowa, has created a three-way alliance among his company, the distributors and their suppliers, as well as the manufacturer in the United States. Accordingly, the three meet to discuss ways to better manage costs up and down the supply chain.[2] Manufacturers may even co-develop new products with business customers, sharing marketing research, production, scheduling, inventory management, and information systems. Although business marketing can be based on collaborative long-term buyer-seller relationships, there are also transactions based on timely exchanges of basic products at highly competitive market prices. For most business marketers, the goal is understanding customer needs and providing a value-added exchange that shifts from attracting customers to keeping customers and developing favorable customer relationships.

The four categories of business markets are producer, reseller, government, and institutional. In the remainder of this section we discuss each of these types of markets.

PRODUCER MARKETS

Individuals and business organizations that purchase products for the purpose of making a profit by using them to produce other products or using them in their operations are classified as **producer markets**. Producer markets include buyers of raw materials, as well as purchasers of semifinished and finished items used to produce other products. For example, manufacturers buy raw materials and component parts for direct use in product production. Supermarkets are part of producer markets for numerous support products such as paper and plastic bags, shelves, counters, and scanners. Farmers are part of producer markets for farm machinery, fertilizer, seed, and livestock. Producer markets include a broad array of industries, ranging from agriculture, forestry, fisheries, and mining to construction, transportation, communications, and utilities. As Table 7.1 indicates, the number of business establishments in national producer markets is enormous.

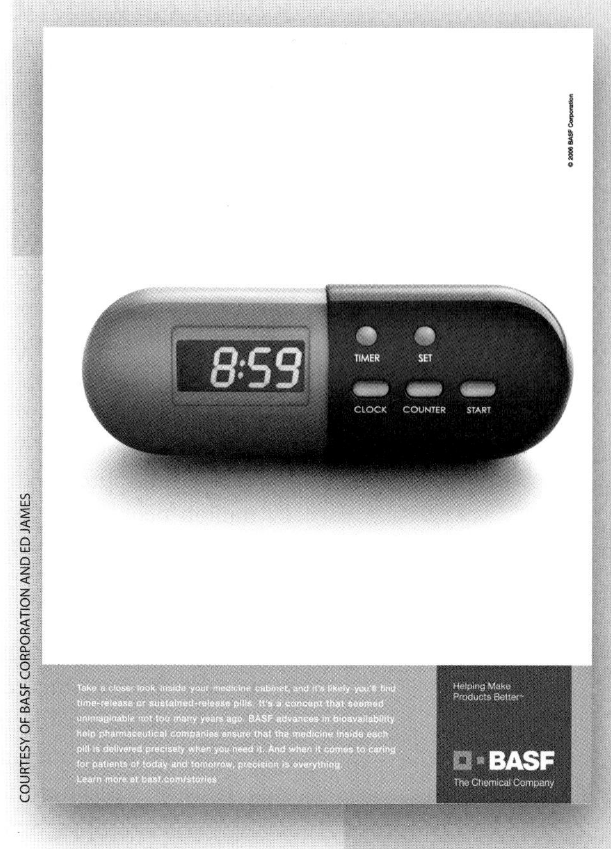

Focused on Producer Market
Some business marketers focus on producer markets. BASF aims the products discussed in this advertisement at manufacturers of pharmaceutical products.

Manufacturers are geographically concentrated. More than half are located in just seven states: California, New York, Texas, Ohio, Illinois, Pennsylvania, and Michigan (arranged in descending order). This concentration sometimes enables businesses that sell to producer markets to serve them more efficiently. Within certain states, production in a specific industry may account for a sizable proportion of that industry's total production.

TABLE 7.1 Number of Establishments in Industry Groups

Industry	Number of Establishments
Agriculture, forestry, fishing, and hunting	24,100
Mining	24,700
Construction	787,700
Manufacturing	333,500
Transportation, warehousing, and utilities	228,500
Finance, insurance, and real estate	847,500
Other services	5,253,700

Source: U.S. Bureau of the Census, *Statistical Abstract of the United States*, 2009 (Washington, DC: U.S. Government Printing Office, 2008), Table 737.

producer markets Individuals and business organizations that purchase products to make profits by using them to produce other products or using them in their operations

RESELLER MARKETS

Reseller markets consist of intermediaries, such as wholesalers and retailers, who buy finished goods and resell them for profit. Aside from making minor alterations, resellers do not change the physical characteristics of the products they handle. Except for items that producers sell directly to consumers, all products sold to consumer markets are first sold to reseller markets, consisting of wholesalers and retailers. Wholesalers purchase products for resale to retailers, to other wholesalers, and to producers, governments, and institutions. Arrow Electronics, for example, buys computer chips and other electronics components and resells them to producers of subsystems for cell phones, computers, and automobiles. Of the 429,823 wholesalers in the United States, a large percentage are located in New York, California, Illinois, Texas, Ohio, Pennsylvania, New Jersey, and Florida.[3] Although some products are sold directly to end users, some manufacturers sell their products to wholesalers, who, in turn, sell the products to other firms in the distribution system. Retailers purchase products and resell them to final consumers. There are approximately 1.1 million retailers in the United States, employing more than 15 million people and generating more than $3.1 trillion in annual sales.[4] Some retailers—Home Depot, PetSmart, and Staples, for example—carry a large number of items. Supermarkets may handle as many as 50,000 different products. In small, individually owned retail stores, owners or managers make purchasing decisions.

When making purchase decisions, resellers consider several factors. They evaluate the level of demand for a product to determine in what quantity and at what prices the product can be resold. Retailers assess the amount of space required to handle a product relative to its potential profit. In fact, they sometimes evaluate products on the basis of sales per square foot of selling area. Because customers often depend on resellers to have products available when needed, resellers typically appraise a supplier's ability to provide adequate quantities when and where wanted. Resellers also take into account the ease of placing orders and the availability of technical assistance and training programs from the producer. These types of concerns distinguish reseller markets from other markets.

GOVERNMENT MARKETS

Federal, state, county, and local governments make up **government markets**. These markets spend billions of dollars annually for a variety of goods and services—ranging from office supplies and health care services to vehicles, heavy equipment, and weapons—to support their internal operations and provide citizens with products such as highways, education, water, energy, and national defense. The federal government spends more than $660 billion annually on national defense alone. Government expenditures annually account for about 19 percent of the U.S. gross domestic product.[5] In addition to the federal government, there are 50 state governments, 3,033 county governments, and 89,476 local governments.[6] The amount spent by federal, state, and local government units over the last 30 years has increased rapidly because the total number of government units and the services they provide have both increased. Costs of providing these services also have risen.

The types and quantities of products bought by government markets reflect societal demands on various government agencies. As citizens' needs for government services change, so does the demand for products by government markets. For example, NIC is the nation's leading provider of official government portals, online services, and secure payment processing solutions. The company's innovative e-Government services help reduce costs and increase efficiencies for government agencies, citizens, and businesses across the country. One of its clients is the Utah state government. Utah state's official website—http://www.utah.gov—provides citizens and businesses access to nearly 800 online services. Last year, the site received over 12 million visits, securely processed 9.6 million online transactions, and launched 37 new

reseller markets
Intermediaries who buy finished goods and resell them for profit

government markets
Federal, state, county, and local governments that buy goods and services to support their internal operations and provide products to their constituencies

services including the new Public Meeting Notice site (http://www.utah.gov/pmn/index.html), which allows visitors to easily search and locate public meetings scheduled by government organizations throughout Utah.[7]

institutional markets Organizations with charitable, educational, community, or other nonbusiness goals

Although it is common to hear of large corporations being awarded government contracts, in fact, businesses of all sizes market to government agencies. In recent years, the Internet has helped small businesses earn more government contracts than ever before by providing venues for small businesses to learn about and bid on government contracting opportunities. For example, ZANA Network is an online marketplace and business development resource for small and medium enterprises (SMEs) worldwide. ZANA Network provides selling, buying, and partnering opportunities, along with trade resources, business guidance, and essential services. It also enables entrepreneurs, inventors, professionals, and other SME business people to come together in a community for mutual benefit. Along with the new government contracts feature, ZANA Network provides a one-stop menu of online services that enables businesses to buy and sell products.[8]

Because government agencies spend public funds to buy the products needed to provide services, they are accountable to the public. This accountability explains their relatively complex set of buying procedures. Some firms do not even try to sell to government buyers because they want to avoid the tangle of red tape. However, many marketers have learned to deal efficiently with government procedures and do not find them to be a stumbling block. For certain products, such as defense-related items, the government may be the only customer. The U.S. Government Printing Office publishes and distributes several documents explaining buying procedures and describing the types of products various federal agencies purchase.

INSTITUTIONAL MARKETS

Organizations with charitable, educational, community, or other nonbusiness goals constitute **institutional markets**. Members of institutional markets include churches, some hospitals, fraternities and sororities, charitable organizations, and private colleges. Institutions purchase millions of dollars' worth of products annually to provide goods, services, and ideas to congregations, students, patients, and others. Because institutions often have different goals and fewer resources than other types of organizations, marketers may use special marketing efforts to serve them. For example, Hussey Seating in Maine sells bleacher stadium seating to schools, colleges, churches, and other institutions, as well as to sports arenas, around the world. The family-owned business shows its support for institutional customers through assistance with school funding and reduced-cost construction of local economic development projects.[9]

© AP IMAGES/PRNEWSFOTO/AMERICAN COLLEGE OF THE BUILDING ARTS

Institutional Markets Some colleges are a part of institutional markets.

Dimensions of Marketing to Business Customers

Having considered different types of business customers, we now look at several dimensions of marketing to them, including transaction characteristics, attributes of business customers, primary concerns of business customers, buying methods, major types of purchases, and the characteristics of demand for business products. (See Figure 7.1.)

FIGURE 7.1 Dimensions of Marketing to Business Customers

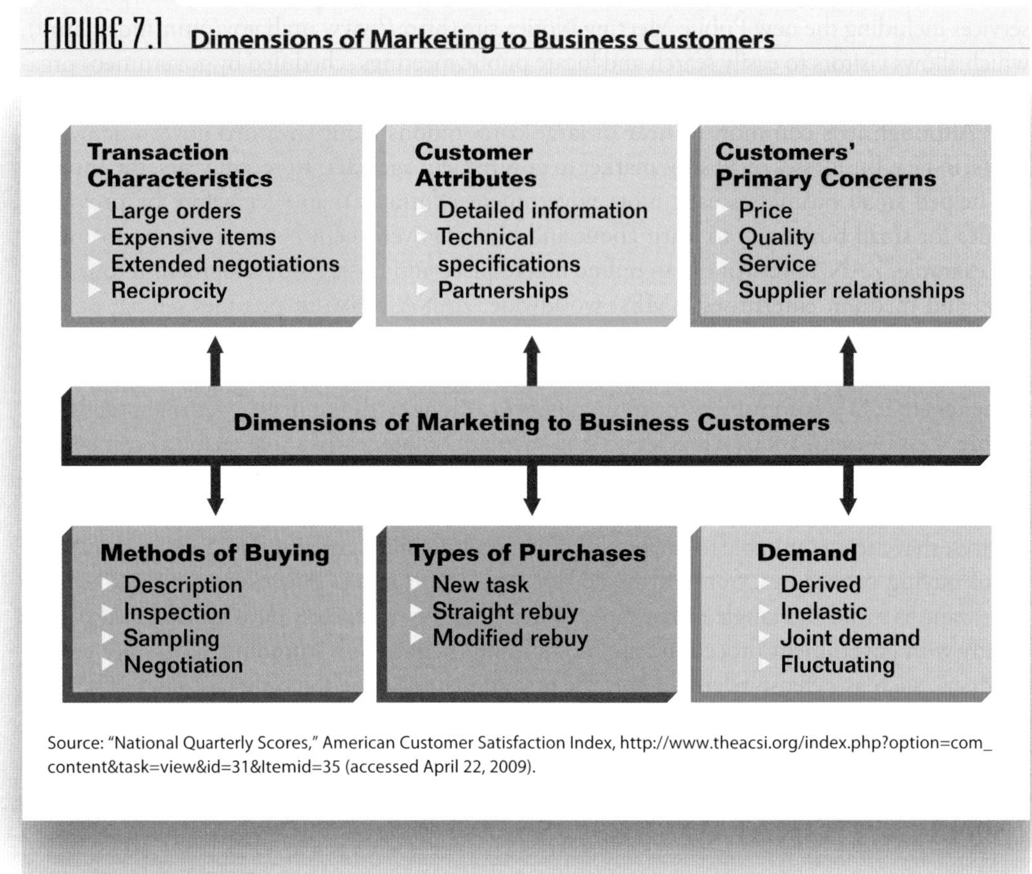

Source: "National Quarterly Scores," American Customer Satisfaction Index, http://www.theacsi.org/index.php?option=com_content&task=view&id=31&Itemid=35 (accessed April 22, 2009).

CHARACTERISTICS OF TRANSACTIONS WITH BUSINESS CUSTOMERS

Transactions between businesses differ from consumer sales in several ways. Orders by business customers tend to be much larger than individual consumer sales. Consider that Ireland's Ryanair, the largest discount airline in Europe, placed an order for 32 Boeing 737-800 jet aircraft at an estimated cost of $2.25 billion to add to its fleet of 281 Boeing 737 aircraft.[10] Suppliers often must sell products in large quantities to make profits; consequently, they prefer not to sell to customers who place small orders. Some business purchases involve expensive items, such as computer systems. Other products, such as raw materials and component items, are used continuously in production, and the supply may need frequent replenishing. The contract regarding terms of sale of these items is likely to be a long-term agreement.

Discussions and negotiations associated with business purchases can require considerable marketing effort. Purchasing decisions often are made by committee. Orders frequently are large and expensive. Products may be custom-built. Several people or departments in the purchasing organization may be involved.

One practice unique to business markets is **reciprocity**, an arrangement in which two organizations agree to buy from each other. Reciprocal agreements that threaten competition are illegal. The Federal Trade Commission and the Justice Department take actions to stop anticompetitive reciprocal practices. Nonetheless, a certain amount of reciprocal activity occurs among small businesses and, to a lesser extent, among larger companies. Because reciprocity influences purchasing agents to deal only with certain suppliers, it can lower morale among agents and lead to less than optimal purchases.

reciprocity
An arrangement unique to business marketing in which two organizations agree to buy from each other

ATTRIBUTES OF BUSINESS CUSTOMERS

Business customers differ from consumers in their purchasing behavior because they are better informed about the products they purchase. They typically demand detailed information about products' functional features and technical specifications to ensure that the products meet the organization's needs. Personal goals, however, also may influence business buying behavior. Most purchasing agents seek the psychological satisfaction that comes with organizational advancement and financial rewards. Agents who consistently exhibit rational business buying behavior are likely to attain these personal goals because they help their firms achieve organizational objectives. Today, many suppliers and their customers build and maintain mutually beneficial relationships, sometimes called *partnerships.* Researchers have found that even in a partnership between a small vendor and a large corporate buyer, a strong partnership exists because high levels of interpersonal trust can lead to higher levels of commitment to the partnership by both organizations.[11]

SNAPSHOT

Source: Data from American Express Fall Small Business Monitor survey of 627 small-business owners/managers of companies with fewer than 100 employees. Margin of error: ±4 percentage points.

PRIMARY CONCERNS OF BUSINESS CUSTOMERS

When making purchasing decisions, business customers take into account a variety of factors. Among their chief considerations are price, product quality, service, and supplier relationships. Obviously, price matters greatly to business customers because it influences operating costs and costs of goods sold, which, in turn, affect selling price, profit margin, and ultimately, the ability to compete. When purchasing major equipment, a business customer views price as the amount of investment necessary to obtain a certain level of return or savings. A business customer is likely to compare the price of a product with the benefits the product will provide to the organization, often over a period of years.

Most business customers try to achieve and maintain a specific level of quality in the products they buy. To achieve this goal, most firms establish standards (usually stated as a percentage of defects allowed) for these products and buy them on the basis of a set of expressed characteristics, commonly called *specifications.* A customer evaluates the quality of the products being considered to determine whether they meet specifications. If a product fails to meet specifications or malfunctions for the ultimate consumer, the customer may drop that product's supplier and switch to a different supplier. On the other hand, business customers are ordinarily cautious about buying products that exceed specifications because such products often cost more, thus increasing the organization's overall costs. Specifications are designed to meet a customer's wants, and anything that does not contribute to meeting those wants may be considered wasteful.

Concerns of Business Customers
In this advertisement, CDW promises excellent and timely service, one of the primary concerns of business customers.

Sustainable Marketing

Business Travelers Want Greener Airlines

Fly faster, fly cheaper, fly greener? Business travelers are demanding customers—and now they've got something else to be demanding about. A growing number of corporate travel coordinators are checking into airlines' environmental activities. Which airlines have a recycling program? What are airlines doing to reduce pollution and conserve natural resources?

© RON T. ENNIS/MCT/LANDOV

When American Airlines began fielding inquiries about its environmental policies, it took the questions a step further and asked its suppliers about *their* environmental policies. As a result, American's business travelers are actually putting green pressure on all the suppliers as well as the airline itself. And flying greener will make the carrier's bottom line greener by cutting waste and shaving costs. Now, as a member of the U.S. Environmental Protection Agency's Climate Leaders program, American plans to cut its greenhouse gas emissions by 30 percent before 2015. It is already replacing older jets with more fuel-efficient models and revamping its offices to save energy.

Other airlines are also taking action to fly greener. British Airways, for example, has set a goal of recycling or reusing 40 percent of the solid waste generated per passenger (such as paper, bottles, and cans) by the end of this decade. Knowing that passengers are concerned about air quality and global warming, the airline put a carbon dioxide calculator on its website. Now passengers can determine the carbon dioxide emissions for their flights and, if they choose, make a donation to offset those emissions by investing in cleaner energy initiatives.[a]

Business buyers value service. Services offered by suppliers directly and indirectly influence customers' costs, sales, and profits. In some instances the mix of customer services is the major means by which marketers gain a competitive advantage. Procter & Gamble, for example, provided Wendy's International with customized videos and laminated guides to show Wendy's employees how to use its industrial cleaning supplies to clean every part of each restaurant.[12] Typical services desired by customers are market information, inventory maintenance, on-time delivery, repair services, and online communication capabilities. Business buyers are likely to need technical product information, data regarding demand, information about general economic conditions, or supply and delivery information. Maintaining adequate inventory is critical because it helps to make products accessible when a customer needs them and reduces customer inventory requirements and costs. Because business customers are usually responsible for ensuring that products are on hand and ready for use when needed, on-time delivery is crucial. Furthermore, reliable, on-time delivery saves business customers money because it enables them to carry less inventory. Purchasers of machinery are especially concerned about obtaining repair services and replacement parts quickly because inoperable equipment is costly. Caterpillar, Inc., manufacturer of earth-moving, construction, and materials-handling machinery, has built an international reputation, as well as a competitive advantage, by providing prompt service and replacement parts for its products around the world. Business customers are likely to resist a supplier's effort to implement a new technology if there are questions about the technology's compatibility, reliability, or other factors that could cause the supplier to fail to deliver on promises.[13]

Communication channels that allow customers to ask questions, voice complaints, submit orders, and trace shipments are indispensable components of service. Marketers should strive for uniformity of service, simplicity, truthfulness, and accuracy. Marketers should develop customer service objectives and monitor customer service programs. Firms can monitor service by formally surveying customers or informally calling on customers and asking questions about the quality of the services they receive. Expending the time and effort to ensure that customers are happy can greatly benefit marketers by increasing customer retention.

Finally, business customers are concerned about the costs of developing and maintaining relationships with their suppliers. By developing relationships and building trust with a particular supplier, buyers can reduce their search effort and uncertainty about monetary price.[14]

Business customers have to keep in mind the overall fit of a purchase, including its potential to reduce inventory and carrying costs, as well as to increase inventory turnover and ability to move the right products to the right place at the right time. The entire business can be affected by a single supplier failing to be a good partner.

METHODS OF BUSINESS BUYING

Although no two business buyers do their jobs the same way, most use one or more of the following purchase methods: description, inspection, sampling, and negotiation. When products are standardized according to certain characteristics (such as size, shape, weight, and color) and graded using such standards, a business buyer may be able to purchase simply by describing or specifying quantity, grade, and other attributes. Agricultural products often fall into this category. Sometimes buyers specify a particular brand or its equivalent when describing the desired product. Purchases on the basis of description are especially common between a buyer and seller with an ongoing relationship built on trust.

Certain products, such as industrial equipment, used vehicles, and buildings, have unique characteristics and may vary with regard to condition. For example, a particular used truck may have a bad transmission. Consequently, business buyers of such products must base purchase decisions on inspection.

Sampling entails taking a specimen of the product from the lot and evaluating it on the assumption that its characteristics represent the entire lot. This method is appropriate when the product is homogeneous—for instance, grain—and examining the entire lot is not physically or economically feasible.

Method of Business Buying
Purchases of aircraft are likely to occur through negotiated contracts.

COURTESY OF INTEL CORPORATION

Derived Demand
The demand for Intel Quad-Core processors derives from the sales to end users of computing equipment containing these processors. In this message, Intel advertises directly to computing equipment users, not to manufacturers of the equipment.

Some purchases by businesses are based on negotiated contracts. In certain instances, buyers describe exactly what they need and ask sellers to submit bids. They then negotiate with the suppliers who submit the most attractive bids. This approach may be used when acquiring commercial vehicles, for example. In other cases, the buyer may be unable to identify specifically what is to be purchased but can provide only a general description, such as might be the case for a piece of custom-made equipment. A buyer and seller might negotiate a contract that specifies a base price and provides for the payment of additional costs and fees. These contracts are used most commonly for one-time projects such as buildings, custom-made equipment, and special projects.

TYPES OF BUSINESS PURCHASES

Most business purchases are one of three types: new-task, straight-rebuy, or modified-rebuy purchase. Each type is subject to different influences and thus requires business marketers to modify their selling approach appropriately.[15] In a **new-task purchase**, an organization makes an initial purchase of an item to be used to perform a new job or solve a new problem. A new-task purchase may require development of product specifications, vendor specifications, and procedures for future purchases of that product. To make the initial purchase, the business buyer usually needs much information. For example, if Heineken were introducing a salty, spicy beer-flavored snack and were purchasing automated packaging equipment, that would be a new-task purchase.

A **straight-rebuy purchase** occurs when buyers purchase the same products routinely under approximately the same terms of sale. Buyers require little information for these routine purchase decisions and tend to use familiar suppliers that have provided satisfactory service and products in the past. These suppliers try to set up automatic reordering systems to make reordering easy and convenient for business buyers.

In a **modified-rebuy purchase**, a new-task purchase is changed the second or third time it is ordered, or requirements associated with a straight-rebuy purchase are modified. A business buyer might seek faster delivery, lower prices, or a different quality level of product specifications. A modified-rebuy situation may cause regular suppliers to become more competitive to keep the account because other suppliers could obtain the business. When a firm changes the terms of a service contract, such as for telecommunication services, it has made a modified purchase.

new-task purchase
An initial purchase by an organization of an item to be used to perform a new job or solve a new problem

straight-rebuy purchase
A routine purchase of the same products under approximately the same terms of sale by a business buyer

modified-rebuy purchase
A new-task purchase that is changed on subsequent orders or when the requirements of a straight-rebuy purchase are modified

DEMAND FOR BUSINESS PRODUCTS

Unlike consumer demand, demand for business products (also called *industrial demand*) can be characterized as (1) derived, (2) inelastic, (3) joint, or (4) fluctuating.

Derived Demand

Because business customers, especially producers, buy products for direct or indirect use in the production of goods and services to satisfy consumers' needs, the demand for business products derives from the demand for consumer products. It is therefore called **derived demand**. In the long run, no demand for business products is totally unrelated to the demand for consumer products. The derived nature of demand is usually multilevel. Business marketers at different levels are affected by a change in consumer demand for a particular product. For instance, consumers have become concerned with health and good nutrition and as a result are purchasing more products with less fat, cholesterol, and sodium. When consumers reduced their purchases of high-fat foods, a change occurred in the demand for products marketed by food processors, equipment manufacturers, and suppliers of raw materials associated with these products. When consumer demand for a product changes, it sets in motion a wave that affects demand for all firms involved in the production of that product.

Entrepreneurial Marketing

Steelcase Wants to Keep Business Customers Healthy

Steelcase received its first patent in 1914 for a steel wastebasket, marketed as a solution to the common business problem of straw wastebaskets catching on fire. Today they are finding solutions to help businesses create office environments that enhance efficiency. Knowing that employee health is a growing concern, Steelcase's marketing experts worked with a doctor at Mayo Clinic to develop a line of office furniture that helps office workers get (or stay) in shape. The Walkstation consists of an adjustable desk and computer workstation attached to a treadmill (matching chair is optional). Steelcase's CEO asks one key question over and over again of his marketing experts: "What's the user insight that led to this product?"[b]

Inelastic Demand

Inelastic demand means that a price increase or decrease will not significantly alter demand for a business product. Because some business products contain a number of parts, price increases affecting only one or two parts may yield only a slightly higher per-unit production cost. When a sizable price increase for a component represents a large proportion of the product's cost, demand may become more elastic because the price increase in the component causes the price at the consumer level to rise sharply. For example, if aircraft engine manufacturers substantially increase the price of engines, forcing Boeing to raise the prices of the aircraft it manufactures, the demand for airliners may become more elastic as airlines reconsider whether they can afford to buy new aircraft. An increase in the price of windshields, however, is unlikely to affect greatly either the price of or the demand for airliners.

Inelasticity applies only to industry demand for business products, not to the demand curve that an individual firm faces. Suppose that a spark plug producer increases the price of spark plugs sold to small-engine manufacturers, but its competitors continue to maintain lower prices. The spark plug company probably will experience reduced unit sales because most small-engine producers will switch to lower-priced brands. A specific firm is vulnerable to elastic demand, even though industry demand for a specific business product is inelastic. We will take another look at price elasticity in Chapter 11.

Joint Demand

Demand for certain business products, especially raw materials and components, is subject to joint demand. **Joint demand** occurs when two or more items are used in combination to produce a product. For example, a firm that manufactures axes needs the same number of ax handles as it does ax blades. These two products thus are demanded jointly. If a shortage of ax handles exists, the producer buys fewer ax blades. Understanding the effects of joint demand is particularly important for a marketer selling multiple, jointly demanded items. Such a marketer realizes that when a customer begins purchasing one of the jointly demanded items, a good opportunity exists to sell related products.

Fluctuating Demand

Because the demand for business products is derived from consumer demand, it may fluctuate enormously. In general, when particular consumer products are in high demand, their producers buy large quantities of raw materials and components to ensure meeting long-run production requirements. In addition, these producers may expand production capacity, which entails acquiring new equipment and machinery, more workers, and more raw materials and component parts. Conversely, a decline in demand for certain consumer goods significantly reduces demand for business products used to produce those goods. Sometimes price changes

derived demand
Demand for industrial products that stems from demand for consumer products

inelastic demand
Demand that is not significantly altered by a price increase or decrease

joint demand
Demand involving the use of two or more items in combination to produce a product

Marketing IN TRANSITION

Now in Aisle 1: Partnering for Profit

Large or small, the companies that supply discount retailers Costco and Walmart are learning new efficiencies by partnering with these retail giants. For example, Costco has insisted that some companies repackage their products so more can fit in every truck and on store shelves, a change that benefits suppliers as well as the retailer. When Costco's buyers ask for something, even the biggest companies pay close attention because the retailer is such a big customer.

© MIRA/ALAMY

Mauna Loa, a division of Hershey, sells 70 percent of its top-quality macadamia nuts to Costco. So when Costco suggested mixing small macadamia nuts into a new chocolate snack, Mauna Loa didn't hesitate. Small nuts ordinarily sell at a low price for little profit. Now Mauna Loa is able to profitably use more of the nut crop, price the new snack attractively, and increase Hershey's overall sales volume with Costco.

The world's largest retailer, Walmart, has a single-minded goal in working with suppliers: "If our customers want to buy it, we want to sell it," says an executive. Suppliers have to comply with specific rules, such as quality-control testing, but the rewards of getting merchandise into even a few Walmart stores make the process worthwhile. So many companies want to sell to Walmart, in fact, that the retailer now holds Business-to-Business Expo meetings around the country to meet with prospective suppliers. Even when Walmart doesn't buy, its feedback can help companies improve their products and prepare for a profitable future.[c]

lead to surprising temporary changes in demand. A price increase for a business product initially may cause business customers to buy more of the item because they expect the price to rise further. Similarly, demand for a business product may be significantly lower following a price cut because buyers are waiting for further price reductions. Fluctuations in demand can be substantial in industries in which prices change frequently.

Business Buying Decisions

Business (organizational) buying behavior refers to the purchase behavior of producers, government units, institutions, and resellers. Although several factors affecting consumer buying behavior (discussed in Chapter 6) also influence business buying behavior, several factors are unique to the latter. We first analyze the buying center to learn who participates in business purchase decisions. We then focus on the stages of the buying decision process and the factors affecting it.

THE BUYING CENTER

Relatively few business purchase decisions are made by just one person; often they are made through a buying center. A **buying center** is a group of people within an organization who make business purchase decisions. They include users, influencers, buyers, deciders, and gatekeepers.[16] One person may perform several roles.

Users are the organization members who actually use the product being acquired. They frequently initiate the purchase process and/or generate purchase specifications. After the purchase, they evaluate product performance relative to the specifications. Influencers are often technical personnel, such as engineers, who help develop the specifications and evaluate alternative products. Technical personnel are especially important influencers when products being considered involve new, advanced technology. Buyers select suppliers and negotiate terms of purchase. They also may become involved in developing specifications. Buyers are sometimes called *purchasing agents* or *purchasing managers*. Their choices of vendors and products, especially for new-task purchases, are heavily influenced by people occupying other roles in the buying center. Deciders actually choose the products. Although buyers may be deciders, it is not unusual for different people to occupy these roles. For routinely purchased items, buyers are commonly deciders. However, a buyer may not be authorized to make purchases exceeding a certain dollar limit, in which case higher-level management personnel are deciders. Gatekeepers, such as secretaries and technical personnel, control the flow of information to and among people occupying other roles in the buying center. Buyers who deal directly with vendors also may be gatekeepers because they can control information flows.

The number and structure of an organization's buying centers are affected by the organization's size and market position, the volume and types of products being purchased, and the firm's overall managerial philosophy regarding exactly who should be involved in purchase decisions. The size of a buying center is influenced by the stage of the buying decision process and the type of purchase (new task, straight rebuy, or modified rebuy). A marketer attempting to sell to a business customer should determine who is in the buying center, the types of decisions each individual makes, and which individuals are most influential in the decision process. Because in some instances many people make up the buying center, marketers cannot feasibly contact all participants. Instead, they must be certain to contact a few of the most influential participants.

business (organizational) buying behavior The purchase behavior of producers, government units, institutions, and resellers

buying center The people within an organization, including users, influencers, buyers, deciders, and gatekeepers, who make business purchase decisions

STAGES OF THE BUSINESS BUYING DECISION PROCESS

Like consumers, businesses follow a buying decision process. This process is summarized in the lower portion of Figure 7.2. In the first stage, one or more individuals recognize that a problem or need exists. Problem recognition may arise under a variety of circumstances—for instance, when machines malfunction or a firm modifies an existing product or introduces a new one. Individuals in the buying center, such as users, influencers, or buyers, may be involved in

FIGURE 7.2 Business (Organizational) Buying Decision Process and Factors that May Influence It

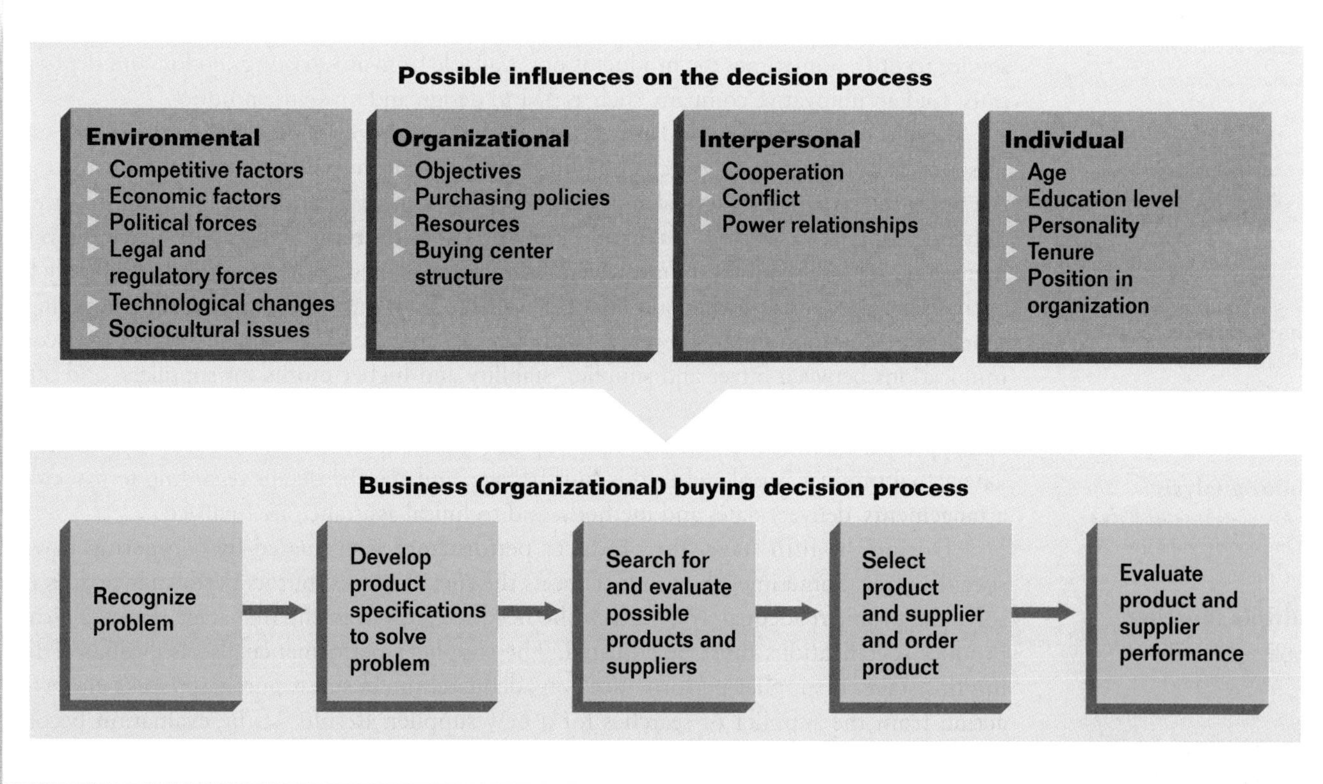

Problem Recognition
This ad aimed at health care providers focuses on problem recognition. Some health care providers may want to update equipment to improve diagnostic capabilities.

problem recognition, but it may be stimulated by external sources, such as sales representatives or advertisements.

The second stage of the process, development of product specifications, requires that buying center participants assess the problem or need and determine what is necessary to resolve or satisfy it. During this stage, users and influencers, such as engineers, often provide information and advice for developing product specifications. By assessing and describing needs, the organization should be able to establish product specifications.

Searching for and evaluating potential products and suppliers constitute the third stage in the decision process. Search activities may involve looking in company files and trade directories, contacting suppliers for information, soliciting proposals from known vendors, and examining websites, catalogs, and trade publications. To facilitate vendor searches, some organizations, such as Walmart, advertise their desire to build partnerships with specific types of vendors, such as those owned by women or by minorities. During this stage, some organizations engage in **value analysis**, an evaluation of each component of a potential purchase. Value analysis examines quality, design, materials, and possibly item reduction or deletion to acquire the product in the most cost-effective way. Products are evaluated to make sure that they meet or exceed product specifications developed in the second stage. Usually suppliers are judged according to multiple criteria. A number of firms employ **vendor analysis**, a formal, systematic evaluation of current and potential vendors focusing on characteristics such as price, product quality, delivery service, product availability, and overall reliability. Some vendors may be deemed unacceptable because they lack the resources to supply needed quantities. Others may be excluded because of poor delivery and service records. Sometimes the product is not available from any existing vendor, and the buyer must find an innovative company such as 3M to design and make the product.

Results of deliberations and assessments in the third stage are used during the fourth stage to select the product to be purchased and the supplier from which to buy it. In some cases the buyer selects and uses several suppliers, a process known as **multiple sourcing**. In others, only one supplier is selected, a situation known as **sole sourcing**. Firms with federal government contracts are required to have several sources for an item. Sole sourcing traditionally has been discouraged, except when a product is available from only one company. Sole sourcing is much more common today, however, partly because such an arrangement means better communications between buyer and supplier, stability and higher profits for suppliers, and often lower prices for buyers. However, many organizations still prefer multiple sourcing because this approach lessens the possibility of disruption caused by strikes, shortages, or bankruptcies. The actual product is ordered in this fourth stage, and specific details regarding terms, credit arrangements, delivery dates and methods, and technical assistance are finalized.

value analysis
An evaluation of each component of a potential purchase

vendor analysis
A formal, systematic evaluation of current and potential vendors

multiple sourcing
An organization's decision to use several suppliers

sole sourcing
An organization's decision to use only one supplier

During the fifth stage, the product's performance is evaluated by comparing it with specifications. Sometimes the product meets the specifications, but its performance does not solve the problem adequately or satisfy the need recognized in the first stage. In such a case, product specifications must be adjusted. The supplier's performance also is evaluated during this stage. If supplier performance is inadequate, the business purchaser seeks corrective action from the supplier or searches for a new supplier. Results of the evaluation become feedback for the other stages in future business purchase decisions.

This business buying decision process is used in its entirety primarily for new-task purchases. Several stages, but not necessarily all, are used for modified-rebuy and straight-rebuy situations.

INFLUENCES ON THE BUSINESS BUYING DECISION PROCESS

Figure 7.2 also lists four major categories of factors that influence business buying decisions: environmental, organizational, interpersonal, and individual.

Environmental factors include competitive and economic factors, political forces, legal and regulatory forces, technological changes, and sociocultural issues. These factors generate considerable uncertainty for an organization, which can make individuals in the buying center apprehensive about certain types of purchases. Changes in one or more environmental forces can create new purchasing opportunities and threats. For example, changes in competition and technology can make buying decisions difficult in the case of such products as software, computers, and telecommunications equipment. On the other hand, many business marketers believe that the Internet can reduce their customer service costs and allow firms to improve relationships with business customers.[17]

Organizational factors influencing the buying decision process include the company's objectives, purchasing policies, and resources, as well as the size and composition of its buying center. An organization may have certain buying policies to which buying center participants must conform. For instance, a firm's policies may mandate unusually long- or short-term contracts, perhaps longer or shorter than most sellers desire. An organization's financial resources may require special credit arrangements. Any of these conditions could affect purchase decisions.

Influences on the Business Buying Decision Process
Numerous business purchases are influenced by environmental forces. Energy savings result in lower costs which, in turn, allow organizations to be more competitive.

Interpersonal factors are the relationships among people in the buying center. Trust among all members of collaborative partnerships is crucial, particularly in purchases involving customized products.[18] Use of power and level of conflict among buying center participants influence business buying decisions. Certain individuals in the buying center may be better communicators than others and may be more persuasive. Often these interpersonal dynamics are hidden, making them difficult for marketers to assess.

Individual factors are personal characteristics of participants in the buying center, such as age, education, personality, and tenure and position in the organization. For example, a 55-year-old manager who has been in the organization for 25 years may affect decisions made by the buying center differently than a 30-year-old person employed only two years. How influential these factors are depends on the buying situation, the type of product being purchased, and whether the purchase is new task, modified rebuy, or straight rebuy. Negotiating styles of people vary within an organization and from one organization to another. To be effective, marketers must know customers well enough to be aware of these individual factors and the effects they may have on purchase decisions.

Industrial Classification Systems

Marketers have access to a considerable amount of information about potential business customers because much of this information is available through government and industry publications and websites. Marketers use this information to identify potential business customers and to estimate their purchase potential.

Much information about business customers is based on industrial classification systems. In the United States, marketers traditionally have relied on the *Standard*

TABLE 7.2 Examples of NAICS Classification

NAICS Hierarchy for AT&T, Inc.		NAICS Hierarchy for Apple, Inc.	
Sector 51	Information	Sector 31-33	Manufacturing
Subsector 517	Telecommunications	Subsector 334	Computer and Electronic Marketing
Industry Group 5171 Industry Group 5172	Wired Telecommunication Carriers Wireless Telecommunication Carriers	Industry Group 3341	Computer and Peripheral Equipment Manufacturing
Industry 51711 Industry 51721	Wired Telecommunication Carriers Wireless Telecommunication Carriers	Industry 33411	Computer and Peripheral Equipment Manufacturing
Industry 517110 Industry 517210	Wired Telecommunication Carriers Wireless Telecommunications Carriers	U.S. Industry 334111	Electronic Computer Manufacturing

Source: NAICS Association, http://www.census.gov/epcd/naics07/ (accessed March 6, 2009).

Industrial Classification (SIC) System, which the federal government developed to classify selected economic characteristics of industrial, commercial, financial, and service organizations. However, the SIC System has been replaced by a new industry classification system called the **North American Industry Classification System (NAICS)**. NAICS is a single-industry classification system used by the United States, Canada, and Mexico to generate comparable statistics among the three partners of the North American Free Trade Agreement (NAFTA). The NAICS classification is based on the types of production activities performed. NAICS is similar to the International Standard Industrial Classification (ISIC) System used in Europe and many other parts of the world. Whereas the SIC System divided industrial activity into 10 divisions, NAICS divides it into 20 sectors (Table 7.2). NAICS contains 1,170 industry classifications compared with 1,004 in the SIC System. NAICS is more comprehensive and more up-to-date and provides considerably more information about service industries and high-tech products.[19] Table 7.2 shows some NAICS codes for Apple, Inc., and AT&T, Inc. Over the next few years, all three NAFTA countries will convert from previously used industrial classification systems to NAICS.

Industrial classification systems are ready-made tools that help marketers to categorize organizations into groups based mainly on the types of goods and services provided. Although an industrial classification system is a vehicle for segmentation, it is used most appropriately in conjunction with other types of data to determine exactly how many and which customers a marketer can reach.

North American Industry Classification System (NAICS)
An industry classification system that will generate comparable statistics among the United States, Canada, and Mexico

A marketer can take several approaches to determine the identities and locations of organizations in specific industrial classification groups. One approach is to use state directories or commercial industrial directories, such as *Standard & Poor's Register* and Dun & Bradstreet's *Million Dollar Directory*. These sources contain information about a firm, such as its name, industrial classification, address, phone number, and annual sales. By referring to one or more of these sources, marketers isolate business customers with industrial classification numbers, determine their locations, and develop lists of potential customers by desired geographic area. A more expedient, although more expensive, approach is to use a commercial data service.

Dun & Bradstreet, for example, can provide a list of organizations that fall into a particular industrial classification group. For each company on the list, Dun & Bradstreet gives the name, location, sales volume, number of employees, types of products handled, names of chief executives, and other pertinent information. Either method can effectively identify and locate a group of potential customers. However, a marketer probably cannot pursue all organizations on the list. Because some companies have greater purchasing potential than others, marketers must determine which customer or customer group to pursue.

To estimate the purchase potential of business customers or groups of customers, a marketer must find a relationship between the size of potential customers' purchases and a variable available in industrial classification data, such as the number of employees. For example, a paint manufacturer might attempt to determine the average number of gallons purchased by a specific type of potential customer relative to the number of employees. A marketer with no previous experience in this market segment probably will have to survey a random sample of potential customers to establish a relationship between purchase sizes and numbers of employees. Once this relationship is established, it can be applied to potential customer groups to estimate their purchases. After deriving these estimates, the marketer is in a position to select the customer groups with the most sales and profit potential.

Despite their usefulness, industrial classification data pose several problems. First, a few industries do not have specific designations. Second, because a transfer of products from one establishment to another is counted as part of total shipments, double counting may occur when products are shipped between two establishments within the same firm. Third, because the U.S. Bureau of the Census is prohibited from providing data that identify specific business organizations, some data, such as value of total shipments, may be understated. Finally, because government agencies provide industrial classification data, a significant lag usually exists between data-collection time and the time the information is released.

CHAPTER REVIEW

OBJECTIVES

Be able to distinguish among the various types of business markets.

Business (B2B) markets consist of individuals and groups that purchase a specific kind of product for resale, direct use in producing other products, or use in day-to-day operations. Producer markets include those individuals and business organizations purchasing products for the purpose of making a profit by using them to produce other products or as part of their operations. Intermediaries that buy finished products and resell them to make a profit are classified as reseller markets. Government markets consist of federal, state, county, and local governments, which spend billions of dollars annually for goods and services to support internal operations and to provide citizens with services. Organizations with charitable, educational, community, or other nonprofit goals constitute institutional markets.

2 Identify the major characteristics of business customers and transactions.

Transactions involving business customers differ from consumer transactions in several ways. Such transactions tend to be larger, and negotiations occur less frequently, although they are often lengthy when they do occur. They often involve more than one person or department in the purchasing organization. They also may involve reciprocity, an arrangement in which two organizations agree to buy from each other. Business customers are usually better informed than ultimate consumers and more likely to seek information about a product's features and technical specifications.

3 Understand several attributes of the demand for business products.

Business customers are particularly concerned about quality, service, price, and supplier relationships. Quality is important because it directly affects the quality of products the buyer's firm produces. To achieve an exact level of quality, organizations often buy products on the basis of a set of expressed characteristics, called *specifications.* Because services have such a direct influence on a firm's costs, sales, and profits, matters such as market information, on-time delivery, availability of parts, and communication capabilities are crucial to a business buyer. Although business customers do not depend solely on price to decide which products to buy, price is of prime concern because it directly influences profitability.

Business buyers use several purchasing methods, including description, inspection, sampling, and negotiation. Most organizational purchases are new task, straight rebuy, or modified rebuy. In a new-task purchase, an organization makes an initial purchase of items to be used to perform new jobs or to solve new problems. A straight-rebuy purchase occurs when a buyer purchases the same products routinely under approximately the same terms of sale. In a modified-rebuy purchase, a new-task purchase is changed the second or third time it is ordered, or requirements associated with a straight-rebuy purchase are modified.

Industrial demand differs from consumer demand along several dimensions. Industrial demand derives from demand for consumer products. At the industry level, industrial demand is inelastic. Some business products are subject to joint demand, which occurs when two or more items are used in combination to make a product. Finally, because organizational demand derives from consumer demand, the demand for business products can fluctuate widely.

4 Become familiar with the major components of a buying center.

Business purchase decisions are made through a buying center, the group of people involved in making such purchase decisions. Users are those in the organization who actually use the product. Influencers help to develop specifications and evaluate alternative products for possible use. Buyers select suppliers and negotiate purchase terms. Deciders choose the products. Gatekeepers control the flow of information to and among individuals occupying other roles in the buying center.

5 Understand the stages of the business buying decision process and the factors that affect this process.

The stages of the business buying decision process are problem recognition, development of product specifications to solve problems, search for and evaluation of products and suppliers, selection and ordering of the most appropriate product, and evaluation of the product's and supplier's performance.

Four categories of factors influence business buying decisions. Environmental factors include competitive forces, economic conditions, political forces, laws and regulations, technological changes, and sociocultural factors. Organizational factors include the company's objectives, purchasing policies, and resources, as well as the size and composition of its buying center. Interpersonal factors are the relationships among people in the buying center. Individual factors are personal characteristics of members of the buying center, such as age, education, personality, tenure, and position in the organization.

6 Describe industrial classification systems and explain how they can be used to identify and analyze business markets.

An industrial classification system—such as the North American Industry Classification System (NAICS) used by the United States, Canada, and Mexico—provides marketers with information needed to identify business customer groups. It is best used for this purpose in conjunction with other information. After identifying target industries, a marketer can obtain the names and locations of potential customers by using government and commercial data sources. Marketers then must estimate potential purchases of business customers by finding a relationship between a potential customer's purchases and a variable available in industrial classification data.

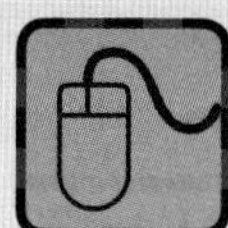

Please visit the student website at www.cengage.com/international for quizzes and games that will help you prepare for exams and help achieve the grade you want.

KEY CONCEPTS

producer markets
reseller markets
government markets
institutional markets
reciprocity
new-task purchase
straight-rebuy purchase
modified-rebuy purchase
derived demand
inelastic demand
joint demand
business (organizational) buying behavior
buying center
value analysis
vendor analysis
multiple sourcing
sole sourcing
North American Industry Classification System (NAICS)

ISSUES FOR DISCUSSION AND REVIEW

1. Identify, describe, and give examples of the four major types of business markets.
2. Regarding purchasing behavior, why might business customers generally be considered more rational than ultimate consumers?
3. What are the primary concerns of business customers?
4. List several characteristics that differentiate transactions involving business customers from consumer transactions.
5. What are the commonly used methods of business buying?
6. Why do buyers involved in a straight-rebuy purchase require less information than those making a new-task purchase?
7. How does demand for business products differ from consumer demand?
8. What are the major components of a firm's buying center?
9. Identify the stages of the business buying decision process. How is this decision process used when making straight rebuys?
10. How do environmental, business, interpersonal, and individual factors affect business purchases?
11. What function does an industrial classification system help marketers perform?
12. List some sources that a business marketer can use to determine the names and addresses of potential customers.

MARKETING APPLICATIONS

1. Identify organizations in your area that fit each business market category—producer, reseller, government, and institutional. Explain your classifications.
2. Indicate the method of buying (description, inspection, sampling, or negotiation) an organization would be most likely to use when purchasing each of the following items. Defend your selection.
   a. A building for the home office of a light bulb manufacturer
   b. Wool for a clothing manufacturer
   c. An Alaskan cruise for a company retreat, assuming a regular travel agency is used
   d. One-inch nails for a building contractor
3. Categorize the following purchase decisions as new task, modified rebuy, or straight rebuy and explain your choice.
   a. Bob has purchased toothpicks from Smith Restaurant Supply for 25 years and recently placed an order for yellow toothpicks rather than the usual white ones.
   b. Jill's investment company has been purchasing envelopes from AAA Office Supply for a year and now needs to purchase boxes to mail year-end portfolio summaries to clients. Jill calls AAA to purchase these boxes.
   c. Reliance Insurance has been supplying its salespeople with small personal computers to assist in their sales efforts. The company recently agreed to begin supplying them with faster, more sophisticated computers.
4. Identifying qualified customers is important to the survival of any organization. NAICS provides helpful information about many different businesses. Find the NAICS manual at the library and identify the NAICS code for the following items.
   a. Chocolate candy bars
   b. Automobile tires
   c. Men's running shoes

ONLINE EXERCISE

5. The Saudi Basic Industries Corporation (SABIC) is a highly diversified, global corporation with many divisions. SABIC Innovative Plastics (purchased from GE Plastics) is the online site for SABIC's resins and plastics business. Visit the site at http://www.sabic-ip.com/gep/Plastics/en/Home/Home/home.html
   a. At what type of business markets are SABIC's resin products targeted?
   b. How does SABIC's website address some of the concerns of business customers?
   c. What environmental factors do you think affect the demand for SABIC resin products?

DEVELOPING YOUR MARKETING PLAN

When developing a marketing strategy for business customers it is essential to understand the process the business goes through when making a buying decision. Knowledge of business buying behavior is important when developing several aspects of the marketing plan. To assist you in relating the information in this chapter to the creation of a marketing plan for business customers, consider the following issues:

1. What are the primary concerns of business customers? Could any of these concerns be addressed with strengths of your company?
2. Determine the type of business purchase your customer will likely be using when purchasing your product. How would this impact the level of information required by the business when moving through the buying decision process?
3. Discuss the different types of demand that the business customer will experience when purchasing your product.

The information obtained from these questions should assist you in developing various aspects of your marketing plan found in the *Interactive Marketing Plan* exercise.

VIDEO CASE 7

Numi Tea Brews Up Business Relationships

Tea—one of the oldest beverages in the world—is a growth industry these days. Served hot or cold, brewed in bags or using loose leaves, tea accounts for $10 billion in U.S. sales every year. Although the business is dominated by corporate giants such as Lipton, companies with unique tea products can compete quite effectively by connecting with key resellers.

Numi Tea of Oakland, California, is riding the wave of tea popularity in just this way. Founded in 1999 by the brother-and-sister team of Ahmed and Reem Rahim, Numi markets only organic full-leaf teas. Many of its teas are Fair Trade-certified, which means that the growers in India, China, and South Africa are paid more than the usual market rate for their leaves. For environmental sustainability, Numi's gift boxes and store displays are made from fast-growing bamboo.

Numi's product offering includes teabags, tea leaf mixtures, herbal teas, and accessories such as teapots and filters. One of its most unusual products is flowering tea. When a hand-sewn bundle of these black, white, or green tea leaves is dropped into boiling water, it releases its fragrant flavor as it expands into a pretty blossom shape. In addition, Numi runs a Tea Garden in downtown Oakland, furnished in eco-friendly materials and featuring Numi's organic teas plus an assortment of cheeses, fruits, and bakery items.

How did Numi bring its sales to a multimillion-dollar boil in only a few years? From the start, the Rahims recognized that their company's growth depended on building long-term relationships with good wholesalers and retailers. For one thing, Numi needed to educate resellers (and help them educate their customers) about the advantages of Numi's tea products. To do this, it created training materials for reseller employees and a series of informational tea cards for resellers to give to customers. It also developed colorful product highlight cards and displays for store shelves and restaurant tables, plus eye-catching posters and banners showcasing the brand.

Service is another important element of Numi's marketing strategy. The company has a brand ambassador who visits restaurants, wholesalers, and retailers to introduce new products and promotions, discuss point-of-purchase displays, conduct product demonstrations, and identify new sales opportunities. It also sends out newsletters and e-mails with product and promotion updates.

Rather than using a "one size fits all" approach, Numi adapts its service to the differing needs of its various resellers. For example, to help upscale restaurants make a good impression on their patrons, Numi provides handsome bamboo tea chests and boxes in which to present tea choices at tableside. Numi also makes glossy presentation folders for luxury hotels to leave Numi teabags in guest rooms as a special amenity.

For the convenience of its resellers, Numi offers a number of ordering options. Depending on the size of their order and where they are located, retailers can buy through a local wholesaler, through Numi's website, or through the wholesaler WorldPantry.com. To make it easy for consumers to find Numi retailers in the United States and Canada, the company's website includes a store locator function.

Careful attention to reseller relationships has helped Numi build annual sales beyond $13 million. No wonder it was recently named one of the San Francisco area's fastest-growing, privately owned businesses. More growth is ahead as the company expands distribution by intensifying its marketing to gourmet grocery stores, quality restaurants, and upscale hotels across North America.

QUESTIONS FOR DISCUSSION

1. What important concerns might retailers and wholesalers have when making decisions about buying from Numi?
2. During vendor analysis, how much weight do you think a buyer for a high-end restaurant is likely to place on Numi's service capabilities? Why?
3. How might local wholesalers react to the policy of allowing retailers to order directly from Numi's website?

"One Minute with Reem Rahim, Numi Tea Inc.," *San Francisco Business Times*, July 14, 2008, http://eastbay.bizjournals.com/eastbay/stories/2008/07/14/smallb2.html; Lisa McLaughlin, "Tea's Got a Brand New Bag," *Time*, March 27, 2008, www.time.com; "Numi Organic Tea," *Beverage Industry*, November 2007, p. 10; "Numi Organic Tea," *Beverage Industry*, June 2007, p. 13; Crystal Detamore-Rodman, "A Perfect Match?" *Entrepreneur*, October 2003, pp. 60+; www.numitea.com.

Global Markets and International Marketing

CHAPTER 8

© CHARLES STURGE/ALAMY

MOBILE PHONES IN DEVELOPING COUNTRIES OFFER LUCRATIVE OPPORTUNITIES FOR MARKETERS

Poorer nations lacking the infrastructure for landlines are finding that cell phones are often the answer, allowing people to make calls, surf the Internet, and conduct business. Cell phone technology is allowing a lot of poor people to leapfrog ahead technologically. For people in emerging markets, the mobile phone will become the primary way of accessing the Internet. In fact, the greatest growth areas for many mobile companies are in developing countries like Indonesia, Egypt, and Russia. The International Telecommunication Union estimates that 4 billion people are already cell phone subscribers, most in developing countries. Cell phones have allowed people to do everything from check their e-mails to engage in online banking. New technology has made accessing the Internet from mobile phones even easier. It is estimated that the number of high-performance mobile phone browsers will increase to 700 million by 2013.

In addition to being convenient, mobile phones may also act to revolutionize the infrastructure in developing countries. The popularity of mobile phones encourages global companies to build towers, power stations, and other types of wireless technology in developing countries. This in turn could lead to the development of more roads and harbors, causing significant economic growth in these nations. Mobile companies like Nokia are also holding competitions urging consumers to develop ways of using mobile phones to better the world. One Ghanaian finalist created a system that uses mobile phones to help detect fake medicines, which could

OBJECTIVES:

1. Understand the nature of global markets and international marketing.
2. Analyze the environmental forces affecting international marketing efforts.
3. Identify several important regional trade alliances, markets, and agreements.
4. Examine modes of entering international markets.
5. Recognize that international marketing strategies fall along a continuum from customization to globalization.

improve the lives of thousands of people in Africa where one of four drugs is fake. The new innovations in mobile phone technology and its increasing use are encouraging the mobile communications industry to step up marketing efforts in the world's poorest nations. These efforts not only can help some people pull themselves out of poverty, but also create job growth and improved quality of life for many millions of people.[1]

Technological advances and rapidly changing political and economic conditions are making it easier than ever for companies like Nokia and other mobile phone producers to market their products overseas as well as at home. With most of the world's population and two-thirds of total purchasing power outside the United States, international markets represent tremendous opportunities for growth. Visa, for example, launched its very first global advertising campaign in 2009. The "More people go with Visa" tagline is meant to reflect Visa's move to a unified global company. Visa is also working to develop a truly global marketing strategy, which will save the company money.[2]

Because of the increasingly global nature of marketing, we devote this chapter to the unique features of global markets and international marketing. We begin by considering the nature of global marketing strategy and exploring the environmental forces that create opportunities and threats for international marketers. Next, we consider several regional trade alliances, markets, and agreements. Finally, we consider the levels of commitment that U.S. firms have toward international marketing and their degree of involvement in it. These factors are significant and must be considered in any marketing plan that includes an international component.

The Nature of Global Marketing Strategy

International marketing involves developing and performing marketing activities across national boundaries. For example, Walmart has 2 million employees and operates 8,100 stores in 15 countries, including large markets like the United States, Brazil, and China; whereas Starbucks has 176,000 employees at its 16,600 stores in 47 countries.[3] Accessing these markets can promote innovation, whereas intensifying global competition spurs companies to market better, less expensive products.

Companies are finding that international markets provide tremendous opportunities for growth. At the same time, governments and industry leaders contend that too few firms take full advantage of international opportunities. To counter this, many countries offer significant practical assistance and valuable benchmarking research that will help their domestic firms become more competitive globally. For example, the U.S. Commercial Service, the global business solutions unit of the U.S. Department of Commerce, offers U.S. firms extensive practical knowledge about international markets and industries, a unique global network, innovative use of information technology, and a focus on small- and medium-sized businesses.[4]

international marketing
Developing and performing marketing activities across national boundaries

Traditionally, most companies—including McDonald's and KFC—have entered the global marketplace incrementally as they gained knowledge about various markets and opportunities. Beginning in the 1990s, however, some firms—such as eBay, Google, and Logitech—were founded with the knowledge and resources to expedite their commitment and investment in the global marketplace. These *born globals*—typically small, technology-based firms earning as much as 70 percent of their sales outside the domestic home market—export their products almost immediately after being established in market niches in which they compete with larger, more established firms.[5] Whether the traditional approach, the born-global approach, or an approach that merges attributes of both is adopted to market the firm's products and services, international marketing strategy is a critical element of a firm's global operations. Today, global competition in most industries is intense and becoming increasingly fierce with the addition of newly emerging markets and firms.

IMAGE COURTESY OF THE ADVERTISING ARCHIVES

International Marketing
This Spanish-language ad for Bounty paper towels is part of an extensive international marketing program.

Environmental Forces in International Markets

Firms that enter foreign markets often find that they must make significant adjustments in their marketing strategies. The environmental forces that affect foreign markets may differ dramatically from those affecting domestic markets. Thus a successful international marketing strategy requires a careful environmental analysis. Conducting research to understand the needs and desires of foreign customers is crucial to international marketing success. Companies have begun to recognize the enormous market potential of poor consumers in developing nations. Unilever, Procter & Gamble, Lipton, and Vaseline have all increased their market presence in poor nations by focusing on value for money, such as small and single-use packaging that even someone living on $2 a day can afford. The strategy was conceived decades ago when Hindustan Lever realized that the prices of its products were out of reach for most Indians.[6] Many firms have demonstrated that such efforts can generate tremendous financial rewards, increase market share, and heighten customer awareness of their products around the world. In this section we explore how differences in the sociocultural; economic; political, legal, and regulatory; social and ethical; competitive; and technological forces of the marketing environment in other countries can profoundly affect marketing activities.

SOCIOCULTURAL FORCES

Cultural and social differences among nations can have significant effects on marketing activities. Because marketing activities are primarily social in purpose, they are influenced by beliefs and values regarding family, religion, education, health, and recreation. By identifying major sociocultural deviations among countries, marketers lay the groundwork for an effective adaptation of marketing strategy. In India, for instance, three-quarters of McDonald's menu was created to appeal to Indian tastes, including many vegetarian items, and the menu does not include pork or beef products at all. In China, however, the fast-food giant has made fewer menu adjustments and even promotes its beef burgers in a sexy ad campaign.[7] Although football is a popular sport in the United States and a major opportunity for many television advertisers, soccer is the most popular televised sport in Europe and Latin America. In order to address its lack of international popularity, the NFL has shifted its marketing strategy. After decades of losing millions trying to export the game, the NFL realized that football has not caught on because non-Americans do not understand the game. To address this problem, marketers created the fictional online Coach Silo. This tough-talking character gives the uninitiated a three-hour-long, eight-chapter tutorial on how football is played. The website also features NFL stars and is available in five languages.[8] And, of course, marketing communications often must be

IMAGE COURTESY OF THE ADVERTISING ARCHIVES

Cultural Differences
Kellogg's is utilizing cultural differences in breakfast food consumption in this ad for Bran Flakes, featuring Olympic gold medal-winning cyclist Chris Hoy.

translated into other languages. Sometimes, however, the true meaning of translated messages can be misinterpreted or lost. Consider some translations that went awry in foreign markets: KFC's long-running slogan, "Finger lickin' good," was translated into Spanish as "Eat your fingers off," whereas Coors' "Turn it loose" campaign was translated into Spanish as "Drink Coors and get diarrhea."[9]

It can be difficult to transfer marketing symbols, trademarks, logos, and even products to international markets, especially if these are associated with objects that have profound religious or cultural significance in a particular culture. For example, when Big Boy opened a new restaurant in Bangkok, it quickly became popular with European and American tourists, but the local Thai refused to eat there. Instead, they placed gifts of rice and incense at the feet of the Big Boy statue—a chubby boy holding a hamburger—which reminded them of Buddha.[10]

Buyers' perceptions of other countries can influence product adoption and use. Research indicates that consumer preferences for domestic products depend on both the country of origin and the product category of competing products.[11] When people are unfamiliar with products from another country, their perceptions of the country itself may affect their attitude toward the product and help determine whether they will buy it. If a country has a reputation for producing quality products and therefore has a positive image in consumers' minds, marketers of products from that country will want to make the country of origin well known. For example, a generally favorable image of Western computer technology has fueled sales in Japan of U.S.-made personal computers by Dell and Apple and software by Microsoft. On the other hand, marketers may want to dissociate themselves from a particular country. Because the world has not always viewed Mexico as producing quality products, Volkswagen may not want to advertise that some of the models it sells in the United States, including the Beetle, are made in Mexico. The extent to which a product's brand image and country of origin influence purchases is subject to considerable variation based on national culture characteristics.[12]

When products are introduced from one nation into another, acceptance is far more likely if similarities exist between the two cultures. In fact, there are many similar cultural characteristics across countries. For international marketers, cultural differences have implications for product development, advertising, packaging, and pricing. Starbucks, for example, has struggled to sell coffee products in China, a nation of tea drinkers; however, the company has been successful in targeting China's younger generations, which like the chain's made-to-order drinks, personal service, and original music. To appeal to China's "little emperors," the generation of children who resulted from China's strict one-child-per-family policy, Starbucks offers formal coffee tastings, generous samples, helpful brochures, and a comfortable, informal gathering place.[13]

ECONOMIC FORCES

Global marketers need to understand the international trade system, particularly the economic stability of individual nations, as well as trade barriers that may stifle marketing efforts. Economic differences among nations—differences in standards of living, credit, buying power, income distribution, national resources, exchange rates, and the like—dictate many of the adjustments that must be made in marketing abroad.

Although in the past, the United States and western Europe have been more economically stable than the rest of the world, the global recession that began in 2008 put economic pressure even on these global powers. However, developing nations were hit the hardest. A global collapse in the demand for goods has hurt countries such as China and Japan, which have largely relied on manufacturing and exports for growth. Singapore, Hong Kong, and Taiwan saw exports plummet as developed nations reduced consumption.[14] The Group of 20 (called the G-20) is a group of 19 of the world's largest economies plus the European Union. The G-20 represents 80 percent of world trade, and in early 2009 agreed on a global financial recovery package that injected $1.1 trillion into the global economy.[15] Recently many countries as diverse as Brazil, Iceland, Pakistan, and Russia have all experienced economic problems such as recession, high unemployment, corporate bankruptcies, instability in currency markets, trade imbalances, and financial systems that need major reforms. Even more stable developing countries, such as Mexico and Brazil, tend to have greater fluctuations in their business cycles than does the United States. Economic instability can disrupt the markets for U.S. products in places that otherwise might be great marketing opportunities. In many countries, consumers are inclined to save considerably more than they spend. This could be because of a culture that values saving, or because of political, economic,

Sustainable Marketing

Long-Distance Wi-Fi Opens Doors to Remote Businesses

Advances in technology are a key force in facilitating international marketing. Wireless technology is not only allowing people to access e-mail and instant messaging services, it is also helping third-world communities provide better health care facilities in areas that are far from mainstream technology and transportation systems. This is all possible through a new product developed by Eric Brewer, a professor at the University of California, Berkeley, and his graduate students. They developed a wireless networking system they called Wildnet. It extends the range of wi-fi technology 100 times further than an airport "hot spot," up to distances of 60 miles.

© PETER BECK/CORBIS

Wildnet utilizes inexpensive components and systems such as the Linux operating system. In addition, one router costs less than $400 and uses just 8 watts of power; it can even be run off a solar panel. Wildnet's most dramatic impact to date has been in southern India, where the high-speed links are bringing better eye care to poor villagers. Some of the local communities' clinics have set up links to regional hospitals to enable local residents to link to doctors without traveling over great distances in person. The Aravind Eye Hospital is a regional hospital that treats 1,400 new patients a month at five remote vision centers that are connected via Wildnet. Wildnet opens up the opportunity for advancing economic development and the well-being of people in developing countries. These advances will create more educated and economically productive members of the global economy.[a]

TABLE 8.1 Comparative Analysis of Selected Countries

Country	Population	GDP (US$)	Exports (US$)	Imports (US$)	Internet Users	Cell Phones	Broadcast Television Stations
Brazil	198,739,269	2.03 trillion	200 billion	176 billion	50 million	120.98 million	138
Canada	33,487,208	1.336 trillion	461.8 billion	436.7 billion	28 million	18.75 million	80
China	1,338,612,968	7.8 trillion	1.465 trillion	1.156 trillion	253 million	547.286 million	3,240
Honduras	7,792,854	28.48 billion	6.236 billion	10.2 billion	424,200	4.185 million	11
India	1,166,079	3.319 trillion	175.7 billion	287.5 billion	80 million	296.08 million	562
Japan	127,078,679	4.487 trillion	776.8 billion	696.2 billion	88.11 million	107.339 million	211
Jordan	6,342,948	31.01 billion	6.521 billion	15.65 billion	1.127 million	4.771 million	22
Kenya	39,002,772	66.48 billion	4.729 billion	9.485 billion	3 million	11.44 million	8
Mexico	11,211,789	1.578 trillion	294 billion	305.9 billion	22.812 million	68.254 million	236
Russia	140,041,247	2.225 trillion	476 billion	302 billion	30 million	170 million	7,306
South Africa	49,052,489	506.1 billion	81.47 billion	87.3 billion	5.1 million	42.3 million	556
Switzerland	7,604,467	309.9 billion	172.7 billion	212.8 billion	4.61 million	8.096 million	106
Turkey	76,805,524	729.4 billion	141.8 billion	204.8 billion	13.15 million	61.976 million	635
Thailand	65,905,410	570.1 billion	178.4 billion	179 billion	13.416 million	51.377 million	111
United States	307,212,123	14.58 trillion	1.377 trillion	2.19 trillion	223 million	255 million	2,218

Source: CIA, *World Fact Book*, https://www.cia.gov/library/publications/the-world-factbook/ (accessed March 30, 2009).

or job instability. During the most recent global recession, with exports in significant decline in some countries, governments scrambled to devise ways to increase consumer spending as a way of stimulating economies. This problem was particularly acute in Asia.[16]

In terms of the value of all products produced by a nation, the United States has the largest gross domestic product in the world, nearly $14.6 trillion. **Gross domestic product (GDP)** is an overall measure of a nation's economic standing; it is the market value of a nation's total output of goods and services for a given period. However, it does not take into account the concept of GDP in relation to population (GDP per capita). The United States has the highest GDP per capita in the world at $48,000. Canada, which is comparable in geographic size to the United States, has a GDP per capita of $40,200. Brazil, the largest economy in Latin America, has a GDP per capita of only $10,300.[17] Table 8.1 provides a comparative economic analysis of 15 countries, including the United States. Knowledge about per capita income, credit, and the distribution of income provides general insights into market potential.

Opportunities for international trade are not limited to countries with the highest incomes. Some nations are progressing at a much faster rate than they were a few years ago, and these countries—especially in Africa, eastern Europe, Latin America, and the Middle East—have great market potential. In Africa, for example, some cell phone service providers concede that they grossly underestimated the potential market for cell phone service in many countries because of their low GDP and low landline telephone use. The cell phone industry in India continues to boom in one demographic—the rural poor. Even though the global recession caused many consumers to curtail spending, these poor buyers have not been affected by collapsing real estate prices, falling stock values, or curtailed lending. In regions where telephone landlines were never installed, cell phones help rural poor farmers and other small businesses

gross domestic product (GDP) The market value of a nation's total output of goods and services for a given period; an overall measure of economic standing

keep in touch with the rest of the world.[18] However, marketers must understand the political and legal environment before they can convert the buying power of customers in these countries into actual demand for specific products.

POLITICAL, LEGAL, AND REGULATORY FORCES

The political, legal, and regulatory forces of the environment are as closely intertwined in many countries as they are in the United States. Typically, legislation is enacted, legal decisions are interpreted, and regulatory agencies are operated by elected or appointed officials. A country's legal and regulatory infrastructure is a direct reflection of its political climate. In some countries this political climate is determined by the people via elections, whereas in others leaders are appointed or have assumed leadership based on certain powers. While laws and regulations have direct effects on a firm's operations in a country, political forces are indirect and often not clearly known in all country markets. For example, a company needs to work with the government of China to enter and establish operations in that country, and that has been a highly political process since the advent of Communist rule.

Some individuals and businesses attempt to take advantage of variations in national tax laws in order to dodge taxes or regulations in their home countries. Allen Stanford, an American financier who is also a knight in Antigua, sold certificates of deposit from his Houston, Texas, offices based on investments made from his Caribbean Bank of Antigua. The government did not insure these certificates, nor did Stanford's operations have much government oversight. He ultimately bilked investors out of an estimated $8 billion. Since the Middle Ages, Swiss banks have been famous for their secrecy. However, the recent global financial crisis has forced countries to reconsider whether to allow Switzerland, Liechtenstein, and Andorra to continue their practice of complete and total banking privacy. Under pressure by the United States, Germany, the United Kingdom, and other countries, the European principalities of Liechtenstein and Andorra, followed by the Swiss, have all agreed to abandon their unusually high protection of depositors accused of tax evasion in their home countries.[19]

A nation's political system, laws, regulatory bodies, special-interest groups, and courts all have great impact on international marketing. A government's policies toward public and private enterprise, consumers, and foreign firms influence marketing across national boundaries. Some countries have established trade restrictions, such as tariffs. An **import tariff** is any duty levied by a nation on goods bought outside its borders and brought in. Because they raise the prices of foreign goods, tariffs impede free trade between nations. Tariffs usually are designed either to raise revenue for a country or to protect domestic products. In response to an ongoing trade dispute between the two countries, the Mexican government placed tariffs on 90 industrial and agricultural products from the United States. Mexico claims that the tariffs were in retaliation for U.S. cancellation of a program that would have allowed Mexican trucks to transport cargo throughout the United States. Unions have long opposed Mexican trucks on U.S. roads, even though the two countries have agreements allowing for their eventual passage.[20] In the United States, tariff revenues account for less than 2 percent of total federal revenues, down from about 50 percent of total federal revenues in the early 1900s.[21]

Nontariff trade restrictions include quotas and embargoes. A **quota** is a limit on the amount of goods an importing country will accept for certain product categories in a specific time period. An **embargo** is a government's suspension of trade in a particular product or with a given country. Embargoes generally are directed at specific goods or countries and are established for political, health, or religious reasons. For example, the United States forbids the importation of uncertified Iberian ham, absinthe, and any product containing dog or cat fur.[22]

Exchange controls, government restrictions on the amount of a particular currency that can be bought or sold, also may limit international trade. They can force businesses to buy and sell foreign products through a central agency, such as a central bank. On the other hand, to

import tariff
A duty levied by a nation on goods bought outside its borders and brought in

quota
A limit on the amount of goods an importing country will accept for certain product categories in a specific time period

embargo
A government's suspension of trade in a particular product or with a given country

exchange controls
Government restrictions on the amount of a particular currency that can be bought or sold

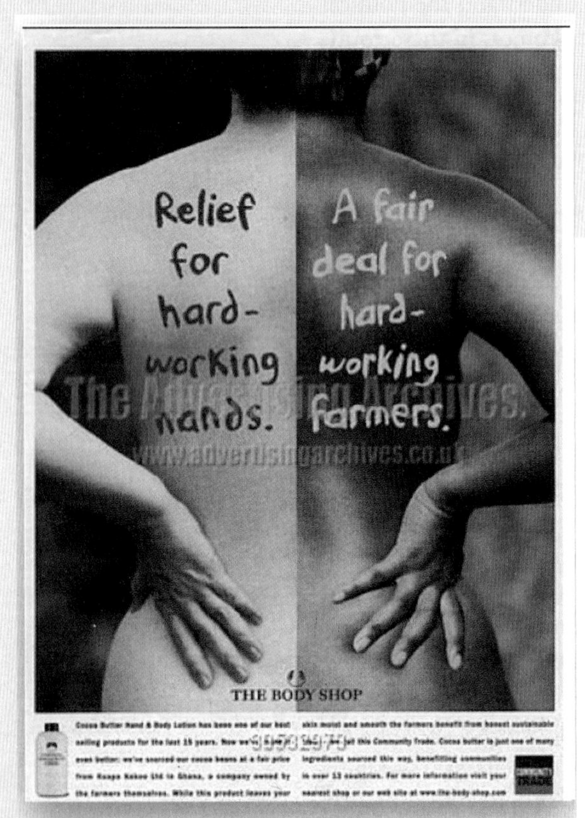

IMAGE COURTESY OF THE ADVERTISING ARCHIVES

Global Diversity
Diversity is a value that can lead to increased competitiveness around the world.

promote international trade, some countries have joined together to form free trade zones—multinational economic communities that eliminate tariffs and other trade barriers. Such regional trade alliances are discussed later in this chapter. Foreign currency exchange rates also affect the prices marketers can charge in foreign markets. Fluctuations in the international monetary market can change the prices charged across national boundaries on a daily basis. Consequently, these fluctuations must be considered in any international marketing strategy.

Countries may limit imports to maintain a favorable balance of trade. The **balance of trade** is the difference in value between a nation's exports and its imports. When a nation exports more products than it imports, a favorable balance of trade exists because money is flowing into the country. The United States has a negative balance of trade—a trade deficit—of around $680 billion.[23] A negative balance of trade is considered harmful because it means that U.S. dollars are supporting foreign economies at the expense of U.S. companies and workers.

Many nontariff barriers, such as quotas and minimum price levels set on imports, taxes, and health and safety requirements, can make it difficult for U.S. companies to export their products. For example, the collectivistic nature of Japanese culture and the high-context nature of Japanese communication make some types of direct marketing messages less effective there and may predispose many Japanese to support greater regulation of direct marketing practices.[24] A government's attitude toward importers has a direct impact on the economic feasibility of exporting to that country.

SOCIAL RESPONSIBILITY AND ETHICS FORCES[25]

Differences in ethical values and legal standards also can affect marketing efforts. China and Vietnam, for example, have different standards regarding intellectual property than does the United States. These differences create an issue for marketers of computer software, music CDs, books, and many other products. In fact, the World Customs Organization and Interpol estimate that the industry for pirated goods represents 5 to 7 percent of worldwide merchandise trade, particularly in China, resulting in lost sales of $512 billion a year. The Chinese government has, however, been taking steps to curb its piracy problem.[26] Among the products routinely counterfeited are consumer electronics, pharmaceuticals, cell phones, cigarettes, watches, shoes, motorcycles, and automobiles.[27]

Some brands are created specifically to have a positive impact. Project RED is a brand created by U2's front man, Bono, to help raise awareness and money for the Global Fund to Fight AIDS, Tuberculosis, and Malaria. Well-known global brands such as American Express, Apple, Converse, Gap Inc., Emporio Armani, Hallmark, and Motorola have all teamed up with Project RED to help contribute to the global fight against HIV and AIDS. Project RED allows corporations to reap profits while simultaneously helping to push the agenda of corporate social responsibility and assisting those in need.[28]

balance of trade
The difference in value between a nation's exports and its imports

When marketers travel and work abroad, they sometimes perceive that cultures in other nations have different modes of operation and different values regarding ethical conduct. Consider that many in the United States hold the perception that U.S. firms are often different from those in other countries. This implied perspective of "us" versus "them" is also widespread in other countries. Table 8.2 indicates the countries that businesspeople, risk analysts, and the

TABLE 8.2 Perceptions of the Least and Most Corrupt Countries

Least Corrupt	Most Corrupt
Denmark	Somalia
New Zealand	Myanmar
Sweden	Iraq
Singapore	Haiti
Finland	Afghanistan
Switzerland	Sudan
Iceland	Guinea
Netherlands	Chad
Australia	Equatorial Guinea
Canada	Democratic Republic of Congo

Note: The United States ranks 18th, tied with Belgium and Japan.
Source: Adapted from the Transparency International, "Corruption Perceptions Index 2008," http://www.transparency.org/policy_research/surveys_indices/cpi/2008 (accessed April 2, 2009).

general public perceived as the most and least corrupt. In marketing, the idea that "we" differ from "them" is called the *self-reference criterion* (SRC)—the unconscious reference to one's own cultural values, experiences, and knowledge. When confronted with a situation, we tend to react on the basis of knowledge we have accumulated over a lifetime, which is usually grounded in our culture of origin (and often rooted in our religious beliefs). Our reactions are based on meanings, values, and symbols that relate to our culture but may not have the same relevance to people of other cultures. However, many marketers adopt the principle of "When in Rome, do as the Romans do." They adapt to the cultural practices of the country they are working in and use that country's cultural practices to rationalize sometimes straying from their own ethical values when doing business internationally. For example, by defending the payment of bribes or "greasing the wheels of business" and other questionable practices in this fashion, some businesspeople are resorting to **cultural relativism**—the concept that morality varies from one culture to another and that business practices are therefore differentially defined as right or wrong by particular cultures.

Differences in national standards are illustrated by what the Mexicans call *la mordida,* "the bite." The use of payoffs and bribes is deeply entrenched in many governments. Because U.S. trade and corporate policy, as well as U.S. law, prohibit direct involvement in payoffs and bribes, U.S. companies may have a hard time competing with foreign firms that do engage in these practices. Some U.S. businesses that refuse to make payoffs are forced to hire local consultants, public relations firms, or advertising agencies, which results in indirect payoffs. The ultimate decision about whether to give small tips or gifts where they are customary must be based on a company's code of ethics. Under the Foreign Corrupt Practices Act of 1977, however, it is illegal for U.S. firms to attempt to make large payments or bribes to influence policy decisions of foreign governments. Nevertheless, facilitating payments, or small payments to support the performance of standard tasks, are often acceptable. The act also subjects all publicly held U.S. corporations to rigorous internal controls and recordkeeping requirements for their overseas operations.

cultural relativism
The concept that morality varies from one culture to another and that business practices are therefore differentially defined as right or wrong by particular cultures

Because of differences in legal and ethical standards, many companies are working both individually and collectively to establish ethics programs and standards for international business conduct.[29] Mattel experienced significant negative press when in 2008 it was forced to

© AP IMAGES/PRNEWSFOTO/AT&T INC.

Staying Ahead of the Competition
AT&T's extensive global network provides a competitive advantage.

recall nearly a million toys made in China because of unsafe lead levels. The company quickly identified the problem and has since implemented more stringent safety standards. The incident served as the impetus for increased regulation of the toy industry so as to avoid a similar public safety disaster in the future. Although regulations increase the cost of making toys, many stakeholders feel that this is a necessary step in keeping children safe.[30] Levi Strauss's code of ethics bars the firm from manufacturing in countries where workers are known to be abused. Starbucks's global code of ethics strives to protect agricultural workers who harvest coffee. Many companies choose to standardize their ethical behavior across national boundaries to maintain a consistent and well-integrated corporate culture.

Monsanto, the giant biotech food corporation, is no stranger to criticisms regarding its commitment to social responsibility and ethics. Monsanto produces 97 percent of soy in the United States, and its insecticides and herbicides are the defaults for most farmers. However, Monsanto is most famous for its genetically modified crops, the health and environmental impact of which are under fierce debate around the world. While GMO crops can help farmers to grow larger yields, many detractors worry about the effects of these lab-engineered plants on insects, other plants, and the health of human beings. Monsanto argues that GMOs can help to solve the growing problem of world hunger, which they believe is the most important concern right now. The argument appears to be persuasive, with over 282 million acres worldwide currently cultivated for biotech crops. The fastest regions of growth are in the developing world, places like India that need high-yield crops to feed their large populations.[31]

COMPETITIVE FORCES

Competition is often viewed as a staple of the global marketplace, with customers thriving on the choices offered by competition and companies continually seeking opportunities to outmaneuver their competition. However, the increasingly interconnected international marketplace and advances in technology have resulted in competitive forces that are unique to the international marketplace. Each country has unique competitive aspects—often founded in the other environmental forces (i.e., sociocultural, technological, political, legal, regulatory, and economic forces)—that are often independent of the competitors in that country's market. The

TABLE 8.3 A Ranking of the Most Competitive Countries in the World

1. United States	**9.** Japan
2. Switzerland	**10.** Canada
3. Denmark	**11.** Hong Kong SAR
4. Sweden	**12.** United Kingdom
5. Singapore	**13.** Korea
6. Finland	**14.** Austria
7. Germany	**15.** Norway
8. Netherlands	

Source: The Global Competitiveness Report 2008–2009, *World Economic Forum*, http://www.weforum.org/pdf/gcr/2008/rankings.pdf (accessed March 31, 2009).

most globally competitive countries are listed in Table 8.3. Although companies drive competition, nations establish and maintain the infrastructure for the types of competition that can take place. For example, Microsoft's near monopoly over software in the United States (and in many other countries) has led the U.S. government and U.S. firms to a long-standing legal battle over the firm's competitive practices. Other countries permit monopoly structures to exist to lesser or greater degrees. In Sweden, for example, most alcohol sales are made through Systembolaget, the government store that is legally supported by the Swedish Alcohol Retail Monopoly.[32]

Beyond the types of competition (i.e., brand, product, generic, and total budget competition) and types of competitive structures (i.e., monopoly, oligopoly, monopolistic competition, and pure competition) that are discussed in Chapter 3, firms operating internationally also need to address the competitive forces in the countries they target, recognize the interdependence of countries and the global competitors in those markets, and be mindful of a new breed of customers—the global customer. Until recently, customers seldom had opportunities to compare products from competitors, learn details about competing product features, and examine other options beyond the local (country or region) markets. Customers today, however, expect to be able to buy the same product in most of the world's countries, and they expect that the product they buy in their local store in Miami will have the same features as similar products sold in London or even in Beijing. In an attempt to bring car ownership to billions of impoverished people in places like India, Tata Motors has produced the world's cheapest mass-produced car at $2,000. Although it does not have the amenities or safety features of more expensive cars, it could be a way for poor people to realize their dream of owning their own car. A U.S. version of the car is in the works, but stricter safety laws mean that consumers in the United States will have to wait to own a Nano of their own. Many people are protesting the release of this car, as it has the potential to greatly worsen greenhouse gas emissions, a problem that is already leading to more extreme weather patterns and global warming.[33]

TECHNOLOGICAL FORCES

Advances in technology have made international marketing much easier. Voice mail, e-mail, fax, cellular phones, and the Internet make international marketing activities more affordable and convenient. Internet usage has accelerated dramatically throughout the world, with an estimated global 1.6 billion users.[34] Japan has over 88 million users, while the United States has the highest penetration rate with 223 million users. Developing nations present a large growth area for Internet companies, with countries like Kenya registering 3 million users and Honduras a mere 424,200.[35] (See Table 8.1.)

Internet marketing can be a smart addition to a firm's international marketing strategy because of the potential to reach large numbers of customers for a relatively low cost. However, issues such as language and localized content can complicate securing international markets through use of the Internet.[36] Many firms do not utilize websites as well as they should in seeking to gain new markets. Four of the practices that are becoming essential on firms' websites are personalized shopping, clear categorization, order tracking, and in-depth product or service-related information.[37]

Countries across the globe are placing innovation at the top of their agendas, using such means as recruiting from a global talent pool, and offering tax credits and regulatory relief as added incentives. Singapore, for example, offers tax credits to firms willing to do research and development in the areas of life sciences, clean energy, and digital media.[38] In many developing countries that lack the level of technological infrastructure found in the United States and Japan, marketers are beginning to capitalize on opportunities to "leapfrog" existing technology. For example, cellular and wireless phone technology is reaching many countries at less expense than traditional hardwired telephone systems. Over half of the world's population uses mobile phones, and growth in cell phone subscriptions has now surpassed that for fixed lines.[39] Opportunities for growth in the cell phone market remain strong in Africa, the Middle East, and Southeast Asia. One opportunity created by the rapid growth in cell phone service contracts in China is the *shouji jiayouzhan,* or "cell phone gas station," which allows consumers to recharge their phone, camera, and personal digital assistant (PDA) batteries quickly for the equivalent of 12 cents, and they can view ads during the 10-minute charging session.[40]

SNAPSHOT

The World's Top Ten Most Admired Companies

1	Apple (U.S.)
2	Berkshire Hathaway (U.S.)
3	Toyota Motor (Japan)
4	Google (U.S.)
5	Johnson & Johnson (U.S.)
6	Procter & Gamble (U.S.)
7	FedEx (U.S.)
8	Southwest Airlines (U.S.)
9	General Electric (U.S.)
10	Microsoft (U.S.)

Source: *Fortune* March 16, 2009, p. 76.

Regional Trade Alliances, Markets, and Agreements

Although many more firms are beginning to view the world as one huge marketplace, various regional trade alliances and specific markets affect companies engaging in international marketing. Some create opportunities; others impose constraints. In this section we examine several regional trade alliances, markets, and changing conditions affecting markets, including the North American Free Trade Agreement among the United States, Canada, and Mexico; the European Union; the Common Market of the Southern Cone; Asia-Pacific Economic Cooperation; the General Agreement on Tariffs and Trade; and the World Trade Organization.

THE NORTH AMERICAN FREE TRADE AGREEMENT (NAFTA)

North American Free Trade Agreement (NAFTA)
An alliance that merges Canada, Mexico, and the United States into a single market

The **North American Free Trade Agreement (NAFTA)**, implemented in 1994, effectively merged Canada, Mexico, and the United States into one market of more than 430 million consumers. NAFTA was created with the goal of eliminating nearly all tariffs on goods produced and traded among Canada, Mexico and the United States, a goal that was achieved in

January 2008.[41] This trade alliance has an estimated annual output of US$15 trillion. NAFTA has made it easier for U.S. businesses to invest in Mexico and Canada; provides protection for intellectual property; expands trade by requiring equal treatment of U.S. firms in all involved countries; and simplifies country-of-origin rules.

Canada's nearly 33.5 million people are quite affluent with a per capita GDP comparable to the United States' at US$40,200. Canada has a sizable trade surplus with the United States, which absorbs 80 percent of Canada's exports each year. Mexico is a much larger nation than Canada, with approximately 111 million people, but per capita GDP is significantly lower at an estimated US$14,200. While the NAFTA countries continue to trade among one another, weakened economies because of the recession that began in 2008 will mean reduced growth.

Many U.S. companies have taken advantage of Mexico's relatively low labor costs and close proximity to the United States to set up factories, sometimes called *maquiladoras*, near the Mexico/U.S. border. Maquiladoras have been an especially popular model in the automotive, electronics, and apparel industries. Because of the high concentration of manufacturing jobs in northern Mexico, the quality of life in the north has made the region increasingly more like Texas, while southern Mexico remains more akin to Central America. In the recent depression, maquiladoras have been particularly affected. Decreased demand for manufactured goods and escalating violence from the drug wars along the U.S./Mexico border have led to concern over the future of Mexico's economy. In fact, Mexico's economy even retracted an estimated 3 percent in 2009.[42]

The governments of the United States and Mexico both hoped that NAFTA would help to foster a healthier trade relationship between the two countries, one in which goods would be exported, not immigrants. One and a half decades after the passage of NAFTA, Mexico's exports to the United States have exploded, but the trade agreement has not been successful in stemming the stream of immigration into the United States. NAFTA has produced unexpected side effects. Mexican farmers cannot compete with cheap subsidized agricultural goods from the United States; domestic industries have also suffered as multinationals increasingly get their parts from cheap Asian manufacturers. While trade has increased astronomically, many rural dwellers and small businesses have lost their jobs, and consequently have sought to migrate to the United States where opportunities are perceived to be greater.[43] Even years into NAFTA, Mexico's job growth has averaged around 3 percent—well below the rate needed to create jobs for millions of young workers entering the job market. To respond to many of the criticisms of NAFTA, President Obama has mentioned a desire for stricter environmental and labor-protection rules—although he has reassured leaders he will be careful not to hinder the free trade agreement or to enact any protectionist measures.[44]

Declining consumption has hurt NAFTA and fueled its critics as well. Early 2009 saw NAFTA experience a record decline in trade of over 27 percent, largely due to the global economic recession.[45] A trucking dispute has also strained U.S./Mexico relations. The United States has imposed a ban on the entry of Mexican trucks into the United States for shipping purposes, citing Mexico's lower standard of driving safety regulations as a reason. Mexico retaliated by imposing tariffs on more than 90 goods commonly shipped into the United States, in direct opposition to NAFTA's aim of doing away with tariffs and trade restrictions.[46]

Mexico's membership in NAFTA links the United States and Canada with other Latin American countries, providing additional opportunities to integrate trade among all the nations in the Western Hemisphere. Indeed, efforts to create a free trade agreement among the 34 nations of North and South America are underway. Like NAFTA, the *Free Trade Area of the Americas* (FTAA) will progressively eliminate trade barriers and create the world's largest free trade zone, with 800 million people. However, the negotiations to complete the agreement have been contentious, and the agreement itself has become a lightning rod for antiglobalization activists. A related trade agreement—the *Central American Dominican Republic Free Trade Agreement* (CAFTA-DR)—among Costa Rica, the Dominican Republic, El Salvador, Guatemala, Honduras, Nicaragua, and the United States also has been ratified

Entrepreneurs Take on Chinese Piracy: The Story of BraBaby

Even inexpensive household products face competitive challenges in global markets. Robert and Laura Engel, founders of Angel Sales, Inc., invented the BraBaby, a plastic device used for laundering bras that preserves and extends their wear. They realized their product was being copied and made available throughout the world without their permission, partnership, licensing, or compensation. The Engels spent nearly $125,000 registering, patenting, and copyrighting the trademark in the United States, the European Community, Australia, New Zealand, Taiwan, Hong Kong, and China, and yet pirates paid no attention to these measures. The Engels learned a valuable lesson about the challenges inherent in developing and marketing a successful product. Inventing the product is the beginning of the battle in global markets with intellectual property standards that are not enforced or culturally accepted.[b]

by all those countries except Costa Rica. The United States has already begun implementing the provisions of the agreement with the countries that have ratified it. When these agreements are fully implemented, they will have a great influence on trade in the region.

THE EUROPEAN UNION (EU)

The **European Union (EU)**, also called the *European Community* or *Common Market,* was established in 1958 to promote trade among its members, which initially included Belgium, France, Italy, West Germany, Luxembourg, and the Netherlands. In 1991, East and West Germany united, and by 2007, the United Kingdom, Spain, Denmark, Greece, Portugal, Ireland, Austria, Finland, Sweden, Cyprus, Poland, Hungary, the Czech Republic, Slovenia, Estonia, Latvia, Lithuania, Slovakia, Malta, Romania, and Bulgaria had joined as well. (Croatia and Turkey also have requested membership.[47]) Until 1993, each nation functioned as a separate market, but at that time, the members officially unified into one of the largest single world markets, which today includes nearly half a billion consumers with a combined GDP of more than $12 trillion.[48]

To facilitate free trade among members, the EU is working toward standardization of business regulations and requirements, import duties, and value-added taxes; the elimination of customs checks; and the creation of a standardized currency for use by all members. Many European nations trade in a common currency, the euro; however, several EU members (e.g., Denmark, Sweden, and the United Kingdom) have rejected use of the euro in their countries. Although the common currency requires many marketers to modify their pricing strategies and will subject them to increased competition, the use of a single currency frees companies that sell goods among European countries from the nuisance of dealing with complex exchange rates.[49] The long-term goals are to eliminate all trade barriers within the EU, improve the economic efficiency of the EU nations, and stimulate economic growth, thus making the union's economy more competitive in global markets, particularly against Japan and other Pacific Rim nations and North America. Several disputes and debates still divide the member nations, however, and many barriers to completely free trade remain. Consequently, it may take many years before the EU is truly one deregulated market.

European Union (EU) An alliance that promotes trade among its member countries in Europe

Common Market of the Southern Cone (MERCOSUR) An alliance that promotes the free circulation of goods, services, and production factors and has a common external tariff and commercial policy among member nations in South America

Asia-Pacific Economic Cooperation (APEC) An alliance that promotes open trade and economic and technical cooperation among member nations throughout the world

As the EU nations attempt to function as one large market, consumers in the EU may become more homogeneous in their needs and wants. Most residents of the EU strongly desire, however, to maintain their national cultures and traditions.[50] As a result, marketers may need to adjust their marketing mixes for customers within each nation to reflect their differences in tastes and preferences as well as primary language. Gathering information about these distinct tastes and preferences is likely to remain a very important factor in developing marketing mixes that satisfy the needs of European customers.

THE COMMON MARKET OF THE SOUTHERN CONE (MERCOSUR)

The **Common Market of the Southern Cone** (also known as *Mercado Comun del Sur* or **MERCOSUR**) was established in 1991 under the Treaty of Asunción to unite Argentina, Brazil, Paraguay, and Uruguay as a free trade alliance; Venezuela joined in 2006, but is not a full member. Bolivia, Chile, Colombia, Ecuador, and Peru are associate members. The alliance represents two-thirds of South America's population and has a combined GDP of US$2.97 trillion, making it the third-largest trading bloc behind NAFTA and the EU. Like NAFTA, MERCOSUR promotes "the free circulation of goods, services and production factors among the countries" and establishes a common external tariff and commercial policy.[51]

ASIA-PACIFIC ECONOMIC COOPERATION (APEC)

The **Asia-Pacific Economic Cooperation (APEC)**, established in 1989, promotes open trade and economic and technical cooperation among member nations, which initially included Australia, Brunei Darussalam, Canada, Indonesia, Japan, Korea, Malaysia, New Zealand, the Philippines, Singapore, Thailand, and the United States. Since then, the alliance has grown to include Chile, China, Chinese Taipei, Hong Kong, Mexico, Papua New Guinea, Peru, Russia, and Vietnam. The 21-member alliance represents 40 percent of the world's population, 54 percent of its GDP, and 44 percent of world trade.[52] APEC differs from other international trade alliances in its commitment to facilitating business and its practice of allowing the business/private sector to participate in a wide range of APEC activities.

Despite economic turmoil and a recession in Asia in recent years, companies of APEC have become increasingly competitive and sophisticated in global business in the last three decades. South Korea, for example, has become the fifth-largest producer of cars and trucks in the world, exporting more than half a million vehicles to the United States. Hyundai and Kia gained market share in the United States by expanding their product lines and improving their quality and brand image. Japanese firms in particular have made tremendous inroads into world markets for automobiles, motorcycles, watches, cameras, and audio and video equipment. Products from Sony, Sanyo, Toyota, Mitsubishi, Canon, Suzuki, and Toshiba are sold all over the world and have set standards of quality by which other products are often judged. The most important emerging economic power is China, which has become one of the most productive manufacturing nations. China, which has become the second-largest trading partner of the United States, has initiated economic reforms to stimulate its economy by privatizing many industries, restructuring its banking system, and increasing public spending on infrastructure. While China's growth rate has been cut from 9 percent to 7 percent, the country still outperforms most other

Marketing IN TRANSITION

"Made in China" Trying to Rebuild Its Reputation

China exports over $1.2 trillion in goods annually and accounts for almost 9 percent of global trade. However, in recent years the phrase "Made in China" has taken on a stigma because of scandals concerning lead paint in children's toys and tainted pet food and milk. A recent survey conducted by Interbrand and *Fortune* indicates that only 6 percent of the more than 700 individuals surveyed were interested in purchasing items made in China. Brand image problems also have impacted Chinese products. They are reputed to be cheap, low-quality, and unsafe. In addition, Chinese brands lack a critical element needed to grab the consumer's interest and loyalty—that emotional connection.

A few Chinese brands are rising above the controversy. Lenovo (the world's fourth-largest PC brand) and Haier (the world's third-largest appliance brand) excel. Lenovo took off after acquiring IBM's PC division. Haier is known for innovation and quality. In fact, in areas such as technology and consumer electronics, analysts expect China will move to the global forefront. China is a country rich in manufacturing, high-end technology, and competitive pricing.

China can become a strong presence by pursuing any or all of the following paths: focusing on markets in which China has a positive reputation (i.e., alternative medicine), manufacturing for reputable global companies under those companies' banners, and acquiring brands. China must strive for greater transparency and must improve regulation. Despite scandals and poor reputation, Chinese companies—such as those producing cars, shoes, and airline travel—are determined to improve. With attention to innovation, product quality, safety, emotional appeal, and value, the phrase "Made in China" might take on a whole new meaning.[c]

countries in the world. The U.S. car market, long deemed attractive by Chinese manufacturers, has thus far eluded them, however, in spite of China being the world's second largest automobile producer. Not a single Chinese car has broken into the U.S. market yet. China has big plans to become the largest electric car producer, however, as a way to gain a global competitive edge in this rapidly changing industry.[53] Nike and Adidas have shifted most of their shoe production to China, and recently, China has become a major producer of CD players, cellular phones, portable stereos, and personal computers.

The markets of APEC offer tremendous opportunities to marketers who understand them. For example, Yum! Brands, the number two fast-food chain after McDonald's, opened its first KFC fast-food restaurant in China in 1987 and has since opened 2,000 KFC and Pizza Hut outlets in China, as well as a new concept store called East Dawning, which serves Chinese fast food. China accounts for about 16 percent of the company's profits.[54]

While APEC countries provide great opportunities for many companies, the sheer size of countries like China and India pose regulatory and safety concerns. Those who remember the Mattel lead-contaminated toys or the toxic melamine-tainted milk scandals of 2008 will see how quickly a problem can escalate when international trade is involved.[55] China's reputation suffered serious blows from those two incidents. Research has shown that all Chinese brands suffered after the coverage of the melamine-tainted milk scandal.[56] Coupled with a decline in world trade and concerns over a bird flu outbreak in early 2009, China's economic health has suffered considerably.[57] A minimum of 20 million Chinese migrants lost their manufacturing jobs in late 2008, and Chinese exports dropped nearly 26 percent in early 2009 from the previous year. Japan fared even worse, with a 35 percent drop in exports. Export powerhouses like Beijing are seeking to slow the decline by cutting taxes and creating incentives to boost trade.[58] All of these problems combined with the global recession spell trouble for Asian APEC countries that will have repercussions for years to come.

THE WORLD TRADE ORGANIZATION (WTO)

The **World Trade Organization (WTO)** is a global trade association that promotes free trade among 149 member nations. The WTO is the successor to the **General Agreement on Tariffs and Trade (GATT)**, originally signed by 23 nations in 1947 to provide a forum for tariff negotiations and a place where international trade problems could be discussed and resolved. Rounds of GATT negotiations reduced trade barriers for most products and established rules to guide international commerce, such as rules to prevent **dumping**, the selling of products at unfairly low prices.

Achieving the WTO's primary goal of free trade requires eliminating trade barriers; educating individuals, companies, and governments about trade rules around the world; and assuring global markets that no sudden changes of policy will occur. The WTO also serves as a forum for trade negotiations and dispute resolution.[59] At the heart of the WTO are agreements that provide legal ground rules for international commerce and trade policy.For example, the United States, Canada, and the EU complained to the WTO that new WTO member China levies tariffs on imported car parts as if they were complete vehicles, putting foreign manufacturers of auto parts at a distinct disadvantage in China. After attempts to resolve the dispute failed, the nations asked the WTO to mediate and rule as to whether China's actions are lawful.[60]

The WTO is facing some of the largest challenges of its existence. A worsening global recession throughout late 2008 and 2009 put tremendous pressures on the organization's mission to promote free trade. Many countries, in an effort to save local jobs and spur growth, enacted quasi-protectionist measures that provided consumers and businesses with incentives for purchasing locally, even if the quality is lower or the price higher. Global trade in 2009 declined by over 9 percent, making it the worst year in the WTO's history. In spite of the pressures

World Trade Organization (WTO)
An entity that promotes free trade among member nations

General Agreement on Tariffs and Trade (GATT)
An agreement among nations to reduce worldwide tariffs and increase international trade

dumping
Selling products at unfairly low prices

to protect local businesses, the WTO's official stance remains that international free trade will lead to the healthiest global economy.[61]

Modes of Entry into International Markets

Marketers enter international markets at several levels of involvement covering a wide spectrum, as Figure 8.1 shows. Domestic marketing involves marketing strategies aimed at markets within the home country; at the other extreme, global marketing entails developing marketing strategies for major regions or for the entire world. Many firms with an international presence start as small companies serving local and regional markets and expand to national markets before considering opportunities in foreign markets. The level of commitment to international marketing is a major variable in international marketing strategies. In this section we examine importing and exporting, trading companies, licensing and franchising, contract manufacturin g, joint ventures, direct ownership, and other approaches to international involvement.

Business Across Borders
Ethos Water supports a cause and exports resources to provide clean water for children in Africa.

IMPORTING AND EXPORTING

Importing and exporting require the least amount of effort and commitment of resources. **Importing** is the purchase of products from a foreign source. **Exporting**, the sale of products to foreign markets, enables businesses of all sizes to participate in global business. Limited exporting may occur even if a firm makes little or no effort to obtain foreign sales. Foreign buyers may seek the company and/or its products, or a distributor may discover the firm's products and export them. A firm may find an exporting intermediary to take over most marketing functions associated with selling to other countries. This approach entails minimal effort and cost. Modifications in packaging, labeling, style, or color may be the major expenses in adapting a product for the foreign market. Having sound objectives and maintaining product quality are important in attaining a competitive advantage in exporting.[62]

Export agents bring together buyers and sellers from different countries and collect a commission for arranging sales. Export houses and export merchants purchase products from different companies and then sell them abroad. They are specialists at understanding foreign customers' needs. Using exporting intermediaries involves limited risk because no direct investment in the foreign country is required.

Even supposedly "recession-proof" industries suffered during the 2008–2009 recession. U.S. department stores cut back on orders from high-end fashion designers in anticipation of slumping demand from their wealthy consumers. In order to make up for these slumping sales in the United States, many fashion houses sought to increase sales through international retailers. Oscar de la Renta, for example, has seen foreign buyer presence at his runway shows increase by 500 percent over pre-2008 numbers. Some designers like Thakoon and Derek Lam have switched to more conservative cuts and fabrics in order to make their products more appealing to Middle Eastern markets. American designers hope to strengthen their global positions in the long term by being more innovative and flexible than their European counterparts.[63]

importing
The purchase of products from a foreign source

exporting
The sale of products to foreign markets

Marketers sometimes employ a trading company, which links buyers and sellers in different countries but is not involved in manufacturing and does not own assets related to manufacturing. Trading companies buy goods in one country at the lowest price consistent

FIGURE 8.1 Levels of Involvement in Global Marketing

with quality and sell them to buyers in another country. The best-known U.S. trading company is Sears World Trade, which specializes in consumer goods, light industrial items, and processed foods. Trading companies reduce the risk for firms seeking to get involved in international marketing. A trading company provides producers with information about products that meet quality and price expectations in domestic and international markets.

LICENSING AND FRANCHISING

When potential markets are found across national boundaries, and when production, technical assistance, or marketing know-how is required, **licensing** is an alternative to direct investment. The licensee (the owner of the foreign operation) pays commissions or royalties on sales or supplies used in manufacturing. The licensee also may pay an initial down payment or fee when the licensing agreement is signed. Exchanges of management techniques or technical assistance are primary reasons for licensing agreements. For example, Questor Corporation owns the Spalding name but produces not a single golf club or tennis ball itself; all Spalding sporting products are licensed worldwide. Likewise, Yoplait is a French yogurt that is licensed for production in the United States; the Yoplait brand tries to maintain a French image.

licensing
An alternative to direct investment requiring a licensee to pay commissions or royalties on sales or supplies used in manufacturing

Licensing is an attractive alternative to direct investment when the political stability of a foreign country is in doubt or when resources are unavailable for direct investment. Licensing also can be a valuable strategy for enhancing a firm's brand while generating additional revenue.

PepsiCo has licensed many products, including T-shirts, men's and women's apparel, footwear, and accessories, under its well-known name. The company views licensing as a significant tool for building awareness of and extending the Pepsi brand.[64]

Franchising is a form of licensing in which a company (the franchiser) grants a franchisee the right to market its product using its name, logo, methods of operation, advertising, products, and other elements associated with the franchiser's business, in return for a financial commitment and an agreement to conduct business in accordance with the franchiser's standard of operations. This arrangement allows franchisers to minimize the risks of international marketing in four ways: (1) The franchiser does not have to put up a large capital investment; (2) the franchiser's revenue stream is fairly consistent because franchisees pay a fixed fee and royalties; (3) the franchiser retains control of its name and increases global penetration of its product; and (4) franchise agreements ensure a certain standard of behavior from franchisees, which protects the franchise name.[65] KFC, Wendy's, McDonald's, Holiday Inn, and Marriott are well-known franchisers with international visibility.

Franchising
Subway offers an extensive global franchise network.

CONTRACT MANUFACTURING

Contract manufacturing occurs when a company hires a foreign firm to produce a designated volume of the firm's product to specification, and the final product carries the domestic firm's name. Gap Inc., for example, relies on contract manufacturing for some of its apparel, and Reebok uses Korean contract manufacturers to manufacture many of its athletic shoes. Marketing may be handled by the contract manufacturer or by the contracting company.

In recent years, outsourcing has become popular. **Outsourcing** involves contracting manufacturing or other tasks (such as customer-service help lines) to companies in countries where labor and supplies are less expensive. Consider that the majority of all footwear is now produced in China regardless of the brand on the shoe. Services also can be outsourced. Tribune, which owns daily newspapers such as *Newsday* and *The Chicago Tribune,* outsourced its customer-service operations to a firm in the Philippines in an effort to improve efficiency and boost customer service at the newspaper chain.[66] Outsourcing has been controversial, however, in large part owing to the number of U.S. jobs that have been lost.

Outsourcing became a volatile issue for aerospace giant Boeing Company. Almost 27,000 machinists walked off their job in September 2008 over disputes regarding their contracts and fears about job security. At the heart of the matter were questions over whether the company should shed unionized workers in order to remain more flexible, and hopefully remain more competitive. Boeing had been utilizing foreign contractors for most of the manufacture and assembly of their 787 Dreamliner, with final assembly done in the United States. However, foreign suppliers fell behind in production, resulting in an order backlog of over a year. Striking American workers argued that the holdup never would have occurred if they had been in charge of production, but Boeing reserves the right to use foreign contractors when it deems it economically beneficial to the company.[67]

franchising
A form of licensing in which a franchiser, in exchange for a financial commitment, grants a franchisee the right to market its product in accordance with the franchiser's standards

contract manufacturing
The practice of hiring a foreign firm to produce a designated volume of product to specification

outsourcing
The practice of contracting manufacturing or other tasks to companies in countries where labor and supplies are less expensive

JOINT VENTURES

In international marketing, a **joint venture** is a partnership between a domestic firm and a foreign firm or government. Joint ventures are especially popular in industries that call for large investments, such as natural resources extraction or automobile manufacturing. Control of the joint venture may be split equally, or one party may control decision making. Joint

joint venture
A partnership between a domestic firm and a foreign firm or government

ventures are often a political necessity because of nationalism and government restrictions on foreign ownership.

In developed nations, multinational firms dominate with high-tech products or by having strong research and development divisions. In emerging markets, on the other hand, local companies can win with low-cost manufacturing and distribution. By developing partnerships or joint ventures, local companies can take advantage of core competencies and use their knowledge of local markets to gain a competitive advantage. In China, multinationals hold the lead in brand-intensive businesses; local companies hold the advantage where distribution and production are important.[68] Joint ventures also provide legitimacy in the eyes of the host country's citizens. Local partners have firsthand knowledge of the economic and sociopolitical environment and of distribution networks, and they may have privileged access to local resources (raw materials, labor management, and so on). Entrepreneurs in many less developed countries actively seek associations with a foreign partner as a ready means of implementing their own corporate strategy.

Joint ventures are assuming greater global importance because of cost advantages and the number of inexperienced firms entering foreign markets. They may be the result of a tradeoff between a firm's desire for completely unambiguous control of an enterprise and its quest for additional resources. They may occur when acquisition or internal development is not feasible or when the risks and constraints leave no other alternative. As project sizes increase in the face of global competition and firms attempt to spread the huge costs of technological innovation, the impetus to form joint ventures is stronger.[69]

Strategic alliances, the newest form of international business structure, are partnerships formed to create competitive advantage on a worldwide basis. They are very similar to joint ventures. What distinguishes international strategic alliances from other business structures is that partners in the alliance may have been traditional rivals competing for market share in the same product class. One such collaboration is the Sky Team Alliance—involving Northwest Airlines, KLM, Aeromexico, Air France, Alitalia, Continental Airlines, CSA Czech Airlines, Delta Air Lines, and Korean Air—which is designed to improve customer service among the nine firms. Another example of such an alliance is New United Motor Manufacturing, Inc. (NUMMI), formed by Toyota and General Motors, which today manufactures the popular Toyota Tacoma compact pickup, as well as the Toyota Corolla and Pontiac Vibe. This alliance united the quality engineering of Japanese cars with the marketing expertise and market access of General Motors.[70] After GM's bankruptcy, Toyota's knowledge of fuel-efficient cars may help the American car maker to recover. Partners in international strategic alliances often retain their distinct identities, and each brings a core competency to the union.

DIRECT OWNERSHIP

strategic alliances
Partnerships formed to create a competitive advantage on a worldwide basis

direct ownership
A situation in which a company owns subsidiaries or other facilities overseas

multinational enterprise
Firms that have operations or subsidiaries in many countries

Once a company makes a long-term commitment to marketing in a foreign nation that has a promising political and economic environment, **direct ownership** of a foreign subsidiary or division is a possibility. Most foreign investment covers only manufacturing equipment or personnel because the expense of developing a separate foreign distribution system can be tremendous. The opening of retail stores in China, India, or Mexico can require a staggering financial investment in facilities, research, and management. In order to cut down on some of these high costs, Dell moved its Irish operations to Poland. This move resulted in the loss of half of Dell's Irish workforce, or 1,900 people. Because Dell was the country's second-largest foreign employer, the layoffs were a serious blow to Limerick, Ireland, where Dell operations are based. The relocation to Poland was part of an organization-wide move that began in 2008 to cut $3 billion in costs.[71]

The term **multinational enterprise**, also called *multinational corporation,* refers to firms that have operations or subsidiaries in many countries. Often the parent company is based in one country and carries on production, management, and marketing activities in other

TABLE 8.4 The Ten Largest Global Corporations

Rank Company	Revenues (in millions US$)
1. Royal Dutch Shell	458,361.0
2. Exxon Mobil	442,851.0
3. Walmart Stores	405,607.0
4. BP	367,053.0
5. Chevron	263,159.0
6. Total	234,674.0
7. Conoco-Phillips	230,764.0
8. ING Group	226,577.0
9. Sinopec	207,814.0
10. Toyota Motor	204,352.0

Source: "The 2009 Fortune Global 500," *Fortune*, http://money.cnn.com/magazines/fortune/global500/2009/full_list/ (accessed October 9, 2009).

countries. The firm's subsidiaries may be mostly autonomous so that they can respond to the needs of individual international markets. Table 8.4 lists the ten largest global corporations.

A wholly owned foreign subsidiary may be allowed to operate independently of the parent company to give its management more freedom to adjust to the local environment. Cooperative arrangements are developed to assist in marketing efforts, production, and management. A wholly owned foreign subsidiary may export products to the home country. Some U.S. automobile manufacturers, for example, import cars built by their foreign subsidiaries. A foreign subsidiary offers important tax, tariff, and other operating advantages. One of the greatest advantages is the cross-cultural approach. A subsidiary usually operates under foreign management so that it can develop a local identity. The greatest danger in such an arrangement comes from political uncertainty: A firm may lose its foreign investment.

Customization Versus Globalization of International Marketing Mixes

Like domestic marketers, international marketers create marketing mixes to serve specific target markets. Table 8.5 provides a sample of international issues related to product, distribution, promotion, and price. Traditionally, international marketing strategies have customized marketing mixes according to cultural, regional, and national differences. Many soap and detergent manufacturers, for example, adapt their products to local water conditions, equipment, and washing habits. Ford Motor Company has customized its F-series trucks to accommodate global differences in roads, product use, and economic conditions. The strategy has been quite successful, with millions of Ford trucks sold around the world. Ford's strategy may best be described as *mass customization,* the use of standard platforms with custom applications. This practice dissolves the oxymoron of efficiency of mass production with effectiveness of customization of a product or service.

At the other end of the spectrum, **globalization** of marketing involves developing marketing strategies as though the entire world (or its major regions) were a single entity; a globalized

globalization
The development of marketing strategies that treat the entire world (or its major regions) as a single entity

TABLE 8.5 International Marketing-Mix Issues

Product Placement	Sample International Issues
Product Element	
Core product	Is there a commonality to customers' needs across countries? How will the product be used and in what context?
Product adoption	How is awareness created for the product in various markets? How and where is the product typically bought?
Managing products	How are truly new products managed in specific international markets in relation to existing products or products that have been modified slightly?
Branding	Is the brand widely accepted around the world? Do perceptions of the home country help or hurt the brand perception of the consumer?
Distribution Element	
Marketing intermediaries	What is the role of marketing intermediaries internationally? Where is value created beyond the domestic borders of the firm?
Physical distribution	What is the most efficient movement of products from the home country to the foreign market?
Retail stores	What types of stores are available in the various countries through which to sell the product to consumers?
Retailing strategy	Where do customers typically shop in the targeted countries—downtown, suburbs, or malls?
Promotion Element	
Advertising	Consumers in some countries expect to see firm-specific advertising instead of product-specific advertising. How does this affect advertising?
Public relations	How is public relations used to manage stakeholders' interests internationally? Are the stakeholders' interests different worldwide?
Personal selling	What product types require personal selling internationally? Does it differ from how those products are sold domestically?
Sales promotion	Is coupon usage a widespread activity in the targeted international markets? What other forms of sales promotion should be used?
Pricing Element	
Core price	Is price a critical component of the value equation of the product in the targeted country markets?
Analysis of demand	Is international demand similar to domestic demand? Will a change in price drastically change demand?
Demand, cost, and profit relationships	What are the costs when marketing the product internationally? Are they similar to the domestic setting?
Determination of price	How do the pricing strategy, environmental forces, business practices, and cultural values affect price?

firm approaches the world market with as much standardization in the marketing strategy as possible. Nike and Adidas shoes, for example, are standardized worldwide. Other examples of globalized products include electronic communications equipment, American clothing, movies, soft drinks, rock and alternative music CDs, cosmetics, and toothpaste. Sony televisions, Starbucks coffee, Levi jeans, and American cigarette brands post year-to-year gains in the

© PRNEWSFOTO/PEPSI-COLA COMPANY

Globalization
Although offering some modifications in packaging, PepsiCo treats the world as one market.

world market. Today, technological advancement, particularly with regard to computers and telecommunications, has the potential to facilitate globalization.[72]

For many years, organizations have attempted to globalize their marketing mixes as much as possible by employing standardized products, promotion campaigns, prices, and distribution channels for all markets. The economic and competitive payoffs for globalized marketing strategies are certainly great. Brand name, product characteristics, packaging, and labeling are among the easiest marketing-mix variables to standardize; media allocation, retail outlets, and price may be more difficult. In the end, the degree of similarity among the various environmental and market conditions determines the feasibility and degree of globalization. A successful globalization strategy often depends on the extent to which a firm can implement the idea of "think globally, act locally."[73] Even takeout food lends itself to globalization: McDonald's, KFC, and Taco Bell restaurants seem to satisfy hungry customers in every hemisphere, although menus are customized to some degree to satisfy local tastes.

International marketing demands some strategic planning if a firm is to incorporate foreign sales into its overall marketing strategy. Although globalization has been viewed as a mechanism for world economic development, advances may be challenging if marketers ignore unique nation-specific factors.[74] International marketing activities often require customized marketing mixes to achieve the firm's goals. Globalization requires a total commitment to the world, regions, or multinational areas as an integral part of the firm's markets; world or regional markets become as important as domestic ones. Regardless of the extent to which a firm chooses to globalize its marketing strategy, extensive environmental analysis and marketing research are necessary to understand the needs and desires of the target market(s) and successfully implement the chosen marketing strategy. A global presence does not automatically result in a global competitive advantage. However, a global presence generates five opportunities for creating value: (1) to adapt to local market differences, (2) to exploit economies of global scale, (3) to exploit economies of global scope, (4) to mine optimal locations for activities and resources, and (5) to maximize the transfer of knowledge across locations.[75] To exploit these opportunities, marketers need to conduct marketing research.

CHAPTER REVIEW

OBJECTIVES

1 Understand the nature of global markets and international marketing.

International marketing involves developing and performing marketing activities across national boundaries. International markets can provide tremendous opportunities for growth.

2 Analyze the environmental forces affecting international marketing efforts.

Environmental aspects of special importance include sociocultural; economic; political, legal, and regulatory; social and ethical; competitive; and technological forces. Because marketing activities are primarily social in purpose, they are influenced by beliefs and values regarding family, religion, education, health, and recreation. Cultural differences may affect decision-making behavior, product adoption, and product use. Gross domestic product (GDP) and GDP per capita are common measures of a nation's economic standing. Political and legal forces include a nation's political and ethics systems, laws, regulatory bodies, special-interest groups, and courts. Significant trade barriers include import tariffs, quotas, embargoes, and exchange controls. In the area of ethics, cultural relativism is the concept that morality varies from one culture to another and that business practices are therefore differentially defined as right or wrong by particular cultures. In addition to considering the types of competition and the types of competitive structures that exist in other countries, marketers also need to consider the competitive forces at work and recognize the importance of the global customer who is well informed about product choices from around the world. Advances in technology have greatly facilitated international marketing.

3 Identify several important regional trade alliances, markets, and agreements.

Various regional trade alliances and specific markets, such as the North American Free Trade Agreement, the European Union, the Common Market of the Southern Cone, Asia-Pacific Economic Cooperation, the General Agreement on Tariffs and Trade, and the World Trade Organization, create both opportunities and constraints for companies engaged in international marketing.

4 Examine modes of entering international markets.

Importing (the purchase of products from a foreign source) and exporting (the sale of products to foreign markets) are the easiest and most flexible methods of entering international markets. Licensing and franchising are arrangements whereby one firm pays fees to another for the use of its name, expertise, and supplies. Contract manufacturing occurs when a company hires a foreign firm to produce a designated volume of the firm's product to specification, and the final product carries the domestic firm's name. Joint ventures are partnerships between a domestic firm and a foreign firm or a government; strategic alliances are partnerships formed to create competitive advantage on a worldwide basis. A firm also can establish its own marketing or production facilities overseas. When companies have direct ownership of facilities in many countries, they may be considered multinational enterprises.

5 Recognize that international marketing strategies fall along a continuum from customization to globalization.

Although most firms adjust their marketing mixes for differences in target markets, some firms standardize their marketing efforts worldwide. Traditional full-scale international marketing involvement is based on products customized according to cultural, regional, and national differences. Globalization, however, involves developing marketing strategies as if the entire world (or regions of it) were a single entity; a globalized firm markets standardized products in the same way everywhere. International marketing demands some strategic planning if a firm is to incorporate foreign sales into its overall marketing strategy.

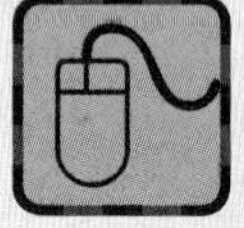

Please visit the student website at www.cengage.com/international for quizzes and games that will help you prepare for exams and help achieve the grade you want.

KEY CONCEPTS

international marketing
gross domestic product (GDP)
import tariff
quota
embargo
exchange controls
balance of trade
cultural relativism
North American Free Trade Agreement (NAFTA)
European Union (EU)
Common Market of the Southern Cone (MERCOSUR)
Asia-Pacific Economic Cooperation (APEC)
World Trade Organization (WTO)
General Agreement on Tariffs and Trade (GATT)
dumping
importing
exporting
licensing
franchising
contract manufacturing
outsourcing
joint venture
strategic alliances
direct ownership
multinational enterprise
globalization

ISSUES FOR DISCUSSION AND REVIEW

1. How does international marketing differ from domestic marketing?
2. What factors must marketers consider as they decide whether to become involved in international marketing?
3. Why do you think this chapter focuses on an analysis of the international marketing environment?
4. A manufacturer recently exported peanut butter with a green label to a nation in Asia. The product failed because it was associated with jungle sickness. How could this mistake have been avoided?
5. If you were asked to provide a small tip (or bribe) to have a document approved in a foreign nation where this practice is customary, what would you do?
6. How will NAFTA affect marketing opportunities for U.S. products in North America (the United States, Mexico, and Canada)?
7. In marketing dog food to Latin America, what aspects of the marketing mix would a U.S. firm need to alter?
8. What should marketers consider as they decide whether to license or enter into a joint venture in a foreign nation?
9. Discuss the impact of strategic alliances on marketing strategies.
10. Contrast globalization with customization of marketing mixes. Is one practice better than the other? Explain.

MARKETING APPLICATIONS

1. Which environmental forces (sociocultural, economic, political/legal/regulatory, social/ethical, competitive, or technological) might a marketer need to consider when marketing the following products in the international marketplace, and why?
   a. Barbie dolls
   b. Beer
   c. Financial services
   d. Televisions
2. Which would be the best organizational approach to international marketing of the following products, and why?
   a. Construction equipment manufacturing
   b. Cosmetics
   c. Automobiles

3. Describe how a shoe manufacturer would go from domestic marketing, to limited exporting, to international marketing, and finally to globalization of marketing. Give examples of some activities that might be involved in this process.

ONLINE EXERCISE

4. Founded in 1910 as Florists' Telegraph Delivery, FTD was the first company to offer a "flowers-by-wire" service. FTD does not itself deliver flowers but depends on local florists to provide this service. In 1994, FTD expanded its toll-free telephone-ordering service by establishing a website. Visit the site at http://www.ftd.com.
   a. Click on "International Shipping." Select a country to which you would like to send flowers. Summarize the delivery and pricing information that would apply to that country.
   b. Determine the cost of sending fresh-cut seasonal flowers to Germany.
   c. What are the benefits of this global distribution system for sending flowers worldwide? What other consumer products could be distributed globally through the Internet?

DEVELOPING YOUR MARKETING PLAN

When formulating marketing strategy, one of the issues a company must consider is whether or not to pursue international markets. While international markets present increased marketing opportunities, they also require more complex decisions when formulating marketing plans. To assist you in relating the information in this chapter to the development of your marketing plan, focus on the following:

1. Review the environmental analysis that was completed in Chapter 3. Extend the analysis for each of the seven factors to include global markets.
2. Using Figure 8.1 as a guide, determine the degree of international involvement that is appropriate for your product and your company.
3. Discuss the concepts of customization and globalization for your product when moving to international markets. Refer to Table 8.5 for guidance in your discussion.

The information obtained from these questions should assist you in developing various aspects of your marketing plan found in the *Interactive Marketing Plan* exercise.

VIDEO CASE 8

Lonely Planet Provides Guidance to Global Explorers

Lonely Planet has been global since before it was even a company—in its audience, its scope, and its foundation. The now ubiquitous guidebook brand got its start in 1973 when Brit Tony Wheeler and his wife, Maureen, holed up in Australia to write a pamphlet on their experiences traveling in Asia. The couple had met in their native Britain, found that they shared a love of adventure, and gotten married soon thereafter. For their honeymoon they chose to make a trip that no one at the time believed was possible—a journey from Britain across Europe and Asia via land all the way to Australia. They made it, but were stuck in Australia with 27 cents between the two of them. Tony made the best of the situation by writing the 94-page *Across Asia on the Cheap,* which sold 8,500 copies. From this suitably adventurous start, Lonely Planet ballooned into one of the powerhouses of the growing guidebook and phrasebook industry, with around 500 titles on 118 countries. Lonely Planet now represents one quarter of all English-language guidebooks sold in the world and has annual revenues in excess of $75 million.

The company has offices in London and Oakland, with its headquarters in Melbourne. It employs 500 office staff and around 300 on-the-road contributors. Thanks to these contributors from dozens of different countries, the company has a global scope and a global perspective, which helps the company successfully market worldwide. The huge diversity of languages, cultures, and interests across their consumer base makes marketing and developing a coherent brand image difficult. To cope with these hurdles, Lonely Planet works on maintaining a balance between consistency in branding and customizing marketing to suit specific target markets.

In 2007, the Wheelers finally relinquished control of the company when they sold it to BBC Worldwide, which is the commercial branch of the British Broadcasting Company. The addition of the BBC's extensive network of distribution channels has helped Lonely Planet to market itself more successfully, and to branch into complementary business areas such as Lonely Planet Images, Lonely Planet Television, Lonely Planet Foreign Rights Team, Lonely Planet Business Solutions unit, and Lonely Planet Foundation (which contributes 5% of all profits to international charities and has established a carbon offset program for printing and the travels of all employees). From the start, one of the fundamental tenets of the Lonely Planet brand has been that travel can truly change the world and make it a better place. Through the Lonely Planet Foundation, the Wheelers have tried to make profound differences in the places they visit. Their far-reaching message is being heard loud and clear as evidenced by the 4.3 million unique visitors clicking on lonelyplanet.com each month.

This marketing strategy of selective customization combined with relentless fact checking and updating, and a focus on hiring the best and most knowledgeable travel writers, has earned Lonely Planet a reputation for quality. Lonely Planet books are not only popular; they are considered by many to be the definitive guidebooks. In fact, Jay Garner, the first American administrator in Iraq, considers Lonely Planet such an authority on global travel that he used the book *Lonely Planet Iraq* to develop a list of historical sites worth saving. Another nod to the success of the brand is the fact that in Asia, imitation Lonely Planet guidebooks are now sold alongside imitation Gucci and Chanel handbags and Rolex watches.

No matter what criticisms people may have of Lonely Planet, this single guidebook brand has been responsible for the soaring popularity of adventure tourism worldwide. Because of Lonely Planet, there are surf camps in El Salvador, foreign-owned luxury resorts in Nicaragua, and remote villages in the heights of the Himalayas with economies based around tourism—monuments to the success of their marketing strategy.

Lonely Planet continues its trek toward boundless success, due largely to the organization's clear vision of its target market. The Lonely Planet traveler is willing to embrace foreign food and culture, but still wants to do it comfortably and cheaply, if possible. The company reaches its market through smart marketing and promotion strategies that balance a recognizable brand with customization to accommodate local tastes. Lonely Planet has never forgotten that there really is no such thing as global—that the world consists of thousands of different local populations. And Lonely Planet, by knowing clearly who comprises its market and by smart marketing strategies, has grown from a pamphlet written in a cheap hostel to a huge global brand loved by millions of travelers the world over.

QUESTIONS FOR DISCUSSION

1. Why is Lonely Planet a global success?
2. How has Lonely Planet been able to provide and market guidebooks that are useful across languages and cultures?
3. How could Lonely Planet guidebooks help marketers to develop effective marketing strategies in targeted foreign markets?

Tad Friend, "The Parachute Artist," *The New Yorker,* April 18, 2005, p. 78–91; Jenny Allen, Chris Charleton, and Ali Jeremy, "BBC Worldwide Acquires Lonely Planet," *BBC.com,* October 1, 2007, http://www.bbc.co.uk/pressoffice/bbcworldwide/worldwidestories/pressreleases/2007/10_october/lonely_planet.shtml (accessed October 27, 2009).

Product Decisions

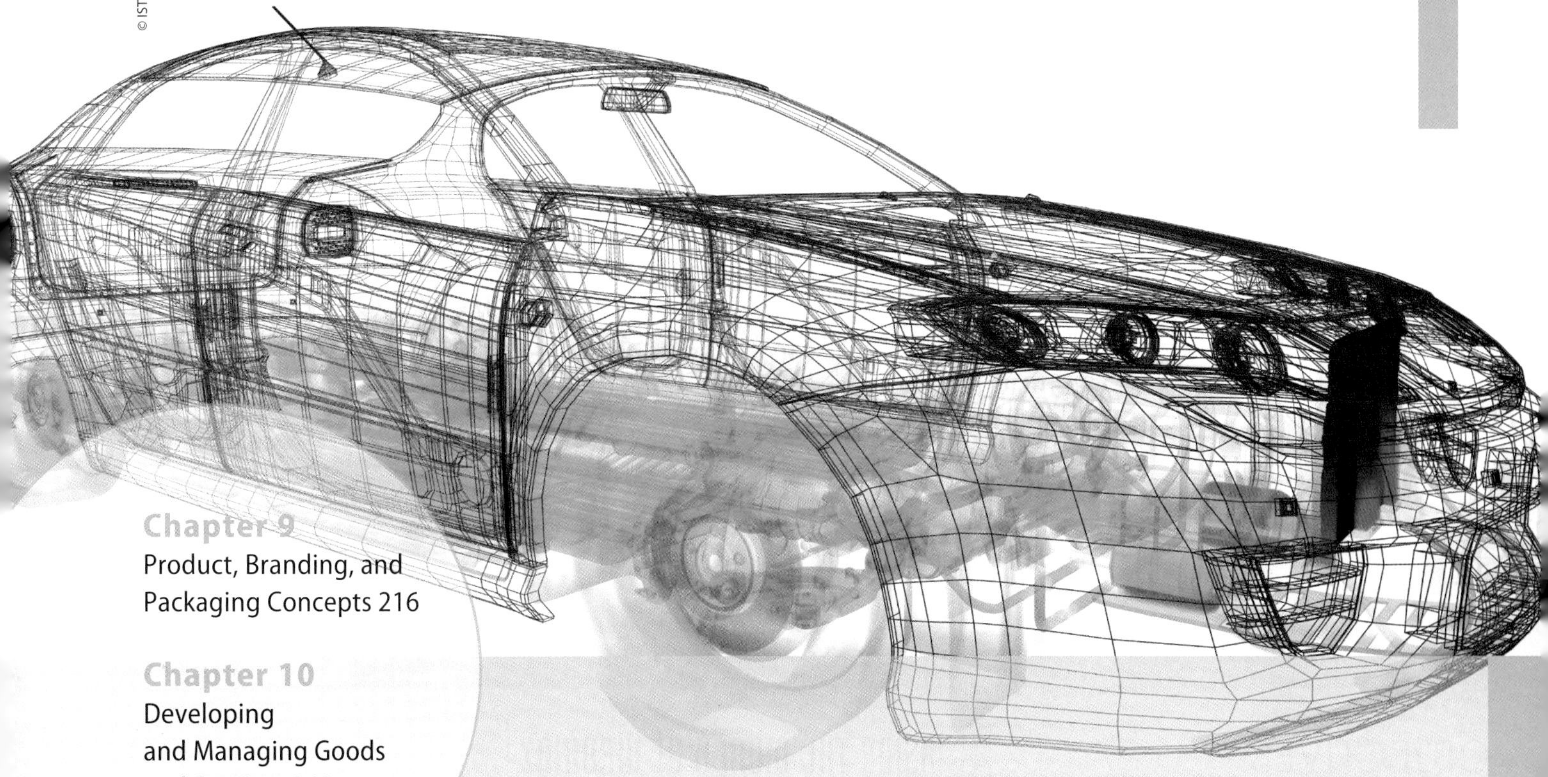

4

We are now prepared to analyze the decisions and activities associated with developing and maintaining effective marketing mixes. In Parts 4 through 7, we focus on the major components of the marketing mix: product, pricing, distribution, and promotion. Part 4 explores the product ingredient of the marketing mix. Chapter 9 focuses on basic product concepts and on branding and packaging decisions. Chapter 10 analyzes various dimensions regarding product management, including line extensions and product modification, new-product development, product deletions, and the management of services as products.

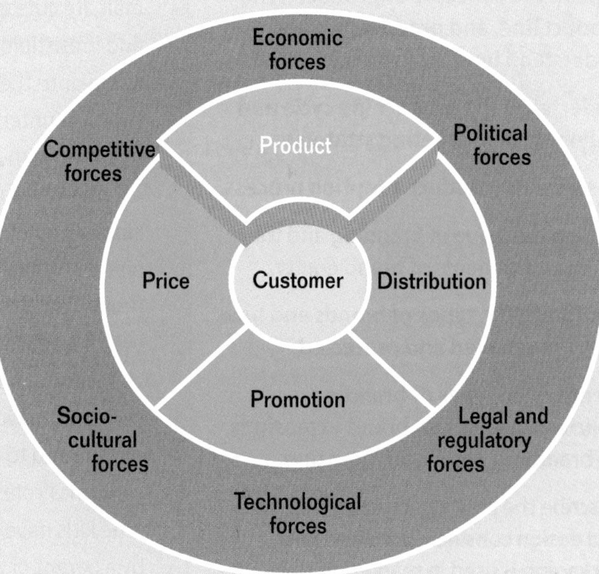

CHAPTER 9 Product, Branding, and Packaging Concepts

© 2008 SUZANNA SMITH

OBJECTIVES:

1. Understand the concept of a product and how products are classified.
2. Explain the concepts of product item, product line, and product mix, and understand how they are connected.
3. Understand the product life cycle and its impact on marketing strategies.
4. Describe the product adoption process.
5. Explain the value of branding and the major components of brand equity.
6. Recognize the types of brands and how they are selected and protected.
7. Identify two types of branding policies, and explain brand extensions, co-branding, and brand licensing.
8. Describe the major packaging functions and design considerations and how packaging is used in marketing strategies.
9. Understand the functions of labeling and selected legal issues.

INSIDE THE WORLD OF WEBKINZ

The stuffed toy business is going to the dogs—and cats, cows, and avatars. Just ask Ganz, the company that built Webkinz into a $2 billion brand. The plush animals are cute and cuddly, but they also have an interactive element that children find irresistible. Each Webkinz toy comes with a secret code that allows the owner to log onto the Webkinz World site, adopt and name the animal, then play with its virtual counterpart. Owners can make online playdates with friends' Webkinz and text-chat with other owners (with parents' consent).

The initial purchase price buys a year's access to Webkinz World plus 2,000 KinzCash for buying virtual extras like pet toys. Ganz wants Webkinz owners to visit often, so it awards KinzCash for entering contests or answering trivia questions. In all, nearly 3 million users log onto Webkinz World every month. After the first year, however, the only way to gain entry is to get a new secret code by buying another Webkinz.

Without advertising, how did Webkinz get launched? "Most of our success comes from word of mouth," says a Ganz spokesperson. "We say it spreads from playground to playground." Word of mouth makes Webkinz especially appealing, confirms Professor LIsa Bolton of Wharton School at University of Pennsylvania: "The kids have discovered it for themselves; they haven't had it pushed on them by a parent or a marketer."

The popularity of Webkinz has prompted competitors to add interactivity to some of their products. For example, buyers of Mattel's Barbie Girls MP3 Player get a code for free entry into http://www.BarbieGirls.com. Each of Hasbro's Littlest

Pet Shop plush pets comes with a password for a special play site. And Disney's Pixie Hollow jewelry products include codes for entering a virtual world of avatars, dress-up, and make-believe. Can Webkinz stay ahead by taking interactive toys to new heights?[1]

Products are an important variable in the marketing mix. The mix of products offered by a company like Ganz, the maker of Webkinz, can be a firm's most important competitive tool. If a company's products do not meet customers' desires and needs, the company will fail unless it makes adjustments. Developing successful products like Dell personal computers requires knowledge of fundamental product concepts.

In this chapter, we first define a product and discuss how products are classified. Next, we examine the concepts of product line and product mix. We then explore the stages of the product life cycle and the effect of each life cycle stage on marketing strategies. Next, we outline the product adoption process. Then we discuss branding, its value to customers and marketers, brand loyalty, and brand equity. Next, we examine the various types of brands. We then consider how companies choose and protect brands, the various branding policies employed, brand extensions, co-branding, and brand licensing. We look at the critical role packaging plays as part of the product. We then explore the functions of packaging, issues to consider in packaging design, and how the package can be a major element in marketing strategy. We conclude with a discussion of labeling.

What Is a Product?

As defined in Chapter 1, a *product* is a good, a service, or an idea received in an exchange. It can be either tangible or intangible and includes functional, social, and psychological utilities or benefits. It also includes supporting services, such as installation, guarantees, product information, and promises of repair or maintenance. Thus the four-year/50,000-mile warranty that covers some new automobiles is part of the product itself. A **good** is a tangible physical entity, such as a Dell personal computer or a Big Mac. A **service**, in contrast, is intangible; it is the result of the application of human and mechanical efforts to people or objects. Examples of services include a concert performance by Beyoncé, online travel agencies, medical examinations, child day care, real estate services, and martial arts lessons. An **idea** is a concept, philosophy, image, or issue. Ideas provide the psychological stimulation that aids in solving problems or adjusting to the environment. For example, Mothers Against Drunk Driving (MADD) promotes safe consumption of alcohol and stricter enforcement of laws against drunk driving.

good
A tangible physical entity

service
An intangible result of the application of human and mechanical efforts to people or objects

idea
A concept, philosophy, image, or issue

It is helpful to think of a total product offering as having three interdependent elements: the core product itself, its supplemental features, and its symbolic or experiential benefits (see Figure 9.1). Consider that some people buy new tires for their basic utility (e.g., Sears' Guardsman III), whereas some look for safety (e.g., Michelin), and others buy on the basis of brand name or exemplary performance (e.g., Pirelli). The core product consists of a product's fundamental utility or main benefit and usually addresses a fundamental need of the consumer. Broadband Internet services, for instance, offer speedy Internet access, but some buyers want additional features, such as wireless connectivity anywhere they go. Supplemental features provide added value or attributes in addition to the core utility or benefit. Supplemental products also can provide installation, delivery, training, and financing. These supplemental attributes are not required to make the core product function effectively, but they help to differentiate one product brand from another. BLOCKBUSTER Online, for example, offers an extra feature—it lets subscribers exchange rented DVDs at its stores regardless of how they received them; rival Netflix customers must return their rentals by mail and wait several days to receive the next DVD in their queue.[2] Finally, customers also receive benefits based on their experiences with the product. In addition, many products have symbolic meaning for buyers. For some consumers, the simple act of shopping gives symbolic value and improves their attitudes. Some stores capitalize on this value by striving to create a special experience for customers. For example, you can buy stuffed toys at many retailers, but at Build-a-Bear you can choose the type of animal, stuff it yourself, give it a heart, create a name complete with a birth certificate, give the toy a bath, and clothe and accessorize it. The atmosphere and decor of a retail store, the variety and depth of product choices, the customer support, and even the sounds and smells all contribute to the experiential element.

When buyers purchase a product, they are really buying the benefits and satisfaction they think the product will provide. A Rolex watch, for example, is often purchased to make a statement of success, not just for telling time. Services in particular are purchased on the basis of expectations. Expectations, suggested by images, promises, and symbols, as well as processes and delivery, help consumers to make judgments about tangible and intangible products. Products are formed by the activities and processes that help to satisfy expectations. For instance, Starbucks did not originate the coffee shop, but it did make high-quality coffee

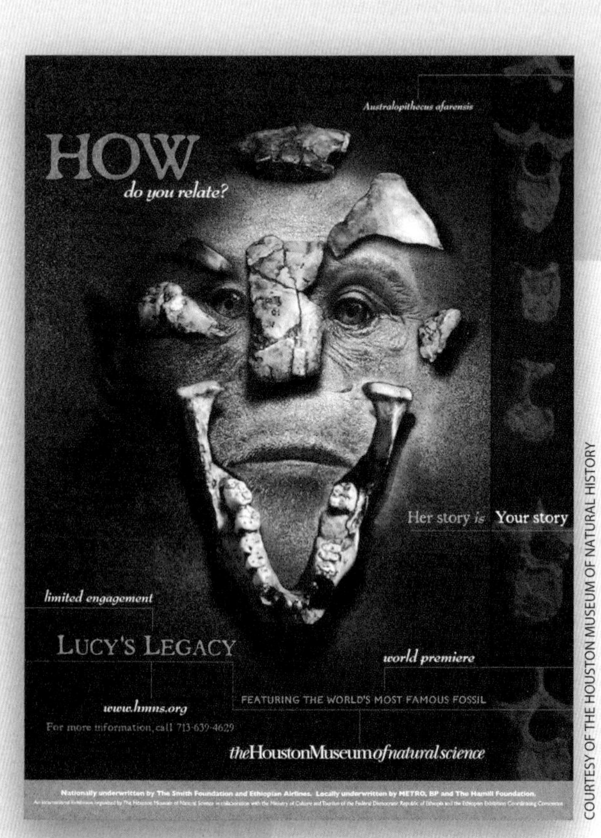

COURTESY OF THE HOUSTON MUSEUM OF NATURAL HISTORY

What Is a Product?
A product is a good, a service, an idea, or a combination of these. The Houston Museum of Natural Science provides a service.

FIGURE 9.1 The Total Product

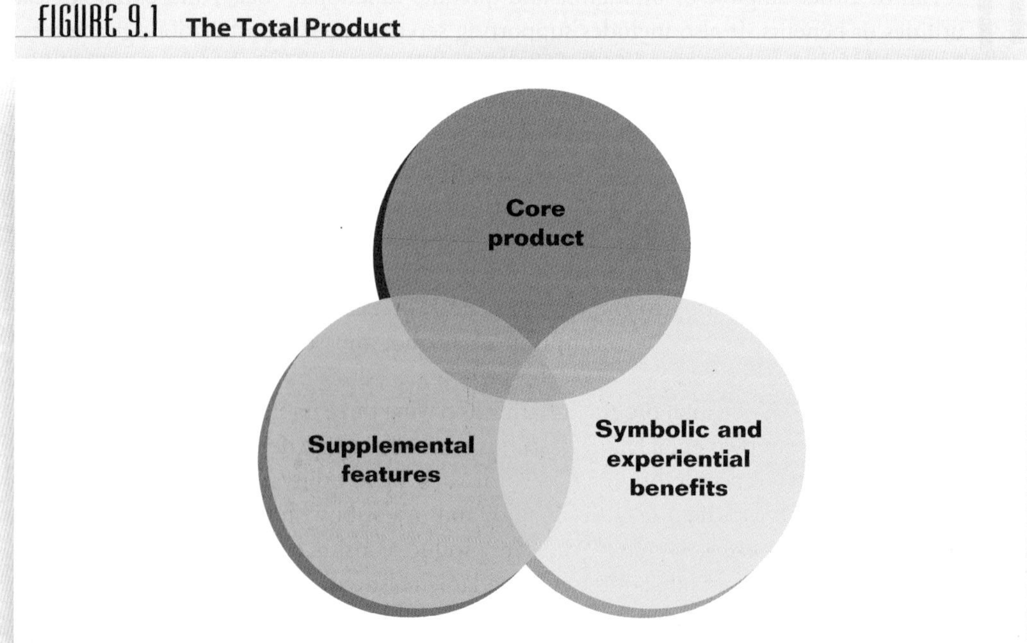

beverages rzadily available around the world with standardized service and in stylish, inviting stores. Often symbols and cues are used to make intangible products more tangible, or real, to the consumer. Allstate Insurance Company, for example, uses giant hands to symbolize security, strength, and friendliness.

Entrepreneurial Marketing

This Is Not Your Grandmother's Circus!

When Guy Laliberté founded Cirque du Soleil in 1984, his goal was to reinvent the circus. Starting with a handful of street performers, today he employs thousands of performers, choreographers, artists, trainers, and planners who concurrently stage 19 distinctly different shows each year. Cirque's scouts travel the world searching for talent to fill the roles for each show. Cast members receive months of training to fine-tune every aspect of their performance before taking the stage.

Meanwhile, Cirque's marketing experts consider the image they want to project as they plan their marketing mix, including print ads and merchandise. These tangible elements help convey Cirque's innovative approach to the circus concept and hint at the memorable experiences that await audience members at every performance.[a]

Classifying Products

Products fall into one of two general categories. Products purchased to satisfy personal and family needs are **consumer products**. Those bought to use in a firm's operations, to resell, or to make other products are **business products**. Consumers buy products to satisfy their personal wants, whereas business buyers seek to satisfy the goals of their organizations. Product classifications are important because they may influence pricing, distribution, and promotion decisions. In this section we examine the characteristics of consumer and business products and explore the marketing activities associated with some of these products.

CONSUMER PRODUCTS

The most widely accepted approach to classifying consumer products is based on characteristics of consumer buying behavior. It divides products into four categories: convenience, shopping, specialty, and unsought products. However, not all buyers behave in the same way when purchasing a specific type of product. Thus a single product can fit into several categories. To minimize this problem, marketers think in terms of how buyers *generally* behave when purchasing a specific item. Examining the four traditional categories of consumer products can provide further insight.

Convenience Products

Convenience products are relatively inexpensive, frequently purchased items for which buyers exert only minimal purchasing effort. They range from bread, soft drinks, and chewing gum to gasoline and newspapers. The buyer spends little time planning the purchase or comparing available brands or sellers. Even a buyer who prefers a specific brand will readily choose a substitute if the preferred brand is not conveniently available. A convenience product is normally marketed through many retail outlets, such as 7-Eleven, Exxon Mobil, and Starbucks. Starbucks, for example, has opened locations inside airports, hotels, and grocery stores to ensure that customers can get coffee whenever or wherever the desire strikes. Because sellers experience high inventory turnover, per-unit gross margins can be relatively low. Producers of convenience products, such as Altoid mints, expect little promotional effort at the retail level and thus must provide it themselves with advertising and sales promotion. Packaging is also important because many convenience items are available only on a self-service basis at the retail level, and thus the package plays a major role in selling the product.

Shopping Products

Shopping products are items for which buyers are willing to expend considerable effort in planning and making the purchase. Buyers spend much time comparing stores and brands with

consumer products Products purchased to satisfy personal and family needs

business products Products bought to use in an organization's operations, to resell, or to make other products

convenience products Relatively inexpensive, frequently purchased items for which buyers exert minimal purchasing effort

shopping products Items for which buyers are willing to expend considerable effort in planning and making purchases

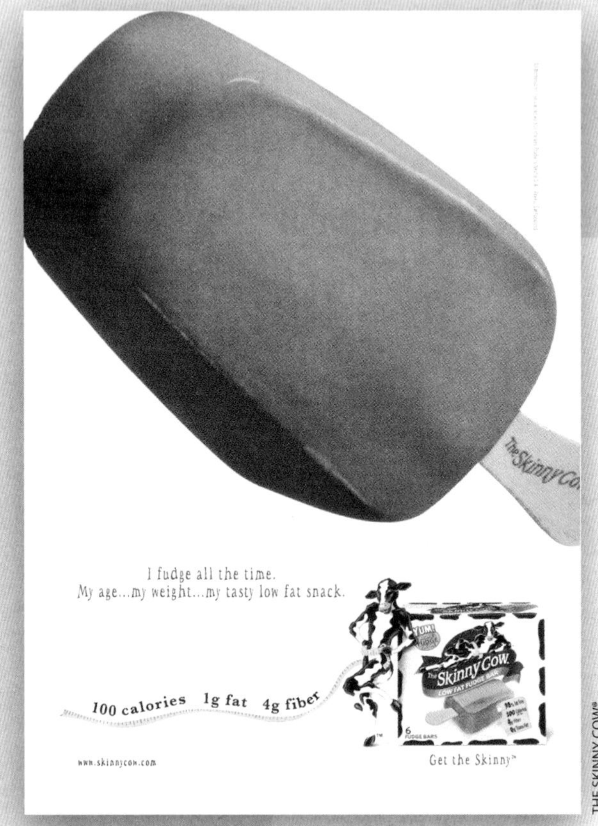

Convenience Product and Shopping Product
An ice cream bar is a convenience product. Hotels are shopping products.

respect to prices, product features, qualities, services, and perhaps warranties. Department stores such as Macy's carry shopping products and often are found in the same shopping centers with competitors so that consumers can shop and compare products and prices. Appliances, bicycles, furniture, stereos, cameras, and shoes exemplify shopping products. These products are expected to last a fairly long time and thus are purchased less frequently than convenience items. Even though shopping products are more expensive than convenience products, few buyers of shopping products are particularly brand-loyal. If they were, they would be unwilling to shop and compare among brands. Shopping products require fewer retail outlets than convenience products. Because shopping products are purchased less frequently, inventory turnover is lower, and marketing channel members expect to receive higher gross margins. In certain situations, both shopping products and convenience products may be marketed in the same location.

specialty products
Items with unique characteristics that buyers are willing to expend considerable effort to obtain

unsought products
Products purchased to solve a sudden problem, products of which customers are unaware, and products that people do not necessarily think about buying

installations
Facilities and nonportable major equipment

Specialty Products

Specialty products possess one or more unique characteristics, and generally buyers are willing to expend considerable effort to obtain them. Buyers actually plan the purchase of a specialty product; they know exactly what they want and will not accept a substitute. Examples of specialty products include a Mont Blanc pen and a one-of-a-kind piece of baseball memorabilia, such as a ball signed by Babe Ruth. When searching for specialty products, buyers do not compare alternatives. They are concerned primarily with finding an outlet that has the preselected product available. Tag Heuer, for example, issued a special Indy 500 watch designed especially for racing fans. Specialty products are often distributed through a limited number of retail outlets. Like shopping products, they are purchased infrequently, causing lower inventory turnover and thus requiring relatively high gross margins.

Unsought Products

Unsought products are products purchased when a sudden problem must be solved, products of which customers are unaware, and products that people do not necessarily think of purchasing. Emergency medical services and automobile repairs are examples of products needed quickly to solve a problem. A consumer who is sick or injured has little time to plan to go to an emergency medical center or hospital. Likewise, in the event of a broken fan belt on the highway, a consumer likely will seek the nearest auto repair facility to get back on the road as quickly as possible. In such cases, speed and problem resolution are far more important than price and other features buyers might normally consider if they had more time for making decisions. Companies such as ServiceMaster, which markets emergency services such as disaster recovery and plumbing repair, are making the purchases of these unsought products more bearable by building trust with consumers through recognizable brands (ServiceMaster Clean and Rescue Rooter) and superior functional performance.

BUSINESS PRODUCTS

Business products are usually purchased on the basis of an organization's goals and objectives. Generally, the functional aspects of the product are more important than the psychological rewards sometimes associated with consumer products. Business products can be classified into seven categories according to their characteristics and intended uses: installations; accessory equipment; raw materials; component parts; process materials; maintenance, repair, and operating (MRO) supplies; and business services.

Installations

Installations include facilities, such as office buildings, factories, and warehouses, and major equipment that are nonportable, such as production lines and very large machines. Normally, installations are expensive and intended to be used for a considerable length of time. Because they are so expensive and typically involve a long-term investment of capital, purchase decisions often are made by high-level management. Marketers of installations frequently must provide a variety of services, including training, repairs, maintenance assistance, and even aid in financing such purchases.

Sustainable Marketing

Digging Deeper into Green Claims

Is a chainsaw "green" when it runs on electricity rather than gasoline? What about a toothpaste that contains natural mint and green tea extract or a paintbrush with a plastic handle? This is a red-hot issue as sales of green products rise and both marketers and consumers try to determine what, exactly, makes a product green.

Consider what happened when Home Depot invited suppliers to nominate green products for special attention in its Eco Options marketing campaign. Suddenly the retailer discovered that of the 176,000 items carried in its stores, suppliers believed more than 60,000 to be worthy of the "green" designation. "In somebody's mind, the products they were selling us were environmentally friendly," remembers Ron Jarvis, the executive in charge of the Eco Options campaign. He adds: "If they say their product makes the sky bluer and the grass greener, that's just not good enough."

© DIGITAL VISION/GETTY IMAGES

After screening the products using standards such as the Environmental Protection Agency's Energy Star designation, Jarvis allowed only 2,500 into the Eco Options program, including items such as solar-powered lawn lights and energy-efficient washing machines. To promote the program, the company gave away 1 million free compact-fluorescent light bulbs and set up a website where customers can read about the products and see their environmental impact.

Shoppers are responding: Within three months, sales of Eco Options products were, on average, 10 percent higher than before the program began. Despite being slightly higher priced than nongreen merchandise, Eco Options items sold very well during the recent economic downturn because customers understood their environmental value. "Customers may pay a little more up front but they see the payoff down the line," Jarvis says.[b]

Business Product
Avantair aircraft are products designed for use by business customers.

REPRINTED WITH PERMISSION OF AVANTAIR®

Accessory Equipment

accessory equipment Equipment that does not become part of the final physical product but is used in production or office activities

Accessory equipment does not become part of the final physical product but is used in production or office activities. Examples include file cabinets, fractional-horsepower motors, calculators, and tools. Compared with major equipment, accessory items usually are much cheaper, purchased routinely with less negotiation, and treated as expense items rather than capital items because they are not expected to last as long. More outlets are required for distributing accessory equipment than for installations, but sellers do not have to provide the multitude of services expected of installations marketers.

Raw Materials

raw materials Basic natural materials that become part of a physical product

Raw materials are the basic natural materials that actually become part of a physical product. They include minerals, chemicals, agricultural products, and materials from forests and oceans. Corn, for example, is a raw material found in many different products, including food, beverages (as corn syrup), and even fuel (ethanol). Indeed, the growing popularity of ethanol as an alternative fuel has caused corn prices to soar.3 Raw materials are usually bought and sold according to grades and specifications and in relatively large quantities.

Component Parts

component parts Items that become part of the physical product and are either finished items ready for assembly or products that need little processing before assembly

Component parts become part of the physical product and are either finished items ready for assembly or products that need little processing before assembly. Although they become part of a larger product, component parts often can be identified and distinguished easily. Spark plugs, tires, clocks, brakes, and switchers are all component parts of an automobile. Buyers purchase such items according to their own specifications or industry standards. They expect the parts to be of specified quality and delivered on time so that production is not slowed or stopped. Producers that are primarily assemblers, such as most lawn mower and computer manufacturers, depend heavily on suppliers of component parts.

Process Materials

process materials Materials that are used directly in the production of other products but are not readily identifiable

MRO supplies Maintenance, repair, and operating items that facilitate production and operations but do not become part of the finished product

Process materials are used directly in the production of other products. Unlike component parts, however, process materials are not readily identifiable. For example, a salad dressing manufacturer includes vinegar in its salad dressing. The vinegar is a process material because it is included in the salad dressing but is not identifiable. As with component parts, process materials are purchased according to industry standards or the purchaser's specifications.

MRO Supplies

MRO supplies are maintenance, repair, and operating items that facilitate production and operations but do not become part of the finished product. Paper, pencils, oils, cleaning agents, and paints are in this category. Although you might be familiar with Tide, Downy, and Febreze as consumer products, to restaurants and hotels, they are MRO supplies needed to wash dishes and launder sheets and towels. Procter & Gamble is increasingly targeting business customers in the $3.2 billion market for janitorial and housekeeping products.[4] MRO supplies are commonly sold through numerous outlets and are purchased routinely. To ensure supplies are available when needed, buyers often deal with more than one seller.

Business Services

Business services are the intangible products that many organizations use in their operations. They include financial, legal, marketing research, information technology, and janitorial services. Firms must decide whether to provide their own services internally or obtain them from outside the organization. This decision depends on the costs associated with each alternative and how frequently the services are needed. For example, few firms have the resources to provide global overnight delivery services efficiently, so most companies rely on FedEx, UPS, DHL, and other service providers.

business services
The intangible products that many organizations use in their operations

product item
A specific version of a product that can be designated as a distinct offering among a firm's products

product line
A group of closely related product items viewed as a unit because of marketing, technical, or end-use considerations

product mix
The total group of products that an organization makes available to customers

width of product mix
The number of product lines a company offers

depth of product mix
The average number of different product items offered in each product line

Product Line and Product Mix

Marketers must understand the relationships among all the products of their organization to coordinate the marketing of the total group of products. The following concepts help to describe the relationships among an organization's products. A **product item** is a specific version of a product that can be designated as a distinct offering among an organization's products. A Gillette M3 Power Nitro razor represents a product item. A **product line** is a group of closely related product items that are considered to be a unit because of marketing, technical, or end-use considerations. For example, Reebok launched a new line of athletic shoes that have the fruity aroma of Kool-Aid flavors. The first shoes in the line, which get their smell from scent-infused sock liners, come in grape, cherry, and strawberry "flavors."5 The exact boundaries of a product line (although sometimes blurred) are usually indicated by using descriptive terms such as frozen dessert product line or shampoo product line. To develop the optimal product line, marketers must understand buyers' goals. Specific product items in a product line usually reflect the desires of different target markets or the different needs of consumers.

A **product mix** is the composite, or total, group of products that an organization makes available to customers. For example, all the health care, beauty care, laundry and cleaning, food and beverage, paper, cosmetic, and fragrance products that Procter & Gamble manufactures constitute its product mix. The **width of product mix** is measured by the number of product lines a company offers. The **depth of product mix** is the average number of different product items offered in each product line. Figure 9.2 shows the width and depth of part of Procter & Gamble's product mix.

IMAGE COURTESY OF THE ADVERTISING ARCHIVES

Product Lines
Burberry produces several product lines, including shoes, purses, sunglasses, watches, and apparel.

FIGURE 9.2 **The Concepts of Product Mix Width and Depth Applied to Selected U.S. Procter & Gamble Products**

Laundry detergents	Toothpastes	Bar soaps	Deodorants	Shampoos	Tissue/Towel
Ivory Snow 1930	Gleem 1952	Ivory 1879	Old Spice 1948	Pantene 1947	Charmin 1928
Dreft 1933	Crest 1955	Camay 1926	Secret 1956	Head & Shoulders 1961	Puffs 1960
Tide 1946		Zest 1952	Sure 1972	Vidal Sassoon 1974	Bounty 1965
Cheer 1950		Safeguard 1963		Pert Plus 1979	
Bold 1965		Oil of Olay 1993		Ivory 1983	
Gain 1966				Infusium 23 1986	
Era 1972				Physique 2000	
Febreze Clean Wash 2000				Herbal Essence 2001	

Depth

Width

Product Life Cycles and Marketing Strategies

Just as biological cycles progress from birth through growth and decline, so do product life cycles. As Figure 9.3 shows, a **product life cycle** has four major stages: introduction, growth, maturity, and decline. As a product moves through its cycle, the strategies relating to competition, pricing, distribution, promotion, and market information must be evaluated periodically and possibly changed. Astute marketing managers use the life cycle concept to make sure that the introduction, alteration, and deletion of a product are timed and executed properly. By understanding the typical life cycle pattern, marketers can maintain profitable product mixes.

product life cycle
The progression of a product through four stages: introduction, growth, maturity, and decline

introduction stage
The initial stage of a product's life cycle—its first appearance in the marketplace—when sales start at zero and profits are negative

INTRODUCTION

The **introduction stage** of the product life cycle begins at a product's first appearance in the marketplace, when sales start at zero and profits are negative. Profits are below zero because initial revenues are low, and the company generally must cover large expenses for product development, promotion, and distribution. Notice in Figure 9.3 how sales should move upward from zero, and profits also should move upward from a position in which they are negative because of high expenses.

Potential buyers must be made aware of new-product features, uses, and advantages. Efforts to highlight a new product's value can create a foundation for building brand loyalty and customer relationships.[6] Two difficulties may arise at this point. First, sellers may lack the resources, technological knowledge, and marketing know-how to launch the product successfully. Entrepreneurs without large budgets still can attract attention, however, by giving away free samples, as Essence of Vali does with its aromatherapy products. Another technique is to gain visibility through media appearances. Second, the initial product price may have to be high to recoup expensive marketing research or development costs. Given these difficulties, it is not surprising that many products never get beyond the introduction stage.

FIGURE 9.3 The Four Stages of the Product Life Cycle

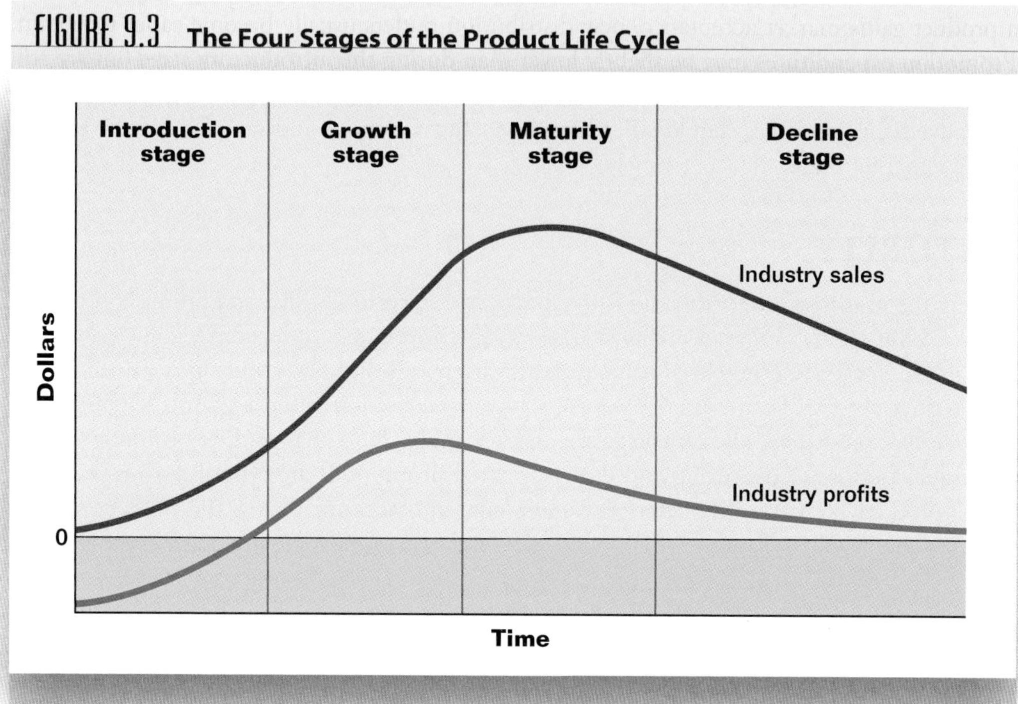

Most new products start off slowly and seldom generate enough sales to bring immediate profits. As buyers learn about the new product, marketers should be alert for product weaknesses and make corrections quickly to prevent the product's early demise. As the sales curve moves upward, the breakeven point is reached, and as competitors enter the market, the growth stage begins.

GROWTH

During the **growth stage**, sales rise rapidly; profits reach a peak and then start to decline (see Figure 9.3). The growth stage is critical to a product's survival because competitive reactions to the product's success during this period will affect the product's life expectancy. Profits begin to decline late in the growth stage as more competitors enter the market, driving prices down.

As sales increase, management must support the momentum by adjusting the marketing strategy. The goal is to establish and fortify the product's market position by encouraging brand loyalty. To achieve greater market penetration, segmentation may have to be used more intensely. This requires developing product variations to satisfy the needs of people in several different market segments. Apple, for example, introduced variations on its wildly popular iPod MP3 player, including the slimmer, colorful mini, the affordable shuffle, the smaller nano, and the iPod video, with a larger screen for viewing downloaded videos; all these variations helped to expand Apple's market penetration in the competitive MP3 player industry. Marketers also should analyze the competing brands' product positions relative to their own brands and take corrective actions, if needed.

As sales volume increases, efficiencies in production may result in lower costs, thus providing an opportunity for lower prices. For example, when flat-panel televisions were introduced, the price was $5,000 or more. As demand soared, manufacturers of both liquid crystal display (LCD) and plasma technologies were able to take advantage of economies of scale to reduce production costs and lower prices to less than $1,000 within several years. If price cuts are feasible, they can help a brand gain market share and discourage new competitors from entering

growth stage
The stage of a product's life cycle when sales rise rapidly and profits reach a peak and then start to decline

maturity stage
The stage of a product's life cycle when the sales curve peaks and starts to decline as profits continue to fall

the market. Gaps in geographic market coverage should be filled during the growth period. As a product gains market acceptance, new distribution outlets usually become easier to obtain. Promotion expenditures may be slightly lower than during the introductory stage but are still quite substantial. As sales increase, promotion costs should drop as a percentage of total sales. The advertising messages should stress brand benefits. Coupons and samples may be used to increase market share.

MATURITY

During the **maturity stage**, the sales curve peaks and starts to decline, and profits continue to fall (see Figure 9.3). This stage is characterized by intense competition because many brands are now in the market. Competitors emphasize improvements and differences in their versions of the product. As a result, during the maturity stage, weaker competitors are squeezed out of the market. The producers who remain in the market are likely to change their promotional and distribution efforts. Advertising and dealer-oriented promotions are typical during this stage of the product life cycle. Marketers also must take into account that as the product reaches maturity, buyers' knowledge of it attains a high level. Consumers are no longer inexperienced generalists. Instead, they are experienced specialists. Marketers of mature products sometimes expand distribution into global markets. Often the products have to be adapted to fit differing needs of global customers more precisely.

IMAGE COURTESY OF THE ADVERTISING ARCHIVES

Product Life Cycle
Notebook computers are in the maturity stage of the product life cycle.

Because many products are in the maturity stage of their life cycles, marketers must know how to deal with these products and be prepared to adjust their marketing strategies. There are many approaches to altering marketing strategies during the maturity stage. To increase the sales of mature products, marketers may suggest new uses for them. Arm & Hammer has boosted demand for its baking soda by this method.

During the maturity stage, three objectives are sometimes pursued, including generating cash flow, maintaining share of market, and increasing share of customer. Generating cash flow is essential for recouping the initial investment and generating excess cash to support new products. For example, General Motors, after years of declining sales in a mature market, is focused on cash flow to support its global operations. Some firms, such as Coca-Cola, simply strive to maintain their current market shares through aggressive promotions and new-product introductions. Companies with marginal market shares must decide whether they have a reasonable chance to improve their position or whether they should drop out. Companies also can focus on boosting their share of their individual customer's purchases. For example, many banks have added new services (brokerage, financial planning, auto leasing, etc.) to gain more of each customer's financial services business. Likewise, many supermarkets are seeking to increase share of customer by adding services such as restaurants, movie rentals, and dry cleaning to provide one-stop shopping for their customers' household needs.[7]

A greater mixture of pricing strategies is used during the maturity stage. Strong price competition is likely and may ignite price wars. Firms also compete in other ways besides price, such as through product quality or services. In addition, marketers develop price flexibility to differentiate offerings in product lines. Markdowns and price incentives are common. Prices may have to be increased, however, if distribution and production costs rise.

During the maturity stage, marketers go to great lengths to serve dealers and to provide incentives for selling their brands. Maintaining market share during the maturity stage requires moderate, and sometimes large, promotion expenditures. Advertising messages focus on differentiating a brand from the field of competitors, and sales promotion efforts may be aimed at both consumers and resellers.

DECLINE

During the **decline stage**, sales fall rapidly (see Figure 9.3). When this happens, the marketer considers pruning items from the product line to eliminate those not earning a profit. The marketer also may cut promotion efforts, eliminate marginal distributors, and finally, plan to phase out the product. For example, although Procter & Gamble's Sure deodorant had been around for nearly three decades, sharply declining sales led the company to sell the well-known brand to Innovative Brands LLC, which had earlier purchased Procter & Gamble's Pert shampoo brand.[8]

In the decline stage, marketers must determine whether to eliminate the product or try to reposition it to extend its life. Usually a declining product has lost its distinctiveness because similar competing products have been introduced. Competition engenders increased substitution and brand switching as buyers become insensitive to minor product differences. For these reasons, marketers do little to change a product's style, design, or other attributes during its decline. New technology or social trends, product substitutes, or environmental considerations also may indicate that the time has come to delete the product.

During a product's decline, outlets with strong sales volumes are maintained, and unprofitable outlets are weeded out. An entire marketing channel may be eliminated if it does not contribute adequately to profits. An outlet not used previously, such as a factory outlet or Internet retailer, sometimes will be used to liquidate remaining inventory of an obsolete product. As sales decline, the product becomes more inaccessible, but loyal buyers seek out dealers who still carry it. Spending on promotion efforts is usually reduced considerably. Advertising of special offers may slow the rate of decline. Sales promotions, such as coupons and premiums, may regain buyers' attention temporarily. As the product continues to decline, the sales staff shifts its emphasis to more profitable products.

Product Adoption Process

Acceptance of new products—especially new-to-the-world products—usually doesn't happen overnight. In fact, it can take a very long time. People are sometimes cautious or even skeptical about adopting new products, as indicated by some of the remarks quoted in Table 9.1.

Customers who eventually accept a new product do so through an adoption process. The stages of the **product adoption process** are as follows:

1. *Awareness.* The buyer becomes aware of the product.
2. *Interest.* The buyer seeks information and is receptive to learning about the product.
3. *Evaluation.* The buyer considers the product's benefits and decides whether to try it.
4. *Trial.* The buyer examines, tests, or tries the product to determine if it meets his or her needs.
5. *Adoption.* The buyer purchases the product and can be expected to use it again whenever the need for this general type of product arises.[9]

In the first stage, when individuals become aware that the product exists, they have little information about it and are not concerned about obtaining more. Consumers enter the interest stage when they are motivated to get information about the product's features, uses,

decline stage
The stage of a product's life cycle when sales fall rapidly

product adoption process
The stages buyers go through in accepting a product

TABLE 9.1 Most New Ideas Have Their Skeptics

"I think there is a world market for maybe five computers."
—Thomas Watson, chairman of IBM, 1943

"This 'telephone' has too many shortcomings to be seriously considered as a means of communication. The device is inherently of no value to us."
—Western Union internal memo, 1876

"The wireless music box has no imaginable commercial value. Who would pay for a message sent to nobody in particular?"
—David Sarnoff's associates in response to his urgings for investment in the radio in the 1920s

"The concept is interesting and well formed, but in order to earn better than a C, the idea must be feasible."
—A Yale University management professor in response to Fred Smith's paper proposing reliable overnight delivery service (Smith went on to found Federal Express Corp.)

"Who the hell wants to hear actors talk?"
—H. M. Warner, Warner Brothers, 1927

"A cookie store is a bad idea. Besides, the market research reports say America likes crispy cookies, not soft and chewy cookies like you make."
—Banker's response to Debbie Fields's idea of starting Mrs. Fields' Cookies

"We don't like their sound, and guitar music is on the way out."
—Decca Recording Company rejecting the Beatles, 1962

advantages, disadvantages, price, or location. During the evaluation stage, individuals consider whether the product will satisfy certain criteria that are crucial to meeting their specific needs. In the trial stage, they use or experience the product for the first time, possibly by purchasing a small quantity, taking advantage of free samples, or borrowing the product from someone. Individuals move into the adoption stage by choosing a specific product when they need a product of that general type. Entering the adoption process does not mean that the person will eventually adopt the new product. Rejection may occur at any stage, including the adoption stage. Both product adoption and product rejection can be temporary or permanent.

When an organization introduces a new product, people do not begin the adoption process at the same time, nor do they move through the process at the same speed. Of those who eventually adopt the product, some enter the adoption process rather quickly, whereas others start considerably later. For most products, there is also a group of nonadopters who never begin the process.

innovators First adopters of new products

early adopters Careful choosers of new products

early majority Those adopting new products just before the average person

late majority Skeptics who adopt new products when they feel it is necessary

laggards The last adopters, who distrust new products

Depending on the length of time it takes them to adopt a new product, consumers fall into one of five major adopter categories: innovators, early adopters, early majority, late majority, and laggards.[10] Figure 9.4 illustrates each adopter category and the percentage of total adopters it typically represents. **Innovators** are the first to adopt a new product; they enjoy trying new products and tend to be venturesome. **Early adopters** choose new products carefully and are viewed as "the people to check with" by those in the remaining adopter categories. People in the **early majority** adopt just prior to the average person; they are deliberate and cautious in trying new products. Individuals in the **late majority** are quite skeptical of new products but eventually adopt them because of economic necessity or social pressure. **Laggards**, the last to adopt a new product, are oriented toward the past. They are suspicious of new products, and when they finally adopt the innovation, it may already have been replaced by a new product.

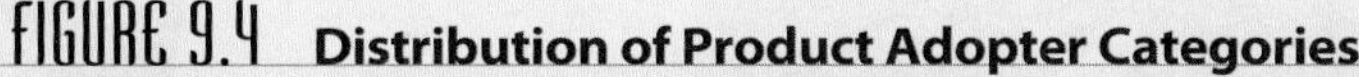

FIGURE 9.4 Distribution of Product Adopter Categories

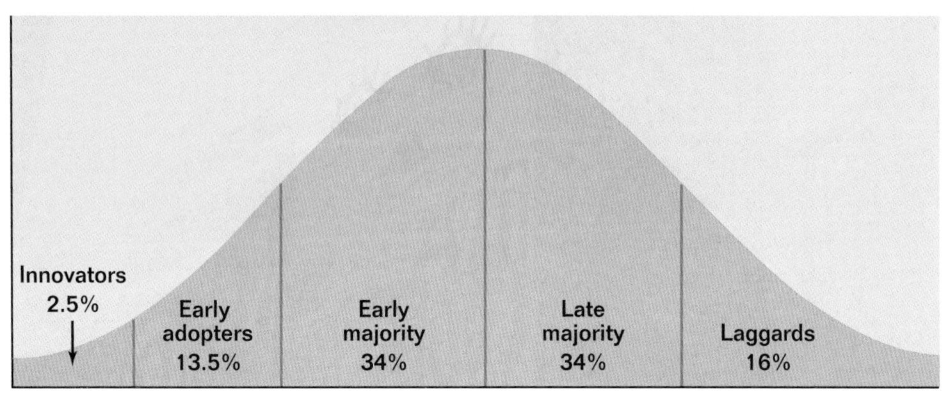

Source: Reprinted with permission of The Free Press, a division of Simon & Schuster Adult Publishing Group, from *Diffusion of Innovations*, Fourth Edition, by Everett M. Rogers. Copyright © 1995 by Everett M. Rogers. Copyright © 1962, 1971, 1983 by The Free Press. All rights reserved.

Branding

Marketers must make many decisions about products, including choices about brands, brand names, brand marks, trademarks, and trade names. A **brand** is a name, term, design, symbol, or any other feature that identifies one marketer's product as distinct from those of other marketers. A brand may identify a single item, a family of items, or all items of that seller.[11] Some have defined a brand as not just the physical good, name, color, logo, or ad campaign but everything associated with the product, including its symbolism and experiences.[12] For example, Hearts on Fire has branded a particular hearts and arrows cut for its diamonds, which maximizes their brilliance and fire—and allows Hearts on Fire diamonds to command a 15- to 20-percent premium over traditional diamonds.[13] A **brand name** is the part of a brand that can be spoken—including letters, words, and numbers—such as 7UP. A brand name is often a product's only distinguishing characteristic. Without the brand name, a firm could not differentiate its products. To consumers, a brand name is as fundamental as the product itself. Indeed, many brand names have become synonymous with the product, such as Scotch Tape and Xerox copiers. Through promotional activities, the owners of these brand names try to protect them from being used as generic names for tape and photocopiers.

The element of a brand that is not made up of words—often a symbol or design—is a **brand mark**. Examples of brand marks include McDonald's Golden Arches, Nike's "swoosh," and the stylized silhouette of Apple's iPod. A **trademark** is a legal designation indicating that the owner has exclusive use of a brand or a part of a brand and that others are prohibited by law from using it. To protect a brand name or brand mark in the United States, an organization must register it as a trademark with the U.S. Patent and Trademark Office. In a typical year, the Patent and Trademark Office registers about 170,000 new trademarks.[14] Finally, a **trade name** is the full and legal name of an organization, such as Ford Motor Company, rather than the name of a specific product.

brand
A name, term, design, symbol, or any other feature that identifies one marketer's product as distinct from those of other marketers

brand name
The part of a brand that can be spoken

brand mark
The part of a brand not made up of words

trademark
A legal designation of exclusive use of a brand

trade name
Full legal name of an organization

VALUE OF BRANDING

Both buyers and sellers benefit from branding. Brands help buyers to identify specific products that they do and do not like, which, in turn, facilitates the purchase of items that satisfy

Brand Mark
The red-and-white target is the brand mark for Target stores.

their needs and reduces the time required to purchase the product. Without brands, product selection would be quite random because buyers could have no assurance that they were purchasing what they preferred. The purchase of certain brands can be a form of self-expression. For example, clothing brand names are important to many consumers. Names such as Tommy Hilfiger, Polo Ralph Lauren, Champion, Nike, and GUESS give manufacturers an advantage in the marketplace. Especially when a customer is unable to judge a product's quality, a brand may symbolize a certain quality level to the customer, and in turn, the person lets that perception of quality represent the quality of the item. A brand helps to reduce a buyer's perceived risk of purchase. In addition, a psychological reward may come from owning a brand that symbolizes status. The Mercedes-Benz brand in the United States is an example.

Sellers benefit from branding because each company's brands identify its products, which makes repeat purchasing easier for customers. Branding helps a firm to introduce a new product that carries the name of one or more of its existing products because buyers are already familiar with the firm's existing brands. It facilitates promotional efforts because the promotion of each branded product indirectly promotes all other similarly branded products. Branding also fosters brand loyalty. To the extent that buyers become loyal to a specific brand, the company's market share for that product achieves a certain level of stability, allowing the firm to use its resources more efficiently. Once a firm develops some degree of customer loyalty for a brand, it can maintain a fairly consistent price rather than continually cutting the price to attract customers.

There is a cultural dimension to branding. Most brand experiences are individual, and each consumer confers his or her own social meaning onto brands. A brand's appeal is largely at an emotional level based on its symbolic image and key associations.[15] For some brands, such

FIGURE 9.5 **Major Elements of Brand Equity**

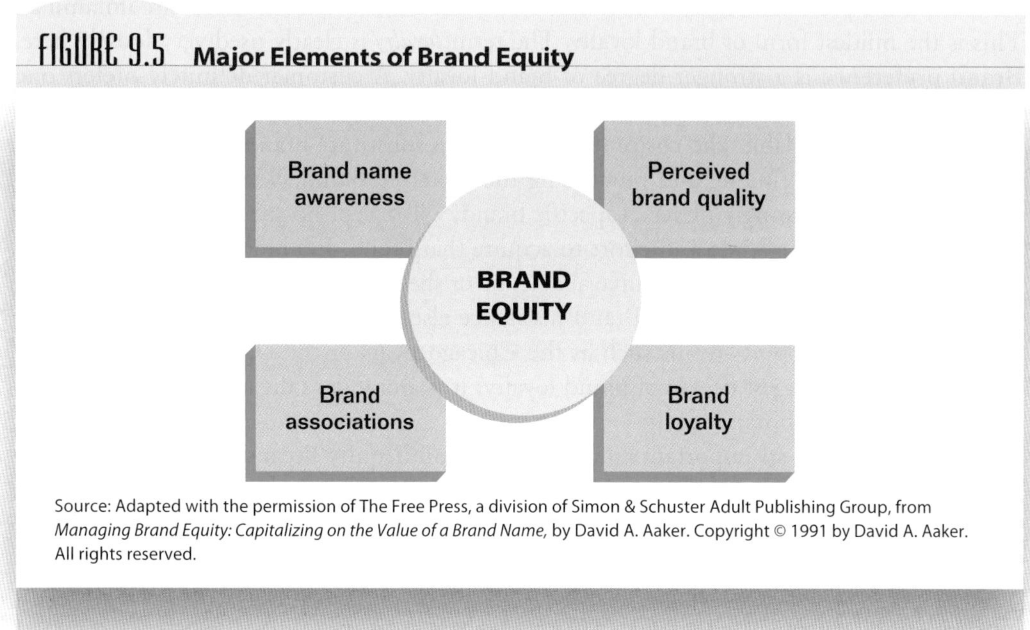

Source: Adapted with the permission of The Free Press, a division of Simon & Schuster Adult Publishing Group, from *Managing Brand Equity: Capitalizing on the Value of a Brand Name,* by David A. Aaker. Copyright © 1991 by David A. Aaker. All rights reserved.

as Harley-Davidson, Google, and Apple, this can result in an almost cultlike following. These brands often develop a community of loyal customers that communicate through get-togethers, online forums, blogs, podcasts, and other means. These brands even may help consumers to develop their identity and self-concept and serve as a form of self-expression. In fact, the term *cultural branding* has been used to explain how a brand conveys a powerful myth that consumers find useful in cementing their identities.[16] It is also important to recognize that because a brand exists independently in the consumer's mind, it is not controlled directly by the marketer. Every aspect of a brand is subject to a consumer's emotional involvement, interpretation, and memory. By understanding how branding influences purchases, marketers can foster customer loyalty.[17]

BRAND EQUITY

A well-managed brand is an asset to an organization. The value of this asset is often referred to as brand equity. **Brand equity** is the marketing and financial value associated with a brand's strength in a market. Besides the actual proprietary brand assets, such as patents and trademarks, four major elements underlie brand equity: brand name awareness, brand loyalty, perceived brand quality, and brand associations[18] (see Figure 9.5).

Being aware of a brand leads to brand familiarity, which, in turn, results in a level of comfort with the brand. A familiar brand is more likely to be selected than an unfamiliar brand because the familiar brand often is viewed as more reliable and of more acceptable quality. The familiar brand is likely to be in a customer's consideration set, whereas the unfamiliar brand is not.

Brand loyalty is a customer's favorable attitude toward a specific brand. If brand loyalty is strong enough, customers may purchase this brand consistently when they need a product in that product category. Customer satisfaction with a brand is the most common reason for loyalty to that brand.[19] Development of brand loyalty in a customer reduces his or her risks and shortens the time spent buying the product. However, the degree of brand loyalty for products varies from one product category to another. It is challenging to develop brand loyalty for some products, such as bananas, because customers can readily judge the quality of these products and do not need to refer to a brand as an indicator of quality. Brand loyalty also varies by country. Customers in France, Germany, and the United Kingdom tend to be less brand-loyal than U.S. customers.

There are three degrees of brand loyalty: recognition, preference, and insistence. **Brand recognition** occurs when a customer is aware that the brand exists and views it as an alternative

brand equity
The marketing and financial value associated with a brand's strength in a market

brand loyalty
A customer's favorable attitude toward a specific brand

brand recognition
A customer's awareness that the brand exists and is an alternative purchase

brand preference The degree of brand loyalty in which a customer prefers one brand over competitive offerings

brand insistence The degree of brand loyalty in which a customer strongly prefers a specific brand and will accept no substitute

manufacturer brands Brands initiated by producers

purchase if the preferred brand is unavailable or if the other available brands are unfamiliar. This is the mildest form of brand loyalty. The term *loyalty* is clearly used very loosely here. **Brand preference** is a stronger degree of brand loyalty. A customer definitely prefers one brand over competitive offerings and will purchase this brand if it is available. However, if the brand is not available, the customer will accept a substitute brand rather than expending additional effort finding and purchasing the preferred brand. When **brand insistence** occurs, a customer strongly prefers a specific brand, will accept no substitute, and is willing to spend a great deal of time and effort to acquire that brand. If a brand-insistent customer goes to a store and finds the brand unavailable, he or she will seek the brand elsewhere rather than purchase a substitute brand. Brand insistence also can apply to service products such as Hilton Hotels or sports teams such as the Chicago Bears or the Dallas Cowboys. Brand insistence is the strongest degree of brand loyalty; it is a brander's dream. However, it is the least common type of brand loyalty.

Brand loyalty is an important component of brand equity because it reduces a brand's vulnerability to competitors' actions. It allows an organization to keep its existing customers and avoid spending significant resources to gain new ones. Loyal customers provide brand visibility and reassurance to potential new customers. And because customers expect their brands to be available when and where they shop, retailers strive to carry the brands known for their strong customer following.

Customers associate a particular brand with a certain level of overall quality. A brand name may be used as a substitute for actual judgment of quality. In many cases, customers can't actually judge the quality of the product for themselves and instead must rely on the brand as a quality indicator. Perceived high brand quality helps to support a premium price, allowing a marketer to avoid severe price competition. Also, favorable perceived brand quality can ease the introduction of brand extensions because the high regard for the brand likely will translate into high regard for the related products.

Stimulating Brand Associations
Geico uses the gecko as a trade character to stimulate favorable brand associations.

The set of associations linked to a brand is another key component of brand equity. At times, a marketer works to connect a particular lifestyle or, in some instances, a certain personality type with a specific brand. For example, customers associate Michelin tires with protecting family members; a DeBeers diamond with a loving, long-lasting relationship ("A Diamond Is Forever"); and Dr Pepper with a unique taste. These types of brand associations contribute significantly to the brand's equity. Brand associations sometimes are facilitated by using trade characters, such as the Jolly Green Giant, the Pillsbury Dough Boy, and Charlie the Tuna. Placing these trade characters in advertisements and on packages helps consumers to link the ads and packages with the brands.

Although difficult to measure, brand equity represents the value of a brand to an organization. Table 9.2 lists the top ten brands with the highest economic value. Any company that owns a brand listed in Table 9.2 would agree that the economic value of that brand is likely to be the greatest single asset in the organization's possession.

TYPES OF BRANDS

There are three categories of brands: manufacturer, private distributor, and generic. **Manufacturer brands** are initiated by producers and ensure that producers are identified with their products at the point of purchase—for example, Green Giant, Dell, Starbucks, and Levi's

TABLE 9.2 **Top Ten Most Valuable Brands in the World**

Brand	Brand Value (in billion $)
Coca-Cola	68.7
IBM	60.2
Microsoft	56.6
GE	47.8
Nokia	34.9
McDonald's	32.3
Google	32.0
Toyota	31.3
Intel	30.6
Disney	28.4

Source: "Best Global Brands, 2009," Interbrand, http://www.interbrand.com/best_global_brands.aspx (accessed October 15, 2009).

jeans. A manufacturer brand usually requires a producer to become involved in distribution, promotion, and to some extent, pricing decisions.

Private distributor brands (also called *private brands, store brands,* or *dealer brands*) are initiated and owned by resellers—wholesalers or retailers. The major characteristic of private brands is that the manufacturers are not identified on the products. Retailers and wholesalers use private distributor brands to develop more efficient promotion, generate higher gross margins, and change store image. Familiar retailer brand names include Sears' Kenmore and JCPenney's Arizona. Some successful private brands, such as Kenmore, are distributed nationally. Sometimes retailers with successful private distributor brands start manufacturing their own products to gain more control over product costs, quality, and design with the hope of increasing profits. Sales of private labels are now growing at more than twice the rate of brand names and account for 20 percent of packaged items sold in supermarkets.[20]

Some marketers of traditionally branded products have embarked on a policy of not branding, often called *generic branding.* **Generic brands** indicate only the product category (such as aluminum foil) and do not include the company name or other identifying terms. Generic brands usually are sold at lower prices than comparable branded items. Although at one time generic brands may have represented as much as 10 percent of all retail grocery sales, today they account for less than one half of 1 percent.

SELECTING A BRAND NAME

Marketers consider several factors in selecting a brand name. First, the name should be easy for customers (including foreign buyers if the firm intends to market its products in other countries) to say, spell, and recall. Short, one-syllable names, such as Cheer, often satisfy this requirement. Second, the brand name should indicate the product's major benefits and, if possible, should suggest in a positive way the product's uses and special characteristics; negative or offensive references should be avoided. For example, the brand names of household cleaning products such as Ajax dishwashing liquid, Vanish toilet bowl cleaner, Formula 409 multipurpose cleaner,

private distributor brands
Brands initiated and owned by resellers

generic brands
Brands indicating only the product category

Cascade dishwasher detergent, and Wisk laundry detergent connote strength and effectiveness. There is evidence that consumers are more likely to recall and to evaluate favorably names that convey positive attributes or benefits.[21] Third, to set it apart from competing brands, the brand should be distinctive. If a marketer intends to use a brand for a product line, that brand must be compatible with all products in the line. Finally, a brand should be designed so that it can be used and recognized in all types of media. Finding the right brand name has become a challenging task because many obvious product names have already been used.

How are brand names devised? Brand names can be created from single or multiple words—for example, Dodge Nitro. Letters and numbers are used to create brands such as Volvo's S60 sedan or Motorola's RAZR V3 phone. Words, numbers, and letters are combined to yield brand names such as Apple's iPhone or BMW's Z4 Roadster. To avoid terms that have negative connotations, marketers sometimes use fabricated words that have absolutely no meaning when created—for example, Kodak and Exxon.

Who actually creates brand names? Brand names can be created internally by the organization. At Del Monte, a team of executives brainstormed 27 ideas for new cat food offerings with names such as "pâté," "soufflé," and "crème brulee."[22] Sometimes a name is suggested by individuals who are close to the development of the product. Some organizations have committees that participate in brand name creation and approval. Large companies that introduce numerous new products annually are likely to have a department that develops brand names. At times, outside consultants and companies that specialize in brand name development are used.

PROTECTING A BRAND

A marketer also should design a brand so that it can be protected easily through registration. A series of court decisions has created a broad hierarchy of protection based on brand type. From most protectable to least protectable, these brand types are fanciful (Exxon), arbitrary (Dr Pepper), suggestive (Spray 'n Wash), descriptive (Minute Rice), and generic (aluminum foil). Generic brands are not protectable. Surnames and descriptive, geographic, or functional names are difficult to protect.[23] However, research shows that overall, consumers prefer descriptive and suggestive brand names and find them easier to recall compared with fanciful and arbitrary brand names.[24] Because of their designs, some brands can be legally infringed on more easily than others. Although registration protects trademarks domestically for ten years, and trademarks can be renewed indefinitely, a firm should develop a system for ensuring that its trademarks are renewed as needed.

To protect its exclusive rights to a brand, a company must ensure that the brand is not likely to be considered an infringement on any brand already registered with the U.S. Patent and Trademark Office. Consider that after Apple launched the iPhone to much fanfare, it was sued by Cisco, which owns the trademark name iPhone, after the two companies failed to reach agreement on Apple's use of the name. This task may be complex because infringement is determined by the courts, which base their decisions on whether a brand causes consumers to be confused, mistaken, or deceived about the source of the product. McDonald's is one company that aggressively protects its trademarks against infringement; it has brought charges against a number of companies with *Mc* names because it fears that use of the prefix will give consumers the impression that these companies are associated with or owned by McDonald's.

A marketer should guard against allowing a brand name to become a generic term used to refer to a general product category. Generic terms cannot be protected as exclusive brand names. For example, *aspirin, escalator,* and *shredded wheat*—all brand names at one time—eventually were declared generic terms that refer to product classes. Thus they could no longer be protected. To keep a brand name from becoming a generic term, the firm should spell the name with a capital letter and use it as an adjective to modify the name of the general product

Protecting a Brand
Companies try to protect their brands by using certain phrases and symbols in their advertisements. Note the term "brand" after Ziploc, and the use of the ® symbol.

class, as in Kool-Aid Brand Soft Drink Mix.[25] Including the word *brand* just after the brand name is also helpful. An organization can deal with this problem directly by advertising that its brand is a trademark and should not be used generically. The firm also can indicate that the brand is a registered trademark by using the symbol®.

A U.S. firm that tries to protect a brand in a foreign country frequently encounters problems. In many countries, brand registration is not possible; the first firm to use a brand in such a country automatically has the rights to it. In some instances, U.S. companies actually have had to buy their own brand rights from a firm in a foreign country because the foreign firm was the first user in that country. Consider the decade-long dispute over Havana Club rum, which is marketed in 183 countries by Pernod Ricard, a French company, in a joint venture with the Cuban government, which nationalized the brand in 1960. However, Bacardi purchased the rights and original recipe from the brand's Cuban originators with the intention of producing it for distribution in the United States. Pernod Ricard sued Bacardi for violating its agreement, but Bacardi insists that the Cuban registration of the trademark in the United States is no longer valid. The dispute has involved U.S. courts and the World Trade Organization.[26]

Marketers trying to protect their brands also must contend with brand counterfeiting. In the United States, for instance, one can purchase counterfeit General Motors parts, Cartier watches, Louis Vuitton handbags, Walt Disney character dolls, Warner Brothers clothing, Mont Blanc pens, and a host of other products illegally marketed by manufacturers that do not own the brands. Losses caused by counterfeit products are estimated to be between $250 billion and $350 billion annually.

In the interest of strengthening trademark protection, Congress enacted the Trademark Law Revision Act in 1988, the only major federal trademark legislation since the Lanham Act of 1946. The purpose of this more recent legislation is to increase the value of the federal registration system for U.S. firms relative to foreign competitors and to protect the public from counterfeiting, confusion, and deception.[27]

BRANDING POLICIES

Before establishing branding policies, a firm must decide whether to brand its products at all. If a company's product is homogeneous and is similar to competitors' products, it may be difficult to brand in a way that will generate brand loyalty. Raw materials such as coal, sand, and farm produce are hard to brand because of the homogeneity of such products and their physical characteristics.

If a firm chooses to brand its products, it may use individual branding, family branding, or a combination. **Individual branding** is a policy of naming each product differently. Sara Lee uses individual branding among its many divisions, which include Hanes underwear, L'eggs pantyhose, Champion sportswear, Bali, Jimmy Dean, Ball Park, and other vastly different brands. A major advantage of individual branding is that if an organization introduces an inferior product, the negative images associated with it do not contaminate the company's other products. An individual branding policy also may facilitate market segmentation when a firm wishes to enter many segments of the same market. Separate, unrelated names can be used, and each brand can be aimed at a specific segment.

When using **family branding**, all of a firm's products are branded with the same name or at least part of the name, such as Kellogg's Frosted Flakes, Kellogg's Rice Krispies, and Kellogg's Corn Flakes. In some cases, a company's name is combined with other words to brand items. Arm & Hammer uses its name on all its products, along with a general description of the item, such as Arm & Hammer Heavy Duty Detergent, Arm & Hammer Pure Baking Soda, and Arm & Hammer Carpet Deodorizer. Unlike individual branding, family branding means that the promotion of one item with the family brand promotes the firm's other products. Examples of other companies that use family branding include Mitsubishi, Heinz, and Sony.

An organization is not limited to a single branding policy. A company that uses primarily individual branding for many of its products also may use family branding for a specific product line. Branding policy is influenced by the number of products and product lines the company produces, the characteristics of its target markets, the number and types of competing products available, and the size of the firm's resources.

BRAND EXTENSIONS

A **brand extension** occurs when an organization uses one of its existing brands to brand a new product in a different product category. An example is when Bic, the maker of disposable pens, introduced Bic disposable razors and Bic lighters. A brand extension should not be confused with a line extension. A line extension refers to using an existing brand on a new product in the same product category, such as new flavors or sizes. For example, when the maker of Tylenol, McNeil Consumer Products, introduced Extra Strength Tylenol P.M., the new product was a line extension because it was in the same category.

Marketers share a common concern that if a brand is extended too many times or extended too far outside its original product category, the brand can be weakened significantly. For example, the Nabisco SnackWell brand initially appeared only on crackers, cookies, and snack bars, all of which fall into the baked-snack category. However, extending the brand to yogurts and gelatin mixes goes further afield. Although some experts might caution Nabisco against extending the SnackWell brand to this degree, some evidence suggests that brands can be extended successfully to less closely related product categories through the use of advertisements that extend customers' perceptions of the original product category.

CO-BRANDING

Co-branding is the use of two or more brands on one product. Marketers employ co-branding to capitalize on the brand equity of multiple brands. Co-branding is popular in several

individual branding
A policy of naming each product differently

family branding
Branding all of a firm's products with the same name

brand extension
Using an existing brand to brand a new product in a different product category

co-branding
Using two or more brands on one product

processed-food categories and in the credit card industry. The brands used for co-branding can be owned by the same company. For example, Kraft's Lunchables product teams the Kraft cheese brand with Oscar Mayer lunchmeats, another Kraft-owned brand. The brands also may be owned by different companies. Credit card companies such as American Express, Visa, and MasterCard, for instance, team up with other brands such as General Motors, AT&T, and many airlines. Effective co-branding capitalizes on the trust and confidence customers have in the brands involved. The brands should not lose their identities, and it should be clear to customers which brand is the main brand. For example, it is fairly obvious that Kellogg owns the brand and is the main brander of Kellogg's Healthy Choice Cereal. It is important for marketers to understand that when a co-branded product is unsuccessful, both brands are implicated in the product failure. To gain customer acceptance, the brands involved must represent a complementary fit in the minds of buyers. Trying to link a brand such as Harley-Davidson with a brand such as Healthy Choice will not achieve co-branding objectives because customers are not likely to perceive these brands as compatible.

BRAND LICENSING

A popular branding strategy involves **brand licensing**, an agreement in which a company permits another organization to use its brand on other products for a licensing fee. Royalties may be as low as 2 percent of wholesale revenues or higher than 10 percent. Kohl's, for example, licensed the Tony Hawk brand for use on a line of casual footwear.[28] The licensee is responsible for all manufacturing, selling, and advertising functions and bears the costs if the licensed product fails. The advantages of licensing range from extra revenues and low-cost or free publicity to new images and trademark protection. The major disadvantages are a lack of manufacturing control, which could hurt the company's name, and bombarding consumers with too many unrelated products bearing the same name.

brand licensing
An agreement whereby a company permits another organization to use its brand on other products for a licensing fee

Co-Branding
Lunchables is a co-branded item consisting of Oscar Mayer and Kraft products.

Packaging

Packaging involves the development of a container and a graphic design for a product. A package can be a vital part of a product, making it more versatile, safer, and easier to use. Like a brand name, a package can influence customers' attitudes toward a product and so affect their purchase decisions. For example, several producers of jellies, sauces, and ketchups have packaged their products in squeezable plastic containers to make use and storage more convenient, whereas several paint manufacturers have introduced easy-to-open and -pour paint cans. Package characteristics help to shape buyers' impressions of a product at the time of purchase or during use. In this section we examine the main functions of packaging and consider several major packaging decisions. We also analyze the role of the package in a marketing strategy.

PACKAGING FUNCTIONS

Effective packaging involves more than simply putting products in containers and covering them with wrappers. First, packaging materials serve the basic purpose of protecting the product and maintaining its functional form. Fluids such as milk and orange juice need packages that preserve and protect them. The packaging should prevent damage that could affect the product's usefulness and thus lead to higher costs. Since product tampering has become a problem, several packaging techniques have been developed to counter this danger. Some packages are also designed to deter shoplifting.

Another function of packaging is to offer convenience to consumers. For example, small, aseptic packages—individual-size boxes or plastic bags that contain liquids and do not require refrigeration—strongly appeal to children and young adults with active lifestyles. The size or shape of a package may relate to the product's storage, convenience of use, or replacement rate. Small, single-serving cans of vegetables, for instance, may prevent waste and make storage easier. A third function of packaging is to promote a product by communicating its features, uses, benefits, and image. Sometimes a reusable package is developed to make the product more desirable. For example, the Cool Whip package doubles as a food-storage container.

MAJOR PACKAGING CONSIDERATIONS

As they develop packages, marketers must take many factors into account. Obviously, one major consideration is cost. Although a number of different packaging materials, processes, and designs are available, costs vary greatly. In recent years, buyers have shown a willingness to pay more for improved packaging, but there are limits.

Marketers should consider how much consistency is desirable among an organization's package designs. No consistency may be the best policy, especially if a firm's products are unrelated or aimed at vastly different target markets. To promote an overall company image, a firm may decide that all packages should be similar or include one major element of the design. This approach is called **family packaging**. Sometimes it is used only for lines of products, as with Campbell's soups, Weight Watchers' foods, and Planters Nuts.

A package's promotional role is an important consideration. Through verbal and nonverbal symbols, the package can inform potential buyers about the product's content, features, uses, advantages, and hazards. A firm can create desirable images and associations by its choice of color, design, shape, and texture. Many cosmetics manufacturers, for example, design their packages to create impressions of richness, luxury, and exclusiveness. To develop a package that has a definite promotional value, a designer must consider size, shape, texture, color, and graphics. Beyond the obvious limitation that the package must be large enough to hold the product, a package can be designed to appear taller or shorter. Light-colored packaging may make a package appear larger, whereas darker colors may minimize the perceived size.

family packaging
Using similar packaging for all of a firm's products or packaging that has one common design element

Colors on packages are often chosen to attract attention, and color can positively influence customers' emotions. People often associate specific colors with certain feelings and experiences. Blue is soothing; it is also associated with wealth, trust, and security. Gray is associated with strength, exclusivity, and success. Orange can stand for low cost. Red connotes excitement and stimulation. Purple is associated with dignity and stateliness. Yellow connotes cheerfulness and joy. Black is associated with being strong and masterful.[29] When opting for color on packaging, marketers must judge whether a particular color will evoke positive or negative feelings when linked to a specific product. Rarely, for example, do processors package meat or bread in green materials because customers may associate green with mold. Marketers also must determine whether a specific target market will respond favorably or unfavorably to a particular color. Packages designed to appeal to children often use primary colors and bold designs.

Packaging also must meet the needs of resellers. Wholesalers and retailers consider whether a package facilitates transportation, storage, and handling. Resellers may refuse to carry certain products if their packages are cumbersome. Concentrated versions of laundry detergents and fabric softeners aid retailers in offering more product diversity within the existing shelf space.

PACKAGING AND MARKETING STRATEGY

Packaging can be a major component of a marketing strategy. A new cap or closure, a better box or wrapper, or a more convenient container may give a product a competitive advantage. The right type of package for a new product can help it to gain market recognition very quickly. Sunsweet Growers, for example, had this in mind when it introduced New Ones dried prunes, targeted at consumers who wanted healthier snacks. Sold in transparent canisters containing 20 individually wrapped pitted prune snacks that look rather like candy, the package protects the product and makes it portable enough for the lunchbox or desk.[30] In the case of existing brands, marketers should reevaluate packages periodically. Marketers should view packaging as a major strategic tool, especially for consumer convenience products. For instance, in the food industry, jumbo and large package sizes for products such as hot dogs, pizzas, English muffins, frozen dinners, and biscuits have been very successful. When considering the strategic uses of packaging, marketers also must analyze the cost of packaging and package changes. In this section we examine several ways in which packaging can be used strategically.

Convenience Packaging
Some companies compete by designing packages that are convenient to use.

Marketing IN TRANSITION

How Green Is That Product? Check the Label

More companies are seeking green certification of their goods, services, and operations to more effectively satisfy their environmentally conscious customers. Some of the best-known green certification labels and designations include:

- Energy Star. Administered by the U.S. Environmental Protection Agency and the U.S. Department of Energy, the Energy Star label identifies energy-efficient home and office equipment such as personal computers, dishwashers, washing machines, and laser printers. Dell has introduced many computers and monitors that comply with Energy Star standards for low power usage, for example.
- Green Seal. This nonprofit organization examines the environmental impact of a product's supplies, production, packaging, consumption, and disposal. Look for the Green Seal logo on paper and other products made from sustainable wood, as well as environmentally friendly household cleaning products.

© AP IMAGES/PRNEWSFOTO/'ALL' LAUNDRY DETERGENT

- Forest Stewardship Council. The Forest Stewardship Council, active in more than 46 nations, labels wood and wood products that originated in forests managed with sustainability in mind. Both Martin and Gibson make guitars from woods that have earned this certification label.
- Sustainable Forestry Initiative. To qualify for this label, all or some of a product's fiber content must come from forests that are managed for sustainability. The label also identifies products that contain recycled materials. One study found that 70 percent of consumers would choose products made from sustainable lumber if the labels explained the environmental benefits.
- Leadership in Energy and Environmental Design (LEED). LEED certification indicates that a building's design, construction, and operation meet green standards established by the U.S. Green Building Council. As an example, the U.S. Postal Service is polishing its green credentials by building LEED-certified distribution centers that conserve energy and water.[c]

Altering the Package

At times, a marketer changes a package because the existing design is no longer in style, especially when compared with the packaging of competitive products. Arm & Hammer now markets a refillable plastic shaker for its baking soda. Quaker Oats hired a package design company to redesign its Rice-A-Roni package to give the product the appearance of having evolved with the times while retaining its traditional taste appeal. A package may be redesigned because new product features need to be highlighted or because new packaging materials have become available. An organization may decide to change a product's packaging to make the product safer or more convenient to use. Oscar Mayer introduced sliced bacon in a redesigned "Stay-Fresh Reclosable Tray" to address consumer complaints that traditional bacon packaging is sometimes messy and can't be sealed to ensure freshness through multiple servings. Developed in cooperation with packaging company Bemis Co., the new package represents the most significant change in bacon packaging since the 1920s.[31]

Secondary-Use Packaging

A secondary-use package is one that can be reused for purposes other than its initial function. For example, a margarine container can be reused to store leftovers, and a jelly container can serve as a drinking glass. Customers often view secondary-use packaging as adding value to products, in which case its use should stimulate unit sales.

Category-Consistent Packaging

With category-consistent packaging, the product is packaged in line with the packaging practices associated with a particular product category. Some product categories—for example, mayonnaise, mustard, ketchup, and peanut butter—have traditional package shapes. Other product categories are characterized by recognizable color combinations, such as red and white for soup and red, yellow, and blue for Ritz-like crackers. When an organization introduces a brand in one of these product categories, marketers often will use traditional package shapes and color combinations to ensure that customers will recognize the new product as being in that specific product category.

Innovative Packaging

Sometimes a marketer employs a unique cap, design, applicator, or other feature to make a product distinctive. Such packaging can be effective when the innovation makes the product safer or easier to use or provides better protection for the product. In some instances, marketers use innovative or unique packages that are inconsistent with traditional packaging practices to make the brand stand out from its competitors. Unusual packaging sometimes requires spending considerable resources not only on package design but also on making customers aware of the unique package and its benefits. Moreover, the findings of a recent study suggest that uniquely shaped packages that attract attention are more likely to be perceived as containing a higher volume of product.[32]

labeling
Providing identifying, promotional, or other information on package labels

Multiple Packaging

Rather than packaging a single unit of a product, marketers sometimes use twin-packs, tri-packs, six-packs, or other forms of multiple packaging. For certain types of products, multiple packaging may increase demand because it increases the amount of the product available at the point of consumption (in one's house, for example). It also may increase consumer acceptance of the product by encouraging the buyer to try the product several times. Multiple packaging can make products easier to handle and store, as in the case of six-packs for soft drinks.

Handling-Improved Packaging

A product's packaging may be changed to make it easier to handle in the distribution channel—for example, by changing the outer carton or using special bundling, shrink-wrapping, or pallets. In some cases, the shape of the package is changed. Outer containers for products are sometimes changed so that they will proceed more easily through automated warehousing systems.

Labeling

Labeling is very closely interrelated with packaging and is used for identification, promotional, informational, and legal purposes. Labels can be small or large relative to the size of the product and carry varying amounts of information. The sticker on a Chiquita banana, for example, is quite small and displays only the brand name of the fruit and perhaps a stock-keeping unit number. A label can be part of the package itself or a separate feature attached to the package. The label on a can of Coke is actually part of the can, whereas the label on a two-liter bottle of Coke is separate and can be removed. Information presented on a label may include the brand name and mark, the registered trademark symbol, package size and content, product features, nutritional information, potential presence of allergens, type and style of the product, number of servings, care instructions, directions for use and safety precautions, the name and address of the manufacturer, expiration dates, seals of approval, and other facts.

Labels can facilitate the identification of a product by displaying the brand name in combination with a unique graphic design. For example, Heinz ketchup is easy to identify on a supermarket shelf because the brand name is easy to read, and the label has a distinctive, crownlike shape. By

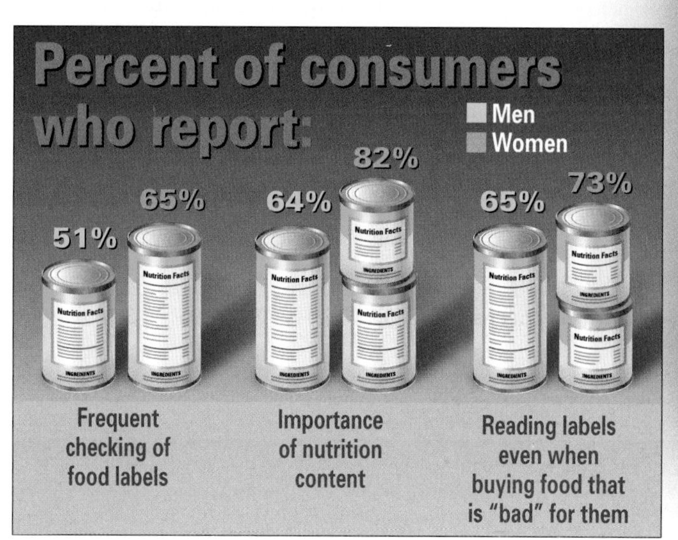

Source: AP-Ipsos

drawing attention to products and their benefits, labels can strengthen an organization's promotional efforts. Labels may contain promotional messages such as the offer of a discount or a larger package size at the same price or information about a new or improved product feature.

Several federal laws and regulations specify information that must be included on the labels of certain products. Garments must be labeled with the name of the manufacturer, country of manufacture, fabric content, and cleaning instructions. Labels on nonedible items such as shampoos and detergents must include both safety precautions and directions for use. The Nutrition Labeling Act of 1990 requires the Food and Drug Administration (FDA) to review food labeling and packaging, focusing on nutrition content, label format, ingredient labeling, food descriptions, and health messages. This act regulates much of the labeling on more than 250,000 products made by 26,000 U.S. companies. Any food product for which a nutritional claim is made must have nutrition labeling that follows a standard format. Food product labels must state the number of servings per container, serving size, number of calories per serving, number of calories derived from fat, number of carbohydrates, and amounts of specific nutrients such as vitamins. In addition, new nutritional labeling requirements focus on the amounts of trans-fatty acids in food products. Although consumers have responded favorably to this type of information on labels, evidence as to whether they actually use it has been mixed. One study reported that 80 percent of American consumers claim to read food labels, yet 44 percent admitted to buying a product even when the information on the label indicated that it was less than healthy.[33]

The use of new technology in the production and processing of food has led to additional food labeling issues. The FDA now requires that a specific irradiation logo be used when labeling irradiated food products. In addition, the FDA has issued voluntary guidelines for food marketers to follow if they opt to label foods as being free of genetically modified organisms or to promote their biotech ingredients.

Of concern to many manufacturers are the Federal Trade Commission's (FTC) guidelines regarding "Made in U.S.A." labels, a growing problem owing to the increasingly global nature of manufacturing. The FTC requires that "all or virtually all" of a product's components be made in the United States if the label says "Made in U.S.A." Although the FTC recently considered changing its guidelines to read "substantially all," it rejected this idea and maintains the "all or virtually all" standard. In light of this decision, the FTC ordered New Balance to stop using the "Made in U.S.A." claim on its athletic shoe labels because some components (rubber soles) are made in China. The "Made in U.S.A." labeling issue has not been totally resolved. The FTC criteria for using "Made in U.S.A." are likely to be challenged and subsequently changed.[34] Table 9.3 provides insight into just how important the "Made in U.S.A" label can be for both Americans and western Europeans. It includes assessments of both quality and value for U.S.A-, Japan-, Korea-, and Chinese-origin labels.

TABLE 9.3 Perceived Quality and Value of Products Based on Country of Origin*

	"Made in U.S.A"		"Made in Japan"		"Made in Korea"		"Made in China"	
	Value	Quality	Value	Quality	Value	Quality	Value	Quality
U.S. adults	4.0	4.2	3.2	3.2	2.6	2.4	2.8	2.4
Western Europeans	3.3	3.4	3.5	3.5	2.8	2.4	2.9	2.4

*On a scale of 1 (low) to 5 (high).
Source: "American Demographics 2006 Consumer Perception Survey," *Advertising Age*, January 2, 2006, p. 9. Data by Synovate.

CHAPTER REVIEW

OBJECTIVES

1 Understand the concept of a product and how products are classified.

A product is a good, a service, an idea, or any combination of the three received in an exchange. It can be either tangible or intangible and includes functional, social, and psychological utilities or benefits. When consumers purchase a product, they are buying the benefits and satisfaction they think the product will provide.

Products can be classified on the basis of the buyer's intentions. Consumer products are those purchased to satisfy personal and family needs. Business products are purchased for use in a firm's operations, to resell, or to make other products. Consumer products can be subdivided into convenience, shopping, specialty, and unsought products. Business products can be classified as installations, accessory equipment, raw materials, component parts, process materials, MRO supplies, and business services.

2 Explain the concepts of product item, product line, and product mix, and understand how they are connected.

A product item is a specific version of a product that can be designated as a distinct offering among an organization's products. A product line is a group of closely related product items that are considered a unit because of marketing, technical, or end-use considerations. The composite, or total, group of products that an organization makes available to customers is called the product mix. The width of the product mix is measured by the number of product lines the company offers. The depth of the product mix is the average number of different products offered in each product line.

3 Understand the product life cycle and its impact on marketing strategies.

The product life cycle describes how product items in an industry move through four stages: introduction, growth, maturity, and decline. The sales curve is at zero at introduction, rises at an increasing rate during growth, peaks during the maturity stage, and then declines. Profits peak toward the end of the growth stage of the product life cycle.

4 Describe the product adoption process.

When customers accept a new product, they usually do so through a five-stage adoption process. The first stage is awareness, when buyers become aware that a product exists. Interest, the second stage, occurs when buyers seek information and are receptive to learning about the product. The third stage is evaluation; buyers consider the product's benefits and decide whether to try it. The fourth stage is trial; during this stage, buyers examine, test, or try the product to determine if it meets their needs. The last stage is adoption, when buyers actually purchase the product and use it whenever a need for this general type of product arises.

5 Explain the value of branding and the major components of brand equity.

A brand is a name, term, design, symbol, or any other feature that identifies one seller's good or service and distinguishes it from those of other sellers. Branding helps buyers to identify and evaluate products, helps sellers to facilitate product introduction and repeat purchasing, and fosters brand loyalty. Brand equity is the marketing and financial value associated with a brand's strength. It represents the value of a brand to an organization. The four major elements underlying brand equity include brand name awareness, brand loyalty, perceived brand quality, and brand associations.

6 Recognize the types of brands and how they are selected and protected.

A manufacturer brand is initiated by a producer. A private distributor brand is initiated and owned by a reseller, sometimes taking on the name of the store or distributor. A generic brand indicates only the product category and does not include the company name or other identifying terms. When selecting a brand name, a marketer should choose one that is easy to say, spell, and recall and that alludes to the product's uses, benefits, or special characteristics. Brand names can be devised from words, letters, numbers, nonsense words, or a combination of these. Companies protect ownership of their brands through registration with the U.S. Patent and Trademark Office.

Identify two types of branding policies, and explain brand extensions, co-branding, and brand licensing.

Individual branding designates a unique name for each of a company's products. Family branding identifies all of a firm's products with a single name. A brand extension is the use of an existing name on a new or improved product in a different product category. Co-branding is the use of two or more brands on one product. Through a licensing agreement and for a licensing fee, a firm may permit another organization to use its brand on other products. Brand licensing enables producers to earn extra revenue, receive low-cost or free publicity, and protect their trademarks.

Describe the major packaging functions and design considerations and how packaging is used in marketing strategies.

Packaging involves the development of a container and a graphic design for a product. Effective packaging offers protection, economy, safety, and convenience. It can influence a customer's purchase decision by promoting features, uses, benefits, and image. When developing a package, marketers must consider the value to the customer of efficient and effective packaging, offset by the price the customer is willing to pay. Other considerations include how to make the package tamper resistant, whether to use multiple packaging and family packaging, how to design the package as an effective promotional tool, and how best to accommodate resellers. Packaging can be an important part of an overall marketing strategy and can be used to target certain market segments. Modifications in packaging can revive a mature product and extend its product life cycle. Producers alter packages to convey new features or to make them safer or more convenient. If a package has a secondary use, the product's value to the consumer may increase. Category-consistent packaging makes products more easily recognized by consumers. Innovative packaging enhances a product's distinctiveness.

Understand the functions of labeling and selected legal issues.

Labeling is closely interrelated with packaging and is used for identification, promotional, and informational and legal purposes. Various federal laws and regulations require that certain products be labeled or marked with warnings, instructions, nutritional information, manufacturer's identification, and perhaps other information.

Please visit the student website at www.cengage.com/international for quizzes and games that will help you prepare for exams and help achieve the grade you want.

KEY CONCEPTS

good
service
idea
consumer products
business products
convenience products
shopping products
specialty products
unsought products
installations
accessory equipment
raw materials
component parts
process materials
MRO supplies
business services
product item
product line
product mix
width of product mix
depth of product mix
product life cycle
introduction stage
growth stage
maturity stage
decline stage
product adoption process
innovators
early adopters
early majority
late majority
laggards
brand
brand name
brand mark
trademark
trade name
brand equity
brand loyalty
brand recognition
brand preference
brand insistence

manufacturer brands
private distributor brands
generic brands
individual branding
family branding
brand extension
co-branding
brand licensing
family packaging
labeling

ISSUES FOR DISCUSSION AND REVIEW

1. Is a personal computer sold at a retail store a consumer product or a business product? Defend your answer.
2. How do convenience products and shopping products differ? What are the distinguishing characteristics of each type of product?
3. How does an organization's product mix relate to its development of a product line? When should an enterprise add depth to its product line rather than width to its product mix?
4. How do industry profits change as a product moves through the four stages of its life cycle?
5. What are the stages in the product adoption process, and how do they affect the commercialization phase?
6. How does branding benefit consumers and marketers?
7. What is brand equity? Identify and explain the major elements of brand equity.
8. What are the three major degrees of brand loyalty?
9. Compare and contrast manufacturer brands, private distributor brands, and generic brands.
10. Identify the factors a marketer should consider in selecting a brand name.
11. What is co-branding? What major issues should be considered when using co-branding?
12. Describe the functions a package can perform. Which function is most important? Why?
13. What are the main factors a marketer should consider when developing a package?
14. In what ways can packaging be used as a strategic tool?
15. What are the major functions of labeling?

MARKETING APPLICATIONS

1. Choose a familiar clothing store. Describe its product mix, including its depth and width. Evaluate the mix and make suggestions to the owner.
2. Tabasco pepper sauce is a product that has entered the maturity stage of the product life cycle. Name products that would fit into each of the four stages (introduction, growth, maturity, and decline). Describe each product and explain why it fits in that stage.
3. Generally, buyers go through a product adoption process before becoming loyal customers. Describe your experience in adopting a product you now use consistently. Did you go through all the stages?
4. Identify two brands for which you are brand insistent. How did you begin using these brands? Why do you no longer use other brands?
5. General Motors introduced the subcompact Geo with a name that appeals to a world market. Invent a brand name for a line of luxury sports cars that also would appeal to an international market. Suggest a name that implies quality, luxury, and value.
6. For each of the following product categories, choose an existing brand. Then, for each selected brand, suggest a co-brand and explain why the co-brand would be effective.
   a. Cookies
   b. Pizza
   c. Long-distance telephone service
   d. A sports drink
7. Identify a package that you believe to be inferior. Explain why you think the package is inferior, and discuss your recommendations for improving it.

ONLINE EXERCISE

8. In addition to providing information about the company's products, Goodyear's website helps consumers find the exact products they want and even directs them to the nearest Goodyear retailer. Visit the Goodyear site at http://www.goodyear.com.
   a. How does Goodyear use its website to communicate information about the quality of its tires?
   b. How does Goodyear's website demonstrate product and design features?
   c. Based on what you learned at the website, describe what Goodyear has done to position its tires.

DEVELOPING YOUR MARKETING PLAN

Identifying the needs of consumer groups and developing products that satisfy those needs is essential when creating a marketing strategy. Successful product development begins with a clear understanding of fundamental product concepts. The product concept is the basis on which many of the marketing plan decisions are made. When relating the information in this chapter to the development of your marketing plan, consider the following:

1. Using Figure 9.2 as a guide, create a matrix of the current product mix for your company.
2. Discuss how the profitability of your product will change as it moves through each of the phases of the product life cycle.
3. Create a brief profile of the type of consumer who is likely to represent each of the product adopter categories for your product.
4. Discuss the factors that could contribute to the failure of your product. How will you define product failure?

The information obtained from these questions should assist you in developing various aspects of your marketing plan found in the *Interactive Marketing Plan* exercise.

VIDEO CASE 9

Brewing Up Profits at New Belgium Brewery

The idea for New Belgium Brewing Company (NBB) began with a bicycling trip through Belgium, known for fine ales. As Jeff Lebesch, a U.S. electrical engineer, cruised around the country on a fat-tired mountain bike, he wondered if he could produce such high-quality ales in his home state of Colorado. After returning home, Lebesch began to experiment in his Fort Collins basement. When his home-brewed experiments earned rave reviews from friends, Lebesch and his wife, Kim Jordan, decided to open NBB in 1991. They named their first brew Fat Tire Amber Ale in honor of Lebesch's Belgian biking adventure.

Today NBB markets a variety of year-round and seasonal ales and pilsners. The standard line includes Sunshine Wheat, Blue Paddle Pilsner, Abbey Ale, and 1554 Black Ale, as well as the original Fat Tire Amber Ale. The company also markets seasonal beers, such as Frambozen and Abbey Grand Cru, released at Thanksgiving and Christmas. The firm occasionally offers one-time-only brews—such as LaFolie, a wood-aged beer—that are sold only until the batch runs out. Bottle label designs employ "good ol' days" nostalgia. The Fat Tire label, for example, features an old-style cruiser bike with wide tires, a padded seat, and a basket hanging from the handlebars.

NBB's beers are premium-priced to reflect their consistently high quality. This quality image differentiates the beers from macrobrews such as Budweiser and Coors and also keeps them competitive with other microbrews, such as Pete's Wicked Ale, Pyramid Pale Ale, and Sierra Nevada. To demonstrate its appreciation for its retailers and business partners, NBB does not sell beer to consumers on-site at the brewhouse for less than the retailers' charge. Although Fat Tire was initially sold only in

Fort Collins, distribution quickly expanded throughout the rest of Colorado. Customers can now find Fat Tire and other New Belgium offerings in 19 western states.

Since its founding, NBB's most effective promotion has been via word-of-mouth communication by devoted customers. The company initially avoided mass advertising, relying instead on small-scale, local promotions, such as print advertisements in alternative magazines, participation in local festivals, and sponsorship of alternative sports events. Through event sponsorships, such as the Tour de Fat and Ride the Rockies, NBB has raised thousands of dollars for various environmental, social, and cycling nonprofit organizations.

With expanding distribution, however, the brewery recognized a need to reach out to far-flung customers. It consulted with Dr. David Holt, an Oxford professor and branding expert. Holt, together with marketing director Greg Owsley, drafted a 70-page "manifesto" describing the brand's attributes, character, cultural relevancy, and promise. In particular, Holt identified in NBB an ethos of pursuing creative activities simply for the joy of doing them well and in harmony with the natural environment. The company then hired an ad agency to target affluent beer drinkers, men ages 25 to 44, with ads positioning the brand as whimsical, thoughtful, and reflective.

NBB has long linked its products and operations with concern for the natural environment. The brewery looks for cost-efficient, energy-saving ways to reduce its impact on the environment. Its employee owners unanimously agreed to invest in a wind turbine, making NBB the first fully wind-powered brewery in the United States. It also recycles as many supplies as possible, including cardboard boxes, keg caps, office materials, and the amber glass used in bottling. The brewery stores spent barley and hop grains in an on-premise silo and invites local farmers to pick up the grains, free of charge, to feed their pigs.

Another way NBB conserves energy is through the use of "sun tubes," which provide natural daytime lighting throughout the brewhouse all year long. NBB also encourages employees to reduce air pollution through alternative transportation. As an incentive, NBB gives each employee a "cruiser bike"—just like the one on the Fat Tire Amber Ale label and in the television ads—after one year of employment to encourage biking to work.

Beyond its use of environment-friendly technologies and innovations, NBB strives to improve communities and enhance lives through corporate giving, event sponsorship, and philanthropic involvement. The company donates $1 per barrel of beer sold to various cultural, social, environmental, and drug and alcohol awareness programs across the 15 western states in which it distributes beer. The brewhouse also maintains a community board where organizations can post community involvement activities and proposals.

NBB's commitment to quality, the environment, and its employees and customers is clearly expressed in its stated purpose: "To operate a profitable brewery which makes our love and talent manifest." This dedication has been well rewarded with loyal customers and industry awards. From cutting-edge environmental programs and high-tech industry advancements to employee-ownership programs and a strong belief in giving back to the community, NBB demonstrates its desire to create a living, learning community.

According to David Edgar, director of the Institute for Brewing Studies, "They've created a very positive image for their company in the beer-consuming public with smart decision making." NBB has set out to prove that for those who make the choice to drink responsibly, the company can do everything possible to contribute to society. With $96 million in annual sales, NBB is brewing up profits and saving the environment at the same time.

QUESTIONS FOR DISCUSSION

1. How do New Belgium Brewing Company's social responsibility initiatives help build its brand?
2. Describe New Belgium's branding policy. How does it use packaging to further its brand image?
3. Assess New Belgium's brand equity.

Mike Taylor, "2008 CEO of the Year: New Belgium's Kim Jordan," *ColoradoBiz,* December 2008, pp. 24+; Peter Asmus, "Goodbye Coal, Hello Wind," *Business Ethics,* July/August 1999, pp. 10–11; Robert Baun, "What's in a Name? Ask the Makers of Fat Tire," *The [Fort Collins] Coloradoan,* October 8, 2000, pp. E1, E3; Rachel Brand, Jeff Cioletti, "Earth's Brewer," *Beverage World,* October 15, 2007, pp. 22+; "Four Businesses Honored with Prestigious International Award for Outstanding Marketplace Ethics," Better Business Bureau, press release, September 23, 2002, www.bbb.org/alerts/2002torchwinners.asp; Julie Gordon, "Lebesch Balances Interests in Business, Community," *The [Fort Collins] Coloradoan,* February 26, 2003; David Kemp, Tour Connoisseur, New Belgium Brewing Company, personal interview by Nikole Haiar, November 21, 2000; "New Belgium Brewing Wins Ethics Award," *Denver Business Journal,* January 2, 2003, http://denver.bizjournals.com/denver/stories/2002/12/30/daily21. html; Lisa Sanders, "This Beer Will Reduce Your Anxiety," *Advertising Age,* January 17, 2005, p. 25; Bryan Simpson, "New Belgium Brewing: Brand Building Through Advertising and Public Relations," http://college.hmco.com/instructors/catalog/misc/new_belgium_brewing.pdf (accessed Feb. 5, 2008).

Developing and Managing Goods and Services

CHAPTER 10

© GARY CRABBE/ALAMY

MARKETING MAGIC BY MERLIN ENTERTAINMENTS

Magic Kingdom, move over: Merlin Entertainments Group, based in the United Kingdom, is making magic in theme parks all over the world. Merlin owns such well-known attractions as the Legoland and Sea Life parks, Madame Tussaud's wax museums, and the London Eye Ferris wheel. It acquired the Gardaland theme park and resort in Italy to extend its customer base by "attracting high volumes of young adults and teens as well as our traditional family market," says the CEO. In all, more than 27 million customers visit Merlin's 58 theme parks worldwide every year.

Bringing in new customers, delivering a memorable experience, and encouraging repeat visits are important when a new theme park costs millions of dollars and competition is fierce. Just as Disney and Universal never stop adding new attractions in their theme parks, Merlin constantly refreshes and expands its attractions. For example, adding 15 new exhibits to Legoland in Carlsbad, California, including the popular Pirate Shores, drove peak-season attendance higher by 20 percent. Inside that Legoland, Merlin has also opened the Land of Adventure and the Lost Kingdom.

In many cases, Merlin combines its brands to create entertainment destinations that draw families for multi-day stays. Next to Legoland in California, Merlin built Sea Life Legoland to showcase underwater creatures native to local waters plus submarines and divers made entirely out of Lego building blocks. The company is also introducing smaller versions of its theme parks, such as the Legoland Discovery Center in Illinois, as affordable one-day outings for families that don't want to spend big for multi-day visits to the big theme parks. Watch for more theme-park magic as Merlin makes the most of its service brands in the future.[1]

OBJECTIVES:

1. **Understand how companies manage existing products through line extensions and product modifications.**
2. **Describe how businesses develop a product idea into a commercial product.**
3. **Know the importance of product differentiation and the elements that differentiate one product from another.**
4. **Explain product positioning and repositioning.**
5. **Understand how product deletion is used to improve product mixes.**
6. **Understand the characteristics of services and how these characteristics present challenges when developing marketing mixes for service products.**
7. **Be familiar with organizational structures used for managing products.**

line extension Development of a product that is closely related to existing products in the line but meets different customer needs

product modification Change in one or more characteristics of a product

To compete effectively and achieve their goals, organizations such as Merlin Entertainments Group must be able to adjust their product mixes in response to changes in customers' needs. A firm often has to introduce new products, modify existing products, or delete products that were successful perhaps only a few years ago. To provide products that satisfy target markets and achieve the organization's objectives, a marketer must develop, alter, and maintain an effective product mix. An organization's product mix may need several types of adjustments. Because customers' attitudes and product preferences change over time, their desire for certain products may wane.

In this chapter we examine several ways to improve an organization's product mix. First, we discuss managing existing products through effective line extension and product modification. Next, we examine the stages of new-product development. Then we go on to discuss the ways companies differentiate their products in the marketplace and follow with a discussion of product positioning and repositioning. Next, we examine the importance of deleting weak products and the methods companies use to eliminate them. Then we explore the characteristics of services as products and how these services' characteristics affect the development of marketing mixes for services. Finally, we look at the organizational structures used to manage products.

Managing Existing Products

An organization can benefit by capitalizing on its existing products. By assessing the composition of the current product mix, a marketer can identify weaknesses and gaps. This analysis then can lead to improvement of the product mix through line extensions and product modifications.

LINE EXTENSIONS

A **line extension** is the development of a product closely related to one or more products in the existing product line but designed specifically to meet somewhat different customer needs. Procter & Gamble, for example, created several line extensions for its Febreze deodorizer, including candles and a travel-size version that fits in a purse or luggage.[2]

Many of the so-called new products introduced each year are in fact line extensions. Line extensions are more common than new products because they are a less expensive, lower-risk alternative for increasing sales. A line extension may focus on a different market segment or may be an attempt to increase sales within the same market segment by more precisely satisfying the needs of people in that segment. However, one side effect of employing a line extension is that it may result in a less positive evaluation of the core product if customers are less satisfied with the line extension.

Line Extension
Chocolate-flavored Chex Mix is a line extension.

PRODUCT MODIFICATIONS

Product modification means changing one or more characteristics of a product. A product modification differs from a line extension because the original product does not remain in the line. For example, automakers use product modifications annually when they create new models of the same brand. Once the new models are introduced, the manufacturers stop producing last year's model. Like line extensions, product modifications entail less risk than developing new products.

Product modification can indeed improve a firm's product mix, but only under certain conditions. First, the product must be modifiable. Second, customers must be able to perceive that a modification has been made. Third, the modification should make the product more consistent with customers' desires so that it provides greater satisfaction. One drawback to modifying a successful product is that the consumer who had experience with the original version of the product may view a modified version as a riskier purchase.[3] There are three major ways to modify products: quality, functional, and aesthetic modifications.

© AP IMAGES/PRNEWSFOTO/UNIWORLD GROUP INC.

Product Modification
Automobile companies employ quality, functional, and aesthetic modifications.

Quality Modifications

Quality modifications are changes relating to a product's dependability and durability. The changes usually are executed by altering the materials or the production process. For example, Continental Tire offers trucking companies commercial tires, including steer, drive, and trailer tires. Continental modified its tires to include features such as a patented stone ejection system that gives a longer casing life, and a full inch of tread depth, which make the tires last longer.[4] For a service, such as a sporting event or air travel, quality modifications may involve enhancing the emotional experience that makes the consumer passionate and loyal to the brand.

Reducing a product's quality may allow an organization to lower its price and direct the item at a different target market. In contrast, increasing the quality of a product may give a firm an advantage over competing brands. Higher quality may enable a company to charge a higher price by creating customer loyalty and lowering customer sensitivity to price. However, higher quality may require the use of more expensive components and processes, thus forcing the organization to cut costs in other areas. Some firms, such as Caterpillar, are finding ways to increase quality while reducing costs.

Functional Modifications

Changes that affect a product's versatility, effectiveness, convenience, or safety are called **functional modifications**; they usually require that the product be redesigned. Product categories that have undergone considerable functional modification include office and farm equipment, appliances, cleaning products, and consumer electronics. Functional modifications can make a product useful to more people and thus enlarge its market. Research in Motion, for example, added GPS chips and navigation features to its BlackBerry smart phones.[5] Functional modifications can place a product in a favorable competitive position by providing benefits that competing brands do not offer. They also can help an organization achieve and maintain a progressive image. Finally, functional modifications are sometimes made to reduce the possibility of product liability lawsuits.

quality modifications Changes relating to a product's dependability and durability

functional modifications Changes affecting a product's versatility, effectiveness, convenience, or safety

Aesthetic Modifications

Aesthetic modifications change the sensory appeal of a product by altering its taste, texture, sound, smell, or appearance. A buyer making a purchase decision is swayed by how a product looks, smells, tastes, feels, or sounds. Cadbury Schweppes, for example, added a new cherry vanilla flavor to its Dr Pepper soft-drink product line. An aesthetic modification may strongly affect purchases. Automobile makers have relied on both quality and aesthetic modifications.

Through aesthetic modifications, a firm can differentiate its product from competing brands and thus gain a sizable market share. The major drawback in using aesthetic modifications is that their value is determined subjectively. Although a firm may strive to improve the

aesthetic modifications Changes to the sensory appeal of a product

product's sensory appeal, customers actually may find the modified product less attractive.

Example of a New Product
Some marketers would consider this to be a new product, while others would view it as a line extension.

Developing New Products

A firm develops new products as a means of enhancing its product mix. Developing and introducing new products is frequently expensive and risky. However, failure to introduce new products is also risky.

The term *new product* can have more than one meaning. A genuinely new product offers innovative benefits. Enviga, a green-tea product offered by a joint venture of Coca-Cola and Nestlé, purports to be "calorie deficient," meaning drinking Enviga causes individuals to burn more calories than consumed per can.[6] But products that are different and distinctly better are often viewed as new. Cascade Lacrosse, for example, introduced a new sports helmet that reduces shock sustained by the brain by 40 percent. Since 40 percent of pro hockey players get at least one concussion a year, this represents a significant new product.[7] The following items are product innovations of the last 30 years: Post-it Notes, fax machines, cell phones, personal computers, personal digital assistants (PDAs), digital music players, satellite radio, and digital video recorders. A new product can be an innovative product that has never been sold by any organization, such as the digital camera when it was introduced for the first time. A radically new product involves a complex developmental process, including an extensive business analysis to determine the possibility of success.[8] A new product also can be one that a specific firm is currently launching even though other firms are already producing and marketing similar products. Finally, a product can be viewed as new when it is brought to one or more markets from another market. For example, making the Saturn VUE SUV available in Japan is viewed as a new-product introduction in Japan.

Before a product is introduced, it goes through the seven phases of the **new-product development process** shown in Figure 10.1: (1) idea generation, (2) screening, (3) concept testing, (4) business analysis, (5) product development, (6) test marketing, and (7) commercialization. A product may be dropped—and many are—at any stage of development. In this section we look at the process through which products are developed from idea inception to fully commercialized product.

IDEA GENERATION

new-product development process
A seven-phase process for introducing products

idea generation
Seeking product ideas to achieve objectives

Businesses and other organizations seek product ideas that will help them to achieve their objectives. This activity is **idea generation**. The fact that only a few ideas are good enough to be successful commercially underscores the challenge of the task. Although some organizations get their ideas almost by chance, firms that try to manage their product mixes effectively usually develop systematic approaches for generating new-product ideas. At the heart of innovation is a purposeful, focused effort to identify new ways to serve a market.

New-product ideas can come from several sources. They may come from internal sources—marketing managers, researchers, sales personnel, engineers, or other organizational personnel. Brainstorming and incentives or rewards for good ideas are typical intrafirm devices for stimulating development of ideas. For example, the idea for 3M Post-it Notes came from an

FIGURE 10.1 Phases of New-Product Development

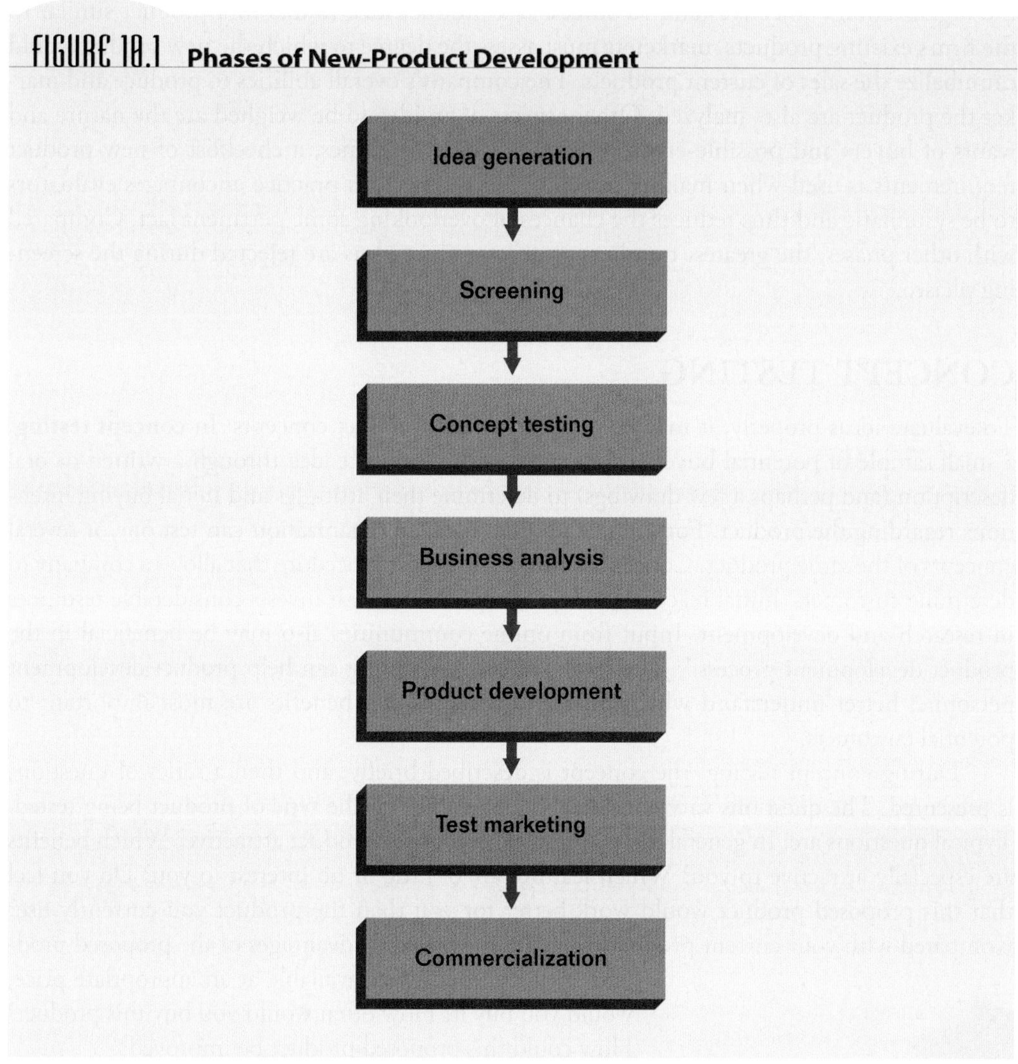

employee. As a church choir member, he used slips of paper to mark songs in his hymnal. Because the pieces of paper fell out, he suggested developing an adhesive-backed note. In the restaurant industry, ideas may come from franchisees. At McDonald's, for example, franchise owners invented the Big Mac and the Egg McMuffin. Today, new McDonald's product ideas often come from corporate chef Dan Coudreaut, who developed the fast-food giant's new snack wrap.[9]

New-product ideas also may arise from sources outside the firm, such as customers, competitors, advertising agencies, management consultants, and research organizations. Procter & Gamble gets 35 percent of its ideas from inventors and outside consultants.[10] Consultants are often used as sources for stimulating new-product ideas. When outsourcing new-product development activities to outside organizations, the best results are achieved from spelling out the specific tasks with detailed contractual specifications.[11] A significant portion of this money is used to assess customers' needs. Asking customers what they want from products and organizations has helped many firms become successful and remain competitive.

SCREENING

screening Choosing the most promising ideas for further review

In the process of **screening**, the ideas with the greatest potential are selected for further review. During screening, product ideas are analyzed to determine whether or not they match

concept testing Seeking potential buyers' responses to a product idea

business analysis Evaluating the potential contribution of a product idea to the firm's sales, costs, and profits

the organization's objectives and resources. If a product idea results in a product similar to the firm's existing products, marketers must assess the degree to which the new product could cannibalize the sales of current products. The company's overall abilities to produce and market the product are also analyzed. Other aspects of an idea to be weighed are the nature and wants of buyers and possible environmental changes. At times, a checklist of new-product requirements is used when making screening decisions. This practice encourages evaluators to be systematic and thus reduces the chances of overlooking some pertinent fact. Compared with other phases, the greatest numbers of new-product ideas are rejected during the screening phase.

CONCEPT TESTING

To evaluate ideas properly, it may be necessary to test product concepts. In **concept testing**, a small sample of potential buyers is presented with a product idea through a written or oral description (and perhaps a few drawings) to determine their attitudes and initial buying intentions regarding the product. For a single product idea, an organization can test one or several concepts of the same product. Concept testing is a low-cost procedure that allows a company to determine customers' initial reactions to a product idea before it invests considerable resources in research and development. Input from online communities also may be beneficial in the product development process.[12] The results of concept testing can help product development personnel better understand which product attributes and benefits are most important to potential customers.

During concept testing, the concept is described briefly, and then a series of questions is presented. The questions vary considerably depending on the type of product being tested. Typical questions are: In general, do you find this proposed product attractive? Which benefits are especially attractive to you? Which features are of little or no interest to you? Do you feel that this proposed product would work better for you than the product you currently use? Compared with your current product, what are the primary advantages of the proposed product? If this product were available at an appropriate price, would you buy it? How often would you buy this product? How could this proposed product be improved?

Entrepreneurial Marketing

"Crazy" Former Comic Laughs All the Way to the Bank—Thanks to Spanx!

When Sara Blakely wanted footless control top pantyhose for a smooth line under tight-fitting pants, she cut the feet off of her pantyhose to get what she wanted. She realized other women were probably seeking solutions to the same problem so she quickly went online to start the lengthy process of patenting her innovative idea.

When she tried to find a manufacturer for her prototype product, she was repeatedly turned down because the idea "made no sense, and would never sell." Finally, one manufacturer called her back and offered to work with her. What made him change his mind? He had two daughters and they didn't think the idea was crazy at all.

Spanx now has annual sales in excess of $150 million.[a]

BUSINESS ANALYSIS

During the **business analysis** stage, the product idea is evaluated to determine its potential contribution to the firm's sales, costs, and profits. In the course of a business analysis, evaluators ask various questions: Does the product fit with the organization's existing product mix? Is demand strong enough to justify entering the market, and will the demand endure? What types of environmental and competitive changes can be expected, and how will these changes affect the product's future sales, costs, and profits? Are the organization's research, development, engineering, and production capabilities adequate to develop the product? If new facilities must be constructed, how quickly can they be built, and how much will they cost? Is the necessary financing for development and commercialization on hand or obtainable at terms consistent with a favorable return on investment?

In the business analysis stage, firms seek market information. The results of consumer polls, along with secondary data, supply the specifics needed to estimate potential sales, costs, and profits. For many products in this stage (when they are still just product ideas), forecasting sales accurately is difficult. This is especially true for innovative and completely new products. Organizations sometimes employ breakeven analysis to determine how many units they would have to sell to begin making a profit. At times, an organization also uses payback analysis, in which marketers compute the time period required to recover the funds that would be invested in developing the new product. Because breakeven and payback analyses are based on estimates, they are usually viewed as useful but not particularly precise tools.

PRODUCT DEVELOPMENT

Product development is the phase in which the organization determines if it is technically feasible to produce the product and if it can be produced at costs low enough to make the final price reasonable. To test its acceptability, the idea or concept is converted into a prototype, or working model. The prototype should reveal tangible and intangible attributes associated with the product in consumers' minds. The product's design, mechanical features, and intangible aspects must be linked to wants in the marketplace. Through marketing research and concept testing, product attributes that are important to buyers are identified. These characteristics must be communicated to customers through the design of the product.

After a prototype is developed, its overall functioning must be tested. Its performance, safety, convenience, and other functional qualities are tested both in a laboratory and in the field. Functional testing should be rigorous and lengthy enough to test the product thoroughly. Manufacturing issues that come to light at this stage may require adjustments. When Cadbury Schweppes was developing its Trident Splash gum, production problems necessitated changes in the ingredients. One combination resulted in a too-soft gum that jammed machines; another combination resulted in the gum's liquid center leaking during trial deliveries. Finding just the right recipe required months.[13]

A crucial question that arises during product development is how much quality to build into the product. For example, a major dimension of quality is durability. Higher quality often calls for better materials and more expensive processing, which increase production costs and, ultimately, the product's price. In determining the specific level of quality, a marketer must ascertain approximately what price the target market views as acceptable. In addition, a marketer usually tries to set a quality level consistent with that of the firm's other products. Obviously, the quality of competing brands is also a consideration.

The development phase of a new product is frequently lengthy and expensive; thus a relatively small number of product ideas are put into development. If the product appears sufficiently successful during this stage to merit test marketing, then, during the latter part of the development stage, marketers begin to make decisions regarding branding, packaging, labeling, pricing, and promotion for use in the test marketing stage.

product development
Determining if producing a product is technically feasible and cost effective

TEST MARKETING

A limited introduction of a product in geographic areas chosen to represent the intended market is called **test marketing**. Procter & Gamble, for example, test marketed Align, a probiotic dietary supplement, in Cincinnati, Dallas, and St. Louis for two years before rolling out the product.[14] The aim of test marketing is to determine the extent to which potential customers will buy the product. Test marketing is not an extension of the development stage; it is a sample launching of the entire marketing mix. Test marketing should be conducted only after the product has gone through development and initial plans regarding the other

test marketing
Introducing a product on a limited basis to measure the extent to which potential customers will actually buy it

TABLE 10.1 Top Ten U.S. Test Market Cities

Rank	City
1	Albany, NY
2	Rochester, NY
3	Greensboro, NC
4	Birmingham, AL
5	Syracuse, NY
6	Charlotte, NC
7	Nashville, TN
8	Eugene, OR
9	Wichita, KS
10	Richmond, VA

Source: "Which American City Provides the Best Consumer Test Market?" *Business Wire*, May 24, 2004.

marketing-mix variables. For example, Swedish Match AB, the parent company of Chesterfield County–based Swedish Match North America, joined hands with cigarette maker Philip Morris International to sell a smokeless tobacco product called Snus, in the United States. Snus is a type of oral, smokeless tobacco that is pasteurized and sold in pouches that consumers place under the lip. The product was test-marketed under the Marlboro brand name in Dallas and Indianapolis.[15]

Companies use test marketing to lessen the risk of product failure. The dangers of introducing an untested product include undercutting already profitable products and, should the new product fail, loss of credibility with distributors and customers.

Selection of appropriate test areas is very important because the validity of test market results depends heavily on selecting test sites that provide accurate representation of the intended target market. The top ten most often used U.S. test market cities appear in Table 10.1.

The criteria used for choosing test cities depend on the product's attributes, the target market's characteristics, and the firm's objectives and resources. Test marketing provides several benefits. It lets marketers expose a product in a natural marketing environment to measure its sales performance. While the product is being marketed in a limited area, the company can strive to identify weaknesses in the product or in other parts of the marketing mix. A product weakness discovered after a nationwide introduction can be expensive to correct. If consumers' early reactions are negative, marketers may be unable to persuade consumers to try the product again. Thus, making adjustments after test marketing can be crucial to the success of a new product. On the other hand, testing results may be positive enough to accelerate introduction of the new product. Test marketing also allows marketers to experiment with variations in advertising, pricing, and packaging in different test areas and to measure the extent of brand awareness, brand switching, and repeat purchases resulting from these alterations in the marketing mix.

Test marketing is not without risks. It is expensive, and competitors may try to interfere. A competitor may attempt to "jam" the test program by increasing its own advertising or promotions, lowering prices, and offering special incentives, all to combat the recognition and purchase of the new brand. Any such tactics can invalidate test results. Sometimes, too, competitors copy the product in the testing stage and rush to introduce a similar product. This is the time to conduct research to identify issues that might drive potential customers to market-leading competitors instead.[16] It is desirable to move to the commercialization phase as soon as possible after successful testing. On the other hand, some firms have been known to promote new products heavily long before they are ready for the market to discourage competitors from developing similar new products.

Because of these risks, many companies use alternative methods to measure customer preferences. One such method is simulated test marketing. Typically, consumers at shopping centers are asked to view an advertisement for a new product and are given a free sample to take home. These consumers are interviewed subsequently over the phone and asked to rate the product. The major advantages of simulated test marketing are greater speed, lower costs, and tighter security, which reduce the flow of information to competitors and reduce jamming. Several marketing research firms, such as ACNielsen Company, offer test marketing services to help provide independent assessment of proposed products.

Clearly, not all products that are test marketed are launched. At times, problems discovered during test marketing cannot be resolved.

COMMERCIALIZATION

During the **commercialization** phase, plans for full-scale manufacturing and marketing must be refined and settled and budgets for the project prepared. Early in the commercialization phase, marketing management analyzes the results of test marketing to find out what changes in the marketing mix are needed before the product is introduced. The results of test marketing may tell marketers to change one or more of the product's physical attributes, modify the distribution plans to include more retail outlets, alter promotional efforts, or change the product's price. However, as more and more changes are made based on test marketing findings, the test marketing projections may become less valid.

During the early part of this stage, marketers not only must gear up for larger-scale production but also must make decisions about warranties, repairs, and replacement parts. The type of warranty a firm provides can be a critical issue for buyers, especially when expensive, technically complex products are involved. Establishing an effective system for providing repair services and replacement parts is necessary to maintain favorable customer relationships. Although the producer may furnish these services directly to buyers, it is more common for the producer to provide such services through regional service centers. Regardless of how services are provided, it is important to customers that they be performed quickly and correctly.

The product enters the market during the commercialization phase. When introducing a product, a firm may spend enormous sums for advertising, personal selling, and other types of promotion, as well as for plant and equipment. Such expenditures may not be recovered for several years. Smaller firms may find this process difficult, but even so, they may use press releases, blogs, podcasts, and other tools to capture quick feedback as well as promote the new product. Another low-cost promotional tool is product reviews in newspapers and magazines, which can be especially helpful when they are positive and target the same customers.

Products are not usually launched nationwide overnight but are introduced through a process called a *rollout*. Through a rollout, a product is introduced in stages, starting in one geographic area and gradually expanding into adjacent areas. It may take several years to market the product nationally. Sometimes the test cities are used as initial marketing areas, and introduction of the product becomes a natural extension of test marketing. A product test marketed in Albany, NY, Birmingham, AL, Eugene, OR, and Wichita, KS, as the map in Figure 10.2 shows, could be introduced first in those cities. After the stage 1 introduction is complete,

commercialization
Deciding on full-scale manufacturing and marketing plans and preparing budgets

stage 2 could include market coverage of the states where the test cities are located. In stage 3, marketing efforts might be extended into adjacent states. All remaining states then would be covered in stage 4. Gradual product introductions do not always occur state by state; other geographic combinations, such as groups of counties that cross state borders, are sometimes used. Products destined for multinational markets also may be rolled out one country or region at a time.

Gradual product introduction is desirable for several reasons. It reduces the risks of introducing a new product. If the product fails, the firm will experience smaller losses if it introduced the item in only a few geographic areas than if it marketed the product nationally. Furthermore, a company cannot introduce a product nationwide overnight because a system of wholesalers and retailers necessary to distribute the product cannot be established so quickly. The development of a distribution network may take considerable time. Also, the number of units needed to satisfy national demand for a successful product can be enormous, and a firm usually cannot produce the required quantities in a short time. Finally, gradual introduction allows for fine-tuning of the marketing mix to better satisfy target customers.

Despite the good reasons for introducing a product gradually, marketers realize that this approach creates some competitive problems. A gradual introduction allows competitors to observe what the firm is doing and to monitor results, just as the firm's own marketers are doing. If competitors see that the newly introduced product is successful, they may quickly enter the same target market with similar products. In addition, as a product is introduced region by region, competitors may expand their marketing efforts to offset promotion of the new product.

FIGURE 10.2 Stages of Expansion into a National Market During Commercialization

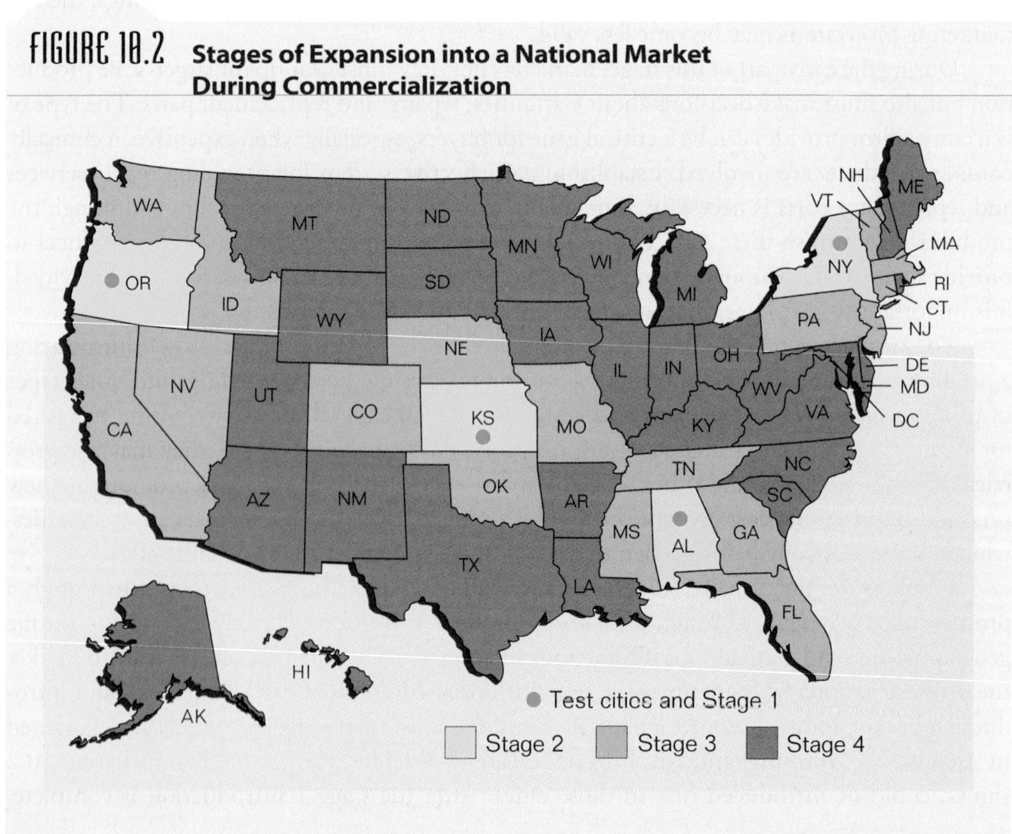

Product Differentiation Through Quality, Design, and Support Services

Some of the most important characteristics of products are the elements that distinguish them from one another. **Product differentiation** is the process of creating and designing products so that customers perceive them as different from competing products. Customer perception is critical in differentiating products. Perceived differences might include quality, features, styling, price, and image. A crucial element used to differentiate one product from another is the brand. In this section we examine three aspects of product differentiation that companies must consider when creating and offering products for sale: product quality, product design and features, and product support services. These aspects involve the company's attempt to create real differences among products. Later in this chapter we discuss how companies position their products in the marketplace based on these three aspects.

PRODUCT QUALITY

Quality refers to the overall characteristics of a product that allow it to perform *as expected* in satisfying customer needs. The words *as expected* are very important to this definition because quality usually means different things to different customers. For some, durability signifies quality. For other customers, a product's ease of use may indicate quality.

The concept of quality also varies between consumer and business markets. For business markets, technical suitability, ease of repair, and company reputation are important characteristics. Unlike consumers, most businesses place far less emphasis on price than on product quality.

One important dimension of quality is **level of quality**, the amount of quality a product possesses. The concept is a relative one because the quality level of one product is difficult to describe unless it is compared with that of other products. For example, most consumers would consider the quality level of Timex watches to be good, but when they compare Timex watches with Rolex watches, most consumers would say that Rolex's level of quality is higher.

product differentiation
Creating and designing products so that customers perceive them as different from competing products

quality
Characteristics of a product that allow it to perform as expected in satisfying customer needs

level of quality
The amount of quality a product possesses

COURTESY OF ROLEX

Product Quality
Select products are designed to have very high quality and to use quality as a major competitive tool.

Sustainable Marketing

Small Businesses Prosper with Green Products

Differentiating products as green has built big profits for small businesses like New Leaf Paper and Carol's Daughter. Entrepreneur Jeff Mendelsohn started New Leaf Paper in 1998 to turn recycled materials into high-quality, eco-friendly paper stock for commercial use. Although first-year sales were $1 million, he continued to expand his green product line and educate both printers and designers about the environmental benefits of New Leaf Paper. In the first decade, Mendelsohn increased annual sales beyond $20 million on the basis of green differentiation. "We have a unique product line and story to tell in the paper industry," he says.

© PETER ADAMS/ZEFA/CORBIS

Carol's Daughter specializes in all-natural personal care products such as shampoo, skin cream, and bath oil. The company's green differentiation sets it apart from much larger corporate competitors targeting the consumer cosmetics market. Lisa Price founded Carol's Daughter in 1994 when she began making beauty products in her kitchen using fresh, natural ingredients. With investments from celebrities like Will Smith and his wife, Jada Pinkett Smith, plus the marketing savvy of Steve Stoute, Carol's Daughter has expanded and now sells through Macy's, Sephora, and other major retailers as well as its own store outlets. Even as annual sales approach $30 million, Stoute emphasizes that "we haven't changed the heritage of the brand"— green remains the primary differentiation.[b]

How high should the level of quality be? It depends on the product and the costs and consequences of a product failure.

A second important dimension is consistency. **Consistency of quality** refers to the degree to which a product has the same level of quality over time. Consistency means giving customers the quality they expect every time they purchase the product. As with level of quality, consistency is a relative concept. It implies a quality comparison within the same brand over time. The quality level of McDonald's french fries is generally consistent from one location to another. The consistency of product quality also can be compared across competing products. At this stage, consistency becomes critical to a company's success. Companies that can provide quality on a consistent basis have a major competitive advantage over rivals.

PRODUCT DESIGN AND FEATURES

Product design refers to how a product is conceived, planned, and produced. Design is a very complex topic because it involves the total sum of all the product's physical characteristics. Many companies are known for the outstanding designs of their products: Sony for personal electronics, Hewlett-Packard for printers, Apple for computers and music players, and JanSport for backpacks. Good design is one of the best competitive advantages any brand can possess.

One component of design is **styling**, or the physical appearance of the product. The style of a product is one design feature that can allow certain products to sell very rapidly. Good design, however, means more than just appearance; it also involves a product's functionality and usefulness. For example, a pair of jeans may look great, but if they fall apart after three washes, clearly the design was poor. Most consumers seek products that both look good and function well.

Product features are specific design characteristics that allow a product to perform certain tasks. By adding or subtracting features, a company can differentiate its products from those of the competition. Chrysler promotes its line of minivans as having more features related to passenger safety—dual air bags, steel-reinforced doors, and integrated child safety seats—than any other auto company. Product features also can be used to differentiate products within the same company. For example, Nike offers both a walking shoe and a run-walk shoe for specific consumer needs. In these cases, the company's products are sold with a wide range of features, from low-priced "base" or "stripped-down" versions to high-priced, prestigious, "feature-packed" ones. The automotive industry regularly sells products with a wide range of features. In general, the more features a product has, the higher is its price, and often, the higher is the perceived quality. For a brand to have a sustainable competitive advantage, marketers must determine the product designs and features that customers desire. Information from marketing research efforts and from databases can help in assessing customers' product design and feature preferences. Being able to meet customers' desires for product design and features at prices they can afford is crucial to a product's long-term success.

SNAPSHOT

Source: BusinessWeek

PRODUCT SUPPORT SERVICES

Many companies differentiate their product offerings by providing support services. Usually referred to as **customer services**, these services include any human or mechanical efforts or activities a company provides that add value to a product.[17] Examples of customer services include delivery and installation, financing arrangements, customer training, warranties and guarantees, repairs, layaway plans, convenient hours of operation, adequate parking, and information through toll-free numbers and websites. For example, Zappos, an online shoe retailer, has earned a reputation for excellent customer service in part owing to its 24-hour service and free, fast returns.[18]

Whether as a major or minor part of the total product offering, all marketers of goods sell customer services. Providing good customer service may be the only way that a company can differentiate its products when all products in a market have essentially the same quality, design, and features. This is especially true in the computer industry. When buying a laptop computer, for example, some customers are more concerned about fast delivery, technical support, warranties, and price than about product quality and design. Through research, a company can discover the types of services customers want and need. The level of customer service a company provides can profoundly affect customer satisfaction.

consistency of quality The degree to which a product has the same level of quality over time

product design How a product is conceived, planned, and produced

styling The physical appearance of a product

product features Specific design characteristics that allow a product to perform certain tasks

customer services Human or mechanical efforts or activities that add value to a product

product positioning Creating and maintaining a certain concept of a product in customers' minds

Product Positioning and Repositioning

Product positioning refers to the decisions and activities intended to create and maintain a certain concept of the firm's product (relative to competitive brands) in customers' minds. When marketers introduce a product, they try to position it so that it appears to have the characteristics that the target market most desires. This projected image is crucial. Crest is positioned as a fluoride toothpaste that fights cavities, and Close-Up is positioned as a whitening toothpaste that enhances the user's sex appeal.

PERCEPTUAL MAPPING

A product's position is the result of customers' perceptions of the product's attributes relative to those of competitive brands. Buyers make numerous purchase decisions on a regular basis. To avoid a continuous reevaluation of numerous products, buyers tend to group, or "position," products in

FIGURE 10.3 Hypothetical Perceptual Map for Pain Relievers

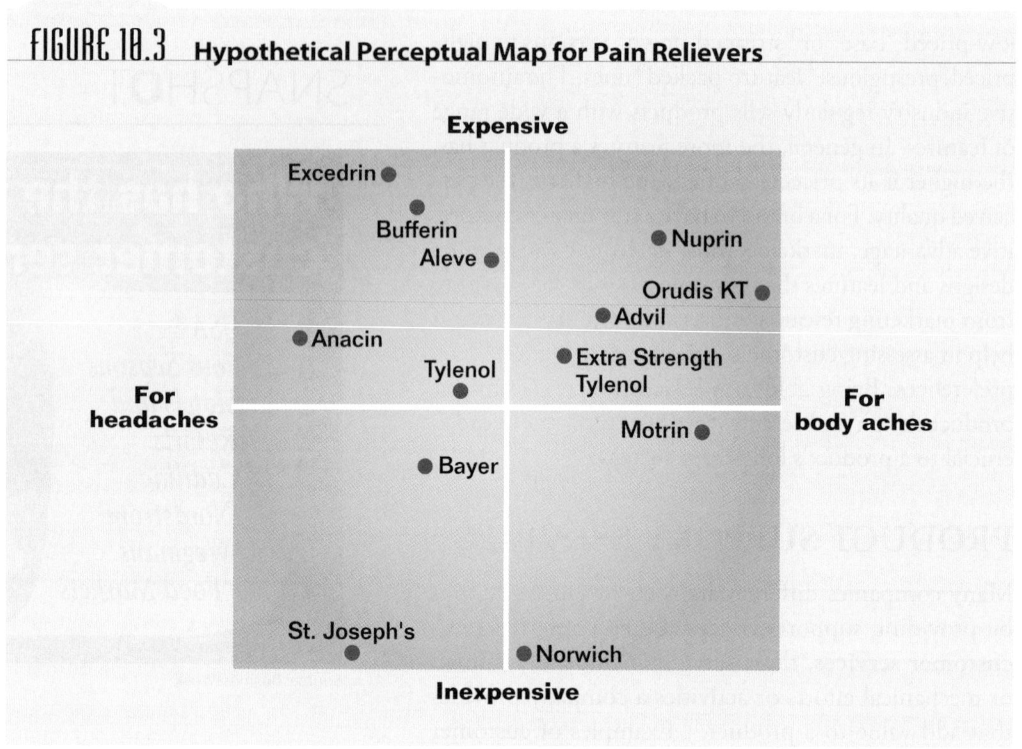

COURTESY OF CORT

Product Support Services
CORT Furniture provides product support services that some other office furniture manufacturers do not.

their minds to simplify buying decisions. Rather than allowing customers to position products independently, marketers often try to influence and shape consumers' concepts or perceptions of products through advertising. Marketers sometimes analyze product positions by developing perceptual maps, as shown in Figure 10.3. Perceptual maps are created by questioning a sample of consumers about their perceptions of products, brands, and organizations with respect to two or more dimensions. To develop a perceptual map like the one in Figure 10.3, respondents would be asked how they perceive selected pain relievers in regard to price and type of pain for which the products are used. Also, respondents would be asked about their preferences for product features to establish "ideal points" or "ideal clusters," which represent a consensus about a specific group of customers' desires in terms of product features. Then marketers can see how their brand is perceived compared with the ideal points.

BASES FOR POSITIONING

Marketers can use several bases for product positioning. A common basis for positioning products is to use competitors. A firm can position a product to compete head-on with another brand, as PepsiCo has done against Coca-Cola, or to avoid competition, as 7UP has done relative to other soft-drink producers. Head-to-head competition may be a marketer's positioning objective if the product's performance characteristics are at least equal to those of competitive brands and if the product is priced lower. Head-to-head positioning may be appropriate even when the price is higher if the product's performance characteristics are superior. For example, Ford has positioned its Fusion sedan head-to-head against the Honda Accord and Toyota Camry through advertisements that highlight the results of a *Car and Driver* magazine driving challenge in which the Fusion earned the top ratings.[19] Conversely, positioning to avoid competition may be best when the product's performance characteristics do not differ significantly from those of competing brands. Moreover, positioning a brand to avoid competition may be appropriate when that brand has unique characteristics that are important to some buyers. Volvo, for example, has for years positioned itself away from competitors by focusing on the safety characteristics of its cars. Whereas some auto companies mention safety issues in their advertisements, many are more likely to focus on style, fuel efficiency, performance, or terms of sale. Avoiding competition is critical when a firm introduces a brand into a market in which the company already has one or more brands. Marketers usually want to avoid cannibalizing sales of their existing brands unless the new brand generates substantially larger profits.

© AP IMAGES/PRNEWSFOTO/DOCKERS

Product Positioning
The maker of Dockers positions its products as being comfortable, flexible, and a reasonable value.

A product's position can be based on specific product attributes or features. For example, the Apple's iPhone is positioned based on product attributes such as its unique shape, its easy-to-use touch screen, and its access to iTunes. If a product has been planned properly, its features will give it the distinct appeal needed. Style, shape, construction, and color help to create the image and the appeal. If buyers can easily identify the benefits, they are, of course, more likely to purchase the product. When the new product does not offer certain preferred attributes, there is room for another new product.

Other bases for product positioning include price, quality level, and benefits provided by the product. For example, Era laundry detergent provides stain treatment and stain removal. Also, the target market can be a positioning basis caused by marketing. This type of positioning relies heavily on promoting the types of people who use the product.

REPOSITIONING

Positioning decisions are not just for new products. Evaluating the positions of existing products is important because a brand's market share and profitability may be strengthened by product repositioning. For example, several years ago Kraft was on the verge of discontinuing Cheez Whiz because its sales had declined considerably. After Kraft marketers repositioned Cheez Whiz as a fast, convenient, microwavable cheese sauce, its sales rebounded to new heights. When introducing a new product into a product line, one or more existing brands may have to be repositioned to minimize cannibalization of established brands and thus ensure a favorable position for the new brand.

Repositioning can be accomplished by physically changing the product, its price, or its distribution. Rather than making any of these changes, marketers sometimes reposition a product by changing its image through promotional efforts. Finally, a marketer may reposition a product by aiming it at a different target market.

Product Deletion

Generally, a product cannot satisfy target market customers and contribute to the achievement of an organization's overall goals indefinitely. **Product deletion** is the process of eliminating a product from the product mix, usually because it no longer satisfies a sufficient number of customers. Condé Naste, for example, discontinued

product deletion
Eliminating a product from the product mix

its century-old *House & Garden* magazine after years of declining ad revenues, due in part to intense competition from other home décor and home life magazines.[20] A declining product reduces an organization's profitability and drains resources that could be used to modify other products or develop new ones. A marginal product may require shorter production runs, which can increase per-unit production costs. Finally, when a dying product completely loses favor with customers, the negative feelings may transfer to some of the company's other products.

Most organizations find it difficult to delete a product. A decision to drop a product may be opposed by managers and other employees who believe that the product is necessary to the product mix. Salespeople who still have some loyal customers are especially upset when a product is dropped. Considerable resources and effort are sometimes spent trying to change a slipping product's marketing mix to improve its sales and thus avoid having to eliminate it.

Some organizations delete products only after the products have become heavy financial burdens. A better approach is some form of systematic review in which each product is evaluated periodically to determine its impact on the overall effectiveness of the firm's product mix. Such a review should analyze the product's contribution to the firm's sales for a given period, as well as estimate future sales, costs, and profits associated with the product. It also should gauge the value of making changes in the marketing strategy to improve the product's performance. A systematic review allows an organization to improve product performance and ascertain when to delete products.

There are three basic ways to delete a product: phase it out, run it out, or drop it immediately (see Figure 10.4). A *phase-out* allows the product to decline without a change in the marketing strategy; no attempt is made to give the product new life. Nikon, for example, simply allowed sales of its discontinued film cameras to continue until their supplies ran out.[21] A *run-out* exploits any strengths left in the product. Intensifying marketing efforts in core markets or eliminating some marketing expenditures, such as advertising, may cause a sudden jump in profits. This approach is commonly taken for technologically obsolete products, such as older models of computers and calculators. Often the price is reduced to get a sales spurt. The third alternative, an *immediate drop* of an unprofitable product, is the best strategy when losses are too great to prolong the product's life.

FIGURE 10.4 Product Deletion Process

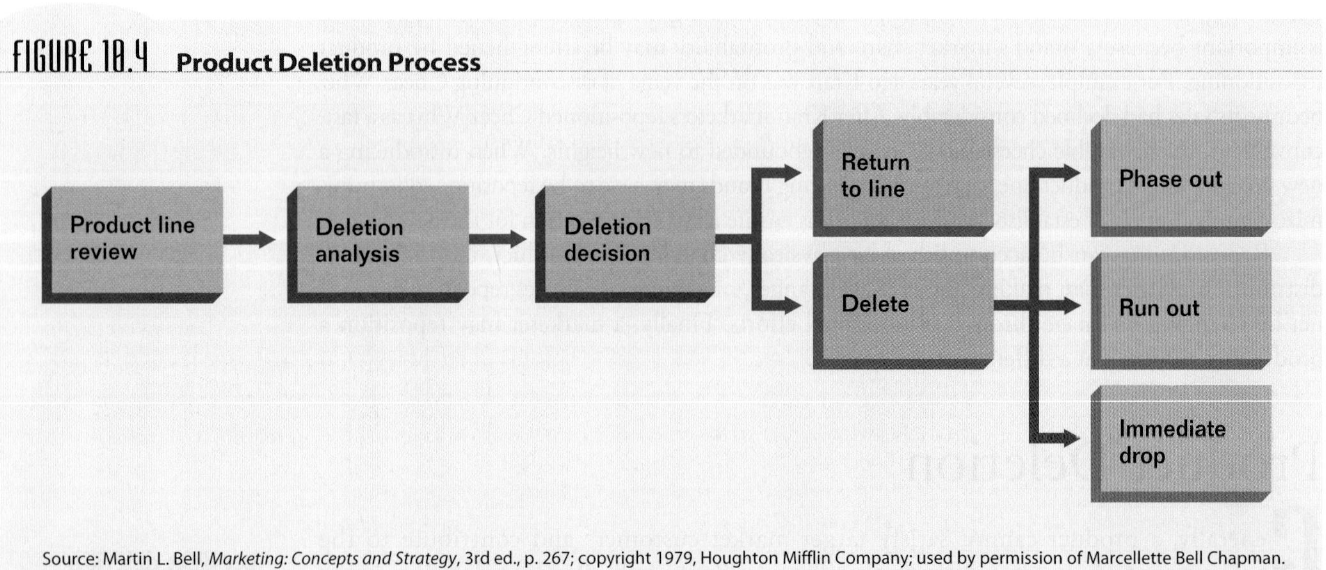

Source: Martin L. Bell, *Marketing: Concepts and Strategy*, 3rd ed., p. 267; copyright 1979, Houghton Mifflin Company; used by permission of Marcellette Bell Chapman.

Managing Services as Products

Many products are services rather than tangible goods. The organizations that market service products include for-profit firms, such as those offering financial, personal, and professional services, and nonprofit organizations, such as educational institutions, churches, charities, and governments. In this section we focus initially on the growing importance of service industries in our economy. Then we address the unique characteristics of services. Finally, we deal with the challenges these characteristics pose in developing and managing marketing mixes for services.

NATURE AND IMPORTANCE OF SERVICES

All products, whether goods, services, or ideas, are to some extent intangible. Services are usually provided through the application of human and/or mechanical efforts directed at people or objects. For example, a service such as education involves the efforts of service providers (teachers) directed at people (students), whereas janitorial and interior decorating services direct their efforts at objects. Services also can involve the use of mechanical efforts directed at people (air or mass transportation) or objects (freight transportation). A wide variety of services, such as health care and landscaping, involve both human and mechanical efforts. Although many services entail the use of tangibles such as tools and machinery, the primary difference between a service and a good is that a service is dominated by the intangible portion of the total product. Services, as products, should not be confused with the related topic of customer services. While customer service is part of the marketing of goods, service marketers also provide customer services.

The increasing importance of services in the U.S. economy has led many people to call the United States the world's first service economy. In most developed countries, including Germany, Japan, Australia, and Canada, services account for about 70 percent of the country's gross domestic product (GDP). More than half of new businesses are service businesses, and service employment is expected to continue to grow. These industries have absorbed much of the influx of women and minorities into the workforce. In the United States, some customer-contact jobs, especially call centers, have been outsourced—into the homes of U.S. workers, especially women. JetBlue, for example, has 1,400 reservation agents who work from their homes.[22]

CHARACTERISTICS OF SERVICES

The issues associated with marketing service products are not exactly the same as those associated with marketing goods. To understand these differences, it is first necessary to understand the distinguishing characteristics of services. Services have six basic characteristics: intangibility, inseparability of production and consumption, perishability, heterogeneity, client-based relationships, and customer contact.[23]

Intangibility

As already noted, the major characteristic that distinguishes a service from a good is intangibility. **Intangibility** means a service is not physical and therefore cannot be touched. For example, it is impossible to touch the education that students derive from attending classes; the intangible benefit is becoming more knowledgeable. In addition, services cannot be physically possessed. Products range from pure goods (tangible) to pure services (intangible). Pure goods, if they exist at all, are rare because practically all marketers of goods also provide customer services. Intangible, service-dominant products such as education and health care are clearly service products. Of course, some products, such as a restaurant meal or a hotel stay, have both tangible and intangible dimensions.

intangibility
A service that is not physical and cannot be touched

Inseparability of Production and Consumption

Another important characteristic of services that creates challenges for marketers is **inseparability**, which refers to the fact that the production of a service cannot be separated from its consumption by customers. For example, air passenger service is produced and consumed simultaneously. In other words, services are often produced, sold, and consumed at the same time. In goods marketing, a customer can purchase a good, take it home, and store it until he or she is ready to use it. The manufacturer of the good may never see an actual customer. Customers, however, often must be present at the production of a service (such as marriage counseling or surgery) and cannot take the service home. Indeed, both the service provider and the customer must work together to provide the service's full value.[24] For instance, customers who use coin-counting machines in their local supermarkets must pour in their coins and then wait until all the change is tallied. Inseparability implies a shared responsibility between the customer and service provider. As a result, training programs for employees should stress the customer's role in the service experience to elevate their perceptions of shared responsibility and positive feelings.[25]

Perishability

Services are characterized by **perishability** because the unused service capacity of one time period cannot be stored for future use. For example, empty seats on an air flight today cannot be stored and sold to passengers at a later date. Other examples of service perishability include unsold basketball tickets, unscheduled dentists' appointment times, and empty hotel rooms. Although some goods, such as meat, milk, and produce, are perishable, goods generally are less perishable than services. If a pair of jeans has been sitting on a department store shelf for a week, someone still can buy them the next day. Goods marketers can handle the supply-demand problem through production scheduling and inventory techniques. Service marketers do not have the same advantage, and they face several hurdles in trying to balance supply and demand. They can, however, plan for demand that fluctuates according to day of the week, time of day, or season.

Heterogeneity

Services delivered by people are susceptible to **heterogeneity**, or variation in quality. Quality of manufactured goods is easier to control with standardized procedures, and mistakes are easier to isolate and correct. Because of the nature of human behavior, however, it is very difficult for service providers to maintain a consistent quality of service delivery. This variation in quality can occur from one organization to another, from one service person to another within the same service facility, and from one service facility to another within the same organization. For example, the retail clerks in one bookstore may be more knowledgeable and therefore more helpful than those in another bookstore owned by the same chain. Heterogeneity usually increases as the degree of labor intensiveness increases. Many services, such as auto repair, education, and hairstyling, rely heavily on human labor. Other services, such as telecommunications, health clubs, and public transportation, are more equipment-intensive. People-based services are often prone to fluctuations in quality from one time period to the next. For example, the fact that a hairstylist gives a customer a good haircut today does not guarantee that customer a haircut of equal quality from the same hairstylist at a later date. Equipment-based services, in contrast, suffer from this problem to a lesser degree than people-based services. For instance, automated teller machines have reduced inconsistency in the quality of teller services at banks, and bar-code scanning has improved the accuracy of service at the checkout counters in grocery stores.

inseparability
Being produced and consumed at the same time

perishability
The inability of unused service capacity to be stored for future use

heterogeneity
Variation in quality

client-based relationships
Interactions that result in satisfied customers who use a service repeatedly over time

Client-Based Relationships

The success of many services depends on creating and maintaining **client-based relationships**, interactions with customers that result in satisfied customers who use a service repeatedly over time.[26] In fact, some service providers, such as lawyers, accountants, and financial advisers, call

© AP IMAGES/PRNEWSFOTO/SILICON VALLEY BANK

Level of Customer Contact
Banking services require a relatively low level of customer contact, especially since a number of services are provided online.

their customers *clients* and often develop and maintain close long-term relationships with them. For such service providers, it is not enough to attract customers. They are successful only to the degree to which they can maintain a group of clients who use their services on an ongoing basis. For example, an accountant may serve a family in his or her area for decades. If the members of this family like the quality of the accountant's services, they are likely to recommend the accountant to other families. If several families repeat this positive word-of-mouth communication, the accountant likely will acquire a long list of satisfied clients. Indeed, research has found that word-of-mouth communication plays a key role in services, particularly for consumers with innovative personalities.[27] This process is the key to creating and maintaining client-based relationships. To ensure that it actually occurs, the service provider must take steps to build trust, demonstrate customer commitment, and satisfy customers so well that they become very loyal to the provider and unlikely to switch to competitors.

Customer Contact

Not all services require a high degree of customer contact, but many do. **Customer contact** refers to the level of interaction between the service provider and the customer that is necessary to deliver the service. High-contact services include health care, real estate, legal, and hair-care services. Examples of low-contact services are tax preparation, auto repair, and dry cleaning. Some service-oriented businesses are reducing their level of customer contact through technology. Alamo Rent A Car, for example, introduced self-service check-in kiosks, where customers can print out their rental agreement and then head straight to the rental vehicle.[28] Note that high-contact services generally involve actions directed toward people, who must be present during production. A hairstylist's customer, for example, must be present during the styling process. When the customer must be present, the process of production may be just as important as its final outcome. Although it is sometimes possible for the service provider to go to the customer, high-contact services typically require that the customer go to the production facility. Thus the physical appearance of the facility may be a major component of the customer's overall evaluation of the service. For example, when the physical setting fosters customer-to-customer interactions, it can lead to greater loyalty to an establishment and positive word-of-mouth communications.[29]

customer contact The level of interaction between provider and customer needed to deliver the service

TABLE 10.2 Service Characteristics and Marketing Challenges

Service Characteristics	Resulting Marketing Challenges
Intangibility	Difficult for customer to evaluate
	Customer does not take physical possession
	Difficult to advertise and display
	Difficult to set and justify prices
	Service process usually not protectable by patents
Inseparability of production and consumption	Service provider cannot mass produce services
	Customer must participate in production
	Other consumers affect service outcomes
	Services are difficult to distribute
Perishability	Services cannot be stored
	Balancing supply and demand is very difficult
	Unused capacity is lost forever
	Demand may be very time-sensitive
Heterogeneity	Service quality is difficult to control
	Service delivery is difficult to standardize
Client-based relationships	Success depends on satisfying and keeping customers over the long term Generating repeat business is challenging
	Relationship marketing becomes critical
Customer contact	Service providers are critical to delivery
	Requires high levels of service employee training and motivation
	Changes a high-contact service into a low-contact service to achieve lower costs without reducing customer satisfaction

Sources: K. Douglas Hoffman and John E. G. Bateson, *Essentials of Services Marketing* (Mason, OH: South-Western, 2001); Valarie A. Zeithaml, A. Parasuraman, and Leonard L. Berry, *Delivering Quality Service: Balancing Customer Perceptions and Expectations* (New York: Free Press, 1990); Leonard L. Berry and A. Parasuraman, *Marketing Services: Competing through Quality* (New York: Free Press, 1991), p. 5.

Employees of high-contact service providers are part of a very important ingredient in creating satisfied customers. A fundamental precept of customer contact is that satisfied employees lead to satisfied customers. In fact, research indicates that employee satisfaction is the single most important factor in providing high service quality. Thus, to minimize the problems that customer contact can create, service organizations must take steps to understand and meet the needs of employees by training them adequately, empowering them to make more decisions, and rewarding them for customer-oriented behavior.[30]

CREATING MARKETING MIXES FOR SERVICES

The characteristics of services create a number of challenges for service marketers (see Table 10.2). These challenges are especially evident in the development and management of marketing mixes for services. Although such mixes contain the four major marketing-mix variables—product, price, distribution, and promotion—the characteristics of services require that marketers consider additional issues.

Development of Services

A service offered by an organization generally is a package, or bundle, of services consisting of a core service and one or more supplementary services. A *core service* is the basic service experience or commodity that a customer expects to receive. A *supplementary service* is a supportive one related to the core service that is used to differentiate the service bundle from that of competitors. For example, Hampton Inns provides a room as a core service. Bundled with the room are supplementary services such as free local phone calls, cable television, and a complimentary continental breakfast.

As discussed earlier, heterogeneity results in variability in service quality and makes it difficult to standardize services. However, heterogeneity provides one advantage to service marketers: It allows them to customize their services to match the specific needs of individual customers. Health care is an example of an extremely customized service; the services provided differ from one patient to the next. Such customized services can be expensive for both provider and customer, and some service marketers therefore face a dilemma: how to provide service at an acceptable level of quality in an efficient and economic manner and still satisfy individual customer needs. To cope with this problem, some service marketers offer standardized packages. For example, a lawyer may offer a divorce package at a specified price for an uncontested divorce. When service bundles are standardized, the specific actions and activities of the service provider usually are highly specified. Automobile quick-lube providers frequently offer a service bundle for a single price; the specific actions to be taken are quite detailed about what will be done to a customer's car. Various other equipment-based services are also often standardized into packages. For instance, cable television providers frequently offer several packages, such as "Basic," "Standard," "Premier," and "Hollywood."

The characteristic of intangibility makes it difficult for customers to evaluate a service prior to purchase. Intangibility requires service marketers, such as hairstylists, to market promises to customers. The customer is forced to place some degree of trust in the service provider to perform the service in a manner that meets or exceeds those promises. Service marketers must guard against making promises that raise customer expectations beyond what they can provide. To cope with the problem of intangibility, marketers employ tangible cues, such as well-groomed, professional-appearing contact personnel and clean, attractive physical facilities, to help assure customers about the quality of the service. Most service providers uniform at least some of

Marketing IN TRANSITION

Blogging and Tweeting for Service

More service marketers are staying in touch with customers through posts on blogs and on Twitter. A *blog* (short for *web log*) is an Internet site where people post messages and images, then invite visitors to comment. Twitter is a microblogging site where users post messages (called *tweets*) of up to 140 characters. By posting messages and responding to what readers say, company bloggers and Twitterers create a personal connection with service customers around the world.

© MARKA/ALAMY

For example, Bill Marriott, CEO of Marriott International, posts audio messages as well as written ideas, photos, and videos on his "Marriott on the Move" blog. The blog's 6,000 weekly visitors can see what Marriott's CEO is doing, read about the hotels and resorts he visits, and add their own comments. It's also a good way to market Marriott's services: Visitors who clicked from the blog to the reservations page have booked $5 million worth of hotel stays.

A growing number of companies are using Twitter to answer customers' questions, help with service issues, and promote special offers in just a sentence or two. For example, JetBlue Airways uses Twitter to communicate about sales, delays, and complaints with the 128,000 customers who follow its tweets. Similarly, the cable company Comcast uses Twitter to gather feedback and provide tips for customers experiencing problems with its service. And Starbucks has 70,000 customers tuned to its Twitter posts about new products and store openings, special events, and more.[c]

their high-contact employees. Uniforms help to make the service experience more tangible, and they serve as physical evidence to signal quality, create consistency, and send cues to suggest a desired image.[31] Consider the professionalism, experience, and competence conveyed by an airline pilot's uniform. Life insurance companies sometimes try to make the quality of their policies more tangible by putting them on very high-quality paper and enclosing them in leather sheaths.

The inseparability of production and consumption and the level of customer contact also influence the development and management of services. The fact that customers are present during the production of a service means that other customers can affect the outcome of the service. For instance, if a nonsmoker dines in a restaurant without a no-smoking section, the overall quality of service experienced by the nonsmoking customer declines. Service marketers can reduce these problems by encouraging customers to share the responsibility of maintaining an environment that allows all participants to receive the intended benefits of the service.

Pricing of Services

Services should be priced so as to reflect consumer price sensitivity, the nature of the transaction, and its costs.[32] Prices for services can be established on several different bases. The prices of pest-control services, dry cleaning, carpet cleaning, and a physician's consultation usually are based on the performance of specific tasks. Other service prices are based on time. For example, attorneys, consultants, counselors, piano teachers, and plumbers often charge by the hour or day.

Some services use demand-based pricing. When demand for a service is high, the price is also high; when demand for a service is low, so is the price. The perishability of services means that when demand is low, the unused capacity cannot be stored and is therefore lost forever. Every empty seat on an airline flight or in a movie theater represents lost revenue. Some services are very time-sensitive because a significant number of customers desire the service at a particular time. This point in time is called *peak demand.* A provider of time-sensitive services brings in most of its revenue during peak demand. For an airline, peak demand is usually early and late in the day. Providers of time-sensitive services often use demand-based pricing to manage the problem of balancing supply and demand. They charge top prices during peak demand and lower prices during off-peak demand to encourage more customers to use the service. This is why the price of a matinee movie is often half the price of the same movie shown at night.

When services are offered to customers in a bundle, marketers must decide whether to offer the services at one price, price them separately, or use a combination of the two methods. For example, some hotels offer a package of services at one price, whereas others charge separately for the room, phone service, and breakfast. Some service providers offer a one-price option for a specific bundle of services and make add-on bundles available at additional charges. For example, telephone services, such as call waiting and caller ID, frequently are bundled and sold as a package for one price.

Because of the intangible nature of services, customers rely heavily at times on price as an indicator of quality. If customers perceive the available services in a service category as being similar in quality, and if the quality of such services is difficult to judge even after these services are purchased, customers may seek out the lowest-priced provider. For example, many customers seek auto insurance providers with the lowest rates. If the quality of different service providers is likely to vary, customers may rely heavily on the price-quality association. For example, if you have to have an appendectomy, will you choose the surgeon who charges an average price of $1,500 or the surgeon who will take your appendix out for $399?

Distribution of Services

Marketers deliver services in various ways. In some instances customers go to a service provider's facility. For example, most health care, dry-cleaning, and spa services are delivered at the service providers' facilities. Some services are provided at the customer's home or business. Lawn care, air-conditioning and heating repair, and carpet cleaning are examples. Some services are delivered primarily at "arm's length," meaning that no face-to-face contact occurs between the customer and the service provider. Several equipment-based services are delivered at arm's length, including electric, Internet, cable television, and telephone services. Providing high-quality customer service at arm's length can be costly but essential in keeping customers satisfied and maintaining market share.

Marketing channels for services usually are short and direct, meaning that the producer delivers the service directly to the end user. Some services, however, use intermediaries. For example, travel agents facilitate the delivery of airline services, independent insurance agents participate in the marketing of various insurance policies, and financial planners market investment services.

Service marketers are less concerned with warehousing and transportation than are goods marketers. They are very concerned, however, about inventory management, especially balancing supply and demand for services. The service characteristics of inseparability and level of customer contact contribute to the challenges of demand management. In some instances service marketers use appointments and reservations as approaches for scheduling the delivery of services. Health care providers, attorneys, accountants, auto mechanics, and restaurants often use reservations or appointments to plan and pace the delivery of their services. To increase the supply of a service, marketers use multiple service sites and also increase the number of contact service providers at each site. National and regional eye-care and hair-care services are examples.

Distribution
FedEx provides some of its services through retail stores.

To make delivery more accessible to customers and to increase the supply of a service, as well as reduce labor costs, some service providers have decreased the use of contact personnel and replaced them with equipment. In other words, they have changed a high-contact service into a low-contact one. The banking industry is an example. By installing ATMs, banks have increased production capacity and reduced customer contact. In addition, numerous automated banking services are now available by telephone 24 hours a day. Such services have helped to lower costs by reducing the need for customer-service representatives. Changing the delivery of services from human to equipment has created some problems, however.

Promotion of Services

The intangibility of services results in several promotion-related challenges to service marketers. Because it may not be possible to depict the actual performance of a service in an advertisement or to display it in a store, explaining a service to customers can be a difficult task. Promotion of services typically includes tangible cues that symbolize the service. For example, Transamerica uses its pyramid-shaped building to symbolize strength, security, and reliability, important features associated with insurance and other financial services. Similarly, the hands Allstate uses in its ads symbolize personalized service and trustworthy, caring representatives. Although these symbols have nothing to do with the actual services, they make it much easier for customers to understand the intangible attributes associated with insurance services. To make a service more tangible, advertisements for services often show pictures of facilities, equipment, and service personnel. Marketers may also promote their services as a tangible expression of consumers' lifestyles. Ameriprise, for example, featured *Easy Rider* actor Dennis Hopper in commercials for retirement financial services targeted at baby boomers nearing retirement age. The company chose Hopper for his "great antihero hero image" to provide an emotional appeal for baby boomers who may not desire a conventional retirement on the golf course.[33]

Compared with goods marketers, service providers are more likely to promote price, guarantees, performance documentation, availability, and training and certification of contact personnel. The International Smart Tan Network, a trade association for indoor tanning salons, offers a certification course in professional standards for tanning facility operators. The association encourages salons to promote their "Smart Tan Certification" in advertising and throughout the salon as a measure of quality training.[34] When preparing advertisements, service marketers are careful to use concrete, specific language to help make services more tangible in the minds of customers. Bear Stearns, for example, once advertised that it was voted "America's most admired securities company." Service companies are also careful not to promise too much regarding their services so that customer expectations do not rise to unattainable levels.

Through their actions, service contact personnel can be directly or indirectly involved in the personal selling of services. Personal selling is often important because personal influence can help the customer visualize the benefits of a given service. Because service contact personnel may engage in personal selling, some companies invest heavily in training.

Because of the heterogeneity and intangibility of services, word-of-mouth communication is important in service promotion. What other people say about a service provider can have a tremendous impact on whether an individual decides to use that provider. Some service marketers attempt to stimulate positive word-of-mouth communication by asking satisfied customers to tell their friends and associates about the service and may even provide incentives for doing so.

Organizing to Develop and Manage Products

After reviewing the concepts of product line and mix, life cycles, positioning, and repositioning, it should be obvious that managing products is a complex task. Often the traditional functional form of organization, in which managers specialize in business functions such as advertising, sales, and distribution, does not fit a company's needs. In this case management must find an organizational approach that accomplishes the tasks necessary to develop and manage products. Alternatives to functional organization include the product or brand manager approach, the market manager approach, and the venture team approach.

A **product manager** is responsible for a product, a product line, or several distinct products that make up an interrelated group within a multiproduct organization. A **brand manager** is responsible for a single brand. General Foods, for example, has one brand manager for Maxim coffee and one for Maxwell House coffee. Both product and brand managers operate cross-functionally to coordinate the activities, information, and strategies involved in marketing an assigned product. Product managers and brand managers plan marketing activities to achieve objectives by coordinating a mix of distribution, promotion (especially sales promotion and advertising), and price. They must consider packaging and branding decisions and work closely with personnel in research and development, engineering, and production. Marketing research helps product managers understand consumers and find target markets. Because luxury brands such as Mercedes-Benz and Jaguar can have their brand image reduced by association with their producers' other mass-market brands, brand managers must balance their brands' independent image with associated brands of the firm.[35] The product or brand manager approach to organization is used by many large, multiple-product companies.

product manager The person within an organization responsible for a product, a product line, or several distinct products that make up a group

brand manager The person responsible for a single brand

market manager The person responsible for managing the marketing activities that serve a particular group of customers

A **market manager** is responsible for managing the marketing activities that serve a particular group of customers. This organizational approach is particularly effective when a firm engages in different types of marketing activities to provide products to diverse customer groups. A company might have one market manager for business markets and another for consumer markets. These broad market categories might be broken down into more limited market responsibilities.

A **venture team** creates entirely new products that may be aimed at new markets. Unlike a product or market manager, a venture team is responsible for all aspects of developing a product: research and development, production and engineering, finance and accounting, and marketing. Venture team members are brought together from different functional areas of the organization. In working outside established divisions, venture teams have greater flexibility to apply inventive approaches to develop new products that can take advantage of opportunities in highly segmented markets. Companies are increasingly using such cross-functional teams for product development in an effort to boost product quality. When a new product has demonstrated commercial potential, team members may return to their functional areas, or they may join a new or existing division to manage the product.

venture team
A cross-functional group that creates entirely new products that may be aimed at new markets

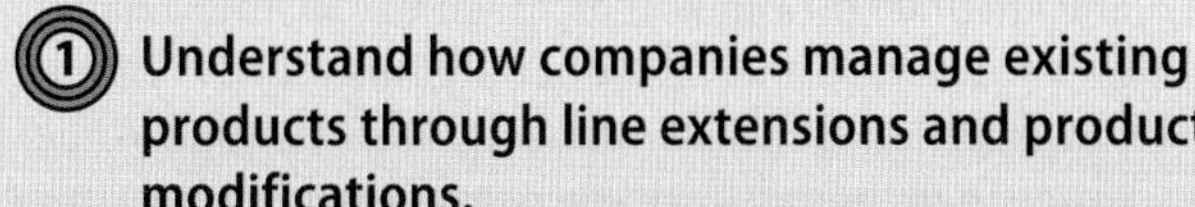

OBJECTIVES

1 Understand how companies manage existing products through line extensions and product modifications.

Organizations must be able to adjust their product mixes to compete effectively and achieve their goals. Using existing products, a product mix can be improved through line extension and through product modification. A line extension is the development of a product closely related to one or more products in the existing line but designed specifically to meet different customer needs. Product modification is the changing of one or more characteristics of a product. This approach can be achieved through quality modifications, functional modifications, and aesthetic modifications.

2 Describe how businesses develop a product idea into a commercial product.

Before a product is introduced, it goes through a seven-phase new-product development process. In the idea-generation phase, new-product ideas may come from internal or external sources. In the process of screening, ideas are evaluated to determine whether they are consistent with the firm's overall objectives and resources. Concept testing, the third phase, involves having a small sample of potential customers review a brief description of the product idea to determine their initial perceptions of the proposed product and their early buying intentions. During the business analysis stage, the product idea is evaluated to determine its potential contribution to the firm's sales, costs, and profits. In the product development stage, the organization determines if it is technically feasible to produce the product and if it can be produced at a cost low enough to make the final price reasonable. Test marketing is a limited introduction of a product in areas chosen to represent the intended market. Finally, in the commercialization phase, full-scale production of the product begins, and a complete marketing strategy is developed.

3 Know the importance of product differentiation and the elements that differentiate one product from another.

Product differentiation is the process of creating and designing products so that customers perceive them as different from competing products. Product quality, product design and features, and product support services are three dimensions of product differentiation that companies consider when creating and marketing products.

4 Explain product positioning and repositioning.

Product positioning refers to the decisions and activities that create and maintain a certain concept of the firm's product in the customer's mind. Organizations can position a product to compete head to head with another brand if the product's performance is at least equal to the competitive brand's and if the product is priced lower. When a brand possesses unique characteristics that are important to some buyers, positioning it to avoid competition is appropriate. Companies also increase an existing brand's market share and profitability through product repositioning.

5 Understand how product deletion is used to improve product mixes.

Product deletion is the process of eliminating a product that no longer satisfies a sufficient number of customers. Although a firm's personnel may oppose product deletion, weak products are unprofitable, consume too much time and effort, may require shorter production runs, and can create an unfavorable impression of the firm's other products. A product mix should be systematically reviewed to determine when to delete products. Products to be deleted can be phased out, run out, or dropped immediately.

6 Understand the characteristics of services and how these characteristics present challenges when developing marketing mixes for service products.

Services are intangible products involving deeds, performances, or efforts that cannot be physically possessed. They have six fundamental characteristics: intangibility, inseparability of production and consumption, perishability, heterogeneity, client-based relationships, and customer contact. Intangibility means that a service cannot be seen, touched, tasted, or smelled. Inseparability refers to the fact that the production of a service cannot be separated from its consumption. Perishability means that unused service capacity of one time period cannot be stored for future use. Heterogeneity is variation in service quality. Client-based relationships are interactions with customers that lead to the repeated use of a service over time. Customer contact is the interaction needed to deliver a service between providers and customers.

7 Be familiar with organizational structures used for managing products.

Often the traditional functional form or organization does not lend itself to the complex task of developing and managing products. Alternative organizational forms include the product or brand manager approach, the market manager approach, and the venture team approach. A product manager is responsible for a product, a product line, or several distinct products that make up an interrelated group within a multiproduct organization. A brand manager is a product manager who is responsible for a single brand. A market manager is responsible for managing the marketing activities that serve a particular group or class of customers. A venture team is sometimes used to create entirely new products that may be aimed at new markets.

Please visit the student website at www.cengage.com/international for quizzes and games that will help you prepare for exams and help achieve the grade you want.

KEY CONCEPTS

line extension
product modification
quality modifications
functional modifications
aesthetic modifications
new-product development process
idea generation
screening
concept testing
business analysis
product development
test marketing
commercialization
product differentiation
quality
level of quality
consistency of quality
product design
styling
product features
customer services
product positioning
product deletion
intangibility
inseparability
perishability
heterogeneity
client-based relationships
customer contact
product manager
brand manager
market manager
venture team

ISSUES FOR DISCUSSION AND REVIEW

1. What is a line extension, and how does it differ from a product modification?
2. Compare and contrast the three major approaches to modifying a product.
3. Identify and briefly explain the seven major phases of the new-product development process.
4. Do small companies that manufacture just a few products need to be concerned about developing and managing products? Why or why not?
5. Why is product development a cross-functional activity within an organization? That is, why must finance, engineering, manufacturing, and other functional areas be involved?
6. What is the major purpose of concept testing, and how is it accomplished?
7. What are the benefits and disadvantages of test marketing?
8. Why can the process of commercialization take a considerable amount of time?
9. What is product differentiation, and how can it be achieved?
10. Explain how the term *quality* has been used to differentiate products in the automobile industry in recent years. What are some makes and models of automobiles that come to mind when you hear the terms *high quality* and *poor quality*?
11. What is product positioning? Under what conditions would head-to-head product positioning be appropriate? When should head-to-head positioning be avoided?
12. What types of problems does a weak product cause in a product mix? Describe the most effective approach for avoiding such problems.
13. How important are services in the U.S. economy?
14. Identify and discuss the major service characteristics.
15. For each marketing-mix element, which service characteristics are most likely to have an impact?
16. What type of organization might use a venture team to develop new products? What are the advantages and disadvantages of such a team?

MARKETING APPLICATIONS

1. A company often test markets a proposed product in a specific area or location. Suppose that you wish to test market your new revolutionary SuperWax car wax, which requires only one application for a lifetime finish. Where and how would you test market your new product?
2. Select an organization that you think should reposition itself in the consumer's eye. Identify where it is currently positioned, and make recommendations for repositioning. Explain and defend your suggestions.
3. Identify a familiar product that recently was modified, categorize the modification (quality, functional, or aesthetic), and describe how you would have modified it differently.
4. The characteristics of services affect the development of marketing mixes for services. Choose a specific service and explain how each marketing-mix element could be affected by these service characteristics.
5. Identify three service organizations you see in outdoor, television, or magazine advertising. What symbols are used to represent their services? What message do the symbols convey to potential customers?
6. Visit a retail store in your area, and ask the manager what products he or she has had to discontinue in the recent past. Find out what factors influenced the decision to delete the product and who was involved in the decision. Ask the manager to identify any

products that should be but have not been deleted, and try to ascertain the reason.

ONLINE EXERCISE

7. Merck, a leading global pharmaceutical company, develops, manufactures, and markets a broad range of health-care products. In addition, the firm's Merck-Medco Managed Care Division manages pharmacy benefits for more than 40 million Americans. The company has established a website to serve as an educational and informational resource for Internet users around the world. Visit Merck at **http://www.merck.com**.
   a. What products has Merck developed and introduced recently?
   b. What role does research play in Merck's success? How does research facilitate new-product development at Merck?
   c. Find Merck's mission statement. Is Merck's focus on research consistent with the firm's mission and values?

DEVELOPING YOUR MARKETING PLAN

A company's marketing strategy may be revised to include new products as it considers its SWOT analysis and the impact of environmental factors on its product mix. When developing a marketing plan, the company must decide whether new products are to be added to the product mix, or if existing ones should be modified. The information in this chapter will assist you in the creation of your marketing plan as you consider the following:

1. Identify whether your product will be the modification of an existing one in your product mix, or the development of a new product.
2. If the product is an extension of one in your current product mix, determine the type(s) of modifications that will be performed.
3. Using Figure 10.1 as a guide, discuss how your product idea would move through the stages of new product development. Examine the idea using the tests and analyses included in the new product development process.
4. Discuss how the management of this product will fit into your current organizational structure.

The information obtained from these questions should assist you in developing various aspects of your marketing plan found in the *Interactive Marketing Plan* exercise.

VIDEO CASE 10

Southwest Airlines Keeps Services Marketing Flying High

Southwest Airlines has risen to the top of the airline industry by making top-quality customer service and no-frills prices its top priorities. Founded in 1971 as a regional airline flying three planes between Dallas, Houston, and San Antonio, Southwest has grown into a national carrier with 3,200 daily flights, 35,000 employees nationwide, and $10 billion in annual revenue. Its stock symbol is LUV, which also sums up the airline's service attitude toward customers.

From the start, Southwest set its airfares low and its service standards high. The airline sees every flight as an opportunity to reinforce its reputation for friendly, attentive service in the sky and on the ground. In recognition of Southwest's financial and service successes, *Fortune* magazine regularly ranks it among the top 20 most admired U.S. companies.

Maintaining a consistently high level of customer service is an ongoing challenge as Southwest adds new destinations and expands its flight schedule year after year. Southwest starts by carefully screening job applicants to hire people who enjoy customer interaction, have good communication skills, and can work cooperatively with colleagues. The airline provides extensive training and allows customer-contact personnel to take the initiative by resolving complaints and service problems on the spot.

Southwest employees, especially those who deal directly with customers, are required to look and behave professionally. They're also encouraged to add a bit of fun to the flying experience, a key element that differentiates Southwest from competitors. For instance, some crew members coax smiles from seat-belted passengers by leading toilet paper games or enlivening routine announcements with gentle humor. Delivering service with a smile shows that Southwest genuinely cares about its customers.

Just as important, Southwest keeps the service spirit alive through a culture committee at headquarters and similar committees in each of its airport and maintenance facilities across the country. These committees celebrate the achievements of employees who provide outstanding service. They also plan customer and employee appreciation events around the country, such as employees surprising incoming flights with cookies and milk for passengers and crew members.

Thanks in part to its service spirit, Southwest has remained at cruising altitude for decades, despite some periods of turbulence. Not long ago, the airline was criticized, and it paid a multimillion-dollar fine for continuing to fly 46 jets that were overdue for a federally mandated fuselage safety inspection. When questioned by officials, Southwest grounded the jets, completed the inspections, and quickly resumed regular flights. The airline also conducted an internal investigation and reassured customers by pointing to its long-standing safety record and its rigorous equipment maintenance schedule.

When the price of jet fuel reached sky-high levels recently, some large carriers began cutting back on flights, parking planes, and withdrawing from certain destinations to save money. Not Southwest. Because of smart negotiating, Southwest had its fuel costs under control and actually expanded to new cities while competitors were shrinking their schedules. Its profits were lower during the recent economic downturn, but it found ways of creatively managing costs without disrupting service delivery.

To offset higher costs, other airlines have been unbundling services and tacking on extra fees for checking baggage and other services that used to be bundled with the ticket price. Southwest has differentiated itself by sticking with its bundle of services and promoting itself as the "no-fee airline." In fact, the airline has created a new "Business Select" airfare for business travelers, bundling priority boarding and a free drink at a slightly higher price. The fare is fully refundable if the traveler is unable to fly as scheduled, another feature that makes the Business Select bundle particularly appealing to businesspeople.

Although running an airline is serious business, Southwest's spirited approach to service keeps customers smiling—and keeps them coming back for more LUV.

QUESTIONS FOR DISCUSSION

1. As a high-contact service provider, how does Southwest Airlines ensure that its employees satisfy customers?
2. Although services are intangible, some aspects of the experience of flying on Southwest Airlines are tangible. What are the implications for the airline's service marketing efforts?
3. What is Southwest Airlines doing to manage customers' service expectations?

Micheline Maynard, "Southwest Posts a Fourth-Quarter Loss," *New York Times,* January 23, 2009, p. B2; Lewis Lazare, "Why Southwest Soars as Other Airlines Sag," *Chicago Sun-Times,* June 20, 2008, www.suntimes.com; Trebor Banstetter, "Southwest's Boss Shuns Fees, Aims for More Fliers," *Fort Worth Star-Telegram,* June 2, 2008, www.dfw.com; Evan Smith, "Texas Monthly Talks: Evan Smith Sits Down with Herb Kelleher," *Texas Monthly,* June 2008, pp. 78+; Del Quentin Wilber, "Groundings Prompt FAA Safety Overhaul," *Washington Post,* April 19, 2008, p. D1; "Southwest Airlines Traffic Up 7% in May," *Orlando Business Journal,* June 4, 2008, orlando.bizjournals.com/orlando/stories/2008/06/02/daily25.html; "Southwest Air," *Business Civic Leadership Center,* U.S. Chamber of Commerce, 2005, www.uschamber.com/bclc/profiles/southwest.htm; www.southwest.com.

Pricing Decisions 5

ISTOCKPHOTO.COM/JIM JURICA

If an organization is to provide a satisfying marketing mix, the price must be acceptable to target-market members. Pricing decisions can have numerous effects on other parts of the marketing mix. For example, price can influence how customers perceive the product, what types of marketing institutions are used to distribute the product, and how the product is promoted. Chapter 11 discusses the importance of price and looks at some characteristics of price and nonprice competition. It explores fundamental concepts such as demand, elasticity, marginal analysis, and breakeven analysis. Then it examines the major factors that affect marketers' pricing decisions. Chapter 12 discusses six major stages in the process marketers use to establish prices.

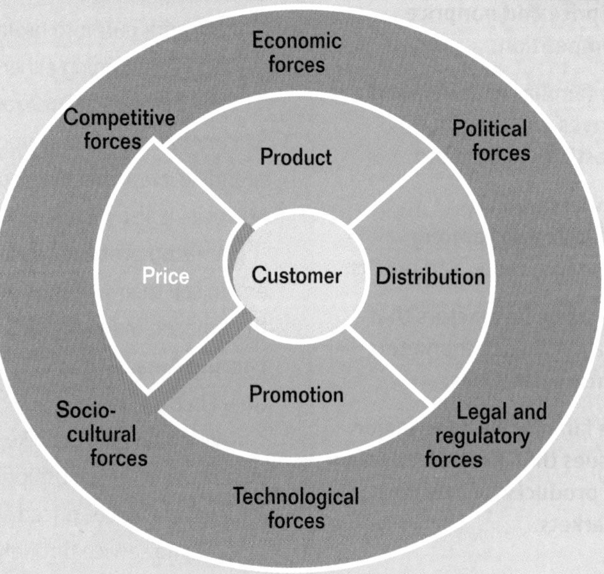

CHAPTER 11 Pricing Fundamentals

©AP IMAGES/MARK LENNIHAN

OBJECTIVES:

1. Understand the role of price.
2. Identify the characteristics of price and nonprice competition.
3. Be familiar with demand curves and the price elasticity of demand.
4. Understand the relationships among demand, costs, and profits.
5. Describe key factors that may influence marketers' pricing decisions.
6. Be familiar with the major issues that affect the pricing of products for business markets.

AMAZON.COM'S BEST-SELLING PRICING IDEAS

Online retail pioneer Amazon.com has built a profitable $14.5 billion business by paying close attention to pricing. Founded as a Web-based discount bookstore, Amazon has expanded into dozens of product categories and countries. Continually investing to improve its sites, systems, and offerings cuts into profit margins, but it helps Amazon attract and retain customers by making the shopping experience fun, fast, and easy.

One hallmark of Amazon's pricing is its long-running offer of free shipping for orders of $25 or more. Because shoppers know they're saving money, they're more inclined to keep spending even after they qualify for free shipping. As popular as this shipping offer has been, however, it also increases Amazon's costs and cuts into profits.

Amazon profits from serving as an online storefront for other merchants (and consumers) to sell their wares, sometimes competing with Amazon itself. Every purchase from the Amazon Marketplace earns Amazon a small fee. The margins are especially attractive because Amazon doesn't pay to buy or store any inventory, and the cost of posting additional items is low.

All-digital products like electronic books, music, and movies are lucrative because they entail no inventory or shipping costs—which is why Amazon has moved more aggressively into such products, priced at or below what other online retailers charge. It also has a video-on-demand service through which customers pay $1.99 or less to rent a movie or television program.

Amazon recently introduced a new version of its Kindle reading device. Users wirelessly connect to Amazon's site and download any of 230,000 books, with best-sellers priced at $9.99. The Kindle has been so successful that orders are backlogged for months. Even if the company is willing to accept a tiny profit margin on a high volume of download purchases, can the Kindle generate the kind of profitability Amazon needs to continue growing?[1]

Like Amazon, many firms use pricing as a tool to compete against major competitors. However, their rivals also may employ pricing as a major competitive tool. In some industries, firms are very successful even if they don't have the lowest prices. The best price is not always the lowest price.

In this chapter we focus first on the role of price. We then consider some characteristics of price and nonprice competition. Next, we discuss several pricing-related concepts such as demand, elasticity, and breakeven analysis. Then we examine in some detail the numerous factors that can influence pricing decisions. Finally, we discuss selected issues related to the pricing of products for business markets.

The Role of Price

The purpose of marketing is to facilitate satisfying exchange relationships between buyer and seller. **Price** is the value exchanged for products in a marketing transaction. Many factors may influence the assessment of value, including time constraints, price levels, perceived quality, and motivations to use available information about prices.[2] However, price does not always take the form of money paid. In fact, trading of products, or **barter**, is the oldest form of exchange. Money may or may not be involved. Barter among businesses accounts for about $9 billion in annual U.S. sales.

Buyers' interest in price stems from their expectations about the usefulness of a product or the satisfaction they may derive from it. Because consumers have limited resources, they must allocate those resources to obtain the products they most desire. They must decide whether the utility gained in an exchange is worth the buying power sacrificed. Almost anything of value—ideas, services, rights, and goods—can be assessed by a price. In our society, financial price is the measurement of value commonly used in exchanges. The purpose of price is to quantify and express the value of the items in marketing exchanges.

As pointed out in Chapter 10, developing a product may be a lengthy process. It takes time to plan promotion and to communicate benefits. Distribution usually requires a long-term commitment to dealers who will handle the product. Often price is the only thing a marketer can change quickly to respond to changes in demand or to actions of competitors. Under certain circumstances, however, the price variable may be relatively inflexible.

Price is a key element in the marketing mix because it relates directly to the generation of total revenue. The following equation is an important one for the entire organization:

$$\text{Profit} = \text{total revenue} - \text{total costs}$$

or

$$\text{Profits} = (\text{price} \times \text{quantity sold}) - \text{total costs}$$

price
Value exchanged for products in a marketing transaction

barter
The trading of products

Prices affect an organization's profits in several ways because price is a key component of the profit equation and can be a major determinant of the quantities sold. For example, price is a top priority for Hewlett-Packard in gaining market share and improving financial performance.[3] Furthermore, total costs are influenced by quantities sold.

Because price has a psychological impact on customers, marketers can use it symbolically. By pricing high, they can emphasize the quality of a product and try to increase the prestige associated with its ownership. By lowering a price, marketers can emphasize a bargain and attract customers who go out of their way to save a small amount of money. Thus, as this chapter details, price can have strong effects on a firm's sales and profitability.

Price and Nonprice Competition

The competitive environment strongly influences the marketing mix decisions associated with a product. Pricing decisions often are made according to the price or nonprice competitive situation in a particular market. Price competition exists when consumers have difficulty distinguishing competitive offerings, and marketers emphasize low prices. Nonprice competition involves a focus on marketing mix elements other than price.

PRICE COMPETITION

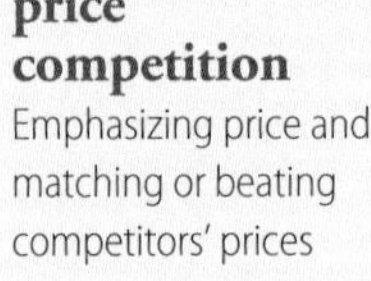

price competition
Emphasizing price and matching or beating competitors' prices

When engaging in **price competition**, a marketer emphasizes price as an issue and matches or beats the prices of competitors. To compete effectively on a price basis, a firm should be the low-cost seller of the product. If all firms producing the same product charge the same price for it, the firm with the lowest costs is the most profitable. Firms that stress low price as a key marketing mix element tend to market standardized products. A seller competing on price may change prices frequently or at least must be willing and able to do so. For example, when increasing numbers of coffee sellers entered the market, competition increased. Starbucks Corp. needed to counter the widespread perception that it was the home of the $4 cup of coffee, especially during the economic downturn. In order to compete with McDonald's inexpensive coffee, Starbucks cut its coffee prices and started selling discounted breakfast foods for

© AP IMAGES/AP PHOTO/NICK UT

Price Competition
Consumer electronics stores compete on the basis of price.

$3.95, including coffee.[4] Whenever competitors change their prices, the seller usually responds quickly and aggressively.

Price competition gives a marketer flexibility. Prices can be altered to account for changes in the firm's costs or in demand for the product. If competitors try to gain market share by cutting prices, an organization competing on a price basis can react quickly to such efforts. However, a major drawback of price competition is that competitors also have the flexibility to adjust prices. If they quickly match or beat a company's price cuts, a price war may ensue. For example, a price war has developed in the market for some generic pharmaceuticals. After Walmart announced that it would offer approximately 300 generic medicines for $4 in some markets, rival Target announced that it would offer $4 generics at every U.S. Target store with a pharmacy.[5] Chronic price wars can weaken organizations substantially.

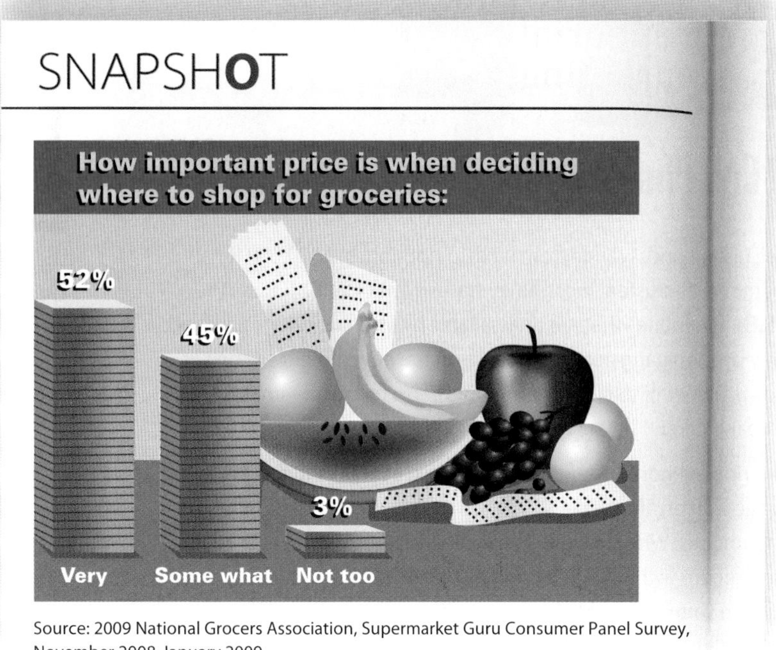

Source: 2009 National Grocers Association, Supermarket Guru Consumer Panel Survey, November 2008-January 2009.

NONPRICE COMPETITION

Nonprice competition occurs when a seller decides not to focus on price and instead emphasizes distinctive product features, service, product quality, promotion, packaging, or other factors to distinguish its product from competing brands. Thus nonprice competition allows a company to increase its brand's unit sales through means other than changing the brand's price. Mars, for example, markets not only Snickers and M&Ms but also has an upscale candy line called Ethel's Chocolate. With the tagline, "No mystery middles," Ethel's Chocolates competes on the basis of taste, attractive appearance, and hip packaging and thus has little need to engage in price competition.[6] A major advantage of nonprice competition is that a firm can build customer loyalty toward its brand. If customers prefer a brand because of nonprice factors, they may not be easily lured away by competing firms and brands. In contrast, when price is the primary reason customers buy a particular brand, a competitor is often able to attract these customers through price cuts.

Nonprice competition is effective only under certain conditions. A company must be able to distinguish its brand through unique product features, higher product quality, promotion, packaging, or excellent customer service. For example, Tulsa-based Fine Airport Parking emphasizes the use of technology to make its customer service better than its competition. It offers a new ticketless entry system for frequent travelers and larger indoor and outdoor parking facilities than competitors, both of which provide convenience for customers.[7] Buyers not only must be able to perceive these distinguishing characteristics, but they also must view them as important. The distinguishing features that set a particular brand apart from competitors should be difficult, if not impossible, for competitors to imitate. Finally, the organization must extensively promote the distinguishing characteristics of the brand to establish its superiority and set it apart from competitors in the minds of buyers.

Even a marketer that is competing on a nonprice basis cannot ignore competitors' prices. It must be aware of them and sometimes be prepared to price its brand near or slightly above competing brands. Therefore, price remains a crucial marketing-mix component even in environments that call for nonprice competition.

nonprice competition
Emphasizing factors other than price to distinguish a product from competing brands

A Cell Phone at Any Cost

Cell phone prices range from next-to-nothing, to $370,000 for a diamond-encrusted, must-have, status symbol Vertu phone, to $1.2M for phones that are unassailable by listening devices, owned only by mob gangsters and people on the government's watch list. Nokia, owner of the highly profitable Vertu brand, dominates the global market.

The Apple iPhone entered the fray priced at $600 and quickly found its niche at an affordable $199—on par with its competitor's high-end phones. While popular in the retail market, Apple must adapt to compete with BlackBerry wireless devices whose reliability and custom software capabilities make them very popular with corporate customers.

At the low end, Samsung is working to increase its market share by launching ultra-low-price cell phones in emerging markets. In contrast to the high-priced Vertu, Samsung's profit margins on low-end phones must be monitored very carefully. Marketing strategy must be flexible if results fall short of expectations.[a]

Analysis of Demand

Determining the demand for a product is the responsibility of marketing managers, who are aided in this task by marketing researchers and forecasters. Marketing research and forecasting techniques yield estimates of sales potential, or the quantity of a product that could be sold during a specific period. These estimates are helpful in establishing the relationship between a product's price and the quantity demanded.

THE DEMAND CURVE

For most products, the quantity demanded goes up as the price goes down, and as the price goes up, the quantity demanded goes down. Intel, for example, knows that lowering prices boosts demand for its processors. Thus an inverse relationship exists between price and quantity demanded. As long as the marketing environment and buyers' needs, ability (purchasing power), willingness, and authority to buy remain stable, this fundamental inverse relationship holds.

Figure 11.1 illustrates the effect of one variable—price—on the quantity demanded. The classic **demand curve** (D_1) is a graph of the quantity of a product taken by buyers in the market at various prices, given that all other factors are held constant.[8] It illustrates that as price falls, the quantity demanded usually rises. Demand depends on other factors in the marketing mix, including product quality, promotion, and distribution. An improvement in any of these factors may cause a shift to, say, demand curve D_2. In such a case, an increased quantity (Q_2) will be sold at the same price (P).

There are many types of demand, and not all conform to the classic demand curve shown in Figure 11.1. Prestige products, such as select perfumes and jewelry, seem to sell better at high prices than at low ones. These products are desirable partly because their expense makes buyers feel elite. If the price fell drastically and many people owned these products, they would lose some of their appeal.

The demand curve in Figure 11.2 shows the relationship between price and quantity demanded for prestige products. Quantity demanded is greater, not less, at higher prices. For a certain price range—from P_1 to P_2—the quantity demanded (Q_1) goes up to Q_2. After a certain point, however, raising the price backfires. If the price goes too high, the quantity demanded goes down. The figure shows that if the price is raised from P_2 to P_3, the quantity demanded goes back down from Q_2 to Q_1.

demand curve
A graph of the quantity of a product taken by buyers in the market at various prices, given that all other factors are held constant

DEMAND FLUCTUATIONS

Changes in buyers' needs, variations in the effectiveness of other marketing mix variables, the presence of substitutes, and dynamic environmental factors can influence demand. Restaurants and utility companies experience large fluctuations in demand daily. Toy manufacturers,

FIGURE 11.1 **Demand Curve Illustrating the Price-Quantity Relationship and Increase in Demand**

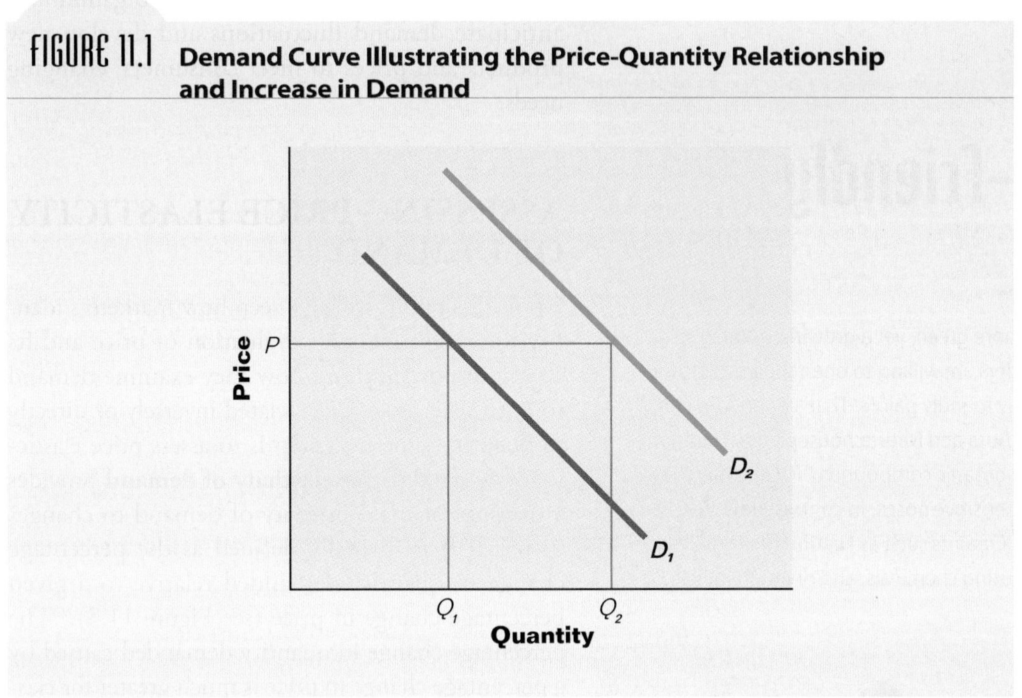

fireworks suppliers, and air-conditioning and heating contractors also face demand fluctuations because of the seasonal nature of their products. The demand for broadband services, beef, and flat-screen TVs has changed over the last few years. In some cases demand fluctuations are predictable. It is no surprise to restaurants and utility company managers that demand fluctuates. However, changes in demand for other products may be less predictable, and this leads to

FIGURE 11.2 **Demand Curve Illustrating the Relationship Between Price and Quantity for Prestige Products**

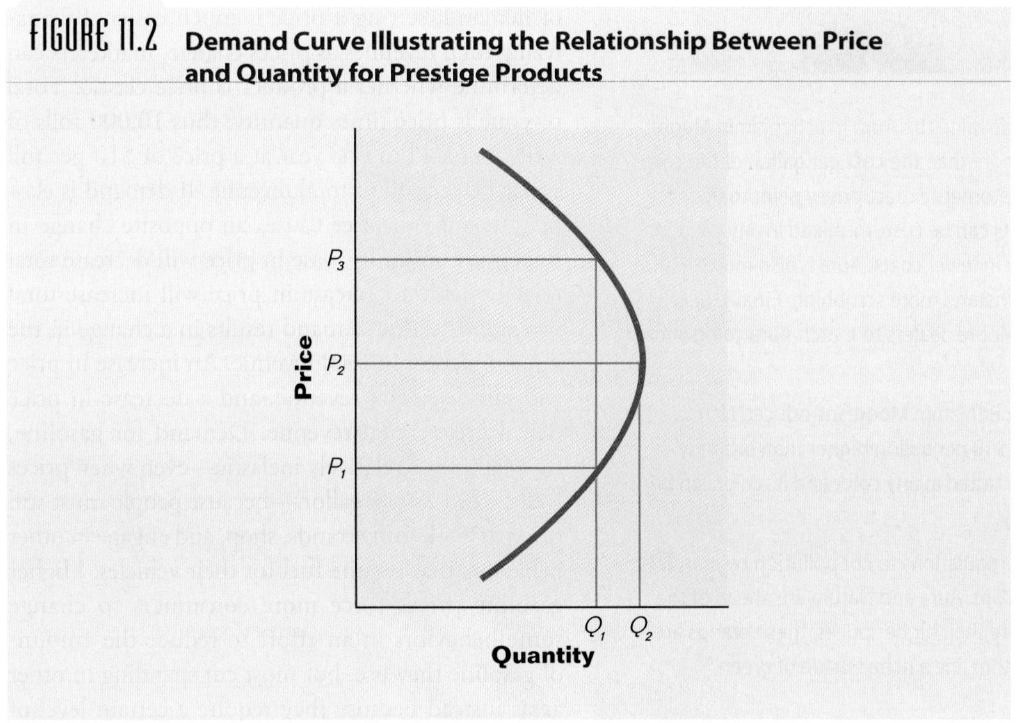

Sustainable Marketing

Pricing Eco-Friendly Paints

Painting it green costs more green, yet a growing number of homeowners and builders are willing to open their wallets for today's environmentally friendly paints. That's good news for Benjamin Moore, which makes Aura and Natura housepaints. Traditional paints release polluting volatile organic compounds (VOCs) while they dry, and their smell can irritate sensitive noses. In contrast, low-VOC paints such as Aura and non-VOC paints such as Natura don't smell as bad, release lower levels of polluting chemicals, and dry more quickly.

© PHOTONICA/GETTY IMAGES

After investing $150 million to develop the Aura line, Benjamin Moore introduced it at a price of $15 more than the cost per gallon of the company's other paints. Because customers expect pricey paint to do more than save the planet, Aura paints can be custom-mixed in any color, dark or light, for good coverage in fewer coats. Aura is also more durable than ordinary paint and can withstand more scrubbing. Finally, new technology enables Benjamin Moore dealers to match Aura colors more accurately.

Two years after launching Aura, Benjamin Moore introduced Natura, a line of VOC-free paints priced $10 per gallon higher than ordinary paints. Like Aura, Natura can be tinted in any color and its color can be computer-matched for accuracy.

Year by year, states are passing regulations to cut pollution by mandating lower VOC levels in house paint. Aura and Natura are ahead of the curve in many states and, despite their higher prices, these brands are painting Benjamin Moore's bottom line a richer shade of green.[b]

problems for some companies. Other organizations anticipate demand fluctuations and develop new products and prices to meet consumers' changing needs.

ASSESSING PRICE ELASTICITY OF DEMAND

Up to this point, we have seen how marketers identify the target market's evaluation of price and its ability to purchase and how they examine demand to learn whether price is related inversely or directly to quantity. The next step is to assess price elasticity of demand. **Price elasticity of demand** provides a measure of the sensitivity of demand to changes in price. It is formally defined as the percentage change in quantity demanded relative to a given percentage change in price (see Figure 11.3).[9] The percentage change in quantity demanded caused by a percentage change in price is much greater for elastic demand than for inelastic demand. For a product such as electricity, demand is relatively inelastic: When its price increases, say, from P_1 to P_2, quantity demanded goes down only a little, from Q_1 to Q_2. For products such as recreational vehicles, demand is relatively elastic: When price rises sharply, from P_1 to P_2, quantity demanded goes down a great deal, from Q_1 to Q_2.

If marketers can determine the price elasticity of demand, setting a price is much easier. By analyzing total revenues as prices change, marketers can determine whether a product is price elastic. Total revenue is price times quantity; thus 10,000 rolls of wallpaper sold in one year at a price of $10 per roll equals $100,000 of total revenue. If demand is elastic, a change in price causes an opposite change in total revenue; an increase in price will decrease total revenue, and a decrease in price will increase total revenue. Inelastic demand results in a change in the same direction in total revenue. An increase in price will increase total revenue, and a decrease in price will decrease total revenue. Demand for gasoline, for example, is relatively inelastic—even when prices well exceed $3 per gallon—because people must still drive to work, run errands, shop, and engage in other behaviors that require fuel for their vehicles. Higher gasoline prices force more consumers to change some behaviors in an effort to reduce the amount of gasoline they use, but most cut spending in other areas instead because they require a certain level of

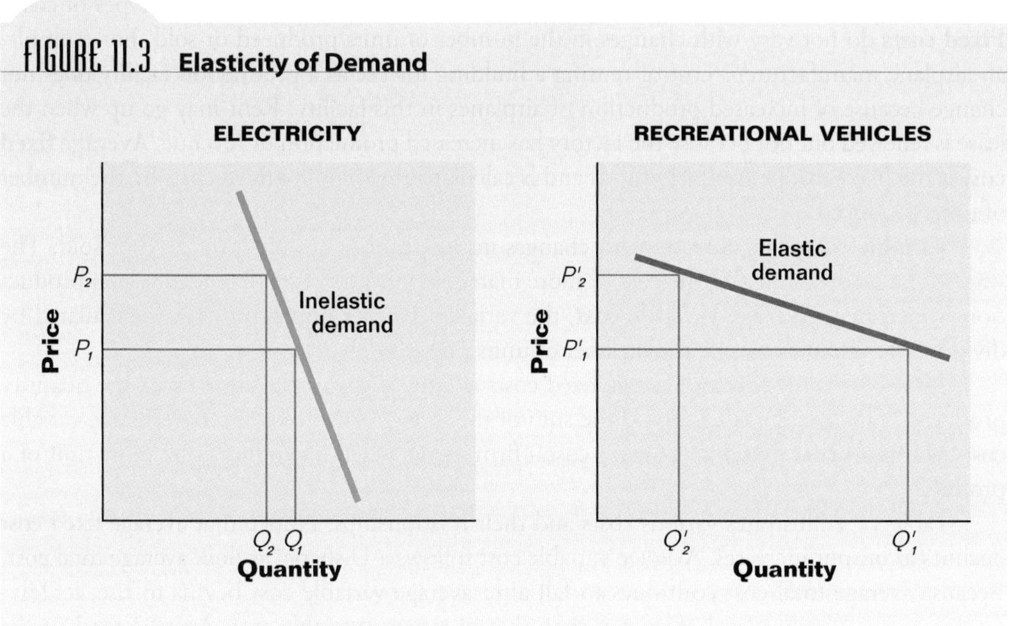

fuel for weekly activities such as commuting to work.[10] The following formula determines the price elasticity of demand:

$$\text{Price elasticity of demand} = \frac{(\text{\% change in quantity demanded})}{(\text{\% change in price})}$$

For example, if demand falls by 8 percent when a seller raises the price by 2 percent, the price elasticity of demand is –4 (the negative sign indicating the inverse relationship between price and demand). If demand falls by 2 percent when price is increased by 4 percent, elasticity is –0.5. The less elastic the demand, the more beneficial it is for the seller to raise the price. Products without readily available substitutes and for which consumers have strong needs, such as electricity or appendectomies, usually have inelastic demand.

Marketers cannot base prices solely on elasticity considerations. They also must examine the costs associated with different sales volumes and evaluate what happens to profits.

Demand, Cost, and Profit Relationships

The analysis of demand, cost, and profit is important because customers are becoming less tolerant of price increases, forcing manufacturers to find new ways to control costs. In the past, many customers desired premium brands and were willing to pay extra for these products. Today, customers pass up certain brand names if they can pay less without sacrificing quality. To stay in business, a company has to set prices that not only cover its costs but also meet customers' expectations. In this section we explore two approaches to understanding demand, cost, and profit relationships: marginal analysis and breakeven analysis.

MARGINAL ANALYSIS

Marginal analysis examines what happens to a firm's costs and revenues when production (or sales volume) changes by one unit. Both production costs and revenues must be evaluated. To

price elasticity of demand
A measure of the sensitivity of demand to changes in price

fixed costs Costs that do not vary with changes in the number of units produced or sold

average fixed cost The fixed cost per unit produced

variable costs Costs that vary directly with changes in the number of units produced or sold

average variable cost The variable cost per unit produced

total cost The sum of average fixed and average variable costs times the quantity produced

determine the costs of production, it is necessary to distinguish among several types of costs. **Fixed costs** do not vary with changes in the number of units produced or sold. For example, an airplane manufacturer's cost of renting a building for use as a production facility does not change because of increased production of airplanes in this facility. Rent may go up when the lease is renewed but not because the factory has increased production or revenue. **Average fixed cost** is the fixed cost per unit produced and is calculated by dividing fixed costs by the number of units produced.

Variable costs vary directly with changes in the number of units produced or sold. The wages for a second shift and the cost of more materials are extra costs that occur when production is increased. **Average variable cost**, the variable cost per unit produced, is calculated by dividing the variable costs by the number of units produced.

Total cost is the sum of average fixed costs and average variable costs times the quantity produced. The **average total cost** is the sum of the average fixed cost and the average variable cost. **Marginal cost (MC)** is the extra cost a firm incurs when it produces one more unit of a product.

Table 11.1 illustrates various costs and their relationships. Notice that average fixed cost declines as output increases. Average variable cost follows a U shape, as does average total cost. Because average total cost continues to fall after average variable cost begins to rise, its lowest point is at a higher level of output than that of average variable cost. Average total cost is lowest at 5 units at a cost of $22, whereas average variable cost is lowest at 3 units at a cost of $10.67. As Figure 11.4 shows, marginal cost equals average total cost at the latter's lowest level. In Table 11.1, this occurs between 5 and 6 units of production. Average total cost decreases as long as marginal cost is less than average total cost, and it increases when marginal cost rises above average total cost.

Marginal revenue (MR) is the change in total revenue that occurs when a firm sells an additional unit of a product. Figure 11.5 depicts marginal revenue and a demand curve. Most

TABLE 11.1 Costs and Their Relationships

1	2	3	4	5	6	
Quantity	Fixed Cost	Average Fixed Cost (2) ÷ (1)	Average Variable Cost	Average Total Cost (3) + (4)	Total Cost (5) × (1)	Marginal Cost
1	$40	$40.00	$20.00	$60.00	$ 60	
						$10
2	40	20.00	15.00	35.00	70	
						2
3	40	13.33	10.67	24.00	72	
						18
4	40	10.00	12.50	22.50	90	
						20
5	40	8.00	14.00	22.00	110	
						30
6	40	6.67	16.67	23.33	140	
						40
7	40	5.71	20.00	25.71	180	

FIGURE 11.4 Typical Marginal Cost and Average Total Cost Relationship

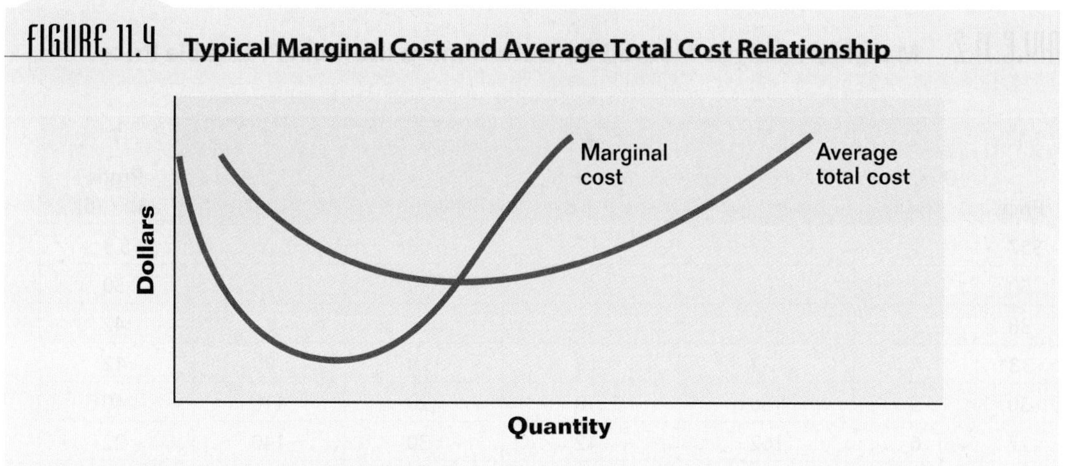

firms in the United States face downward-sloping demand curves for their products. They must lower their prices to sell additional units. This situation means that each additional unit of product sold provides the firm with less revenue than the previous unit sold. MR then becomes less than average revenue, as Figure 11.5 shows. Eventually, MR reaches zero, and the sale of additional units actually hurts the firm.

Before the firm can determine whether a unit makes a profit, it must know its cost, as well as its revenue, because profit equals revenue minus cost. If MR is a unit's addition to revenue and MC is a unit's addition to cost, MR minus MC tells us whether the unit is profitable. Table 11.2 illustrates the relationships among price, quantity sold, total revenue, marginal revenue, marginal cost, total cost, and profit for various combinations of price and quantity. Notice that the total cost and the marginal cost figures in Table 11.2 are calculated and appear in Table 11.1.

Profit is the highest where MC = MR (see Table 11.2). In this table, note that at a quantity of 4 units, profit is the highest, and MR − MC = 0. The best price is $33, and the profit is $42. Up to this point, the additional revenue generated from an extra unit sold exceeds the additional cost of producing it. Beyond this point, the additional cost of producing another unit exceeds the additional revenue generated, and profits decrease. If the price were based on

average total cost
The sum of the average fixed cost and the average variable cost

marginal cost (MC)
The extra cost a firm incurs by producing one more unit of a product

marginal revenue (MR)
The change in total revenue resulting from the sale of an additional unit of a product

FIGURE 11.5 Typical Marginal Revenue and Average Revenue Relationship

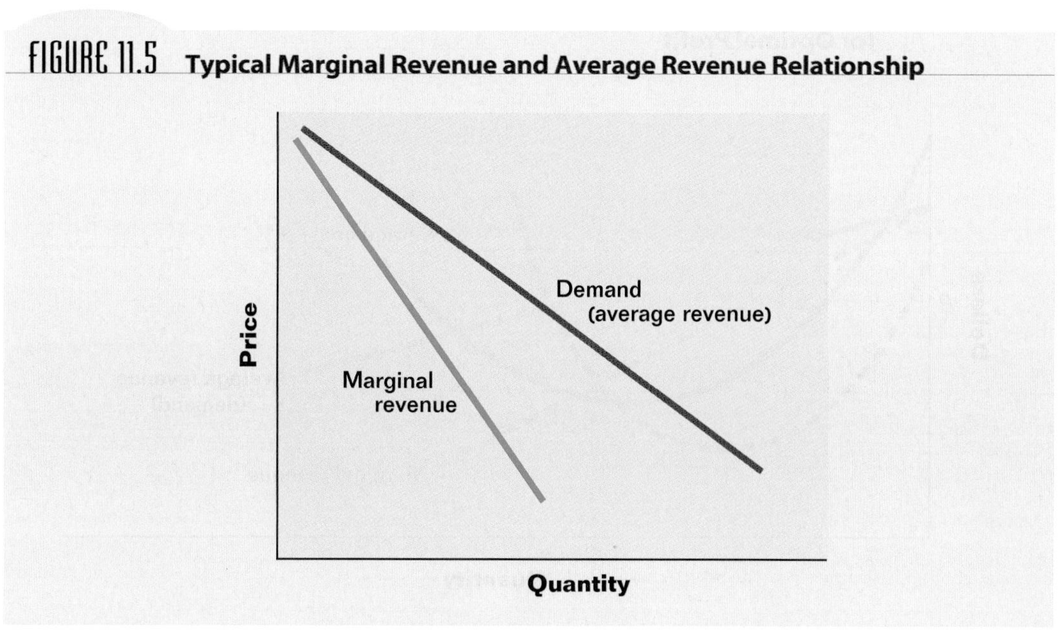

TABLE 11.2 **Marginal Analysis Method for Determining the Most Profitable Price**

1 Price	2 Quantity Sold	3 Total Revenue (1) × (2)	4 Marginal Revenue	5 Marginal Cost	6 Total Cost	7 Profit (3) − (6)
$57	1	$ 57	$ 57	$ 60	$ 60	−$ 3
50	2	100	43	10	70	30
38	3	114	14	2	72	42
33*	**4**	**132**	**18**	**18**	**90**	**42**
30	5	150	18	20	110	40
27	6	162	12	30	140	22
25	7	175	13	40	180	−5

*Boldface indicates the best price-profit combination.

minimum average total cost—$22 (see Table 11.1)—it would result in a lower profit of $40 (see Table 11.2) for 5 units priced at $30 versus a profit of $42 for 4 units priced at $33.

Graphically combining Figures 11.4 and 11.5 into Figure 11.6 shows that any unit for which MR exceeds MC adds to a firm's profits, and any unit for which MC exceeds MR subtracts from profits. The firm should produce at the point where MR equals MC because this is the most profitable level of production.

This discussion of marginal analysis may give the false impression that pricing can be highly precise. If revenue (demand) and cost (supply) remained constant, prices could be set for maximum profits. In practice, however, cost and revenue change frequently. The competitive

FIGURE 11.6 **Combining the Marginal Cost and Marginal Revenue Concepts for Optimal Profit**

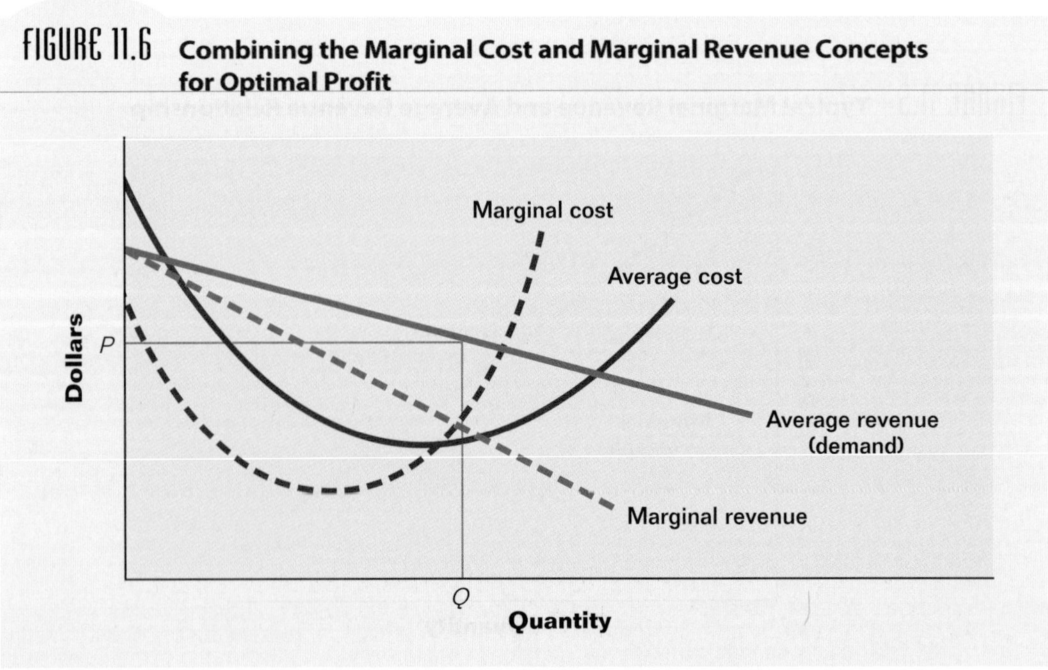

tactics of other firms or government action can quickly undermine a company's expectations of revenue. Thus marginal analysis is only a model from which to work. It offers little help in pricing new products before costs and revenues are established. On the other hand, in setting prices of existing products, especially in competitive situations, most marketers can benefit by understanding the relationship between marginal cost and marginal revenue.

BREAKEVEN ANALYSIS

The point at which the costs of producing a product equal the revenue made from selling the product is the **breakeven point**. If a wallpaper manufacturer has total annual costs of $100,000 and sells $100,000 worth of wallpaper in the same year, the company has broken even.

Figure 11.7 illustrates the relationships among costs, revenue, profits, and losses involved in determining the breakeven point. Knowing the number of units necessary to break even is important in setting the price. If a product priced at $100 per unit has an average variable cost of $60 per unit, the contribution to fixed costs is $40. If total fixed costs are $120,000, the breakeven point in units is determined as follows:

$$\text{Breakeven point} = \frac{\text{fixed costs}}{\text{per-unit contribution to fixed costs}}$$
$$= \frac{\text{fixed costs}}{\text{price-variable costs}}$$
$$= \$120{,}000/\$40$$
$$= 3{,}000 \text{ units}$$

To calculate the breakeven point in terms of dollar sales volume, multiply the breakeven point in units by the price per unit. In the preceding example, the breakeven point in terms of dollar sales volume is 3,000 (units) times $100, or $300,000.

breakeven point
The point at which the costs of producing a product equal the revenue made from selling the product

To use breakeven analysis effectively, a marketer should determine the breakeven point for each of several alternative prices. This determination allows the marketer to compare the effects on total revenue, total costs, and the breakeven point for each price under consideration.

FIGURE 11.7 **Determining the Breakeven Point**

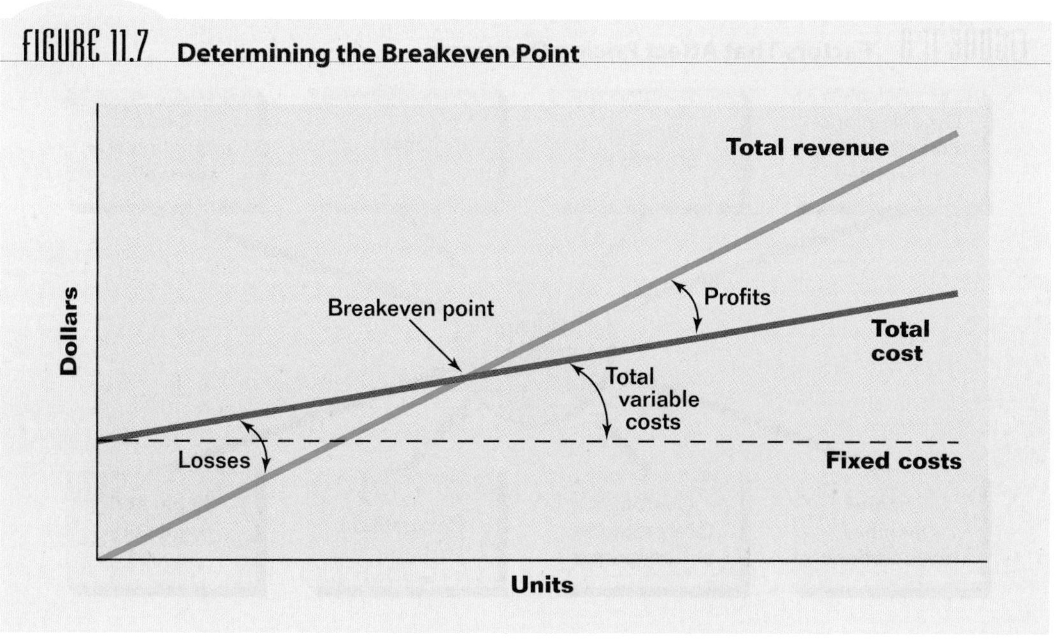

Although this comparative analysis may not tell the marketer exactly what price to charge, it will identify highly undesirable price alternatives that definitely should be avoided.

Breakeven analysis is simple and straightforward. It does assume, however, that the quantity demanded is basically fixed (inelastic) and that the major task in setting prices is to recover costs. It focuses more on how to break even than on how to achieve a pricing objective, such as percentage of market share or return on investment. Nonetheless, marketing managers can use this concept to determine whether a product will achieve at least a breakeven volume.

Factors Affecting Pricing Decisions

Pricing decisions can be complex because of the number of factors to be considered. Frequently, there is considerable uncertainty about the reactions to price among buyers, distribution channel members, and competitors. Price is also an important consideration in marketing planning, market analysis, and sales forecasting. It is a major issue when assessing a brand's position relative to competing brands. Most factors that affect pricing decisions can be grouped into one of the eight categories shown in Figure 11.8. In this section we explore how each of these eight groups of factors enters into price decision making.

ORGANIZATIONAL AND MARKETING OBJECTIVES

Marketers should set prices that are consistent with the organization's goals and mission. For example, a retailer trying to position itself as value-oriented may wish to set prices that are quite reasonable relative to product quality. In this case a marketer would not want to set premium prices on products but would strive to price products in line with this overall organizational goal.

Pricing decisions also should be compatible with the organization's marketing objectives. For instance, suppose that one of a producer's marketing objectives is a 12 percent increase

FIGURE 11.8 Factors That Affect Pricing Decisions

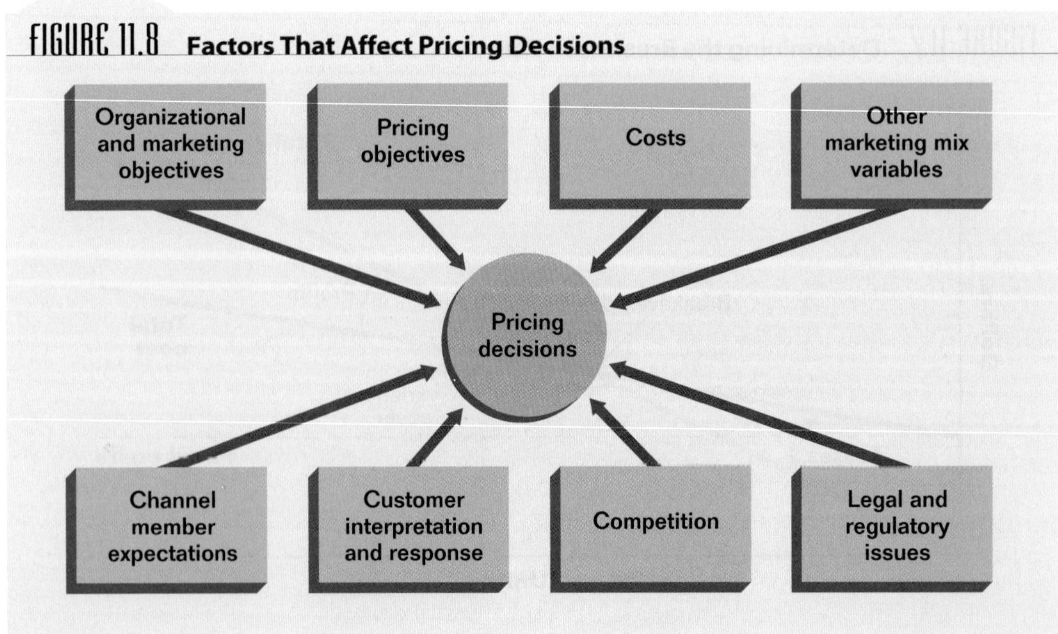

in unit sales by the end of the next year. Assuming that buyers are price-sensitive, increasing the price or setting a price above the average market price would not be in line with this objective.

TYPES OF PRICING OBJECTIVES

The types of pricing objectives a marketer uses obviously have considerable bearing on the determination of prices. For example, an organization that uses pricing to increase its market share likely would set the brand's price below those of competing brands of similar quality to attract competitors' customers. A marketer sometimes uses temporary price reductions in the hope of gaining market share. If a business needs to raise cash quickly, it likely will use temporary price reductions such as sales, rebates, and special discounts. We examine pricing objectives in more detail in the next chapter.

COSTS

Clearly, costs must be an issue when establishing price. A firm temporarily may sell products below cost to match competition, to generate cash flow, or even to increase market share, but in the long run it cannot survive by selling its products below cost. Even when a firm has a high-volume business, it cannot survive if each item is sold slightly below what it costs. A marketer should be careful to analyze all costs so that they can be included in the total cost associated with a product.

To maintain market share and revenue in an increasingly price-sensitive market, many marketers have concentrated on reducing costs. In the highly competitive computer industry, for example, Sun Microsystems constantly looks for ways to lower the cost of developing, producing, and marketing computers, software, and related products. As a cost-cutting move, the company recently laid off 3,700 employees and shrunk its real estate holdings.[11] Labor-saving technologies, a focus on quality, and efficient manufacturing processes have brought productivity gains that translate into reduced costs and lower prices for customers.

Besides considering the costs associated with a particular product, marketers must take into account the costs that the product shares with others in the product line. Products often share some costs, particularly the costs of research and development, production, and distribution. Most marketers view a product's cost as a minimum, or floor, below which the product cannot be priced.

Marketing IN TRANSITION

Anytime, Anywhere: Customers Dare to Compare

Thanks to technology, customers can now compare product prices at any hour and from any place. One recent survey found that 38 percent of consumers were comparing prices online and 27 percent were downloading online coupons before they set out to shop for back-to-school supplies in local stores. Here are a few ways that customers are comparing prices from home, in stores, or on the phone:

- Websites such as MySimon.com, Shopping.com, and PriceGrabber.com allow price comparisons by type of product, retailer, and other criteria. Research shows that such price-comparison sites are drawing particularly heavy traffic during the year-end holiday buying season.
- Websites such as FreeShipping.org and DealCatcher.com help customers find special pricing promotions such as free shipping or discount coupons.
- Mobile phone services such as Frucall let customers compare store prices with online prices before they buy. Customers punch in the product name or code and Frucall finds the best online price for that item. If the online price is lower, customers can place an immediate order using Frucall.

Customers who compare prices may not necessarily choose the lowest-priced offer, but they do weigh their alternatives in light of internal and external reference prices. "For financial products and services, people tend to use comparison sites as a starting point for the quote process," says one marketing expert. "This sets the standard and can trigger brand-related searches." This is true in many other product categories, meaning that customers respond to pricing based on many factors, not just by which is the biggest bargain.[c]

Price Affects Promotion Decisions
Most fragrance advertisements do not include prices.

OTHER MARKETING MIX VARIABLES

All marketing mix variables are highly interrelated. Pricing decisions can influence decisions and activities associated with product, distribution, and promotion variables. A product's price frequently affects the demand for that item. A high price, for instance, may result in low unit sales, which, in turn, may lead to higher production costs per unit. Conversely, lower per-unit production costs may result from a low price. For many products, buyers associate better product quality with a high price and poorer product quality with a low price. This perceived price–quality relationship influences customers' overall image of products or brands. Sony, for example, prices its televisions higher than average to help communicate that Sony televisions are high-quality electronic products. Consumers recognize the Sony brand name, its reputation for quality, and the prestige associated with buying Sony products.

The price of a product is linked to several dimensions of its distribution. Premium-priced products—a Bentley or a Rolls-Royce automobile, for example—are often marketed through selective or exclusive distribution. Lower-priced products in the same product category may be sold through intensive distribution. For example, Cross pens are distributed through selective distribution and Bic pens through intensive distribution. Moreover, an increase in physical distribution costs, such as shipping, may have to be passed on to customers. After fuel prices soared in 2005 and 2006, many firms were forced to pass the cost onto their customers in the form of higher prices or fuel surcharges. Big Sky Airlines, for example, had to increase fares by 25 to 40 percent, whereas Briggs Distributing Company had to levy a fuel surcharge of $3 on every delivery of beer and other beverages to its retail customers.[12] When setting a price, the profit margins of marketing channel members, such as wholesalers and retailers, must be considered. Channel members must be compensated adequately for the functions they perform.

Price may determine how a product is promoted. Bargain prices are often included in advertisements. Premium prices are less likely to be advertised, although they are sometimes included in advertisements for upscale items such as luxury cars or fine jewelry. Higher-priced products are more likely than lower-priced ones to require personal selling. Furthermore, the price structure can affect a salesperson's relationship with customers. A complex pricing structure takes longer to explain to customers, is more likely to confuse potential buyers, and may cause misunderstandings that result in long-term customer dissatisfaction. For example, the pricing structures of many airlines are complex and frequently confuse ticket sales agents and travelers alike.

CHANNEL MEMBER EXPECTATIONS

When making price decisions, a producer must consider what members of the distribution channel expect. A channel member certainly expects to receive a profit for the functions it performs. The amount of profit expected depends on what the intermediary could make if it were handling a competing product instead. Also, the amount of time and the resources required to carry the product influence intermediaries' expectations. Failure to understand channel member expectations can have negative consequences. For example, Food Lion and several other grocery store chains dropped over 300 Unilever products because the products were priced too high and Unilever increased their prices during the recent recession.[13]

Channel members often expect producers to give discounts for large orders and prompt payment. At times, resellers expect producers to provide several support activities such as sales training, service training, repair advisory service, cooperative advertising, sales promotions, and perhaps a program for returning unsold merchandise to the producer. These support activities clearly have associated costs that a producer must consider when determining prices.

CUSTOMER INTERPRETATION AND RESPONSE

When making pricing decisions, marketers should be concerned with a vital question: How will our customers interpret our prices and respond to them? *Interpretation* in this context refers to what the price means or what it communicates to customers. Does the price mean "high quality," "low quality," or "great deal," "fair price," or "rip-off"? Customer *response* refers to whether the price will move customers closer to the purchase of the product and the degree to which the price enhances their satisfaction with the purchase experience and with the product after purchase.

Customers' interpretation of and response to a price are determined to some degree by their assessment of value, or what they receive compared with what they give up to make the purchase. In evaluating what they receive, customers will consider product attributes, benefits, advantages, disadvantages, the probability of using the product, and possibly the status associated with the product. In assessing the cost of the product, customers likely will consider its price, the amount of time and effort required to obtain it, and perhaps the resources required to maintain it after purchase.

At times, customers interpret a higher price as an indication of higher product quality. They are especially likely to make this price–quality association when they cannot judge the quality of the product themselves. This is not always the case, however. Whether price is equated with quality depends on the types of customers and products involved. Obviously, marketers who rely on customers making a price–quality association and who provide moderate- or low-quality products at high prices will be unable to build long-term customer relationships.

When interpreting and responding to prices, how do customers determine if the price is too high, too low, or about right? In general, they compare prices with internal or external reference prices. An **internal reference price** is a price developed in the buyer's mind through experience with the product. It is a belief that a product should cost approximately a certain amount. To arrive at an internal reference price, consumers may consider one or more values, including what they think the product "ought" to cost, the price usually charged for it, the last price they paid, the highest and lowest amounts they would be willing to pay, the price of the brand they usually buy, the average price of similar products, the expected future price, and the typical discounted price.[14] Research has found that less-confident consumers tend to have higher internal reference prices than consumers with greater confidence, and frequent buyers—perhaps because of their experience and confidence—are more likely to judge high prices unfairly.[15] As consumers, our experiences have given each of us internal reference prices for several products. For example, most of us have a reasonable idea of how much to pay for a six-pack of soft drinks, a loaf of bread, or a gallon of milk. For the product categories with which we have less experience, we rely more heavily on external reference prices. An **external reference price** is a comparison price provided by others, such as retailers or producers. Customers' perceptions of prices are also influenced by their expectations about future price increases, by what they paid for the product recently, and by what they would like to pay for the product. Other factors affecting customers' perception of whether the price is right include time or financial constraints, the costs associated with searching for lower-priced products, and expectations that products will go on sale.

internal reference price
A price developed in the buyer's mind through experience with the product

external reference price
A comparison price provided by others

Buyers' perceptions of a product relative to competing products may allow the firm to set a price that differs significantly from rivals' prices. If the product is deemed superior to most of

© ROBERT BRENNER/PHOTOEDIT INC.

Customer Interpretation of Price
What does the price in this ad mean to customers?

the competition, a premium price may be feasible. However, even products with superior quality can be overpriced. Strong brand loyalty sometimes provides the opportunity to charge a premium price. On the other hand, if buyers view a product less than favorably (although not extremely negatively), a lower price may generate sales.

In the context of price, buyers can be characterized according to their degree of value consciousness, price consciousness, and prestige sensitivity. Marketers who understand these characteristics are better able to set pricing objectives and policies. **Value-conscious** consumers are concerned about both price and quality of a product.[16] These consumers may perceive value as quality per unit of price or as not only economic savings but also the additional gains expected from one product over a competitor's brand. The first view is appropriate for commodities such as bottled water, bananas, and gasoline. If a value-conscious consumer perceives the quality of gasoline to be the same for Exxon and Shell, he or she will go to the station with the lower price. For consumers looking not just for economic value but additional gains they expect from one brand over another, a product differentiation value could be associated with benefits and features that are believed to be unique.[17] **Price-conscious** individuals strive to pay low prices.[18] A price-conscious pet food buyer, for example, probably would purchase Walmart's Ol' Roy brand because it is the lowest-priced dog food and satisfies a basic need. Research has found that bargain-hunting price-conscious consumers comprise just 1.2 percent of all shoppers and in general reduce profits by less than 1 percent.[19] **Prestige-sensitive** buyers focus on purchasing products that signify prominence and status.[20] For example, Coty, Inc., a major producer of fragrances and beauty products for prestige-sensitive buyers, recently partnered with the Home Shopping Network (HSN) to offer select Coty products. One such product is the Lancaster 365 Cellular Elixer, an advanced anti-aging product from Coty Prestige's Lancaster brand, which costs $95 for a 1.7 fluid ounce bottle.[21] It is important to recognize that some consumers vary in their degree of value, price, and prestige consciousness. In some segments, moreover, consumers are increasingly "trading up" to higher-status products in categories such as automobiles, home appliances, restaurants, and even pet food; yet they remain price conscious regarding cleaning and grocery products.

COMPETITION

A marketer needs to know competitors' prices so that it can adjust its own prices accordingly. This does not mean that a company will necessarily match competitors' prices; it may set its price above or below theirs. For some organizations, however, matching competitors' prices is an important strategy for survival.

When adjusting prices, a marketer must assess how competitors will respond. Will competitors change their prices, and if so, will they raise or lower them? In Chapter 3 we described several types of competitive market structures. The structure that characterizes the industry to which a firm belongs affects the flexibility of price setting. For example, because of reduced pricing regulation, firms in the telecommunications industry have moved from a monopolistic market structure to an oligopolistic one, which has resulted in significant price competition.

When an organization operates as a monopoly and is unregulated, it can set whatever prices the market will bear. However, the company may not price the product at the highest

value conscious
Concerned about price and quality of a product

price-conscious
Striving to pay low prices

prestige-sensitive
Drawn to products that signify prominence and status

possible level to avoid government regulation or to penetrate a market by using a lower price. If the monopoly is regulated, it normally has less pricing flexibility; the regulatory body lets it set prices that generate a reasonable, but not excessive, return. A government-owned monopoly may price products below cost to make them accessible to people who otherwise could not afford them. Transit systems, for example, sometimes operate this way. However, government-owned monopolies sometimes charge higher prices to control demand. In some states with state-owned liquor stores, the price of liquor is higher than in states where liquor stores are not owned by a government body.

The automotive and airline industries exemplify oligopolies, in which there are only a few sellers and the barriers to competitive entry are high. Companies in such industries can raise their prices, hoping competitors will do the same. When an organization cuts its price to gain a competitive edge, other companies are likely to follow suit. Thus very little advantage is gained through price cuts in an oligopolistic market structure.

A monopolistic competition market structure consists of numerous sellers with product offerings that are differentiated by physical characteristics, features, quality, and brand images. The distinguishing characteristics of its product may allow a company to set a different price than its competitors. However, firms in a monopolistic competitive market structure are likely to practice nonprice competition, discussed earlier in this chapter.

© AP IMAGES/PRNEWSFOTO/TALLYGENICOM

Impact of Market Structure
The setting and establishing of Tally Genicom printer prices are affected by the fact that the printer industry is an oligopoly.

Under conditions of perfect competition, many sellers exist. Buyers view all sellers' products as the same. All firms sell their products at the going market price, and buyers will not pay more than that. Thus this type of market structure gives a marketer no flexibility in setting prices. Farming, as an industry, has some characteristics of perfect competition. Farmers sell their products at the going market price. At times, for example, corn, soybean, and wheat growers have had bumper crops and have been forced to sell them at depressed market prices.

LEGAL AND REGULATORY ISSUES

Legal and regulatory issues influence pricing decisions. To curb inflation, the federal government can invoke price controls, freeze prices at certain levels, or determine the rates at which prices may be increased. In some states, regulatory agencies set prices on products such as insurance, dairy products, and liquor.

Many regulations and laws affect pricing decisions and activities. The Sherman Antitrust Act prohibits conspiracies to control prices, and in interpreting the act, courts have ruled that price fixing among firms in an industry is illegal. Marketers must refrain from fixing prices by developing independent pricing policies and setting prices in ways that do not even suggest collusion. Both the Federal Trade Commission Act and the Wheeler-Lea Act prohibit deceptive pricing. Some other nations and trade agreements have similar prohibitions. The European Commission, for example, is investigating allegations of price fixing in the global candy industry, asking numerous candy makers, including U.S.-based Hershey and Mars, to provide it with information on their pricing practices.[22]

The Robinson-Patman Act has had a strong impact on pricing decisions. For various reasons, marketers may wish to sell the same type of product at different prices. Provisions in the Robinson-Patman Act, as well as those in the Clayton Act, limit the use of such price differentials. The practice of providing price differentials that tend to injure competition by giving one or more buyers a competitive advantage over other buyers is called **price discrimination** and is prohibited by law. However, not all price differentials are discriminatory. A marketer can use price differentials if they do not hinder competition, if they result from differences in the costs of selling or transportation to various customers, or if they arise because the firm has had to cut its price to a particular buyer to meet competitors' prices. Airlines, for example, may charge different customers different prices for the same flights based on the availability of seats at the time of purchase. As a result, fliers sitting in adjacent seats may have paid vastly different fares because one passenger booked weeks ahead, whereas the other booked on the spur of the moment a few days before, when only a few seats remained on the flight.

Pricing for Business Markets
Network Solutions offers computer-based marketing services to small businesses. These services include web site design tools, real-person customer service, personalized email, and online sales and marketing tools, starting at $24.95 per month.

Pricing for Business Markets

Business markets consist of individuals and organizations that purchase products for resale, for use in their own operations, or for producing other products. Establishing prices for this category of buyers sometimes differs from setting prices for consumers. Differences in the size of purchases, geographic factors, and transportation considerations require sellers to adjust prices. In this section we discuss several issues unique to the pricing of business products, including discounts, geographic pricing, and transfer pricing.

PRICE DISCOUNTING

Producers commonly provide intermediaries with discounts, or reductions, from list prices. Although there are many types of discounts, they usually fall into one of five categories: trade, quantity, cash, seasonal, and allowance. Table 11.3 summarizes some reasons to use each type of discount and provides examples. Such discounts can be a significant element in a marketing strategy.

Trade Discounts

A reduction off the list price given by a producer to an intermediary for performing certain functions is called a **trade**, or **functional**, **discount**. A trade discount is usually stated in terms of a percentage or series of percentages off the list price. Intermediaries are given trade discounts as compensation for performing various functions, such as selling, transporting, storing, final processing, and perhaps providing credit services. Although certain trade discounts are often a standard practice within an industry, discounts vary considerably among industries. It is important that a manufacturer provide a trade discount large enough to offset the intermediary's costs, plus a reasonable profit, to entice the reseller to carry the product.

price discrimination
Providing price differentials that injure competition by giving one or more buyers a competitive advantage

trade (functional) discount
A reduction off the list price given by a producer to an intermediary for performing certain functions

quantity discounts
Deductions from list price for purchasing large quantities

Quantity Discounts

Deductions from list price that reflect the economies of purchasing in large quantities are called **quantity discounts**. Quantity discounts are used in many industries and pass on to the buyer cost savings gained through economies of scale.

Quantity discounts can be either cumulative or noncumulative. **Cumulative discounts** are quantity discounts aggregated over a stated time period. Purchases totaling $10,000 in

TABLE 11.3 Discounts Used for Business Markets

Type	Reasons for Use	Examples
Trade (functional)	To attract and keep effective resellers by compensating them for performing certain functions, such as transportation, warehousing, selling, and providing credit	A college bookstore pays about one-third less for a new textbook than the retail price a student pays.
Quantity	To encourage customers to buy large quantities when making purchases and, in the case of cumulative discounts, to encourage customer loyalty	Large department store chains purchase some women's apparel at lower prices than do individually owned specialty stores.
Cash	To reduce expenses associated with accounts receivable and collection by encouraging prompt payment of accounts	Numerous companies serving business markets allow a 2 percent discount if an account is paid within ten days.
Seasonal	To allow a marketer to use resources more efficiently by stimulating sales during off-peak periods	Florida hotels provide companies holding national and regional sales meetings with deeply discounted accommodations during the summer months.
Allowance	In the case of a trade-in allowance, to assist the buyer in making the purchase and potentially earn a profit on the resale of used equipment; in the case of a promotional allowance, to ensure that dealers participate in advertising and sales support programs	A farm equipment dealer takes a farmer's used tractor as a trade-in on a new one. Nabisco pays a promotional allowance to a supermarket for setting up and maintaining a large end-of-aisle display for a two-week period.

a three-month period, for example, might entitle the buyer to a 5 percent, or $500, rebate. Such discounts are supposed to reflect economies in selling and to encourage the buyer to purchase from one seller. **Noncumulative discounts** are one-time reductions in prices based on the number of units purchased, the dollar value of the order, or the product mix purchased. Like cumulative discounts, these discounts should reflect some economies in selling or trade functions.

cumulative discounts Quantity discounts aggregated over a stated period

noncumulative discounts One-time reductions in price based on specific factors

Cash Discounts

A **cash discount**, or price reduction, is given to a buyer for prompt payment or cash payment. Accounts receivable are an expense and a collection problem for many organizations. A policy to encourage prompt payment is a popular practice and sometimes a major concern in setting prices.

Discounts are based on cash payments or cash paid within a stated time. For example, "2/10 net 30" means that a 2 percent discount will be allowed if the account is paid within ten days. If the buyer does not make payment within the ten-day period, the entire balance is due within 30 days without a discount. If the account is not paid within 30 days, interest may be charged.

cash discount Price reduction given to buyers for prompt payment or cash payment

Seasonal Discounts

A price reduction to buyers who purchase goods or services out of season is a **seasonal discount**. These discounts let the seller maintain steadier production during the year. For example, automobile rental agencies offer seasonal discounts in winter and early

seasonal discount A price reduction given to buyers for purchasing goods or services out of season

spring to encourage firms to use automobiles during the slow months of the automobile rental business.

Allowances

Another type of reduction from the list price is an **allowance**, or a concession in price to achieve a desired goal. Trade-in allowances, for example, are price reductions granted for turning in a used item when purchasing a new one. Allowances help to make the buyer better able to make the new purchase. This type of discount is popular in the aircraft industry. Another example is a *promotional allowance,* a price reduction granted to dealers for participating in advertising and sales support programs intended to increase sales of a particular item.

allowance
A concession in price to achieve a desired goal

GEOGRAPHIC PRICING

Geographic pricing involves reductions for transportation costs or other costs associated with the physical distance between buyer and seller. Prices may be quoted as F.O.B. (free-on-board) factory or destination. An **F.O.B. factory** price indicates the price of the merchandise at the factory, before it is loaded onto the carrier, and thus excludes transportation costs. The buyer must pay for shipping. An **F.O.B. destination** price means that the producer absorbs the costs of shipping the merchandise to the customer. This policy may be used to attract distant customers. Although F.O.B. pricing is an easy way to price products, it is sometimes difficult for marketers to administer, especially when a firm has a wide product mix or when customers are widely dispersed. Because customers will want to know about the most economical method of shipping, the seller must be informed about shipping rates.

To avoid the problems involved in charging different prices to each customer, **uniform geographic pricing**, sometimes called *postage-stamp pricing,* may be used. The same price is charged to all customers regardless of geographic location, and the price is based on average shipping costs for all customers. Paper products and office equipment are often priced on a uniform basis.

Zone pricing sets uniform prices for each of several major geographic zones; as the transportation costs across zones increase, so do the prices. For example, a Florida manufacturer's prices may be higher for buyers on the Pacific Coast and in Canada than for buyers in Georgia.

Base-point pricing is a geographic pricing policy that includes the price at the factory plus freight charges from the base point nearest the buyer. This approach to pricing has virtually been abandoned because of its questionable legal status. The policy resulted in all buyers paying freight charges from one location, such as Detroit or Pittsburgh, regardless of where the product was manufactured.

When the seller absorbs all or part of the actual freight costs, **freight absorption pricing** is being used. The seller might choose this method because it wishes to do business with a particular customer or to get more business; more business will cause the average cost to fall and counterbalance the extra freight cost. This strategy is used to improve market penetration and to retain a hold in an increasingly competitive market.

geographic pricing
Reductions for transportation and other costs related to the physical distance between buyer and seller

F.O.B. factory
The price of the merchandise at the factory, before shipment

F.O.B. destination
A price indicating the producer is absorbing shipping costs

uniform geographic pricing
Charging all customers the same price, regardless of geographic location

zone pricing
Pricing based on transportation costs within major geographic zones

base-point pricing
Geographic pricing combining factory price and freight charges from the base point nearest the buyer

freight absorption pricing
Absorption of all or part of actual freight costs by the seller

TRANSFER PRICING

Transfer pricing occurs when one unit in an organization sells a product to another unit. The price is determined by one of several methods. *Actual full cost* is calculated by dividing all fixed and variable expenses for a period into the number of units produced. *Standard full cost* is computed based on what it would cost to produce the goods at full plant capacity. *Cost plus investment* is full cost plus the cost of a portion of the selling unit's assets used for internal needs. *Market-based cost* is the market price less a small discount to reflect the lack of sales effort and other expenses. The choice of transfer-pricing method depends on the company's management strategy and the nature of the units' interaction. An organization also must ensure that transfer pricing is fair to all units involved in the purchases.

transfer pricing
Setting prices on products sold by one unit to another unit in the same company

CHAPTER REVIEW

OBJECTIVES

1 Understand the role of price.

Price is the value exchanged for products in marketing transactions. Price is not always money paid; barter, the trading of products, is the oldest form of exchange. Price is a key element in the marketing mix because it relates directly to the generation of total revenue. The profit factor can be determined mathematically by multiplying price by quantity sold to get total revenue and then subtracting total costs. Price is the marketing mix variable that usually can be adjusted quickly and easily to respond to changes in the external environment.

2 Identify the characteristics of price and nonprice competition.

Price competition emphasizes price as the major product differential. Prices fluctuate frequently, and price competition among sellers is aggressive. Nonprice competition emphasizes product differentiation through distinctive features, services, product quality, or other factors. Establishing brand loyalty by using nonprice competition works best when the product can be physically differentiated and the customer can recognize these differences.

3 Be familiar with demand curves and the price elasticity of demand.

The classic demand curve is a graph of the quantity of products expected to be sold at various prices if other factors hold constant. It illustrates that as price falls, the quantity demanded usually increases. For prestige products, however, there is a direct positive relationship between price and quantity demanded; demand increases as price increases. Price elasticity of demand—the percentage change in quantity demanded relative to a given percentage change in price—must be determined. If demand is elastic, a change in price causes an opposite change in total revenue. Inelastic demand results in a parallel change in total revenue when a product's price is changed.

4 Understand the relationships among demand, costs, and profits.

Analysis of demand, cost, and profit relationships can be accomplished through marginal analysis or breakeven analysis. Marginal analysis examines what happens to a firm's costs and revenues when production (or sales volume) is changed by one unit. Marginal analysis combines the demand curve with the firm's costs to develop a price that yields maximum profit. Fixed costs do not vary with changes in the number of units produced or sold; average fixed cost is the fixed cost per unit produced. Variable costs vary directly with changes in the number of units produced or sold. Average variable cost is the variable cost per unit produced. Total cost is the sum of average fixed cost and average variable costs times the quantity produced. The optimal price is the point at which marginal cost (the cost associated with producing one more unit of the product) equals marginal revenue (the change in total revenue that occurs when one additional unit of the product is sold).

Breakeven analysis—determining the number of units that must be sold to break even—is important in setting prices. The point at which the cost of production equals the revenue from selling the product is the breakeven point. To use breakeven analysis effectively, a marketer should determine the breakeven point for each of several alternative prices. This determination makes it possible to compare the effects on total revenue, total costs, and the breakeven point for each price under consideration.

5 Describe key factors that may influence marketers' pricing decisions.

Eight factors affect price decision making: organizational and marketing objectives, pricing objectives, costs, other marketing mix variables, channel member expectations, customer interpretation and response, competition, and legal and regulatory issues. When setting prices, marketers should make decisions consistent with the organization's goals and mission. Pricing objectives heavily influence price-setting decisions. Most marketers view a product's cost as the floor below which a product cannot be priced. Because of the interrelation among the marketing mix variables, price can affect product, promotion, and distribution decisions. The revenue that channel members expect for their functions also should be considered when making price decisions. Buyers' perceptions of price vary. Some consumer segments are sensitive to price, but others may not be. Knowledge of the prices charged for competing brands is essential so that the firm can adjust its prices relative to competitors. Government regulations and legislation influence pricing decisions.

Be familiar with the major issues that affect the pricing of products for business markets.

The categories of discounts offered to business customers include trade, quantity, cash, seasonal, and allowance. A trade discount is a price reduction for performing functions such as storing, transporting, final processing, or providing credit services. If an intermediary purchases in large enough quantities, the producer gives a quantity discount, which can be either cumulative or noncumulative. A cash discount is a price reduction for prompt payment or payment in cash. Buyers who purchase goods or services out of season may be granted a seasonal discount. A final type of reduction from the list price is an allowance, such as a trade-in allowance.

Geographic pricing involves reductions for transportation costs or other costs associated with the physical distance between buyer and seller. A price quoted as F.O.B. factory means that the buyer pays for shipping from the factory. An F.O.B. destination price means that the producer pays for shipping. This is the easiest way to price products, but it is difficult for marketers to administer. When the seller charges a fixed average cost for transportation, it is using uniform geographic pricing. Zone prices are uniform within major geographic zones; they increase by zone as the transportation costs increase. With base-point pricing, prices are adjusted for shipping expenses incurred by the seller from the base point nearest the buyer. Freight absorption pricing occurs when a seller absorbs all or part of the freight costs.

Transfer pricing occurs when a unit in an organization sells products to another unit in the same organization. Methods used for transfer pricing include actual full cost, standard full cost, cost plus investment, and market-based cost.

Please visit the student website at www.cengage.com/international for quizzes and games that will help you prepare for exams and help achieve the grade you want.

KEY CONCEPTS

price
barter
price competition
nonprice competition
demand curve
price elasticity of demand
fixed costs
average fixed cost
variable costs
average variable cost
total cost
average total cost
marginal cost (MC)
marginal revenue (MR)
breakeven point
internal reference price
external reference price
value-conscious
price-conscious
prestige-sensitive
price discrimination
trade (functional) discount
quantity discounts
cumulative discounts
noncumulative discounts
cash discount
seasonal discount
allowance
geographic pricing
F.O.B. factory
F.O.B. destination
uniform geographic pricing
zone pricing
base-point pricing
freight absorption pricing
transfer pricing

ISSUES FOR DISCUSSION AND REVIEW

1. Why are pricing decisions important to an organization?
2. Compare and contrast price and nonprice competition. Describe the conditions under which each form works best.
3. Why do most demand curves demonstrate an inverse relationship between price and quantity?
4. List the characteristics of products that have inelastic demand, and give several examples of such products.

5. Explain why optimal profits should occur when marginal cost equals marginal revenue.
6. Chambers Company has just gathered estimates for conducting a breakeven analysis for a new product. Variable costs are $7 a unit. The additional plant will cost $48,000. The new product will be charged $18,000 a year for its share of general overhead. Advertising expenditures will be $80,000, and $55,000 will be spent on distribution. If the product sells for $12, what is the breakeven point in units? What is the breakeven point in dollar sales volume?
7. In what ways do other marketing mix variables affect pricing decisions?
8. What types of expectations may channel members have about producers' prices? How might these expectations affect pricing decisions?
9. How do legal and regulatory forces influence pricing decisions?
10. Compare and contrast a trade discount and a quantity discount.
11. What is the reason for using the term *F.O.B.?*
12. What are the major methods used for transfer pricing?

MARKETING APPLICATIONS

1. Price competition is intense in the fast-food, air travel, and personal computer industries. Discuss a recent situation in which companies had to meet or beat a competitor's price in a price-competitive industry. Did you benefit from this situation? Did it change your perception of the companies and/or their products?
2. Customers' interpretations and responses regarding a product and its price are an important influence on marketers' pricing decisions. Perceptions of price are affected by the degree to which customers are value conscious, price conscious, or prestige sensitive. Discuss how these factors influence the buying decision process for the following products:
   a. A new house
   b. Weekly groceries for a family of five
   c. An airline ticket
   d. A soft-drink from a vending machine

ONLINE EXERCISE

3. Autosite offers car buyers a free, comprehensive website to find the invoice prices for almost all car models. The browser also can access a listing of all the latest new-car rebates and incentives. Visit this site at http://www.autosite.com.
   a. Which Lexus dealer is closest to you? Find the lowest-priced Lexus available today and examine its features.
   b. If you wanted to purchase this Lexus, what are the lowest monthly payments you could make over the longest time period?
   c. Is this free site more credible than a "pay" site? Why or why not?

DEVELOPING YOUR MARKETING PLAN

The appropriate pricing of a product is an important factor in developing a successful marketing strategy. The price contributes to the profitability of the product and can deter competition from entering the market. A clear understanding of pricing concepts is essential in developing strategy and the marketing plan. Consider the information in this chapter when focusing on the following issues:

1. Does your company currently compete based on price or non-price factors? Should your new product continue with this approach?
2. Discuss the level of elasticity of demand for your product. Is additional information needed in order for you to determine its elasticity?
3. At various price points, calculate the break-even point for sales of your product.
4. Using Figure 11.8 as a guide, discuss the various factors that affect the pricing of your product.

The information obtained from these questions should assist you in developing various aspects of your marketing plan found in the *Interactive Marketing Plan* exercise.

VIDEO CASE 11

Washburn Guitars Plays a Multiple Pricing Tune

Chicago-based Washburn Guitars has been making guitars, banjos, and mandolins for every kind of music and every kind of budget since 1883. Whether they play blues or bluegrass, heavy metal or hard rock, musicians and music students buy Washburn instruments for their sound quality, solid craftsmanship, and good looks. Professionals especially appreciate the way Washburn guitars stand up to the wear and tear of lengthy concert tours.

Washburn offers six product lines: electric guitars, acoustic guitars, bass guitars, bluegrass instruments, classical guitars, and travel guitars. More than two dozen of its guitars are designated as "Signature" models designed by well-known musicians such as Dan Donegan of Disturbed, Scott Ian of Anthrax, Joe Trohman of Fall Out Boy, Nick Catanese of Black Label Society, Paul Stanley of Kiss, Nuno Bettencourt of Extreme, and Greg Tribbett of Mudvayne. These names add luster to the Washburn brand and enhance the perceived value of the specially designed Signature models.

In setting the manufacturers' suggested retail price for each product, the company has established four broad price points. At the low end, products that sell for $349 or less are entry level. Products that sell for $350 to $999 are intermediate level and products that sell for $1,000 to $3,000 are professional level. At the high end, products that sell for more than $3,000 are collectors' level. At every level, Washburn promises that each of its instruments "represents the finest quality at the best possible price."

The guitars made in Washburn's U.S. factory are priced at $2,259 and more, reflecting the high cost of handcrafting. These guitars are perceived to be high quality and are therefore in high demand among professional musicians. In fact, Washburn has a six- to nine-month backlog of orders for its U.S.-made guitars. Its very highest-priced guitars—the few Signature models that sell for $5,000 or more—not only influence customers' perceptions of Washburn quality but also attract attention and get people talking about the brand. Similarly, the Limited Edition Rare Wood Series guitars are priced to reflect the unusual woods that make up the guitar bodies.

Apart from the high-end models, Washburn's instruments are machine manufactured outside the United States. This keeps both fixed and variable costs lower than those in the U.S. factories. Although Washburn's variable costs go down as its manufacturing volume rises, the company has found that changing equipment to make different models takes time and adds to its costs.

Washburn sells its instruments through independent retailers in the United States, Canada, and several dozen countries worldwide. These stores receive quantity discounts for large orders and expect to earn a certain profit margin based on a percentage of the manufacturer's suggested retail price for each product. Although the stores now face intense price competition from online-only retailers that have lower fixed costs, Washburn insists that its authorized retailers not offer discounts below certain minimum prices. Stores that price Washburn products lower than the company's minimum receive a warning and, if they don't change their prices, are removed from the list of authorized retailers and receive no more shipments.

Washburn's advertising campaigns include magazine and television commercials spotlighting the star quality of the performers and the particular Washburn guitars they prefer, without mentioning prices. Washburn has a strong online presence, including a virtual catalog, podcasts, video tours on YouTube, and brand pages on MySpace and Facebook. Even after more than 125 years in the music business, Washburn still keeps its marketing—including its pricing—as fresh as the newest number-one hit song.

QUESTIONS FOR DISCUSSION

1. Is Washburn using price or nonprice competition? Explain your answer.
2. What effect do you think a manufacturer's suggested retail price is likely to have on customers who buy Washburn guitars from a local music store?
3. Which factors shown in Figure 11.8 of your text are likely to have a major impact on pricing decisions at Washburn?

Mark C. Davis, "Washburn Guitars: D49SPK," *Guitar Player*, April 2009, p. 28; Washburn Guitar website, www.washburn.com; Washburn Guitar video.

CHAPTER 12 Pricing Management

© ANTHONY DEVLIN/PA WIRE URN:6131482 (PRESS ASSOCIATION VIA AP IMAGES)

OBJECTIVES:

1. Understand the six major stages of the process used to establish prices.
2. Know the issues that are related to developing pricing objectives.
3. Understand the importance of identifying the target market's evaluation of price.
4. Describe how marketers analyze competitive prices.
5. Be familiar with the bases used for setting prices.
6. Explain the different types of pricing strategies.
7. Understand how a final, specific price is determined.

APPLE ANSWERS THE CALL FOR iPHONE PRICING

Days before the first Apple iPhones went on sale, thousands of buyers lined up outside Apple stores, eager to try the cell phone's user-friendly touch screen and multimedia capabilities. Like Apple's iconic iPod media player, the stylish iPhone immediately became a must-have status symbol for tech-savvy consumers. However, within two months after the iPhone's release, Apple drew criticism and controversy for changing its pricing.

Traditionally, Apple has set high prices for new products. One reason is to reinforce the brand's high-end positioning and special cachet. Another is to start recouping development costs and build profits from the very start of each product's life. This pricing strategy has worked well with Apple's Macintosh computers and its iPods.

Following this strategy, the iPhone was initially priced at $599, not including the cost of phone service through an exclusive deal with AT&T. Two months later, in a break from its usual pattern, Apple abruptly cut $200 from the iPhone's price to make it more affordable as the year-end gift-giving holidays approached.

Apple's pricing decision provoked angry protests from customers who had bought at the higher price, and the CEO quickly conceded that customers had a point. "Our early customers trusted us, and we must live up to that trust with our actions in moments like these," he said. The company offered a $100 Apple store credit to each customer who had bought an iPhone before the price cut.

Since then, Apple has launched a number of new iPhone models with more features, more power, and lower prices. Walmart now sells iPhones at a $2 discount off the official price of $199 for the basic model and $299 for the advanced model. All this buzz has polished the Apple brand and helped it gain share in the highly competitive market for smartphones.[1]

Apple, like most companies, has developed a specific approach to pricing to attract and retain customers. Selecting pricing strategies is one of the fundamental steps in the process of setting prices. Indeed, some firms have developed products, especially software, to help client companies set the best price for their own products.

In this chapter we examine six stages of a process marketers can use when setting prices (Figure 12.1). Stage 1 is the development of a pricing objective that is compatible with the organization's overall objectives and its marketing objectives. Stage 2 entails assessing the target market's evaluation of price. Stage 3 involves evaluating competitors' prices, which helps to determine the role of price in the marketing strategy. Stage 4 involves choosing a basis for setting prices. Stage 5 is the selection of a pricing strategy, or the guidelines for using price in the marketing mix. Stage 6, determining the final price, depends on environmental forces and marketers' understanding and use of a systematic approach to establishing prices. These stages are not rigid steps that all marketers must follow; rather, they are guidelines that provide a logical sequence for establishing prices.

FIGURE 12.1 Stages for Establishing Prices

1 Development of pricing objectives

2 Assessment of target market's evaluation of price

3 Evaluation of competitors' prices

4 Selection of a basis for pricing

5 Selection of a pricing strategy

6 Determination of a specific price

Development of Pricing Objectives

The first step in setting prices is developing **pricing objectives**, goals that describe what a firm wants to achieve through pricing. Developing pricing objectives is an important task because pricing objectives form the basis for decisions about other stages of pricing. Thus pricing objectives must be stated explicitly, and the statement should include the time frame for accomplishing them.

Marketers must make sure that the pricing objectives are consistent with the organization's marketing objectives and with its overall objectives because pricing objectives influence decisions in many functional areas, including finance, accounting, and production. A marketer can use both short- and long-term pricing objectives and can employ one or multiple pricing objectives. For instance, a firm may wish to increase market share by 18 percent over the next three years, achieve a 15 percent return on investment, and promote an image of quality in the marketplace. In this section we examine some of the pricing objectives that companies might set for themselves (Table 12.1).

SURVIVAL

pricing objectives Goals that describe what a firm wants to achieve through pricing

A fundamental pricing objective is survival. Most organizations will tolerate problems such as short-run losses and internal upheaval if necessary for survival. For example, many builders like D.R. Horton and KB Homes slashed prices on brand-new homes by as much as six figures to stimulate sales during a severe housing slump and to slim down an expensive inventory of unsold homes.[2] Because price is a flexible variable, it is sometimes used to keep a company afloat by increasing sales volume to levels that match expenses. For example, a women's apparel retailer may run a three-day 60-percent-off sale to generate enough cash to pay creditors, employees, and rent.

TABLE 12.1 Pricing Objectives and Typical Actions Taken to Achieve Them

Objective	Possible Action
Survival	Adjust price levels so that the firm can increase sales volume to match organizational expenses
Profit	Identify price and cost levels that allow the firm to maximize profit
Return on investment	Identify price levels that enable the firm to yield targeted return on investment
Market share	Adjust price levels so that the firm can maintain or increase sales relative to competitors' sales
Cash flow	Set price levels to encourage rapid sales
Status quo	Identify price levels that help stabilize demand and sales
Product quality	Set prices to recover research and development expenditures and establish a high-quality image

PROFIT

Although a business may claim that its objective is to maximize profits for its owners, the objective of profit maximization is rarely operational because its achievement is difficult to measure. Because of this difficulty, profit objectives tend to be set at levels that the owners and top-level decision makers view as satisfactory. Specific profit objectives may be stated in terms of actual dollar amounts or in terms of a percentage of sales revenues. For example, when Procter & Gamble introduced the Gillette Fusion five-blade razor, it set a price 30 percent higher than its Mach 3 three-blade products. With an overall 72 percent market share, P&G hopes that the Fusion family of shaving products will help to boost profits.[3]

RETURN ON INVESTMENT

Pricing to attain a specified rate of return on the company's investment is a profit-related pricing objective. Most pricing objectives based on return on investment (ROI) are achieved by trial and error because not all cost and revenue data needed to project the ROI are available when prices are set. General Motors uses ROI pricing objectives. Many pharmaceutical companies also use ROI pricing objectives because of their great investment in research and development.

MARKET SHARE

Many firms establish pricing objectives to maintain or increase market share, a product's sales in relation to total industry sales. Many firms recognize that high relative market shares often translate into higher profits. The Profit Impact of Market Strategies (PIMS) studies, conducted over the last 30 years, have shown that both market share and product quality heavily influence profitability. Thus marketers often use an increase in market share as a primary pricing objective.

Maintaining or increasing market share need not depend on growth in industry sales. Remember that an organization can increase its market share even if sales for the total industry are flat or decreasing. On the other hand, a firm's sales volume may increase while its market share decreases if total industry sales are growing.

Sustainable Marketing

Homemade Energy

From energy-generating solar panels to nature-friendly building materials, new homes are getting greener by the day. According to the National Association of Home Builders, nine out of ten home builders now incorporate good-for-the-environment features in new construction. However, cutting-edge products such as solar panels and decking made from recycled plastics are often marketed using a price-skimming strategy. As a result, even people who want to own a green home hesitate when they see the price tag of these extra features.

© ISTOCKPHOTO.COM/OTMAR SMIT

For instance, the average cost of installing solar panels to generate electricity when the sun shines can range from $8,000 to $40,000 per home. This investment will pay for itself by drastically reducing the owner's energy costs in the long run. One Maryland homeowner pays less than $30 monthly for electricity—sometimes as little as $3—thanks to solar panels and other energy-efficient house improvements. Yet, of the new homes sold annually, less than 1 percent are equipped with solar panels.

Little by little, prices are starting to move lower as more competitors enter the market. In addition, state and federal government–sponsored incentives are making green home features more affordable for buyers. Finally, no matter how high the price tag, builders and buyers in many communities will soon have no choice but to go greener to comply with local building codes.[a]

Product Quality
This ad for Kellogg's Corn Flakes focuses on high product quality. A part of Kellogg's message in many of its advertisements is "bringing our best to you."

CASH FLOW

Some companies set prices so that they can recover cash as quickly as possible. Financial managers understandably seek to quickly recover capital spent to develop products. This objective may have the support of a marketing manager who anticipates a short product life cycle.

Although it may be acceptable in some situations, the use of cash flow and recovery as an objective oversimplifies the value of price in contributing to profits. If this pricing objective results in high prices, competitors with lower prices may gain a large share of the market.

STATUS QUO

In some cases an organization is in a favorable position and, desiring nothing more, may set an objective of status quo. Status quo objectives can focus on several dimensions, such as maintaining a certain market share, meeting (but not beating) competitors' prices, achieving price stability, and maintaining a favorable public image. A status quo pricing objective can reduce a firm's risks by helping to stabilize demand for its products. The use of status quo pricing objectives sometimes minimizes pricing as a competitive tool, leading to a climate of nonprice competition in an industry.

PRODUCT QUALITY

A company may have the objective of leading its industry in product quality. This goal normally dictates a high price to cover the high product quality and, in some instances, the high cost of research and development. For example, Bentley Motors uses premium prices to help signal the quality of its hand-made cars, which can cost from $190,000 to well over $260,000 depending on accessories and options.[4] As mentioned previously, the PIMS studies have shown that both product quality and market share are good indicators of profitability. The products and brands that customers perceive to be of high quality are more likely to survive in a competitive marketplace. High quality usually enables a marketer to charge higher prices for the product.

Assessment of the Target Market's Evaluation of Price

After developing pricing objectives, marketers next need to assess the target market's evaluation of price. Despite the general assumption that price is a major issue for buyers, the importance of price depends on the type of product, the type of target market, and the purchase situation. For example, buyers are probably more sensitive to gasoline prices than to luggage prices. With respect to the type of target market, adults may have to pay more than children for certain products. The purchase situation also affects the buyer's view of price. In other situations, most moviegoers would never pay the prices charged for soft drinks, popcorn, and candy at movie concession stands. By assessing the target market's evaluation of price, a marketer is in a better position to know how much emphasis to put on price in the overall marketing strategy. Information about the target market's price evaluation also may help a marketer to determine how far above the competition the firm can set its prices.

Because some consumers today are seeking less expensive products and shopping more selectively, some manufacturers and retailers are focusing on the value of their products. Value combines a product's price and quality attributes, which customers use to differentiate among competing brands. Consumers are looking for good deals on products that provide better value for their money. They also may view products that have highly desirable attributes, such as organic content or time-saving features, as having great value. Companies that offer both low prices and high quality, such as Target and Best Buy, have altered consumers' expectations about how much quality they must sacrifice for low prices.[5] Understanding the importance of a product to customers, as well as their expectations about quality and value, helps marketers to correctly assess the target market's evaluation of price.

SNAPSHOT

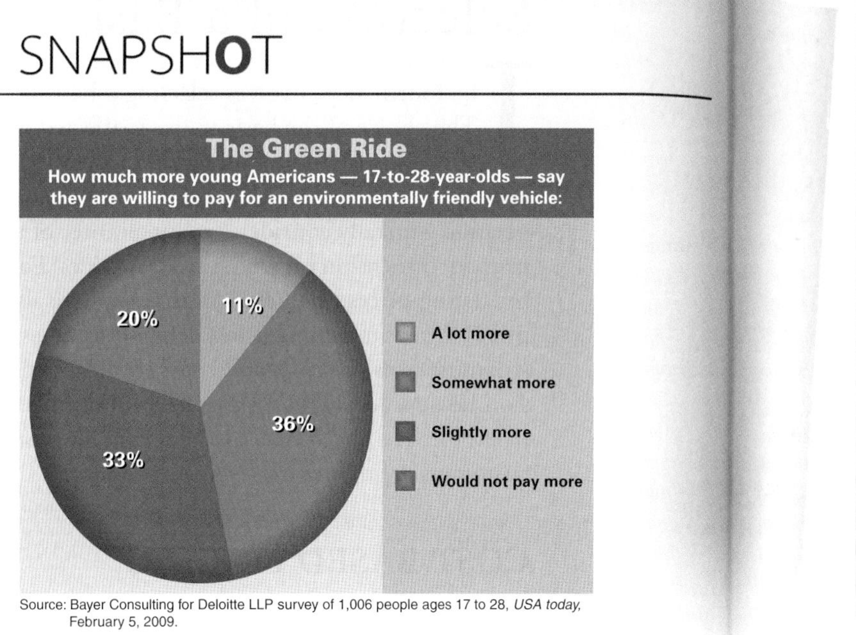

Source: Bayer Consulting for Deloitte LLP survey of 1,006 people ages 17 to 28, *USA today,* February 5, 2009.

Evaluation of Competitors' Prices

In most cases marketers are in a better position to establish prices when they know the prices charged for competing brands, the third step in establishing prices. Discovering competitors' prices may be a regular function of marketing research. Some grocery and department stores, for example, have full-time comparative shoppers who systematically collect data on prices. However, uncovering competitors' prices is not always easy, especially in producer and reseller markets. Competitors' price lists are often closely guarded. Even if a marketer has access to competitors' price lists, these lists may not reflect the actual prices at which competitive products are sold because those prices may be established through negotiation.

Knowing the prices of competing brands can be very important for a marketer. Competitors' prices and the marketing-mix variables they emphasize partly determine how important price will be to customers. A marketer in an industry in which price competition prevails needs competitive price information to ensure that its prices are the same as, or lower than, competitors' prices. In some instances an organization's prices are designed to be slightly above competitors' prices to give its products an exclusive image. In contrast, another company may use price as a competitive tool and price its products below those of competitors.

Selection of a Basis for Pricing

The fourth step involves selecting a basis for pricing: cost, demand, and/or competition. The choice of the basis to use is affected by the type of product, the market structure of the industry, the brand's market share position relative to competing brands, and customer characteristics. Although we discuss each basis separately in this section, an organization generally considers two or all three of these dimensions, even though one may be the primary dimension on which it bases prices. For example, if a company is using cost as a basis for setting prices, marketers in that firm are also aware of and concerned about competitors' prices. If a company is using demand as a basis for pricing, those making pricing decisions still must consider costs and competitors' prices. Indeed, cost is a factor in every pricing decision because it establishes a price minimum below which the firm will not be able to recoup its production and other costs; demand likewise sets an effective price maximum above which customers are unlikely to buy the product.

COST-BASED PRICING

With **cost-based pricing**, a dollar amount or percentage is added to the cost of the product. This approach thus involves calculations of desired profit margins. Cost-based pricing does not necessarily take into account the economic aspects of supply and demand, nor must it relate to just one pricing strategy or pricing objective. Cost-based pricing is straightforward and easy to implement. Two common forms of cost-based pricing are cost-plus and markup pricing.

Cost-Plus Pricing

In **cost-plus pricing**, the seller's costs are determined (usually during a project or after a project is completed), and then a specified dollar amount or percentage of the cost is added to the seller's cost to establish the price. Cost-plus pricing and competition-based pricing are in fact the most common bases for pricing services.[6] When production costs are difficult to predict, cost-plus pricing is appropriate. Projects involving custom-made equipment and commercial construction are often priced by this technique. The government frequently uses such cost-based pricing in granting defense contracts. One pitfall for the buyer is that the seller may increase costs to establish a larger profit base. Furthermore, some costs, such as overhead, may be difficult to determine. In periods of rapid inflation, cost-plus pricing is popular, especially when the producer must use raw materials that are fluctuating in price.

Markup Pricing

A common pricing approach among retailers is **markup pricing**, in which a product's price is derived by adding a predetermined percentage of the cost, called *markup*, to the cost of the product. Although the percentage markup in a retail store varies from one category of goods to another—35 percent of cost for hardware items and 100 percent of cost for greeting cards, for example—the same percentage often is used to determine the price on items within a single product category, and the percentage markup may be largely standardized across an industry at the retail level. Using a standard percentage markup for a specific product category reduces pricing to a routine task that can be performed quickly. This is one of the major reasons that many retailers use markup pricing.

Markup can be stated as a percentage of the cost or as a percentage of the selling price. The following example illustrates how percentage markups are determined and points out the differences in the two methods. Assume that a retailer purchases a can of tuna at 45 cents, adds 15 cents to the cost, and then prices the tuna at 60 cents. Here are the figures:

cost-based pricing
Adding a dollar amount or percentage to the cost of the product

cost-plus pricing
Adding a specified dollar amount or percentage to the seller's cost

markup pricing
Adding to the cost of the product a predetermined percentage of that cost

$$\text{Markup as percentage of cost} = \frac{\text{markup}}{\text{cost}} = \frac{15}{45} = 33.3 \text{ percent}$$

$$\text{Markup as percentage of selling price} = \frac{\text{markup}}{\text{selling price}} = \frac{15}{60} = 25.0 \text{ percent}$$

Obviously, when discussing a percentage markup, it is important to know whether the markup is based on cost or selling price.

demand-based pricing Pricing based on the level of demand for the product

competition-based pricing Pricing influenced primarily by competitors' prices

DEMAND-BASED PRICING

Marketers sometimes base prices on the level of demand for the product. When **demand-based pricing** is used, customers pay a higher price when demand for the product is strong and a lower price when demand is weak. For example, hotels that otherwise attract numerous travelers often offer reduced rates during lower-demand periods. Some long-distance telephone companies, such as Sprint and Verizon, also use demand-based pricing by charging peak and off-peak rates or offering free cell phone minutes during off-peak times. To use this pricing basis, a marketer must be able to estimate the amounts of a product consumers will demand at different prices. The marketer then chooses the price that generates the highest total revenue. Obviously, the effectiveness of demand-based pricing depends on the marketer's ability to estimate demand accurately. Compared with cost-based pricing, demand-based pricing places a firm in a better position to reach higher profit levels, assuming that buyers value the product at levels sufficiently above the product's cost.

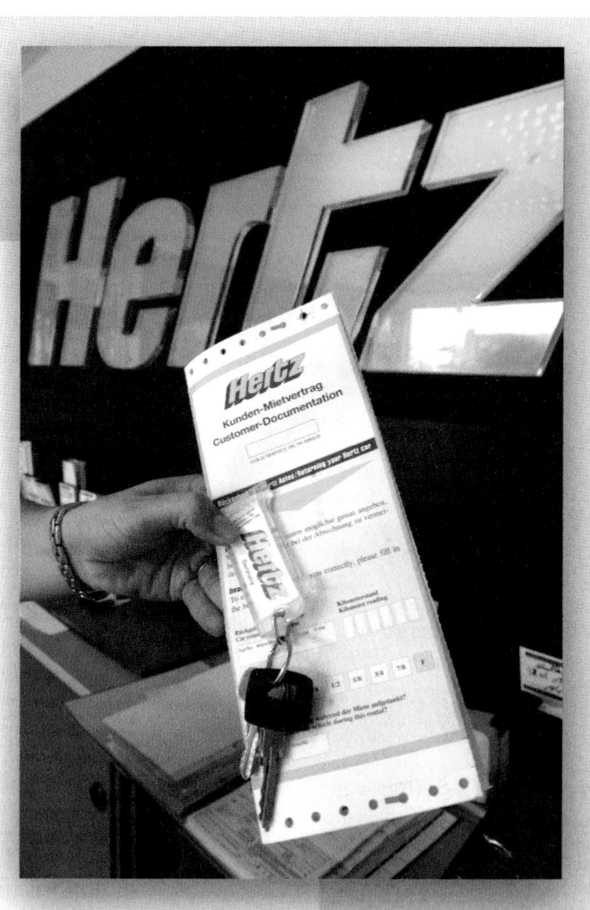

Demand-Based Pricing Rental car rates are frequently based on demand. High demand results in higher prices. Prices are lower when demand is low.

COMPETITION-BASED PRICING

In **competition-based pricing,** an organization considers costs as secondary to competitors' prices. The importance of this method increases when competing products are relatively homogeneous, and the organization is serving markets in which price is a key purchase consideration. A firm that uses competition-based pricing may choose to price below competitors' prices, above competitors' prices, or at the same level. Airlines use competition-based pricing, often charging identical fares on the same routes. Also, online travel services such as Orbitz, Expedia, and Priceline.com employ competition-based pricing.

Although not all introductory marketing texts have exactly the same price, they do have similar prices. The price the bookstore paid to the publishing company for this textbook was determined on the basis of competitors' prices. Competition-based pricing can help a firm achieve the pricing objective of increasing sales or market share. Competition-based pricing may necessitate frequent price adjustments. For example, for many competitive airline routes, fares are adjusted often.

TerraCycle Turns Trash into Cash

Back in 2001, two Princeton University students founded TerraCycle, selling organic plant food made from worm castings. Their latest product line includes tote bags, umbrellas, and shower curtains made from recycled trash.

TerraCycle's raw materials come from thousands of local "brigades"—recycling programs who receive postage-paid collection bags from sponsors, such as Stonyfield Farm and Coca-Cola, in which to send bundles of used containers to TerraCycle. Their products are made from trash, so their raw material prices aren't going up. As a result, TerraCycle can set highly competitive prices for its products and build profits while helping the environment. Annual sales are headed past $15 million as the company expands its recycling brigades, designs new products, and gears up to turn more trash into cash.[b]

Selection of a Pricing Strategy

The next step after choosing a basis for pricing is to select a pricing strategy, an approach or a course of action designed to achieve pricing and marketing objectives. Generally, pricing strategies help marketers to solve the practical problems of establishing prices. Table 12.2 lists the most common pricing strategies, which we discuss in this section.

DIFFERENTIAL PRICING

An important issue in pricing decisions is whether to use a single price or different prices for the same product. Using a single price has several benefits. A primary advantage is simplicity. A single price is easily understood by both employees and customers, and since many salespeople and customers do not like having to negotiate a price, it reduces the chance of an adversarial relationship developing between marketer and customer. The use of a single price does create some challenges, however. If the single price is too high, some potential customers may be unable to afford the product. If it is too low, the firm loses revenue from customers who would have paid more if the price had been higher.

Differential pricing means charging different prices to different buyers for the same quality and quantity of product. For differential pricing to be effective, the market must consist of multiple segments with different price sensitivities, and the method should be used in a way that avoids confusing or antagonizing customers. Customers paying the lower prices should not be able to resell the product to the individuals and organizations paying higher prices, unless that is the intention of the seller. Differential pricing can occur in several ways, including negotiated pricing, secondary-market discounting, periodic discounting, and random discounting.

differential pricing Charging different prices to different buyers for the same quality and quantity of product

Negotiated Pricing

Negotiated pricing occurs when the final price is established through bargaining between seller and customer. If you buy a house, for example, you are likely to negotiate the final price with the seller. Negotiated pricing occurs in numerous industries and at all levels of distribution. During an economic downturn, there is a greater use of negotiated pricing.[7] Even when there is a predetermined stated price or a price list, manufacturers, wholesalers, and retailers still may negotiate to establish the final sales price. Consumers commonly negotiate prices for houses, cars, and used equipment.

negotiated pricing Establishing a final price through bargaining

Secondary-Market Pricing

Secondary-market pricing means setting one price for the primary target market and a different price for another market. Often the price charged in the secondary market is lower. However, when the costs of serving a secondary market are higher than normal, secondary-market customers may have to pay a higher price. Examples of secondary markets include a geographically isolated domestic market, a market in a foreign country, and a segment willing to purchase a product during off-peak times. For example, some restaurants offer special "early

secondary-market pricing Setting one price for the primary target market and a different price for another market

TABLE 12.2 Common Pricing Strategies

Differential Pricing	Psychological Pricing
Negotiated pricing	Reference pricing
Secondary-market pricing	Bundle pricing
Periodic discounting	Multiple-unit pricing
Random discounting	Everyday low prices
New-Product Pricing	Odd-even pricing
Price skimming	Customary pricing
Penetration pricing	Prestige pricing
Product-Line Pricing	**Promotional Pricing**
Captive pricing	Price leaders
Premium pricing	Special-event pricing
Bait pricing	Comparison discounting
Price lining	**Professional Pricing**

bird" prices during the early evening hours, movie theaters offer senior-citizen discounts, and some textbooks and pharmaceutical products are sold for considerably less in certain foreign countries than in the United States. Secondary markets give an organization an opportunity to use excess capacity and to stabilize the allocation of resources.

Periodic Discounting

Periodic discounting is the temporary reduction of prices on a patterned or systematic basis. For example, most retailers have annual holiday sales. Automobile dealers regularly discount prices on current models when the next year's models are introduced. From the marketer's point of view, a major problem with periodic discounting is that because the discounts follow a pattern, customers can predict when the reductions will occur and may delay their purchases until they can take advantage of the lower prices.

Random Discounting

To alleviate the problem of customers knowing when discounting will occur, some organizations employ **random discounting**; that is, they temporarily reduce their prices on an unsystematic basis. When price reductions of a product occur randomly, current users of that brand are likely to be unable to predict when the reductions will occur and so will not delay their purchases. However, in the automobile industry, with its increasing dependence on sales, rebates, and incentives such as 0 percent financing, random discounting has become nearly continuous discounting, and some analysts have warned that automakers will find it increasingly difficult to cease generous incentives that consumers have come to expect. Marketers also use random discounting to attract new customers.

Regardless of whether periodic discounting or random discounting is used, retailers often employ tensile pricing when putting products on sale. *Tensile pricing* refers to a broad statement about price reductions as opposed to detailing specific price discounts. Examples of tensile pricing would be statements such as "20 to 50 percent off," "up to 75 percent off," and "save 10 percent or more." Generally, using and advertising the tensile price that mentions only the maximum reduction (such as "up to 50 percent off") generates the highest customer response.[8]

periodic discounting Temporary reduction of prices on a patterned or systematic basis

random discounting Temporary reduction of prices on an unsystematic basis

Random Discounting
Retailers use random discounting to attract customers to its stores. Consumers cannot predict when discounts will be available.

© JEFF GREENBERG/PHOTOEDIT

NEW-PRODUCT PRICING

Setting the base price for a new product is a necessary part of formulating a marketing strategy. The base price is easily adjusted (in the absence of government price controls), and its establishment is one of the most fundamental decisions in the marketing mix. When a marketer sets base prices, it also considers how quickly competitors will enter the market, whether they will mount a strong campaign on entry, and what effect their entry will have on the development of primary demand. Two strategies used in new-product pricing are price skimming and penetration pricing.

Price Skimming

price skimming Charging the highest possible price that buyers who most desire the product will pay

penetration pricing Setting prices below those of competing brands to penetrate a market and gain a significant market share quickly

Price skimming is charging the highest possible price that buyers who most desire the product will pay. The Apple iPhone, for example, was introduced through AT&T with a starting price of $599 for a smartphone with 8 gigabytes of memory, $200 more than the next most expensive phone offered by AT&T.[9] This approach provides the most flexible introductory base price. Price skimming can provide several benefits, especially when a product is in the introductory stage of its life cycle. A skimming policy can generate much-needed initial cash flows to help offset sizable developmental costs. When introducing a new pharmaceutical, most drug makers such as Merck and Pfizer often use a skimming price to defray large research and development costs and to help fund further research and development into other drugs. Price skimming protects the marketer from problems that arise when the price is set too low to cover costs. When a firm introduces a product, its production capacity may be limited. A skimming price can help to keep demand consistent with the firm's production capabilities. The use of a skimming price may attract competition into an industry because the high price makes that type of business appear to be quite lucrative.

Penetration Pricing

In **penetration pricing**, prices are set below those of competing brands to penetrate a market and gain a large market share quickly. This approach is less flexible for a marketer than price skimming because it is more difficult to raise a penetration price than to lower or discount a skimming price. It is not unusual for a firm to use a penetration price after having skimmed the market with a higher price.

Penetration pricing can be especially beneficial when a marketer suspects that competitors could enter the market easily. If penetration pricing allows the marketer to gain a large market share quickly, competitors may be discouraged from entering the market. In addition, because the lower per-unit penetration price results in lower per-unit profit, the market may not appear to be especially lucrative to potential new entrants.

product-line pricing
Establishing and adjusting prices of multiple products within a product line

captive pricing
Pricing the basic product in a produce line low while pricing related items at a higher level

premium pricing
Pricing the highest-quality or most versatile products higher than other models in the product line

PRODUCT-LINE PRICING

Rather than considering products on an item-by-item basis when determining pricing strategies, some marketers employ product-line pricing. **Product-line pricing** means establishing and adjusting the prices of multiple products within a product line. When marketers use product-line pricing, their goal is to maximize profits for an entire product line rather than focusing on the profitability of an individual product. Product-line pricing can provide marketers with flexibility in price setting. For example, marketers can set prices so that one product is quite profitable, while another increases market share by virtue of having a lower price than competing products. When marketers employ product-line pricing, they have several strategies from which to choose, including captive pricing, premium pricing, bait pricing, and price lining.

Captive Pricing

With **captive pricing**, the basic product in a product line is priced low, whereas the price on the items required to operate or enhance it may be higher. Printer companies such as Hewlett-Packard and Canon have used this pricing strategy, providing relatively low-cost, low-margin printers and selling ink cartridges to generate significant profits. Likewise, Sony set an introduction price for its PlayStation 3 video game console at $599—$240 below cost—with the anticipation of selling accessories and games to generate profits.[10]

IMAGE COURTESY OF THE ADVERTISING ARCHIVES

Captive Pricing
The Gillette razor is inexpensive. To use this razor on a regular basis, customers must buy the replacement blade cartridges. The annual cost of the replacement blade cartridges is significant. Gillette is using captive pricing.

Premium Pricing

Premium pricing is often used when a product line contains several versions of the same product; the highest-quality products or those with the most versatility are given the highest prices. Chevrolet, for example, set an initial price of $100,000 for its fastest, most powerful Corvette ZR1. The company expects the muscle car, with its hand-built 620-horsepower V8 engine, to compete with the performance of a Ferrari.[11] Other products in the line are priced to appeal to price-sensitive shoppers or to those who seek product-specific features.

Marketers who use a premium strategy often realize a significant portion of their profits from premium-priced products. Examples of product categories that commonly use premium pricing are small kitchen appliances, beer, ice cream, and cable television service.

Cable Bites
Price bundling is commonly used in the communications industry, including phone, TV cable, and internet services.

Bait Pricing

To attract customers, marketers may put a low price on one item in a product line, with the intention of selling a higher-priced item in the line; this strategy is known as **bait pricing**. For example, a computer retailer might advertise its lowest-priced computer model, hoping that when customers come to the store, they will purchase a higher-priced one. This strategy can facilitate sales of a line's higher-priced products. As long as a retailer has sufficient quantities of the advertised low-priced model available for sale, this strategy is considered acceptable. However, *bait and switch* is an activity in which retailers have no intention of selling the bait product; they use the low price merely to entice customers into the store to sell them higher-priced products. Bait and switch is considered unethical, and in some states it is illegal as well.

Price Lining

When an organization sets a limited number of prices for selected groups or lines of merchandise, it is using **price lining**. A retailer may have various styles and brands of similar-quality men's shirts that sell for $15 and another line of higher-quality shirts that sell for $22. Price lining simplifies customers' decision making by holding constant one key variable in the final selection of style and brand within a line. Another type of price lining is subscription services. Cable or satellite TV subscribers choose different packages or groupings of channels with different prices. Likewise, subscribers to subscription DVD rental services such as Netflix can choose a membership price based on the number of DVDs they want to receive at one time.

The basic assumption in price lining is that the demand for various groups or sets of products is inelastic. If the prices are attractive, customers will concentrate their purchases without responding to slight changes in price. Thus a women's dress shop that carries dresses priced at $85, $55, and $35 may not attract many more sales with a drop to, say, $83, $53, and $33. The "space" between the price of $85 and $55, however, can stir changes in consumer response.

bait pricing
Pricing an item in the product line low with the intention of selling a higher-priced item in the line

price lining
Setting a limited number of prices for selected groups or lines of merchandise

psychological pricing
Pricing that attempts to influence a customer's perception of price to make a product's price more attractive

reference pricing
Pricing a product at a moderate level and displaying it next to a more expensive model or brand

PSYCHOLOGICAL PRICING

Learning the price of a product is not always a pleasant experience for customers. It can sometimes be surprising (as at a movie concession stand) and sometimes downright horrifying. Most of us have been afflicted with "sticker shock." **Psychological pricing** attempts to influence a customer's perception of price to make a product's price more attractive. In this section we consider several forms of psychological pricing: reference pricing, bundle pricing, multiple-unit pricing, everyday low prices (EDLP), odd-even pricing, customary pricing, and prestige pricing.

Reference Pricing

Reference pricing means pricing a product at a moderate level and displaying it next to a more expensive model or brand in the hope that the customer will use the higher price as an external reference price (i.e., a comparison price). Because of the comparison, the customer is expected to view the moderate price favorably. Reference pricing is based on the "isolation effect," meaning an alternative is less attractive when viewed by itself than when compared with other alternatives. When you go to Best Buy to buy a DVD player, a moderately priced DVD player may appear especially attractive because it offers most of the important attributes of the more expensive alternatives on display and at a lower price. It is not unusual for an organization's moderately priced private brands to be positioned alongside more expensive, better-known manufacturer brands.

Bundle Pricing

Bundle pricing is packaging together two or more products, usually complementary ones, to be sold for a single price. Many fast-food restaurants, for example, offer combination meals at a price that is lower than the combined prices of each item priced separately. Most telephone and cable television providers bundle local telephone service, broadband Internet access, and digital cable or satellite television for one monthly fee. To attract customers, the single price is usually considerably less than the sum of the prices of the individual products. Bundle pricing facilitates customer satisfaction and, when slow-moving products are bundled with products with higher turnover, can help a company stimulate sales and increase revenues. It also may help to foster customer loyalty and improve customer retention. Selling products as a package rather than individually also may result in cost savings. Bundle pricing is commonly used for banking and travel services, computers, and automobiles with option packages.

Some organizations, however, are unbundling in favor of a more itemized approach sometimes called *à la carte pricing*. This provides customers with the opportunity to pick and choose the products they want without having to purchase bundles that may not be the right mix for their purposes. Furthermore, with the help of the Internet, comparison shopping has become more convenient than ever, allowing customers to price items and create their own mixes. Nevertheless, bundle pricing continues to appeal to customers who prefer the convenience of a package.

Everyday Low Price
Walmart is well-known for using the Everyday Low Prices strategy.

Multiple-Unit Pricing

Multiple-unit pricing occurs when two or more identical products are packaged together and sold for a single price. This normally results in a lower per-unit price than the one regularly charged. Multiple-unit pricing is used commonly for twin-packs of potato chips, four-packs of light bulbs, and six- and twelve-packs of soft drinks. Customers benefit from the cost saving and convenience this pricing strategy affords. A company may use multiple-unit pricing to attract new customers to its brand and, in some instances, to increase consumption of its brands. When customers buy in larger quantities, their consumption of the product may increase. For example, multiple-unit pricing may encourage a customer to buy larger quantities of snacks, which are likely to be consumed in higher volume at the point of consumption simply because they are available. However, this is not true for all products. For instance, greater availability at the point of consumption of light bulbs, bar soap, and table salt is not likely to increase usage.

Discount stores and especially warehouse clubs, such as Sam's Club and Costco, are major users of multiple-unit pricing. For certain products in these stores, customers receive significant per-unit price reductions when they buy packages containing multiple units of the same product, such as an eight-pack of canned tuna fish.

Everyday Low Prices (EDLP)

To reduce or eliminate the use of frequent short-term price reductions, some organizations use an approach referred to as **everyday low prices (EDLP)**. With EDLP, a marketer sets a low price for its products on a consistent basis rather than setting higher prices and frequently discounting them. Everyday low prices, though not deeply discounted, are set far enough below competitors' prices to make customers feel confident they are receiving a fair price. EDLP is employed by retailers such as Walmart. Indeed, Walmart, which has already trademarked the phrase, "Always Low Prices. Always," sought to trademark the acronym EDLP because of its extensive use of the practice. Vociferous opposition from the National Grocers Association and SUPERVALU,

bundle pricing
Packaging together two or more complementary products and selling them for a single price

multiple-unit pricing
Packaging together two or more identical products and selling them for a single price

everyday low prices (EDLP)
Setting a low price for products on a consistent basis

Prestige Pricing
Organiztions employ prestige pricing to help support and communicate a premium, high-quality product.

a supermarket chain, as well as other firms, may prevent the retail giant from registering the term, however.[12] A company that uses EDLP benefits from reduced losses from frequent markdowns, greater stability in sales, and reduced promotional costs.

A major problem with EDLP is that customers have mixed responses to it. Over the last several years, many marketers have "trained" customers to seek and expect deeply discounted prices. In some product categories, such as apparel, finding the deepest discount has become almost a national consumer sport. Thus failure to provide deep discounts can be a problem for certain marketers. In some instances customers simply don't believe that everyday low prices are what marketers claim they are but are instead a marketing gimmick.

Odd-Even Pricing

Through **odd-even pricing**—ending the price with certain numbers—marketers try to influence buyers' perceptions of the price or the product. Odd pricing assumes that more of a product will be sold at $99.95 than at $100. Theoretically, customers will think, or at least tell friends, that the product is a bargain—not $100, but $99 and change. Also, customers will supposedly think that the store could have charged $100 but instead cut the price to the last cent, to $99.95. Some claim, too, that certain types of customers are more attracted by odd prices than by even ones. Research indicates that women are more likely to respond to odd-ending prices than men.[13] Nonetheless, odd prices are far more common today than even prices.

Even prices are often used to give a product an exclusive or upscale image. An even price supposedly will influence a customer to view the product as being a high-quality premium brand. A shirt maker, for example, may print on a premium shirt package a suggested retail price of $42.00 instead of $41.95; the even price of the shirt is used to enhance its upscale image.

odd-even pricing
Ending the price with certain numbers to influence buyers' perceptions of the price or product

customary pricing
Pricing on the basis of tradition

prestige pricing
Setting prices at an artificially high level to convey prestige or a quality image

professional pricing
Fees set by people with great skill or experience in a particular field

price leaders
Product priced below the usual markup, near cost, or below cost

Customary Pricing

In **customary pricing**, certain goods are priced primarily on the basis of tradition. Recent economic uncertainties have made most prices fluctuate fairly widely, but the classic example of the customary, or traditional, price is the price of a candy bar. For years, a candy bar cost 5 cents. A new candy bar would have had to be something very special to sell for more than a nickel. This price was so sacred that rather than change it, manufacturers increased or decreased the size of the candy bar itself as chocolate prices fluctuated. Today, of course, the nickel candy bar has disappeared. Yet most candy bars still sell at a consistent, but obviously higher, price. Thus customary pricing remains the standard for this market.

Prestige Pricing

In **prestige pricing**, prices are set at an artificially high level to convey prestige or a quality image. Prestige pricing is used especially when buyers associate a higher price with higher quality. Pharmacists report that some consumers complain when a prescription does not cost enough; apparently some consumers associate a drug's price with its potency. Research confirms that many consumers believe a more expensive medicine works better than a less costly one.[14]

Typical product categories in which selected products are prestige priced include perfumes, liquor, jewelry, and cars. Although traditionally appliances have not been prestige priced, upscale appliances have appeared in recent years to capitalize on the willingness of some consumer segments to "trade up" for high-quality products. These consumers do not mind paying extra for a Sub-Zero refrigerator, a Viking commercial range, or a Whirlpool Duet washer and dryer because these products offer high quality as well as a level of prestige. If producers who use prestige pricing lowered their prices dramatically, the new prices would be inconsistent with the perceived high-quality images of their products. From golf clubs to handbags, prestige products are selling at record levels. Consider some of the prestige products shown in Table 12.3 that were selected as the best by *Smart Money* magazine. For example, spending on pets has escalated to $36 billion a year, rivaling what some families spend on their children. Some consumers are willing to pay as much as $1,000 for designer dogs like the "puggle," a beagle-pug mix, for their nice dispositions, intelligence, and smaller size.[15]

PROFESSIONAL PRICING

Professional pricing is used by people who have great skill or experience in a particular field. Professionals often believe their fees (prices) should not relate directly to the time and effort spent in specific cases; rather, a standard fee is charged regardless of the problems involved in performing the job. Some doctors' and lawyers' fees are prime examples: $75 for a checkup, $1,500 for an appendectomy, and $399 for a divorce. Other professionals set prices in other ways. Like other marketers, professionals have costs associated with facilities, labor, insurance, equipment, and supplies. Certainly, costs are considered when setting professional prices.

The concept of professional pricing carries the idea that professionals have an ethical responsibility not to overcharge customers. In some situations a seller can charge customers a high price and continue to sell many units of the product. If a diabetic requires one insulin treatment per day to survive, the individual probably will buy that treatment whether its price is $1 or $10. In fact, the patient surely would purchase the treatment even if the price went higher. In these situations, sellers could charge exorbitant fees.

PROMOTIONAL PRICING

As an ingredient in the marketing mix, price is often coordinated with promotion. The two variables sometimes are so interrelated that the pricing policy is promotion-oriented. Types of promotional pricing include price leaders, special-event pricing, and comparison discounting.

Price Leaders

Sometimes a firm prices a few products below the usual markup, near cost, or below cost, which results in prices known as **price leaders**. This type of pricing is used most often in supermarkets and restaurants to attract customers by giving them especially low prices on a few items. Management hopes that sales of regularly priced products will more than offset the reduced revenues from the price leaders.

Marketing IN TRANSITION

Will Mixing Up Pricing Strategies Mix Up Customers?

Will customers buy everyday low pricing (EDLP)? Many types of retailers—especially supermarkets—are grappling with this question as they plan their pricing in today's challenging economic and competitive environment.

Grocery chains often use promotional pricing to attract customers with limited-time bargains. Yet these pricing ups and downs may limit a supermarket's ability to successfully implement EDLP, according to the senior vice president of marketing for the Stop & Shop and Giant grocery chains. "Based on the multiple price campaigns that have been conducted throughout the years in supermarkets, consumers really have a pretty low opinion of the likely credibility of supermarket price claims," he says.

© ISTOCKPHOTO.COM/DIEGO CERVO

As a result, a growing number of supermarkets are combining targeted EDLP with highly visible promotional pricing on selected merchandise. Stop & Shop, for example, started a changeover to EDLP by lower prices in several departments and used advertising and in-store signage to alert customers to the new pricing. It also continued its weekly sales specials, lowering prices temporarily on different seasonal, produce, food, and household items.

SUPERVALU is adopting EDLP in particular departments of its Shaw's and Acme grocery chains. The CEO observes that supermarkets "have trained consumers to buy only when the items are on sale" in certain categories. Therefore, SUPERVALU expects to benefit from introducing EDLP in those categories instead of relying on promotional pricing to compete with supermarket rivals who run frequent sales in those categories. Still, like Stop & Shop, SUPERVALU is not doing away with weekly pricing specials, knowing that value-hungry shoppers are always looking for savings.[c]

TABLE 12.3 Sample Prestige Product Prices

Mail-order beef	Niman Ranch Grass-Fed Prime Filet	$63/pound
Automobiles	Lexus LFA	$375,000
Winter adventures	Week at Lake Placid Lodge's Owl's Head Cabin	$4,480/couple
Champagne	House of Salon's Salon Le Mesnil 1996	$350

Source: Kristen Bellstrom, "The Best of Everything," *Smart Money*, November 13, 2007, http://www.smartmoney.com.

Special-Event Pricing

To increase sales volume, many organizations coordinate price with advertising or sales promotions for seasonal or special situations. **Special-event pricing** involves advertised sales or price cutting linked to a holiday, season, or event. If the pricing objective is survival, special sales events may be designed to generate the necessary operating capital. Special-event pricing entails coordination of production, scheduling, storage, and physical distribution. Whenever a sales lag occurs, special-event pricing is an alternative that marketers should consider.

Comparison Discounting

Comparison discounting sets the price of a product at a specific level and simultaneously compares it with a higher price. The higher price may be the product's previous price, the price of a competing brand, the product's price at another retail outlet, or a manufacturer's suggested retail price. Customers may find comparative discounting informative, and it can have a significant impact on their purchases.

Because this pricing strategy has on occasion led to deceptive pricing practices, the Federal Trade Commission has established guidelines for comparison discounting. If the higher price against which the comparison is made is the price formerly charged for the product, the seller must have made the previous price available to customers for a reasonable period of time. If the seller presents the higher price as the one charged by other retailers in the same trade area, it must be able to demonstrate that this claim is true. When the seller presents the higher price as the manufacturer's suggested retail price, the higher price must be similar to the price at which a reasonable proportion of the product was sold. Some manufacturers' suggested retail prices are so high that very few products are actually sold at those prices. In such cases, comparison discounting would be deceptive.

special-event pricing Advertised sales or price cutting linked to a holiday, season, or event

comparison discounting Setting a price at a specific level and comparing it with a higher price

Determination of a Specific Price

A pricing strategy will yield a certain price. However, this price may need refinement to make it consistent with circumstances as well as pricing practices in a particular market or industry.

In the absence of government price controls, pricing remains a flexible and convenient way to adjust the marketing mix. In many situations, prices can be adjusted quickly—in a matter of minutes or over a few days. Such flexibility is unique to this component of the marketing mix.

To set the final price, it is important for marketers to establish pricing objectives; have considerable knowledge about target-market customers; and determine demand, price elasticity, costs, and competitive factors.

CHAPTER REVIEW

OBJECTIVES

1 Understand the six major stages of the process used to establish prices.

The six stages in the process of setting prices are (1) developing pricing objectives, (2) assessing the target market's evaluation of price, (3) evaluating competitors' prices, (4) choosing a basis for pricing, (5) selecting a pricing strategy, and (6) determining a specific price.

2 Know the issues that are related to developing pricing objectives.

Setting pricing objectives is critical because pricing objectives form a foundation on which the decisions of subsequent stages are based. Organizations may use numerous pricing objectives, including short- and long-term ones, and different ones for different products and market segments. Pricing objectives are overall goals that describe the role of price in a firm's long-range plans. There are several major types of pricing objectives. The most fundamental pricing objective is the organization's survival. Price usually can be easily adjusted to increase sales volume or combat competition to help the organization stay alive. Profit objectives, which are usually stated in terms of sales dollar volume or percentage change, are normally set at a satisfactory level rather than at a level designed for profit maximization. A sales growth objective focuses on increasing the profit base by increasing sales volume. Pricing for return on investment (ROI) has a specified profit as its objective. A pricing objective to maintain or increase market share implies that market position is linked to success. Other types of pricing objectives include cash flow, status quo, and product quality.

3 Understand the importance of identifying the target market's evaluation of price.

Assessing the target market's evaluation of price tells the marketer how much emphasis to place on price and may help to determine how far above the competition the firm can set its prices. Understanding how important a product is to customers relative to other products, as well as customers' expectations of quality, helps marketers to correctly assess the target market's evaluation of price.

4 Describe how marketers analyze competitive prices.

A marketer needs to be aware of the prices charged for competing brands. This allows the firm to keep its prices in line with competitors' prices when non-price competition is used. If a company uses price as a competitive tool, it can price its brand below competing brands.

5 Be familiar with the bases used for setting prices.

The three major dimensions on which prices can be based are cost, demand, and competition. When using cost-based pricing, the firm determines price by adding a dollar amount or percentage to the cost of the product. Two common cost-based pricing methods are cost-plus and markup pricing. Demand-based pricing is based on the level of demand for the product. To use this method, a marketer must be able to estimate the amounts of a product that buyers will demand at different prices. Demand-based pricing results in a high price when demand for a product is strong and a low price when demand is weak. In the case of competition-based pricing, costs and revenues are secondary to competitors' prices.

6 Explain the different types of pricing strategies.

A pricing strategy is an approach or a course of action designed to achieve pricing and marketing objectives. The major categories of pricing strategies are differential pricing, new-product pricing, product-line pricing, psychological pricing, professional pricing, and promotional pricing. When marketers employ differential pricing, they charge different buyers different prices for the same quality and quantity of products. Negotiated pricing, secondary-market discounting, periodic discounting, and random discounting are forms of differential pricing. Two strategies used in new-product pricing are price skimming and penetration pricing. With price skimming, the organization charges the highest price that buyers who most desire the product will pay. A penetration price is a low price designed to penetrate a market and gain a significant market share quickly. Product-line pricing establishes and adjusts the prices of multiple products within a product line. This category of strategies includes captive pricing, premium pricing, bait pricing, and price lining. Psychological pricing attempts to influence customer's perceptions of price to make a product's price more attractive. Psychological pricing strategies include reference pricing, bundle pricing, multiple-unit pricing, everyday low prices, odd-even pricing, customary pricing, and prestige pricing. Professional pricing is used by people who have great skill or experience in a particular field, therefore allowing them to set the price. This concept carries the idea that professionals have an ethical responsibility not to overcharge customers. As an ingredient in the marketing mix, price is often coordinated with promotion. The two variables are sometimes so interrelated that the pricing policy is promotion-oriented. Promotional pricing includes price leaders, special-event pricing, and comparison discounting. Price leaders are products that are priced below the usual markup, near cost, or below cost. Special-event pricing involves advertised sales or price-cutting linked to a holiday, season, or event. Marketers who use a comparison discounting strategy price a product at a specific level and compare it with a higher price.

Understand how a final, specific price is determined.

Once a price is determined by using one or more pricing strategies, it will need to be refined to a final price consistent with the pricing practices in a particular market or industry. Using pricing strategies helps in setting a final price. The way that pricing is used in the marketing mix affects the final price. Because pricing is flexible, it is a convenient way to adjust the marketing mix.

Please visit the student website at www.cengage.com/international for quizzes and games that will help you prepare for exams and help achieve the grade you want.

KEY CONCEPTS

pricing objectives
cost-based pricing
cost-plus pricing
markup pricing
demand-based pricing
competition-based pricing
differential pricing
negotiated pricing
secondary-market pricing
periodic discounting
random discounting
price skimming
penetration pricing
product-line pricing
captive pricing
premium pricing
bait pricing
price lining
psychological pricing
reference pricing
bundle pricing
multiple-unit pricing
everyday low prices (EDLP)
odd-even pricing
customary pricing
prestige pricing
professional pricing
price leaders
special-event pricing
comparison discounting

ISSUES FOR DISCUSSION AND REVIEW

1. Identify the six stages involved in the process of establishing prices.
2. How does a return on investment pricing objective differ from an objective of increasing market share?
3. Why must marketing objectives and pricing objectives be considered when making pricing decisions?
4. Why should a marketer be aware of competitors' prices?
5. What are the benefits of cost-based pricing?
6. Under what conditions is cost-plus pricing most appropriate?
7. A retailer purchases a can of soup for 24 cents and sells it for 36 cents. Calculate the markup as a percentage of cost and as a percentage of selling price.
8. What is differential pricing? In what ways can it be achieved?
9. For what types of products would price skimming be most appropriate? For what types of products would penetration pricing be more effective?
10. Describe bundle pricing, and give three examples using different industries.
11. What are the advantages and disadvantages of using everyday low prices?
12. Why do customers associate price with quality? When should prestige pricing be used?
13. Are price leaders a realistic approach to pricing? Explain your answer.

MARKETING APPLICATIONS

1. Which strategy—price skimming or penetration pricing—is more appropriate for the following products? Explain.
   a. Short airline flights between cities in Florida
   b. A DVD player
   c. A backpack or book bag with a lifetime warranty
   d. Season tickets for a newly franchised NBA team
2. Visit a few local retail stores to find examples of price lining. For what types of products and stores is this practice most common? For what products and stores is price lining not typical or usable?
3. Find examples (advertisements, personal contacts) that reflect a professional-pricing policy. How is the price established? Are there any restrictions on the services performed at that price?
4. Locate an organization that uses several pricing objectives, and discuss how this approach influences the company's marketing-mix decisions. Are some objectives oriented toward the short term and others toward the long term? How does the marketing environment influence these objectives?

ONLINE EXERCISE

5. T-Mobile has attempted to position itself as a low-cost cell phone service provider. A person can purchase a calling plan, a cellular phone, and phone accessories at its website. Visit the T-Mobile website at http://www.t-mobile.com.
   a. Determine the various nationwide rates available in your area.
   b. How many different calling plans are available in your area?
   c. What type of pricing strategy is T-Mobile using on its rate plans for your area?

Setting the right price for a product is a crucial part of marketing strategy. Price helps to establish a product's

DEVELOPING YOUR MARKETING PLAN

position in the mind of the consumer and can differentiate a product from its competition. Several decisions in the marketing plan will be affected by the pricing strategy that is selected. To assist you in relating the information in this chapter to the development of your marketing plan, focus on the following:

1. Using Table 12.1 as a guide, discuss each of the seven pricing objectives. Which pricing objectives will you use for your product? Consider the product life cycle, competition, and product positioning for your target market during your discussion.
2. Review the various types of pricing strategies in Table 12.2. Which of these is the most appropriate for your product?
3. Select a basis for pricing your product (cost, demand, and/or competition). How will you know when it is time to revise your pricing strategy?

The information obtained from these questions should assist you in developing various aspects of your marketing plan found in the *Interactive Marketing Plan* exercise.

VIDEO CASE 12

Tiny Price Tag for Tiny Smart Car

Tiny car, tiny price tag, tiny gasoline bill. The Smart Car, made by Daimler's Mercedes Car Group in Hambach, France, first appeared on U.S. roads in 2008, just as gas prices were soaring. The timing could not have been better. Tired of emptying their wallets every time they filled their gas tanks, many U.S. drivers were thinking about downsizing from a big sport-utility vehicle or pickup truck to a smaller vehicle. But were they ready for a 106-inch-long car that seats only two people? Daimler was ready to find out.

From 1998 to 2008, Daimler sold more than 900,000 Smart Cars in Europe, the Middle East, Asia, Australia, Mexico, and Canada. The car was cute, nimble, and unconventional, a good size for getting through crowded, narrow city streets and fitting into any tight parking spot. Not only was the purchase price highly affordable, the excellent fuel efficiency made the car especially popular in countries where gas prices were generally high.

To bring the Smart Car to the United States, Daimler redesigned the body and engineering to meet U.S. safety standards. It added six inches to the car's length and included four air bags, an antilock braking system, a collapsing steering column, and other safety features. It also installed a fuel-saving 71-horsepower engine so that the Smart Car would go about 40 highway miles on a gallon of gasoline.

Daimler set the list price of the Smart Fortwo Pure model—the basic version of the two-seater—at $11,590. The list price of the Smart Fortwo Passion Coupe, equipped with more features, was $13,590. The list price of the Smart Fortwo Passion Cabriolet, a convertible with leather seats, was $16,590. Buyers had the option of ordering extras, such as a metallic paint finish or an alarm system, for an additional fee. Keeping the list price as tiny as the car would allow Daimler to build market share quickly.

Rather than selling Smart Cars through its regular dealer network, Daimler contracted with the Penske Automotive Group to handle distribution and sales. In another unusual move, Daimler set up a website to let buyers reserve the model of their choice and choose from six interior colors and six exterior colors on the car body's removable panels. Three of the exterior colors were offered as part of the purchase price, while the three metallic exterior colors were offered at an extra cost. The $99 reservation fee was applied to the buyer's purchase price once the ordered model became available. By the time Smart Cars arrived in U.S. showrooms, 30,000 people had paid for reservations.

To build customer interest prior to the introduction, Daimler sent a number of Smart Cars on a 50-city U.S. tour. Nearly 50,000 members of the media and prospective car buyers took test drives. Although many reporters couldn't resist poking fun at the tiny car (*USA Today* called it a "breadbox on wheels"), they all noted its high fuel efficiency and low purchase price.

Soon demand became so strong that even buyers who had reserved their cars well in advance had to wait months for delivery. During the first full year of sales in the United States, Daimler sold 24,600 Smart Cars. Down the road, as more auto manufacturers gear up to bring gas-sipping cars to U.S. markets, will the Smart Car maintain its popularity?

QUESTIONS FOR DISCUSSION

1. Why is bundle pricing appropriate for the various models of Smart Cars?
2. How is demand likely to affect dealers' willingness to negotiate prices with Smart Car buyers?
3. Imagine that Daimler is considering selling unpainted Smart Cars and reducing the list price by $1,500. The Smart Car exterior consists of ten removable panels that can be easily painted. Buyers could paint their own panels, leave the panels unpainted, or pay the dealer an additional fee to personalize their cars by having the panels custom-finished in almost any color or design. What are the advantages and disadvantages of this pricing idea?

Doron Levin, "Online Sales Fuel Smart Car's Success," *The Record (Bergen Cty, N.J.)*, February 8, 2009, p. B1; Steve Miller, "Vroom for Two," *Brandweek*, June 2, 2008, pp. 20+; Bill Marsh, "Welcome, Little Smart Car, to the Big American Road," *New York Times*, January 6, 2008, sec. 4, p. 3; Chris Woodyard, "America Crazy about Breadbox on Wheels Called Smart Car," *USA Today*, November 11, 2007, www.usatoday.com/money/autos/2007-11-11-smartcar_N.htm; Royal Ford, "Smallest Car, Biggest Market," *Boston Globe*, December 6, 2007, p. E1.

Distribution Decisions 6

Developing products that satisfy customers is important, but it is not enough to guarantee successful marketing strategies. Products must also be available in adequate quantities in accessible locations at the times when customers desire them. Part 6 deals with the distribution of products and the marketing channels and institutions that help to make products available. **Chapter 13** discusses supply-chain management, marketing channels, and the decisions and activities associated with the physical distribution of products, such as order processing, materials handling, warehousing, inventory management, and transportation. **Chapter 14** explores retailing and wholesaling, including types of retailers and wholesalers, direct marketing and selling, and strategic retailing issues.

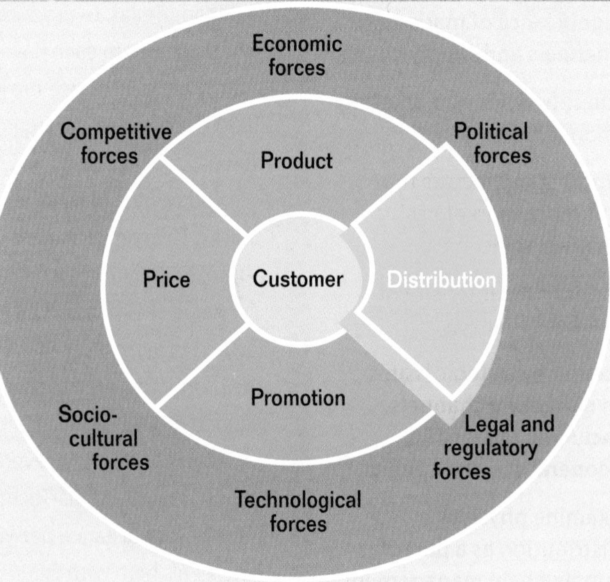

CHAPTER 13 Marketing Channels and Supply-Chain Management

© JEFF GREENBERG/ALAMY

OBJECTIVES:

1. **Describe the foundations of supply-chain management.**
2. **Explore the role and significance of marketing channels and supply chains.**
3. **Identify types of marketing channels.**
4. **Understand factors that influence marketing channel selection.**
5. **Identify the intensity of market coverage.**
6. **Examine strategic issues in marketing channels, including leadership, cooperation, and conflict.**
7. **Examine physical distribution as a part of supply-chain management.**
8. **Explore legal issues in channel management.**

GROWTH BRINGS DISTRIBUTION CHALLENGES TO BLUE BELL CREAMERIES

Blue Bell Creameries originated in 1907 as the Brenham Creamery Company, founded in Brenham, Texas, to produce butter. By 1911, the company was also hand-cranking two gallons of ice cream each day, buying ingredients from local farmers and delivering ice cream to nearby areas via horse-drawn wagon. The ice cream quickly became a local favorite, and in 1930 the company changed its name to Blue Bell Creameries, after the Texas bluebell wildflower.

Today, Blue Bell is a Texas icon, producing more than 66 ice cream flavors and 250 frozen snacks. The company distributes its products throughout 17 states, and its products represent approximately 20 percent of all frozen products nationwide.

Years of expansion brought new challenges to Blue Bell. At its main distribution center, located in Sylacauga, Alabama, 200 people were working two shifts to move ice cream from the production area to storage and then out to retailers or distribution centers. The company needed more storage.

After considering several options, Blue Bell chose an automated storage retrieval system (ASRS) from Westfalia Technologies. First, Westfalia set up a pallet-conveying system to cover the 400-foot distance between the production line and the new ASRS. Next, it built the ASRS nine levels high with 7,000 pallet storage locations, including two storage retrieval machines for redundancy. If one machine isn't working, the second takes over so the production line never shuts down. The system also handles different pallet sizes, which allows Blue Bell to diversify its packaging sizes.

Because Blue Bell previously handled all these operations manually, this system represents a big improvement. Blue Bell's general manager says, "The system helped us reduce forklift traffic by 80 percent. . . .There is also less product damage and huge labor savings." Now the company can continue its expansion and maintain the product quality its loyal customers expect.[1]

Decisions like those made at Blue Bell Creameries relate to the **distribution** component of the marketing mix, which focuses on the decisions and activities involved in making products available to customers when and where they want to purchase them. Choosing which channels of distribution to use is a major decision in the development of marketing strategies.

In this chapter, we focus on marketing channels and supply-chain management. First, we explore the concept of the supply chain and its various activities. Second, we elaborate on marketing channels and the need for intermediaries and then analyze the primary functions they perform. We then consider supply-chain management, including behavioral patterns within marketing channels and forms of channel integration. Next, we outline the types of marketing channels, discuss how they are selected, and explore how marketers determine the appropriate intensity of market coverage for a product. We also look at the role of physical distribution within the supply chain, including its objectives and basic functions. Finally, we look at several legal issues affecting channel management.

distribution
The decisions and activities that make products available to customers when and where they want to purchase them

supply chain
All the activities associated with the flow and transformation of products from raw materials through delivery to the end customer

operations management
The total set of managerial activities used by an organization to transform resource inputs into products

logistics management
Planning, implementing, and controlling the efficient and effective flow and storage of products and information from the point of origin to consumption in order to meet customers' needs and wants

supply management
In its broadest form, refers to the processes that enable the progress of value from raw material to final customer and back to redesign and final disposition

supply-chain management
A set of approaches used to integrate the functions of operations management, logistics management, supply management, and marketing channel management so that products are produced and distributed in the right quantities, to the right locations, and at the right time

Foundations of the Supply Chain

An important function of distribution is the joint effort of all involved organizations to be part of creating an effective **supply chain,** which refers to all the activities associated with the flow and transformation of products from raw materials through delivery to the end customer. This results in a total distribution system that involves firms that are "upstream" in the supply chain (e.g., suppliers) as well as "downstream" (e.g., wholesalers, retailers) to serve customers and generate competitive advantage. Historically, marketing focused only on select downstream activities of supply chains, but today marketing professionals are recognizing that important marketplace advantages can be secured by effectively integrating important activities in the supply chain. These include operations, logistics, sourcing, and marketing channels. Integrating these activities requires marketing managers to work with their counterparts in operations management, logistics management, and supply management.[2] **Operations management** is the total set of managerial activities used by an organization to transform resource inputs into products.[3] **Logistics management** involves planning, implementing, and controlling the efficient and effective flow and storage of products and information from the point of origin to consumption in order to meet customers' needs and wants. **Supply management** (e.g., purchasing, procurement, sourcing) in its broadest form refers to the processes that enable the progress of value from raw material to final customer and back to redesign and final disposition.

Supply-chain management (SCM) is therefore a set of approaches used to integrate the functions of operations management, logistics management, supply management, and marketing channel management so that products are produced and distributed in the right quantities, to the right locations, and at the right time. It includes activities such as manufacturing, research, sales, advertising, shipping, and most of all, cooperating and understanding of tradeoffs throughout the whole chain to achieve optimal levels of efficiency and service. Table 13.1 outlines the key tasks involved in supply-chain management. The supply chain also includes suppliers of raw materials and other components to make goods and services, logistics and transportation firms, communication firms, and other firms that indirectly take part in marketing exchanges. Thus, the supply chain includes all entities that facilitate product distribution and benefit from cooperative efforts. Consider that Intel, the computer chip maker, spends $3 billion to build a new semiconductor facility, and it loses $1 million a day if an assembly line goes down due to system failures or part shortages. Consequently, Intel requires its equipment suppliers to respond to failures within 15 minutes.[4] Worldwide spending on supply-chain management systems is more than $25 billion.[5]

Technology has improved supply-chain management capabilities on a global basis. Information technology in particular has created an almost seamless distribution process for matching inventory needs to manufacturer requirements in the upstream portion of the supply chain and to customers' requirements in the downstream portion of the chain. With integrated information sharing among chain members, costs can be reduced, service can be improved, and increased value can be provided to the end customer. Indeed, information is crucial in operating supply chains efficiently and effectively.

As demand for innovative goods and services has escalated in recent years, marketers have had to increase their flexibility and responsiveness to develop new products and modify existing ones to meet the ever-changing needs of customers. Suppliers now provide material and service inputs to meet customer needs in the "upstream" portion of the supply chain. Customers are increasingly a knowledge source in developing the right product in the "downstream" portion of the supply chain. This means that the entire supply chain is critically important in ensuring that customers get the products when, where, and how they want.

Firms must therefore be involved in the management of their own supply chains in partnership with the network of upstream and downstream organizations in the supply chain. Upstream firms provide direct or indirect input to make the product. Downstream firms are responsible for delivery of the product and after-market services to the end customers. The management of the upstream and downstream in the supply-chain activities is what is involved in managing supply chains.

Effective supply chain management is closely linked to a marketing orientation. All functional areas of business (marketing, management, production, finance, and information

TABLE 13.1 Key Tasks in Supply-Chain Management

Operations management	Organizational and systemwide coordination of operations and partnerships to meet customers' product needs
Supply management	Sourcing of necessary resources, products, and services from suppliers to support all supply-chain members
Logistics management	All activities designed to move the product through the marketing channel to the end user, including warehousing and inventory management
Channel management	All activities related to selling, service, and the development of long-term customer relationships

Technology Facilitates Supply-Chain Management
BAX Global provides services and technology to facilitate supply chain management for business customers.

systems) are involved in executing a customer orientation and supply-chain management. Both of these activities overlap with operations management, logistics management, and supply management. If a firm has established a marketing strategy based on continuous customer-focused leadership, then supply-chain management will be driven by cooperation and strategic coordination to ensure customer satisfaction. Managers should recognize that supply-chain management is critical to fulfilling customer requirements and requires coordination with all areas of the business. This logical association between marketing orientation and supply-chain management should lead to increased firm performance.[6]

The Role of Marketing Channels in Supply Chains

A **marketing channel** (also called a *channel of distribution* or *distribution channel*) is a group of individuals and organizations that direct the flow of products from producers to customers within the supply chain. The major role of marketing channels—in concert with operations management, logistics management, and supply management—is to make products available at the right time at the right place in the right quantities. Providing customer satisfaction should be the driving force behind marketing channel decisions. Buyers' needs and behavior are therefore important concerns of channel members.

marketing channel
A group of individuals and organizations that direct the flow of products from producers to customers within the supply chain

Some marketing channels are direct, meaning that the product goes directly from the producer to the customer. For example, when a customer orders food online from Omaha Steaks (http://www.omahasteaks.com), the product is sent from the manufacturer to the customer. Most channels, however, have one or more **marketing intermediaries** that link producers to other intermediaries or to ultimate consumers through contractual arrangements or through the purchase and resale of products. Marketing intermediaries perform the activities described in Table 13.2. They also play key roles in customer relationship management, not only through

marketing intermediaries
Middlemen that link producers to other intermediaries or ultimate consumers through contractual arrangements or through the purchase and resale of products

TABLE 13.2 **Marketing Channel Activities Performed by Intermediaries**

Marketing Activities	Sample Activities
Marketing information	Analyze sales data and other information in databases and information systems Perform or commission marketing research
Marketing management	Establish strategic and tactical plans for developing customer relationships and organizational productivity
Facilitating exchanges	Choose product assortments that match the needs of customers Cooperate with channel members to develop partnerships
Promotion	Set promotional objectives Coordinate advertising, personal selling, sales promotion, publicity, and packaging
Price	Establish pricing policies and terms of sales
Physical distribution	Manage transportation, warehousing, materials handling, inventory control, and communication

their distribution activities but also by maintaining databases and information systems to help all members of the marketing channel maintain effective customer relationships. For example, eBay serves as a marketing intermediary between Internet sellers and buyers. eBay not only provides a forum for these exchanges, but also helps facilitate relationships among eBay channel members and eases payment issues through its PayPal subsidiary.

Wholesalers and retailers are examples of intermediaries. Wholesalers buy and resell products to other wholesalers, to retailers, and to industrial customers. Retailers purchase products and resell them to the end consumers. For example, your local supermarket probably purchased the Tylenol or Advil on its shelves from a wholesaler, which purchased that pain medicine, along with other over-the-counter and prescription drugs, from manufacturers such as McNeil Consumer Labs and Whitehall-Robins. Chapter 14 discusses the functions of wholesalers and retailers in marketing channels in greater detail.

Supply chains start with the customer and require the cooperation of channel members to satisfy customer requirements. All members should focus on cooperation to reduce the costs of all channel members and thereby improve profits. When the buyer, the seller, marketing intermediaries, and facilitating agencies work together, the cooperative relationship results in compromise and adjustments that meet customers' needs regarding delivery, scheduling, packaging, or other requirements.

Each supply-chain member requires information from other channel members. For example, suppliers need order and forecast information from the manufacturer; they also may need availability information from their own suppliers. Customer relationship management (CRM) systems exploit the information from supply-chain partners' information systems to help all channel members make marketing strategy decisions that develop and sustain desirable customer relationships. Thus, managing relationships with supply-chain partners is crucial to satisfying customers. CRM is gaining popularity, with big companies such as Hewlett-Packard and Amazon.com spending large sums of money on implementation and support for data mining and CRM analytical applications.

THE SIGNIFICANCE OF MARKETING CHANNELS

Although marketing-channel decisions do not need to precede other marketing decisions, they are a powerful influence on the rest of the marketing mix (i.e., product, promotion, and pricing). Channel decisions are critical because they determine a product's market presence and buyers' accessibility to the product. Without effective marketing channel operations, even the best goods and services will not be successful. Consider that small businesses are more likely to purchase computers from chain specialty stores such as Best Buy and Office Depot, putting computer companies without distribution through these outlets at a disadvantage. In fact, even Dell—which pioneered the direct sales model in the computer industry—is now selling its computers at Best Buy. The option of buying Dell systems directly from Dell or in retail stores such as Best Buy means that customers can purchase what they need when and where they want while also allowing customers to "test drive" a computer system of their choice.

Marketing channel decisions have additional strategic significance because they generally entail long-term commitments among a variety of firms (e.g., suppliers, logistics providers, and operations firms). It is usually easier to change prices or promotional strategies than to change marketing channels. Marketing channels also serve many functions, including creating utility and facilitating exchange efficiencies. Although some of these functions may be performed by a single channel member, most functions are accomplished through both independent and joint efforts of channel members.

Marketing Channels Create Utility

Marketing channels create four types of utility: time, place, possession, and form. *Time utility* is having products available when the customer wants them. *Place utility* is created by making products available in locations where customers wish to purchase them. *Possession utility* means that the customer has access to the product to use or to store for future use. Possession utility can occur through ownership or through arrangements that give the customer the right to use the product, such as a lease or rental agreement. Channel members sometimes create *form utility* by assembling, preparing, or otherwise refining the product to suit individual customer needs.

Marketing Channels Facilitate Exchange Efficiencies

Marketing intermediaries can reduce the costs of exchanges by performing certain services or functions efficiently. Even if producers and buyers are located in the same city, there are costs associated with exchanges. As Figure 13.1 shows, when four buyers seek products from four producers, 16 transactions are possible. If one intermediary serves both producers and buyers, the number of transactions can be reduced to eight. Intermediaries are specialists in facilitating exchanges. They provide valuable assistance because of their access to and control over important resources used in the proper functioning of marketing channels.

Nevertheless, the press, consumers, public officials, and even other marketers freely criticize intermediaries, especially wholesalers. Critics accuse wholesalers of being inefficient and parasitic. Buyers often wish to make the distribution channel as short as possible, assuming that the fewer the intermediaries, the lower the price will be.

Critics who suggest that eliminating wholesalers would lower customer prices fail to recognize that this would not eliminate the need for the services that wholesalers provide. Although wholesalers can be eliminated, their functions cannot. Other channel members would have to perform those functions, and customers still would have to pay for them. In addition, all producers would have to deal directly with retailers or customers, meaning that every producer would have to keep voluminous records and hire enough personnel to deal with a multitude of customers. Customers might end up paying a great deal more for products because prices would reflect the costs of less efficient channel members.

Because suggestions to eliminate wholesalers come from both ends of the marketing channel, wholesalers must be careful to perform only those marketing activities that are truly desired. To survive, they must be more efficient and more customer-focused than other marketing institutions. Indeed, research suggests that lower wholesale prices may result in higher sales volume when combined with low retailing costs at discount firms such as Walmart.[7]

FIGURE 13.1 Efficiency in Exchanges Provided by an Intermediary

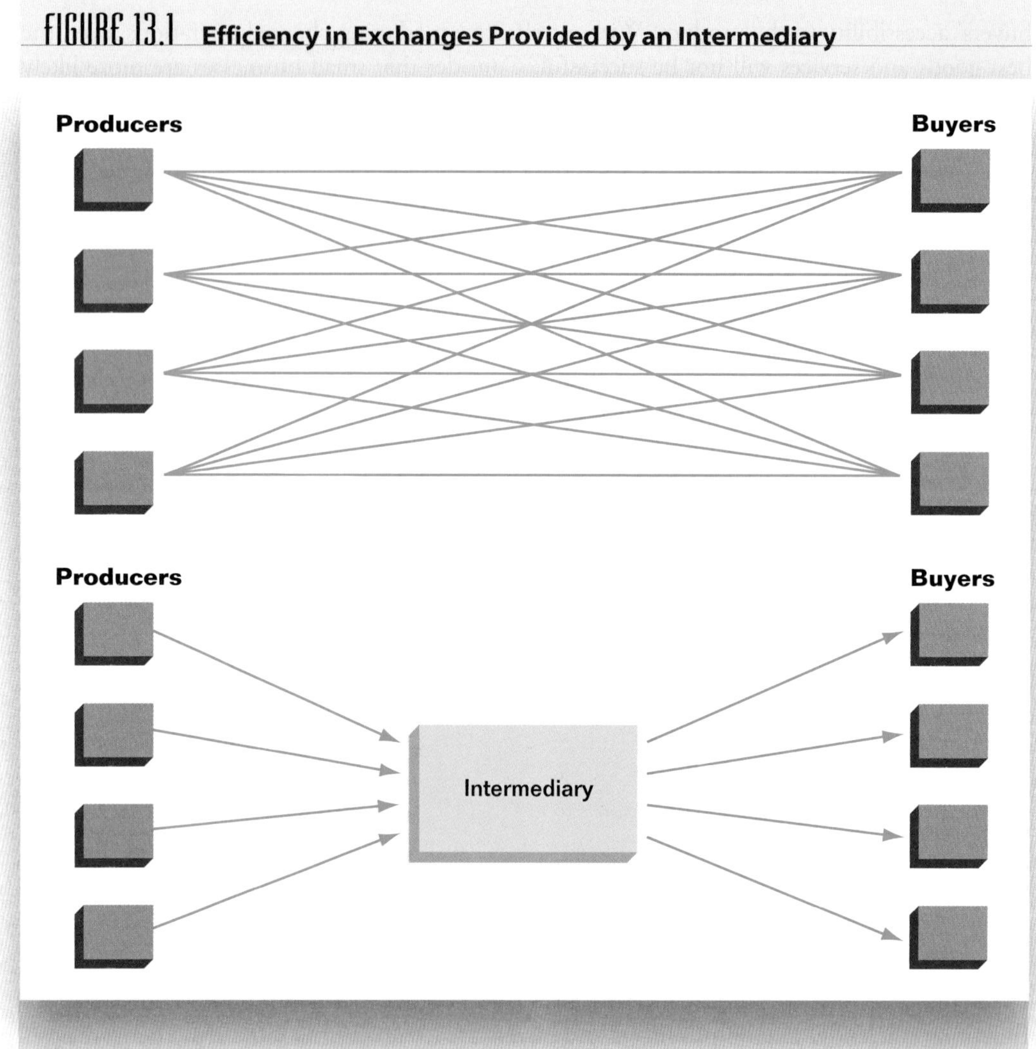

TYPES OF MARKETING CHANNELS

Because marketing channels appropriate for one product may be less suitable for others, many different distribution paths have been developed. The various marketing channels can be classified generally as channels for consumer products and channels for business products.

Channels for Consumer Products

Figure 13.2 illustrates several channels used in the distribution of consumer products. Channel A depicts the direct movement of products from producer to consumers. For example, the legal advice given by attorneys moves through Channel A. Producers that sell products directly from their factories to end users use direct marketing channels, as do companies that sell their own products via the Internet, such as Omaha Steaks. Direct marketing via the Internet has become a critically important part of some companies' distribution strategies, often as a complement to their products being sold in traditional retail stores. Faced with the strategic choice of going directly to the customer or using intermediaries, a firm must evaluate the benefits of going direct versus the transaction costs involved in using intermediaries.

Channel B, which moves goods from the producer to a retailer and then to customers, is a frequent choice of large retailers since it allows them to buy in quantity from manufacturers.

FIGURE 13.2 Typical Marketing Channels for Consumer Products

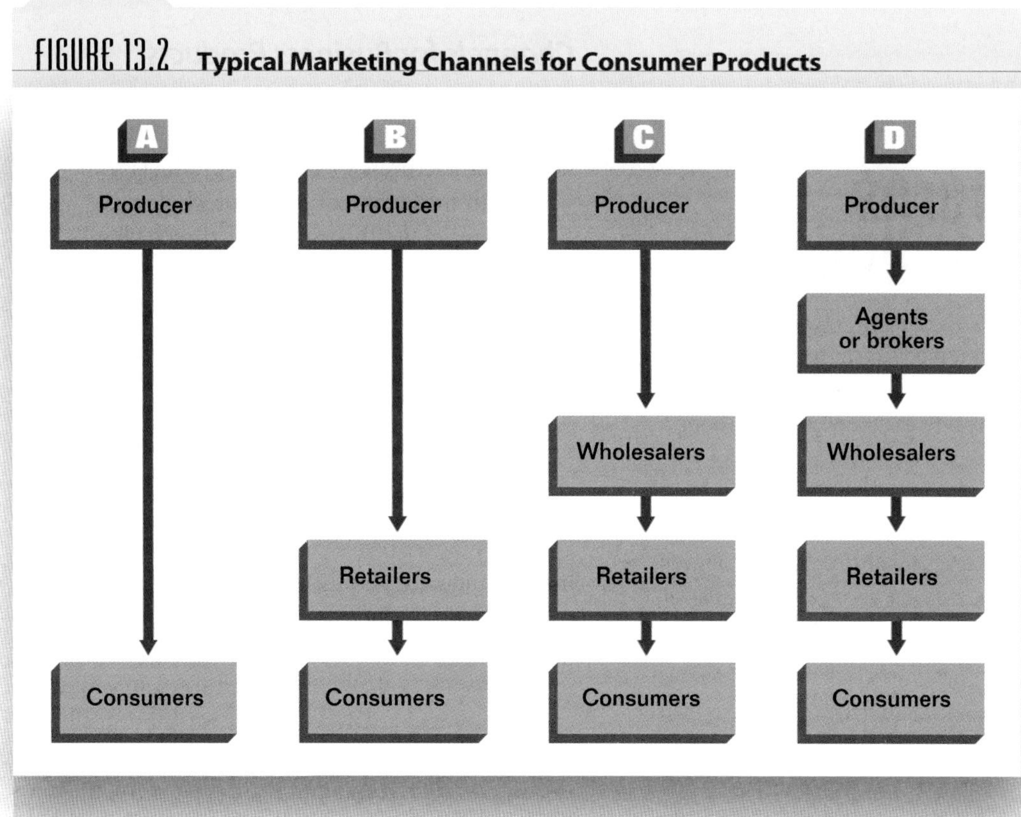

Retailers such as Kmart and Walmart sell clothing, stereos, and many other items purchased directly from producers. New automobiles and new college textbooks are also sold through this type of marketing channel. Primarily nonstore retailers, such as L.L.Bean and J.Crew, also use this type of channel.

Channel C represents a long-standing distribution channel, especially for consumer products. It takes goods from the producer to a wholesaler, then to a retailer, and finally to consumers. It is a practical option for producers that sell to hundreds of thousands of customers through thousands of retailers. Consider the number of retailers marketing Wrigley's chewing gum. It would be extremely difficult, if not impossible, for Wrigley to deal directly with each retailer that sells its brand of gum. Manufacturers of tobacco products, some home appliances, hardware, and many convenience goods sell their products to wholesalers, which then sell to retailers, which in turn do business with individual consumers.

Channel D, through which goods pass from producer to agents to wholesalers to retailers and then to consumers, is used frequently for products intended for mass distribution, such as processed foods. For example, to place its cracker line in specific retail outlets, a food processor may hire an agent (or a food broker) to sell the crackers to wholesalers. Wholesalers then sell the crackers to supermarkets, vending machine operators, and other retail outlets.

Contrary to popular opinion, a long channel may be the most efficient distribution channel for some consumer goods. When several channel intermediaries perform specialized functions, costs may be lower than when one channel member tries to perform them all. In essence, this logic is similar to outsourcing part of the production to firms in low-cost countries. For the marketing channel, it means that firms specializing in certain elements of producing a product or moving it through the channel are more effective and efficient at performing specialized tasks than the manufacturer. This results in cost efficiencies and added value to customers.

Sustainable Marketing

Wind Power Turns the Turbines at Home

Marketing channels for some products can gain incredible efficiency if the source of distribution can be at the point of consumption. One such case is electricity generated from one's own wind turbines, which are becoming smaller and cheaper. As technology becomes more efficient at harnessing energy at even low wind speeds, more small-scale users—even residences—will be able to enjoy the advantages of wind power. Companies around the world are already jumping on the renewable energy bandwagon, as consumers are demanding environmentally friendly alternatives to traditional coal-fired electricity.

© ISTOCKPHOTO.COM/FOTOVOYAGER

Southwest Windpower, based in Flagstaff, Arizona, has recognized this tremendous market niche and introduced a wind turbine for residential homes. To further help Southwest's endeavors, the national government and many state governments are offering substantial rebates as an additional incentive, often up to 30 percent of the wind turbines' cost. As global demand for energy increases and the cost of residential turbines decreases, it may not be long before a house in every neighborhood has one.

The Skystream 3.7 is the newest creation from Southwest to hit the markets. Ranging between 34 and 70 feet tall with 12-foot rotors, the Skystream 3.7 can generate enough electricity to power a house, while any extra electricity produced can, in some areas, be sold back to power companies. The Skystream 3.7 is designed for very low winds—it begins producing power in an 8-mph breeze and achieves maximum output at 23 mph. Because costs per turbine range from $12,000 to $15,000, the current market for the product is not quite the average consumer. However, depending on installation costs, wind speed average, rebates, and local electricity costs, the Skystream 3.7 can pay for itself in as quickly as five years.

While electricity may thus be supplied at the point of consumption, consumers find a marketing channel or supply chain to obtain a Skystream 3.7. Southwest Windpower sells exclusively through its global network of dealers. In the United States, for example, Conergy and SunWize are regional wholesalers who make the 3.7 turbines available to local dealers. Local dealers such as Affordable Solar in Albuquerque, New Mexico, work directly with customers, selling the units and offering services such as delivery. Because potential buyers of wind turbines are so scattered, it is much more efficient for Southwest Windpower to depend on wholesalers and dealers to sell its alternative energy products. If demand for these residential turbines continues to grow, one or more companies may invest in mass production, further lowering the cost of the turbine. This in turn could create a new version of Henry Ford's vision: a wind turbine for every family.[a]

Channels for Business Products

Figure 13.3 shows four of the most common channels for business products. As with consumer products, manufacturers of business products sometimes work with more than one level of wholesalers.

Channel E illustrates the direct channel for business products. In contrast to consumer goods, more than half of all business products, especially expensive equipment, are sold through direct channels. Business customers prefer to communicate directly with producers, especially when expensive or technically complex products are involved. For example, buyers prefer to purchase expensive and highly complex SQL server computers directly from Dell. Similarly, Intel has established direct marketing channels for selling its microprocessor chips to computer manufacturers. In these circumstances, a customer wants the technical assistance and personal assurances that only a producer can provide.

In channel F, an industrial distributor facilitates exchanges between the producer and customer. An **industrial distributor** is an independent business that takes title to products and carries inventories. Industrial distributors usually sell standardized items such as maintenance supplies, production tools, and small operating equipment. Some industrial distributors carry a wide variety of product lines. W.W. Grainger, for example, sells more than $6.4 billion of power and hand tools, pumps, janitorial supplies, and many other products to producer, government, and institutional markets around the world.[8] Other industrial distributors specialize in one or a small number of lines. Industrial distributors are carrying an increasing percentage of business products. Overall, these distributors can be most effectively used when a product has broad market appeal, is easily stocked and serviced, is sold in small quantities, and is needed on demand to avoid high losses.

Industrial distributors offer sellers several advantages. They can perform the needed selling activities in local markets at a relatively low cost to a manufacturer and reduce a producer's financial burden by providing customers with credit services. Also, because industrial distributors usually maintain close relationships with their customers, they are aware of local needs and can pass on market information to producers. By holding adequate inventories in their local markets, industrial distributors reduce producers' capital requirements.

Using industrial distributors has several disadvantages, however. Industrial distributors may

FIGURE 13.3 Typical Marketing Channels for Business Products

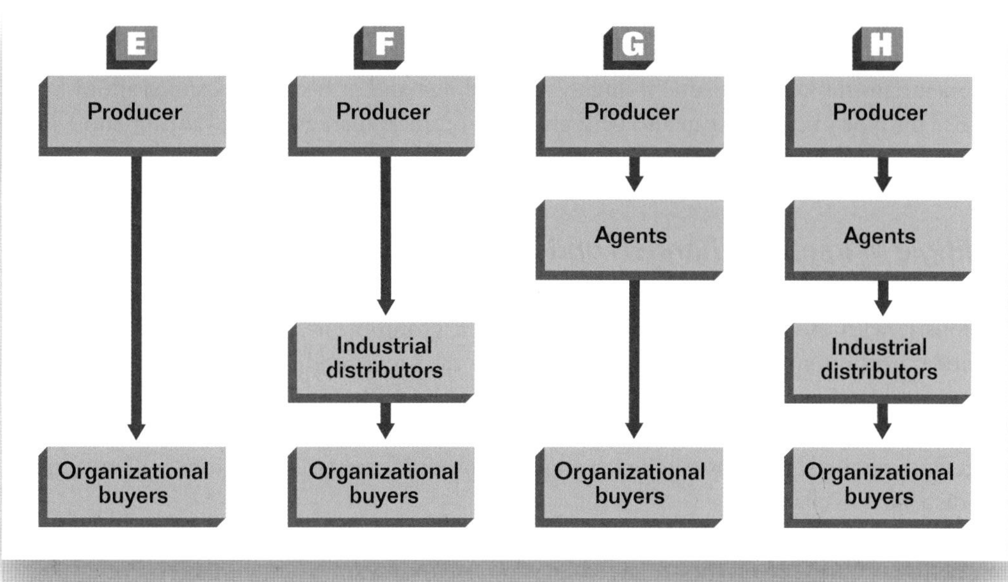

industrial distributor An independent business organization that takes title to industrial products and carries inventories

be difficult to control since they are independent firms. Because they often stock competing brands, a producer cannot depend on them to sell its brand aggressively. Furthermore, since industrial distributors maintain inventories, they incur numerous expenses; consequently they are less likely to handle bulky or slow-selling items or items that need specialized facilities or extraordinary selling efforts. In some cases, industrial distributors lack the technical knowledge necessary to sell and service certain products.

The third channel for business products, channel G, employs a *manufacturers' agent,* an independent businessperson who sells complementary products of several producers in assigned territories and is compensated through commissions. Unlike an industrial distributor, a manufacturers' agent does not acquire title to the products and usually does not take possession. Acting as a salesperson on behalf of the producers, a manufacturers' agent has little or no latitude in negotiating prices or sales terms.

Using manufacturers' agents can benefit an organizational marketer. These agents usually possess considerable technical and market information and have an established set of customers. For an organizational seller with highly seasonal demand, a manufacturers' agent can be an asset because the seller does not have to support a year-round sales force. The fact that manufacturers' agents are typically paid on a commission basis may also be an economical alternative for a firm that has highly limited resources and cannot afford a full-time sales force.

The use of manufacturers' agents is not problem-free. Even though straight commissions may be more financially viable, the seller may have little control over manufacturers' agents. Because of the compensation method, manufacturers' agents generally prefer to concentrate on their larger accounts. They are often reluctant to spend time following up sales, putting forth special selling efforts, or providing sellers with market information when such activities reduce the amount of productive selling time. Because they rarely

Direct Channel for Business Products Dell uses a direct marketing channel to reach business customers.

dual distribution The use of two or more marketing channels to distribute the same products to the same target market

strategic channel alliance An agreement whereby the products of one organization are distributed through the marketing channels of another

maintain inventories, manufacturers' agents have a limited ability to provide customers with parts or repair services quickly.

Finally, channel H includes both a manufacturers' agent and an industrial distributor. This channel may be appropriate when the producer wishes to cover a large geographic area but maintains no sales force due to highly seasonal demand or because it cannot afford a sales force. This type of channel can also be useful for a business marketer that wants to enter a new geographic market without expanding its existing sales force.

Multiple Marketing Channels and Channel Alliances

To reach diverse target markets, manufacturers may use several marketing channels simultaneously, with each channel involving a different group of intermediaries. In particular, a manufacturer often uses multiple channels when the same product is directed to both consumers and business customers. For example, when Del Monte markets ketchup for household use, the product is sold to supermarkets through grocery wholesalers or, in some cases, directly to retailers, whereas ketchup being sold to restaurants or institutions follows a different distribution channel.

In some instances, a producer may prefer **dual distribution,** the use of two or more marketing channels to distribute the same products to the same target market. For example, Kellogg sells its cereal directly to large retail organizations, such as Walmart (Channel B), and to food brokers, or wholesalers (Channel C). Another example of dual distribution is a firm that sells products through retail outlets and its own mail-order catalog or website. Dual distribution, however, can cause dissatisfaction among wholesalers and smaller retailers when they must compete with large retail grocery chains that make direct purchases from manufacturers such as Kellogg. Another example is State Farm Insurance, which has decided to maintain its "old" business model of using agents as the primary vehicle for customer interaction, potentially losing sales to other insurance companies by not offering insurance policies online in the same way as others (e.g., Progressive).

A **strategic channel alliance** exists when the products of one organization are distributed through the marketing channels of another. The products of the two firms are often similar with respect to target markets or uses, but they are not direct competitors. A brand of bottled water might be distributed through a marketing channel for soft drinks, or a domestic cereal producer might form a strategic channel alliance with a European food processor. Ocean Spray and PepsiCo formed such an alliance whereby Pepsi manufactured, bottled, and distributed single-serve cranberry juice products under the Ocean Spray name.[9] Such alliances can provide benefits for both the organization that owns the marketing channel and the company whose brand is being distributed through the channel.

Using Multiple Marketing Channels Major soft drink companies, like Coca-Cola, employ multiple marketing channels.

SELECTING MARKETING CHANNELS

Selecting appropriate marketing channels is important. While the process varies across organizations, channel selection decisions usually are significantly affected by one or more of the following factors: customer characteristics, product attributes, type of organization, competition, marketing environmental forces, and characteristics of intermediaries (see Figure 13.4).

FIGURE 13.4 Selecting Marketing Channels

Customer Characteristics

Marketing managers must consider the characteristics of target-market members in channel selection. As we have discussed, the channels appropriate for consumers are different from those for business customers. A different marketing channel will be required for business customers purchasing carpet for commercial buildings compared with consumers purchasing carpet for their homes. As already mentioned, business customers often prefer to deal directly with producers (or very knowledgeable channel intermediaries such as industrial distributors), especially for highly technical or expensive products such as mainframe computers, jet airplanes, and large mining machines. Moreover, business customers are more likely to buy complex products requiring strict specifications and technical assistance and/or to buy in considerable quantities.

Consumers, on the other hand, generally buy limited quantities of a product, purchase from retailers, and often do not mind limited customer service. Additionally, when customers are concentrated in a small geographic area, a more direct channel may be ideal, but when many customers are spread across an entire state or nation, distribution through multiple intermediaries is likely to be more efficient.

Product Attributes

The attributes of the product can have a strong influence on the choice of marketing channels. Marketers of complex and expensive products such as automobiles likely will employ short channels, as will marketers of perishable products such as dairy and produce. Less expensive, more standardized products such as soft drinks and canned goods can employ longer channels with many intermediaries. In addition, channel decisions may be affected by a product's sturdiness: Fragile products that require special handling are more likely to be distributed through shorter channels to minimize the risk of damage. Firms that desire to convey an exclusive image for their products may wish to limit the number of outlets available.

Type of Organization

Clearly, the characteristics of the organization will have a great impact on the distribution channels chosen. Owing to their sheer size, larger firms may be better able to negotiate better deals with vendors or other channel members. Compared with small firms, they may be in better positions to have more distribution centers, which may reduce delivery times to customers. A smaller regional company using regional or local channel members may be in a position to better serve customers in that region compared with a larger, less flexible organization. Compared with smaller organizations, large companies can use an extensive product mix as a competitive tool. Smaller firms may not have the resources to develop their own sales force, to ship their products long distances, to store or own products, or to extend credit. In such cases, they may have to include other channel members that have the resources to provide these services to customers efficiently and cost effectively.

Competition

Competition is another important factor for supply-chain managers to consider. The success or failure of a competitor's marketing channel may encourage or dissuade an organization from considering a similar approach. A firm also may be forced to adopt a similar strategy to remain competitive. In a highly competitive market, it is important for a company to keep its costs low so that it can underprice its competitors if necessary.

SNAPSHOT

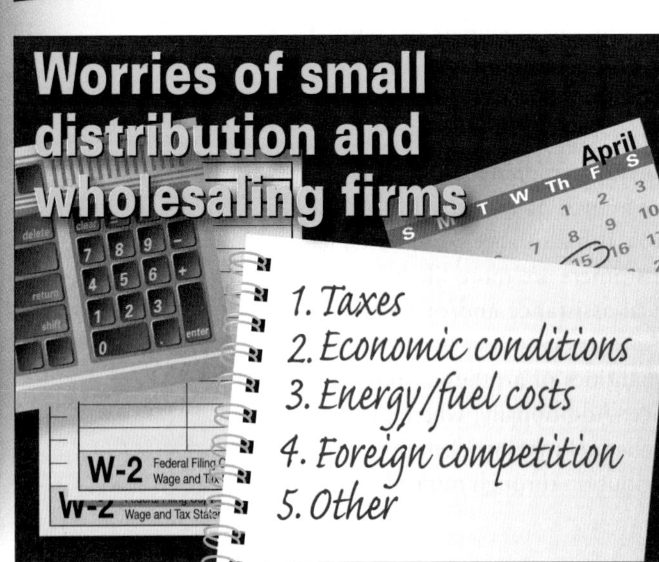

Source: Small Business Research Board study, in "Top 5 Business Concerns," Inbound Logistics, September 2007, p. 20.

Environmental Forces

Environmental forces also can play a role in channel selection. Adverse economic conditions might force an organization to use a low-cost channel, even though customer satisfaction is reduced. In contrast, a booming economy might allow a company to choose a channel that previously had been too costly to consider. The introduction of new technology might cause an organization to add or modify its channel strategy. For instance, as the Internet became a powerful marketing communication tool, many companies were forced to go online to remain competitive. Government regulations also can affect channel selection. As new labor and environmental regulations are passed, an organization may be forced to modify its existing distribution channel structure. Firms may choose to make the changes before regulations are passed in order to appear compliant or to avoid legal issues. Governmental regulations also can include trade agreements with other countries that complicate the supply chain.

Characteristics of Intermediaries

When an organization believes that a current intermediary is not promoting the organization's products adequately, it may reconsider its channel choices. In these instances the company may choose another channel member to handle its products, or it may choose to eliminate intermediaries altogether and perform the eliminated intermediaries' functions itself. Alternatively, an existing intermediary may not offer an appropriate mix of services, forcing an organization to change to another intermediary.

Intensity of Market Coverage

In addition to deciding which marketing channels to use to distribute a product, marketers must determine the intensity of coverage that a product should get, that is, the number and kinds of outlets in which it will be sold. This decision depends on the characteristics of the product and the target market. To achieve the desired intensity of market coverage, distribution must correspond to behavior patterns of buyers. In Chapter 9, we divided consumer products into four categories—convenience products, shopping products, specialty products, and unsought products—according to how consumers make purchases. In considering products for purchase, consumers take into account replacement rate, product adjustment (services), duration of consumption, time required to find the product, and similar factors.[10] These variables directly affect the intensity of market coverage. As shown in Figure 13.5, the three major levels of market coverage are intensive, selective, and exclusive distribution.

FIGURE 13.5 **Intensity of Market Coverage**

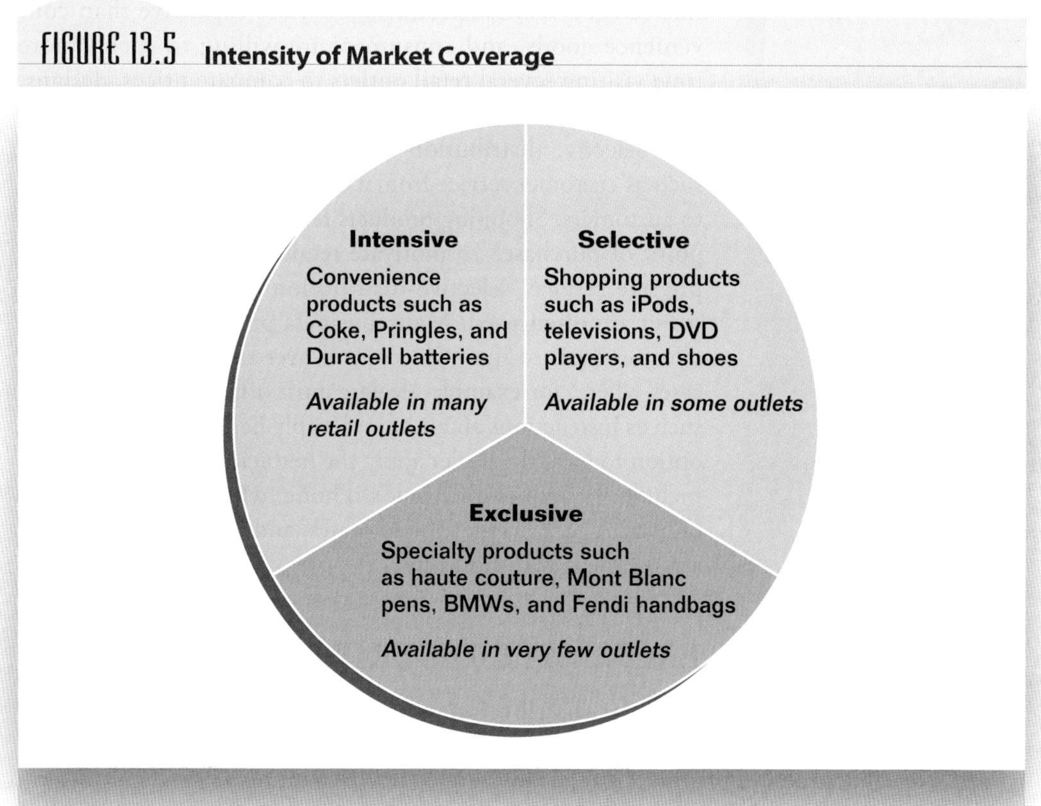

intensive distribution Using all available outlets to distribute a product

selective distribution Using only some available outlets to distribute a product

exclusive distribution Using a single outlet in a fairly large geographic area to distribute a product

INTENSIVE DISTRIBUTION

Intensive distribution uses all available outlets for distributing a product. Intensive distribution is appropriate for most convenience products such as bread, chewing gum, soft drinks, and newspapers. Convenience products have a high replacement rate, require almost no service, and are often bought based on price cues. To meet these demands, intensive distribution is necessary, and multiple channels may be used to sell through all possible outlets. For example, soft drinks, snacks, laundry detergent, and pain relievers are available at convenience stores, service stations, supermarkets, discount stores, and other types of retailers. To consumers, availability means a store is located nearby and minimum time is necessary to search for the product at the store. This ensures that consumers are provided with the greatest speed in obtaining the product, the quality they have come to expect of a certain convenience product, the flexibility to buy the product wherever it is convenient to them, and at the lowest cost possible.

Sales may have a direct relationship to product availability. The successful sale of convenience products such as bread and milk at service stations or gasoline at convenience grocery stores illustrates that the availability of these products is more important than the nature of the outlet. Companies such as Procter & Gamble that produce consumer packaged items rely on intensive distribution for many of their products (for example, soaps, detergents, food and juice products, and personal-care products) because consumers want ready availability.

SELECTIVE DISTRIBUTION

Intensive Distribution Most brands of bottled water, like Aquafina, are distributed through intensive distribution.

Selective distribution uses only some available outlets in an area to distribute a product. Selective distribution is appropriate for shopping products; durable goods such as televisions, stereos, and home computers usually fall into this category. These products are more expensive than convenience goods, and consumers are willing to spend more time visiting several retail outlets to compare prices, designs, styles, and other features.

Selective distribution is desirable when a special effort, such as customer service from a channel member, is important to customers. Shopping products require differentiation at the point of purchase. To motivate retailers to provide adequate pre-sale service, selective distribution and company-owned stores are often used. Many business products are sold on a selective basis to maintain control over the products (e.g., in cases where, for example, dealers must offer services to buyers such as instructions about how to apply herbicides safely or the option to have the dealer apply the herbicide). Other examples include the launch of Apple's iPhone, which was distributed only by AT&T in the United States, and Dell's exclusive retail arrangement with Best Buy.

EXCLUSIVE DISTRIBUTION

Exclusive distribution uses only one outlet in a relatively large geographic area. Exclusive distribution is suitable for products purchased infrequently, consumed over a long period of time, or requiring service or information to fit them to buyers' needs. It is also used for expensive, high-quality products, such as Porsche, BMW, and other luxury automobiles. It is not appropriate for convenience products and many shopping products.

Exclusive distribution is often used as an incentive to sellers when only a limited market is available for products. For example, like luxury automobiles, Patek Philippe watches, which may sell for $10,000 or more, are available in only a few select locations. A producer using exclusive distribution generally expects dealers to carry a complete inventory, send personnel for sales and service training, participate in promotional programs, and provide excellent customer service. Some products are appropriate for exclusive distribution when first introduced, but as competitors enter the market and the product moves through its life cycle, other types of market coverage and distribution channels often become necessary (e.g., Dell expanding from exclusive online distribution to being offered through Best Buy retail stores as well). A problem that can arise with exclusive distribution (and selective distribution) is that unauthorized resellers acquire and sell products, violating the agreement between a manufacturer and its exclusive authorized dealers. This has been a problem for Rolex, a manufacturer of luxury watches.

Strategic Issues in Marketing Channels

To fulfill the potential of effective supply-chain management and ensure customer satisfaction, marketing channels require a strategic focus on certain competitive priorities and the development of channel leadership, cooperation, and the management of channel conflict. They may also require consolidation of marketing channels through channel integration.

COMPETITIVE PRIORITIES IN MARKETING CHANNELS

There is much evidence that supply chains can provide a competitive advantage for many marketers. As mentioned earlier, effective supply chain management has been linked to a marketing orientation. Because supply chain decisions cut across all functional areas of the business, it is a competitive priority. Building the most effective and efficient supply chain can sustain a business in a variety of competitive environments.

It is estimated that a significant supply-chain problem can reduce a firm's market value by more than 10 percent. Deloitte Touche Tohmatsu has reported that just 7 percent of companies today are managing their supply chains effectively; however, these companies are 73 percent more profitable than other firms. Many well-known firms including Amazom.com, Dell, FedEx, Toyota, and Walmart owe much of their success to outmaneuvering rivals with unique supply-chain capabilities.

If supply chain activities are not integrated, functions exist without coordination. As supply chains integrate functions, the reward is efficiency and effectiveness as well as a holistic view of the supply chain.

Goal-driven supply chains, by direction of their firms, focus on the "competitive priorities" of speed, quality, cost, or flexibility as the performance objective. For example, before Domino's got into legal trouble for its 30-minute-or-free promise of delivering pizza, speed was its main concern. The quality, cost, and the variety of toppings on the pizza were secondary to the time it took to get a hot pizza delivered to the customer's door. Other companies (e.g., Rolls-Royce) focus on different competitive priorities, such as delivering top-notch quality products, where neither cost nor speed is an issue. Rolls-Royce still stresses certain flexibility in the product customization, however. Walmart is the poster example of stressing low cost, often at the "cost" of speed, quality, and flexibility. Yet, some firms thrive on being flexible. For example, L.L.Bean provides almost endless flexibility, particularly in return policies. However, they have very few stores where customers can get their products, so the speed is slower than for some of their competitors. Cost is higher than the industry average, but their products are usually of high quality.

CHANNEL LEADERSHIP, COOPERATION, AND CONFLICT

Each channel member performs a different role in the distribution system and agrees (implicitly or explicitly) to accept certain rights, responsibilities, rewards, and sanctions for nonconformity. Moreover, each channel member holds certain expectations of other channel members. Retailers, for instance, expect wholesalers to maintain adequate inventories and deliver goods on time. Wholesalers expect retailers to honor payment agreements and keep them informed of inventory needs.

Channel partnerships facilitate effective supply-chain management when partners agree on objectives, policies, and procedures for physical distribution efforts associated with the supplier's products. Such partnerships eliminate redundancies and reassign tasks for maximum systemwide efficiency.

One of the best-known partnerships is that between Walmart and Procter & Gamble. Procter & Gamble locates some of its staff near Walmart's purchasing department in Bentonville, Arkansas, to establish and maintain the supply chain. Sharing information through a cooperative information system, P&G monitors Walmart's inventory and additional data to determine production and distribution plans for its products. The results are increased efficiency, decreased inventory costs, and greater satisfaction for the customers of both companies. In this section we discuss channel member behavior, including leadership, cooperation, and conflict, that marketers must understand to make effective channel decisions.

Channel Leadership

Many marketing channel decisions are determined by give and take among channel partners, with the idea that the overall channel ultimately will benefit. Some marketing channels, however, are organized and controlled by a single leader, or **channel captain** (also called *channel leader*). The channel captain may be a producer, wholesaler, or retailer. Channel captains may establish channel policies and coordinate development of the marketing mix. Walmart, for example, dominates the supply chain for its retail stores by virtue of the magnitude of its resources (especially information management) and strong, nationwide customer base. To attain desired objectives, the captain must possess **channel power**, the ability to influence another channel member's goal achievement. The member that becomes the channel captain will accept the responsibilities and exercise the power associated with this role.

When a manufacturer's large-scale production efficiency demands that it increase sales volume, the manufacturer may exercise power by giving channel members financing, business advice, ordering assistance, advertising services, sales and service training, and support materials. For example, U.S. automakers provide these services to retail automobile dealerships. However, these manufacturers also place numerous requirements on their retail dealerships with respect to sales volume, sales and service training, and customer satisfaction.

channel captain
The dominant member of a marketing channel or supply chain

channel power
The ability of one channel member to influence another member's goal achievement

Retailers may also function as channel captains. With the rise in power of national chain stores and private-brand merchandise, many large retailers such as Walmart are taking a leadership role in the channel. Small retailers too may assume leadership roles when they gain strong customer loyalty in local or regional markets. These retailers control many brands and sometimes replace uncooperative producers. Increasingly, leading retailers are concentrating their buying power with fewer suppliers and, in the process, improving their marketing effectiveness and efficiency. Long-term commitments enable retailers to place smaller and more frequent orders as needed rather than waiting for large volume discounts or placing huge orders and assuming the risks associated with carrying a larger inventory.

Wholesalers assume channel leadership roles as well, although they were more powerful decades ago, when many manufacturers and retailers were smaller, underfinanced, and widely scattered. Today wholesaler leaders may form voluntary chains with several retailers, which they supply with bulk buying or management services; these chains may also market their own brands. In return, the retailers shift most of their purchasing to the wholesaler leader. The Independent Grocers Alliance (IGA) is one of the best-known wholesaler leaders in the United States. IGA's power is based on its expertise in advertising, pricing, and purchasing knowledge that it makes available to independent business owners. Other wholesaler leaders help retailers with store layouts, accounting, and inventory control.

Channel Leadership
The producer of Candie's products provides channel leadership.

Channel Cooperation

Channel cooperation is vital if each member is to gain something from other members. Cooperation enables retailers, wholesalers, suppliers, and logistics providers to speed up inventory replenishment, improve customer service, and cut the costs of bringing products to the consumer.[11] Without cooperation, neither overall channel goals nor individual member goals can be realized. All channel members must recognize that the success of one firm in the channel depends in part on other member firms. Thus, marketing channel members should make a coordinated effort to satisfy market requirements. Channel cooperation leads to greater trust among channel members and improves the overall functioning of the channel. It also leads to more satisfying relationships among channel members.

There are several ways to improve channel cooperation. If a marketing channel is viewed as a unified supply chain competing with other systems, individual members will be less likely to take actions that create disadvantages for other members. Similarly, channel members should agree to direct efforts toward common objectives so channel roles can be structured for maximum marketing effectiveness, which in turn can help members achieve individual objectives. A critical component in cooperation is a precise definition of each channel member's tasks. This provides a basis for reviewing the intermediaries' performance and helps reduce conflicts because each channel member knows exactly what is expected of it.

Channel Conflict

Although all channel members work toward the same general goal—distributing products profitably and efficiently—members sometimes may disagree about the best methods for attaining this goal. However, if self-interest creates misunderstanding about role expectations, the end result is frustration and conflict for the whole channel. Consider what happened when the New England–based Hannaford Bros. supermarket chain introduced a new system that rated the nutritional content of every single product on the stores' shelves for the benefit of consumers looking for the healthiest products. Although Hannaford Bros.'s executives insisted that they simply wanted to offer confused shoppers more guidance on finding healthful choices, many of its suppliers grumbled when the supermarket gave their products a lower than expected rating, especially those marketing products touted as "healthy" but with significant salt or sugar content.[12] For individual organizations to function together, each channel member must clearly communicate and understand role expectations. Communication difficulties are a potential form of channel conflict because ineffective communication leads to frustration, misunderstandings, and ill-coordinated strategies, jeopardizing further coordination.

The increased use of multiple channels of distribution, driven partly by new technology, has increased the potential for conflict between manufacturers and intermediaries. For example, Hewlett-Packard makes products available directly to consumers through its website, thereby competing directly with existing distributors and retailers, such as Best Buy and CompUSA. Channel conflicts also arise when intermediaries overemphasize competing products or diversify into product lines traditionally handled by other intermediaries. Sometimes conflict develops because producers strive to increase efficiency by circumventing intermediaries. Such conflict is occurring in marketing channels for computer software. A number of software-only stores are establishing direct relationships with software producers, bypassing wholesale distributors altogether.

When a producer that has traditionally used franchised dealers broadens its retailer base to include other types of retail outlets, considerable conflict can arise. When Goodyear intensified its market coverage by allowing Sears and Discount Tire to market Goodyear tires, its action antagonized 2,500 independent Goodyear dealers.

Although there is no single method for resolving conflict, partnerships can be reestablished if two conditions are met. First, the role of each channel member must be specified. To minimize misunderstanding, all members must be able to expect unambiguous, agreed-on performance levels from one another. Second, members of channel partnerships must institute certain measures of channel coordination, which requires leadership and benevolent exercise of control. To prevent channel conflict from arising, producers or other channel members may provide competing resellers with different brands, allocate markets among resellers, define policies for direct sales to avoid potential conflict over large accounts, negotiate territorial issues among regional distributors, and provide recognition to certain resellers for their importance in distributing to others.

CHANNEL INTEGRATION

Channel members can either combine and control most activities or pass them on to another channel member. Channel functions may be transferred between intermediaries and to producers and even to customers. However, a channel member cannot eliminate supply-chain functions; unless buyers themselves perform the functions, they must pay for the labor and resources needed to perform them.

Various channel stages may be combined under the management of a channel captain either horizontally or vertically. Such integration may stabilize supply, reduce costs, and increase coordination of channel members.

Vertical Channel Integration

vertical channel integration Combining two or more stages of the marketing channel under one management

Vertical channel integration combines two or more stages of the channel under one management. This may occur when one member of a marketing channel purchases the operations of another member or simply performs the functions of another member, eliminating the need for that intermediary. For example, Smithfield Foods, a leading U.S. food processor, acquired Premium Standard Farms, Inc., the number two U.S. hog farmer. Although the purchase may trigger antitrust concerns, it reflects a trend among large meat processors to grow and slaughter their own livestock instead of obtaining them from independent farmers.[13]

Unlike conventional channel systems, participants in vertical channel integration coordinate efforts to reach a desired target market. In this more progressive approach to distribution, channel members regard other members as extensions of their own operations. Vertically integrated channels are often more effective against competition because of increased bargaining power and the sharing of information and responsibilities. At one end of a vertically integrated channel, a manufacturer might provide advertising and training assistance, and the retailer at the other end might buy the manufacturer's products in large quantities and actively promote them.

Integration has been successfully institutionalized in marketing channels called **vertical marketing systems (VMSs),** in which a single channel member coordinates or manages channel activities to achieve efficient, low-cost distribution aimed at satisfying target-market customers. Vertical integration brings most or all stages of the marketing channel under common control or ownership. The Limited, a retail clothing chain, uses a wholly owned subsidiary, Mast Industries, as its primary supply source. Radio Shack operates as a VMS, encompassing both wholesale and retail functions. Because efforts of individual channel members are combined in a VMS, marketing activities can be coordinated for maximum effectiveness and economy without duplication of services. VMSs are competitive, accounting for a share of retail sales in consumer goods.

Most vertical marketing systems take one of three forms: corporate, administered, or contractual. A *corporate VMS* combines all stages of the marketing channel, from producers to consumers, under a single owner. For example, The Limited established a corporate VMS that operates corporate-owned production facilities and retail stores. Supermarket chains that own food-processing plants and large retailers that purchase wholesaling and production facilities are other examples of corporate VMSs.

In an *administered VMS,* channel members are independent, but a high level of interorganizational management is achieved through informal coordination. Members of an administered VMS, for example, may adopt uniform accounting and ordering procedures and cooperate in promotional activities for the benefit of all partners. Although individual channel members maintain autonomy, as in conventional marketing channels, one channel member (such as a producer or large retailer) dominates the administered VMS so that distribution decisions take the whole system into account. Because of its size and power, Intel exercises a strong influence over distributors and manufacturers in its marketing channels, as do Kellogg (cereal) and MAGNAVOX (televisions and other electronic products).

Under a *contractual VMS,* the most popular type of vertical marketing system, channel members are linked by legal agreements spelling out each member's rights and obligations. Franchise organizations, such as McDonald's and KFC, are contractual VMSs. Other contractual VMSs include wholesaler-sponsored groups, such as IGA (Independent Grocers Alliance) stores, in which independent retailers band together under the contractual leadership of a wholesaler. Retailer-sponsored cooperatives, which own and operate their own wholesalers, are a third type of contractual VMS.

vertical marketing systems (VMSs)
A marketing channel managed by a single channel member to achieve efficient, low-cost distribution aimed at satisfying target-market customers

Horizontal Channel Integration

Combining organizations at the same level of operation under one management constitutes **horizontal channel integration.** An organization may integrate horizontally by merging with other organizations at the same level in the marketing channel. The owner of a dry-cleaning firm, for example, might buy and combine several other existing dry-cleaning establishments. Japan Tobacco, the world's third largest cigarette maker, acquired Britain's Gallaher Group Plc., which owns several upscale cigarette brands and has a strong presence in Russia and eastern Europe, for about $14.7 billion. The purchase boosted Japan Tobacco's global market share from 3 to 11 percent.[14] Horizontal integration may enable a firm to generate sufficient sales revenue to integrate vertically as well.

horizontal channel integration
Combining organizations at the same level of operation under one management

Although horizontal integration permits efficiencies and economies of scale in purchasing, marketing research, advertising, and specialized personnel, it is not always the most effective method of improving distribution. Problems of size often follow, resulting in decreased flexibility, difficulties in coordination, and the need for additional marketing research and large-scale planning. Unless distribution functions for the various units can be performed more efficiently under unified management than under the previously separate managements, horizontal integration will neither reduce costs nor improve the competitive position of the integrating firm.

Physical Distribution in Supply-Chain Management

Physical distribution, also known as *logistics,* refers to the activities used to move products from producers to consumers and other end users. Physical distribution systems must meet the needs of both the supply chain and customers. Distribution activities are thus an important part of supply-chain planning and require the cooperation of all partners.

Within the marketing channel, physical distribution activities may be performed by a producer, a wholesaler, or a retailer, or they may be outsourced. In the context of distribution, **outsourcing** is the contracting of physical distribution tasks to third parties who do not have managerial authority within the marketing channel. Most physical distribution activities can be outsourced to third-party firms that have special expertise in areas such as warehousing, transportation, inventory management, and information technology. Some manufacturing firms, for example, outsource delivery services to Penske Truck Leasing, a joint venture between General Electric and Penske Corp. Penske Truck, in turn, has outsourced some of its own activities, including some scheduling, billing, and invoicing services to contractors in Mexico and India. Outsourcing has saved Penske $15 million and helped the company to improve efficiency and customer service.[15] Cooperative relationships with third-party organizations, such as trucking companies, warehouses, and data-service providers, can help to reduce marketing-channel costs and boost service and customer satisfaction for all supply-chain partners. When choosing companies through which to outsource, marketers must be cautious and use efficient firms that help the outsourcing company provide excellent customer service. They need to recognize as well the importance of logistics functions such as warehousing and information technology in reducing physical distribution costs associated with outsourcing.[16]

Planning an efficient physical distribution system is crucial to developing an effective marketing strategy because it can decrease costs and increase customer satisfaction. Speed of delivery, flexibility, and quality of service are often as important to customers as costs. Companies that have the right goods, in the right place, at the right time, in the right quantity, and with the right support services are able to sell more than competitors that do not. Even when the demand for products is unpredictable, suppliers must be able to respond quickly to inventory needs. In such cases, physical distribution costs may be a minor consideration when compared with service, dependability, and timeliness.

Customer relationship management systems exploit the information from supply-chain partners' database systems to help logistics managers identify and root out inefficiencies in the supply chain for the benefit of all marketing-channel members—from the producer to the ultimate consumer. Indeed, technology is playing a larger and larger role in physical distribution within marketing channels. It has transformed physical distribution by facilitating just-in-time delivery, precise inventory visibility, and instant shipment tracking capabilities, which help companies to avoid expensive mistakes, reduce costs, and even generate revenues. Information technology brings visibility to the supply chain by allowing all marketing-channel members to

physical distribution
Activities used to move products from producers to consumers and other end users

outsourcing
The contracting of physical distribution tasks to third parties who do not have managerial authority within the marketing channel

cycle time
The time needed to complete a process

order processing
The receipt and transmission of sales order information

see precisely where an item is within the supply chain at any time.[17]

Although physical distribution managers try to minimize the costs associated with order processing, inventory management, materials handling, warehousing, and transportation, decreasing the costs in one area often raises them in another. Figure 13.6 shows the percentage of total costs that physical distribution functions represent. A total-cost approach to physical distribution enables managers to view physical distribution as a system rather than a collection of unrelated activities. This approach shifts the emphasis from lowering the separate costs of individual activities to minimizing overall distribution costs.

Physical distribution managers must be sensitive to the issue of cost tradeoffs. Higher costs in one functional area of a distribution system may be necessary to achieve lower costs in another. Tradeoffs are strategic decisions to combine (and recombine) resources for greatest cost-effectiveness. When distribution managers regard the system as a network of integrated functions, tradeoffs become useful tools in implementing a unified, cost-effective distribution strategy.

Another important goal of physical distribution involves **cycle time,** the time needed to complete a process. For example, reducing cycle time while maintaining or reducing costs and/or maintaining or increasing customer service is a winning combination in supply chains—ultimately leading to greater end-customer satisfaction.

In the rest of this section, we take a closer look at a variety of physical distribution activities, including order processing, inventory management, materials handling, warehousing, and transportation.

ORDER PROCESSING

Order processing is the receipt and transmission of sales-order information. Although management sometimes overlooks the importance of these activities, efficient order processing facilitates product flow. Computerized order processing provides a database for all supply-chain members to increase their productivity. When carried out quickly and accurately, order processing contributes to customer satisfaction, decreased costs and cycle time, and increased profits.

Order processing entails three main tasks: order entry, order handling, and order delivery. Order entry begins when customers or salespeople place purchase orders via telephone, mail, e-mail, or website. Electronic ordering is less time-consuming than a manual,

Marketing IN TRANSITION

Streamlining Physical Distribution to Profit in Style

Fashion firms are profiting in style by streamlining physical distribution. For example, the global retailer Zara, owned by Spain's Inditex, can rush a new design from sketch to finished product and into stores within two weeks. To start, Zara's store managers track sales of every item, ask customers what they like, and report the latest trends to Inditex.

© PETER HORREE/ALAMY

Based on these details, company designers quickly create new styles, have them manufactured in Inditex's European factories, and warehouse everything in Spain. Small batches of each style can be trucked to Zara's European stores within a day and sent by air cargo to Zara stores outside Europe within two days. The result: Zara's 1,500 stores in 72 countries have a steady stream of new fashions to bring customers back again and again.

Valentino Fashion Group, owner of the Valentino, HUGO BOSS, and M Missoni brands, has also revamped physical distribution to get the right fashions to the right stores at the right time. With its inventory management system connected to the sales systems of the department stores it supplies, Valentino can see immediately what's hot and what's not. This helps management decide which merchandise to send where—and when.[b]

FIGURE 13.6 **Proportional Cost of Each Physical Distribution Function as a Percentage of Total Distribution Costs**

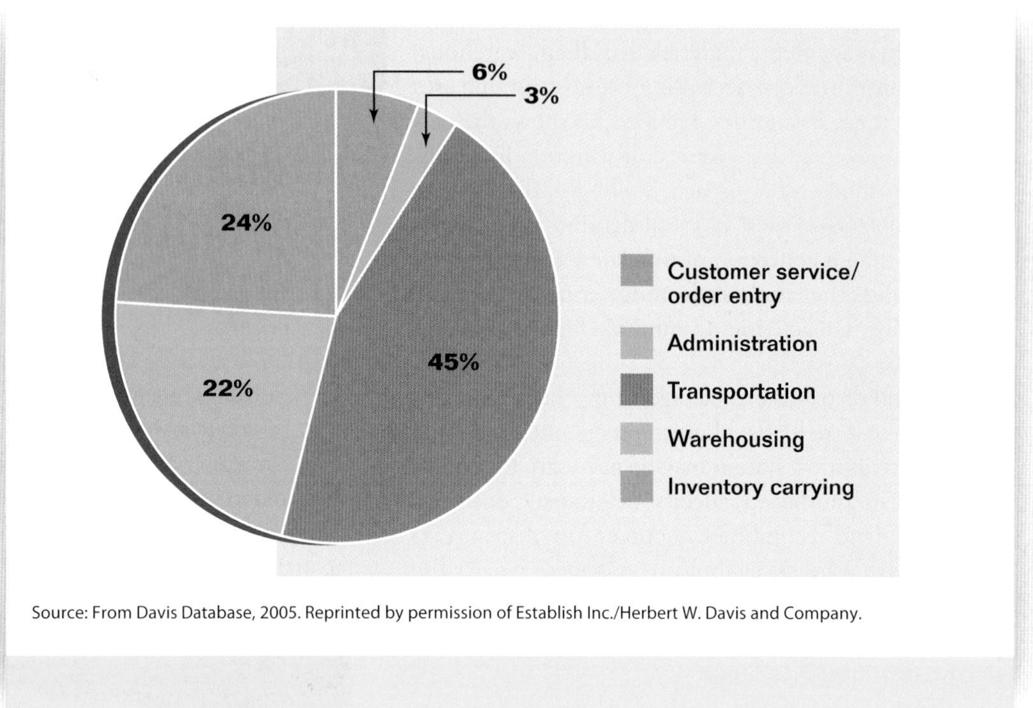

Source: From Davis Database, 2005. Reprinted by permission of Establish Inc./Herbert W. Davis and Company.

paper-based ordering system and reduces costs. In some companies, sales representatives receive and enter orders personally and also handle complaints, prepare progress reports, and forward sales order information.

Order handling involves several tasks. Once an order is entered, it is transmitted to a warehouse, where product availability is verified, and to the credit department, where prices, terms, and the customer's credit rating are checked. If the credit department approves the purchase, warehouse personnel (sometimes assisted by automated equipment) pick and assemble the order. If the requested product is not in stock, a production order is sent to the factory, or the customer is offered a substitute.

When the order has been assembled and packed for shipment, the warehouse schedules delivery with an appropriate carrier. If the customer pays for rush service, overnight delivery by FedEx, UPS, DHL, or another overnight carrier is used. The customer is sent an invoice, inventory records are adjusted, and the order is delivered.

Whether to use a manual or an electronic order-processing system depends on which method provides the greater speed and accuracy within cost limits. Manual processing suffices for small-volume orders and is more flexible in certain situations. Most companies, however, use **electronic data interchange (EDI)**, which uses computer technology to integrate order processing with production, inventory, accounting, and transportation. Within the supply chain, EDI functions as an information system that links marketing-channel members and outsourcing firms together. It reduces paperwork for all members of the supply chain and allows them to share information on invoices, orders, payments, inquiries, and scheduling. Consequently, many companies have pushed their suppliers toward EDI to reduce distribution costs and cycle times. Walmart and Home Depot, for example, strongly urge their suppliers to use EDI systems like those produced by RedTail Solutions, which focuses on developing EDI software for medium-sized suppliers.[18]

electronic data interchange (EDI) A computerized means of integrating order processing with production, inventory, accounting, and transportation

INVENTORY MANAGEMENT

Inventory management involves developing and maintaining adequate assortments of products to meet customers' needs. It is a key component of any effective physical distribution system. Inventory decisions have a major impact on physical distribution costs and the level of customer service provided. When too few products are carried in inventory, the result is *stock-outs,* or shortages of products, which, in turn, can result in brand switching, lower sales, and loss of customers. When too many products (or too many slow-moving products) are carried, costs increase, as do risks of product obsolescence, pilferage, and damage. The objective of inventory management is to minimize inventory costs while maintaining an adequate supply of goods to satisfy customers. To achieve this objective, marketers focus on two major issues: when to order and how much to order.

To determine when to order, a marketer calculates the *reorder point,* the inventory level that signals the need to place a new order. To calculate the reorder point, the marketer must know the order lead time, the usage rate, and the amount of safety stock required. The *order lead time* refers to the average time lapse between placing the order and receiving it. The *usage rate* is the rate at which a product's inventory is used or sold during a specific time period. *Safety stock* is the amount of extra inventory a firm keeps to guard against stockouts resulting from above-average usage rates and/or longer-than-expected lead times. The reorder point can be calculated using the following formula:

© AP IMAGES/KEVIN RIVOLI

Inventory Management
This handheld inventory management device allows employees to have an instant overview of every item – and its price – in the warehouse at any given time.

$$\text{Reorder point} = (\text{order lead time} \times \text{usage rate}) + \text{safety stock}$$

Thus, if order lead time is 10 days, usage rate is 3 units per day, and safety stock is 20 units, the reorder point is 50 units.

Efficient inventory management with accurate reorder points is crucial for firms that use a **just-in-time (JIT)** approach, in which supplies arrive just as they are needed for use in production or for resale. When using JIT, companies maintain low inventory levels and purchase products and materials in small quantities whenever they need them. Usually there is no safety stock, and suppliers are expected to provide consistently high-quality products. JIT inventory management requires a high level of coordination between producers and suppliers, but it eliminates waste and reduces inventory costs significantly. This approach has been used successfully by many well-known firms, including Chrysler, Harley-Davidson, and Dell, to reduce costs and boost customer satisfaction. When a JIT approach is used in a supply chain, suppliers often move close to their customers.

inventory management
Developing and maintaining adequate assortments of products to meet customers' needs

just-in-time (JIT)
An inventory-management approach in which supplies arrive just when needed for production or resale

MATERIALS HANDLING

Materials handling, the physical handling of tangible goods, supplies, and resources, is an important factor in warehouse operations, as well as in transportation from points of production to points of consumption. Efficient procedures and techniques for materials handling minimize inventory management costs, reduce the number of times a good is handled, improve customer service, and increase customer satisfaction. Systems for packaging, labeling, loading, and movement must be coordinated to maximize cost reduction and customer satisfaction.

materials handling
Physical handling of tangible goods, supplies, and resources

A growing number of firms are turning to radio waves to track materials tagged with radio frequency ID (RFID) through every phase of handling. Daisy Brand, for example, is using RFID to track its dairy products throughout the supply chain, which helps the firm recognize when a retailer has run out of product and needs to be replenished.[19] The rise of RFID technology is especially pronounced in China, where it is used in transportation, cash replacement, and secure access cards. The system is even being used in China's national ID card system.[20]

Product characteristics often determine handling. For example, the characteristics of bulk liquids and gases determine how they can be moved and stored. Internal packaging is also an important consideration in materials handling; goods must be packaged correctly to prevent damage or breakage during handling and transportation. Most companies employ packaging consultants during the product design process to help them decide which packaging materials and methods will result in the most efficient handling.

Unit loading and containerization are two common methods used in materials handling. With *unit loading,* one or more boxes are placed on a pallet or skid; these units then can be loaded efficiently by mechanical means such as forklifts, trucks, or conveyer systems. *Containerization* is the consolidation of many items into a single, large container that is sealed at its point of origin and opened at its destination. Containers are usually 8 feet wide, 8 feet high, and 10 to 40 feet long. They can be conveniently stacked and shipped via train, barge, or ship. Once containers reach their destinations, wheel assemblies can be added to make them suitable for ground transportation. Because individual items are not handled in transit, containerization greatly increases efficiency and security in shipping.

WAREHOUSING

Warehousing, the design and operation of facilities for storing and moving goods, is another important physical distribution function. Warehousing provides time utility by enabling firms to compensate for dissimilar production and consumption rates. When mass production creates a greater stock of goods than can be sold immediately, companies may warehouse the surplus until customers are ready to buy. Warehousing also helps to stabilize prices and the availability of seasonal items.

The choice of warehouse facilities is an important strategic consideration. The right type of warehouse allows a company to reduce transportation and inventory costs or improve service to customers. The wrong type of warehouse may drain company resources. Beyond deciding how many facilities to operate and where to locate them, a company must determine which type of warehouse is most appropriate. Warehouses fall into two general categories: private and public. In many cases a combination of private and public facilities provides the most flexible warehousing approach.

Companies operate **private warehouses** for shipping and storing their own products. A firm usually leases or purchases a private warehouse when its warehousing needs in a given geographic market are substantial and stable enough to warrant a long-term commitment to a fixed facility. Private warehouses are also appropriate for firms that require special handling and storage and that want control of warehouse design and operation. Retailers such as Sears and Radio Shack find it economical to integrate private warehousing with purchasing and distribution for their retail outlets. When sales volumes are fairly stable, ownership and control of a private warehouse may provide benefits such as property appreciation. Private warehouses, however, face fixed costs such as insurance, taxes, maintenance, and debt expense. They also limit flexibility when firms wish to move inventories to more strategic locations. Many private warehouses are being eliminated by direct links between producers and customers, reduced cycle times, and outsourcing to public warehouses.

warehousing
The design and operation of facilities for storing and moving goods

private warehouses
Company-operated facilities for storing and shipping products

Public warehouses lease storage space and related physical distribution facilities to other companies. They sometimes provide distribution services such as receiving, unloading, inspecting, and reshipping products; filling orders; providing financing; displaying products; and coordinating shipments. ODW, for example, offers a wide range of such services through its 3 million square feet of warehouse space at 11 facilities.[21] Public warehouses are especially useful to firms that have seasonal production or low-volume storage needs, have inventories that must be maintained in many locations, are testing or entering new markets, or own private warehouses but occasionally require additional storage space. Public warehouses also serve as collection points during product-recall programs. Whereas private warehouses have fixed costs, public warehouses offer variable (and often lower) costs because users rent space and purchase warehousing services only as needed.

Many public warehouses furnish security for products being used as collateral for loans, a service provided at either the warehouse or the site of the owner's inventory. *Field public warehouses* are established by public warehouses at the owner's inventory location. The warehouser becomes custodian of the products and issues a receipt that can be used as collateral for a loan. Public warehouses also provide *bonded storage,* a warehousing arrangement in which imported or taxable products are not released until the products' owners pay U.S. customs duties, taxes, or other fees. Bonded warehouses enable firms to defer tax payments on such items until they are delivered to customers.

Distribution centers are large, centralized warehouses that receive goods from factories and suppliers, regroup them into orders, and ship them to customers quickly, the focus being on movement of goods rather than storage.[22] Distribution centers are specially designed for rapid flow of products. They are usually one-story buildings (to eliminate elevators) with access to transportation networks such as major highways and/or railway lines. Many distribution centers are highly automated, with computer-directed robots, forklifts, and hoists that collect and move products to loading docks. American Eagle Outfitters, for example, operates three distribution centers to serve the needs of its 913 U.S. and Canadian American Eagle Outfitter and Martin + Osa stores, which market apparel to the 15- to 25-year-old market, as well as a direct sales channel. Efficiency and creativity in distribution operations helps the firm to keep up with a high volume of merchandise moving through the centers and stay on top of busy holiday seasons.[23] Although some public warehouses offer such specialized services, most distribution centers are privately owned. They serve customers in regional markets and, in some cases, function as consolidation points for a company's branch warehouses.

TRANSPORTATION

Transportation, the movement of products from where they are made to intermediaries and end users, is the most expensive physical distribution function. Because product availability and timely deliveries depend on transportation functions, transportation decisions directly affect customer service. A firm even may build its distribution and marketing strategy around a unique transportation system if that system can ensure on-time deliveries and thereby give the firm a competitive edge. Companies may build their own transportation fleets (private carriers) or outsource the transportation function to a common or contract carrier.

public warehouses
Storage space and related physical distribution facilities that can be leased by companies

distribution centers
Large, centralized warehouses that focus on moving rather than storing goods

transportation
The movement of products from where they are made to intermediaries and end users

Transportation Modes

There are five basic transportation modes for moving physical goods: railroads, trucks, waterways, airways, and pipelines. Each mode offers distinct advantages. Many companies adopt physical handling procedures that facilitate the use of two or more modes in combination. Table 13.3 indicates the percentage of intercity freight carried by each transportation mode.

Railroads such as Union Pacific and Canadian National carry heavy, bulky freight that must be shipped long distances over land. Railroads commonly haul minerals, sand, lumber, chemicals, and farm products, as well as low-value manufactured goods and an increasing number of automobiles. They are especially efficient for transporting full carloads, which can be shipped at lower rates than smaller quantities because they require less handling. Many companies locate factories or warehouses near rail lines for convenient loading and unloading.

Trucks provide the most flexible schedules and routes of all major transportation modes in the United States because they can go almost anywhere. Because trucks have a unique ability to move goods directly from factory or warehouse to customer, they are often used in conjunction with other forms of transport that cannot provide door-to-door deliveries. Trucks are more expensive and somewhat more vulnerable to bad weather than trains. They are also subject to size and weight restrictions on the products they carry. Trucks are sometimes criticized for high levels of loss and damage to freight and for delays caused by the rehandling of small shipments.

Waterways are the cheapest method of shipping heavy, low-value, nonperishable goods such as ore, coal, grain, and petroleum products. Water carriers offer considerable capacity. Powered by tugboats and towboats, barges that travel along intracoastal canals, inland rivers,

TABLE 13.3 Characteristics and Ratings of Transportation Modes by Selection Criteria

	Railroads	Trucks	Pipelines	Waterways	Airplanes
Selection Criteria					
Cost	Moderate	High	Low	Very low	Very high
Speed	Average	Fast	Slow	Very slow	Very fast
Dependability	Average	High	High	Average	High
Load flexibility	High	Average	Very low	Very high	Low
Accessibility	High	Very high	Very limited	Limited	Average
Frequency	Low	High	Very high	Very low	Average
% Ton-miles transported	38.2	28.5	19.9	13.0	0.3
Products carried	Coal, grain, lumber, heavy equipment, paper and pulp products, chemicals	Clothing, computers, books, groceries and produce, livestock	Oil, processed coal, natural gas	Chemicals, bauxite, grain, motor vehicles, agricultural implements	Flowers, food (highly perishable), technical instruments, emergency parts and equipment, overnight mail

Source: U.S. Bureau of Transportation Statistics, *National Transportation Statistics* (Washington, DC: U.S. Government Printing Office), http://www.bts.gov/publications/national_transportation_statistics/html/table_01_46b.html (accessed April 8, 2009).

and navigation systems can haul at least ten times the weight of one rail car, and ocean-going vessels can haul thousands of containers. More than 95 percent of international cargo is transported by water. However, many markets are inaccessible by water transportation unless supplemented by rail or truck. Droughts and floods also may create difficulties for users of inland waterway transportation. Nevertheless, the extreme fuel efficiency of water transportation and the continuing globalization of marketing likely will increase its use in the future.

Air transportation is the fastest but most expensive form of shipping. It is used most often for perishable goods; for high-value, low-bulk items; and for products requiring quick delivery over long distances, such as emergency shipments. Some air carriers transport combinations of passengers, freight, and mail. Despite its expense, air transit can reduce warehousing and packaging costs and losses from theft and damage, thus helping to lower total costs (but truck transportation needed for pickup and final delivery adds to cost and transit time). Although air transport accounts for less than 1 percent of total ton-miles carried, its importance as a mode of transportation is growing. In fact, the success of many businesses is now based on the availability of overnight air delivery service provided by organizations such as UPS, FedEx, DHL, RPS Air, and the U.S. Postal Service. Amazon.com, for example, ships many products ordered online via UPS within a day of order.

Entrepreneurial Marketing

French Fries Go Back to the Future—by Rail!

Efficient physical distribution—minimizing costs and increasing value—is crucial to marketing strategy.

Back when Martin-Brower Company trucked all their frozen potato products for 600 McDonald's around Virginia, they faced skyrocketing transportation costs. They decided to go back to the future and make all of their incoming frozen fries ride the rails! Many thought it couldn't be done, because few railroads offered refrigerated service. But through cooperation with Cryo-Trans, builder of refrigerated rail cars, they created a solution that even included tracking capabilities to make inventory visible during the entire shipping process. They were able to slash transportation costs, decrease congestion at loading docks, and reduce their carbon footprint.

Today, Martin-Brower ships all its frozen products by rail and has become McDonald's largest distributor in the Americas.[c]

Pipelines, the most automated transportation mode, usually belong to the shipper and carry the shipper's products. Most pipelines carry petroleum products or chemicals. The Trans-Alaska Pipeline, owned and operated by a consortium of oil companies that includes ExxonMobil and BP Amoco, transports crude oil from remote oil-drilling sites in central Alaska to shipping terminals on the coast. Slurry pipelines carry pulverized coal, grain, or wood chips suspended in water. Pipelines move products slowly but continuously and at relatively low cost. They are dependable and minimize the problems of product damage and theft. However, contents are subject to as much as 1 percent shrinkage, usually from evaporation. Pipelines also have been a concern to environmentalists, who fear installation and leaks could harm plants and animals.

Choosing Transportation Modes

Logistics managers select a transportation mode based on the combination of cost, speed, dependability, load flexibility, accessibility, and frequency that is most appropriate for their products and generates the desired level of customer service. Table 13.3 shows relative ratings of each transportation mode by these selection criteria.

Marketers compare alternative transportation modes to determine whether benefits from a more expensive mode are worth higher costs. Companies such as Accuship can assist marketers in analyzing various transportation options. This Internet firm's software gives corporate users, such as Coca-Cola and the Home Shopping Network, information about the speed and cost of different transportation modes and allows them to order shipping and then track shipments online. Accuship processes almost a million shipments every day.[24]

Transportation
Waterway transportation is used to move heavy, nonperishable products, such as large equipment, grain, motor vehicles, and chemicals.

© AP IMAGES/SETH PERLMAN

Coordinating Transportation

To take advantage of the benefits offered by various transportation modes and compensate for deficiencies, marketers often combine and coordinate two or more modes. In recent years, **intermodal transportation,** as this integrated approach is sometimes called, has become easier because of new developments within the transportation industry. Several kinds of intermodal shipping are available. All combine the flexibility of trucking with the low cost or speed of other forms of transport. Containerization facilitates intermodal transportation by consolidating shipments into sealed containers for transport by *piggyback* (shipping that uses both truck trailers and railway flatcars), *fishyback* (truck trailers and water carriers), and *birdyback* (truck trailers and air carriers). As transportation costs have increased, intermodal shipping has gained popularity.

Specialized outsource agencies provide other forms of transport coordination. Known as **freight forwarders,** these firms combine shipments from several organizations into efficient lot sizes. Small loads (less than 500 pounds) are much more expensive to ship than full carloads or truckloads, which frequently require consolidation. Freight forwarders take small loads from various marketers, buy transport space from carriers, and arrange for goods to be delivered to buyers. Freight forwarders' profits come from the margin between the higher, less-than-carload rates they charge each marketer and the lower carload rates they themselves pay. Because large shipments require less handling, use of freight forwarders can speed delivery. Freight forwarders also can determine the most efficient carriers and routes and are useful for shipping goods to foreign markets. Some companies prefer to outsource their shipping to freight forwarders because the latter provide door-to-door service.

Another transportation innovation is the development of **megacarriers,** freight transportation companies that offer several shipment methods, including rail, truck, and air service. CSX, for example, has trains, barges, container ships, trucks, and pipelines, thus offering a multitude of transportation services. In addition, air carriers have increased their ground-transportation services. As they expand the range of transportation alternatives, carriers too put greater stress on customer service.

intermodal transportation
Two or more transportation modes used in combination

freight forwarders
Organizations that consolidate shipments from several firms into efficient lot sizes

megacarriers
Freight transportation firms that provide several modes of shipment

Legal Issues in Channel Management

The numerous federal, state, and local laws governing channel management are based on the general principle that the public is best served by protecting competition and free trade. Under the authority of such federal legislation as the Sherman Antitrust Act and the Federal Trade Commission Act, courts and regulatory agencies determine under what circumstances channel management practices violate this underlying principle and must be restricted. Although channel managers are not expected to be legal experts, they should be aware that attempts to control distribution functions may have legal repercussions. The following practices are among those frequently subject to legal restraint.

DUAL DISTRIBUTION

Earlier, we noted that some companies may use dual distribution by using two or more marketing channels to distribute the same products to the same target market. Hewlett-Packard, for example, sells computers directly to consumers through a toll-free telephone line and a website, as well as through electronics retailers such as Best Buy. Courts do not consider this practice illegal when it promotes competition. A manufacturer can also legally open its own retail outlets. But the courts view as a threat to competition a manufacturer that uses company-owned outlets to dominate or drive out of business independent retailers or distributors that handle its products. In such cases, dual distribution violates the law. To avoid this interpretation, producers should use outlet prices that do not severely undercut independent retailers' prices.

RESTRICTED SALES TERRITORIES

To tighten control over distribution of its products, a manufacturer may try to prohibit intermediaries from selling its products outside designated sales territories. Intermediaries themselves often favor this practice because it gives them exclusive territories, allowing them to avoid competition for the producer's brands within these territories. In recent years, the courts have adopted conflicting positions in regard to restricted sales territories. Although the courts have deemed restricted sales territories a restraint of trade among intermediaries handling the same brands (except for small or newly established companies), they have also held that exclusive territories can actually promote competition among dealers handling different brands. At present, the producer's intent in establishing restricted territories and the overall effect of doing so on the market must be evaluated for each individual case.

TYING AGREEMENTS

When a supplier (usually a manufacturer or franchiser) furnishes a product to a channel member with the stipulation that the channel member must purchase other products as well, a **tying agreement** exists. Suppliers may institute tying agreements to move weaker products along with more popular items, or a franchiser may tie purchase of equipment and supplies to the sale of franchises, justifying the policy as necessary for quality control and protection of the franchiser's reputation.

A related practice is *full-line forcing,* in which a supplier requires that channel members purchase the supplier's entire line to obtain any of the supplier's products. Manufacturers sometimes use full-line forcing to ensure that intermediaries accept new products and that a suitable range of products is available to customers.

tying agreement
An agreement in which a supplier furnishes a product to a channel member with the stipulation that the channel member must purchase other products as well

The courts accept tying agreements when the supplier alone can provide products of a certain quality, when the intermediary is free to carry competing products as well, and when a company has just entered the market. Most other tying agreements are considered illegal.

EXCLUSIVE DEALING

When a manufacturer forbids an intermediary to carry products of competing manufacturers, the arrangement is called **exclusive dealing.** Manufacturers receive considerable market protection in an exclusive-dealing arrangement and may cut off shipments to intermediaries that violate the agreement.

The legality of an exclusive-dealing contract is generally determined by applying three tests. If the exclusive dealing blocks competitors from as much as 10 percent of the market, if the sales revenue involved is sizable, and if the manufacturer is much larger (and thus more intimidating) than the dealer, the arrangement is considered anticompetitive.[25] If dealers and customers in a given market have access to similar products or if the exclusive-dealing contract strengthens an otherwise weak competitor, the arrangement is allowed.

REFUSAL TO DEAL

exclusive dealing
A situation in which a manufacturer forbids an intermediary to carry products of competing manufacturers

For more than 75 years, the courts have held that producers have the right to choose channel members with which they will do business (and the right to reject others). Within existing distribution channels, however, suppliers may not legally refuse to deal with wholesalers or dealers merely because these wholesalers or dealers resist policies that are anticompetitive or in restraint of trade. Suppliers are further prohibited from organizing some channel members in refusal-to-deal actions against other members that choose not to comply with illegal policies.

CHAPTER REVIEW

OBJECTIVES

Describe the foundations of supply-chain management.

The distribution component of the marketing mix focuses on the decisions and activities involved in making products available to customers when and where they want to purchase them. An important function of distribution is the joint effort of all involved organizations to be part of creating an effective supply chain, which refers to all the activities associated with the flow and transformation of products from raw materials through to the end customer. Operations management is the total set of managerial activities used by an organization to transform resource inputs into products. Logistics management involves planning, implementation, and controlling the efficient and effective flow and storage of goods, services, and information from the point of origin to consumption in order to meet customers' needs and wants. Supply management in its broadest form refers to the processes that enable the progress of value from raw material to final customer and back to redesign and final disposition. Supply-chain management therefore refers to a set of approaches used to integrate the functions of operations management, logistics management, supply management, and marketing channel management so that products and services are produced and distributed in the right quantities, to the right locations, and at the right time. The supply chain includes all entities—shippers and other firms that facilitate distribution, as well as producers, wholesalers, and retailers—that distribute products and benefit from cooperative efforts.

2 Explore the role and significance of marketing channels and supply chains.

A marketing channel, or channel of distribution, is a group of individuals and organizations that direct the flow of products from producers to customers. The major role of marketing channels is to make products available at the right time at the right place and in the right amounts. In most channels of distribution, producers and consumers are linked by marketing intermediaries. The two major types of intermediaries are retailers, which purchase products and resell them to ultimate consumers, and wholesalers, which buy and resell products to other wholesalers, retailers, and business customers.

Marketing channels serve many functions. They create time, place, and possession utilities by making products available when and where customers want them and providing customers with access to product use through sale or rental. Marketing intermediaries facilitate exchange efficiencies, often reducing the costs of exchanges by performing certain services and functions. Although some critics suggest eliminating wholesalers, the functions of the intermediaries in the marketing channel must be performed. As such, eliminating one or more intermediaries result in other organizations in the channel having to do more. Because intermediaries serve both producers and buyers, they reduce the total number of transactions that otherwise would be needed to move products from producer to the end customer.

3 Identify types of marketing channels.

Channels of distribution are broadly classified as channels for consumer products and channels for business products. Within these two broad categories, different channels are used for different products. Although consumer goods can move directly from producer to consumers, consumer channels that include wholesalers and retailers are usually more economical and knowledge efficient. Distribution of business products differs from that of consumer products in the types of channels used. A direct distribution channel is common in business marketing. Also used are channels containing industrial distributors, manufacturers' agents, and a combination of agents and distributors. Most producers have multiple or dual channels so the distribution system can be adjusted for various target markets.

4 Understand factors that influence marketing channel selection.

Selecting an appropriate marketing channel is a crucial decision for supply-chain managers. To determine which channel is most appropriate, managers must think about customer characteristics, the type of organization, product attributes, competition, environmental forces, and the availability and characteristics of intermediaries. Careful consideration of these factors will assist a supply-chain manager in selecting the correct channel.

5 Identify the intensity of market coverage.

A marketing channel is managed such that products receive appropriate market coverage. In choosing intensive distribution, producers strive to make a product available to all possible dealers. In selective distribution, only some outlets in an area are chosen to distribute a product. Exclusive distribution usually gives a single dealer rights to sell a product in a large geographic area.

6 Examine strategic issues in marketing channels, including leadership, cooperation, and conflict.

Each channel member performs a different role in the system and agrees to accept certain rights, responsibilities, rewards, and sanctions for nonconformance. Although many marketing channels are determined by consensus, some are organized and controlled by a single leader, or channel captain. A channel captain may be a producer, wholesaler, or retailer. A marketing channel functions most effectively when members cooperate; when they deviate from their roles, channel conflict can arise.

Integration of marketing channels brings various activities under one channel member's management. Vertical integration combines two or more stages of the channel under one management. The vertical marketing system (VMS) is managed centrally for the mutual benefit of all channel members. Vertical marketing systems may be corporate, administered, or contractual. Horizontal integration combines institutions at the same level of channel operation under a single management.

7 Examine physical distribution as a part of supply-chain management.

Physical distribution, or logistics, refers to the activities used to move products from producers to customers and other end users. These activities include order processing, inventory management, materials handling, warehousing, and transportation. An efficient physical distribution system is an important component of an overall marketing strategy because it can decrease costs and increase customer satisfaction. Within the marketing channel, physical distribution activities are often performed by a wholesaler, but they may also be performed by a producer or retailer or outsourced to a third party. Efficient physical distribution systems can decrease costs and transit time while increasing customer service.

Order processing is the receipt and transmission of sales order information. It consists of three main tasks—order entry, order handling, and order delivery—which may be done manually but are more often handled through electronic data interchange systems. Inventory management involves developing and maintaining adequate assortments of products to meet customers' needs. Logistics managers must strive to find the optimal level of inventory to satisfy customer needs while keeping costs down. Materials handling, the physical handling of products, is a crucial element in warehousing and transporting products. Warehousing involves the design and operation of facilities for storing and moving goods; such facilities may be privately owned or public. Transportation, the movement of products from where they are made to where they are purchased and used, is the most expensive physical distribution function. The basic modes of transporting goods include railroads, trucks, waterways, airways, and pipelines.

Explore legal issues in channel management.

Federal, state, and local laws regulate channel management to protect competition and free trade. Courts may prohibit or permit a practice depending on whether it violates this underlying principle. Procompetitive legislation applies to distribution practices. Channel management practices frequently subject to legal restraint include dual distribution, restricted sales territories, tying agreements, exclusive dealing, and refusal to deal. When these practices strengthen weak competitors or increase competition among dealers, they may be permitted; in most other cases, when competition may be weakened considerably, they are deemed illegal.

Please visit the student website at www.cengage.com/international for quizzes and games that will help you prepare for exams and help achieve the grade you want.

KEY CONCEPTS

distribution
supply chain
operations management
logistics management
supply management
supply-chain management
marketing channel
marketing intermediaries
industrial distributor
dual distribution
strategic channel alliance
intensive distribution
selective distribution
exclusive distribution
channel captain
channel power
vertical channel integration
vertical marketing systems (VMSs)
horizontal channel integration
physical distribution
outsourcing
cycle time
order processing
electronic data interchange (EDI)
inventory management
just-in-time (JIT)
materials handling
warehousing
private warehouses
public warehouses
distribution centers
transportation
intermodal transportation
freight forwarders
megacarriers
tying agreement
exclusive dealing

ISSUES FOR DISCUSSION AND REVIEW

1. Define supply-chain management. Why is it important?
2. Describe the major functions of marketing channels. Why are these functions better accomplished through the combined efforts of channel members?
3. List several reasons consumers often blame intermediaries for distribution inefficiencies.
4. Compare and contrast the four major types of marketing channels for consumer products. Through which type of channel is each of the following products most likely to be distributed?
   a. New automobiles
   b. Saltine crackers
   c. Cut-your-own Christmas trees
   d. New textbooks
   e. Sofas
   f. Soft drinks
5. Outline the four most common channels for business products. Describe the products or situations that lead marketers to choose each channel.
6. Describe an industrial distributor. What types of products are marketed through an industrial distributor?
7. Under what conditions is a producer most likely to use more than one marketing channel?
8. Identify and describe the factors that may influence marketing channel selection decisions.
9. Explain the differences among intensive, selective, and exclusive methods of distribution.
10. "Channel cooperation requires that members support the overall channel goals to achieve individual goals." Comment on this statement.
11. Explain the major characteristics of each of the three types of vertical marketing systems (VMSs): corporate, administered, and contractual.
12. Discuss the cost and service tradeoffs involved in developing a physical distribution system.
13. What are the main tasks involved in order processing?
14. Explain the tradeoffs inventory managers face when reordering products or supplies. How is the reorder point computed?
15. Explain the major differences between private and public warehouses. How do they differ from a distribution center?
16. Compare and contrast the five major transportation modes in terms of cost, speed, and dependability.
17. Under what conditions are tying agreements, exclusive dealing, and dual distribution judged illegal?

MARKETING APPLICATIONS

1. *Supply-chain management* involves long-term partnerships among channel members working together to reduce inefficiencies, costs, and redundancies and to develop innovative approaches to satisfy customers. Select one of the following companies and explain how supply-chain management could increase marketing productivity.
   a. Dell
   b. FedEx
   c. Nike
   d. Taco Bell
2. Marketers can select from three major levels of marketing coverage when determining the number and kinds of outlets in which to sell a product: intensive, selective, or exclusive distribution. Characteristics of the product and its target market determine the intensity of coverage a product should receive. Indicate the intensity level best suited for the following products, and explain why it is appropriate.
   a. Personal computer
   b. Deodorant
   c. Canon digital cameras
   d. Nike athletic shoes

3. Describe the decision process you might go through if you were attempting to determine the most appropriate distribution channel for one of the following:
   a. Shotguns for hunters
   b. Women's lingerie
   c. Telephone systems for small businesses
   d. Toy trucks for 2-year-olds

4. Assume that you are responsible for the physical distribution of computers at a Web-based company. What would you do to ensure product availability, timely delivery, and quality service for your customers?

ONLINE EXERCISE

5. Distribution bottlenecks can be an expensive problem for any business. Trying to prevent such problems is iSuppli, an Internet supply-chain management tool that links all members of a supply chain, from the supplier's system to the retailer's storefront system. Learn more about this innovative tool at http://www.isuppli.com.
   a. Does iSuppli represent a new type of marketing channel? Why or why not?
   b. Why would firms be cautious when deciding whether to use iSuppli?
   c. Do you think iSuppli represents the future of supply-chain management? Why or why not?

DEVELOPING YOUR MARKETING PLAN

One of the key components in a successful marketing strategy is the plan for getting the products to your customer. In order to make the best decisions about where, when, and how your products will be made available to the customer, you will need to know more about how these distribution decisions relate to other marketing-mix elements in your marketing plan. To assist you in relating the information in this chapter to your marketing plan, consider the following issues:

1. Marketing intermediaries perform many activities. Using Table 13.2 as a guide, discuss the types of activities where a channel member could provide needed assistance.

2. Using Figure 13.2 (or 13.3 if your product is a business product), determine which of the channel distribution paths is most appropriate for your product. Given the nature of your product, could it be distributed through more than one of these paths?

3. Determine the level of distribution intensity that is appropriate for your product. Consider the characteristics of your target market(s), the product attributes, and environmental factors in your deliberation.

4. Discuss the physical functions that will be required for distributing your product, focusing on materials handling, warehousing, and transportation.

The information obtained from these questions should assist you in developing various aspects of your marketing plan found in the *Interactive Marketing Plan* exercise.

VIDEO CASE 13

Netflix Looks for the Next High-Tech Distribution Channel

Netflix, founded in 1997, was originally nothing more than an online version of a traditional video rental store. Customers visited the Netflix website, clicked to select a DVD, and paid $4, along with a $2 shipping fee and late fees, if applicable, for each rental. The company quickly realized that this model was not very cost-competitive or efficient compared to in-store rental businesses such as Blockbuster. By 1999, Netflix had switched to an all-subscription business renting DVDs by mail and using both technological advances and ever-wider selection in its quest to dominate the $8 billion movie rental industry.

Today, Netflix's members can subscribe to various packages based on the number of DVDs they want to rent per month. The least expensive subscription package includes two rentals per month, while the most expensive offers unlimited rentals with eight DVDs at home at any given time. Members click to create a list of movies they would like to see in order of preference, and Netflix delivers them by mail in its distinctive red envelopes. Customers can keep each DVD as long as they like with no late fees, but they are not sent their next choice until the previous choice has been received at one of Netflix's 55 distribution centers.

As the company's services become more popular, it is expanding its rental collection to include classic movies, new and classic television shows, and DVD formats such as Blu-Ray. In all, Netflix's rental collection includes 100,000 DVDs. To stay ahead of competitors such as Blockbuster, which allow customers to rent online or in a local store, Netflix has also added a "Play Instantly" feature. Now subscribers can download and immediately watch any of 12,000 movies and programs from the Netflix website.

In addition, Netflix offers direct-to-television streaming through the Roku digital video player, which costs about $100. Apple and Vudu offer similar products, but their boxes are more expensive than the Roku. Encouraging customers to watch instantly is highly cost-effective for Netflix—its cost for downloading a movie is about 6 cents, compared to 80 cents for mailing a movie to and from subscribers.

Blockbuster, a company that has been struggling to reinvent itself as consumers move away from renting out of brick-and-mortar stores, continues to be one of Netflix's toughest competitors now that it offers both in-store and online rentals. Another competitor is Redbox, which operates 12,000 DVD vending machines in supermarkets, McDonald's restaurants, and other retail locations. Customers simply swipe a credit or debit card, select a DVD to rent, and pay $1 per night until they return the DVD (to any Redbox location).

Despite the competition, Netflix's rising popularity shows no sign of abating. The company serves more than 12 million subscribers and rings up $1.3 billion in annual revenue from all its rental activities. With ever-evolving technologies improving the distribution process and the customer experience, the company sees plenty of room to grow in the coming years.

QUESTIONS FOR DISCUSSION

1. Why was Netflix's rent-by-mail distribution strategy a competitive advantage over traditional brick-and-mortar video rental competitors?
2. What technological innovations might strengthen or threaten Netflix's distribution practices?
3. How much channel power do you think Netflix has and why is this important?

Dan Frommer, "Netflix Pays About a Nickel to Stream Each Movie Online," *The Business Insider*, March 18, 2009, http://www.businessinsider.com/netflix-pays-about-a-nickel-to-stream-each-move-online-2009-3; *Netflix*, www.netflix.com; Associated Press Staff Writer, "Movie Rental Giant Netflix Rolls Out Its Post-postal Plan," *New York Daily News*, May 21, 2008, http://www.nydailynews.com/money/2008/05/21/2008-05-21_movie_rental_giant_netflix_rolls_out_its-1.html; Associated Press Staff Writer, "Microsoft's Xbox 360 to Stream Netflix movies," *New York Daily News*, July 14, 2008, http://www.nydailynews.com/money/2008/07/14/2008-07-14_ microsofts_xbox_360_to_stream_netflix_mo.html.

Retailing, Direct Marketing, and Wholesaling

CHAPTER 14

© RICK WILKING/REUTERS/LANDOV

TARGET REFOCUSES ITS RETAILING STRATEGY

A new era of retailing began in 1962, when Target, Walmart, and Kmart all opened as discount stores. Target grew so quickly that by 1975, it was bringing in more sales revenue than its parent company's department stores. Discount retailing continued to gain momentum all over the United States, and in 2000, the parent company renamed itself Target.

Rather than trying to be all things to all shoppers, Target has differentiated itself on the basis of good design at discount prices. For example, architect Michael Graves has developed stylish housewares and home décor products for Target. Even the ClearRx bottles in which Target sells prescription drugs have an entirely new look. In short, the retailer's red-and-white bull's-eye logo has come to stand for "cheap chic."

Target also uses limited-time "pop-up" shops to promote certain product categories or specific designers. In business for a few days or as long as a few weeks, these temporary stand-alone shops give Target a brief but high-profile presence to attract targeted customer segments.

However, recent economic turmoil and a decline in consumer spending have cut into both sales and profits. In response, the company is opening fewer stores and, to compete more effectively with Walmart, intensified its marketing focus on low prices. "The customer is very cash-strapped right now and in some ways, our greatest strength has become something of a challenge," said Target's president. "During these tough times, some of our consumers don't want to be tempted as much as they have in the past." The company is also expanding its offerings of fresh food and basic household products. Will this retail refocusing encourage customers to shop Target more often?[1]

OBJECTIVES:

1. Understand the purpose and function of retailers in the marketing channel.
2. Identify the major types of retailers.
3. Explore strategic issues in retailing.
4. Recognize the various forms of direct marketing and selling.
5. Examine franchising and its benefits and weaknesses.
6. Understand the nature and functions of wholesalers.
7. Understand how wholesalers are classified.

Retailers such as Target are the most visible and accessible marketing-channel members to consumers. They are an important link in the marketing channel because they are both marketers for and customers of producers and wholesalers. They perform many supply-chain functions, such as buying, selling, grading, risk taking, and developing and maintaining information databases about customers. Retailers are in a strategic position to develop relationships with consumers and partnerships with producers and intermediaries in the marketing channel.

In this chapter, we examine the nature of retailing, direct marketing, and wholesaling and their importance in supplying consumers with goods and services. First, we explore the major types of retail stores and consider strategic issues in retailing: location, retail positioning, store image, scrambled merchandising, and the wheel of retailing. Next, we discuss direct marketing, including catalog marketing, direct response marketing, telemarketing, television home shopping, online retailing, and direct selling. Then we look at franchising, a retailing form that continues to grow in popularity. Finally, we examine the importance of wholesalers in marketing channels, including their functions and classifications.

Retailing

Retailing includes all transactions in which the buyer intends to consume the product through personal, family, or household use. Buyers in retail transactions are therefore the ultimate consumers. A **retailer** is an organization that purchases products for the purpose of reselling them to ultimate consumers. Although most retailers' sales are made directly to the consumer, nonretail transactions occur occasionally when retailers sell products to other businesses. Retailing often takes place in stores or service establishments, but it also occurs through direct selling, direct marketing, and vending machines outside stores.

Retailing is important to the national economy. Approximately 1.1 million retailers operate in the United States.[2] This number has remained relatively constant for the past 25 years, but sales volume has increased more than fourfold. Most personal income is spent in retail stores, and nearly one of every eight people employed in the United States works in a retail operation.

Retailers add value, provide services, and assist in making product selections. They can enhance the value of products by making buyers' shopping experiences more convenient, as in home shopping. Through their locations, retailers can facilitate comparison shopping; for example, car dealerships often cluster in the same general vicinity, as do furniture stores. Product value is also enhanced when retailers offer services, such as technical advice, delivery, credit, and repair. Finally, retail sales personnel can demonstrate to customers how products can satisfy their needs or solve problems.

The value added by retailers is significant for both producers and ultimate consumers. Retailers are the critical link between producers and ultimate consumers because they provide the environment in which exchanges with ultimate consumers occur. Ultimate consumers benefit through retailers' performance of marketing functions that result in the availability of broader arrays of products. Retailers play a major role in creating time, place, and possession utility and, in some cases, form utility.

Leading retailers such as Walmart, Home Depot, Macy's, Staples, and Best Buy offer consumers a place to browse and compare merchandise to find just what they need. However, such traditional retailing is being challenged by direct marketing channels that provide home shopping through catalogs, television, and the Internet. "Bricks and mortar" retailers are responding to this change in the retail environment in various ways. Walmart, for example, has established a website for online shopping and joined forces with fast-food giants McDonald's and KFC to attract consumers and offer them the added convenience of eating where they shop.

retailing
All transactions in which the buyer intends to consume the product through personal, family, or household use

retailer
An organization that purchases products for the purpose of reselling them to ultimate consumers

New store formats and advances in information technology are making the retail environment highly dynamic and competitive. Instant-messaging technology is enabling online retailers to converse in real time with customers so that they don't click away to another site. For example, shoppers on the Lands' End website can click to chat, via keyboard, directly with a customer-service representative about sizes, colors, or other product details. The key to success in retailing is to have a strong customer focus with a retail strategy that provides the level of service, product quality, and innovation that consumers desire. Partnerships among noncompeting retailers and other marketing-channel members are providing new opportunities for retailers. For example, airports are leasing space to retailers such as The Sharper Image, McDonald's, Sunglass Hut, and The Body Shop. Kroger and Nordstrom have developed joint co-branded credit cards that offer rebates to customers at participating stores.

SNAPSHOT

U.S. Bureau of the Census, *Statistical Abstract of the United States, 2008* (Washington, DC: U.S. Government Printing Office, 2007), pp. 431, 496, 647, 650.

Retailers are also finding global opportunities. For example, both McDonald's and Gap Inc. are now opening more international stores than domestic ones, a trend that is likely to continue for the foreseeable future. Starbucks has opened hundreds of stores in Japan and Southeast Asia. Increasingly, retailers from abroad, such as IKEA, Zara, and BP, are opening stores in the United States.

MAJOR TYPES OF RETAIL STORES

Many types of retail stores exist. One way to classify them is by the breadth of products offered. Two general categories include general merchandise retailers and specialty retailers.

General Merchandise Retailers

A retail establishment that offers a variety of product lines stocked in considerable depth is referred to as a **general merchandise retailer**. The types of product offerings, mixes of customer services, and operating styles of retailers in this category vary considerably. The primary types of general merchandise retailers are department stores, discount stores, convenience stores, supermarkets, superstores, hypermarkets, warehouse clubs, and warehouse showrooms (see Table 14.1).

general merchandise retailer
A retail establishment that offers a variety of product lines that are stocked in considerable depth

DEPARTMENT STORES. **Department stores** are large retail organizations characterized by wide product mixes and organized into separate departments, such as cosmetics, housewares, apparel, home furnishings, and appliances, to facilitate marketing and internal management. Often each department functions as a self-contained business, and buyers for individual departments are fairly autonomous. Typical department stores, such as Macy's, Sears, Dillard's, and Neiman Marcus, obtain a large proportion of sales from apparel, accessories, and cosmetics. Other products that these stores carry include gift items, luggage, electronics, home accessories, and sports equipment. Some department stores offer services such as automobile insurance, hair care, income tax preparation, and travel and optical services. In some cases, space for these specialized services is leased out, with proprietors managing their own operations and paying rent to the department store. Many department stores also sell products through their websites.

department stores
Large retail organizations characterized by wide product mixes and organized into separate departments to facilitate marketing and internal management

TABLE 14.1 General Merchandise Retailers

Type of Retailer	Description	Examples
Department store	Large organization offering wide product mix and organized into separate departments	Macy's, Sears, JCPenney
Discount store	Self-service general merchandise store offering brand name and private brand products at low prices	Walmart, Target, Kmart
Convenience store	Small self-service store offering narrow product assortment in convenient locations	7-Eleven, Circle K, Stripes
Supermarket	Self-service store offering complete line of food products and some nonfood products	Kroger, Albertsons, Winn-Dixie
Superstore	Giant outlet offering all food and nonfood products found in supermarkets, as well as most routinely purchased products	Walmart Supercenters
Hypermarket	Combination supermarket and discount store; larger than a superstore	Carrefour
Warehouse club	Large-scale members-only establishments combining cash-and-carry wholesaling with discount retailing	Sam's Club, Costco
Warehouse showroom	Facility in a large, low-cost building with large on-premises inventories and minimal service	IKEA

© ROBERT HARDING PICTURE LIBRARY LTD/ALAMY

Department Store
Because of its size, wide product mix, and services provided, Macy's is classified as a department store.

Department stores are somewhat service-oriented. Their total product may include credit, delivery, personal assistance, merchandise returns, and a pleasant atmosphere. Although some so-called department stores are actually large, departmentalized specialty stores, most department stores are shopping stores. Consumers can compare price, quality, and service at one store with those at competing stores. Along with large discount stores, department stores are often considered retailing leaders in a community and are found in most places with populations of more than 50,000.

DISCOUNT STORES. In recent years, department stores have been losing market share to discount stores. **Discount stores** are self-service, general merchandise outlets that regularly offer brand name and private brand products at low prices. Discounters accept lower margins than conventional retailers in exchange for high sales volume. To keep inventory turnover high, they carry a wide but carefully selected assortment of products, from appliances to housewares and clothing. Major discount establishments also offer food products, toys, automotive services, garden supplies, and sports equipment. Walmart and Target are the two largest discount stores. Walmart has grown to 7,250 stores worldwide and brings in more than $378 billion in sales annually.[3] During a recent economic downturn, discount stores like Bealls Outlet Stores, Ross Stores, and Dollar Stores saw an opportunity to provide customers with low-priced value products. Department stores and some independent apparel stores experienced reduced sales and profits during this time.[4] Some discounters such as Meijer, Inc., are regional organizations. Most operate in large (50,000 to 80,000 square feet), no-frills facilities. Discount stores usually offer everyday low prices rather than relying on sales events.

CONVENIENCE STORES. A **convenience store** is a small self-service store that is open long hours and carries a narrow assortment of products, usually convenience items such as soft drinks and other beverages, snacks, newspapers, tobacco, and gasoline, as well as services such as automated teller machines. The primary product offered by the "corner store" is convenience. According to the National Association of Convenience Stores, there are 146,294 convenience stores in the United States with 1.5 million employees. They are typically less than 5,000 square feet, and they are open 24 hours a day, 7 days a week, and stock about 500 items. In addition to many national chains, there are many family-owned independent convenience stores in operation.[5]

SUPERMARKETS. **Supermarkets** are large self-service stores that carry a complete line of food products, as well as some nonfood products such as cosmetics and nonprescription drugs. Supermarkets are arranged in departments for maximum efficiency in stocking and handling products but have central checkout facilities. They offer lower prices than smaller neighborhood grocery stores, usually provide free parking, and also may cash checks. Today, consumers make more than three-quarters of all grocery purchases in supermarkets. Even so, supermarkets' total share of the food market is declining because consumers now have widely varying food preferences and buying habits, and in many communities, shoppers can choose from several convenience stores, discount stores, and specialty food stores, as well as a wide variety of restaurants. Walmart, for example, expects to generate in its "supermarket-type" stores more revenue than the top three U.S. supermarket chains—Kroger, Albertsons, and Safeway—combined.

SUPERSTORES. **Superstores**, which originated in Europe, are giant retail outlets that carry not only food and nonfood products ordinarily found in supermarkets but also routinely purchased consumer products. Superstores combine features of discount stores and supermarkets. Examples include Walmart Supercenters and some Kroger stores. Besides a complete food line, superstores sell housewares, hardware, small appliances, clothing, personal-care products, garden products, and tires—about four times as many items as supermarkets. Services available at superstores include dry cleaning, automotive repair, check cashing, bill paying, and snack bars. To cut handling and inventory costs, they use sophisticated operating techniques and often have tall shelving that displays entire assortments of products. Superstores can have an area of as much as 200,000 square feet (compared with 20,000 square feet in traditional supermarkets). Sales volume is two to three times that of supermarkets partly because locations near good transportation networks help to generate the in-store traffic needed for profitability. Costco, Walgreens, Safeway, and Kroger boast weekly shopper counts of 20 million, 30 million, 44 million, and 68 million, respectively. Passing through the doors of Walmart locations each week are 150 million people.[6]

HYPERMARKETS. **Hypermarkets** combine supermarket and discount store shopping in one location. Larger than superstores, they range from 225,000 to 325,000 square feet and offer 45,000 to 60,000 different types of low-priced products. They commonly allocate 40 to 50 percent of their space to grocery products and the remainder to general merchandise, including athletic shoes, designer jeans, and other apparel; refrigerators, televisions, and other appliances; housewares; cameras; toys; jewelry; hardware; and automotive supplies. Many lease space to noncompeting businesses such as banks, optical shops, and fast-food restaurants. All hypermarkets focus on low prices and vast selections. Although Kmart, Walmart, and Carrefour (a French retailer) have operated hypermarkets in the United States, most of these stores were unsuccessful and closed. Such stores may be too big for time-constrained U.S. shoppers. However, hypermarkets are more successful in Europe, South America, and Mexico.

WAREHOUSE CLUBS. **Warehouse clubs**, a rapidly growing form of mass merchandising, are large-scale members-only selling operations combining cash-and-carry wholesaling with

discount stores
Self-service, general merchandise stores offering brand name and private brand products at low prices

convenience store
A small self-service store that is open long hours and carries a narrow assortment of products, usually convenience items

supermarkets
Large, self-service stores that carry a complete line of food products, along with some nonfood products

superstores
Giant retail outlets that carry food and nonfood products found in supermarkets, as well as most routinely purchased consumer products

hypermarkets
Stores that combine supermarket and discount store shopping in one location

warehouse clubs
Large-scale members-only establishments that combine features of cash-and-carry wholesaling with discount retailing

warehouse showrooms Retail facilities in large, low-cost buildings with large on-premises inventories and minimal services

traditional specialty retailers Stores that carry a narrow product mix with deep product lines

discount retailing. Sometimes called *buying clubs,* warehouse clubs offer the same types of products as discount stores but in a limited range of sizes and styles. Whereas most discount stores carry around 40,000 items, a warehouse club handles only 3,500 to 5,000 products, usually acknowledged brand leaders. Sam's Club stores, for example, stock about 4,000 items, with 1,400 available most of the time and the rest being one-time buys. Costco leads the warehouse club industry with sales of $72.5 billion. Sam's Club is second with nearly $45 billion in store sales. A third company, BJ's Wholesale Club, which operates in the Northeast and Florida, has a much smaller market.[7] All these establishments offer a broad product mix, including food, beverages, books, appliances, housewares, automotive parts, hardware, and furniture.

To keep prices lower than those of supermarkets and discount stores, warehouse clubs provide few services. They generally do not advertise, except through direct mail. Their facilities, often located in industrial areas, have concrete floors and aisles wide enough for forklifts. Merchandise is stacked on pallets or displayed on pipe racks. Customers must transport purchases themselves. Warehouse clubs appeal to many price-conscious consumers and small retailers unable to obtain wholesaling services from large distributors. The average warehouse club shopper has more education, a higher income, and a larger household than the average supermarket shopper.

WAREHOUSE SHOWROOMS. **Warehouse showrooms** are retail facilities with five basic characteristics: large, low-cost buildings; warehouse materials-handling technology; vertical merchandise displays; large on-premises inventories; and minimal services. IKEA, a Swedish company, sells furniture, household goods, and kitchen accessories in warehouse showrooms and through catalogs around the world, including China and Russia. These high-volume, low-overhead operations stress fewer personnel and services. Lower costs are possible because some marketing functions have been shifted to consumers, who must transport, finance, and perhaps store larger quantities of products. Most consumers carry away purchases in the manufacturer's carton, although stores will deliver for a fee.

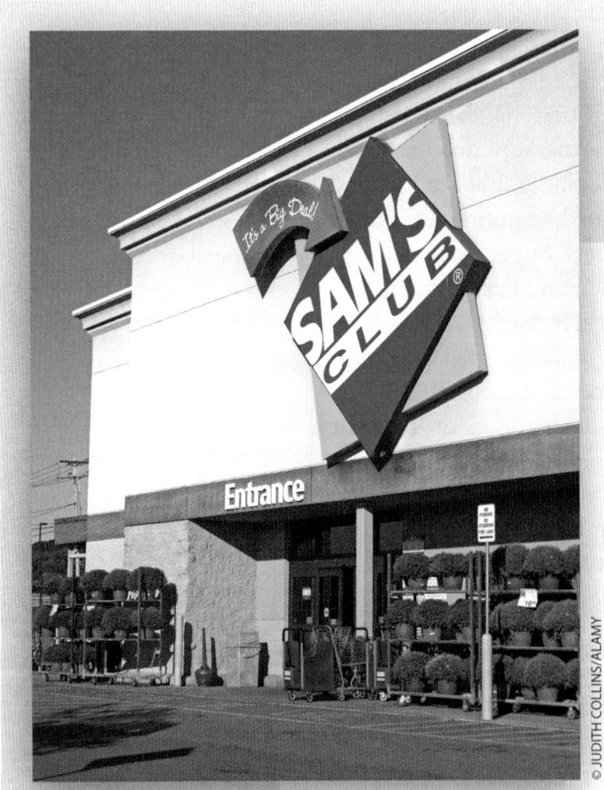

© JUDITH COLLINS/ALAMY

Warehouse Club
Sam's Club is a warehouse club that markets many product lines. Most of Sam's Club product lines have limited depth.

Specialty Retailers

In contrast to general merchandise retailers with their broad product mixes, specialty retailers emphasize narrow and deep assortments. Despite their name, specialty retailers do not sell specialty items (except when specialty goods complement the overall product mix). Instead, they offer substantial assortments in a few product lines. We examine three types of specialty retailers: traditional specialty retailers, category killers, and off-price retailers.

Traditional specialty retailers are stores that carry a narrow product mix with deep product lines. Sometimes called *limited-line retailers,* they may be referred to as *single-line retailers* if they carry unusual depth in one main product category. Traditional specialty retailers commonly sell shopping products such as apparel, jewelry, sporting goods, fabrics, computers, toys, and pet supplies. The Limited, Radio Shack, Hickory Farms, Gap Inc., and Foot Locker are examples of retailers offering limited product lines but great depth within those lines. Many traditional specialty retailers are small businesses with just one or a few outlets.

Because they are usually small, specialty stores may have high costs in proportion to sales, and satisfying customers may require carrying some products with low turnover rates. However, these stores sometimes obtain lower prices from suppliers by purchasing limited lines of merchandise in large quantities. Successful traditional specialty stores understand their customer types and know what products to carry, thus reducing the risk of unsold merchandise. Traditional specialty stores usually offer better selections and more sales expertise than department stores, their main competitors. By capitalizing on fashion, service, personnel, atmosphere, and location, these retailers position themselves strategically to attract customers in specific market segments. Tiffany & Co., for example, put its contemporary foot forward with a new, smaller retail format. The 2,600-square-foot store spotlights Tiffany pieces in a comfortable, airy environment meant to exemplify the opposite of buttoned-down selling. Customers are encouraged to try on the jewelry, with price points beginning at $80.[8]

© AP IMAGES/PRNEWSFOTO/ANN TAYLOR

Traditional Specialty Store
Traditional specialty stores, like Ann Taylor, have narrow but deep product mixes.

Over the last 15 years, a new breed of specialty retailer, the category killer, has evolved. A **category killer** is a very large specialty store that concentrates on a major product category and competes on the basis of low prices and enormous product availability. These stores are referred to as category killers because they expand rapidly and gain sizable market shares, taking business away from smaller, high-cost retail outlets. Examples of category killers include Home Depot and Lowe's (home-improvement chains); Staples, Office Depot, and OfficeMax (office-supply chains); Borders and Barnes & Noble (booksellers); PETCO and PetSmart (pet-supply chains); and Best Buy (consumer electronics).

Off-price retailers are stores that buy manufacturers' seconds, overruns, returns, and off-season production runs at below-wholesale prices for resale to consumers at deep discounts. Unlike true discount stores, which pay regular wholesale prices for goods and usually carry second-line brand names, off-price retailers offer limited lines of national-brand and designer merchandise, usually clothing, shoes, or housewares. The number of off-price retailers such as T.J. Maxx, Marshalls, Stein Mart, and Burlington Coat Factory has grown since the mid-1980s. Off-price stores charge 20 to 50 percent less than do department stores for comparable merchandise but offer few customer services. They often feature community dressing rooms and central checkout counters. Some of these stores do not take returns or allow exchanges. Off-price stores may or may not sell goods with the original labels intact. They turn over their inventory nine to twelve times a year, three times as often as traditional specialty stores. They compete with department stores for the same customers: price-conscious customers who are knowledgeable about brand names.

category killer
A very large specialty store concentrating on a major product category and competing on the basis of low prices and product availability

STRATEGIC ISSUES IN RETAILING

Whereas most business purchases are based on economic planning and necessity, consumer purchases may result from social and psychological influences. Because consumers shop for various reasons—to search for specific items, escape boredom, or learn about something new—retailers must do more than simply fill space with merchandise. They must make desired products available, create stimulating shopping environments, and develop marketing strategies that increase store patronage. In this section we discuss how store location, retail positioning, store image, and category management are used to help achieve retailing objectives.

off-price retailers
Stores that buy manufacturers' seconds, overruns, returns, and off-season merchandise for resale to consumers at deep discounts

Entrepreneurial Marketing

Tara's Organic Ice Cream: A Growing Niche Business

When Santa Fe artist Tara Esperanza's friends gave her a home ice cream maker, they had no idea how it would inspire her creativity and entrepreneurial spirit. Tara experimented with unique flavors such as lemongrass, lavender, and garam masala, which friends willingly tasted, and told her, "You should sell this!" Tara did and became New Mexico's Emerging Entrepreneur of the Year selling organic ice cream in Santa Fe. Good distribution is necessary for success, so she also started selling her product to retailers and online.

Tara emphasizes environmentally friendly business practices. In addition to using all organic ingredients, her new shop in Berkeley, CA (where she moved to be closer to her source of organic dairy products) serves ice cream in compostable containers with spoons made from potato starch.[a]

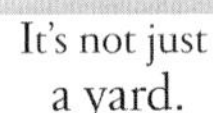

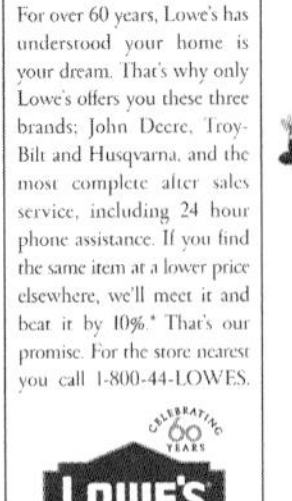

COURTESY: LOWE'S COMPANIES, INC.

Category Killer
Sometimes, stores, like Lowe's, are referred to as category killers because of their enormous product mixes and their relatively low prices.

Location, Location, Location

Location, the least flexible of the strategic retailing issues, is one of the most important because location dictates the limited geographic trading area from which a store draws its customers. Retailers consider various factors when evaluating potential locations, including location of the firm's target market within the trading area, kinds of products being sold, availability of public transportation, customer characteristics, and competitors' locations. In choosing a location, a retailer evaluates the relative ease of movement to and from the site, including factors such as pedestrian and vehicular traffic, parking, and transportation. Retailers also evaluate the characteristics of the site itself: types of stores in the area; size, shape, and visibility of the lot or building under consideration; and rental, leasing, or ownership terms. Retailers look for compatibility with nearby retailers because stores that complement one another draw more customers for everyone.

Many retailers choose to locate in downtown central business districts, whereas others prefer sites within various types of planned shopping centers. Some retailers, including Toys"R"Us, Walmart, Home Depot, and many fast-food restaurants, opt for freestanding structures that are not connected to other buildings, but many chain stores are found in planned shopping centers and malls. Some retailers choose to locate in less orthodox settings. McDonald's, for example, has opened several stores inside hospitals, whereas Subway has franchise locations inside churches, laundromats, and hospitals.[9] Planned shopping centers include neighborhood, community, regional, superregional, lifestyle, and power shopping centers.

Neighborhood shopping centers usually consist of several small convenience and specialty stores, such as small grocery stores, gas stations, and fast-food restaurants. Many of these retailers consider their target markets to be consumers who live within two to three miles of their stores, or ten minutes' driving time. Because most purchases are based on convenience or personal contact, there is usually little coordination of selling efforts within a neighborhood shopping center. Generally, product mixes consist of essential products, and depth of the product lines is limited.

Community shopping centers include one or two department stores and some specialty stores, as well as convenience stores. They draw consumers looking for shopping and specialty products not available in neighborhood shopping centers. Because these centers serve larger geographic areas, consumers must drive longer distances to community shopping centers than to neighborhood centers. Community shopping centers are planned and coordinated to attract shoppers. Special events, such as art exhibits, automobile shows, and sidewalk sales, stimulate traffic. Managers of community shopping centers look for tenants that complement the centers' total assortment of products. Such centers have wide product mixes and deep product lines.

Regional shopping centers usually have the largest department stores, the widest product mixes, and the deepest product lines of all shopping centers. Many shopping malls are regional shopping centers, although some are community shopping centers. With 150,000 or more consumers in their target market, regional shopping centers must have well-coordinated management and marketing activities. Target markets may include consumers traveling from a distance to find products and prices not available in their hometowns. Because of the expense of leasing space in regional shopping centers, tenants are more likely to be national chains than small, independent stores. Large centers usually advertise, have special events, furnish transportation to some consumer groups, maintain their own security forces, and carefully select the mix of stores. The largest of these centers, sometimes called **superregional shopping centers**, have the widest and deepest product mixes and attract customers from many miles away. Superregional centers often have special attractions beyond stores, such as skating rinks, amusement centers, or upscale restaurants. Mall of America, in the Minneapolis area, is the largest shopping mall in the United States with 520 stores, including Nordstrom and Bloomingdale's, and 50 restaurants. The shopping center also includes a walk-through aquarium, museum, theme parks, 14-screen movie theater, hotels, and many special events.[10]

Retail Location
Many retailers, like McDonald's, spend considerable time and resources to place stores in the right locations.

With traditional mall sales declining, some shopping center developers are looking to new formats that differ significantly from traditional shopping centers. A **lifestyle shopping center** is typically an open-air shopping center that features upscale specialty, dining, and entertainment stores, usually owned by national chains. They are often located near affluent neighborhoods and may have fountains, benches, and other amenities that encourage "casual browsing." Indeed, architectural design is an important aspect of these "minicities," which may include urban streets or parks, and is intended to encourage consumer loyalty by creating a sense of place. Some lifestyle centers are designed to resemble traditional "Main Street" shopping centers or may have a central theme evidenced by architecture.[11]

Some shopping center developers are bypassing the traditional department store anchor and combining off-price stores and small stores with category killers in **power shopping center** formats. These centers may be anchored by a store such as Gap Inc., Toys"R"Us, PetSmart, and Home Depot. The number of power shopping centers is growing, resulting in a variety of formats vying for the same retail dollar.

Factory outlet malls feature discount and factory outlet stores carrying traditional manufacturer brands, such as Quicksilver, Liz Claiborne, Reebok, and Le Creuset. Some outlet centers feature upscale products. Manufacturers own these stores and make a special effort to avoid conflict with traditional retailers of their products. Manufacturers claim that their stores are in noncompetitive locations; indeed, most factory outlet centers are located outside metropolitan areas. Not all factory outlets stock closeouts and irregulars, but most avoid comparison with discount houses. Factory outlet centers attract value-conscious customers seeking quality and major brand names. They operate in much the same way as regional shopping centers but usually draw customers, some of which may be tourists, from a larger shopping radius. Promotional activity is at the heart of these shopping centers. Craft and antique shows, contests, and special events attract a great deal of traffic.

neighborhood shopping centers
Shopping centers usually consisting of several small convenience and specialty stores

community shopping centers
Shopping centers with one or two department stores, some specialty stores, and convenience stores

regional shopping centers
A type of shopping center with the largest department stores, the widest product mix, and the deepest product lines of all shopping centers

Lifestyle Shopping Centers
Many lifestyle shopping centers consist of stores such as Banana Republic, Apple Store, and Ann Taylor Lofts.

© AP PHOTO/JERRY S. MENDOZA

superregional shopping centers
A type of shopping center with the widest and deepest product mixes that attracts customers from many miles away

lifestyle shopping centers
A type of shopping center that is typically open air and features upscale specialty, dining, and entertainment stores

power shopping centers
A type of shopping center that combines off-price stores with category killers

retail positioning
Identifying an unserved or underserved market segment and serving it through a strategy that distinguishes the retailer from others in the minds of consumers in that segment

atmospherics
The physical elements in a store's design that appeal to consumers' emotions and encourage buying

Retail Positioning

The large variety of shopping centers and the expansion of product offerings by traditional stores have intensified retailing competition. Retail positioning is therefore an important consideration. **Retail positioning** involves identifying an unserved or underserved market segment and serving it through a strategy that distinguishes the retailer from others in the minds of those customers. For example, Payless ShoeSource, a specialty store chain, has built a reputation for providing a wide variety of low-price shoes in a warehouse-like environment. The retailer is attempting to reposition itself as a purveyor of stylish and trendy shoes with a wider price range (going as high as $60) by expanding its merchandise mix and sprucing up its 4,500 stores. Targeting more women interested as much in fashion as in low prices, Payless has even opened a New York design office to focus on original styles and has introduced a line of shoes designed by Laura Poretzky.[12] Many discount and specialty store chains are positioning themselves to appeal to time- and cash-strapped consumers with convenient locations and layouts as well as low prices. This strategy has helped discount and specialty stores gain market share at the expense of large department stores.[13]

Store Image

To attract customers, a retail store must project an image—a functional and psychological picture in the consumer's mind—that appeals to its target market. Store environment, merchandise quality, and service quality are key determinants of store image. To improve service quality and store image, a Mercedes-Benz dealership in Atlanta is now using RFID technology automated welcoming and messaging when customers drive into the dealership service department. As customers approach dealership service lanes, an RFID tag affixed to the front of sold or previously serviced vehicles' rearview mirrors beam signals that allow staffers to quickly obtain computer-store information, such as the owner's name and the car's service history. Two 50-inch ceiling-suspended plasma monitors provide automated personalized welcoming in conjunction with automated internal messaging of the customer's arrival.[14]

Atmospherics, the physical elements in a store's design that appeal to consumers' emotions and encourage buying, help to create an image and position a retailer. Barnes & Noble, for example, uses murals of authors and framed pictures of classic book covers to convey a literary image. Studies show that retailers can use different elements—music, color, and complexity of layout and merchandise presentation—to influence customer arousal based on their shopping motivation. Supermarkets, for example, should use cooler colors and simple layout and presentations because their customers tend to be task-motivated, whereas specialty retailers may be able to use more complex layouts and brighter colors to stimulate their more recreationally motivated customers.[15]

Exterior atmospheric elements include the appearance of the storefront, display windows, store entrances, and degree of traffic congestion. Exterior atmospherics are particularly important to new customers, who tend to judge an unfamiliar store by its outside appearance and may not enter if they feel intimidated by the building or inconvenienced by the parking lot. Interior atmospheric elements include aesthetic considerations such as lighting, wall and floor coverings, dressing facilities, and store fixtures. Interior sensory elements contribute significantly to atmosphere. Color can attract shoppers to a retail display. Many fast-food restaurants use bright colors, such as red and yellow, because these have been shown to make customers feel hungrier and eat faster, which increases turnover. Sound is another important sensory component of atmosphere and may range from silence to subdued background music. Pottery Barn, for example, plays 1950s cocktail bar music, whereas JCPenney varies the music in its stores—even within departments—based on local demographics.[16] Many retailers employ scent, especially food aromas, to attract customers. Research suggests that consumer evaluations of a product are affected by scent, but only when the scent employed is congruent with the product.[17]

Marketing IN TRANSITION

Store Bags Go Green

Many retailers are helping to preserve the planet by encouraging customers to choose reusable shopping bags instead of use-once plastic bags. Although shoppers carry home purchases in 100 billion plastic bags every year, they recycle fewer than 1 billion bags. And because most plastic bags are not biodegradable, the discards remain in landfills forever. That's why a few cities and countries no longer allow large retailers to offer free plastic bags. In fact, Ireland taxes every plastic bag, as does Toronto, a strategy so successful that similar measures are being considered in many other areas.

© ADRIAN BROOKS/PA PHOTOS/LANDOV

Meanwhile, major retailers are saying goodbye to plastic. IKEA, based in Sweden, has eliminated plastic bags throughout its retail network. Customers can bring their own bags, take purchases home without bags, or buy IKEA's reusable bags for 59 cents each. Any customer who insists on plastic must pay 5 cents per bag, which IKEA donates to a nonprofit forest restoration group.

Walmart, the world's largest retailer, has cut back on plastic bags and sells reusable bags for 50 cents each, moves that will keep 9 billion bags out of landfills. Finally, every Earth Day, a growing number of retailers—including Walmart and Home Depot—give away thousands of reusable bags to encourage customers to go green.[b]

Category Management

Category management is a retail strategy of managing groups of similar, often substitutable products produced by different manufacturers. For example, supermarkets such as Safeway use category management to determine space for products such as cosmetics, cereals, and soups. An assortment of merchandise is both customer and strategically driven to improve performance. Category management developed in the food industry because supermarkets were concerned about highly competitive behavior among manufacturers. Category management is a move toward a collaborative supply-chain initiative to enhance customer value. Successful category management requires the acquisition, analysis, and sharing of sales and consumer information between the retailer and manufacturer. Walmart, for example, has developed strong supplier relationships with manufacturers such as Procter & Gamble. The development of information about demand, consumer behavior, and optimal allocations of products should be available from one source. Firms such as SAS provide software to manage data associated with each step of the category management decision cycle. The key is cooperative interaction between the manufacturers of category products and the retailer to create maximum success for all parties in the supply chain.

category management
A retail strategy of managing groups of similar, often substitutable products produced by different manufacturers

Store Image
Restaurants, like Red Lobster, spend considerable resources to enhance the customer experience through store design and décor.

Direct Marketing and Direct Selling

Although retailers are the most visible members of the supply chain, many products are sold outside the confines of a retail store. Direct selling and direct marketing account for an increasing percentage of product sales. Products also may be sold in automatic vending machines, but these account for less than 2 percent of all retail sales.

DIRECT MARKETING

Direct marketing is the use of telecommunications and nonpersonal media to communicate product and organizational information to customers, who then can purchase products via mail, telephone, or the Internet. Direct marketing can occur through catalog marketing, direct response marketing, telemarketing, television home shopping, and online retailing. Sales through direct marketing activities amount to $2 trillion per year.[18] In the auto industry alone, $77.8 billion in sales stemmed from the $8 billion spent on direct marketing campaigns recently.[19]

direct marketing
The use of telecommunications and nonpersonal media to introduce products to consumers, who then can purchase them via mail, telephone, or the Internet

Catalog Marketing

catalog marketing
A type of marketing in which an organization provides a catalog from which customers make selections and place orders by mail, telephone, or the Internet

In **catalog marketing**, an organization provides a catalog from which customers make selections and place orders by mail, telephone, or the Internet. Catalog marketing began in 1872, when Montgomery Ward issued its first catalog to rural families. Today there are more than 7,000 catalog marketing companies in the United States, as well as several retail stores, such as JCPenney, that engage in catalog marketing. Some organizations, including Spiegel and JCPenney, offer a broad array of products spread over multiple product lines. Catalog companies such as Lands' End, Pottery Barn, and J.Crew offer considerable depth in one major line of products. Still other catalog companies specialize in only a few products within a single line. Some catalog retailers—for instance, Crate and Barrel and The Sharper Image—have stores in major metropolitan areas.

The advantages of catalog retailing include efficiency and convenience for customers. The retailer benefits by being able to locate in remote, low-cost areas; save on expensive store fixtures; and reduce both personal selling and store operating expenses. On the other hand, catalog retailing is inflexible, provides limited service, and is most effective for a selected set of products.

Direct Response Marketing

Direct response marketing occurs when a retailer advertises a product and makes it available through mail or telephone orders. Generally, a purchaser may use a credit card, but other forms of payment are acceptable. Examples of direct response marketing include a television commercial offering a recording artist's musical collection available through a toll-free number, a newspaper or magazine advertisement for a series of children's books available by filling out the form in the ad or calling a toll-free number, and even a billboard promoting floral services available by calling 1-800-FLOWERS. Direct response marketing is also conducted by sending letters, samples, brochures, or booklets to prospects on a mailing list and asking that they order the advertised products by mail or telephone. In general, products must be priced above $20 to justify the advertising and distribution costs associated with direct response marketing.

Telemarketing

A number of organizations use the telephone to strengthen the effectiveness of traditional marketing methods. **Telemarketing** is the performance of marketing-related activities by telephone. Some organizations use a prescreened list of prospective clients. Telemarketing can help to generate sales leads, improve customer service, speed up payments on past-due accounts, raise funds for nonprofit organizations, and gather marketing data.

Currently, the laws and regulations regarding telemarketing, while in a state of flux, are becoming more restrictive. Many states have established do-not-call lists of customers who do not want to receive telemarketing calls from companies operating in their state. Congress implemented a national do-not-call registry for consumers who do not wish to receive telemarketing calls. So far, more than 172 million phone numbers in the United States have been listed on the registry.[20] The national registry is enforced by the Federal Trade Commission and the Federal Communications Commission, and companies are subject to a fine of up to $11,000 for each call made to a consumer listed on the registry.[21] Since the registry went into effect, the two federal agencies have collected over $16 million in penalties and $8 million in restitution from violators.[22] Certain exceptions apply to do-not-call lists. A company still can use telemarketing to communicate with existing customers. In addition, charitable, political, and telephone survey organizations are not restricted by the national registry.

Television Home Shopping

Television home shopping presents products to television viewers, encouraging them to order through toll-free numbers and pay with credit cards. The Home Shopping Network in Florida originated and popularized this format. The most popular products sold through television home shopping are jewelry (40 percent of total sales), clothing, housewares, and electronics. Home shopping channels have grown so rapidly in recent years that more than 60 percent of U.S. households have access to home shopping programs. Home Shopping Network and QVC are two of the largest home shopping networks. Approximately 60 percent of home shopping sales revenues come from repeat purchasers.

The television home shopping format offers several benefits. Products can be demonstrated easily, and an adequate amount of time can be spent showing the product so that viewers are well informed. The length of time a product is shown depends not only on the time required for doing demonstrations but also on whether the product is selling. Once the calls peak and begin to decline, a new product is shown. Other benefits are that customers can shop at their convenience and from the comfort of their homes.

direct response marketing
A type of marketing that occurs when a retailer advertises a product and makes it available through mail or telephone orders

telemarketing
The performance of marketing-related activities by telephone

television home shopping
A form of selling in which products are presented to television viewers, who can buy them by calling a toll-free number and paying with a credit card

COURTESY OF TRAVELOCITY/PHOTOGRAPHER: CHARLES HARRIS

Online Retailing
Travelocity is an online retailer that offers a broad assortment of travel services.

Online Retailing

Online retailing makes products available to buyers through computer connections. The phenomenal growth of Internet use and online information services such as AOL has created new retailing opportunities. Many retailers have set up websites to disseminate information about their companies and products. Although most retailers with websites use them primarily to promote products, a number of companies, including Barnes & Noble, REI, Lands' End, and OfficeMax, sell goods online. Consumers can purchase hard-to-find items, such as PEZ Candy Dispensers and Elvis memorabilia, on eBay. They can buy upscale items for their dogs at SitStay.com, a Web retailer specializing in high-end dog supplies that carries a carefully screened selection of 1,500 products. Banks and brokerage firms have established websites to give customers direct access to manage their accounts and enable them to trade online. Forrester Research projects that online retail sales in the United States will climb to $335 billion by 2012, up from $175 billion in 2007.[23] With advances in computer technology continuing and consumers ever more pressed for time, online retailing will continue to escalate.

Although online retailing represents a major retailing venue, security remains an issue. In a recent survey conducted by the Business Software Alliance, about 75 percent of Internet users expressed concerns about shopping online. The major issues are identity theft and credit card theft.

DIRECT SELLING

Direct selling is the marketing of products to ultimate consumers through face-to-face sales presentations at home or in the workplace. Traditionally called *door-to-door selling,* direct selling in the United States began with peddlers more than a century ago and has since grown into a sizable industry of several hundred firms. Although direct sellers historically used a cold-canvass, door-to-door approach for finding prospects, many companies today, such as Kirby, Amway, Mary Kay, and Avon, use other approaches. They initially identify customers through the mail, telephone, Internet, or shopping-mall intercepts and then set up appointments.

While the majority of direct selling takes place on an individual, or person-to-person, basis, it sometimes also includes the use of a group, or "party," plan. With a party plan, a consumer acts as a host and invites friends and associates to view merchandise in a group setting, where a salesperson demonstrates products. The congenial party atmosphere helps to overcome customers' reluctance and encourages them to buy.

Direct selling has both benefits and limitations. It gives the marketer an opportunity to demonstrate the product in an environment—usually customers' homes—where it most likely would be used. The door-to-door seller can give the customer personal attention, and the product can be presented to the customer at a convenient time and location. Personal attention to the customer is the foundation on which some direct sellers, such as Mary Kay, have built their businesses. Because commissions for salespeople are so high, ranging from 30 to 50 percent of the sales price, and great effort is required to isolate promising prospects, overall costs of direct selling make it the most expensive form of retailing. Furthermore, some customers view direct selling negatively, owing to unscrupulous and fraudulent practices used by some direct sellers in the past. Some communities even have local ordinances that

online retailing
Retailing that makes products available to buyers through computer connections

direct selling
The marketing of products to ultimate consumers through face-to-face sales presentations at home or in the workplace

franchising
An arrangement in which a supplier (franchiser) grants a dealer (franchisee) the right to sell products in exchange for some type of consideration

control or, in some cases, prohibit direct selling. Despite these negative views held by some individuals, direct selling is still alive and well, bringing in revenues of $32 billion a year.[24]

Franchising

Franchising is an arrangement in which a supplier, or franchiser, grants a dealer, or franchisee, the right to sell products in exchange for some type of consideration. The franchiser may receive some percentage of total sales in exchange for furnishing equipment, buildings, management know-how, and marketing assistance to the franchisee. The franchisee supplies labor and capital, operates the franchised business, and agrees to abide by the provisions of the franchise agreement. Table 14.2 lists the leading U.S. franchises, types of products, and startup costs.

Because of changes in the international marketplace, shifting employment options in the United States, the expanding U.S. service economy, and corporate interest in more joint-venture activity, franchising is increasing rapidly. There are 909,253 franchised small businesses in 103 industries. Franchised businesses produce an estimated $881 billion in output per year and employ nearly 10 million people.[25]

Franchising offers advantages to both the franchisee and the franchiser. It enables a franchisee to start a business with limited capital and benefit from the business experience of others. Moreover, nationally advertised franchises, such as ServiceMaster and Burger King, are often assured of customers as soon as they open. If business problems arise, the franchisee can obtain guidance and advice from the franchiser at little or no cost. Franchised outlets are generally more successful than independently owned businesses. Fewer than 10 percent of franchised retail businesses fail during the first two years of operation compared with approximately 50 percent of independent retail businesses. Also, the franchisee receives materials to use in local advertising and can benefit from national promotional campaigns sponsored by the franchiser.

Through franchise arrangements, the franchiser gains fast and selective product distribution without incurring the high cost of constructing and operating its own outlets. The franchiser therefore

Sustainable Marketing

Walmart Has Sustainability in Store

Walmart, the world's largest retailer, has launched a comprehensive green program to encourage sustainability of the world's fisheries, forests, and communities; slash energy use; reduce carbon emissions; recycle waste; and push its 60,000 suppliers to produce in an environmentally friendly way. Thanks to its size and its success, the company has become an environmental leader within the retail industry and beyond—and boosted profits along the way.

© TIME & LIFE PICTURES/GETTY IMAGES

For example, Walmart saved 3,000 tons of material and $3.5 million in transportation costs by changing the packaging of its private-label toys. By tuning up its trucking operations and phasing in hybrid diesel-electric trucks and alternative-fuel trucks, the company improved its fleet efficiency by 25 percent in just three years. And, store-by-store, the company is reducing greenhouse gas emissions and waste. As it remodels its existing stores, it adds eco-friendly lighting, heating, and other systems to cut energy use by 30 percent and produce 30 percent fewer greenhouse emissions. In China, it will soon introduce a store prototype that cuts energy use by 40 percent.

Walmart has joined the Clinton Climate Initiative partnership to help create environmentally friendly cities across the United States and around the world. Its Green Jobs Council, a partnership with suppliers, is finding new ways to create green jobs in the domestic market. The company's supply-chain power and public profile put muscle behind these green initiatives and show that going green is right for the environment and right for the bottom line.[c]

TABLE 14.2 Top U.S. Franchisers and Their Startup Costs

Rank*	Franchise	Description	No. of Franchise Outlets Worldwide	Startup Costs
1	Subway	Sandwiches, salads	29,612	$78.6K–238.3K
2	McDonald's	Hamburgers, chicken, salads	25,465	$950.2K–1.8M
3	Liberty Tax Service	Income-tax preparation	2,579	$53.8K–66.9K
4	Sonic Drive In	Drive-in restaurant	2,768	$1.2M–3.2M
5	InterContinental Hotels	Hotels	3,498	Varies
6	Ace Hardware Corp.	Hardware & home improvement store	4,581	$400K–1.1M
7	Pizza Hut	Pizza	10,239	$638K–2.97M
8	UPS Store, The/Mail Boxes Etc.	Postal, business, & communications services	6,034	$171.2K–280K
9	Circle K	Convenience store	4,143	$161K–1.4M
10	Papa John's	Pizza	2,615	$135.8K–491.6K

*Ranking is based primarily on financial strength and stability, growth rate, size of the system, number of years in business, startup costs, litigation, percentage of terminations, and whether the company provides financing.
Source: "2009 Franchise 500® Rankings," http://www.entrepreneur.com/franchises/rankings/franchise500-115608/2009,.html (accessed March 17, 2009).

has more capital for expanding production and advertising. It also can ensure, through the franchise agreement, that outlets are maintained and operated according to its own standards. Some franchisers, however, permit their franchisees to modify their menus, hours, or other operating elements to better match their target market's needs. For example, Wings Over, a buffalo-style chicken wing franchise, has permitted menu variations to match local tastes and allowed some franchisees located near colleges and universities to open at 4 p.m. and close at 3 a.m.[26] The franchiser benefits from the fact that the franchisee, being a sole proprietor in most cases, is likely to be very highly motivated to succeed. Success of the franchise means more sales, which translate into higher income for the franchiser.

Franchise arrangements also have several drawbacks. The franchiser can dictate many aspects of the business: decor, design of employees' uniforms, types of signs, and numerous details of business operations. In addition, franchisees must pay to use the franchiser's name, products, and assistance. Usually there is a one-time franchise fee and continuing royalty and advertising fees, often collected as a percentage of sales. Franchisees often must work very hard, putting in 10- to 12-hour days, six or seven days a week. In some cases, franchise agreements are not uniform; one franchisee may pay more than another for the same services. Finally, the franchiser gives up a certain amount of control when entering into a franchise agreement. Consequently, individual establishments may not be operated exactly according to the franchiser's standards.

wholesaling
Transactions in which products are bought for resale, for making other products, or for general business operations

wholesaler
An individual or organization that sells products that are bought for resale, for making other products, or for general business operations

Wholesaling

Wholesaling refers to all transactions in which products are bought for resale, for making other products, or for general business operations. It does not include exchanges with ultimate consumers. A **wholesaler** is an individual or organization that sells products that are bought for resale, for making other products, or for general business operations. In other words, wholesalers buy products and resell them to reseller, government, and institutional users. For example, Sysco, the nation's number 1 food-service distributor, supplies restaurants, hotels, schools, industrial caterers, and hospitals with everything from frozen and fresh food and paper products to medical and cleaning supplies. Wholesaling activities are not limited to goods; service companies, such as financial institutions, also use active wholesale networks. For example, some banks buy loans in bulk from other financial institutions, as well as making loans to their own retail customers. There are more than 430,000 wholesaling establishments in the United States,[27] and more than half of all products sold in this country pass through these firms.

Wholesalers may engage in many supply-chain management activities, including warehousing, shipping and product handling, inventory control, information system management and data processing, risk taking, financing, budgeting, and even marketing research and promotion. Regardless of whether there is a wholesaling firm involved in the supply chain, all product distribution requires the performance of these activities. In addition to bearing the primary responsibility for the physical distribution of products from manufacturers to retailers, wholesalers may establish information systems that help producers and retailers better manage the supply chain from producer to customer. Many wholesalers are using information technology and the Internet to allow their employees, customers, and suppliers to share information between intermediaries and facilitating agencies such as trucking companies and warehouse firms. Other firms are making their databases and marketing information systems available to their supply-chain partners to facilitate order processing, shipping, and product development and to share information about changing market conditions and customer desires. As a result, some wholesalers play a key role in supply-chain management decisions.

SERVICES PROVIDED BY WHOLESALERS

Wholesalers provide essential services to both producers and retailers. By initiating sales contacts with a producer and selling diverse products to retailers, wholesalers serve as an extension of the producer's sales force. Wholesalers also provide financial assistance. They often pay for transporting goods; they reduce a producer's warehousing expenses and inventory investment by holding goods in inventory; they extend credit and assume losses from buyers who turn out to be poor credit risks; and when they buy a producer's entire output and pay promptly or in cash, they are a source of working capital. Wholesalers also serve as conduits for information within the marketing channel, keeping producers up to date on market developments and passing along the manufacturers' promotional plans to other intermediaries. Using wholesalers therefore gives producers a distinct advantage because the specialized services wholesalers perform allow producers to concentrate on developing and manufacturing products that match customers' needs and wants.

Wholesalers support retailers by assisting with marketing strategy, especially the distribution component. Wholesalers also help retailers to select inventory. They are often specialists on market conditions and experts at negotiating final purchases. In industries in which obtaining supplies is important, skilled buying is indispensable. For example, Atlanta-based Genuine Parts Company (GPC), the nation's top automotive parts wholesaler, has more than 80 years of experience in the auto parts business, which helps it serve its customers effectively. GPC supplies more than 300,000 replacement parts (from 150 different suppliers) to 6,000 NAPA AUTO PARTS stores.[28] Effective wholesalers make an effort to understand the businesses of their customers. They can reduce a retailer's burden of looking for and coordinating supply sources. If the wholesaler purchases for several different buyers, expenses can be shared by all customers. Furthermore, whereas a manufacturer's salesperson offers retailers only a few products at a time, independent wholesalers always have a wide range of products available. Thus, through partnerships, wholesalers and retailers can forge successful relationships for the benefit of customers.

The distinction between services performed by wholesalers and those provided by other businesses has blurred in recent years. Changes in the competitive nature of business, especially the growth of strong retail chains like Walmart, Home Depot, and Best Buy, are changing supply-chain relationships. In many product categories, such as electronics, furniture, and even food products, retailers have discovered that they can deal directly with producers, performing wholesaling activities themselves at a lower cost. An increasing number of retailers are relying on computer technology to expedite ordering, delivery, and handling of goods. Technology thus is allowing retailers to take over many wholesaling functions. However, when a wholesaler is eliminated from a marketing channel, wholesaling activities still have to be performed by a member of the supply chain, whether a producer, retailer, or facilitating agency. These wholesaling activities are critical components of supply-chain management.

TYPES OF WHOLESALERS

Wholesalers are classified according to several criteria. Whether a wholesaler is independently owned or owned by a producer influences how it is classified. Wholesalers also can be grouped according to whether they take title to (own) the products they handle. The range of services provided is another criterion used for classification. Finally, wholesalers are classified according to the breadth and depth of their product lines. Using these criteria, we discuss three general types of wholesaling establishments: merchant wholesalers, agents and brokers, and manufacturers' sales branches and offices.

Merchant Wholesalers

merchant wholesalers Independently owned businesses that take title to goods, assume ownership risks, and buy and resell products to other wholesalers, business customers, or retailers

Merchant wholesalers are independently owned businesses that take title to goods, assume risks associated with ownership, and generally buy and resell products to other wholesalers, business customers, or retailers. A producer is likely to rely on merchant wholesalers when selling directly to customers would be economically unfeasible. Merchant wholesalers are also useful for providing market coverage, making sales contacts, storing inventory, handling orders, collecting market information, and furnishing customer support. Some merchant wholesalers are even involved in packaging and developing private brands to help retail customers be

FIGURE 14.1 **Types of Merchant Wholesalers**

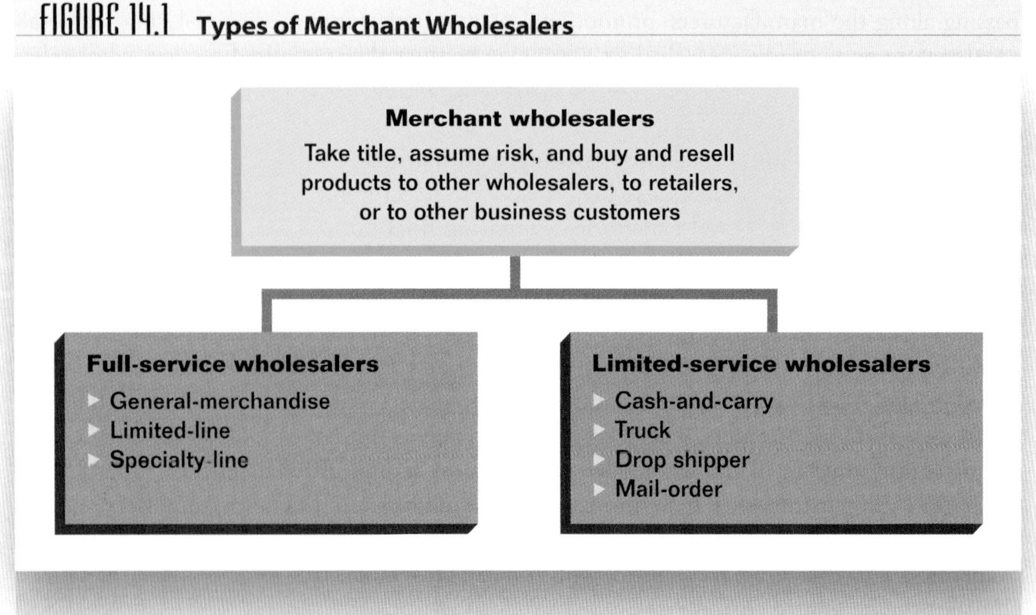

competitive. Merchant wholesalers go by various names, including *wholesaler, jobber, distributor, assembler, exporter,* and *importer.* They fall into one of two broad categories: full-service and limited-service (see Figure 14.1).

Full-service wholesalers perform the widest possible range of wholesaling functions. Customers rely on them for product availability, suitable assortments, breaking large quantities into smaller ones, financial assistance, and technical advice and service. Universal Corporation, the world's largest buyer and processor of leaf tobacco, is an example of a full-service wholesaler. Based in Richmond, Virginia, the firm buys, processes, resells, and ships tobacco and provides financing for its customers, which include cigarette manufacturers such as Philip Morris (which accounts for a significant portion of Universal's sales). Universal is also involved in sales of lumber, building products, and other agricultural products and has operations in 35 countries.[29] Full-service wholesalers handle either consumer or business products and provide numerous marketing services to their customers. Many large grocery wholesalers help retailers with store design, site selection, personnel training, financing, merchandising, advertising, coupon redemption, and scanning. Although full-service wholesalers often earn higher gross margins than other wholesalers, their operating expenses are also higher because they perform a wider range of functions.

full-service wholesalers Merchant wholesalers that perform the widest range of wholesaling functions

Full-service wholesalers are categorized as general merchandise, general-line, and specialty-line wholesalers and as rack jobbers. **General merchandise wholesalers** carry a wide product mix but offer limited depth within product lines. They deal in products such as drugs, nonperishable foods, cosmetics, detergents, and tobacco. **General-line wholesalers** carry only a few product lines, such as groceries, lighting fixtures, or oil-well drilling equipment, but offer an extensive assortment of products within those lines. Bergen Brunswig Corporation, for example, is a general-line wholesaler of pharmaceuticals and health and beauty aids. General-line wholesalers provide a range of services similar to those of general merchandise wholesalers. **Specialty-line wholesalers** offer the narrowest range of products, usually a single product line or a few items within a product line. Red River Commodities, Inc., for example, is the leading importer (specialty-line wholesaler) of nuts, seeds, and dried fruits in the United States.[30] **Rack jobbers** are full-service, specialty-line wholesalers that own and maintain display racks in supermarkets, drugstores, and discount and variety stores. They set up displays, mark merchandise, stock shelves, and keep billing and inventory records; retailers need furnish only space. Rack jobbers specialize in nonfood items with high profit margins, such as health and beauty aids, books, magazines, hosiery, and greeting cards.

general merchandise wholesalers Full-service wholesalers with a wide product mix but limited depth within product lines

general-line wholesalers Full-service wholesalers that carry only a few product lines but many products within those lines

specialty-line wholesalers Full-service wholesalers that carry only a single product line or a few items within a product line

rack jobbers Full-service, specialty-line wholesalers that own and maintain display racks in stores

Limited-service wholesalers provide fewer marketing services than do full-service wholesalers and specialize in just a few functions. Producers perform the remaining functions or pass them on to customers or to other intermediaries. Limited-service wholesalers take title to merchandise but often do not deliver merchandise, grant credit, provide marketing information, store inventory, or plan ahead for customers' future needs. Because they offer restricted services, limited-service wholesalers are compensated with lower rates and have smaller profit margins than full-service wholesalers. The decision about whether to use a limited-service or a full-service wholesaler depends on the structure of the marketing channel and the need to manage the supply chain to provide competitive advantage. Although certain types of limited-service wholesalers are few in number, they are important in the distribution of products such as specialty foods, perishable items, construction materials, and coal. Table 14.3 summarizes the services provided by four typical limited-service wholesalers: cash-and-carry wholesalers, truck wholesalers, drop shippers, and mail-order wholesalers.

limited-service wholesalers Merchant wholesalers that provide some services and specialize in a few functions

Cash-and-carry wholesalers are intermediaries whose customers—usually small businesses—pay cash and furnish transportation. Cash-and-carry wholesalers usually handle a limited line of products with a high turnover rate, such as groceries, building materials, and electrical or office supplies. Many small retailers whose accounts are refused by other wholesalers survive because of cash-and-carry wholesalers. **Truck wholesalers**, sometimes called

cash-and-carry wholesalers Limited-service wholesalers whose customers pay cash and furnish transportation

truck wholesalers Limited-service wholesalers that transport products directly to customers for inspection and selection

TABLE 14.3 **Services That Limited-Service Wholesalers Provide**

Services	Cash-and-Carry	Truck	Drop Shipper	Mail-Order
Physical possession of merchandise	Yes	Yes	No	Yes
Personal sales calls on customers	No	Yes	No	No
Information about market conditions	No	Some	Yes	Yes
Advice to customers	No	Some	Yes	No
Stocking and maintenance of merchandise in customers' stores	No	No	No	No
Credit to customers	No	No	Yes	Some
Delivery of merchandise to customers	No	Yes	No	No

truck jobbers, transport a limited line of products directly to customers for on-the-spot inspection and selection. They are often small operators who own and drive their own trucks. They usually have regular routes, calling on retailers and other institutions to determine their needs. **Drop shippers**, also known as *desk jobbers,* take title to products and negotiate sales but never take actual possession of products. They forward orders from retailers, business buyers, or other wholesalers to manufacturers and arrange for carload shipments of items to be delivered directly from producers to these customers. They assume responsibility for products during the entire transaction, including the costs of any unsold goods. **Mail-order wholesalers** use catalogs instead of sales forces to sell products to retail and business buyers. Wholesale mail-order houses generally feature cosmetics, specialty foods, sporting goods, office supplies, and automotive parts. Mail-order wholesaling enables buyers to choose and order particular catalog items for delivery through United Parcel Service, the U.S. Postal Service, or other carriers. This is a convenient and effective method of selling small items to customers in remote areas that other wholesalers might find unprofitable to serve. The Internet has provided an opportunity for mail-order wholesalers to sell products over their own websites and have the products shipped by the manufacturers.

drop shippers
Limited-service wholesalers that take title to products and negotiate sales but never take actual possession of products

mail-order wholesalers
Limited-service wholesalers that sell products through catalogs

Agents and Brokers

Agents and brokers negotiate purchases and expedite sales but do not take title to products (see Figure 14.2). Sometimes called *functional middlemen,* they perform a limited number of services in exchange for a commission, which generally is based on the product's selling price. **Agents** represent either buyers or sellers on a permanent basis, whereas **brokers** are intermediaries that buyers or sellers employ temporarily.

agents
Intermediaries that represent either buyers or sellers on a permanent basis

brokers
Intermediaries that bring buyers and sellers together temporarily

Although agents and brokers perform even fewer functions than limited-service wholesalers, they are usually specialists in particular products or types of customers and can provide valuable sales expertise. They know their markets well and often form long-lasting associations with customers. Agents and brokers enable manufacturers to expand sales when resources are limited, to benefit from the services of a trained sales force, and to hold down personal selling costs. Table 14.4 summarizes the services provided by agents and brokers.

manufacturers' agents
Independent intermediaries that represent two or more sellers and offer complete product lines

Manufacturers' agents, which account for more than half of all agent wholesalers, are independent intermediaries that represent two or more sellers and usually offer customers complete product lines. They sell and take orders year round, much as a manufacturer's sales

FIGURE 14.2 Types of Agents and Brokers

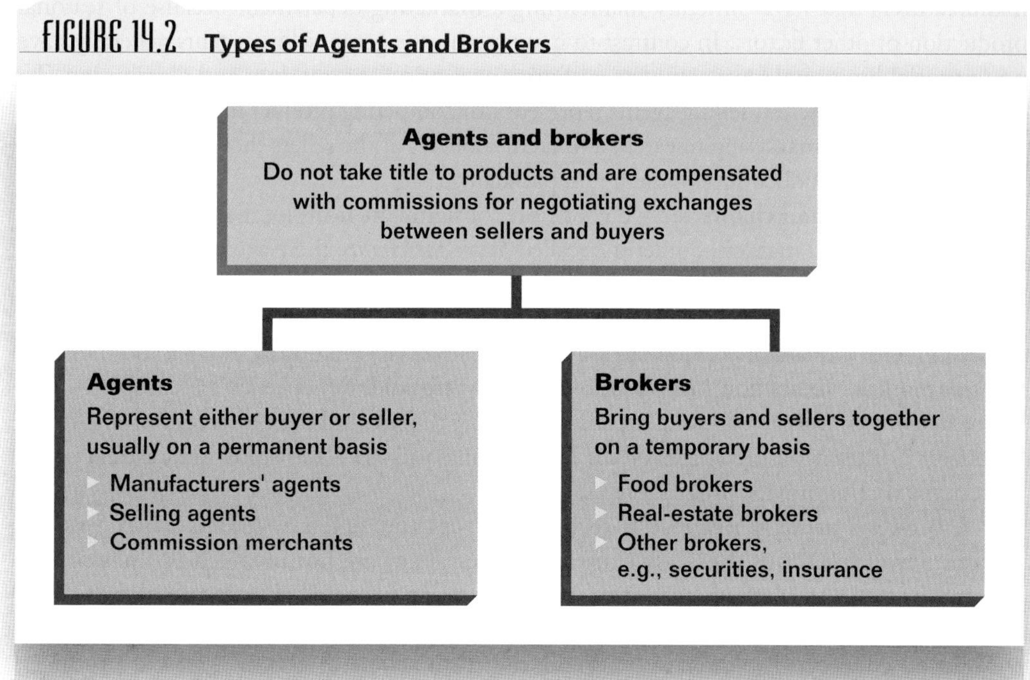

force does. Restricted to a particular territory, a manufacturer's agent handles noncompeting and complementary products. The relationship between the agent and the manufacturer is governed by written contracts that outline territories, selling price, order handling, and terms of sale relating to delivery, service, and warranties. Manufacturers' agents have little or no control over producers' pricing and marketing policies. They do not extend credit and may be unable to provide technical advice. Manufacturers' agents are commonly used in sales of apparel, machinery and equipment, steel, furniture, automotive products, electrical goods, and certain food items.

Selling agents market either all of a specified product line or a manufacturer's entire output. They perform every wholesaling activity except taking title to products. Selling agents usually assume the sales function for several producers simultaneously and are used often in place of marketing departments. In fact, selling agents are used most often by small producers or by

selling agents
Intermediaries that market a whole product line or a manufacturer's entire output

TABLE 14.4 Services That Agents and Brokers Provide

Services	Manufacturers' Agents	Selling Agents	Commission Merchants	Brokers
Physical possession of merchandise	Some	Some	Yes	No
Long-term relationship with buyers or sellers	Yes	Yes	Yes	No
Representation of competing product lines	No	No	Yes	Yes
Limited geographic territory	Yes	No	No	No
Credit to customers	No	Yes	Some	No
Delivery of merchandise to customers	Some	Yes	Yes	No

manufacturers that have difficulty maintaining a marketing department because of seasonal production or other factors. In contrast to manufacturers' agents, selling agents generally have no territorial limits and have complete authority over prices, promotion, and distribution. To avoid conflicts of interest, selling agents represent noncompeting product lines. They play a key role in advertising, marketing research, and credit policies of the sellers they represent, at times even advising on product development and packaging.

Commission merchants receive goods on consignment from local sellers and negotiate sales in large, central markets. Sometimes called *factor merchants,* these agents have broad powers regarding prices and terms of sale. They specialize in obtaining the best price possible under market conditions. Most often found in agricultural marketing, commission merchants take possession of truckloads of commodities, arrange for necessary grading or storage, and transport the commodities to auction or markets where they are sold. When sales are completed, the agents deduct commission and the expense of making the sale and then turn over profits to the producer. Commission merchants also offer planning assistance and sometimes extend credit but usually do not provide promotional support.

A broker's primary purpose is to bring buyers and sellers together. Thus, brokers perform fewer functions than other intermediaries. They are not involved in financing or physical possession, have no authority to set prices, and assume almost no risks. Instead, they offer customers specialized knowledge of a particular commodity and a network of established contacts. Brokers are especially useful to sellers of certain types of products, such as supermarket products and real estate. Food brokers, for example, sell food and general merchandise to retailer-owned and merchant wholesalers, grocery chains, food processors, and business buyers.

Manufacturers' Sales Branches and Offices

Sometimes called *manufacturers' wholesalers,* manufacturers' sales branches and offices resemble merchant wholesalers' operations. **Sales branches** are manufacturer-owned intermediaries that sell products and provide support services to the manufacturer's sales force. Situated away from the manufacturing plant, they are usually located where large customers are concentrated and demand is high. They offer credit, deliver goods, give promotional assistance, and furnish other services. Customers include retailers, business buyers, and other wholesalers. Manufacturers of electrical supplies, such as Westinghouse Electric, and of plumbing supplies, such as American Standard, often have branch operations. They are also common in the lumber and automotive parts industries.

Sales offices are manufacturer-owned operations that provide services normally associated with agents. Like sales branches, they are located away from manufacturing plants, but unlike sales branches, they carry no inventory. A manufacturer's sales office (or branch) may sell products that enhance the manufacturer's own product line.

Manufacturers may set up these branches or offices to reach their customers more effectively by performing wholesaling functions themselves. A manufacturer also may set up such a facility when specialized wholesaling services are not available through existing intermediaries. A manufacturer's performance of wholesaling and physical distribution activities through its sales branch or office may strengthen supply-chain efficiency. In some situations, though, a manufacturer may bypass its sales office or branches entirely—for example, if the producer decides to serve large retailer customers directly.

commission merchants
Agents that receive goods on consignment and negotiate sales in large, central markets

sales branches
Manufacturer-owned intermediaries that sell products and provide support services to the manufacturer's sales force

sales offices
Manufacturer-owned operations that provide services normally associated with agents

CHAPTER REVIEW

OBJECTIVES

1 Understand the purpose and function of retailers in the marketing channel.

Retailing includes all transactions in which buyers intend to consume products through personal, family, or household use. Retailers, organizations that sell products primarily to ultimate consumers, are important links in the marketing channel because they are both marketers for and customers of wholesalers and producers. They add value, provide services, and assist in making product selections.

2 Identify the major types of retailers.

Retail stores can be classified according to the breadth of products offered. Two broad categories are general merchandise retailers and specialty retailers. The primary types of general merchandise retailers include department stores, which are large retail organizations organized by departments and characterized by wide product mixes in considerable depth; discount stores, which are self-service, low-price, general merchandise outlets; convenience stores, which are small self-service stores that are open long hours and carry a narrow assortment of products, usually convenience items; supermarkets, which are large self-service food stores that carry some nonfood products; superstores, which are giant retail outlets that carry all the products found in supermarkets and most consumer products purchased on a routine basis; hypermarkets, which offer supermarket and discount store shopping at one location; warehouse clubs, which are large-scale, members-only discount operations; and warehouse and catalog showrooms, which are low-cost operations characterized by warehouse methods of materials handling and display, large inventories, and minimal services. Specialty retailers offer substantial assortments in a few product lines. They include traditional specialty retailers, which carry narrow product mixes with deep product lines; category killers, large specialty stores that concentrate on a major product category and compete on the basis of low prices and enormous product availability; and off-price retailers, which sell brand name manufacturers' seconds and product overruns at deep discounts.

3 Explore strategic issues in retailing.

Location, the least flexible of the strategic retailing issues, determines the trading area from which a store draws its customers and therefore should be evaluated carefully. When evaluating potential sites, retailers take into account various factors, including the location of the firm's target market within the trading area, customer characteristics, kinds of products sold, availability of public transportation and/or parking, and competitors' locations. Retailers can choose among several types of locations, including freestanding structures, traditional business districts, traditional planned shopping centers (neighborhood, community, regional, and superregional), or nontraditional shopping centers (lifestyle, power, and outlet).

Retail positioning involves identifying an unserved or underserved market segment and serving it through a strategy that distinguishes the retailer from others in those customers' minds. Store image, which should facilitate positioning, derives not only from atmosphere but also from location, products offered, customer services, prices, promotion, and the store's overall reputation. Atmospherics refers to the physical elements of a store's design that can be adjusted to appeal to consumers' emotions and thus induce them to buy. Scrambled merchandising adds unrelated product lines to an existing product mix and is being used by a growing number of stores to generate sales.

4 Recognize the various forms of direct marketing and selling.

Direct marketing is the use of telecommunications and nonpersonal media to communicate product and organizational information to consumers, who then can purchase products by mail, telephone, or Internet. Such communication may occur through a catalog (catalog marketing), advertising (direct response marketing), telephone (telemarketing), television (television home shopping), or online (online retailing). Direct selling markets products to ultimate consumers through face-to-face sales presentations at home or in the workplace.

5 Examine franchising and its benefits and weaknesses.

Franchising is an arrangement in which a supplier grants a dealer the right to sell products in exchange for some type of consideration. Franchise arrangements have a number of advantages and disadvantages over traditional business forms, and their use is increasing.

Understand the nature and functions of wholesalers.

Wholesaling consists of all transactions in which products are bought for resale, for making other products, or for general business operations. Wholesalers are individuals or organizations that facilitate and expedite exchanges that are primarily wholesale transactions. For producers, wholesalers are a source of financial assistance and information; by performing specialized accumulation and allocation functions, they allow producers to concentrate on manufacturing products. Wholesalers provide retailers with buying expertise, wide product lines, efficient distribution, and warehousing and storage.

Understand how wholesalers are classified.

Merchant wholesalers are independently owned businesses that take title to goods and assume ownership risks. They are either full-service wholesalers, offering the widest possible range of wholesaling functions, or limited-service wholesalers, providing only some marketing services and specializing in a few functions. Full-service merchant wholesalers include general merchandise wholesalers, which offer a wide but relatively shallow product mix; general-line wholesalers, which offer extensive assortments within a few product lines; specialty-line wholesalers, which carry only a single product line or a few items within a line; and rack jobbers, which own and service display racks in supermarkets and other stores. Limited-service merchant wholesalers include cash-and-carry wholesalers, which sell to small businesses, require payment in cash, and do not deliver; truck wholesalers, which sell a limited line of products from their own trucks directly to customers; drop shippers, which own goods and negotiate sales but never take possession of products; and mail-order wholesalers, which sell to retail and business buyers through direct mail catalogs.

Agents and brokers negotiate purchases and expedite sales in exchange for a commission, but they do not take title to products. Whereas agents represent buyers or sellers on a permanent basis, brokers are intermediaries employed by buyers and sellers on a temporary basis to negotiate exchanges. Manufacturers' agents market the complete product lines of two or more sellers. Selling agents market a complete product line or a producer's entire output and perform every wholesaling function except taking title to products. Commission merchants are agents that receive goods on consignment from local sellers and negotiate sales in large, central markets.

Manufacturers' sales branches and offices are owned by manufacturers. Sales branches sell products and provide support services for the manufacturer's sales force in a given location. Sales offices carry no inventory and function much as agents do.

Please visit the student website at www.cengage.com/international for quizzes and games that will help you prepare for exams and help achieve the grade you want.

KEY CONCEPTS

retailing
retailer
general merchandise retailer
department stores
discount stores
convenience store
supermarkets
superstores
hypermarkets
warehouse clubs
warehouse showrooms
traditional specialty retailers
category killer
off-price retailers
neighborhood shopping centers
community shopping centers
regional shopping centers
superregional shopping centers
lifestyle shopping centers
power shopping centers
retail positioning
atmospherics
category management
direct marketing
catalog marketing
direct response marketing
telemarketing
television home shopping
online retailing
direct selling
franchising
wholesaling
wholesaler
merchant wholesalers
full-service wholesalers
general merchandise wholesalers

general-line wholesalers
specialty-line wholesalers
rack jobbers
limited-service wholesalers
cash-and-carry wholesalers
truck wholesalers
drop shippers
mail-order wholesalers
agents
brokers
manufacturers' agents
selling agents
commission merchants
sales branches
sales offices

ISSUES FOR DISCUSSION AND REVIEW

1. What value is added to a product by retailers? What value is added by retailers for producers and for ultimate consumers?
2. What are the major differences between discount stores and department stores?
3. In what ways are traditional specialty stores and off-price retailers similar? How do they differ?
4. What major issues should be considered when determining a retail site location?
5. Describe the three major types of traditional shopping centers. Give an example of each type in your area.
6. Discuss the major factors that help to determine a retail store's image. How does atmosphere add value to products sold in a store?
7. How is door-to-door selling a form of retailing? Some consumers believe that direct response orders bypass the retailer. Is this true?
8. If you were opening a retail business, would you prefer to open an independent store or own a store under a franchise arrangement? Explain your preference.
9. What services do wholesalers provide to producers and retailers?
10. What is the difference between a full-service merchant wholesaler and a limited-service merchant wholesaler?
11. Drop shippers take title to products but do not accept physical possession of them, whereas commission merchants take physical possession of products but do not accept title. Defend the logic of classifying drop shippers as wholesale merchants and commission merchants as agents.
12. Why are manufacturers' sales offices and branches classified as wholesalers? Which independent wholesalers are replaced by manufacturers' sales branches? By sales offices?

MARKETING APPLICATIONS

1. Juanita wants to open a small retail store that specializes in high-quality, high-priced children's clothing. What types of competitors should she be concerned about in this competitive retail environment? Why?
2. Location of retail outlets is an issue in strategic planning. What initial steps would you recommend to Juanita (see Marketing Application 1) when she considers a location for her store?
3. Visit a retail store you shop in regularly or one in which you would like to shop. Identify the store, and describe its atmospherics. Be specific about both exterior and interior elements, and indicate how the store is being positioned through its use of atmospherics.
4. Contact a local retailer you patronize, and ask the store manager to describe the store's relationship with one of its wholesalers. Using your text as a guide, identify the distribution activities performed by the wholesaler. Are any of these activities shared by both the retailer and the wholesaler? How do these activities benefit the retailer? How do they benefit you as a consumer?

ONLINE EXERCISE

5. Walmart provides a website from which customers can shop for products, search for a nearby store, and even preorder new products. The website lets customers browse what's on sale and view company

information. Access Walmart's website at http://www.walmart.com.

a. How does Walmart attempt to position itself on its website?

b. Compare the atmospherics of Walmart's website to the atmospherics of a traditional Walmart store. Are they consistent? If not, should they be?

DEVELOPING YOUR MARKETING PLAN

Distribution decisions in the marketing plan entail the movement of your product from the producer until it reaches the final consumer. An understanding of how and where your customer prefers to purchase products is critical to the development of the marketing plan. As you apply the information in this chapter to your plan, focus on the following issues:

1. Considering your product's attributes and your target market(s)' buying behavior, will your product likely be sold to the ultimate customer or to another member of the marketing channel?
2. If your product will be sold to the ultimate customer, what type of retailing establishment is most suitable for your product? Consider the product's characteristics and your target market's buying behavior. Refer to Table 14.1 for retailer types.
3. Discuss how the characteristics of the retail establishment, such as location, store image, and scrambled merchandising, have an impact on the consumer's perception of your product.
4. Are direct marketing or direct selling methods appropriate for your product and target market?
5. If your product will be sold to another member in the marketing channel, discuss whether a merchant wholesaler, agent, or broker is most suitable as your channel customer.

The information obtained from these questions should assist you in developing various aspects of your marketing plan found in the *Interactive Marketing Plan* exercise.

VIDEO CASE 14

Eastern Mountain Sports Goes Back to Its Retail Roots

One of the original outdoor specialty retailers, Eastern Mountain Sports (EMS) was founded by two Massachusetts-based rock climbers, Alan McDonough and Roger Furst, in 1967. Frustrated when trying to buy ice-climbing axes, they saw a market need and decided to fill it themselves. Shortly after opening their retail outlet, McDonough and Furst also opened the first U.S. mountain climbing school, the Eastern Mountain Sports Rock Climbing School.

McDonough and Furst sold EMS in 1979 and the company went through several sets of owners in the next 25 years. The changes in ownership didn't stunt the company's growth. However, the retailer's financial results veered up and down as various owners moved away from the original vision of equipping extreme sport enthusiasts and toward more mainstream products. By 2003, the year CEO Will Manzer took over, the company had become a "Gap with climbing ropes," as he described it.

After leading a management buyout in 2004, Manzer took the company back to its roots by stocking top-quality specialty gear to regain a loyal customer base of climbers, hikers, bikers, and others who enjoy outdoor activities. For example, EMS will stock $1,400 sea kayaks with ergonomic foot contours. It may not sell many, but it establishes EMS as the place to buy specialized equipment and accessories not found in many other stores.

EMS's online operations are becoming vital to the organization. In fact, the top management expects that online shopping will drive much of the company's future revenue growth. EMS uses software to track consumer preferences and see what consumers at each area would like and in what quantity. Everyone from the

CEO to the store managers have access to the same data and can see which products and promotions are successful in order to do a better job with promotions, store layouts, and stock decisions.

Today EMS operates more than 80 stores in 16 states and teaches climbing, kayaking, and skiing. New locations offer a wider variety of products, an updated store design, and services such as custom bike shops with around-the-clock technicians. Every store has an outreach coordinator to connect with sports enthusiasts in the local area, such as through fundraisers where new gear is demonstrated to benefit a community cause. Can EMS continue to profit even in tough economic times?

QUESTIONS FOR DISCUSSION

1. What changes occurred at EMS that caused the company to lose its unique retail positioning?
2. How would you categorize EMS among specialty retailers?
3. Would you recommend that EMS enhance its differentiation by opening schools to teach other extreme sports? Explain your answer.

Tim O'Brien, "Snowshoe Session Planned to Support Habitat Projects," *Times Union (Albany, NY)*, January 29, 2009, n.p.; Lynette Carpiet, "EMS Expands in Northeast," *Bicycle Retailer and Industry News*, May 1, 2008, n.p.; Lucas Conley, "Climbing Back Up the Mountain," *Fast Company*, April 2005; Eastern Mountain Sports Climbing School, http://www.emsclimb.com; Drew Robb, "Eastern Mountain Sports: Getting Smarter with Each Sale," *Computer World*, September 18, 2006, http://www.computerworld.com/action/article.do?command=viewArticleBasic&articleId=112778; "JDA Announces New Software for Softlines Retailers," Business Services Industry, August 7, 1996, http://findarticles.com/p/articles/mi_m0EIN/is_1996_August_7/ai_18568223.

Promotion Decisions 7

© BILL ARON/PHOTOEDIT

Part 7 focuses on communication with target market members and, at times, other groups. A specific marketing mix cannot satisfy people in a particular target market unless they are aware of the product and know where to find it. Some promotion decisions relate to a specific marketing mix; others are geared toward promoting the entire organization. **Chapter 15** discusses integrated marketing communications. It describes the communication process and the major promotional methods that can be included in promotion mixes. **Chapter 16** analyzes the major steps in developing an advertising campaign. It also explains what public relations is and how it can be used. **Chapter 17** deals with personal selling and the role it can play in a firm's promotional efforts. This chapter also explores the general characteristics of sales promotion and describes sales promotion techniques.

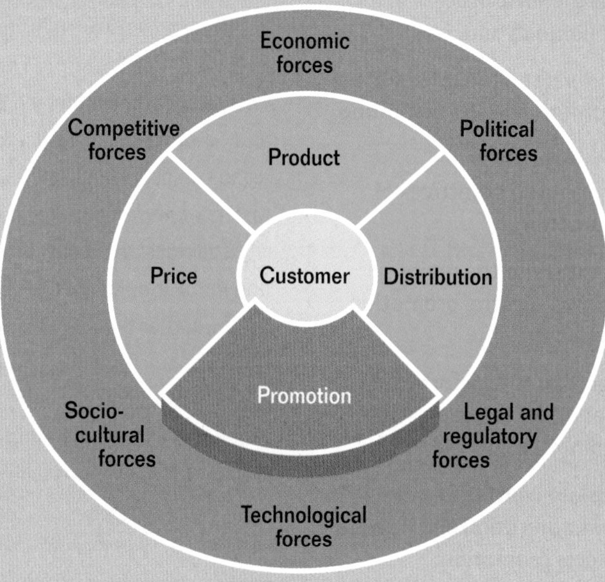

CHAPTER 15 Integrated Marketing Communications

© AP IMAGES/PRNEWSFOTO/BURGER KING CORPORATION

OBJECTIVES:

1. Discuss the nature of integrated marketing communications.
2. Describe the process of communication.
3. Understand the role of promotion in the marketing mix.
4. Explain the objectives of promotion.
5. Understand the major elements of the promotion mix.
6. Describe the factors that affect the choice of promotion-mix elements.
7. Explore word-of-mouth communication and how it affects promotion.
8. Understand the criticisms and defenses of promotion.

"WHOPPER VIRGINS": INVENTIVE MARKETING CAMPAIGN OR TASTELESS EXPLOITATION?

Is it possible that there are people in the world who have never tasted a hamburger? The burger is so ubiquitous that one might think that finding these people would be impossible. Yet this is exactly what Burger King did in a bold marketing move that generated much publicity and some criticism. In December 2008, Burger King launched an ad campaign called "The Whopper Virgins" in which BK researchers traveled to remote areas in Transylvania, Thailand, and Greenland to conduct a taste test between the McDonald's Big Mac and their Whopper using subjects who had never tasted a burger before. According to Burger King, the majority of tasters preferred the Whopper.

Calling it "the world's purest taste test," Russ Klein, president of global marketing, strategy, and innovation of Burger King Corp., said, ". . . with this new campaign, we sought the purest proof that the flame-broiled WHOPPER® sandwich is a favorite." However, many criticized the company for exploiting people in developing countries for profit, pushing burgers on people who are not used to this type of food in their diet. Others saw a problem with the fact that Burger King was spending so much money on an advertising campaign to promote their burger in poor regions where hunger and malnutrition is an issue.

Yet Klein defends his company's actions, saying they performed the project with the utmost care and that none of the communities they chose were places where food was scarce. Additionally, Burger King made donations in the communities to improve the lives of its inhabitants, including donating toys, increasing learning opportunities, and even renovating old churches. Whether or not people agreed with Burger King's actions, the publicity generated by the campaign caused sales to increase for the burger giant by 20 percent. One thing for sure, the controversy has made the Whopper name more visible among the public.[1]

Organizations such as Burger King employ various promotional methods to communicate with their target markets. Providing information to customers and other stakeholders is vital to initiating and developing long-term relationships with them. In this chapter we look at the general dimensions of promotion. First, we discuss the nature of integrated marketing communications. We then define and examine the role of promotion. Next, we analyze the meaning and process of communication and explore some of the reasons promotion is used. After that, we consider major promotional methods and the factors that influence marketers' decisions to use particular methods. Finally, we examine criticisms and defenses of promotion.

integrated marketing communications (IMC) Coordination of promotional efforts for maximum informational and persuasive impact

What Is Integrated Marketing Communications?

Integrated marketing communications (IMC) refers to the coordination of promotional efforts to ensure maximum informational and persuasive impact on customers. Coordinating multiple marketing tools to produce this synergistic effect requires a marketer to employ a broad perspective. A major goal of integrated marketing communications is to send a consistent message to customers. When Chicago bid for the 2016 promotion, they used a variety of tactics to position the city as "Olympic worthy." A website was developed, http://www.chicago2016.org, to talk about the attractions of the city, rally support for the bid and venue development plan, and do fundraising. In addition, Olympics and sport celebrities such as Michael Jordan made videos for the visitation committee when they arrived at the United Center, where Jordan played for the Chicago Bulls. Other sports and Olympics celebrities supporting the effort included Bart Conner, Greg Louganis, and Nadia Comaneci. When the committee arrived at the site of the proposed Olympic stadium, 205 volunteers surrounded the facility holding flags and representing each of the Olympic nations.[2]

COURTESY OF TACO BELL CORP.

Integrated Marketing Communications
Taco Bell uses several marketing communication tools. These promotional efforts are coordinated in an attempt to maximize their informational and persuasive impact.

Because various units both inside and outside most companies traditionally have planned and implemented promotional efforts, customers have not always received consistent messages. Integrated marketing communications allow a firm to coordinate and manage its promotional efforts to transmit consistent messages. This approach fosters not only long-term customer relationships but also the efficient use of promotional resources.

The concept of integrated marketing communications has been increasingly accepted for several reasons. Advertising to a mass audience, a very popular promotional method in the past, is used less today because of its high cost and unpredictable audience size. Marketers now can take advantage of more precisely targeted promotional tools such as cable and satellite TV, direct mail, the Internet, special-interest magazines, CDs and DVDs, cell phones, and even iPods. Database marketing is also allowing marketers to target individual customers more precisely. Until recently, suppliers of marketing communications were specialists. Advertising agencies developed advertising campaigns, sales promotion companies provided sales promotion activities and materials, and public relations firms engaged in publicity efforts. Today, several promotion-related companies provide one-stop shopping to the client seeking advertising, sales promotion, and public relations, thus reducing coordination problems for the sponsoring company. Because the overall cost of marketing communications has risen significantly, upper management demands systematic evaluations of communication efforts and a reasonable return on investment. Although a survey indicated that 74 percent of firms use IMC approaches, only 25 percent rated these approaches as excellent or very good.[3]

The specific communication vehicles employed and the precision with which they are used are changing as both information technology and customer interests become increasingly dynamic. For example, the website Hulu.com, a joint venture between NBC Universal and News Corporation, makes TV episodes available for free with embedded ads. This "on demand" website is attractive to a more mobile and busy target audience who want their entertainment when they have time, not on the network's schedule. Some companies are even creating their own branded content to exploit the many vehicles through which consumers obtain information.

Partnering with Seth McFarlane, "Family Guy" creator, Burger King has short, humorous, cartoon videos available on YouTube. **Branded entertainment** or branded content is designed to combine electronic media (TV, radio, the Internet) with an advertiser to create an entertaining product. In 2008, branded entertainment was more than a $25 billion business. This category of promotion consists of product placement and integration, events, sponsorship, and other branded projects.[4] Such branded content does not replace traditional advertising but gives marketers new, controlled avenues for reaching consumers who have more entertainment choices today than ever before.

Today, marketers and customers have almost unlimited access to data about each other. Integrating and customizing marketing communications while protecting customer privacy has become a major challenge. Through the Internet, companies can provide product information and services that are coordinated with traditional promotional activities. Communication relationships with customers actually can determine the nature of the product. For example, Prescriptives provides custom-blended makeup for different skin types and colors based on informational exchanges with customers. The sharing of information and use of technology to facilitate communication between buyers and sellers are necessary for successful customer relationship management.

branded entertainment
Branded content, which includes product placement, that is designed to combine electronic media with an advertiser to create an integrated, entertaining product

The Communication Process

Communication is essentially the transmission of information. For communication to take place, both the sender and the receiver of information must share some common ground. They must have a common understanding of the symbols, words, and pictures used to transmit information. Thus we define **communication** as a sharing of meaning.[5] Implicit in this definition is the notion of transmission of information because sharing necessitates transmission.

communication
A sharing of meaning

FIGURE 15.1 The Communication Process

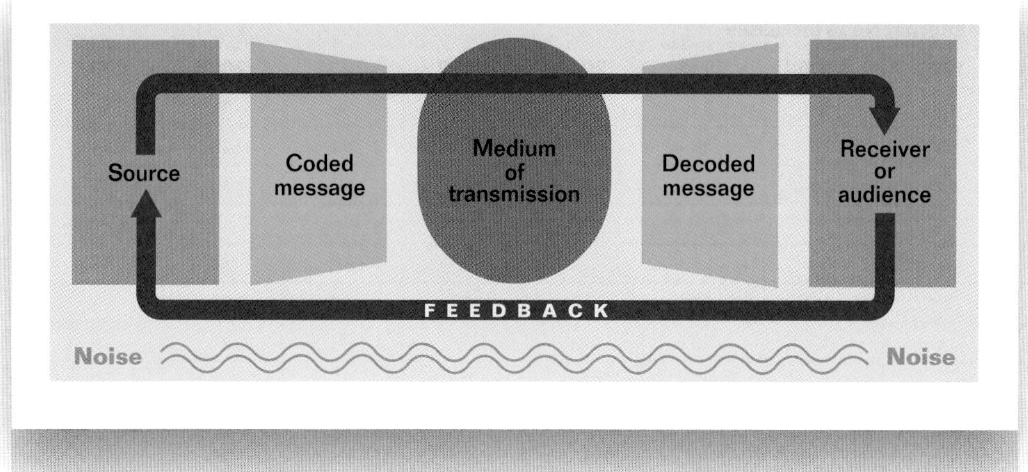

As Figure 15.1 shows, communication begins with a source. A **source** is a person, group, or organization with a meaning it attempts to share with an audience. A source could be a salesperson wishing to communicate a sales message or an organization wanting to send a message to thousands of customers through an advertisement. Developing a strategy can enhance the effectiveness of the source's communication. A **receiver** is the individual, group, or organization that decodes a coded message, and an *audience* is two or more receivers. The intended receivers, or audience, of an advertisement for POM Wonderful pomegranate juice, for example, would probably be consumers who are health conscious. Nearly $25 million in medical research shows pomegranate promotes heart health as well as prostate health.[6]

To share meaning, a source must convert the meaning into a series of signs or symbols representing ideas or concepts. This is called the **coding process**, or *encoding*. When coding meaning into a message, the source must consider certain characteristics of the receiver or audience. To share meaning, the source should use signs or symbols familiar to the receiver or audience. Research has shown that persuasive messages from a source are more effective when the appeal matches an individual's personality.[7] Marketers who understand this realize the importance of knowing their target market and ensuring that an advertisement, for example, uses language the target market understands. Thus, when General Mills advertises Cheerios, it does not mention in its advertising all the ingredients used to make the cereal because some ingredients would have little meaning to consumers. Some notable problems have occurred in translating English advertisements into other languages to communicate with customers in global markets. For example, Budweiser has been advertised in Spain as the "Queen of Beers," and the Chinese have been encouraged to "eat their fingers off" when receiving KFC's slogan "Finger-Lickin' Good."[8] Clearly, it is important that people understand the language used in promotion.

When coding a meaning, a source needs to use signs or symbols that the receiver or audience uses for referring to the concepts the source intends to convey. Instead of technical jargon, explanatory language that helps consumers to understand is more likely to result in positive attitudes and purchase intentions.[9] Marketers try to avoid signs or symbols that may have several meanings for an audience. For example, *soda* as a general term for soft drinks might not work well in national advertisements. Although in some parts of the United States the word means "soft drink," in other regions it may connote bicarbonate of soda, an ice cream drink, or something one mixes with Scotch whiskey.

source
A person, group, or organization with a meaning it tries to share

receiver
The individual, group, or organization that decodes a coded message

coding process
Converting meaning into a series of signs or symbols

TABLE 15.1 Changing Sources of News and Information

Newspaper Readership Declines; Internet News Increases

	1993	1996	1998	2000	2002	2004	2006	2008
Listened/read yesterday...	%	%	%	%	%	%	%	%
Newspaper	58*	50	48	47	41	42	40	34
Radio news	47*	44	49	43	41	40	36	35
Regularly watch...								
Cable TV news	–	–	–	–	33	38	34	39
Local TV News	77	65	64	56	57	59	54	52
Nightly network news	60	42	38	30	32	34	28	29
Network morning news	–	–	23	20	22	22	23	22
Online for news three or more days a week	–	2**	13	23	25	29	31	37

* From 1994; ** From 1995.
Source: "Key News Audiences Now Blend Online and Traditional Sources," August 17, 2008, http://people-press.org/report/444/news-media (accessed April 8, 2009).

To share a coded meaning with the receiver or audience, a source selects and uses a medium of transmission. A **communications channel**, the medium of transmission, carries the coded message from the source to the receiver or audience. Transmission media include ink on paper, air-wave vibrations produced by vocal cords, chalk marks on a chalkboard, and electronically produced vibrations of air waves (in radio and television signals, for example). Table 15.1 summarizes the leading communications channels from which people obtain news and information.

When a source chooses an inappropriate communications channel, several problems may arise. The coded message may reach some receivers, but the wrong ones. Coded messages also may reach intended receivers in incomplete form because the intensity of the transmission is weak. For example, radio and broadcast television signals are received effectively only over a limited range, which varies depending on climatic conditions. Members of the target audience living on the fringe of the broadcast area may receive a weak signal; others well within the broadcast area also may receive an incomplete message if, for example, they listen to the radio while driving or studying.

communications channel The medium of transmission that carries the coded message from the source to the receiver or audience

In the **decoding process**, signs or symbols are converted into concepts and ideas. When a message contradicts a receiver's beliefs or attitudes, the nature of the source will influence the decoding process (credibility, legitimacy, power). Seldom does a receiver decode exactly the same meaning that the source coded. When the result of decoding differs from what was coded, noise exists. **Noise** is anything that reduces the clarity and accuracy of the communication; it has many sources and may affect any or all parts of the communication process. Noise sometimes arises within the communications channel itself. Radio static, poor or slow Internet connections, and laryngitis are sources of noise. Noise also occurs when a source uses signs or symbols that are unfamiliar to the receiver or have a different meaning from the one intended. Noise also may originate in the receiver; a receiver may be unaware of a coded message when perceptual processes block it out.

decoding process Converting signs or symbols into concepts and ideas

noise Anything that reduces a communication's clarity and accuracy

The receiver's response to a message is **feedback** to the source. The source usually expects and normally receives feedback, although perhaps not immediately. During feedback, the receiver or audience is the source of a message directed toward the original source, which then becomes a receiver. Feedback is coded, sent through a communications channel, and decoded by the receiver, the source of the original communication. Thus, communication is a circular process, as indicated in Figure 15.1.

During face-to-face communication, such as occurs in personal selling and product sampling, verbal and nonverbal feedback can be immediate. Instant feedback lets communicators adjust messages quickly to improve the effectiveness of their communication. For example, when a salesperson realizes through feedback that a customer does not understand a sales presentation, the salesperson adapts the presentation to make it more meaningful to the customer. This may be why face-to-face sales presentations create higher behavioral intentions to purchase services than do telemarketing sales contacts.[10] In interpersonal communication, feedback occurs through talking, touching, smiling, nodding, eye movements, and other body movements and postures.

When mass communication such as advertising is used, feedback is often slow and difficult to recognize. In 2008, 4.8 million viewers tuned in to watch CBS's March Madness on Demand on their computers, PDAs, and netbooks. The website generated over $30 million in advertising revenue for the tournament in 2009. The website also features a controversial "boss button," which projects an Excel spreadsheet when a supervisor or co-worker approaches.[11] It may be several years, however, before the effects of this promotion will be known. Feedback does exist for mass communication in the form of measures of changes in sales volume or in consumers' attitudes and awareness levels.

Each communication channel has a limit on the volume of information it can handle effectively. This limit, called **channel capacity**, is determined by the least efficient component of the communication process. Consider communications that depend on speech. An individual source can speak only so fast, and there is a limit to how much an individual receiver can take in aurally. Beyond that point, additional messages cannot be decoded; thus meaning cannot be shared. Although a radio announcer can read several hundred words a minute, a one-minute advertising message should not exceed about 150 words because most announcers cannot articulate words into understandable messages at a rate beyond 150 words per minute.

The Role and Objectives of Promotion

Promotion is communication that builds and maintains favorable relationships by informing and persuading one or more audiences to view an organization more positively and to accept its products. While a company may pursue several promotional objectives (discussed later in this chapter), the overall role of promotion is to stimulate product demand. Toward this end, many organizations spend considerable resources on promotion to build and enhance relationships with current and potential customers. For example, the egg ("The Incredible Edible Egg"), pork ("Pork: The Other White Meat"), and milk ("Got Milk?") industries promote the use of these products to stimulate demand. Marketing campaigns funded by the almond industry promoted the nut as good at combating everything from obesity and heart disease to cancer. Exports of almonds reached nearly $2 billion a year at the high point and domestic sales rose in response to the advertising.[12] Marketers also indirectly facilitate favorable relationships by focusing information about company activities and products on interest groups (such as environmental and consumer groups), current and potential investors, regulatory agencies, and society in general. For example, some organizations promote

feedback
The receiver's response to a message

channel capacity
The limit on the volume of information a communication channel can handle effectively

promotion
Communication to build and maintain relationships by informing and persuading one or more audiences

Objectives for Promotion
Marketers use advertising and other promotion methods to achieve a variety of promotion objectives. What are the objectives of this advertisement?

© AP IMAGES/PRNEWSFOTO/HAWKER BEECHCRAFT CORPORATION

responsible use of products criticized by society, such as tobacco, alcohol, and violent movies. Companies sometimes promote programs that help selected groups. Häagen-Dazs linked its brand to an issue of concern to many in the food industry, the notable disappearance of honeybees. Working with Penn State University and University of California-Davis, factual information was disseminated on this issue. Vanilla Honey Bee ice cream, with a bee logo, was created along with a website, HelpTheHoneybees.com. The goal was to promote and educate consumers on how to support honeybee habitats and spur the public to get involved in planting 1 million seeds. The response exceeded expectations with over 1.2 million plantings and a 5.2 percent increase in sales in a single month.[13] Such *cause-related marketing* efforts link the purchase of products to philanthropic efforts for one or more causes. By contributing to causes that its target markets support, cause-related marketing can help marketers to boost sales and generate goodwill. Marketers also sponsor special events, often leading to news coverage and positive promotion of organizations and their brands. Fendi, for example, held a star-studded hip-hop party in Tokyo to promote the designer label's new B.Mix line of bags.[14]

For maximum benefit from promotional efforts, marketers strive for proper planning, implementation, coordination, and control of communications. Effective management of integrated marketing communications is based on information about and feedback from customers and the marketing environment, often obtained from an organization's marketing information system (see Figure 15.2). How successfully marketers use promotion to maintain positive relationships depends largely on the quantity and quality of information the organization receives. Because customers derive information and opinions from many different sources, integrated marketing communications planning also takes into account informal methods of communication such as word of mouth and independent information sources on the Internet.

Promotional objectives vary considerably from one organization to another and within organizations over time. Large firms with multiple promotional programs operating simultaneously may have quite varied promotional objectives. For the purpose of analysis, we focus on eight promotional objectives. Although this set of possible promotional objectives is not exhaustive, one or more of these objectives underlie many promotional programs.

FIGURE 15.2 Information Flows Are Important in Integrated Marketing Communications

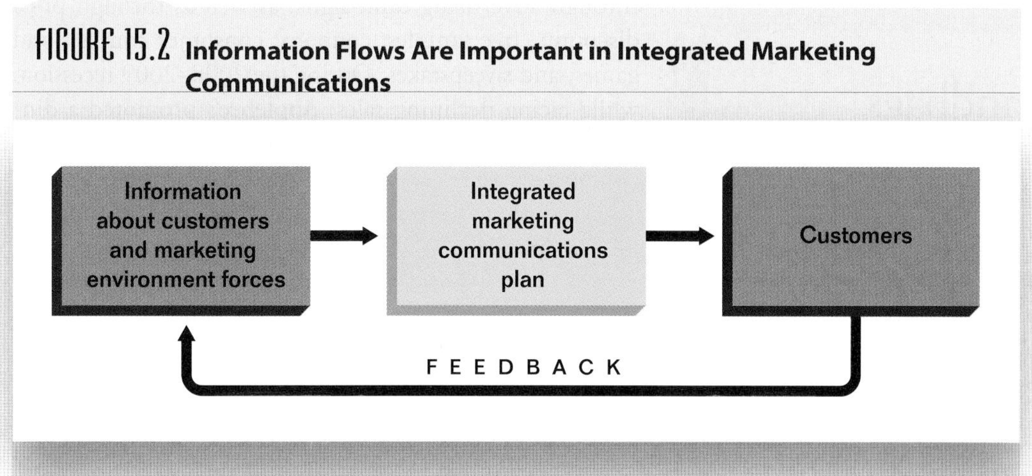

CREATE AWARENESS

A considerable amount of promotion focuses on creating awareness. For an organization introducing a new product or a line extension, making customers aware of the product is crucial to initiating the product adoption process. A marketer that has invested heavily in product development strives to create product awareness quickly to generate revenues to offset the high costs of product development and introduction. One of the most successful new product launches was Gatorade's G2. G2 is a lower calorie version of the popular Gatorade sports drink. Pulling in sales of nearly $160 million in its first year, G2 succeeded whereas 75 percent of new products fail to earn $7.5 million or less in their first year. To create awareness, Super Bowl ads, social and digital media, as well as event marketing strategies were employed.[15]

Creating awareness is important for existing products, too. Promotional efforts may aim to increase awareness of brands, product features, image-related issues (such as organizational size or socially responsive behavior), or operational characteristics (such as store hours, locations, and credit availability). Some promotional programs are unsuccessful because marketers fail to generate awareness of critical issues among a significant portion of target-market members or because the programs do not target the right audience.

STIMULATE DEMAND

When an organization is the first to introduce an innovative product, it tries to stimulate **primary demand**—demand for a product category rather than for a specific brand of product—through pioneer promotion. **Pioneer promotion** informs potential customers about the product: what it is, what it does, how it can be used, and where it can be purchased. Because pioneer promotion is used in the introductory stage of the product life cycle, which means there are no competing brands, it neither emphasizes brand names nor compares brands. The first company to introduce the digital video recorder, for instance, initially attempted to stimulate primary demand by emphasizing the benefits of digital video recorders in general rather than the benefit of its specific brand. Primary-demand stimulation is not just for new products. At times, an industry trade association rather than a single firm uses promotional efforts to stimulate primary demand.

To build **selective demand**, demand for a specific brand, a marketer employs promotional efforts that point out the strengths and benefits of a specific brand. Building selective demand also requires singling out attributes important to potential buyers. Selective demand can be stimulated by differentiating the product from competing brands in the minds of potential buyers. It also can be stimulated by increasing the number of product uses and promoting them

primary demand Demand for a product category rather than for a specific brand

pioneer promotion Promotion that informs consumers about a new product

selective demand Demand for a specific brand

© AP IMAGES/PRNEWSFOTO/PIPERLIME

Selective Demand
Gap Inc. uses ads like this one to build selective demand for Piperlime clothes, shoes, and purses, available only at its Piperlime online stores.

through advertising campaigns, as well as through price discounts, free samples, coupons, consumer contests and games, and sweepstakes. During the 2008–2009 recession, while facing declining sales, Applebee's promoted a dinner for two for $20. The meal included two entrees and an appetizer to attract families impacted by the economic decline.[16] Promotions for large package sizes or multiple-product packages are directed at increasing consumption, which, in turn, can stimulate demand. In addition, selective demand can be stimulated by encouraging existing customers to use more of the product.

ENCOURAGE PRODUCT TRIAL

When attempting to move customers through the product adoption process, a marketer may successfully create awareness and interest, but customers may stall during the evaluation stage. In this case, certain types of promotion, such as free samples, coupons, test drives or limited free-use offers, contests, and games, are employed to encourage product trial. Successful sampling tactics by McDonald's generated awareness of their Southern Style chicken biscuits. McDonald's encouraged customers to evaluate the product line by giving away over 2 million samples of the Southern Style chicken biscuits and 6 million Southern Style chicken sandwiches.[17] Whether a marketer's product is the first of a new product category, a new brand in an existing category, or simply an existing brand seeking customers, trial-inducing promotional efforts aim to make product trial convenient and low risk for potential customers.

IDENTIFY PROSPECTS

Certain types of promotional efforts are directed at identifying customers who are interested in the firm's product and are most likely to buy it. A marketer may use a magazine advertisement with a direct-response information form, requesting the reader to complete and mail the form to receive additional information. Some advertisements have toll-free numbers to facilitate direct customer response. Customers who fill out information blanks or call the organization usually have higher interest in the product, which makes them likely sales prospects. The organization can respond with phone calls, follow-up letters, or personal contact by salespeople. Dun & Bradstreet, for example, offered a free article on customer relationship management to businesspeople who mailed in a card or called a toll-free number. This helped the consulting firm identify prospects to sell data used to develop and maintain customer relationships.

RETAIN LOYAL CUSTOMERS

Clearly, maintaining long-term customer relationships is a major goal of most marketers. Such relationships are quite valuable. Promotional efforts directed at customer retention can help an organization control its costs because the costs of retaining customers are usually considerably lower than those of acquiring new ones. Frequent-user programs, such as those sponsored by airlines, car rental agencies, and hotels, seek to reward loyal customers and encourage them to remain loyal. Delta Air Lines offers frequent flyers benefits for flying 25,000 miles (silver status), 50,000 miles (gold status), and 75,000 miles (platinum status). Benefits can include free upgrades to first class, first notice of promotional programs, and other travel benefits to create commitment and brand loyalty. Some organizations employ special offers that only their existing customers can use. To retain loyal customers, marketers not only advertise loyalty programs but also use reinforcement advertising, which assures current users that they have made the right brand choice and tells them how to get the most satisfaction from the product.

FACILITATE RESELLER SUPPORT

Reseller support is a two-way street. Producers generally want to provide support to resellers to maintain sound working relationships, and in turn, they expect resellers to support their products. When a manufacturer advertises a product to consumers, resellers should view this promotion as a form of strong manufacturer support. In some instances, a producer agrees to pay a certain proportion of retailers' advertising expenses for promoting its products. When a manufacturer is introducing a new consumer brand in a highly competitive product category, it may be difficult to persuade supermarket managers to carry this brand. However, if the manufacturer promotes the new brand with free samples and coupon distribution in the retailer's area, a supermarket manager views these actions as strong support and is much more likely to handle the product. To encourage wholesalers and retailers to market its products more aggressively, a manufacturer may provide them with special offers, buying allowances, and contests. In certain industries, a producer's salesperson may provide support to a wholesaler by working with the wholesaler's customers (retailers) in the presentation and promotion of the products. Strong relationships with resellers are important to a firm's ability to maintain a sustainable competitive advantage. The use of various promotional methods can help an organization achieve this goal.

© DAVID YOUNG-WOLFF/PHOTOEDIT

Encouraging Product Trial
Papa John's uses this special promotional offer to stimulate product trial of one of its specialty pizzas.

COMBAT COMPETITIVE PROMOTIONAL EFFORTS

At times, a marketer's objective in using promotion is to offset or lessen the effect of a competitor's promotional program. This type of promotional activity does not necessarily increase the organization's sales or market share, but it may prevent a sales or market share loss. A combative promotional objective is used most often by firms in extremely competitive consumer markets, such as the fast-food and automobile industries. When some automakers began advertising their automobiles' ability to withstand collisions, as determined by crash tests conducted by various federal and private agencies, Volkswagen, Volvo, and other firms quickly launched their own safety ads to combat their competitors' advertising. Although these ads were trying to promote safety records, the companies also were trying to prevent market share loss in a very competitive market.

REDUCE SALES FLUCTUATIONS

Demand for many products varies from one month to another because of factors such as climate, holidays, and seasons. A business, however, cannot operate at peak efficiency when sales fluctuate rapidly. Changes in sales volume translate into changes in production, inventory levels, personnel needs, and financial resources. When promotional techniques reduce fluctuations by generating sales during slow periods, a firm can use its resources more efficiently.

Promotional techniques are often designed to stimulate sales during sales slumps. For example, advertisements promoting price reduction of lawn-care equipment can increase sales during fall and winter months. During peak periods, a marketer may refrain from advertising to prevent stimulating sales to the point where the firm cannot handle all the demand. On occasion, an organization advertises that customers can be better served by coming in on certain days. A pizza outlet, for example, might distribute coupons that are valid only Monday through Thursday because on Friday through Sunday the restaurant is extremely busy.

To achieve the major objectives of promotion discussed here, companies must develop appropriate promotional programs. In the next section we consider the basic components of such programs, referred to as the *promotion-mix elements.*

The Promotion Mix

Several promotional methods can be used to communicate with individuals, groups, and organizations. When an organization combines specific methods to manage the integrated marketing communications for a particular product, that combination constitutes the **promotion mix** for that product. The four possible elements of a promotion mix are advertising, personal selling, public relations, and sales promotion (see Figure 15.3). For some products, firms use all four ingredients; for others, they use only two or three.

promotion mix
A combination of promotional methods used to promote a specific product

ADVERTISING

Advertising is a paid nonpersonal communication about an organization and its products transmitted to a target audience through mass media, including television, radio, the Internet, newspapers, magazines, direct mail, outdoor displays, and signs on mass-transit vehicles. Individuals and organizations use advertising to promote goods, services, ideas, issues, and people. Being highly flexible, advertising can reach an extremely large target audience or focus on a small, precisely defined segment. For instance, Wendy's advertising focuses on a large audience of potential fast-food customers, ranging from children to adults, whereas advertising for Gulfstream jets aims at a much smaller and more specialized target market.

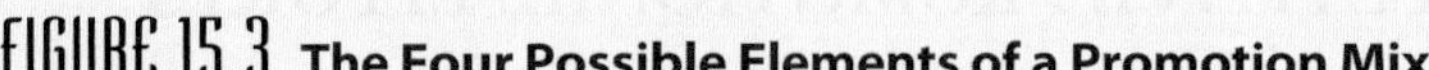
FIGURE 15.3 The Four Possible Elements of a Promotion Mix

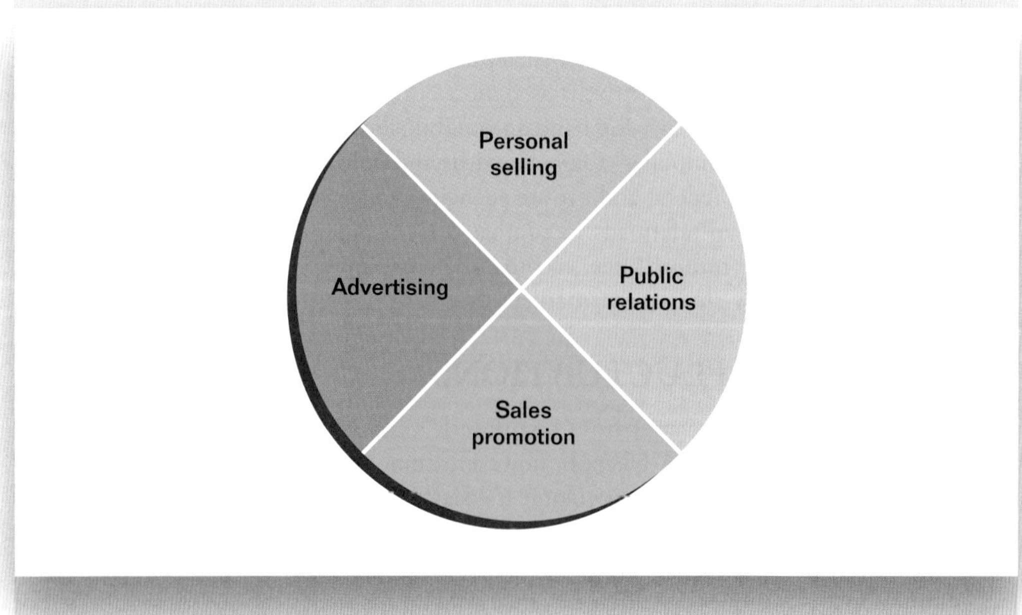

Advertising offers several benefits. It is extremely cost-efficient when it reaches a vast number of people at a low cost per person. For example, the cost of a four-color, one-page ad in *TIME* magazine is $273,750. The magazine has a circulation of over 3.3 million, translating to a guaranteed audience of 19.5 million readers (because of multiple readers per issue). Therefore, the cost of reaching *TIME's* subscribers is approximately $83 per 1,000.[18] Advertising also lets the source repeat the message several times. Levi Strauss, for example, advertises on television, in magazines, and in outdoor displays. Furthermore, advertising a product a certain way can add to its value, and the visibility an organization gains from advertising can enhance its image. For example, research suggests that incorporating touchable elements that generate a positive sensory feedback in mail and print advertising can be a positive persuasive tool.[19] At times, a firm tries to enhance its own or its product's image by including celebrity endorsers in advertisements. Sometimes this strategy can backfire, if the celebrity becomes involved in controversial behavior. For example, singer Chris Brown's commercial for Wrigley's Doublemint gum was suspended due to charges of violent behavior toward his girlfriend, Rihanna. Many celebrity endorsement contracts include "morality clauses" which allow the advertiser to suspend contract obligations.[20]

© AP IMAGES/PRNEWSFOTO/MINNESOTA PARTNERSHIP FOR ACTION AGAINST TOBACCO

Advertising Aimed at Prevention
This ad focuses on one of the many health risks associated with secondhand smoke.

Advertising has disadvantages as well. Even though the cost per person reached may be low, the absolute dollar outlay can be extremely high, especially for commercials during popular television shows. High costs can limit, and sometimes prevent, the use of advertising in a promotion mix. Advertising rarely provides rapid feedback. Measuring its effect on sales is difficult, and it is ordinarily less persuasive than personal selling. In most instances, the time available to communicate a message to customers is limited to seconds because people look at a print advertisement for only a few seconds, and most broadcast commercials are 30 seconds or less long. Of course, the use of "infomercials" can increase exposure time for viewers. We discuss advertising in considerable detail in Chapter 16.

PERSONAL SELLING

Personal selling is a paid personal communication that seeks to inform customers and persuade them to purchase products in an exchange situation. The phrase *purchase products* is interpreted broadly to encompass acceptance of ideas and issues. Telemarketing, direct marketing over the telephone, relies heavily on personal selling.

Personal selling has both advantages and limitations when compared with advertising. Advertising is general communication aimed at a relatively large target audience, whereas personal selling involves more specific communication directed at one or several persons. Reaching one person through personal selling costs considerably more than through advertising, but personal selling efforts often have greater impact on customers. Personal selling also provides immediate feedback, allowing marketers to adjust their messages to improve communication. It helps them to determine and respond to customers' information needs.

When a salesperson and a customer meet face to face, they use several types of interpersonal communication. The predominant communication form is language, both spoken and written. A salesperson and customer frequently use **kinesic communication**, or communication through the movement of head, eyes, arms, hands, legs, or torso. Winking, head nodding, hand gestures, and arm motions are forms of kinesic communication. A good salesperson

kinesic communication Communicating through the movement of head, eyes, arms, hands, legs, or torso

Marketing IN TRANSITION

PureSport Finds Both Pros and Cons in Phelps Endorsement

PureSport, a protein mix created by Texas company Human Performance Labs, LLC, seemed to score big with its use of Olympic swimming champion Michael Phelps as its endorser. Each time Phelps exited the pool in the Beijing Olympics, his coach handed him a bottle of PureSport's protein drink. Fans took notice, and soon began knocking on Phelps' door asking what he was drinking. This major endorsement put this relatively new company among such high-name brands as Hilton Hotel Corp., Visa, and Kellogg Co., all brands that Phelps was endorsing. Some experts believe that Phelps is taking a risk by associating himself with a start-up company since it has no guarantee for success.

However, PureSport now realizes the trouble that one lapse in a celebrity's behavior can cause. A photo recently came out of Phelps smoking a bong at a party on the University of South Carolina campus. Bongs are often used to smoke marijuana, and a local sheriff threatened to pursue criminal charges against Phelps if the evidence showed that he was smoking marijuana. Although there was not enough evidence to pursue charges, damage had been done. USA Swimming suspended Michael Phelps for three months, and Kellogg, along with some other major companies, dropped their sponsorship of Phelps after the story became public. Kellogg maintained that Phelps's behavior was "not consistent with the image of Kellogg." However, the PureSport company is sticking with its star endorser. Although backlash against Phelps has lessened somewhat, Phelps's reputation has been tarnished. It just goes to show that when it comes to celebrity endorsements, the risk goes both ways.[a]

© AP IMAGES/PRNEWSFOTO/H2O AUDIO

often can evaluate a prospect's interest in a product or presentation by noting eye contact and head nodding. **Proxemic communication**, a less obvious form of communication used in personal selling situations, occurs when either person varies the physical distance separating them. When a customer backs away from a salesperson, for example, he or she may be displaying a lack of interest in the product or expressing dislike for the salesperson. Touching, or **tactile communication**, is also a form of communication, although less popular in the United States than in many other countries. Handshaking is a common form of tactile communication both in the United States and elsewhere. We discuss personal selling in more detail in Chapter 17.

PUBLIC RELATIONS

While many promotional activities are focused on a firm's customers, other stakeholders—suppliers, employees, stockholders, the media, educators, potential investors, government officials, and society in general—are important to an organization as well. To communicate with customers and stakeholders, a company employs public relations. Public relations is a broad set of communication efforts used to create and maintain favorable relationships between an organization and its stakeholders. Maintaining a positive relationship with one or more stakeholders can affect a firm's current sales and profits, as well as its long-term survival.

Public relations uses various tools, including annual reports, brochures, event sponsorship, and sponsorship of socially responsible programs aimed at protecting the environment or helping disadvantaged individuals. When President Obama first took office he used a widespread public relations campaign to support his economic plan. President Obama appeared on NBC's *Tonight Show* (the first sitting president to do so), *60 Minutes*, and a prime-time press conference. Even First Lady Michelle Obama appeared on numerous magazine covers. In addition, cabinet members and colleagues supported the president's message in the media.

TrueNorth, a division of Frito-Lay, used press releases and websites to announce an essay contest for inspirational stories that could potentially be the subject of an upcoming ad. Lisa Nigro, the founder of the Inspiration Café in Chicago, was the winner of one of these contests. Lisa delivered food to the homeless first by way of a red wagon, then by car, and eventually by bus, her goal being to treat homeless people with dignity and respect and provide them with training and resources to improve their situation. The resulting advertisement generated significant positive publicity for TrueNorth as well as Lisa's cause.[21]

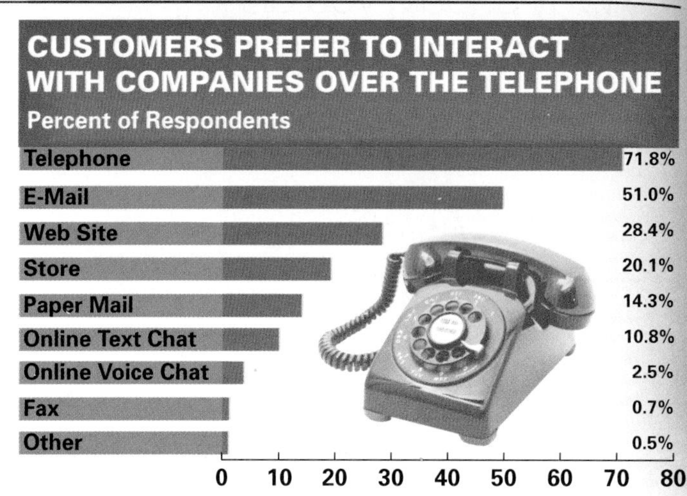

Yankee Group, *Balancing Live Service and Self-Service in the Anywhere Enterprise*, September 2007.

Other tools arise from the use of publicity, which is a component of public relations. Publicity is nonpersonal communication in news story form about an organization or its products, or both, transmitted through a mass medium at no charge. A few examples of publicity-based public relations tools are news releases, press conferences, and feature articles. Ordinarily, public relations efforts are planned and implemented to be consistent with and support other elements of the promotion mix. Public relations efforts may be the responsibility of an individual or of a department within the organization, or the organization may hire an independent public relations agency.

Unpleasant situations and negative events such as product tampering or an environmental disaster may provoke unfavorable public relations for an organization. To minimize the damaging effects of unfavorable coverage, effective marketers have policies and procedures in place to help manage any public relations problems. For example, Wal-Mart responded to negative publicity owing to news stories and lawsuits related to its hiring practices, union management, and aggressive expansion policies with a television ad campaign promoting the entrepreneurial vision of its founder, the savings it offers families, and its employee-benefit packages.[22]

Public relations should not be viewed as a set of tools to be used only during crises. To get the most from public relations, an organization should have someone responsible for public relations either internally or externally and should have an ongoing public relations program. We discuss public relations and publicity in considerable detail in Chapter 16.

SALES PROMOTION

Sales promotion is an activity or material that acts as a direct inducement, offering added value or incentive for the product to resellers, salespeople, or consumers.[23] Examples include free samples, games, rebates, displays, sweepstakes, contests, premiums, and coupons. Some websites help consumers manage their access to coupons. One popular site, RetailMeNot.com, allows you to search by retailer for available coupon codes. Individuals with current codes share them with others and users can report on their success rate with each code or offer. *Sales promotion* should not be confused with *promotion;* sales promotion is just one part of the comprehensive area of promotion. Marketers spend more on sales promotion than on advertising, and sales promotion appears to be a faster-growing area than advertising.

Generally, when companies employ advertising or personal selling, they depend on them either continuously or cyclically. However, a marketer's use of sales promotion tends to be irregular. Many products are seasonal. A company such as Toro may offer more sales promotions in August than in the peak selling season of April or May, when more people buy tractors, lawn mowers, and other gardening equipment. Marketers frequently rely on sales promotion to improve the effectiveness of other promotion-mix elements, especially advertising and personal selling. Decisions to cut sales promotion can have significant negative effects on a company. Increasingly, sales promotion is being linked to target markets through strategic integration into related television programming. Company sponsorship of programming can

proxemic communication Communicating by varying the physical distance in face-to-face interactions

tactile communication Communicating through touching

allow a close connection between brand and target market. Bravo's *Top Chef* has successfully partnered with Toyota, Clorox, *Food & Wine* magazine, Campbell's Soup, Diet Dr Pepper, and Quaker Oats. Are these sponsorship opportunities working? If brand recall is any indicator the answer is yes. Toyota had a 67 percent brand recall (versus a cable average of 49 percent), GLAD had a 77 percent brand recall (versus a cable average of 73 percent), and *Food & Wine* had a brand recall of 77 percent (versus a cable average of 70 percent). More detail on product placements will follow later in this chapter and Chapter 17 will give a more comprehensive discussion of sales promotion.[24]

Sales Promotion
The coupon in this advertisement is a sales promotion technique.

Selecting Promotion-Mix Elements

Marketers vary the composition of promotion mixes for many reasons. Although a promotion mix can include all four elements, frequently a marketer selects fewer than four. Many firms that market multiple product lines use several promotion mixes simultaneously.

An effective promotion mix requires the right combination of components. To see how such a mix is created, we now examine the factors and conditions affecting the selection of promotion-mix elements that an organization uses for a specific promotion mix.

PROMOTIONAL RESOURCES, OBJECTIVES, AND POLICIES

The size of an organization's promotional budget affects the number and relative intensity of promotional methods included in a promotion mix. If a company's promotional budget is extremely limited, the firm is likely to rely on personal selling because it is easier to measure a salesperson's contribution to sales than to measure the sales effectiveness of advertising. Businesses generally must have sizable promotional budgets to use regional or national advertising. Procter & Gamble, for example, the largest advertiser in the United States, spends nearly $2.85 billion a year on advertising.[25] Organizations with extensive promotional resources generally include more elements in their promotion mixes, but having more promotional dollars to spend does not necessarily mean using more promotional methods. Research indicates that resources spent on promotion activities have a positive influence on shareholder value.[26]

An organization's promotional objectives and policies also influence the types of promotion selected. If a company's objective is to create mass awareness of a new convenience good, such as a breakfast cereal, its promotion mix probably leans heavily toward advertising, sales promotion, and possibly public relations. Pepsi's launch of the no-calorie, vitamin-enhanced sparkling beverage Tava involved a broad promotional strategy. Online advertising and product sampling were favored over more traditional print and television advertising. The target market for the beverage was the "reborn digital," age 35–49 men and women who spend considerable amounts of time online, mostly e-mailing and accessing product, travel, music and food information.[27] If a company hopes to educate customers about the features of a durable good, such as a home appliance, its promotion mix may combine a moderate amount of advertising, possibly some sales promotion designed to attract customers to retail stores, and a great deal of personal selling because this is an excellent method to inform customers about such products.

CHARACTERISTICS OF THE TARGET MARKET

Size, geographic distribution, and demographic characteristics of a firm's target market help to dictate the methods to include in a product's promotion mix. To some degree, market size determines composition of the mix. If the size is limited, the promotion mix probably will emphasize personal selling, which can be very effective for reaching small numbers of people. Firms selling to business markets and firms marketing products through only a few wholesalers frequently make personal selling the major component of their promotion mixes. When a product's market consists of millions of customers, businesses rely on advertising and sales promotion because these methods reach masses of people at a low cost per person.

Geographic distribution of a firm's customers also affects the choice of promotional methods. Personal selling is more feasible if a company's customers are concentrated in a small area than if they are dispersed across a vast region. When the company's customers are numerous and dispersed, advertising may be more practical. Distribution of a target market's demographic characteristics, such as age, income, or education, may affect the types of promotional techniques a marketer selects, as well as the messages and images employed.

CHARACTERISTICS OF THE PRODUCT

Generally, promotion mixes for business products concentrate on personal selling, whereas advertising plays a major role in promoting consumer goods. This generalization should be treated cautiously, though. Marketers of business products use some advertising to promote products. Personal selling is used extensively for consumer durables, such as home appliances, automobiles, and houses, whereas consumer convenience items are promoted mainly through advertising and sales promotion. Public relations appears in promotion mixes for both business and consumer products. Marketers of highly seasonal products often emphasize advertising, and sometimes sales promotion as well, because off-season sales generally will not support an extensive year-round sales force. Although most toy producers have sales forces to sell to resellers, many of these companies depend chiefly on advertising to promote their products.

A product's price also influences the composition of the promotion mix. High-priced products call for personal selling because consumers associate greater risk with the purchase of such products and usually want information from a salesperson. Few people, for example, are willing to purchase a refrigerator from a self-service establishment. For low-priced convenience items, marketers use advertising rather than personal selling. When products are marketed through intensive distribution, firms depend strongly on advertising and sales promotion. Many convenience products, such as lotions, cereals, and coffee, are promoted through samples, coupons, and money refunds. When marketers choose selective distribution, promotion mixes vary considerably. Items handled through exclusive distribution, such as expensive watches, furs, and high-quality furniture, typically require a significant amount of

Product Characteristics
Inexpensive, frequently purchased convenience products usually require the manufacturers to include significant levels of advertising in their promotion mixes.

personal selling. Manufacturers of highly personal products, such as laxatives, nonprescription contraceptives, and feminine hygiene products, depend on advertising because many customers do not want to talk with salespeople about these products.

COSTS AND AVAILABILITY OF PROMOTIONAL METHODS

Costs of promotional methods are major factors to analyze when developing a promotion mix. National advertising and sales promotion require large expenditures. If these efforts succeed in reaching extremely large audiences, however, the cost per individual reached may be quite small, possibly a few pennies. Some forms of advertising are relatively inexpensive. Many small, local businesses advertise goods and services through local newspapers, radio and television stations, outdoor displays, search engine result ads, and signs on mass-transit vehicles.

Another consideration that marketers explore when formulating a promotion mix is availability of promotional techniques. Despite the tremendous number of media vehicles in the United States, a firm may find that no available advertising medium effectively reaches a certain target market. The problem of media availability becomes more pronounced when marketers advertise in some foreign countries. Some media, such as television, simply may not be available, or it may be illegal to advertise on television. In China, the State Administration for Radio, Film, and Television banned a Nike commercial that featured basketball star LeBron James besting a kung fu master and a pair of dragons in a video game. In recent years, the agency has cracked down on U.S. and Japanese advertisements that fail to "uphold national dignity and interest, and respect the motherland's culture" of China.[28] Available media may not be open to certain types of advertisements. In some countries, advertisers are forbidden to make brand comparisons on television.

push policy
Promoting a product only to the next institution down the marketing channel

PUSH AND PULL CHANNEL POLICIES

Another element marketers consider when planning a promotion mix is whether to use a push policy or a pull policy. With a **push policy**, the producer promotes the product only to the next

FIGURE 15.4 **Comparison of Push and Pull Promotional Strategies**

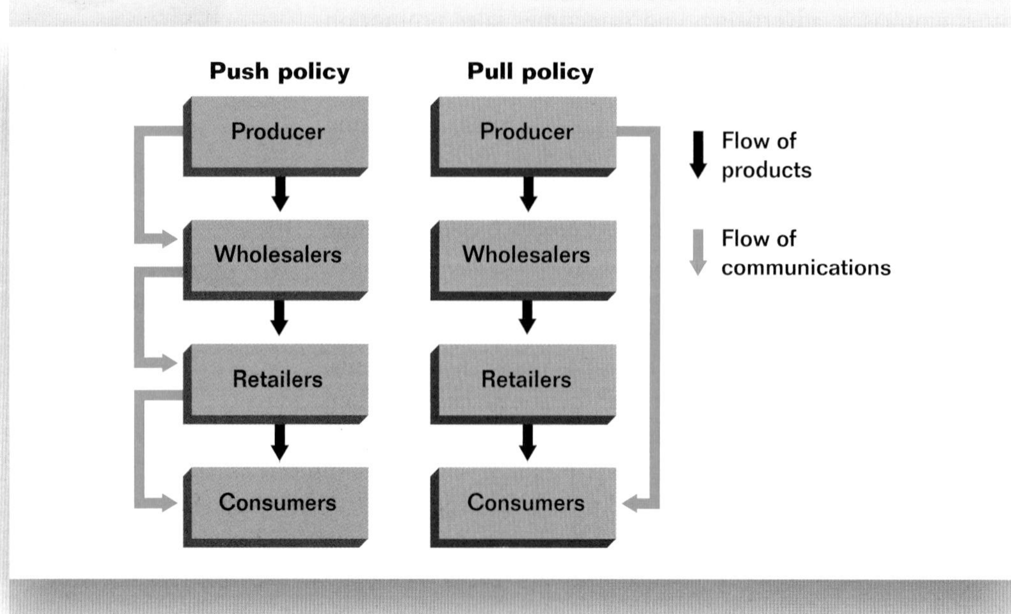

institution down the marketing channel. In a marketing channel with wholesalers and retailers, the producer promotes to the wholesaler because in this case the wholesaler is the channel member just below the producer (see Figure 15.4). Each channel member, in turn, promotes to the next channel member. A push policy normally stresses personal selling. Sometimes sales promotion and advertising are used in conjunction with personal selling to push the products down through the channel.

As Figure 15.4 shows, a firm using a **pull policy** promotes directly to consumers to develop strong consumer demand for its products. It does so primarily through advertising and sales promotion. Because consumers are persuaded to seek the products in retail stores, retailers, in turn, go to wholesalers or the producers to buy the products. This policy is intended to pull the goods down through the channel by creating demand at the consumer level. Consumers are told that if the stores don't have it, ask them to get it. Push and pull policies are not mutually exclusive. At times, an organization uses both simultaneously.

The Growing Importance of Word-of-Mouth Communications

When making decisions about the composition of promotion mixes, marketers should recognize that commercial messages, whether from advertising, personal selling, sales promotion, or public relations, are limited in the extent to which they can inform and persuade customers and move them closer to making purchases. Depending on the type of customers and the products involved, buyers to some extent rely on word-of-mouth communication from personal sources such as family members and friends. **Word-of-mouth communication** is personal, informal exchanges in which customers share with one another information about products, brands, and companies.[29] Most consumers are likely to seek information from knowledgeable friends, family members, and experts when buying medical, legal, and auto repair services. Word-of-mouth communication is also very important when people are selecting restaurants and entertainment, as well as automotive, banking, and personal services such as hair care. Effective marketers who understand the importance of word-of-mouth communication attempt to identify advice givers and opinion leaders and to encourage them to try their products in the hope that they will spread a favorable word about them.

Customers increasingly are going online to share their opinions about goods and services as well as about the companies that market them. At a number of consumer-oriented websites, such as Epinions.com and ConsumerReview.com, consumers can learn about other consumers' feelings toward and experiences with specific products. Users also can search within product categories and compare consumers' viewpoints on various brands and models. Buyers can peruse Internet-based newsgroups, forums, and blogs to find word-of-mouth information. A consumer looking for a new cell phone service, for example, might inquire in forums about other participants' experiences and level of satisfaction to gain more information before making a purchase decision. A study by Forrester and Intelliseek found that more than 90 percent of consumers trust such recommendations they get from other consumers.[30]

The term **social media** describes technology that links people to networks and allows the exchange of personal information, professional information, and common interests such as product and brand preferences. Facebook, LinkedIn, YouTube, Twitter, and others allow marketers to make information available to interested groups. For now, marketers have yet to determine the most effective use of social media. Of 400 executives surveyed, 56 percent said they have no mechanism for tracking positive word-of-mouth via social networks. Only 16 percent of those responding indicated systems to monitor consumer comments on their brands. Procter & Gamble

pull policy
Promoting a product directly to consumers to develop strong consumer demand that pulls products through the marketing channel

word-of-mouth communication
Personal, informal exchanges of information that customers share with one another about products, brands, and companies

social media
Involves electronic technologies that link people to networks and allow the exchange of personal and professional information as well as common interests such as product and brand preferences

Entrepreneurial Marketing

Comic Book Marketing Creates Buzz

Andrew Sinkov got into comic books as an adult and now is in charge of marketing for CoreStreet, a Cambridge, Massachusetts, security software company that markets PIVMAN™, a handheld computer system for emergency workers. Not the most exciting technology product, the PIVMAN™ required a creative communications strategy to build good buzz or word-of-mouth hype about the product. So he hired an artist to draw a 12-page comic book that explained technical information about the product and included characters for educational training. In fact, CoreStreet's popular comic book is generating potential buyers at twice the rate of other marketing materials. The company was able to land part of a security contract with the City of Los Angeles as well as getting many other customers through comic book buzz.[b]

has developed a Social Media Lab to better understand the impact of social media on brands.[31]

Electronic word of mouth is particularly important to consumers staying abreast of trends. At Facebook.com, a feature called The Pulse tracks trends relating to each school. Students, for instance, can see which band is the most popular on their campus and how it compares with bands at other schools. At "social news" websites such as Digg.com, Reddit.com, and Delicious.com, trend-setting consumers can share bookmarks of their favorite websites or Internet stories. These sites have become so influential in introducing consumers to new products and shaping their views about them that marketers are increasingly monitoring them to identify new trends; some firms have even attempted to affect users' votes on their favorite items.[32]

Through an approach called **buzz marketing**, marketers attempt to incite publicity and public excitement surrounding a product through a creative event. OfficeMax, in an attempt to create a buzz around its brand, created a marketing stunt called "Elf Yourself." For the past three years, consumers have been able to animate themselves into elves using their own photo images and send the result to friends, who were also invited to try. In one year, there were over 17 million unique visits to the "Elf Yourself" website, generating significant publicity and buzz.[33] The idea behind buzz marketing is that an accepted member of a social group will always be more credible than any other form of paid communication.[34]

Buzz marketing works best as a part of an integrated marketing communication program that also uses advertising, personal selling, sales promotion, and publicity. However, marketers also should take care that buzz marketing campaigns do not violate any laws or have the potential to be misconstrued and cause undue alarm. Consider that after a buzz effort to promote Cartoon Network's *Aqua Teen Hunger Force* show using electronic devices with flashing lights caused a widespread terrorism scare in the city of Boston, the performance artists hired to implement the campaign were arrested and charged with disorderly conduct. In light of the "botched PR stunt," Ted Turner and Turner Broadcasting apologized and paid the city of Boston $2 million for the time and cost associated with the police and other city personnel engaged in the response.[35]

buzz marketing An attempt to incite publicity and public excitement surrounding a product through a creative event

viral marketing A strategy to get consumers to share a marketer's message, often through e-mail or online video, in a way that spreads dramatically and quickly

product placement The strategic location of products or product promotions within television program content to reach the product's target market

Viral marketing is a strategy to get consumers to share a marketer's message, often through e-mail or online video, in a way that spreads dramatically and quickly. Burger King, for example, created the "Subservient Chicken" website, where Web surfers seem to be able to control a person in a chicken suit by typing in commands. Viral communications resulted in nearly 52 million visitors to the website in less than a year.[36]

Word of mouth, no matter how it's transmitted, is not effective in all product categories. It seems to be most effective for new-to-market and more expensive products. Despite the obvious benefits of positive word of mouth, marketers also must recognize the potential dangers of negative word of mouth. This is particularly important in dealing with online platforms that can reach more people and encourage consumers to "gang up" on a company or product. For example, music giant Sony BMG received negative press over a protest campaign that moved from online to the front of its office building. Sony had stopped production on the third album of its artist Fiona Apple after it decided the record was not radio-friendly. A copy of the album was mysteriously "leaked" on the Internet and soon became one of the most downloaded items online. Fans organized at websites and online forums to create petitions and mail apples to Sony's executives every day for several months. Sony agreed to release the album to stores after members of the online campaign picketed Sony's offices in New York and the story reached the mainstream media.[37] In any case, marketers should not underestimate the importance of word-of-mouth communications and personal influence, nor should they have unrealistic expectations about the performance of commercial messages.

Product Placement

A growing technique for reaching consumers is the selective placement of products within the context of television programs viewed by the target market. **Product placement** is the strategic location of products or product promotions within television programs, movies, video games, or other entertainment venues to reach the product's target market. The hit NBC show *The Office,* for example, has integrated products from Hewlett-Packard and Staples within storylines. Such product placement has become more important owing to the increasing fragmentation of television viewers who have ever-expanding viewing options and technology that can screen advertisements (e.g., digital video recorders such as TiVo). More than 25 percent of TV households currently use a digital video recorder (DVR). This number is expected to double by 2014. A vast majority of DVR users fast-forward through commercials when replaying programs.[38]

In-program product placements have been successful in reaching consumers as they are being entertained rather than in the competitive commercial break time periods. Table 15.2 identifies some of the top ten brands in product placement and the top 10 shows for product placement. For example, the NBC hit comedy show *30 Rock* has included numerous product placements, including rather obvious placements for Verizon's wireless services and Snapple beverages. Reality programming in particular has been a natural fit for product placement because of the close interchange between the participants and the products, for example, Sears and *Extreme Makeover: Home Edition*; Levi's, Burger King, Marquis Jet, and Dove in *The Apprentice*; Coca-Cola and *American Idol.*

Product placement is not limited to U.S. television shows. The European Parliament recently

Sustainable Marketing

There Are Plenty of Fish

Whether or not you believe there are plenty of fish in the sea, one man has discovered how to turn people's search for love into a strong business. In 1999, Markus Frind graduated from technical school as a computer programmer but had a hard time keeping a job as the dot-com bubble was bursting. After moving around for years, Frind grew tired of being laid off and decided to increase his skills by learning ASP.net (a Microsoft web building tool). To challenge himself, he built an online dating site entitled Plenty of Fish.

© ISTOCKPHOTO.COM/ONUR KOCAMAZ

Frind wanted to create a stable income source while saving time and money working from home. Aware of intense competition, he knew his site needed to stand out. Plenty of Fish's competitive advantage is that it offers matchmaking services for free. The target market is people curious about online dating but unwilling to pay for the privilege. Frind, however, had to figure out how to make a living off a free dating site. He used Google's AdSense (which allows users to display Google ads and to earn each time an ad is viewed), and, within his first year, he was earning over $3,300 monthly. He also discovered he could make money selling ad space to other dating sites that assumed Frind's free users would prefer to upgrade (although many never have). Plenty of Fish was designed and run, until recently, by Frind out of his apartment. His success is largely due to minimal costs and a tiny staff. In five years, Frind has accomplished his goals. Plenty of Fish serves 1.6 billion webpages monthly and is set to hit $10 million in revenues. Best of all, Frind says he works a maximum of 10 hours each week. People can save a lot of time, energy, and gasoline getting fixed up online.[c]

TABLE 15.2 Top 10 Brands with TV Product Placement

Top 10 Brands with TV Product Placement		
Brand	**Category**	**Total # Occurrences**
Coca-Cola	Soft Drinks	58
24 Hour Fitness	Fitness Centers	33
Ford	Autos	24
AT&T	Wireless Products/Services	20
Kodak	Cameras	20
Apple	Computer Systems	19
Chevrolet	Autos	14
Mercedes-Benz	Autos	13
Star Trac	Exercise Equipment	13
Everlast	Sporting Equipment	12
Top 10 Shows with Product Placement		
Program	**Network**	**Total # Occurrences**
American Idol	Fox	116
The Biggest Loser	NBC	94
The Amazing Race 14	CBS	67
Extreme Makeover: Home Edition	ABC	48
The Celebrity Apprentice	NBC	40
The Academy Awards	ABC	39
Friday Night Lights	NBC	38
Chuck	NBC	35
The Oscars Red Carpet 2009	ABC	34
90210	CW	32

Source: The Nielsen Company, March 5, 2009, http://adage.com/madisonandvine/article?article_id=135045, accessed April 10, 2009.

green-lighted product placement, but left it up to individual European nations to decide whether and how to permit the practice in their own countries. Moreover, European broadcasters will have to alert viewers that products have been placed in a particular show episode. In general, the notion of product placement has not been viewed favorably in Europe and has been particularly controversial in the United Kingdom. However, British viewers have already been exposed to product placement in shows imported from the United States, including *Desperate Housewives* and *American Idol*.[39]

Criticisms and Defenses of Promotion

Even though promotional activities can help customers to make informed purchasing decisions, social scientists, consumer groups, government agencies, and members of society in general have long criticized promotion. There are two main reasons for such criticism: Promotion does have some flaws, and it is a highly visible business activity that pervades

TABLE 15.3 Criticisms and Defenses of Promotion

Issue	Discussion
Is promotion deceptive?	Although no longer widespread, some deceptive promotion still occurs; laws, government regulations, and industry self-regulation have helped to decrease intentionally deceptive promotion; customers may be unintentionally misled because some words have diverse meanings.
Does promotion increase prices?	When promotion stimulates demand, higher production levels may result in lower per-unit production costs, which keeps prices lower; when demand is not stimulated, however, prices increase owing to the added costs of promotion; promotion fuels price competition, which helps to keep prices lower.
Does promotion create needs?	Many marketers capitalize on people's needs by basing their promotional appeals on these needs; however, marketers do not actually create these needs; if there were no promotion, people would still have basic needs such as those suggested by Maslow.
Does promotion encourage materialism?	Because promotion creates awareness and visibility for products, it may contribute to materialism in the same way that movies, sports, theater, art, and literature may contribute to materialism; if there were no promotion, it is likely that there would still be materialism among some groups, as evidenced by the existence of materialism among some ancient groups of people.
Does promotion help customers without costing too much?	Customers learn about products and services through promotion, allowing them to make more intelligent buying decisions.
Should potentially harmful products be advertised?	Some critics suggest that the promotion of possibly unhealthy products should not be allowed at all; others argue that as long as it is legal to sell such products, promoting those products should be allowed.

our daily lives. Although people almost universally complain that there is simply too much promotional activity, several more specific issues have been raised. Promotional efforts have been called deceptive. Promotion has been blamed for increasing prices. Other criticisms of promotion are that it manipulates consumers into buying products they do not need, that it leads to a more materialistic society, that customers do not benefit sufficiently from promotion to justify its high costs, and that promotion is used to market potentially harmful products. These issues are discussed in Table 15.3.

CHAPTER REVIEW

OBJECTIVES

1 Discuss the nature of integrated marketing communications.

Integrated marketing communications is the coordination of promotion and other marketing efforts to ensure the maximum informational and persuasive impact on customers. Sending consistent messages to customers is a major goal of integrated marketing communications. As both information technology and customer interests become increasingly dynamic, the specific communication vehicles employed and the precision with which they are used are changing.

2 Describe the process of communication.

Communication is a sharing of meaning. The communication process involves several steps. First, the source translates meaning into code, a process known as coding or encoding. The source should employ signs or symbols familiar to the receiver or audience. The coded message is sent through a communications channel to the receiver or audience. The receiver or audience then decodes the message and usually supplies feedback to the source. When the decoded message differs from the encoded one, a condition called noise exists.

3 Understand the role of promotion in the marketing mix.

Promotion is communication to build and maintain relationships by informing and persuading one or more audiences. The overall role of promotion is to stimulate product demand, although a company might pursue several promotional objectives. Cause-related marketing efforts link the purchase of products to philanthropic efforts for one or more causes. Marketers strive for proper planning, implementation, coordination, and control of communications for maximum benefit from promotional efforts. Integrated marketing communications planning takes into account informal methods of communication because customers derive information and opinions from many different sources.

4 Explain the objectives of promotion.

Eight primary objectives underlie many promotional programs. Promotion aims to create awareness of a new product, new brand, or existing product; to stimulate primary and selective demand; to encourage product trial through the use of free samples, coupons, limited free-use offers, contests, and games; to identify prospects; to retain loyal customers; to facilitate reseller support; to combat competitive promotional efforts; and to reduce sales fluctuations.

5 Understand the major elements of the promotion mix.

The promotion mix for a product may include four major promotional methods: advertising, personal selling, public relations, and sales promotion. Advertising is paid nonpersonal communication about an organization and its products transmitted to a target audience through a mass medium. Personal selling is paid personal communication that attempts to inform customers and persuade them to purchase products in an exchange situation. Public relations is a broad set of communication efforts used to create and maintain favorable relationships between an organization and its stakeholders. Sales promotion is an activity or material that acts as a direct inducement, offering added value or incentive for the product, to resellers, salespeople, or consumers.

6 Describe the factors that affect the choice of promotion-mix elements.

Major determinants of which promotional methods to include in a product's promotion mix are the organization's promotional resources, objectives, and policies; characteristics of the target market; characteristics of the product; and cost and availability of promotional methods. Marketers also consider whether to use a push policy or a pull policy. With a push policy, the producer promotes the product only to the next institution down the marketing channel. Normally, a push policy stresses personal selling. Firms that use a pull policy promote directly to consumers, with the intention of developing strong consumer demand for the products. Once consumers are persuaded to seek the products in retail stores, retailers go to wholesalers or the producer to buy the products.

Explore word-of-mouth communication and how it affects promotion.

Most customers are likely to be influenced by friends and family members when making purchases. Word-of-mouth communication is personal, informal exchanges of information that customers share with one another about products, brands, and companies. Customers also may choose to go online to find electronic word of mouth about products or companies. Buzz marketing is an attempt to incite publicity and public excitement surrounding a product through a creative event. Viral marketing is a strategy to get consumers to share a marketer's message, often through e-mail or online video, in a way that spreads dramatically and quickly. A related concept, product placement is the strategic location of products or product promotions within television program content to reach the product's target market.

Understand the criticisms and defenses of promotion.

Promotional activities can help consumers to make informed purchasing decisions, but they also have evoked many criticisms. Promotion has been accused of deception. Although some deceiving or misleading promotions do exist, laws, government regulation, and industry self-regulation minimize deceptive promotion. Promotion has been blamed for increasing prices, but it usually tends to lower them. When demand is high, production and marketing costs decrease, which can result in lower prices. Promotion also helps to keep prices lower by facilitating price competition. Other criticisms of promotional activity are that it manipulates consumers into buying products they do not need, that it leads to a more materialistic society, and that consumers do not benefit sufficiently from promotional activity to justify its high cost. Finally, some critics of promotion suggest that potentially harmful products, especially those associated with violence, sex, and unhealthy activities, should not be promoted at all.

Please visit the student website at www.cengage.com/international for quizzes and games that will help you prepare for exams and help achieve the grade you want.

KEY CONCEPTS

integrated marketing communications
branded entertainment
communication
source
receiver
coding process
communications channel
decoding process
noise
feedback
channel capacity
promotion
primary demand
pioneer promotion
selective demand
promotion mix
kinesic communication
proxemic communication
tactile communication
push policy
pull policy
word-of-mouth communication
social media
buzz marketing
viral marketing
product placement

ISSUES FOR DISCUSSION AND REVIEW

1. What does *integrated marketing communications* mean?
2. What is the major task of promotion? Do firms ever use promotion to accomplish this task and fail? If so, give several examples.
3. What is communication? Describe the communication process. Is it possible to communicate without using all the elements in the communication process? If so, which ones can be omitted?

4. Identify several causes of noise. How can a source reduce noise?
5. Describe the possible objectives of promotion, and discuss the circumstances under which each objective might be used.
6. Identify and briefly describe the four promotional methods an organization can use in its promotion mix.
7. What forms of interpersonal communication besides language can be used in personal selling?
8. How do target-market characteristics determine which promotional methods to include in a promotion mix? Assume that a company is planning to promote a cereal to both adults and children. Along what major dimensions would these two promotional efforts have to differ from each other?
9. How can a product's characteristics affect the composition of its promotion mix?
10. Evaluate the following statement: "Appropriate advertising media are always available if a company can afford them."
11. Explain the difference between a pull policy and a push policy. Under what conditions should each policy be used?
12. In which ways can word-of-mouth communication influence the effectiveness of a promotion mix for a product? How can marketers use word-of-mouth communication to create "buzz" for a product?
13. Which criticisms of promotion do you believe are the most valid? Why?
14. Should organizations be allowed to promote offensive, violent, sexual, or unhealthy products that can be sold and purchased legally? Support your answer.

MARKETING APPLICATIONS

1. Identify two television commercials, one aimed at stimulating primary demand and one aimed at stimulating selective demand. Describe each commercial, and discuss how each attempts to achieve its objective.
2. Which of the four promotional methods—advertising, personal selling, public relations, or sales promotion—would you emphasize if you were developing the promotion mix for the following products? Explain your answers.
   a. Washing machine
   b. Cereal
   c. Halloween candy
   d. Compact disc
3. Suppose that marketers at Falcon International Corporation have come to you for recommendations on how they should promote their products. They want to develop a comprehensive promotional campaign and have a generous budget with which to implement their plans. What questions would you ask them, and what would you suggest they consider before developing a promotional program?
4. Identify two products for which marketers should use a push policy and a pull policy and a third product that might best be promoted using a mix of the two policies. Explain your answers.

ONLINE EXERCISE

5. MySpace isn't just for friends—it's also a unique promotional platform for musical artists, especially unsigned and independent artists. By creating a MySpace page, musicians can share their songs, post important dates, or even blog. MySpace music pages are different from record company websites because they feel more personal. Artists also take advantage of MySpace's viral nature by allowing other MySpace members to post their pictures, songs, and music videos on their own MySpace profile pages. Visit the website at http://music.myspace.com and look for your favorite artist or explore a new one.
   a. Who is the target market for members?
   b. What is being promoted to these individuals?
   c. What are the promotional objectives of the website?

DEVELOPING YOUR MARKETING PLAN

A vital component of a successful marketing strategy is the company's plan for communication to its stakeholders. One segment of the communication plan is included in the marketing mix as the promotional element. A clear understanding of the role that promotion plays, as well as the various methods of promotion, is important in developing the promotional plan. The following questions should assist you in relating the information in this chapter to several decisions in your marketing plan.

1. Review the communication process in Figure 15.1. Identify the various players in the communication process for promotion of your product.
2. What are your objectives for promotion?
3. Which of the four elements of the promotional mix are most appropriate for accomplishing your objectives? Discuss the advantages and disadvantages of each.
4. What role should word-of-mouth communications, buzz marketing, or product placement play in your promotional plan?

The information obtained from these questions should assist you in developing various aspects of your marketing plan found in the *Interactive Marketing Plan* exercise.

VIDEO CASE 15

The Toledo Mud Hens Make Marketing Fun

Since their dismal beginnings in 1896 when they played near a swamp (earning the name Mud Hens in honor of the coots inhabiting the marshy land), the Triple-A Toledo Mud Hens have become one of the most successful minor league baseball teams in the country, and their games some of the best attended. How did they leverage their climb from such a murky start? In a word: marketing. With their two slogans, "Toledo's Family Fun Park" and "Experience the Joy of Mudville," the Mud Hens harness the twin themes of family and history. These days the Mud Hens are the Triple-A affiliate of the major league team the Detroit Tigers. Because the Tigers do all of the hiring and firing of players, trainers, and medical staff, the Mud Hens' home office can focus all of its energy on improving the image and profitability of the Mud Hens enterprise.

The Mud Hens do not have the star power of the major league teams (aside from their popular bird mascots, Muddy and Muddonna), so marketers must seek another way to promote the games. They advertise the games as wholesome, affordable family fun—an alternative to bowling or going to the movies. People of all ages can come to the games and socialize, while watching potential up-and-coming baseball stars develop into mature athletes. Because there is no star paraphernalia to sell, most of the marketing attention is paid to promoting Mud Hens merchandise, like T-shirts and hats, and food and beverage sales. In fact, the team has been the league leader in ballpark merchandise sales since 2000 and ranks second in the minor league for overall merchandise sales. The on-premise Swampshop offers 50 styles of T-shirts and 60 styles of baseball caps in all sizes. Truly avid fans can shop online from anywhere in the world as well.

The league's continued sales and revenue growth stand in contrast to an overall downturn in attendance and purchases at minor league baseball games. This statistic attests to the strength of the Mud Hens' marketing strategy. They market directly to advance ticket buyers in order to target those people who are apt to buy tickets early, buy in quantity, and spend cash at the games. Other marketing channels are the more traditional radio, television, and print media. The Mud Hens enjoy an especially close relationship with local newspapers, where a prominent story about the team is almost guaranteed whenever the Mud Hens have a home game.

When the team decided to build the new Fifth Third Field in downtown Toledo, they knew that the move would generate additional excitement about the team. To accommodate and encourage increased spending at games, planners mapped out a huge 3,000-square-foot Swampshop to comfortably accommodate all consumers. The move to the downtown area has dramatically increased overall attendance rates, which have doubled. All of these strategic maneuvers are part of integrated marketing communications, which entails coordinating promotional and marketing efforts so as to have maximum impact on customers.

Clearly, the Toledo Mud Hens know their market, because they are consistently one of the high revenue generators in the minor leagues. Because the Tigers take care of most of the administrative tasks, the Mud Hens' staff can focus nearly all of their efforts on successfully using the promotion mix (advertising, personal selling, public relations, and promotion) and buzz to get people flocking to the park. The promise of affordable, wholesome family fun has clearly struck a chord with people in this working-class section of Ohio. Games have also been a big hit with corporate season ticket holders as a way to reward employees or to provide a congenial atmosphere for meeting with clients.

The Mud Hens go beyond mere marketing, however, and this is one of the keys to the organization's success. The team has become an integral part of the community—through direct marketing and regular media coverage, but also through charitable endeavors. Because the marketing focus is so much on family fun, community, and socializing, the organization does its best to give back to the community that so avidly supports them. The organization engages in educational and community outreach through various programs such as Muddy's Knothole Club, which provides tickets to underprivileged kids; regular fundraisers and auctions; and donations to local charities. Even pro-bono activities such as these can be part of a well-managed, integrated marketing communications strategy because they increase goodwill toward the organization and encourage people to attend games.

QUESTIONS FOR DISCUSSION

1. How do the Toledo Mud Hens use integrated marketing communications to promote their enterprise?
2. How do the Mud Hens identify and market to their target audience?
3. Suggest how the Mud Hens can gain publicity in order to maintain and increase attendance.

The Toledo Mud Hens, www.mudhens.com (accessed October 27, 2009); The Detroit Tigers, http://tigers.mlb.com (accessed October 27, 2009).

CHAPTER 16 Advertising and Public Relations

© AP IMAGES/PRNEWSFOTO/SOBE

OBJECTIVES:

1. Describe the nature and types of advertising.
2. Explain the major steps in developing an advertising campaign.
3. Identify who is responsible for developing advertising campaigns.
4. Recognize the tools used in public relations.
5. Understand how public relations is used and evaluated.

"DORITOS CONSUMERS OUTWIT MADISON AVENUE EXECUTIVES"

Some of the greatest marketing successes have come from those who think outside the box, like the creators of the SOBE Super Bowl ad. This type of thinking recently paid off for two unemployed brothers whose Doritos commercial won the Ad Meter award in the 2009 Super Bowl. The brother's success foreshadows some fierce competition for advertising agencies from an unlikely source: amateur ad-makers. For under $2,000, two men from an Indiana town filmed an ad that upstaged 50 advertisements by the nation's top advertising agencies. The brothers, Joe and Dave Herbert, were invited along with other amateur filmmakers to create their own advertisements for a possible spot in the Super Bowl. The contest was sponsored by PepsiCo's Frito-Lay division. The contestants had an added incentive to participate: Frito-Lay would award the lucky contestants $1 million if their commercial won the annual Ad Meter survey conducted by *USA Today*.

That's just what the brothers did. Armed with a small amount of money, the brothers filmed their commercial, "Free Doritos," at a local YMCA. The actors received their pay in the form of free food. The brothers' commercial was aired in the first quarter of the Super Bowl and proceeded to best its professional competitors and break Anheuser-Busch's winning streak of 10 Ad Meter contests in a row. "This is going to be the best million dollars we've spent at Frito-Lay," says Ann Mukherjee, group vice president at Frito-Lay. This success might not bode as well for professional advertising agencies that will now have to regard the amateur filmmaker as a formidable foe for the first time.[1]

Like Frito-Lay, many organizations, both for-profit and nonprofit, use advertising and public relations tools to stimulate demand, launch new products, promote current brands, improve organizational images, or boost awareness of public issues. In this chapter we explore several dimensions of advertising and public relations. First, we focus on the nature and types of advertising. Next, we examine the major steps in developing an advertising campaign and describe who is responsible for developing such campaigns. We then discuss the nature of public relations and how public relations is used. We examine various public relations tools and ways to evaluate the effectiveness of public relations. Finally, we focus on how companies deal with unfavorable public relations.

The Nature and Types of Advertising

Advertising permeates our daily lives. At times, we may view it positively; at other times, we avoid it. Some advertising informs, persuades, or entertains us; some bores and even offends us.

As mentioned in Chapter 15, **advertising** is a paid form of nonpersonal communication transmitted to a target audience through mass media, such as television, radio, the Internet, newspapers, magazines, direct mail, outdoor displays, and signs on mass-transit vehicles. In Boston, for example, some taxicabs are sporting a cup of Starbucks coffee magnetically attached to their roofs.[2] Organizations use advertising to reach different audiences ranging from small, specific groups, such as stamp collectors in Idaho, to extremely large groups, such as all athletic-shoe purchasers in the United States.

When asked to name major advertisers, most people immediately mention business organizations. However, many nonbusiness types of organizations, including governments, churches, universities, and charitable organizations, employ advertising to communicate with stakeholders. For example, the government of the United Kingdom spends more than $350 million a year on advertising to advise, influence, or gently chastise its citizens to act appropriately.[3] In 2007, the U.S. government was the 34th largest advertiser in the country, spending $1.1 billion on advertising.[4] Although we analyze advertising in the context of business organizations here, much of the material applies to all types of organizations.

Advertising is used to promote goods, services, ideas, images, issues, people, and anything else that advertisers want to publicize or foster. Depending on what is being promoted, advertising can be classified as institutional or product advertising. **Institutional advertising** promotes organizational images, ideas, and political issues. It can be used to create or maintain an organizational image. Institutional advertisements may deal with broad image issues, such as organizational strength or the friendliness of employees. Institutional advertising also may aim to create a more favorable view of an organization in the eyes of stakeholders, such as shareholders, consumer advocacy groups, potential shareholders, or the general public. When a company promotes its position on a public issue—for instance, a tax increase, abortion, gun control, or international trade coalitions—institutional advertising is referred to as **advocacy advertising**. Institutional advertising may be used to promote socially approved behavior such as recycling and moderation in the consumption of alcoholic beverages. Philip Morris, for example, has run television advertisements urging parents to talk to their children about not smoking. This type of advertising not only has societal benefits but also helps to build an organization's image.

Product advertising promotes the uses, features, and benefits of products. There are two types of product advertising: pioneer and competitive. **Pioneer advertising** focuses on stimulating demand for a product category (rather than a specific brand) by informing potential customers about the product's features, uses, and benefits. This type of advertising is employed when the product is in the introductory stage of the product life cycle. **Competitive advertising**

advertising
Paid nonpersonal communication about an organization and its products transmitted to a target audience through mass media

institutional advertising
Promotes organizational images, ideas, and political issues

advocacy advertising
Promotes a company's position on a public issue

product advertising
Promotes products' uses, features, and benefits

pioneer advertising
Tries to stimulate demand for a product category (rather than a specific brand) by informing potential buyers about the product

competitive advertising
Tries to stimulate demand for a specific brand by promoting its features, uses, and advantages

attempts to stimulate demand for a specific brand by promoting the brand's features, uses, and advantages, sometimes through indirect or direct comparisons with competing brands. To make direct product comparisons, marketers use a form of competitive advertising called **comparative advertising**, which compares the sponsored brand with one or more identified brands on the basis of one or more product characteristics. In response to Subway's $5 foot-long sub sandwich promotion, Quiznos offered their 12-inch Toasty Torpedo for $4. Subway dominates the sub sandwich business and Quiznos attempts to use comparative advertising to gain market share.[5] Often the brands promoted through comparative advertisements have low market shares and are compared with competitors that have the highest market shares in the product category. Product categories that commonly use comparative advertising include soft drinks, toothpaste, pain relievers, foods, tires, automobiles, and detergents. Under the provisions of the 1988 Trademark Law Revision Act, marketers using comparative advertisements must not misrepresent the qualities or characteristics of competing products. Other forms of competitive advertising include reminder and reinforcement advertising. **Reminder advertising** tells customers that an established brand is still around and still offers certain characteristics, uses, and advantages. **Reinforcement advertising** assures current users they have made the right brand choice and tells them how to get the most satisfaction from that brand.

comparative advertising Compares the sponsored brand with one or more identified brands on the basis of one or more product characteristics

reminder advertising Reminds consumers about an established brand's uses, characteristics, and benefits

reinforcement advertising Assures users they chose the right brand and tells them how to get the most satisfaction from it

advertising campaign Designing a series of advertisements and placing them in various advertising media to reach a particular target audience

Developing an Advertising Campaign

An **advertising campaign** involves designing a series of advertisements and placing them in various advertising media to reach a particular target audience. As Figure 16.1 indicates, the major steps in creating an advertising campaign are (1) identifying and analyzing the target audience, (2) defining the advertising objectives, (3) creating the advertising platform, (4) determining the advertising appropriation, (5) developing the media plan,

FIGURE 16.1 General Steps in Developing and Implementing an Advertising Campaign

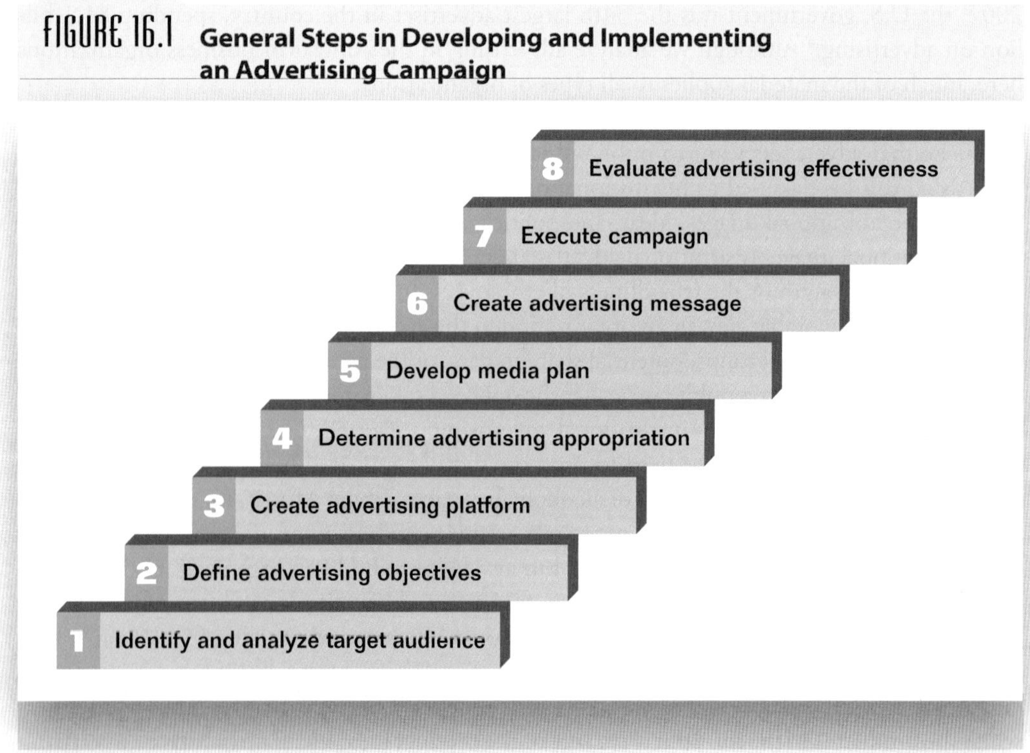

(6) creating the advertising message, (7) executing the campaign, and (8) evaluating advertising effectiveness. The number of steps and the exact order in which they are carried out may vary according to an organization's resources, the nature of its product, and the type of target audience to be reached. Nevertheless, these general guidelines for developing an advertising campaign are appropriate for all types of organizations.

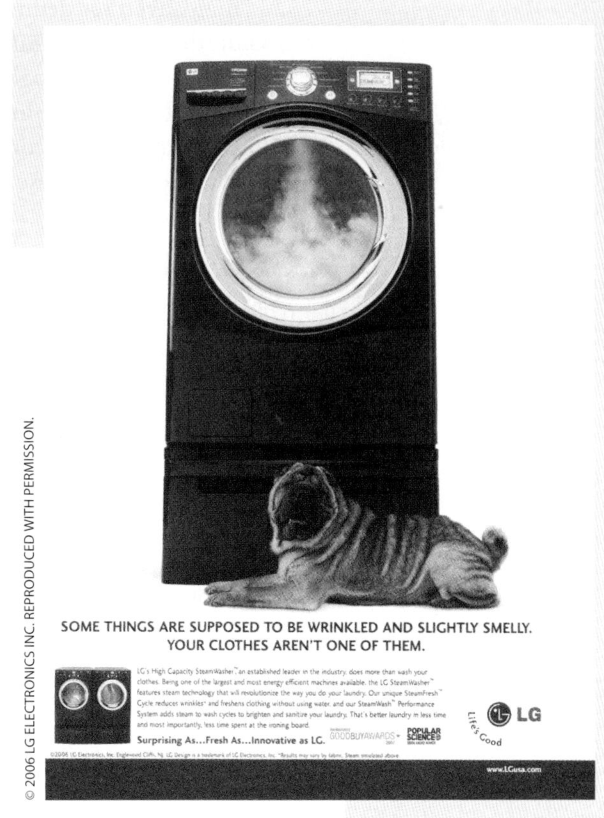

Target Audience
LG produces a front-loading, high-efficiency steam washer. Who is the target audience for this ad?

IDENTIFYING AND ANALYZING THE TARGET AUDIENCE

The **target audience** is the group of people at whom advertisements are aimed. Advertisements for Barbie cereal are targeted toward young girls who play with Barbie dolls, whereas those for Special K cereal are directed at health-conscious adults. Identifying and analyzing the target audience are critical actions. The information yielded helps to determine other steps in developing the campaign. The target audience for a campaign may include everyone in the firm's target market or only a portion of the target market. Tesla's Model S, to be introduced in 2011, will go 300 miles on a single charge and cost around $50,000 after a $7,500 federal tax credit for electric vehicles. The car will target upper-middle-class, energy-conscious consumers and will provide greater affordability than Tesla's Roadster, which sells for over $100,000.[6]

Advertisers research and analyze advertising targets to establish an information base for a campaign. Information commonly needed includes location and geographic distribution of the target group; the distribution of demographic factors such as age, income, race, sex, and education; lifestyle information; and consumer attitudes regarding purchase and use of both the advertiser's products and competing products. The exact kind of information an organization finds useful depends on the type of product being advertised, the characteristics of the target audience, and the type and amount of competition. Generally, the more an advertiser knows about the target audience, the more likely the firm is to develop an effective advertising campaign. When the advertising target is not precisely identified and properly analyzed, the campaign may fail.

DEFINING THE ADVERTISING OBJECTIVES

The advertiser's next step is to determine what the firm hopes to accomplish with the campaign. Because advertising objectives guide campaign development, advertisers should define objectives carefully. Advertising objectives should be stated clearly, precisely, and in measurable terms. Precision and measurability allow advertisers to evaluate advertising success at the end of the campaign in terms of whether or not objectives have been met. To provide precision and measurability, advertising objectives should contain benchmarks and indicate how far the advertiser wishes to move from these standards. If the goal is to increase sales, the advertiser should state the current sales level (the benchmark) and the amount of sales increase sought through advertising. An advertising objective also should specify a time frame so that advertisers know exactly how long they have to accomplish the objective. An advertiser with average monthly sales of $450,000 (the benchmark) might set the following objective: "Our primary advertising objective is to increase average monthly sales from $450,000 to $540,000 within 12 months."

target audience The group of people at whom advertisements are aimed

If an advertiser defines objectives on the basis of sales, the objectives focus on increasing absolute dollar sales or unit sales, increasing sales by a certain percentage, or increasing the firm's market share. Even though an advertiser's long-run goal is to increase sales, not all campaigns are designed to produce immediate sales. Some campaigns are designed to increase product or brand awareness, make consumers' attitudes more favorable, or increase consumers' knowledge of product features. These types of objectives are stated in terms of communication.

CREATING THE ADVERTISING PLATFORM

Before launching a political campaign, party leaders develop a political platform stating the major issues that are the basis of the campaign. Like a political platform, an **advertising platform** consists of the basic issues or selling points that an advertiser wishes to include in the advertising campaign. For example, at half the price of a traditional laptop computer, netbooks have a growing share of the market and interesting positioning. The low price, small size, and light weight make these computers of interest to travelers, students, and increasingly, traditional laptop computer consumers as the performance of these ultra-portable computers improves.[7] A single advertisement in an advertising campaign may contain one or several issues from the platform. Although the platform sets forth the basic issues, it does not indicate how to present them.

An advertising platform should consist of issues important to customers. One of the best ways to determine those issues is to survey customers about what they consider most important in the selection and use of the product involved. Selling features must not only be important to customers, but they also should be strongly competitive features of the advertised brand. For example, New Balance's "Love or Money" campaign stemmed in part from Internet research that found that many people have become disturbed by the behavior of well-known professional athletes, some of whom receive millions of dollars a year in endorsements from New Balance's competitors.[8]

advertising platform
Basic issues or selling points to be included in the advertising campaign

Although research is the most effective method for determining what issues to include in an advertising platform, it is expensive. Therefore, an advertising platform is based most commonly on opinions of personnel within the firm and of individuals in the advertising agency, if an agency is used. This trial-and-error approach generally leads to some successes and some failures.

Advertising Platform Issues
An advertising platform contains multiple issues or selling points. Usually, all of the platform issues are not included in one ad. What platform issues are in this ad?

Because the advertising platform is a base on which to build the advertising message, marketers should analyze this stage carefully. A campaign can be perfect in terms of selection and analysis of its target audience, statement of its objectives, its media strategy, and the form of its message. But the campaign ultimately will fail if the advertisements communicate information that consumers do not deem important when selecting and using the product.

SNAPSHOT

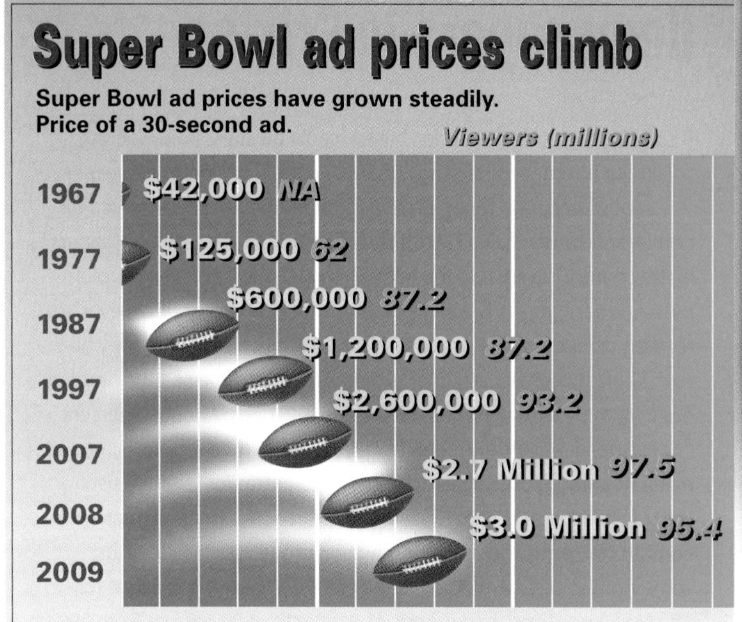

DETERMINING THE ADVERTISING APPROPRIATION

The **advertising appropriation** is the total amount of money a marketer allocates for advertising for a specific time period. New Balance, for example, planned to spend $21 million on its "Love or Money" campaign.[9] It is hard to decide how much to spend on advertising for a specific period because the potential effects of advertising are so difficult to measure precisely.

Many factors affect a firm's decision about how much to appropriate for advertising. Geographic size of the market and the distribution of buyers within the market have a great bearing on this decision. Table 16.1 shows the top ten national advertisers and their expenditures. Advertising appropriations for business products are usually quite small relative to product sales, whereas consumer convenience items, such as soft drinks, soaps, and cosmetics, generally have large advertising expenditures relative to sales.

Of the many techniques used to determine the advertising appropriation, one of the most logical is the **objective-and-task approach**. Using this approach, marketers determine the

advertising appropriation Advertising budget for a specified period

objective-and-task approach Budgeting for an advertising campaign by first determining its objectives and then calculating the cost of all the tasks needed to attain them

TABLE 16.1 Top Ten National Advertisers

Organization	Advertising Expenditures ($ millions)
1. Procter & Gamble	4,898.0
2. AT&T	3,344.7
3. General Motors Corp.	3,296.1
4. Time Warner	3,088.8
5. Verizon	2,821.8
6. Ford Motor Co.	2,576.8
7. GlaxoSmithKline	2,444.2
8. Walt Disney	2,320.0
9. Johnson & Johnson	2,290.5
10. Unilever	2,098.3

Source: *Advertising Age*, June 23, 2008, Vol. 79, Issue 25, p. C10.

Marketing IN TRANSITION

Read All About It: Newspapers in Crisis

It is no secret that the print-based media business is foundering. In our Internet-focused age, many see the traditional newspaper as outdated. As a result, dozens of papers have folded, moved to online-only formats, and laid off staff. Some of the largest newspapers in the country have filed for bankruptcy protection as revenues plummet. And yet, despite the bleak picture, more consumers than ever are reading stories produced in today's newsrooms. How can money be in such short supply when so many people follow the news? The problem has a lot to do with declining advertising revenues. About 90 percent of newspaper advertising sales come from print media, not online, and many newsroom executives admit that their sales forces are resisting the transition to a heavier focus on online content. However, with print editions shrinking and online production growing, revenues must come from somewhere. At the end of 2008, advertising revenue for *The New York Times* had dropped by more than 20 percent from 2007.

© ISTOCKPHOTO.COM/ALEX SLOBODKIN

A few newspaper companies are embracing the changes. The World Company, which owns The *Lawrence Journal-World* and others, stresses the need to focus on local advertisers, just as news is becoming more community oriented. The company has created Marketplace—software enabling local companies to post online information such as profiles, store hours, photos, and commercials. This creation netted the company $500,000 in one year, mostly in new advertising dollars. In the online environment, newspapers also face new competitors for advertising dollars. Companies are going to advertise where the viewers are, which means that newspapers must compete with entertainment and chat sites. It is clear that newspapers must make changes to survive. Cutting staff, paper size, areas covered, and more may serve as a temporary fix, but it is necessary to look for new ways to entice advertisers and create new revenue streams in order to ensure long-term survival.[a]

objectives a campaign is to achieve and then attempt to list the tasks required to accomplish them. The costs of the tasks are calculated and added to arrive at the total appropriation. This approach has one main problem: Marketers sometimes have trouble accurately estimating the level of effort needed to attain certain objectives. A coffee marketer, for example, may find it extremely difficult to determine how much of an increase in television advertising is needed to raise a brand's market share from 8 to 10 percent.

In the more widely used **percent-of-sales approach**, marketers simply multiply the firm's past sales, plus a factor for planned sales growth or decline, by a standard percentage based on what the firm traditionally spends on advertising and perhaps on the industry average. This approach is flawed because it is based on the incorrect assumption that sales create advertising rather than the reverse. A marketer using this approach during declining sales will reduce the amount spent on advertising, but such a reduction may further diminish sales. Though illogical, this technique has been used widely because it is easy to implement.

Another way to determine the advertising appropriation is the **competition-matching approach**. Marketers following this approach try to match their major competitors' appropriations in absolute dollars or to allocate the same percentage of sales for advertising that their competitors do. Although a marketer should be aware of what competitors spend on advertising, this technique should not be used alone because the firm's competitors probably have different advertising objectives and different resources available for advertising. Many companies and advertising agencies review competitive spending on a quarterly basis, comparing competitors' dollar expenditures on print, radio, and television with their own spending levels.

At times, marketers use the **arbitrary approach**, which usually means a high-level executive in the firm states how much to spend on advertising for a certain period. The arbitrary approach often leads to underspending or overspending. Although hardly a scientific budgeting technique, it is expedient.

DEVELOPING THE MEDIA PLAN

As Figure 16.2 shows, advertisers spend tremendous amounts on advertising media. These amounts have grown rapidly during the past two decades. To derive maximum results from media expenditures, marketers must develop effective media plans. A **media plan** sets forth the exact media vehicles to be used (specific

FIGURE 16.2 **Advertising Expenditures by Media Type (In billions US$)**

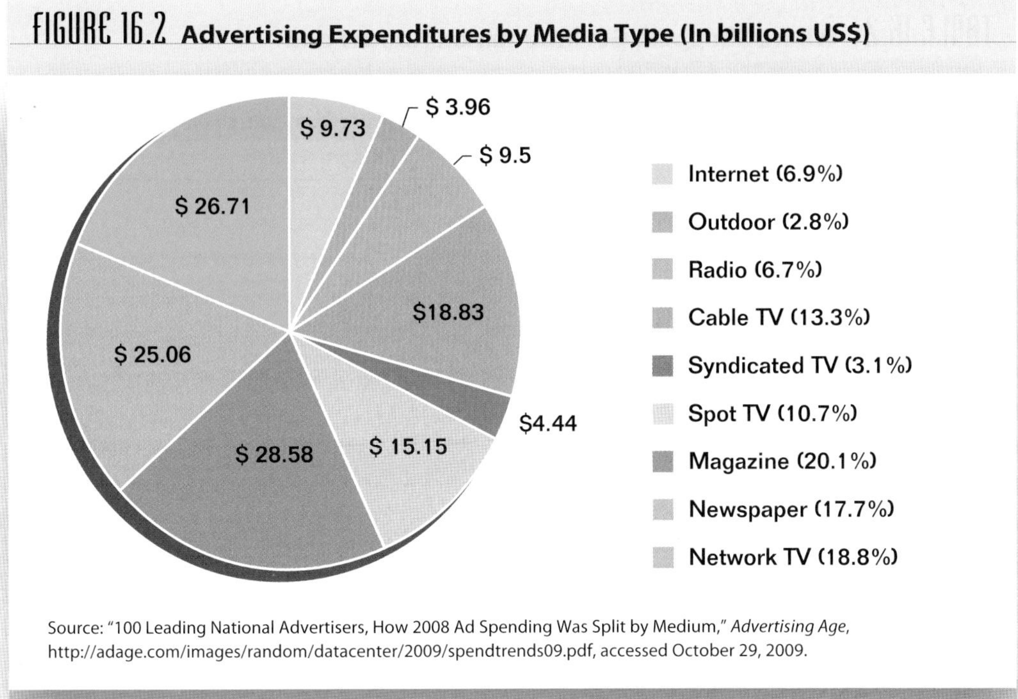

Source: "100 Leading National Advertisers, How 2008 Ad Spending Was Split by Medium," *Advertising Age*, http://adage.com/images/random/datacenter/2009/spendtrends09.pdf, accessed October 29, 2009.

magazines, television stations, newspapers, and so forth) and the dates and times the advertisements will appear. The plan focuses on how many people in the target audience will be exposed to a message and the frequency of exposure. It also determines, to some degree, the effects of the message on those individuals. Media planning is a complex task requiring thorough analysis of the target audience. Sophisticated computer models have been developed to attempt to maximize the effectiveness of media plans.

To formulate a media plan, the planners select the media for the campaign and prepare a time schedule for each medium. The media planner's primary goal is to reach the largest number of people in the advertising target audience that the budget will allow. A secondary goal is to achieve the appropriate message reach and frequency for the target audience while staying within budget. *Reach* refers to the percentage of consumers in the target audience actually exposed to a particular advertisement in a stated period. *Frequency* is the number of times these targeted consumers are exposed to the advertisement.

Media planners begin with broad decisions but eventually make very specific ones. They first decide which kinds of media to use: radio, television, the Internet, newspapers, magazines, direct mail, outdoor displays, or signs on mass-transit vehicles. Although Internet advertising has been growing, it increased only .4 percent in the fourth quarter of 2008 and the projection for the first quarter of 2009 showed a 5 percent decrease, the first decline in online advertising revenue since the 2001 dot-com bubble burst.[10] Media planners assess different formats and approaches to determine which are the most effective. Some media plans are quite focused and use just one medium. The media plans of manufacturers of consumer packaged goods can be quite complex and dynamic.

Media planners take many factors into account when devising a media plan. They analyze location and the demographic characteristics of people in the target audience because people's tastes in media differ according to demographic groups and locations. Figure 16.2 shows traditional advertising expenditures for various media. Note the overall increase in spending on advertising. Spending on television has more than tripled, and spending on the Internet was non-existent in 1985. There are radio stations especially for teenagers, magazines for men ages 18 to 34, and television cable channels aimed at women in various age groups. Media planners also consider the

percent-of-sales approach
Budgeting for an advertising campaign by multiplying the firm's past or expected sales by a standard percentage

competition-matching approach
Determining an advertising budget by trying to match competitors' ad outlays

arbitrary approach
Budgeting for an advertising campaign as specified by a high-level executive in the firm

media plan
Specifies media vehicles and schedule for running the advertisements

TABLE 16.2 Where Shoppers Get Information About Food

Category	Percent of Traffic (Visits from Search Engines)
Newspaper food section	53
Website about food	17
Cable TV food channel	14
Food magazine	12
Food section of magazine	5

Source: Gallup & Robinson, in "Food Shoppers Have Strong Appetite for Newspaper Food Sections," advertisement, *Advertising Age*, January 1, 2007.

cost comparison indicator
A means of comparing the cost of vehicles in a specific medium in relation to the number of people reached

sizes and types of audiences that specific media reach. When T. Boone Pickens introduced his "Pickens Plan" to reduce dependence on foreign oil, he used a variety of media, public relations and networking elements as part of his $58 million media plan. Specifically, the media buy consisted of CNN and MSNBC, as well as full-page ads in *USA Today* and *The Wall Street Journal*. There is also a Facebook account with thousands of friends of the cause. At http://www.pickensplan.com, there is a Facebook-style signup tool with over 50,000 members as well as video blogs. This diversified media strategy was designed to penetrate the marketplace and use new and emerging media tools as well as traditional ones.[11] Declining broadcast television ratings have led many companies to explore alternative media, including not only cable television and Internet advertising but also ads on cell phones and product placements in video games. Several data services collect and periodically provide information about circulations and audiences of various media.

The content of the message sometimes affects media choice. Print media can be used more effectively than broadcast media to present complex issues or numerous details in single advertisements. If an advertiser wants to promote beautiful colors, patterns, or textures, media offering high-quality color reproduction—magazines or television—should be used instead of newspapers. For example, food can be promoted effectively in full-color magazine advertisements but far less effectively in black and white.

The cost of media is an important but troublesome consideration. Planners try to obtain the best coverage possible for each dollar spent. But there is no accurate way to compare the cost and impact of a television commercial with the cost and impact of a newspaper advertisement. A **cost comparison indicator** lets an advertiser compare the costs of several vehicles within a specific medium (such as two magazines) in relation to the number of people each vehicle reaches. The *cost per thousand* (CPM) is the cost comparison indicator for magazines; it shows the cost of exposing a thousand people to a one-page advertisement. Figure 16.2 shows the extent to which each medium is used. Media are selected by weighing the various advantages and disadvantages of each (see Table 16.3).

Media Selection
Valpak selected magazines as one of the media in its media plan.

Like media selection decisions, media scheduling decisions are affected by numerous factors, such as target-audience characteristics, product attributes, product seasonality, customer media behavior, and size of the advertising budget. There are three general types of media

TABLE 16.3 **Advantages and Disadvantages of Major Advertising Media**

Medium	Advantages	Disadvantages
Newspapers	Reaches large audience; purchased to be read; geographic flexibility; short lead time; frequent publication; favorable for cooperative advertising, merchandising services.	Not selective for socioeconomic groups or target market; short life; limited reproduction capabilities; large advertising volume limits exposure to any one advertisement.
Magazines	Demographic selectivity; good reproduction; long life; prestige; geographic selectivity when regional issues are available; read in leisurely manner.	High costs; 30- to 90-day average lead time; high level of competition; limited reach; communicates less frequently.
Direct mail	Little wasted circulation; highly selective; circulation controlled by advertiser; few distractions; personal; stimulates actions; use of novelty; relatively easy to measure performance; hidden from competitors.	Very expensive; lacks editorial content to attract readers; often thrown away unread as junk mail; criticized as invasion of privacy; consumers must choose to read the ad.
Radio	Reaches 95% of consumers; highly mobile and flexible; very low relative costs; ad can be changed quickly; high level of geographic and demographic selectivity; encourages use of imagination.	Lacks visual imagery; short life of message; listeners' attention limited because of other activities; market fragmentation; difficult buying procedures; limited media and audience research.
Television	Reaches large audiences; high frequency available; dual impact of audio and video; highly visible; high prestige; geographic and demographic selectivity; difficult to ignore.	Very expensive; highly perishable message; size of audience not guaranteed; amount of prime time limited; lack of selectivity in target market.
Internet	Immediate response; potential to reach a precisely targeted audience; ability to track customers and build databases; highly interactive medium.	Costs of precise targeting are high; inappropriate ad placement; effects difficult to measure; concerns about security and privacy.
Yellow Pages	Wide availability; action and product category oriented; low relative costs; ad frequency and longevity; nonintrusive.	Market fragmentation; extremely localized; slow updating; lack of creativity; long lead times; requires large space to be noticed.
Outdoor	Allows for frequent repetition; low cost; message can be placed close to point of sale; geographic selectivity; operable 24 hours a day; high creativity and effectiveness.	Message must be short and simple; no demographic selectivity; seldom attracts readers' full attention; criticized as traffic hazard and blight on countryside; much wasted coverage; limited capabilities.

Source: Information from Christian Arens, Michael F. Weigold, and William Arens, *Contemporary Advertising* (Burr Ridge, IL: Irwin/ McGraw-Hill, 2009); George E. Belch and Michael Belch, *Advertising and Promotion* (Burr Ridge, IL: Irwin/McGraw-Hill, 2008).

schedules: continuous, flighting, and pulsing. When a *continuous* schedule is used, advertising runs at a constant level with little variation throughout the campaign period. With a *flighting* schedule, advertisements run for set periods of time, alternating with periods in which no ads run. For example, an advertising campaign might have an ad run for two weeks, then suspend it for two weeks, and then run it again for two weeks. A *pulsing* schedule combines continuous and flighting schedules. During the entire campaign, a certain portion of advertising runs continuously, and during specific time periods of the campaign, additional advertising is used to intensify the level of communication with the target audience.

CREATING THE ADVERTISING MESSAGE

The basic content and form of an advertising message are functions of several factors. A product's features, uses, and benefits affect the content of the message. Characteristics of the people in the target audience—gender, age, education, race, income, occupation, lifestyle, and other

regional issues Versions of a magazine that differ across geographic regions

copy The verbal portion of advertisements

attributes—influence both content and form. For example, gender affects how people respond to advertising claims that use hedging words such as *may* and *probably* and pledging words such as *definitely* and *absolutely*. Researchers have found that women respond negatively to both types of claims, but pledging claims have little effect on men.[12] When Procter & Gamble promotes Crest toothpaste to children, the company emphasizes daily brushing and cavity control. When Crest is marketed to adults, tartar and plaque control are emphasized. To communicate effectively, advertisers use words, symbols, and illustrations that are meaningful, familiar, and attractive to people in the target audience.

An advertising campaign's objectives and platform also affect the content and form of its messages. If a firm's advertising objectives involve large sales increases, the message may include hard-hitting, high-impact language and symbols. When campaign objectives aim at increasing brand awareness, the message may use much repetition of the brand name and words and illustrations associated with it.

Choice of media obviously influences the content and form of the message. Effective outdoor displays and short broadcast spot announcements require concise, simple messages. Magazine and newspaper advertisements can include considerable detail and long explanations. Because several kinds of media offer geographic selectivity, a precise message can be tailored to a particular geographic section of the target audience. Some magazine publishers produce **regional issues**, in which advertisements and editorial content of copies appearing in one geographic area differ from those appearing in other areas. For example, *TIME* magazine publishes eight regional issues. A company advertising in *TIME* might decide to use one message in the New England region and another in the rest of the nation. A company also may choose to advertise in only one region. Such geographic selectivity lets a firm use the same message in different regions at different times.

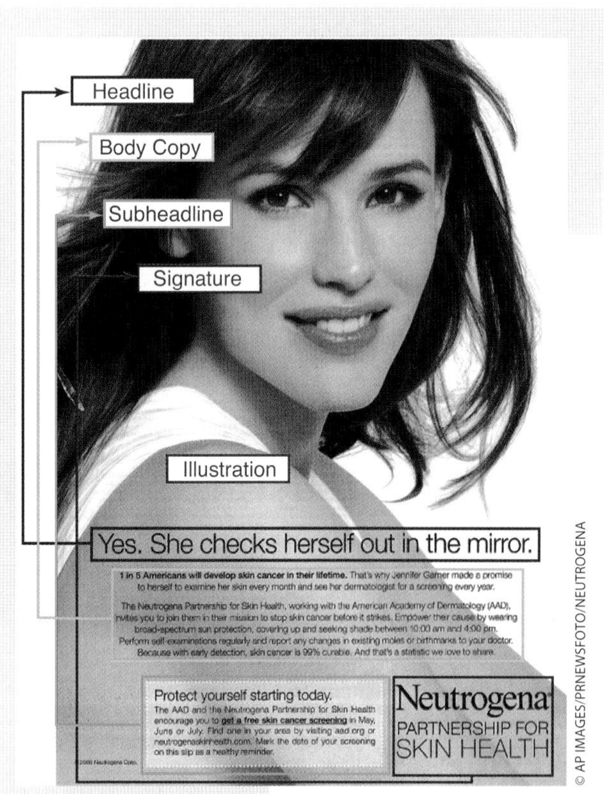

Components of a Print Ad
This Neutrogena ad contains all of the components of a print ad, including a headline, body copy, subheadline, signature, and illustration. Not all print ads contain all of these components.

Copy

Copy is the verbal portion of an advertisement and may include headlines, subheadlines, body copy, and signature. Not all advertising contains all these copy elements. Even handwritten notes on direct-mail advertising that say, "Try this. It works!" seem to increase requests for free samples.[13] The headline is critical because often it is the only part of the copy that people read. It should attract readers' attention and create enough interest to make them want to read the body copy. Bed Bath & Beyond developed a highly effective coupon with the headline "How much do you love saving 20%" with kisses carefully placed on the coupon and promo piece. The glimpse of emotion enhanced the effectiveness of this advertising execution. The subheadline, if there is one, links the headline to the body copy and sometimes is used to explain the headline.

Body copy for most advertisements consists of an introductory statement or paragraph, several explanatory paragraphs, and a closing paragraph. Some copywriters have adopted guidelines for developing body copy systematically: (1) Identify a specific desire or problem, (2) recommend the product as the best way to satisfy that desire or solve that problem, (3) state product benefits and indicate why the product is best for the buyer's particular situation, (4) substantiate advertising claims, and (5) ask the buyer to take action. When substantiating claims, it is important to present the substantiation in a credible manner. The proof of claims should help strengthen the image of the product and company integrity. Kodak has captured consumers' attention with a $30 million ad campaign educating consumers on how much they are wasting on printer ink. With the headline "Last year America paid $5 billion too much for ink," and taglines such as, "The world's most expensive liquid isn't found in the Middle East," Kodak is capturing attention for its efficient printers and diversifying from its core film business, which is on the decline.[14]

The signature identifies the advertisement's sponsor. It may contain several elements, including the firm's trademark, logo, name, and address. The signature should be attractive, legible, distinctive, and easy to identify in a variety of sizes.

Because radio listeners often are not fully "tuned in" mentally, radio copy should be informal and conversational to attract listeners' attention, resulting in greater impact. Radio messages are highly perishable and should consist of short, familiar terms. The length should not require a rate of speech exceeding approximately two and one-half words per second.

In television copy, the audio material must not overpower the visual material, and vice versa. However, a television message should make optimal use of its visual portion, which can be very effective for product demonstrations. Copy for a television commercial is sometimes initially written in parallel script form. Video is described in the left column and audio in the right. When the parallel script is approved, the copywriter and artist combine copy with visual material by using a **storyboard**, which depicts a series of miniature television screens showing the sequence of major scenes in the commercial. Beneath each screen is a description of the audio portion to be used with that video segment. Technical personnel use the storyboard as a blueprint when producing the commercial.

storyboard
A mockup combining copy and visual material to show the sequence of major scenes in a commercial

Artwork

Artwork consists of an advertisement's illustrations and layout. Although **illustrations** are often photographs, they also can be drawings, graphs, charts, and tables. Illustrations can be more important in capturing attention than text or brand elements, independent of size.[15] They are used to attract attention, encourage audiences to read or listen to the copy, communicate an idea quickly, or communicate ideas that are difficult to put into words.[16] Advertisers use various illustration techniques. They may show the product alone, in a setting, or in use, or they may show the results of its use. Illustrations also can be in the form of comparisons, contrasts, and diagrams.

artwork
An ad's illustrations and layout

illustrations
Photos, drawings, graphs, charts, and tables used to spark audience interest

The **layout** of an advertisement is the physical arrangement of the illustration and the copy—headline, subheadline, body copy, and signature. These elements can be arranged in

layout
The physical arrangement of an ad's illustration and copy

Color vs. Black-and-White
This ad highlights the importance of using color when advertising certain products.

many ways. The final layout is the result of several stages of layout preparation. As it moves through these stages, the layout promotes an exchange of ideas among people developing the advertising campaign and provides instructions for production personnel.

EXECUTING THE CAMPAIGN

Execution of an advertising campaign requires extensive planning and coordination because many tasks must be completed on time and many people and firms are involved. Production companies, research organizations, media firms, printers, photoengravers, and commercial artists are just a few of the people and firms contributing to a campaign.

Implementation requires detailed schedules to ensure that various phases of the work are done on time. Advertising management personnel must evaluate the quality of the work and take corrective action when necessary. Citibank, for example, pulled the plug on ads for its credit card rewards program featuring an annoying pair of fictional eastern Europeans because of criticism in the media and the blog world.[17] In some instances, changes are made during the campaign so that it meets objectives more effectively. Sometimes one firm develops a campaign, and another executes it.

EVALUATING ADVERTISING EFFECTIVENESS

Advertising can be evaluated before, during, and after the campaign. An evaluation performed before the campaign begins is called a **pretest**. A pretest usually attempts to evaluate the effectiveness of one or more elements of the message. To pretest advertisements, marketers sometimes use a **consumer jury**, a panel of actual or potential buyers of the advertised product. Jurors judge one or several dimensions of two or more advertisements. Such tests are based on the belief that consumers are more likely than advertising experts to know what influences them.

pretest
Evaluation of ads performed before a campaign begins

consumer jury
A panel of a product's actual or potential buyers who pretest ads

posttest
Evaluation of advertising effectiveness after the campaign

recognition test
A posttest in which individuals are shown the actual ad and asked if they recognize it

unaided recall test
A posttest in which respondents identify ads they have recently seen but are given no recall clues

aided recall test
A posttest that asks respondents to identify recent ads and provides clues to jog their memories

To measure advertising effectiveness during a campaign, marketers sometimes use "inquiries." In a campaign's initial stages, an advertiser may use several advertisements simultaneously, each containing a coupon, form, or toll-free phone number through which potential customers can request information. The advertiser records the number of inquiries returned from each type of advertisement. If an advertiser receives 78,528 inquiries from advertisement A, 37,072 from advertisement B, and 47,932 from advertisement C, advertisement A is judged superior to advertisements B and C.

Evaluation of advertising effectiveness after the campaign is called a **posttest**. Advertising objectives often determine what kind of posttest is appropriate. If the objectives focus on communication—to increase awareness of product features or brands or to create more favorable customer attitudes—the posttest should measure changes in these dimensions. Advertisers sometimes use consumer surveys or experiments to evaluate a campaign based on communication objectives.

For campaign objectives stated in terms of sales, advertisers should determine the change in sales or market share attributable to the campaign. For example, Kroger experienced a 6 percent increase in same-store sales, but they had many promotional messages and tactics in the marketplace, making it hard to isolate a direct cause and effect. In addition to the traditional newspaper inserts, Kroger offered 10 percent off the price of groceries if consumers spent their tax rebate checks at Kroger (the amount of tax rebates redeemed and resulting sales could be tracked), gas discounts, free groceries in exchange for points earned through its loyalty program, targeted ads to consumers through direct marketing (related to loyalty card information), and other personalized discounting.[18] However, changes in sales or market share brought about by advertising cannot be measured precisely. Many factors independent of advertisements affect a firm's sales and market share. Competitors' actions, government actions, and changes in economic conditions, consumer preferences, and weather are only a few factors that might enhance or diminish a company's sales or market share. By using data about past and current sales and advertising expenditures, advertisers can make gross estimates of the effects of a campaign on sales or market share.

Because it is difficult to determine the direct effects of advertising on sales, some advertisers evaluate print advertisements according to how well consumers can remember them. Posttest methods based on memory include recognition and recall tests. Such tests usually are performed by research organizations through surveys. In a **recognition test**, respondents are shown the actual advertisement and asked whether they recognize it. If they do, the interviewer asks additional questions to determine how much of the advertisement each respondent read. When recall is evaluated, the respondents are not shown the actual advertisement but instead are asked about what they have seen or heard recently. Recall can be measured through either unaided or aided recall methods. In an **unaided recall test**, respondents identify advertisements they have seen recently but are not shown any clues to help them remember. A Gallup & Robinson study of 12 years of recall and likability of Super Bowl ads revealed that when consumer confidence is weak, recall is 11 percent lower than the average and 35 percent lower than in good economic times.[19] A similar procedure is used with an **aided recall test**, but respondents are shown a list of products, brands, company names, or trademarks to jog their memories. The Canadian government ran a national anti-drug campaign targeting 13- to 15-year-olds and their parents. In an evaluation of the impact on the parent component, parents had a very high aided recall of 73 percent of the television ad and 25 percent said they did something as a result of the ad campaign.[20] Several research organizations, such as Daniel Starch, provide research services that test recognition and recall of advertisements. The major justification for using recognition and recall methods is that people are more likely to buy a product if they can remember an advertisement about it than if they cannot. Researchers also use sophisticated techniques based on *single-source data* to help evaluate advertisements. With this technique, individuals' behaviors are tracked from televisions to checkout counters. Monitors are placed in preselected homes, and computers record when the television is on and which station is being viewed. At the supermarket checkout, the individual in the sample household presents an identification card. Checkers then record the purchases by scanner, and data are sent to the research facility. Some single

Sustainable Marketing

Would You Like to Buy a Recycled Toothbrush?

Although many eco-responsible entrepreneurs are looking at new products based on recycling technology, probably the last thing you would think about being recycled is your toothbrush. Recycline, Inc., which has been recognized as one of *Inc.* magazine's "50 Green Entrepreneurial Companies," markets the Preserve line of toothbrushes, tongue cleaners, and razors from recycled #5 plastics, the kind in items such as yogurt cups. In the last year, the company has seen its sales jump 45 percent based on public relations, especially publicity.

© DALE DURFEE/STONE/GETTY IMAGES

While public relations is used to maintain a favorable image of a product including positive attitude of the organization with stakeholders, publicity is the communication about the organization and its products that gets transmitted through mass media at no charge. Preserve's products have received such free publicity in movies and in magazines. However, even high-profile exposure did not help this company maintain strong performance through the recent recession. As people began to cut back on more expensive purchases in favor of cheaper options, Preserve partnered with one of its distributors, Whole Foods Market, to devise a new promotional campaign called "Gimme 5." Preserve prominently displayed #5 plastic recycling stations (the type of plastic used in yogurt containers and Brita water filters, which is not easily recyclable) in Whole Foods stores. The stations help consumers feel good about recycling a material they would otherwise throw away, give Preserve a free source of plastics for their products, and create buzz around Preserve, Whole Foods Market, Stonyfield Farm, and other companies that use #5 plastic containers.

Preserve executives hope that as consumers think twice about spending money, they will continue to make feel-good, environmentally responsible choices. They are confident that as long as going green remains affordable, consumers will do the right thing.[b]

source data companies provide sample households with scanning equipment for use at home to record purchases after returning from shopping trips. Single-source data provide information that links exposure to advertisements with purchase behavior.

Who Develops the Advertising Campaign?

An advertising campaign may be handled by an individual or by a few persons within a firm, by a firm's own advertising department, or by an advertising agency. In very small firms, one or two individuals are responsible for advertising (and for many other activities as well). Usually these individuals depend heavily on personnel at local newspapers and broadcast stations for copywriting, artwork, and advice about scheduling media.

In certain large businesses—especially large retail organizations—advertising departments create and implement advertising campaigns. Depending on the size of the advertising program, an advertising department may consist of a few multiskilled persons or a sizable number of specialists, such as copywriters, artists, media buyers, and technical production coordinators. Advertising departments sometimes obtain the services of independent research organizations and hire freelance specialists when a particular project requires it.

Many firms employ an advertising agency to develop advertising campaigns. When Volkswagen introduced its new minivan, the Routan, it used award-winning ad agency Crispin Porter & Bogusky. With the support of spokesperson Brooke Shields, the campaign was launched on TV and the Web. The integrated marketing campaign targeted growing families and offered the website http://babymaker3000.com. More than 140,000 virtual babies were created by uploading pictures of the mother and father and "creating the virtual baby." The rate at which these photos were created was very similar to the actual birthrate at that time.[21] When an organization uses an advertising agency, the firm and the agency usually develop the advertising campaign jointly. Advertising agencies assist businesses in several ways. An agency, especially a large one, can supply the services of highly skilled specialists—not only copywriters, artists, and production coordinators but also media experts, researchers, and legal advisers. Agency personnel often have broad advertising experience and are usually more objective than a firm's employees about the organization's products. Because an agency traditionally receives most of its compensation from a 15 percent commission paid by the media from which it makes purchases, firms can obtain some agency services at low or moderate costs. If an agency contracts for $400,000 of television time for a firm, it receives a commission of $60,000 from the television station. Although the traditional compensation method for agencies is changing and now includes other factors, media commissions still offset some costs of using an agency. Table 16.4 lists some of the leading ad agencies.

Public Relations

Public relations is a broad set of communication efforts used to create and maintain favorable relationships between an organization and its stakeholders. Bank of America maintains an online newsroom that provides press releases, speeches, executive biographies, and facts about the company. This online newsroom became an extremely important source of information during the 2008–2009 recession, when the bank's reputation was damaged by the world financial crisis. An organization communicates with various stakeholders, both internal and external, and public relations efforts can be directed toward any and all of these. A firm's stakeholders can include customers, suppliers, employees, stockholders, the media, educators, potential investors, government officials, and society in general.

public relations
Communication efforts used to create and maintain favorable relations between an organization and its stakeholders

Public relations can be used to promote people, places, ideas, activities, and even countries. It focuses on enhancing the image of the total organization. Assessing public attitudes and creating a favorable image are no less important than direct promotion of the organization's products. Because the public's attitudes toward a firm are likely to affect the sales of its products, it is very important

TABLE 16.4 Top Ten Ad Agencies

1. Crispin, Porter & Bogusky
2. TBWA\Chiat\Day
3. Goodby, Silverstein & Partners
4. R/GA
5. Tribal DDB
6. Mindshare
7. Martin Agency
8. Vidal Partnership
9. RAPP
10. Deutsch

Source: Rupal Parekh, "Agency of the Year: Crispin, Porter & Bogusky," *Advertising Age,* January 19, 2009, http://adage.com/agencya-list08/article?article_id=133815 (accessed April 11, 2009).

for firms to maintain positive public perceptions. In addition, employee morale is strengthened if the public perceives the firm positively.[22] Although public relations can make people aware of a company's products, brands, or activities, it also can create specific company images, such as innovativeness or dependability. Companies such as Green Mountain Coffee Roasters, Patagonia, Sustainable Harvest, and Honest Tea have earned reputations for being socially responsible not just because they strive to act in a socially responsible manner but also because their efforts are reported through news stories and other public relations efforts. By getting the media to report on a firm's accomplishments, public relations helps the company maintain positive public visibility.

Annual Reports
Annual reports, when appropriately designed, can generate favorable public relations.

PUBLIC RELATIONS TOOLS

Companies use various public relations tools to convey messages and create images. Public relations professionals prepare written materials, such as brochures, newsletters, company magazines, news releases, websites, blogs, and annual reports, that reach and influence their various stakeholders. Justin Vernon, a musician from Eau Claire, Wisconsin, recorded nine songs while staying at his parents' hunting cabin. He used a desktop computer and recording software. After placing his songs on MySpace, an online buzz grew that resulted in an appearance on *The Late Show with David Letterman* and a recording contract.[23] Public relations personnel also create corporate identity materials, such as logos, business cards, stationery, and signs, that make firms immediately recognizable. Speeches are another public relations tool. Because what a company executive says publicly at meetings or to the media can affect the organization's image, his or her speech must convey the desired message clearly.

Event sponsorship, in which a company pays for part or all of a special event, such as a benefit concert or a tennis tournament, is another public relations tool. Examples are Home Depot's sponsorship of NASCAR and the U.S. Olympic teams. Sponsoring special events can

Womenkind: An Advertising Agency for Women

Since experts estimate that most purchasing power in the United States is in women's hands, a man named Jerry Judge decided to create an advertising company for women. Called Womenkind, the company provides many marketing services to companies targeting women. Judge employs female freelancers and assembles groups of small businesswomen, mothers, and activists that function as a focus group and communicate via a website and in informal communication like phone conversations. Judge's venture has already attracted attention from marketers like Procter & Gamble. The company has also created a research project called WomIntuition. The function is to measure the difference between men and women when they view ads. Womenkind provides an opportunity for marketers to send the right message to women.[c]

be an effective means of increasing company or brand recognition with relatively minimal expenditures. Event sponsorship can gain companies considerable amounts of free media coverage. McDonald's is one of the largest corporate sponsors in the sports world. From the Olympics to grassroots youth programs, McDonald's has donated large sums of money to help promote sporting events, even throughout the 2008–2009 recession.[24] An organization tries to make sure that its product and the sponsored event target a similar audience and that the two are easily associated in customers' minds. Public relations personnel also organize unique events to "create news" about the company. These may include grand openings with celebrities, prizes, hot-air balloon rides, and other attractions that appeal to a firm's audience.

Publicity is part of public relations. **Publicity** is communication in news story form about the organization, its products, or both transmitted through a mass medium at no charge. By 2009, JetBlue Airways, for example, was ranked third in a consumer airline quality ranking, ahead of all the major carriers. Only Hawaiian Airlines and AirTran Airways ranked above JetBlue.[25] Although public relations has a larger, more comprehensive communication function than publicity, publicity is a very important aspect of public relations. Publicity can be used to provide information about goods or services; to announce expansions, acquisitions, research, or new-product launches; or to enhance a company's image.

The most common publicity-based public relations tool is the **news release**, sometimes called a *press release,* which is usually a single page of typewritten copy containing fewer than 300 words and describing a company event or product. A news release gives the firm's or agency's name, address, phone number, and contact person. News releases can tackle a multitude of specific issues, as suggested in Table 16.5. A **feature article** is a manuscript of up to 3,000 words prepared for a specific publication. A **captioned photograph** is a photograph with a brief description explaining the picture's content. Captioned photographs are effective for illustrating new or improved products with highly visible features.

There are several other kinds of publicity-based public relations tools. A **press conference** is a meeting called to announce major news events. Media personnel are invited to a press conference and are usually supplied with written materials and photographs. Letters to the editor and editorials are sometimes prepared and sent to newspapers and magazines. Videos and audiotapes may be distributed to broadcast stations in the hope that they will be aired.

Publicity-based public relations tools offer several advantages, including credibility, news value, significant word-of-mouth communications, and a perception of being endorsed by the media. The public may consider news coverage more truthful and credible than an advertisement because the media are not paid to provide the information. In addition, stories regarding a new-product introduction or a new environmentally responsible company policy, for example, are handled as news items and are likely to receive notice. Finally, the cost of publicity is low compared with the cost of advertising.[26]

Publicity-based public relations tools have some limitations. Media personnel must judge company messages to be newsworthy if the messages are to be published or broadcast at all. Consequently, messages must be timely, interesting, accurate, and in the public interest. Many communications do not qualify. It may take a great deal of time and effort to

publicity
A news story type of communication transmitted through a mass medium at no charge

news release
A short piece of copy publicizing an event or a product

feature article
A manuscript of up to 3,000 words prepared for a specific publication

captioned photograph
A photo with a brief description of its contents

press conference
A meeting used to announce major news events

TABLE 16.5 Possible Issues for News Releases

Changes in marketing personnel	Packaging changes
Support of a social cause	New products
Improved warranties	New slogan
Reports on industry conditions	Research developments
New uses for established products	Company's history and development
Product endorsements	Employment, production, and sales records
Quality awards	Award of contracts
Company name changes	Opening of new markets
Interviews with company officials	Improvements in financial position
Improved distribution policies	Opening of an exhibit
International business efforts	History of a brand
Athletic event sponsorship	Winners of company contests
Visits by celebrities	Logo changes
Reports on new discoveries	Speeches of top management
Innovative marketing activities	Merit awards
Economic forecasts	Anniversary of inventions

convince media personnel of the news value of publicity releases. Although public relations personnel usually encourage the media to air publicity releases at certain times, they control neither the content nor the timing of the communication. Media personnel alter length and content of publicity releases to fit publishers' or broadcasters' requirements and may even delete the parts of messages that company personnel view as most important. Furthermore, media personnel use publicity releases in time slots or positions most convenient for them. Thus messages sometimes appear in locations or at times that may not reach the firm's target audiences. Although these limitations can be frustrating, properly managed publicity-based public relations tools offer an organization substantial benefits.

EVALUATING PUBLIC RELATIONS EFFECTIVENESS

Because of the potential benefits of good public relations, it is essential that organizations evaluate the effectiveness of their public relations campaigns. Research can be conducted to determine how well a firm is communicating its messages or image to its target audiences. *Environmental monitoring* identifies changes in public opinion affecting an organization. A *public relations audit* is used to assess an organization's image among the public or to evaluate the effect of a specific public relations program. A communications audit may include a content analysis of messages, a readability study, or a readership survey. If an organization wants to measure the extent to which stakeholders view it as being socially responsible, it can conduct a *social audit.*

One approach to measuring the effectiveness of publicity-based public relations is to count the number of exposures in the media. To determine which releases are published in print media and how often, an organization can hire a clipping service, a firm that clips and sends news releases to client companies. To measure the effectiveness of television coverage, a firm can enclose a card with its publicity releases requesting that the television station record its name and the dates when the news item is broadcast (although station personnel do not always comply). Although some television and radio tracking services exist, they are extremely costly.

Ben & Jerry's Global Free Cone Day!

Scoop-Shop Only Flavor & Social Mission Campaigns Highlight Annual Event on April 29th

BURLINGTON, Vt.--(BUSINESS WIRE)--As Ben & Jerry's celebrates its 30th anniversary across the globe, the socially-minded ice cream maker, with the fun and funky flavors, asks what better way to share the love? They're giving it away.

No, this is not one of those internet pranks that makes you send ten emails to your friends for a free pair jeans. This is as plain and simple as vanilla. "Jerry and Ben started their first Free Cone Day as a thank you to their customers," said Debra Heintz, Retail Operations Director. "It's cool," added Heintz with full pun intended, "we get to continue the peace, love and FREE ice cream tradition every year across the world." **Free Cone Day is Tuesday, April 29th, 2008**.

Certainly you can try one of your old favorites such as the legend-dairy classic Cherry Garcia, Phish Food or Chocolate Fudge Brownie. However, if you're looking for a little something new to tickle your ice cream funny-bone the company is introducing a few brand new flavors to bring joy to your belly and soul.

- **Imagine Whirled Peace™** – Continuing in a long lineage of rock and roll flavors, we're honored to introduce Imagine Whirled Peace. John Lennon imagined a world without war, and asked us all to "Give Peace a Chance." We're proud to partner with Peace One Day to act globally and take one step closer to making our planet one of peace and love. Imagine Whirled Peace is a tongue-pleasing concoction of caramel and sweet cream ice creams mixed with fudge peace signs and toffee.

- **Coconut Seven Layer Bar** – What can we say, except we know you'll go coconuts for our latest and greatest flavor, based on the popular dessert: coconut ice cream with coconut & fudge flakes, walnuts & swirls of graham cracker & butterscotch. This is a treat solely for our Scoop Shop fans, as it is the only place in the world that you can get this flavor!
- **ONE Cheesecake Brownie™** - This top-testing new flavor is a decadent cheesecake ice cream with cheesecake brownie chunks. The amazing thing is the taste is only the half of it! We're partnering with ONE.org to "make poverty history." To find out all the campaign info, visit ONE.org/benjerry.

COURTESY OF BEN & JERRY'S

Press Release
Press releases are often used to spread news about a company or its products.

Counting the number of media exposures does not reveal how many people actually have read or heard the company's message or what they thought about the message afterward. However, measuring changes in product awareness, knowledge, and attitudes resulting from the publicity campaign does. To assess these changes, companies must measure these levels before and after public relations campaigns. Although precise measures are difficult to obtain, a firm's marketers should attempt to assess the impact of public relations efforts on the organization's sales.

DEALING WITH UNFAVORABLE PUBLIC RELATIONS

We have thus far discussed public relations as a planned element of the promotion mix. However, companies may have to deal with unexpected and unfavorable publicity resulting from an unsafe product, an accident, controversial actions of employees, or some other negative event or situation. For example, an airline that experiences a plane crash faces a very tragic and distressing situation. Unfavorable coverage can have quick and dramatic effects. After JetBlue, a low-cost airline, left nine planes full of passengers stranded for six hours or more while waiting for a weather break during an ice storm, many negative news stories appeared on TV, in print, and online, and the company's stock plummeted.[27] As it did with JetBlue, a single negative event that produces public relations can wipe out a company's favorable image and destroy positive customer attitudes established through years of expensive advertising campaigns and other promotional efforts. Today's mass media, including online services and the Internet, disseminate information faster than ever before, and bad news generally receives considerable media attention.

To protect its image, an organization needs to prevent unfavorable public relations or at least lessen its effect if it occurs. First and foremost, the organization should try to prevent negative incidents and events through safety programs, inspections, and effective quality-control procedures. Experts insist that sending consistent brand messages and images throughout all communications at all times can help a brand maintain its strength even during a crisis.[28] However, because negative events can befall even the most cautious firms, an organization should have predetermined plans in place to handle them when they do occur. Firms need to establish policies and procedures for reducing the adverse impact of news coverage of a crisis or controversy. In most cases, organizations should expedite news coverage of negative events rather than trying to discourage or block it. If news coverage is suppressed, rumors and other misinformation may replace facts and be passed along anyway. An unfavorable event easily can balloon into serious problems or public issues and become quite damaging. By being forthright with the press and public and taking prompt action, firms may be able to convince the public of their honest attempts to deal with the situation, and news personnel may be more willing to help explain complex issues to the public. Dealing effectively with a negative event allows an organization to lessen the unfavorable impact on its image. Consider that after news reports about JetBlue leaving nine planes of passengers stranded on runways, the company offered the passengers full refunds and vouchers for free flights in the future. JetBlue founder and CEO David Neeleman, who said he was "humiliated and mortified" by the incident, immediately implemented plans to add and train staff to remedy communications and operations issues that contributed to the crisis. He also pledged to enact a customer bill of rights that would penalize the airline and reward passengers should such a scenario recur.[29] Experts generally advise that companies confronting negative publicity respond quickly and honestly to the situation and keep the lines of communications with all stakeholders open.

CHAPTER REVIEW

OBJECTIVES

① Describe the nature and types of advertising.

Advertising is a paid form of nonpersonal communication transmitted to consumers through mass media such as television, radio, the Internet, newspapers, magazines, direct mail, outdoor displays, and signs on mass-transit vehicles. Both nonbusiness and business organizations use advertising. Institutional advertising promotes organizational images, ideas, and political issues. When a company promotes its position on a public issue such as taxation, institutional advertising is referred to as advocacy advertising. Product advertising promotes uses, features, and benefits of products. The two types of product advertising are pioneer advertising, which focuses on stimulating demand for a product category rather than a specific brand, and competitive advertising, which attempts to stimulate demand for a specific brand by indicating the brand's features, uses, and advantages. To make direct product comparisons, marketers use comparative advertising, in which two or more brands are compared. Two other forms of competitive advertising are reminder advertising, which tells customers that an established brand is still around, and reinforcement advertising, which assures current users they have made the right brand choice.

② Explain the major steps in developing an advertising campaign.

Although marketers may vary in how they develop advertising campaigns, they should follow a general pattern. First, they must identify and analyze the target audience, the group of people at whom advertisements are aimed. Second, they should establish what they want the campaign to accomplish by defining advertising objectives. Objectives should be clear, precise, and presented in measurable terms. Third, marketers must create the advertising platform, which contains basic issues to be presented in the campaign. Advertising platforms should consist of issues important to consumers. Fourth, advertisers must decide how much money to spend on the campaign; they arrive at this decision through the objective-and-task approach, percent-of-sales approach, competition-matching approach, or arbitrary approach.

Advertisers then must develop a media plan by selecting and scheduling media to use in the campaign. Some of the factors affecting the media plan are location and demographic characteristics of the target audience, content of the message, and cost of the various media. The basic content and form of the advertising message are affected by product features, uses, and benefits; characteristics of the people in the target audience; the campaign's objectives and platform; and the choice of media. Advertisers use copy and artwork to create the message. The execution of an advertising campaign requires extensive planning and coordination.

Finally, advertisers must devise one or more methods for evaluating advertisement effectiveness. Evaluations performed before the campaign begins are called pretests; those conducted after the campaign are called posttests. Two types of posttests are a recognition test, in which respondents are shown the actual advertisement and asked whether they recognize it, and a recall test. In aided recall tests, respondents are shown a list of products, brands, company names, or trademarks to jog their memories. In unaided tests, no clues are given.

③ Identify who is responsible for developing advertising campaigns.

Advertising campaigns can be developed by personnel within the firm or in conjunction with advertising agencies. When a campaign is created by the firm's personnel, it may be developed by one or more individuals or by an advertising department within the firm. Use of an advertising agency may be advantageous because an agency provides highly skilled, objective specialists with broad experience in advertising at low to moderate costs to the firm.

④ Recognize the tools used in public relations.

Public relations is a broad set of communication efforts used to create and maintain favorable relationships between an organization and its stakeholders. Public relations can be used to promote people, places, ideas, activities, and countries and to create and maintain a positive company image. Public relations tools include written materials, such as brochures, newsletters, and annual reports; corporate identity materials, such as business cards and signs; speeches; event sponsorships; and special events. Publicity is communication in news-story form about an organization, its products, or both transmitted through a mass medium at no charge. Publicity-based public relations tools include news releases, feature articles, captioned photographs, and press conferences. Problems that organizations confront in using publicity-based public relations include reluctance of media personnel to print or air releases and lack of control over timing and content of messages.

Understand how public relations is used and evaluated.

To evaluate the effectiveness of their public relations programs, companies conduct research to determine how well their messages are reaching their audiences. Environmental monitoring, public relations audits, and counting the number of media exposures are all means of evaluating public relations effectiveness. Organizations should avoid negative public relations by taking steps to prevent negative events that result in unfavorable publicity. To diminish the impact of unfavorable public relations, organizations should institute policies and procedures for dealing with news personnel and the public when negative events occur.

Please visit the student website at www.cengage.com/international for quizzes and games that will help you prepare for exams and help achieve the grade you want.

KEY CONCEPTS

advertising
institutional advertising
advocacy advertising
product advertising
pioneer advertising
competitive advertising
comparative advertising
reminder advertising
reinforcement advertising
advertising campaign
target audience
advertising platform
advertising appropriation
objective-and-task approach
percent-of-sales approach
competition-matching approach
arbitrary approach
media plan
cost comparison indicator
regional issues
copy
storyboard
artwork
illustrations
layout
pretest
consumer jury
posttest
recognition test
unaided recall test
aided recall test
public relations
publicity
news release
feature article
captioned photograph
press conference

ISSUES FOR DISCUSSION AND REVIEW

1. What is the difference between institutional and product advertising?
2. What is the difference between competitive advertising and comparative advertising?
3. What are the major steps in creating an advertising campaign?
4. What is a target audience? How does a marketer analyze the target audience after identifying it?
5. Why is it necessary to define advertising objectives?
6. What is an advertising platform, and how is it used?
7. What factors affect the size of an advertising budget? What techniques are used to determine an advertising budget?
8. Describe the steps in developing a media plan.
9. What is the function of copy in an advertising message?
10. Discuss several ways to posttest the effectiveness of advertising.
11. What role does an advertising agency play in developing an advertising campaign?
12. What is public relations? Whom can an organization reach through public relations?
13. How do organizations use public relations tools? Give several examples that you have observed recently.
14. Explain the problems and limitations associated with publicity-based public relations.

15. In what ways is the effectiveness of public relations evaluated?

16. What are some sources of negative public relations? How should an organization deal with unfavorable public relations?

MARKETING APPLICATIONS

1. Which of the following advertising objectives would be most useful for a company, and why?
   a. The organization will spend $1 million to move from second in market share to market leader.
   b. The organization wants to increase sales from $1.2 million to $1.5 million this year to gain the lead in market share.
   c. The advertising objective is to gain as much market share as possible within the next 12 months.
   d. The advertising objective is to increase sales by 15 percent.
2. Select a print ad and identify how it (a) identifies a specific problem, (b) recommends the product as the best solution to the problem, (c) states the product's advantages and benefits, (d) substantiates the ad's claims, and (e) asks the reader to take action.
3. Look through several recent newspapers and magazines or use an Internet search engine and identify a news release, a feature article, or a captioned photograph used to publicize a product. Describe the type of product.
4. Identify a company that recently was the target of negative public relations. Describe the situation, and discuss the company's response. What did marketers at this company do well? What, if anything, would you recommend that they change about their response?

ONLINE EXERCISE

5. The LEGO company has been making toys since 1932 and has become one of the most recognized brand names in the toy industry. With the company motto "Only the best is good enough," it is no surprise that the LEGO company has developed such an exciting and interactive website. See how the company promotes the LEGO products as well as encourages consumer involvement with the brand by visiting http://www.lego.com.
   a. Which type of advertising is LEGO using on its website?
   b. What target audience is the LEGO company intending to reach?
   c. Identify the advertising objectives that the LEGO company is attempting to achieve through this website.

DEVELOPING YOUR MARKETING PLAN

Determining the message that advertising is to communicate to the customer is an important part of developing a marketing strategy. A sound understanding of the various types of advertising and different forms of media is essential in selecting the appropriate methods for communicating the message. These decisions form a critical segment of the marketing plan. To assist you in relating the information in this chapter to the development of your marketing plan, consider the following issues:

1. What class and type of advertising would be most appropriate for your product?
2. Discuss the different methods for determining the advertising appropriation.
3. Using Table 16.3 as a guide, evaluate the different types of media and determine which would be most effective in meeting your promotional objectives (from Chapter 15).
4. What methods would you use to evaluate the effectiveness of your advertising campaign?
5. Review Table 16.5 and discuss possible uses for publicity in your promotional plan.

The information obtained from these questions should assist you in developing various aspects of your marketing plan found in the *Interactive Marketing Plan* exercise.

VIDEO CASE 16

Vans Leverages Athletes in Its Advertising Platform

For most people, surfing and skateboarding come to mind immediately when they think of southern California culture. For forty years Vans has embodied the California lifestyle and remains one of the preeminent skater-shoe companies. Founded in Los Angeles in 1966 by Paul Van Doren, his brother Steve, and Belgian investor Serge D'Elia, Vans quickly became a staple in southern California. Starting with a few versions of the traditional lace-up deck shoe sold out of a factory, the style of shoe became popular almost immediately. Vans rapidly increased its level of popularity by customizing shoes in all different fabrics and designs. The Van Dorens secured their local customized shoe business by selling plaid shoes to Catholic schools and sneakers with school colors to high school athletes. But, when the checkered slip-on was donned by Sean Penn and his surfer buddies in the film *Fast Times at Ridgemont High,* skaters all over the country were demanding their own pairs of Vans. The shoes went from local wear to iconic symbol in just a few years.

Contrary to many corporate success stories, the Vans company never spent much money on advertising. Paul Van Doren knew that he offered a superior product, and he relied on word of mouth to popularize the high-quality, extremely durable shoes. The most marketing Van Doren did at first was to have his children canvas their neighborhood with flyers. At all early Vans stores, signs encouraged customers to "tell a friend about Vans." For years, Van Doren focused mostly on the manufacturing aspect of the company so that even with a minimal amount of advertising, popularity grew because Vans were, quite simply, quality shoes. It wasn't until the late 1980s and early 1990s, when manufacturing was taken overseas, that Vans turned its attention to marketing.

One of Vans's earliest forays into promotion came about by chance. As skateboarders began to discover Vans shoes, the company responded by creating styles more amenable to skating. With their skater following growing, Vans paid a few top skaters a few hundred dollars apiece to wear their shoes at skating events. In 1989, Vans produced its first signature skateboarding shoe, the Steve Caballero shoe. Since then, Vans has partnered with numerous athletes such as Geoff Rowley, who has the best-selling signature Vans shoe to date, and Johnny Layton. As skateboarding culture has continued to flourish over the decades, Vans's connection to the scene has remained strong.

Vans's two-man marketing and promotional team focuses on spreading interest in Vans by doing its best to remain plugged into the youth culture and by fueling teenage interest in Vans products. To this end, the company advertises through print, online, TV, and sporting and music events. Currently, the key to Vans's marketing strategy is developing advertising partnerships with athletes, artists, and media outlets. People immersed in this culture want to own Vans products. Vans is not just a shoe; it is a lifestyle.

Young extreme-sports athletes, like skaters and surfers, remain Vans's most important customer base. In 1995, Vans hosted its first Triple Crown event. The Triple Crown spotlights skateboarding, surfing, snowboarding, BMX, FMX, and wakeboarding. Tony Hawk won the skateboarding competition that first year and has since become a household name. Also in 1995, Vans launched its first annual Warped Tour, blending skating with music through concerts and competitions. These types of events allow Vans to build brand recognition, cement its integral place in the skating lifestyle, and connect with customers via giveaways and promotions such as designing custom shoes.

In addition to events, Vans connects with its audience through magazine advertisements, television, and the Internet, especially to attract young female consumers, who represent a growing part of the Vans consumer base. In the past, the company has partnered with magazines such as *Teen Vogue* and *CosmoGirl* to reach the female demographic. In addition, the company works with some of television's action-sports networks and hosts a weekly show, *Vans Off the Wall Hour,* on FSN. Although it is over forty years old, Vans still connects with youth culture as well as ever—and shows no signs of slowing down.

QUESTIONS FOR DISCUSSION

1. Evaluate Vans's early word-of-mouth marketing strategy.
2. Why were the early Vans advertising activities related to skateboard shoes so successful?
3. How does Vans continue to capture its target market?

Vans Shoes, www.vans.com (accessed October 27, 2009); Jason Lee, "The History of Vans," Sneaker Freaker, http://www.sneakerfreaker.com/feature/history-of-vans/1/ (accessed October 27, 2009); Vans: 40 Years of Originality, www.vans40.com (accessed October 27, 2009).

CHAPTER 17 Personal Selling and Sales Promotion

© AP PHOTO/ADRIAN BIMMER

OBJECTIVES:

1. Define personal selling and understand its purpose.
2. Describe the basic steps in the personal selling process.
3. Identify the types of sales force personnel.
4. Understand sales management decisions and activities.
5. Explain what sales promotion activities are and how they are used.
6. Recognize specific consumer and trade sales promotion methods.

IBM'S CELEBRITY SALESMAN

In Vivek Gupta's opinion, making a sale is similar to a courtship. In India's fast-growing telecom industry, Gupta has made the courtship of the customer an art form. Ever since he started working for IBM five years ago, Gupta has become one of its top salesmen. His 17 years in the telecom industry has given him the expertise to form relationships with some of India's biggest telecom companies. Among his many sales victories, Gupta has secured for IBM a five-year contract with Vodafone, India's fourth-largest cellular phone company. At first, the prospects of a contract with Vodafone weren't that good.

Even though Vodafone explicitly told Gupta that the company intended never to do business with IBM, Gupta managed to convince Vodafone to transfer much of its information technology–related responsibilities to IBM. The secret to Gupta's sales success is his strategy. He works on studying his customers to discover their underlying needs, or what he terms the customer's "pain points." During this study period, Gupta familiarizes himself with the company so well that he often knows more about it than its employees do. Once he understands what his customers want, he finds the best way for IBM to meet those needs. He has also become adept at recognizing key signals his prospects give off. When first meeting with Vodafone, Gupta could tell when his prospects were losing interest. This is where his courtship analogy came in. "Look, this customer is not prepared for marriage, he is prepared for courtship, so let's spend some time on courtship," he told his sales team. Eventually, Gupta was able to sell Vodafone a $600 million contract. With millions of dollars of sales under his belt and opportunities to expand his sales globally, Gupta is the epitome of a super salesman.[1]

For many organizations, programs that motivate employees, especially sales staff, to find creative ways to maintain long-term, satisfying customer relationships contribute to the company's success. As we saw in Chapter 16, personal selling and sales promotion are two possible elements in a promotion mix. Sales promotion is sometimes a company's sole promotional tool, although it is generally used in conjunction with other promotion-mix elements. It is playing an increasingly important role in marketing strategies. Personal selling is becoming more professional and sophisticated, with sales personnel acting more as consultants and advisers.

In this chapter, we focus on personal selling and sales promotion. We first consider the purposes of personal selling and then its basic steps. Next, we look at types of salespeople and how they are selected. We then discuss major sales force management decisions, including setting objectives for the sales force and determining its size; recruiting, selecting, training, compensating, and motivating salespeople; managing sales territories; and controlling and evaluating sales force performance. Then we examine several characteristics of sales promotion, reasons for using sales promotion, and sales promotion methods available for use in a promotion mix.

Nature of Personal Selling
State Farm provides professional sales career opportunities to serve local communities.

What Is Personal Selling?

Personal selling is paid personal communication that attempts to inform customers and persuade them to purchase products in an exchange situation. For example, a salesperson from Baxter International calling on a hospital pharmacist to explain the company's new portfolio of frozen premixed intravenous (IV) drugs is engaged in personal selling.[2] Personal selling goals vary from one firm to another. However, they usually involve finding prospects, persuading prospects to buy, and keeping customers satisfied. Although the public may harbor negative perceptions of personal selling, unfavorable stereotypes of salespeople are changing thanks to the efforts of major corporations, professional sales associations, and academic institutions. Research indicates that personal selling will continue to gain respect as professional sales associations develop and enforce ethical codes of conduct.[3]

Personal selling gives marketers the greatest freedom to adjust a message so that it will satisfy customers' information needs. Compared with other promotion methods, personal selling is the most precise, enabling marketers to focus on the most promising sales prospects. Other promotion-mix elements are aimed at groups of people, some of whom may not be prospective customers. However, personal selling is generally the most expensive element in the promotion mix. The average cost of a business sales call is more than $400.[4]

Millions of people, including increasing numbers of women, earn their living through personal selling. Sales careers can offer high income, a great deal of freedom, a high level of training, and a high degree of job satisfaction.

personal selling
Paid personal communication that attempts to inform customers and persuade them to buy products in an exchange situation

Sustainable Marketing

Selling Green Homes

Today's building industry is going green in Atlanta, and around the south. EarthCraft House, founded in 1999, has garnered praise for being a green building company that builds comfortable and affordable homes. EarthCraft House has certified over 4,000 single-family homes and 1,500 multifamily dwelling units. Atlanta even boasts six EarthCraft communities.

To be certified by EarthCraft, a house must meet guidelines in energy efficiency, durability, indoor air quality, resource efficiency, waste management, and water conservation. EarthCraft houses reduce more than 1,100 pounds of greenhouse gas emissions yearly, are built with as much renewable materials as possible, and can conserve water. Additionally, EarthCraft houses can reduce mildew and virtually obliterate airborne dust. Money saved in utility bills can offset monthly mortgage payments. EarthCraft predicts that by 2010 about 10 percent of all homes will be green—up from 2 percent in 2006. Even during the 2008–2009 recession, EarthCraft House continued to do good business. Cash-strapped homeowners began to understand that going green can be more than just good for the environment. Adding green features to a house can be inexpensive and can save homeowners hundreds of dollars annually on energy bills. Green homes are also healthier to live in than many other new homes.

© ISTOCKPHOTO.COM/BLUESTOCKING

Despite their benefits, EarthCraft-certified homes do not sell themselves automatically. Both personal selling and sales promotion help reach potential buyers in many environments. Sponsors like Georgia-Pacific, Home Depot, and Whirlpool help out by providing point-of-purchase materials and demonstrations in their stores or sales offices. Salespeople who want to see their products used in a green building explain the many reasons why a green house is good for society and how it can save families money over the long run. However, it is up to the homebuilder to inform and persuade a potential buyer about the benefits of an EarthCraft home. Personal selling and sales promotion are necessary for the EarthCraft House program to make a difference.[a]

Salespeople must be aware of their competitors. They must monitor the development of new products and know about competitors' sales efforts in their sales territories, how often and when the competition calls on their accounts, and what the competition is saying about their product in relation to its own. Salespeople must emphasize the benefits that their products provide, especially when competitors' products do not offer those specific benefits.

Identifying potential buyers interested in the organization's products is critical. Because most potential buyers seek information before making purchases, salespeople can ascertain prospects' informational needs and then provide relevant information. To do so, sales personnel must be well trained regarding both their products and the selling process in general.

Few businesses survive solely on profits from one-time customers. For long-run survival, most marketers depend on repeat sales, and thus need to keep their customers satisfied. In addition, satisfied customers supply favorable word-of-mouth communications, thus attracting new customers. Although the whole organization is responsible for achieving customer satisfaction, much of the burden falls on salespeople because they are almost always closer to customers than anyone else in the company and often provide buyers with information and service after the sale. Indeed, research shows that a firm's marketing orientation has a positive influence on salespeople's attitudes, commitment, and influence on customer purchasing intentions. Such contact gives salespeople an opportunity to generate additional sales and offers them a good vantage point for evaluating the strengths and weaknesses of the company's products and other marketing mix components. Their observations help develop and maintain a marketing mix that better satisfies both the firm and its customers.[5]

THE PERSONAL SELLING PROCESS

The specific activities involved in the selling process vary among salespeople, selling situations, and cultures. No two salespeople use exactly the same selling methods. Nonetheless, many salespeople move through a general selling process as they sell

FIGURE 17.1 **General Steps in the Personal Selling Process**

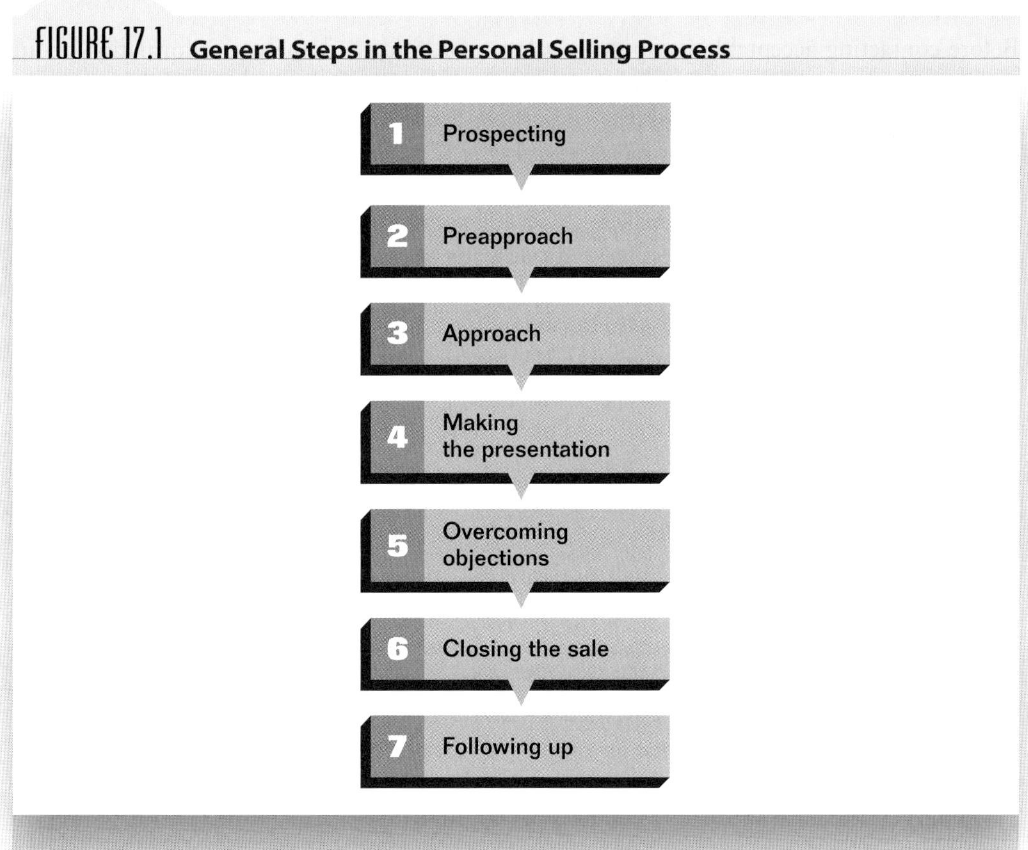

products. This process consists of seven steps, outlined in Figure 17.1: prospecting, preapproach, approach, making the presentation, overcoming objections, closing the sale, and following up.

Prospecting for Customers

Developing a list of potential customers is called **prospecting**. Salespeople seek names of prospects from company sales records, trade shows, commercial databases, newspaper announcements (of marriages, births, deaths, and so on), public records, telephone directories, trade association directories, and many other sources. Sales personnel also use responses to traditional and online advertisements that encourage interested persons to send in information request forms. Seminars and meetings targeted at particular types of clients, such as attorneys or accountants, also may produce leads.

Most salespeople prefer to use referrals—recommendations from current customers—to find prospects. Obtaining referrals requires that the salesperson have a good relationship with the current customer and so must have performed well before asking the customer for help. Research shows that one referral is as valuable as 12 cold calls. Also, 80 percent of clients are willing to give referrals, but only 20 percent are ever asked. Sales experts indicate that the advantages of using referrals are that the resulting sales leads are highly qualified, the sales rates are higher, initial transactions are larger, and the sales cycle is shorter.[6]

Consistent activity is critical to successful prospecting. Salespeople must actively search the customer base for qualified prospects who fit the target-market profile. After developing the prospect list, a salesperson evaluates whether each prospect is able, willing, and authorized to buy the product. Based on this evaluation, prospects are ranked according to desirability or potential.

prospecting
Developing a list of potential customers

Preapproaching Prospects

Before contacting acceptable prospects, a salesperson finds and analyzes information about each prospect's specific product needs, current use of brands, feelings about available brands, and personal characteristics. In short, salespeople need to know what potential buyers and decision makers consider most important and why they need a specific product.[7] The most successful salespeople are thorough in their evaluations of prospects. This *preapproach* step involves identifying key decision makers, reviewing account histories and problems, contacting other clients for information, assessing credit histories, preparing sales presentations, and identifying product needs. Marketers are increasingly using information technology and customer relationship management (CRM) systems to comb through their databases and identify their most profitable products and customers. CRM systems also can help sales departments manage leads, track customers, forecast sales, and assess performance. A salesperson with a lot of information about a prospect is better equipped to develop a presentation that communicates precisely with the prospect.

Approaching the Customer

The **approach**, the manner in which a salesperson contacts a potential customer, is a critical step in the sales process. In more than 80 percent of initial sales calls, the purpose is to gather information about the buyer's needs and objectives. Creating a favorable impression and building rapport with prospective clients are important tasks in the approach. During the initial contact, the salesperson strives to develop a relationship rather than just push a product. The salesperson may have to call on a prospect several times before the product is considered. The approach must be designed to deliver value to targeted customers. If the sales approach is inappropriate, the salesperson's efforts are likely to have poor results.

As mentioned earlier, one type of approach is based on referrals: The salesperson approaches the prospect and explains that an acquaintance, associate, or relative suggested the call. Another type of approach is the "cold canvass," in which a salesperson calls on potential customers without prior consent. The exact type of approach depends on the salesperson's preferences, the product being sold, the firm's resources, and the prospect's characteristics.

Making the Presentation

During the sales presentation, the salesperson must attract and hold the prospect's attention, stimulate interest, and spark a desire for the product. Research indicates that salespersons who carefully monitor the selling situation and adapt their presentations to meet the needs of prospects are associated with effective sales performance.[8] Salespeople should match their influencing tactics—such as information exchange, recommendations, threats, promises, ingratiation, and inspirational appeals—to their prospects. Different types of buyers respond to different tactics, but most prospects respond well to information exchange and recommendations, and virtually no prospects respond to threats.[9] The salesperson should have the prospect touch, hold, or use the product. If possible, the salesperson should demonstrate the product. Audiovisual equipment and software also may enhance the presentation.

During the presentation, the salesperson not only must talk but also listen. Nonverbal modes of communication are especially beneficial in building trust during the presentation.[10] The sales presentation gives the salesperson the greatest opportunity to determine the prospect's specific needs by listening to questions and comments and observing responses. Even though the salesperson plans the presentation in advance, he or she must be able to adjust the message to meet the prospect's informational needs.

approach
The manner in which a salesperson contacts a potential customer

Overcoming Objections

An effective salesperson usually seeks out a prospect's objections so that he or she can address them. If they are not apparent, the salesperson cannot deal with them, and the prospect may not buy. One of the best ways to overcome objections is to anticipate and counter them before the prospect raises them. However, this approach can be risky because the salesperson may mention objections that the prospect would not have raised. If possible, the salesperson should handle objections as they arise. They also can be addressed at the end of the presentation. Research demonstrates that adapting the message in response to the customer's needs generally enhances performance, particularly in new-task or modified rebuy purchase situations.[11]

Closing the Sale

Closing is the stage of the selling process when the salesperson asks the prospect to buy the product. During the presentation, the salesperson may use a "trial close" by asking questions that assume that the prospect will buy the product. The salesperson might ask the potential customer about financial terms, desired colors or sizes, or delivery arrangements. One questioning approach uses broad questions (*what, how,* and *why*) to probe or gather information and focused questions (*who, when,* and *where*) to clarify and close the sale. Reactions to such questions usually indicate how close the prospect is to buying. A trial close allows prospects to indicate indirectly that they will buy the product without having to say those sometimes difficult words, "I'll take it."

A salesperson should try to close at several points during the presentation because the prospect may be ready to buy. One closing strategy involves asking the potential customer to place a low-risk tryout order. An attempt to close the sale may result in objections. Thus, closing can uncover hidden objections, which the salesperson then can address.

Following Up

After a successful closing, the salesperson must follow up the sale. In the follow-up stage, the salesperson determines whether the order was delivered on time and installed properly, if installation was required. He or she should contact the customer to learn if any problems or questions regarding the product have arisen. The follow-up stage is also used to determine customers' future product needs.

TYPES OF SALESPEOPLE

To develop a sales force, a marketing manager decides what kind of salesperson will sell the firm's products most effectively. Most organizations use several different kinds of sales personnel. Based on the functions performed, salespeople can be classified into three groups: order getters, order takers, and support personnel. One salesperson can, and often does, perform all three functions.

Order Getters

To obtain orders, a salesperson informs prospects and persuades them to buy the product. The role of the **order getter** is to increase sales by selling to new customers and increasing sales to current customers. This task sometimes is called *creative selling.* It requires that salespeople recognize potential buyers' needs and give them necessary information. Order getting is sometimes divided into two categories: current-customer sales and new-business sales.

CURRENT-CUSTOMER SALES. Sales personnel who concentrate on current customers call on people and organizations that have purchased products from the firm before. These salespeople

closing
The stage in the selling process when the salesperson asks the prospect to buy the product

order getter
The salesperson who sells to new customers and increases sales to current ones

seek more sales from existing customers by following up on previous sales. Current customers can also be sources of leads for new prospects.

NEW-BUSINESS SALES. Business organizations depend to some degree on sales to new customers. New-business sales personnel locate prospects and convert them into buyers. In many organizations, salespeople help generate new business, but organizations that sell real estate, insurance, appliances, heavy industrial machinery, and automobiles depend in large part on new-customer sales.

Order Takers

Salespeople take orders to perpetuate long-lasting, satisfying customer relationships. **Order takers** seek repeat sales. They generate the bulk of many organizations' total sales. One major objective is to be certain that customers have sufficient product quantities where and when needed. Most order takers handle orders for standardized products purchased routinely and not requiring extensive sales efforts. The role of order takers is evolving, however. In the future they probably will serve more as identifiers and problem solvers to meet the needs of their customers. There are two groups of order takers: inside order takers and field order takers.

In many businesses, *inside order takers,* who work in sales offices, receive orders by mail, telephone, and the Internet. Certain producers, wholesalers, and retailers have sales personnel who sell from within the firm rather than in the field. This does not mean that inside order takers never communicate with customers face to face. For example, retail salespeople are classified as inside order takers. As more orders are placed through the Internet, the role of the inside order taker will continue to change.

Salespeople who travel to customers are *outside*, or *field, order takers.* Often customers and field order takers develop interdependent relationships. The buyer relies on the salesperson to take orders periodically (and sometimes to deliver them), and the salesperson counts on the buyer to purchase a certain quantity of products periodically. Use of notebook and handheld computers has improved the field order taker's inventory and order-tracking capabilities.

order takers
Salespersons who primarily seek repeat sales

support personnel
Sales staff members who facilitate selling but usually are not involved solely with making sales

missionary salespeople
Support salespersons who assist the producer's customers in selling to their own customers

trade salespeople
Salespersons involved mainly in helping a producer's customers promote a product

technical salespeople
Support salespersons who give technical assistance to a firm's current customers

Support Personnel

Support personnel facilitate selling but usually are not involved solely with making sales. They are engaged primarily in marketing industrial products, locating prospects, educating customers, building goodwill, and providing service after the sale. There are many kinds of sales support personnel; the three most common are missionary, trade, and technical salespeople.

Missionary salespeople, usually employed by manufacturers, assist the producer's customers in selling to their own customers. Missionary salespeople may call on retailers to inform and persuade them to buy the manufacturer's products. When they succeed, retailers purchase products from wholesalers, who are the producer's customers. Manufacturers of medical supplies and pharmaceuticals often use missionary salespeople, called *detail reps,* to promote their products to physicians, hospitals, and retail druggists.

Trade salespeople are not strictly support personnel because they usually take orders as well. However, they direct much effort toward helping customers, especially retail stores, promote the product. They are likely to restock shelves, obtain more shelf space, set up displays, provide in-store demonstrations, and distribute samples to store customers. Food producers and processors commonly employ trade salespeople.

Technical salespeople give technical assistance to the organization's current customers, advising them on product characteristics and applications, system designs, and installation procedures. Because this job is often highly technical, the salesperson usually has formal training in one of the physical sciences or in engineering. Technical sales personnel often sell technical industrial products, such as computers, heavy equipment, and steel.

When hiring sales personnel, marketers seldom restrict themselves to a single category because most firms require different types of salespeople. Several factors dictate how many of each type a particular company should have. Product use, characteristics, complexity, and price influence the kind of sales personnel used, as do the number and characteristics of customers. The types of marketing channels and the intensity and type of advertising also affect the composition of a sales force.

team selling
The use of a team of experts from all functional areas of a firm, led by a salesperson, to conduct the personal selling process

relationship selling
The building of mutually beneficial long-term associations with a customer through regular communications over prolonged periods of time

TYPES OF SELLING

Personal selling has become an increasingly complex process owing in large part to rapid technological innovation. Most important, the focus of personal selling is shifting from selling a specific product to building long-term relationships with customers by finding solutions to their needs, problems, and challenges. As a result, the roles of salespeople are changing. Among the new philosophies for personal selling are team selling and relationship selling.

Many products, particularly expensive high-tech business products, have become so complex that a single salesperson can no longer be expert in every aspect of the product and purchase process. **Team selling**, which involves the salesperson joining with people from the firm's financial, engineering, and other functional areas, is appropriate for such products. The salesperson takes the lead in the personal selling process, but other members of the team bring their unique skills, knowledge, and resources to the process to help customers find solutions to their own business challenges. Selling teams may be created to address a particular short-term situation, or they may be formal, ongoing teams. Team selling is advantageous in situations calling for detailed knowledge of new, complex, and dynamic technologies such as jet aircraft and medical equipment. It can be difficult, however, for highly competitive salespersons to adapt to a team-selling environment.

Relationship selling, also known as *consultative* or *solution selling,* involves building mutually beneficial long-term associations with a customer through regular communications over prolonged periods of time. Like team selling, it is used especially in business-to-business (B2B) marketing. Relationship selling involves finding solutions to customers' needs by listening to them, gaining a detailed understanding of their organization, understanding and caring about their needs and challenges, and providing support after the sale. Relationship selling efforts can be enhanced through sales automation technology tools that enhance interactive communication.[12] Using social media to learn about customers' wants and needs can also be beneficial. While companies can respond to online comments, marketers need assurance that the company is going to go the extra mile to listen to customers or potential customers. In many cases, marketers need to listen to customers, and then probe even further to get necessary information.[13]

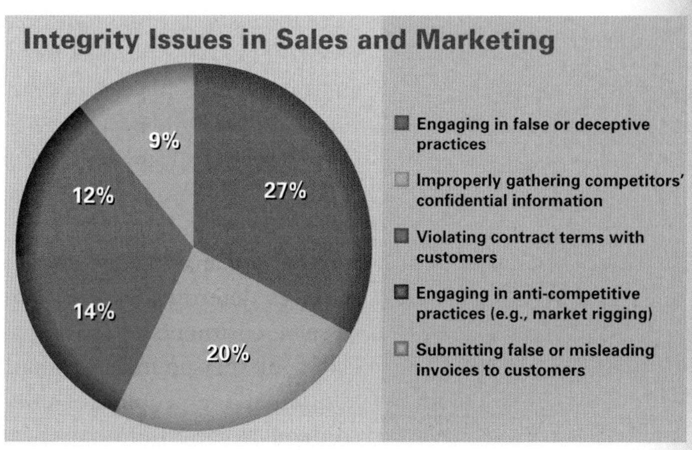

Source: KPMG Forensic Integrity Survey, KPMG LLP (U.S.), 2008–2009.

MANAGING THE SALES FORCE

The sales force is directly responsible for generating one of an organization's primary inputs—sales revenue. Without adequate sales revenue, businesses cannot survive. In addition, a firm's reputation is often determined by the ethical conduct of its sales force. A positive ethical climate, which is one component of corporate culture, has been linked with decreased role stress and turnover retention, and improved job attitudes and performance in sales.[14] The morale and ultimately the success of a firm's sales force depend in large part on adequate compensation, room for advancement, adequate training, and management support—all key areas of sales management. Salespeople who are not satisfied with these elements may leave. Evaluating the input of salespeople is an important part of sales force management because of its strong bearing on a firm's success.

We explore eight general areas of sales management: establishing sales force objectives, determining sales force size, recruiting and selecting salespeople, training sales personnel, compensating salespeople, motivating salespeople, managing sales territories, and controlling and evaluating sales force performance.

Establishing Sales Force Objectives

To manage a sales force effectively, sales managers must develop sales objectives. Sales objectives tell salespeople what they are expected to accomplish during a specified time period. They give the sales force direction and purpose and serve as standards for evaluating and controlling the performance of sales personnel. Research indicates that a focus on sales performance increases efforts to achieve sales objectives.[15] Sales objectives should be stated in precise, measurable terms and should specify the time period and geographic areas involved.

Sales objectives usually are developed for both the total sales force and each salesperson. Objectives for the entire force normally are stated in terms of sales volume, market share, or profit. Volume objectives refer to dollar or unit sales. For example, the objective for an electric drill producer's sales force might be to sell $18 million worth of drills, or 600,000 drills, annually. When sales goals are stated in terms of market share, they usually call for an increase in the proportion of the firm's sales relative to the total number of products sold by all businesses in that industry. When sales objectives are based on profit, they generally are stated in terms of dollar amounts or return on investment.

Sales objectives, or quotas, for individual salespeople commonly are stated in terms of dollar or unit sales volume. Other bases used for individual sales objectives include average order size, average number of calls per time period, and ratio of orders to calls.

Determining Sales Force Size

Sales force size is important because it influences the company's ability to generate sales and profits. The size of the sales force affects the compensation methods used, salespeople's morale, and overall sales force management. Sales force size must be adjusted periodically because a firm's marketing plans change along with markets and forces in the marketing environment. One danger in cutting back the size of the sales force to increase profits is that the sales organization may lose strength, preventing it from rebounding when growth occurs or better market conditions prevail.

Several analytical methods can help to determine optimal sales force size. One method involves determining how many sales calls per year are necessary for the organization to serve customers effectively and then dividing this total by the average number of sales calls a salesperson makes annually. A second method is based on marginal analysis, whereby additional salespeople are added to the sales force until the cost of an additional salesperson equals the additional sales generated by that person. Although marketing managers may use one or several analytical methods, they normally temper decisions with subjective judgments.

Recruiting and Selecting Salespeople

To create and maintain an effective sales force, sales managers must recruit the right type of salespeople. Effective recruiting efforts are a vital part of implementing the strategic sales force plan and can help to ensure successful organizational performance.[16] In recruiting, the sales manager develops a list of qualified applicants for sales positions. To ensure that the recruiting process results in a pool of qualified salespeople from which to hire, a sales manager establishes a set of qualifications before beginning to recruit. Two activities help to establish this set of required attributes. First, the sales manager should prepare a job description listing specific tasks salespeople are to perform. Second, the manager should analyze characteristics of the firm's successful salespeople, as well as those of ineffective sales personnel. From the job description and analysis of traits, the sales manager should be able to develop a set of specific requirements and be aware of potential weaknesses that could lead to failure.

A sales manager generally recruits applicants from several sources: departments within the firm, other firms, employment agencies, educational institutions, respondents to advertisements, and individuals recommended by current employees. The specific sources depend on the type of salesperson required and the manager's experiences with particular sources.

Recruiting and Selecting Salespeople
Careerbuilder.com assists in recruiting the right sales professionals.

The process of recruiting and selecting salespeople varies considerably from one company to another. Companies intent on reducing sales force turnover are likely to have strict recruiting and selection procedures. Some organizations use the specialized services of other companies to hire sales personnel. Recruitment should not be sporadic. It should be a continuous activity aimed at reaching the best applicants. The selection process should systematically and effectively match applicants' characteristics and needs with the requirements of specific selling tasks. Finally, the selection process should ensure that new sales personnel are available where and when needed.

Training Sales Personnel

Many organizations have formal training programs; others depend on informal, on-the-job training. Some systematic training programs are quite extensive, whereas others are rather short and rudimentary. Whether the training program is complex or simple, developers must consider what to teach, whom to train, and how to train them.

A sales training program can concentrate on the company, its products, or selling methods. Training programs often cover all three. Such programs can be aimed at newly hired salespeople, experienced salespeople, or both. Training for experienced company salespeople usually emphasizes product information, although salespeople also must be informed about new selling techniques and changes in company plans, policies, and procedures. Honda, for example, designed a sales training program that involved going to 21 cities to train 7,500 sales associates about the automaker's new entry-level auto, the Fit. The training program introduced sales reps not only to the features and benefits of the new car but also to the car's target market: young buyers who are comfortable finding their own car information online.[17]

Training Sales Personnel
Sales training occurs in numerous ways. Here, sales training is occurring on-site, in a small group, and supported through technology.

Ordinarily, new sales personnel require comprehensive training, whereas experienced personnel need both refresher courses on established products and training regarding new-product information.

Sales training may be done in the field, at educational institutions, in company facilities, and/or online using Web-based technology. For many companies, training online saves time and money and helps salespeople learn about new products quickly. Some firms train new employees before assigning them to a specific sales position. Others put them in the field immediately, providing formal training only after they have gained some experience. Training programs for new personnel can be as short as several days or as long as three years; some are even longer. Because experienced salespeople usually need periodic retraining, a firm's sales management must determine the frequency, sequencing, and duration of these efforts.

Materials for sales training programs range from videos, texts, online materials, manuals, and cases to programmed learning devices and audio- and videocassettes. Lectures, demonstrations, simulation exercises, and on-the-job training all can be effective teaching methods. Self-directed learning to supplement traditional sales training has the potential to improve sales performance.[18] Choice of methods and materials for a particular sales training program depends on type and number of trainees, program content and complexity, length and location, size of the training budget, number of teachers, and teacher preferences.

Compensating Salespeople

To develop and maintain a highly productive sales force, a business must formulate and administer a compensation plan that attracts, motivates, and retains the most effective individuals. The plan should give sales management the desired level of control and provide sales personnel with acceptable levels of income, freedom, and incentive. It should be flexible, equitable, easy to administer, and easy to understand. Good compensation programs facilitate and encourage proper treatment of customers. Obviously, it is quite difficult to incorporate all these requirements into a single program.

Developers of compensation programs must determine the general level of compensation required and the most desirable method of calculating it. In analyzing the required compensation level, sales management must ascertain a salesperson's value to the company on the basis of the tasks and responsibilities associated with the sales position. Sales managers may consider a number of factors, including salaries of other types of personnel in the firm, competitors' compensation plans, costs of sales force turnover, and nonsalary selling expenses. The average low-level salesperson earns about $65,000 annually (including commissions and bonuses), whereas a high-level, high-performing salesperson can make as much as $157,000 a year (Figure 17.2).[19]

Sales compensation programs usually reimburse salespeople for selling expenses, provide some fringe benefits, and deliver the required compensation level. To achieve this, a firm may use one or more of three basic compensation methods: straight salary, straight commission, or a combination of salary and commission. Table 17.1 lists the pros and cons of each. In a **straight salary compensation plan**, salespeople are paid a specified amount per time period, regardless of selling effort. This sum remains the same until they receive a pay increase or decrease. Although this method is easy to administer and affords salespeople financial security, it provides little incentive for them to boost selling efforts. In a **straight commission compensation plan**, salespeople's compensation is determined solely by sales for a given period. A commission may be based on a single percentage of sales or on a sliding scale involving several sales levels and percentage rates. While this method motivates sales personnel to escalate their selling efforts, it offers them little financial security, and it can be difficult for sales managers to maintain control over the sales force. For these reasons, many firms offer a **combination compensation plan** in which salespeople receive a fixed salary

straight salary compensation plan Paying salespeople a specific amount per time period, regardless of selling effort

straight commission compensation plan Paying salespeople according to the amount of their sales in a given time period

combination compensation plan Paying salespeople a fixed salary plus a commission based on sales volume

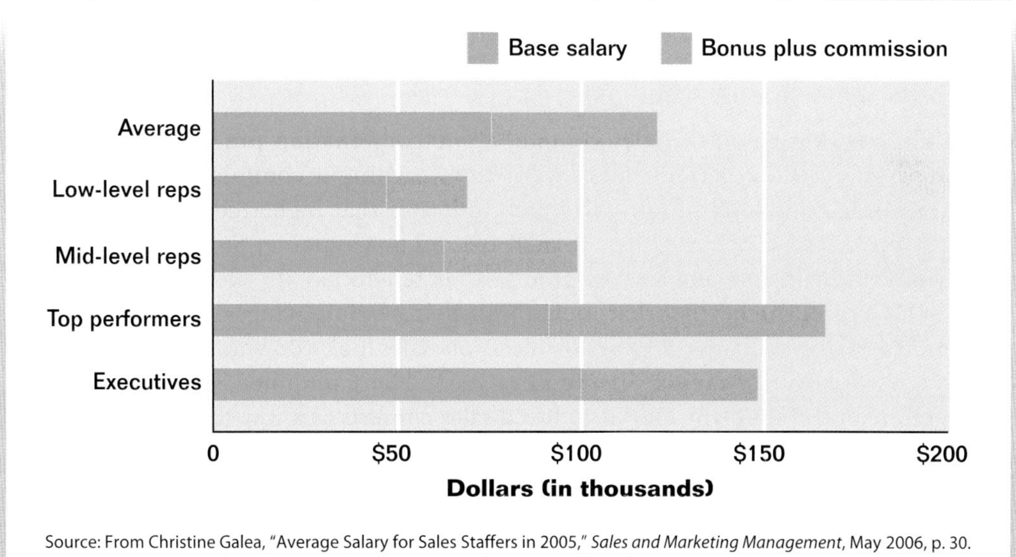

Source: From Christine Galea, "Average Salary for Sales Staffers in 2005," *Sales and Marketing Management*, May 2006, p. 30. 2004 VNU Business Media, Inc. Reprinted with permission from Sales and Marketing Management.

TABLE 17.1 Characteristics of Sales Force Compensation Methods

Compensation Method	Frequency of Use (%)*	When Especially Useful	Advantages	Disadvantages
Straight salary	17.5	Compensating new salespersons; firm moves into new sales territories that require developmental work; sales requiring lengthy presale and postsale services.	Gives salesperson security; gives sales manager control over salespersons; easy to administer; yields more predictable selling expenses.	Provides no incentive; necessitates closer supervision of salespersons; during sales declines, selling expenses remain constant.
Straight commission	14.0	Highly aggressive selling is required; nonselling tasks are minimized; company uses contractors and part-timers.	Provides maximum amount of incentive; by increasing commission rate, sales managers can encourage salespersons to sell certain items; selling expenses relate directly to sales resources.	Salespersons have little financial security; sales manager has minimum control over sales force; may cause salespeople to give inadequate service to smaller accounts; selling costs less predictable.
Combination	68.5	Sales territories have relatively similar sales potential; firm wishes to provide incentive but still control sales force activities.	Provides certain level of financial security; provides some incentive; can move sales force efforts in profitable direction.	Selling expenses less predictable; may be difficult to administer.

*The figures are computed from *Dartnell's 30th Sales Force Compensation Survey*, Dartnell Corporation, Chicago, 1999.

Source: Charles Futrell, *Sales Management* (Ft. Worth: Dryden Press, 2001), pp. 307–316.

plus a commission based on sales volume. Some combination programs require that a salesperson exceed a certain sales level before earning a commission; others offer commissions for any level of sales. Research indicates that higher commissions are the most preferred reward followed by pay increases.[20] The Container Store, which markets do-it-yourself organizing and storage products, prefers to pay its sales staff salaries that are 50 to 100 percent higher than that offered by rivals instead of paying salespeople according to commission plans.[21] In the 2008–2009 recession, sales took a downturn for the first time in 30 years. Instead of laying off the sales staff, The Container Store froze salaries for everyone in the company and introduced sales contests as a way to motivate staff.[22]

Motivating Salespeople

Although financial compensation is an important incentive, additional programs are necessary for motivating sales personnel. A sales manager should develop a systematic approach for motivating salespeople to be productive. Effective sales force motivation is achieved through an organized set of activities performed continuously by the company's sales management.

Sales personnel, like other people, join organizations to satisfy personal needs and achieve personal goals. Sales managers must identify these needs and goals and strive to create an organizational climate that allows each salesperson to fulfill them. Enjoyable working conditions, power and authority, job security, and opportunity to excel are effective motivators, as are company efforts to make sales jobs more productive and efficient. At The Container Store, for example, sales personnel receive 241 hours of training every year about the company's products so that they can help customers solve their organization and storage problems.[23] Research has shown that a strong corporate culture leads to higher levels of job satisfaction and organizational commitment and lower levels of job stress.[24] A positive ethical climate, one component of corporate culture, has been associated with decreased role stress and turnover intention and improved job attitudes and job performance in sales.[25] Sales contests and other incentive programs can be effective motivators. Sales contests can motivate salespeople to increase sales or add new accounts, promote special items, achieve greater volume per sales call, and cover territories more thoroughly. However, companies need to understand salespersons' preferences when designing contests in order to make them effective in increasing sales.[26] Some companies find such contests powerful tools for motivating sales personnel to achieve company goals.

Properly designed incentive programs pay for themselves many times over, and sales managers are relying on incentives more than ever. Recognition programs that acknowledge outstanding performance with symbolic awards, such as plaques, can be very effective when carried out in a peer setting. The most common incentive offered by companies is cash, followed by gift cards and travel.[27] Other common awards include meals, merchandise, and recognition through special parking spaces. Travel reward programs can confer a high-profile honor, provide a unique experience that makes recipients feel special, and build camaraderie among award-winning salespeople. However, some recipients of travel awards may feel that they already travel too much on the job. Cash rewards are easy to administer, are always appreciated by recipients, and appeal to all demographic groups. However, cash has no visible "trophy" value and provides few "bragging rights." The benefits of awarding merchandise are that the items have visible trophy value, recipients who are allowed to select the merchandise feel more control, and merchandise awards can help to build momentum for the sales force. The disadvantages of using merchandise are that employees may have lower perceived value of the merchandise and that the company may experience greater administrative problems. Some companies outsource their incentive programs to companies that specialize in the creation and management of such programs.

Managing Sales Territories

The effectiveness of a sales force that must travel to customers is somewhat influenced by management's decisions regarding sales territories. When deciding on territories, sales managers must consider size, shape, routing, and scheduling.

Several factors enter into the design of a sales territory's size and shape. First, sales managers must construct territories so that sales potential can be measured. Sales territories often consist of several geographic units, such as census tracts, cities, counties, or states, for which market data are obtainable. Sales managers usually try to create territories with similar sales potential or that require about the same amount of work. If territories have equal sales potential, they almost always will be unequal in geographic size. Salespeople with larger territories have to work longer and harder to generate a certain sales volume. Conversely, if sales territories requiring equal amounts of work are created, sales potential for those territories often will vary. At times, sales managers use commercial programs to help them balance sales territories. Although a sales

Motivating Salespeople
Mary Kay cosmetics has a long history of recognizing and rewarding salespeople.

© AP IMAGES/DAILY PRESS, BUDDY NORRIS

manager seeks equity when developing and maintaining sales territories, some inequities always prevail. A territory's size and shape also should help the sales force provide the best possible customer coverage and should minimize selling costs. Customer density and distribution are important factors.

The geographic size and shape of a sales territory are the most important factors affecting the routing and scheduling of sales calls. Next in importance are the number and distribution of customers within the territory, followed by sales call frequency and duration. In some firms, salespeople plan their own routes and schedules with little or no assistance from the sales manager; in other organizations, the sales manager draws up the routes and schedules. No matter who plans the routing and scheduling, the major goals should be to minimize salespeople's nonselling time (time spent traveling and waiting) and maximize their selling time. Planners should try to achieve these goals so that a salesperson's travel and lodging costs are held to a minimum.

Controlling and Evaluating Sales Force Performance

To control and evaluate sales force performance properly, sales managers need information. A sales manager can use call reports, customer feedback, and invoices. Call reports identify the customers called on and present detailed information about interaction with those clients. Web-enabled smart phones also can help sales managers to keep abreast of a salesperson's activities. Data about a salesperson's interactions with customers and prospects can be included in the company's CRM system. This information provides insights about the salesperson's performance.

Dimensions used to measure a salesperson's performance are determined largely by sales objectives, normally set by the sales manager. If an individual's sales objective is stated in terms of sales volume, that person should be evaluated on the basis of sales volume generated. Sales managers often evaluate many performance indicators, including average number of calls per day, average sales per customer, actual sales relative to sales potential, number of new-customer orders, average cost per call, and average gross profit per customer.

To evaluate a salesperson, a sales manager may compare one or more of these dimensions with predetermined performance standards. However, sales managers commonly compare a salesperson's performance with that of other employees operating under similar selling conditions or the salesperson's current performance with past performance. Sometimes management judges factors that have less direct bearing on sales performance, such as personal appearance and product knowledge. The positive relationship between organizational commitment and job performance is stronger for sales personnel than for nonsales employees.[28]

After evaluating salespeople, sales managers take any needed corrective action to improve sales force performance. They may adjust performance standards, provide additional training, or try other motivational methods. Corrective action may demand comprehensive changes in the sales force.

Entrepreneurial Marketing

Selling Sports Celebrities

John Caponigro of Sports Management Network, Inc., uses personal selling in a unique way: to promote sports celebrities. Over the past 20 years, Caponigro has developed a sports management firm that uses personal selling to enhance the career of sports celebrities. To achieve his client's goals, he is relentless in his personal communications with companies, sports, and marketing sponsorship agencies. To him, 99 percent of the work involves maximizing the celebrity's value through sponsorships, endorsements, and licensing.

Racing legend Mario Andretti is one celebrity promoted by Caponigro's company. Andretti is solicited by would-be representatives, but remains loyal to Caponigro. Sports Management Network has tailored its service offerings specifically for the sports and entertainment industries. By building long-term relationships, Caponigro masters personal selling and celebrity promotions.[b]

What Is Sales Promotion?

Sales promotion is an activity or material, or both, that acts as a direct inducement, offering added value or incentive for the product, to resellers, salespeople, or consumers. It encompasses all promotional activities and materials other than personal selling, advertising, and public relations. Wendy's has used an online reverse auction to attract consumers to three value sandwiches that sell for 99 cents each. The auction sold various high-end items, including an Xbox 360 console and game chair, to bidders for 99 cents each. The auction was promoted virally online and aimed to reach out to consumers in the 18–24 age range. The auction idea comes at a time when consumers are dining out less and competition has grown fierce in the casual dining and fast-food industry.[29] In competitive markets, where products are very similar, sales promotion provides additional inducements that encourage product trial and purchase.

Marketers often use sales promotion to facilitate personal selling, advertising, or both. Companies also employ advertising and personal selling to support sales promotion activities. For example, marketers frequently use advertising to promote contests, free samples, and premiums. The most effective sales promotion efforts are highly interrelated with other promotional activities. Decisions regarding sales promotion often affect advertising and personal selling decisions, and vice versa.

Sales promotion can increase sales by providing extra purchasing incentives. Many opportunities exist to motivate consumers, resellers, and salespeople to take desired actions. Some kinds of sales promotion are designed specifically to stimulate resellers' demand and effectiveness, some are directed at increasing consumer demand, and some focus on both consumers and resellers. Regardless of the purpose, marketers must ensure that sales promotion objectives are consistent with the organization's overall objectives, as well as with its marketing and promotion objectives.

sales promotion
An activity and/or material meant to induce resellers or salespeople to sell a product or consumers to buy it

© AP IMAGES/PRNEWSFOTO/DENTEK ORAL CARE COMPANY

Sales Promotion
DenTek included a sample and a coupon in this sales promotion program.

When deciding which sales promotion methods to use, marketers must consider several factors, particularly product characteristics (price, size, weight, costs, durability, uses, features, and hazards) and target-market characteristics (age, gender, income, location, density, usage rate, and shopping patterns). How products are distributed and the number and types of resellers may determine the type of method used. The competitive and legal environments also may influence the choice.

The use of sales promotion has increased dramatically over the last 20 years, primarily at the expense of advertising. This shift in how promotional dollars are used has occurred for several reasons. Heightened concerns about value have made customers more responsive to promotional offers, especially price discounts and point-of-purchase displays. Thanks to their size and access to checkout scanner data, retailers have gained considerable power in the supply chain and are demanding greater promotional efforts from manufacturers to boost retail profits. Declines in brand loyalty have produced an environment in which sales promotions aimed at persuading customers to switch brands are more effective. Finally, the stronger emphasis placed on improving short-term performance results calls for greater use of sales promotion methods that yield quick (albeit perhaps short-lived) sales increases.[30]

In the remainder of this chapter, we examine several consumer and trade sales promotion methods, including what they entail and what goals they can help marketers achieve.

CONSUMER SALES PROMOTION METHODS

Consumer sales promotion methods encourage or stimulate consumers to patronize specific retail stores or try particular products. These methods initiated by retailers often aim to attract customers to specific locations, whereas those used by manufacturers generally introduce new products or promote established brands. In this section we discuss coupons, cents-off offers, money refunds and rebates, frequent-user incentives, demonstrations, point-of-purchase displays, free samples, premiums, consumer contests and games, and consumer sweepstakes.

Coupons and Cents-Off Offers

consumer sales promotion methods Ways of encouraging consumers to patronize specific stores or try particular products

coupons Written price reductions used to encourage consumers to buy a specific product

Coupons reduce a product's price and are used to prompt customers to try new or established products, increase sales volume quickly, attract repeat purchasers, or introduce new package sizes or features. Savings may be deducted from the purchase price or offered as cash. Research indicates that coupons are most effective when a small-face-value coupon is used in conjunction with a lower product price available for all consumers.[31] Coupons are the most widely used consumer sales promotion. Consumer packaged-goods manufacturers distribute about 253 billion coupons, of which about 1 percent are redeemed, saving consumers an estimated $3 billion. Nearly 80 percent of all consumers use coupons.[32] While consumers can find coupons for a wide variety of products and services, Table 17.2 shows the product categories with the greatest coupon distributions.

For best results, the coupons should be easy to recognize and state the offer clearly. The nature of the product (seasonal demand for it, life cycle stage, and frequency of purchase) is

TABLE 17.2 Top Ten Coupon Categories

1	Ready-to-eat cereal
2	Yogurt
3	Salty snacks
4	Personal care
5	Portable snacks
6	Baking ingredients
7	Frozen vegetables
8	Nutritional/diet
9	Carbonated soft drinks
10	Bathroom tissue

Source: "Cereal Tops February List of Most Popular Coupon Categories According to Coupons.com," *Coupons Inc.*, March 16, 2009.

the prime consideration in setting up a coupon promotion. Paper coupons are distributed on and in packages, through freestanding inserts (FSIs), in print advertising, and through direct mail. Electronic coupons are distributed online, via in-store kiosks, through shelf dispensers in stores, and at checkout counters. As shown in Figure 17.3, young people overwhelmingly prefer online coupons to traditional printed coupons. When deciding on the distribution method for coupons, marketers should consider strategies and objectives, redemption rates, availability, circulation, and exclusivity. The coupon distribution and redemption arena has become very competitive. To draw customers to their stores, some grocers double and sometimes even triple the value of customers' coupons.

Coupons offer several advantages. Print advertisements with coupons are often more effective at generating brand awareness than are print ads without coupons. In China, research has found that coupons positively influence consumer attitudes toward a brand.[33] Generally, the larger the coupon's cash offer, the better is the recognition generated. Coupons reward present product users, win back former users, and encourage purchases in larger quantities. Because they are returned, coupons also help a manufacturer determine whether it reached the intended target market. The advantages of using electronic coupons over paper coupons include lower cost per redemption, greater targeting ability, improved data-gathering capabilities, and improved experimentation capabilities to determine optimal face values and expiration cycles.[34] On the other hand, motivated consumers are likely to consider information in a print coupon more carefully than in an online coupon.[35]

Drawbacks of coupon use include fraud and misredemption, which can be expensive for manufacturers. The Coupon Information Council estimates that coupon fraud—including counterfeit Internet coupons as well as coupons cashed in under false retailer names—amounts to $500 million a year in the United States.[36] Another disadvantage, according to some experts, is that coupons are losing their value; because so many manufacturers offer them, consumers have learned not to buy without some incentive, whether it is a coupon, rebate, or refund. Furthermore, brand loyalty among heavy coupon users has diminished, and many consumers redeem coupons only for products they normally buy. It is believed

FIGURE 17.3 Younger Consumers Prefer Online Coupons

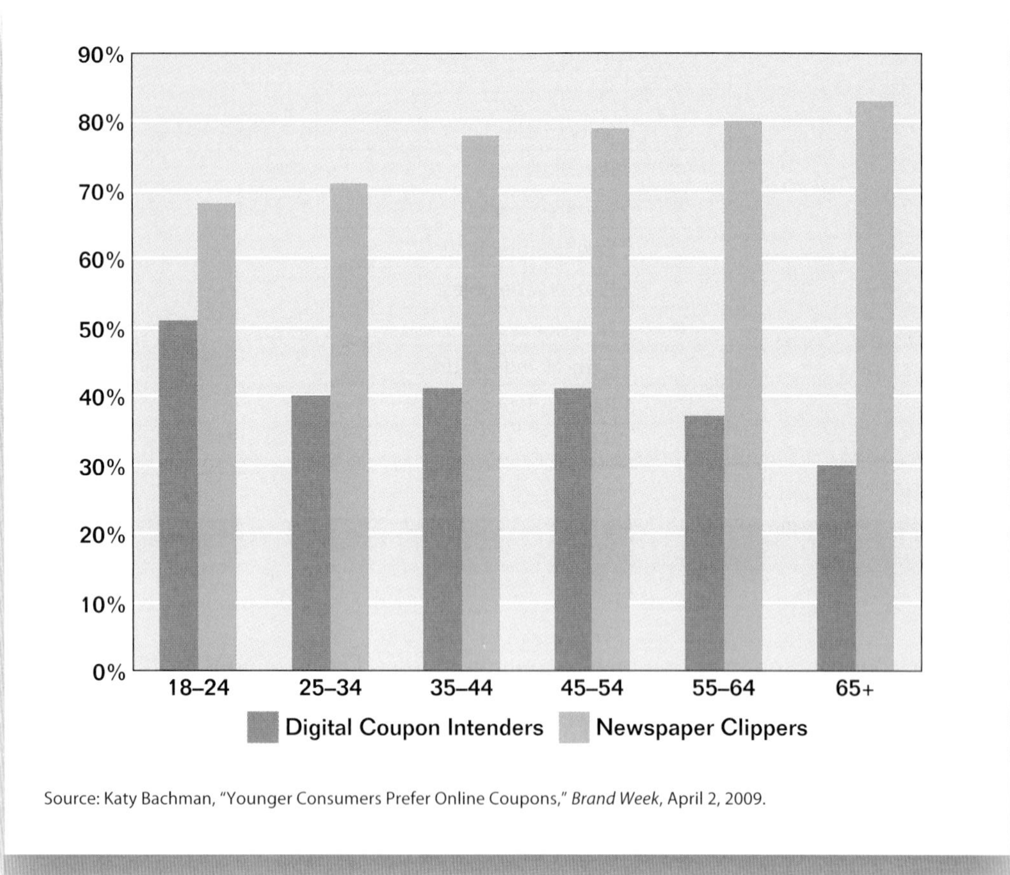

Source: Katy Bachman, "Younger Consumers Prefer Online Coupons," *Brand Week*, April 2, 2009.

that about three-fourths of coupons are redeemed by people already using the brand on the coupon. Thus coupons have questionable success as an incentive for consumers to try a new brand or product. An additional problem with coupons is that stores often do not have enough of the coupon item in stock. This situation generates ill will toward both the store and the product.

cents-off offer
A promotion that lets buyers pay less than the regular price to encourage purchase

money refunds
A sales promotion technique offering consumers money when they mail in a proof of purchase, usually for multiple product purchases

rebates
A sales promotion technique whereby a customer is sent a specific amount of money for purchasing a single product

With a **cents-off offer**, buyers pay a certain amount less than the regular price shown on the label or package. Similar to coupons, this method can serve as a strong incentive for trying new or unfamiliar products. Commonly used in product introductions, cents-off offers can stimulate product sales, yield short-lived sales increases, and promote products in off-seasons. It is an easy method to control and is often used for specific purposes. If used on an ongoing basis, however, cents-off offers reduce the price for customers who would buy at the regular price and also may cheapen a product's image. In addition, the method often requires special handling by retailers who are responsible for giving the discount at the point of sale.

Refunds and Rebates

With **money refunds**, consumers submit proof of purchase and are mailed a specific amount of money. Usually manufacturers demand multiple product purchases before consumers qualify for refunds. Money refunds, used primarily to promote trial use of a product, are relatively low in cost, but because they sometimes generate a low response rate, they have limited impact on sales. With **rebates**, the customer is sent a specified amount of money for making a single purchase. Rebates generally are given on more expensive products than money refunds and are used to encourage customers. Marketers also use rebates to reinforce brand loyalty, provide promotion buzz for salespeople, and as advertisements for the product. On larger items, such as cars, rebates are often given at the point of sale. Most rebates, however, especially on smaller items, offer a delayed discount because it takes time for the customer to receive the rebate.

One problem with money refunds and rebates is that many people perceive the redemption process as too complicated. Only about 40 percent of individuals who purchase rebated products actually apply for the rebates.[37] Consequently, marketers are increasingly encouraging customers to apply for rebates online, eliminating the need for forms that may confuse customers and frustrate retailers. Consumers also may have negative perceptions of manufacturers' reasons for offering rebates. They may believe the products are new, are untested, or haven't sold well. If these perceptions are not changed, rebate offers actually may degrade the image and desirability of the products.

Frequent-User Incentives

Greeting cards are not Hallmark's only product. To reward loyal customers, the company offers the Hallmark Gold Crown Card, which allows frequent buyers to accrue points that are redeemable for merchandise and discounts.[38] Many firms develop incentive programs to reward customers who engage in repeat (frequent) purchases. As mentioned earlier, most major airlines offer frequent-flier programs that reward customers who have flown a specified number of miles with free tickets for additional travel. Frequent-user incentives foster customer loyalty to a specific company or group of cooperating companies. They are favored by service businesses, such as airlines, auto rental agencies, hotels, and restaurants. At Neiman Marcus, for example, the InCircle Rewards program rewards loyal shoppers with dollar-for-dollar-spent benefits, but they must spend $5,000 per year to be eligible. Indeed, research shows that 93 percent of consumers with household incomes above $100,000 participate in frequent-user programs, whereas only 58 percent of shoppers with incomes below $50,000 participate.[39]

Marketing IN TRANSITION

Aggressive "Don't Dew It" Sales Promotion Provides Free Vault

While sales promotion can provide extra purchasing incentives such as coupons, cents off, and rebates, Coca-Cola took sales promotion to an unprecedented level with its "Don't Dew It" promotion. Coca-Cola's Vault brand competes with Mountain Dew but significantly lags behind in the caffeinated citrus beverage market. In fact, Mountain Dew maintains an 80 percent market share compared to Vault's 4 percent. As consumers were in a down economy in 2009, coupon redemption rose 10 percent, with 94 percent of consumers surveyed indicating that they use coupons. This was the ideal environment for the "Don't Dew It" attack.

In an innovative and audacious move, Coca-Cola offered to give away a coupon redeemable for a free sample of its Vault brand citrus beverage to consumers of Pepsi's Mountain Dew. Coca-Cola's promotion gave anyone who purchased a 20-ounce Mountain Dew a free 16-, 20-, or 24-ounce Vault for free.

© TERRI MILLER/E-VISUAL COMMUNICATIONS, INC.

Vault, an artificially flavored hybrid energy drink, contains 70.5 milligrams of caffeine per 12 ounces compared with Mountain Dew's 55 mg per 12 ounces. Coca-Cola's marketing managers believe that when Mountain Dew consumers get a taste of Vault, they will prefer it. Coca-Cola timed the promotion right after Mountain Dew changed its name to Mtn Dew and introduced a new package design. While most consumers will enjoy getting a free Vault, Coca-Cola will have to wait to see if their new promotion picks up market share for the company. While the several million dollars spent on the campaign comes at a time when consumers are anxious to get a free drink, Mtn Dew has the vast majority of consumers in this market and has strong brand loyalty on its side.[c]

Point-of-Purchase Materials and Demonstrations

Point-of-purchase (P-O-P) materials include outdoor signs, window displays, counter pieces, display racks, and self-service cartons. Innovations in P-O-P displays include sniff-teasers, which give off a product's aroma in the store as consumers walk within a radius of four feet, and computerized interactive displays. These items, often supplied by producers, attract attention, inform customers, and encourage retailers to carry particular products. A retailer is likely to make use of P-O-P materials if they are attractive, informative, well constructed, and in harmony with the store's image.

Demonstrations are excellent attention getters. Manufacturers offer them temporarily to encourage trial use and purchase of a product or to show how a product works. Because labor costs can be extremely high, demonstrations are not used widely. They can be highly effective for promoting certain types of products, such as appliances, cosmetics, and cleaning supplies. For example, many Whole Foods stores provide cooking classes and demonstrations to teach consumers how to prepare different cuisines and to give them ideas on how to use products sold in the stores.

Free Samples and Premiums

Marketers use **free samples** to stimulate trial of a product, increase sales volume in the early stages of a product's life cycle, and obtain desirable distribution. Sampling is the most expensive sales promotion method because production and distribution—at local events, by mail or door-to-door delivery, online, in stores, and on packages—entail high costs. Coca-Cola often gives out free samples of products such as Vitamin Water at business conventions, concerts, and sporting events, for example. Many consumers prefer to get their samples by mail. Other consumers like to sample new food products at supermarkets or to try samples of new recipes featuring foods they already like. In designing a free sample, marketers should consider factors such as seasonal demand for the product, market characteristics, and prior advertising. Free samples usually are not appropriate for slow-turnover products. Despite high costs, use of sampling is increasing. In a given year, almost three-fourths of consumer product companies may use sampling. Distribution of free samples through websites such as StartSampling.com and FreeSamples.com is growing.

Premiums are items offered free or at minimal cost as a bonus for purchasing a product. Like the prize in a Cracker Jack box, premiums are used to attract competitors' customers, introduce different sizes of established products, add variety to other promotional efforts, and stimulate consumer loyalty. Creativity is essential when using premiums; to stand out and achieve a significant number of redemptions, the premium must match both the target audience and the brand's image. Premiums also must be easily recognizable and desirable. Premiums are placed on or in packages and also can be distributed by retailers or through the mail. Examples include a service station giving a free carwash with a fill-up, a free toothbrush available with a tube of toothpaste, and a free plastic storage box given with the purchase of Kraft Cheese Singles.

Consumer Games, Contests, and Sweepstakes

In **consumer contests,** individuals compete for prizes based on analytical or creative skills. This method can be used to generate retail traffic and frequency of exposure to promotional messages. Contestants are usually more highly involved in consumer contests than in games or sweepstakes, even though total participation may be lower. Contests also may be used in conjunction with other sales promotional methods, such as coupons. For example, Borders invited its Reward loyalty club members to submit essays about New Orleans in order to win a trip to the New Orleans Jazz & Heritage Festival.[40]

In **consumer games**, individuals compete for prizes based primarily on chance—often by collecting game pieces such as bottle caps or a sticker on the side of a packet of french fries. Because collecting multiple pieces may be necessary to win or increase an individual's chances of winning, the game stimulates repeated business. Games typically are conducted over a long

point-of-purchase (P-O-P) materials
Signs, window displays, display racks, and similar means used to attract customers

demonstrations
A sales promotion method manufacturers use temporarily to encourage trial use and purchase of a product or to show how a product works

free samples
Samples of a product given out to encourage trial and purchase

premiums
Items offered free or at a minimal cost as a bonus for purchasing a product

consumer contests
Sales promotion methods in which individuals compete for prizes based on analytical or creative skills

consumer games
Sales promotion method in which individuals compete for prizes based primarily on chance

period of time and are commonly used by fast-food chains, soft-drink companies, and hotels to stimulate traffic and repeat business. Development and management of consumer games often are outsourced to an independent public relations firm, which can help marketers to navigate federal and state laws applying to games. Although games may stimulate sales temporarily, there is no evidence to suggest that they affect a company's long-term sales. Marketers should exercise care in developing and administering games: Problems or errors may anger customers and could result in lawsuits. Consider that McDonald's popular Monopoly game promotion, in which customers collect Monopoly real estate pieces on drink and fry packages, has been tarnished by both fraud and lawsuits. After six successful years, McDonald's was forced to end the annual promotion after a crime ring, which included employees of the promotional firm running the game, was convicted of stealing millions of dollars in winning game pieces. After McDonald's reintroduced the Monopoly game with improved security, it once again came under scrutiny as the focus of a class-action lawsuit filed by Burger King franchisees, who contended that their customers were lured away by the false promises of McDonald's game.[41]

Entrants in a **consumer sweepstakes** submit their names for inclusion in a drawing for prizes. Advil pain reliever created the "Live Life to the Fullest" sweepstakes, with a chance to win a grand prize of $25,000 and a trip for two to see a live taping of the Ellen DeGeneres show in Los Angeles. Sweepstakes are employed more often than consumer contests and tend to attract a greater number of participants. Contests, games, and sweepstakes may be used in conjunction with other sales promotion methods, such as coupons. It is important to know regulations and laws for contests and sweepstakes because some state laws may view some types of events as forms of gambling or lotteries.[42]

consumer sweepstakes
Sales promotion in which entrants submit their names for inclusion in a drawing for prizes

trade sales promotion methods
Ways of persuading wholesalers and retailers to carry a producer's products and market them aggressively

buying allowance
A temporary price reduction to resellers for purchasing specified quantities of a product

buy-back allowance
A sum of money given to a reseller for each unit bought after an initial promotion deal is over

TRADE SALES PROMOTION METHODS

To encourage resellers, especially retailers, to carry their products and to promote them effectively, producers use sales promotion methods. **Trade sales promotion methods** stimulate wholesalers and retailers to carry a producer's products and market those products more aggressively. These methods include buying allowances, buy-back allowances, scan-back allowances, merchandise allowances, cooperative advertising, dealer listings, free merchandise, dealer loaders, premium or push money, and sales contests.

Trade Allowances

Many manufacturers offer trade allowances to encourage resellers to carry a product or stock more of it. One such trade allowance is a **buying allowance**, which is a temporary price reduction offered to resellers for purchasing specified quantities of a product. A soap producer, for example, might give retailers $1 for each case of soap purchased. Such offers provide an incentive for resellers to handle new products, achieve temporary price reductions, or stimulate purchase of items in larger than normal quantities. The buying allowance, which takes the form of money, yields profits to resellers and is simple and straightforward. There are no restrictions on how resellers use the money, which increases the method's effectiveness. One drawback of buying allowances is that customers may buy "forward," meaning that they buy large amounts that keep them supplied for many months. Another problem is that competitors may match (or beat) the reduced price, which can lower profits for all sellers.

© AP IMAGES/PRNEWSFOTO/CONTINENTAL TIRE NORTH AMERICA, INC.

Rebate
General Tire offered a $50 rebate, in the form of a VISA gift card, to tire purchasers.

A **buy-back allowance** is a sum of money that a producer gives to a reseller for each unit the reseller buys after an initial promotional deal is over. This method is a secondary incentive in which the total amount of money that resellers receive is proportional to their purchases during an initial consumer promotion, such as a coupon offer. Buy-back allowances foster cooperation during an initial sales promotion effort and stimulate repurchase afterward. The main disadvantage of this method is expense.

A **scan-back allowance** is a manufacturer's reward to retailers based on the number of pieces moved through the retailers' scanners during a specific time period. To participate in scan-back programs, retailers usually are expected to pass along savings to consumers through special pricing. Scan-backs are becoming widely used by manufacturers because they link trade spending directly to product movement at the retail level.

scan-back allowance A manufacturer's reward to retailers based on the number of pieces scanned

A **merchandise allowance** is a manufacturer's agreement to pay resellers certain amounts of money for providing promotional efforts such as advertising or P-O-P displays. This method is best suited to high-volume, high-profit, easily handled products. A drawback is that some retailers perform activities at a minimally acceptable level simply to obtain allowances. Before paying retailers, manufacturers usually verify their performance. Manufacturers hope that retailers' additional promotional efforts will yield substantial sales increases.

merchandise allowance A manufacturer's agreement to pay resellers certain amounts of money for providing special promotional efforts

Cooperative Advertising and Dealer Listings

Cooperative advertising is an arrangement whereby a manufacturer agrees to pay a certain amount of a retailer's media costs for advertising the manufacturer's products. The amount allowed is usually based on the quantities purchased. As with merchandise allowances, a retailer must show proof that advertisements did appear before the manufacturer pays the agreed-on portion of the advertising costs. These payments give retailers additional funds for advertising. Some retailers exploit cooperative advertising agreements by crowding too many products into one advertisement. Not all available cooperative advertising dollars are used. Some retailers cannot afford to advertise, whereas others can afford it but do not want to advertise. A large proportion of all cooperative advertising dollars are spent on newspaper advertisements.

cooperative advertising An arrangement in which a manufacturer agrees to pay a certain amount of a retailer's media costs for advertising the manufacturer's products

Dealer listings are advertisements promoting a product and identifying participating retailers that sell the product. Dealer listings can influence retailers to carry the product, build traffic at the retail level, and encourage consumers to buy the product at participating dealers.

dealer listings Advertisements that promote a product and identify the names of participating retailers that sell the product

Free Merchandise and Gifts

Manufacturers sometimes offer **free merchandise** to resellers that purchase a stated quantity of products. Occasionally, free merchandise is used as payment for allowances provided through other sales promotion methods. To avoid handling and bookkeeping problems, the "free" merchandise usually takes the form of a reduced invoice.

free merchandise A manufacturer's reward given to resellers for purchasing a stated quantity of products

A **dealer loader** is a gift to a retailer who purchases a specified quantity of merchandise. Dealer loaders are often used to obtain special display efforts from retailers by offering essential display parts as premiums. For example, a manufacturer might design a display that includes a sterling silver tray as a major component and give the tray to the retailer. Marketers use dealer loaders to obtain new distributors and to push larger quantities of goods.

dealer loader A gift, often part of a display, given to a retailer purchasing a specified quantity of merchandise

Premium (Push) Money

Premium money (*or* **push money**) is additional compensation to salespeople offered by the manufacturer as an incentive to push a line of goods. This method is appropriate when personal selling is an important part of the marketing effort; it is not effective for promoting products sold through self-service. The method often helps manufacturers obtain a commitment from the sales force, but it can be very expensive.

premium money (*or* push money) Extra compensation to salespeople for pushing a line of goods

Sales Contests

A **sales contest** is designed to motivate distributors, retailers, and sales personnel by recognizing outstanding achievements. To be effective, this method must be equitable for all persons involved. One advantage is that it can achieve participation at all distribution levels. Positive effects may be temporary, however, and prizes are usually expensive.

sales contest A promotion method used to motivate distributors, retailers, and sales personnel through recognition of outstanding achievements

CHAPTER REVIEW

OBJECTIVES

1 Define personal selling and understand its purpose.

Personal selling is paid personal communication that attempts to inform customers and persuade them to purchase products in an exchange situation. Three general purposes of personal selling are finding prospects, persuading them to buy, and keeping customers satisfied.

2 Describe the basic steps in the personal selling process.

Many salespeople move through a general selling process when they sell products. In prospecting, the salesperson develops a list of potential customers. Before contacting prospects, the salesperson conducts a preapproach that involves finding and analyzing information about prospects and their needs. The approach is the way in which a salesperson contacts potential customers. During the sales presentation, the salesperson must attract and hold the prospect's attention to stimulate interest in and desire for the product. If possible, the salesperson should handle objections as they arise. During the closing, the salesperson asks the prospect to buy the product or products. After a successful closing, the salesperson must follow up the sale.

3 Identify the types of sales force personnel.

In developing a sales force, marketing managers consider which types of salespeople will sell the firm's products most effectively. The five classifications of salespeople are order getters, current-customer salespeople, new-business salespeople, order takers, and support personnel. Order getters inform both current customers and new prospects and persuade them to buy. Order takers seek repeat sales and fall into two categories: inside order takers and field order takers. Sales support personnel facilitate selling, but their duties usually extend beyond making sales. The three types of support personnel are missionary, trade, and technical salespeople. The roles of salespeople are changing. Team selling involves the salesperson joining with people from the firm's financial, engineering, and other functional areas. Relationship selling involves building mutually beneficial long-term associations with a customer through regular communications over prolonged periods of time.

4 Understand sales management decisions and activities.

Sales force management is an important determinant of a firm's success because the sales force is directly responsible for generating the organization's sales revenue. Major decision areas and activities include establishing sales force objectives; determining sales force size; recruiting, selecting, training, compensating, and motivating salespeople; managing sales territories; and controlling and evaluating sales force performance.

5 Explain what sales promotion activities are and how they are used.

Sales promotion is an activity or a material (or both) that acts as a direct inducement, offering added value or incentive for the product to resellers, salespeople, or consumers. Marketers use sales promotion to identify and attract new customers, introduce new products, and increase reseller inventories.

6 Recognize specific consumer and trade sales promotion methods.

Sales promotion techniques fall into two general categories: consumer and trade. Consumer sales promotion methods encourage consumers to trade at specific stores or try a specific product. These sales promotion methods include coupons, cents-off offers, money refunds and rebates, frequent-user incentives, point-of-purchase displays, demonstrations, free samples, premiums, and consumer contests, games, and sweepstakes. Trade sales promotion techniques can motivate resellers to handle a manufacturer's products and market those products aggressively. These sales promotion techniques include buying allowances, buy-back allowances, scan-back allowances, merchandise allowances, cooperative advertising, dealer listings, free merchandise, dealer loaders, premium (or push) money, and sales contests.

Please visit the student website at www.cengage.com/international for quizzes and games that will help you prepare for exams and help achieve the grade you want.

KEY CONCEPTS

personal selling
prospecting
approach
closing
order getter
order takers
support personnel
missionary salespeople
trade salespeople
technical salespeople
team selling
relationship selling
straight salary compensation plan
straight comission compensation plan
combination compensation plan
sales promotion
consumer sales promotion methods
coupons
cents-off offer
money refunds
rebates
point-of-purchase (P-O-P) materials
demonstrations
free samples
premiums
consumer contests
consumer games
consumer sweepstakes
trade sales promotion methods
buying allowance
buy-back allowance
scan-back allowance
merchandise allowance
cooperative advertising
dealer listings
free merchandise
dealer loader
premium money (*or* push money)
sales contest

ISSUES FOR DISCUSSION AND REVIEW

1. What is personal selling? How does personal selling relate to other types of promotional activities?
2. Identify the elements of the personal selling process. Must a salesperson include all these elements when selling a product to a customer? Why or why not?
3. How does a salesperson find and evaluate prospects? Do you consider any of these methods to be ethically questionable? Explain.
4. Are order getters more aggressive or creative than order takers? Why or why not?
5. Why are team selling and relationship selling becoming more prevalent?
6. How should a sales manager establish criteria for selecting sales personnel? What do you think are the general characteristics of a good salesperson?
7. What major issues or questions should management consider when developing a training program for the sales force?
8. Explain the major advantages and disadvantages of the three basic methods of compensating salespeople. In general, which method would you prefer? Why?
9. How does a sales manager, who cannot be with each salesperson in the field on a daily basis, control the performance of sales personnel?
10. What is sales promotion? Why is it used?
11. For each of the following, identify and describe three techniques and give several examples: (a) consumer sales promotion methods, and (b) trade sales promotion methods.

MARKETING APPLICATIONS

1. Briefly describe an experience you have had with a salesperson at a clothing store or an automobile dealership. Describe the steps used by the salesperson. Did the salesperson skip any steps? What did the salesperson do well? Not so well?
2. Refer to your answer to Marketing Application question 1. Would you describe the salesperson as an order getter, an order taker, or a support salesperson? Why? Did the salesperson perform more than one of these functions?

3. Identify a familiar type of retail store or product. Recommend at least three sales promotion methods that should be used to promote the store or product. Explain why you would use these methods.

4. Identify which method or methods of sales promotion a producer might use in the following situations, and explain why the method would be appropriate.
   a. A golf ball manufacturer wants to encourage retailers to add a new type of golf ball to current product offerings.
   b. A life insurance company wants to increase sales of its universal life products, which have been lagging recently (the company has little control over sales activities).
   c. A light bulb manufacturer with an overproduction of 100-watt bulbs wants to encourage its grocery store chain resellers to increase their bulb inventories.

ONLINE EXERCISE

5. TerrAlign offers consulting services and software products designed to help a firm maximize control and deployment of its field sales representatives. Review its website at http://www.terralign.com.
   a. Identify three features of TerrAlign software that are likely to benefit salespeople.
   b. Identify three features of TerrAlign software that are likely to benefit sales managers.
   c. Why might field sales professionals object to the use of software from TerrAlign?

DEVELOPING YOUR MARKETING PLAN

When developing its marketing strategy, a company must consider the different forms of communication that are necessary to reach a variety of customers. Several types of promotion may be required. Knowledge of the advantages and disadvantages of each promotional element is necessary when developing the marketing plan. Consider the information in this chapter when evaluating your promotional mix:

1. Review the various types of salespeople described in this chapter. Given your promotional objectives (from Chapter 15), do any of these types of salespeople have a place in your promotional plan?
2. Identify the resellers in your distribution channel. Discuss the role that trade sales promotions to these resellers could play in the development of your promotional plan.
3. Evaluate each type of consumer sales promotion as it relates to accomplishing your promotional objectives.

The information obtained from these questions should assist you in developing various aspects of your marketing plan found in the *Interactive Marketing Plan* exercise.

VIDEO CASE 17

IBM Sales Force Sells Solutions

In recent years, IBM has worked hard to reposition itself from a supplier of information technology hardware and software to a company that provides business solution services. In their own words, "We measure ourselves today by how well we help clients solve their biggest and most pressing problems." Obviously, successful problem solving leads to an increase in customers and an increase in goods and services sold.

Although IBM is still the world's largest provider of IT hardware and software, it regards this as the means to an end. The company relies heavily on its global sales force to make the transition from a goods to a solution services provider. The enormous task of changing the company's focus cannot be overstated.

Personal selling has always been a fundamental aspect of IBM's business philosophy and is one of the foundations of the company's success: IBM has customers in 174 countries who speak 165 languages. The company's sales force makes 18 billion client contacts a year and addresses 350,000 sales opportunities per day.

As in all organizations, IBM's change comes from the top. Last year Samuel J. Palmisano, IBM's chair, president, and chief executive officer, led a process of examining and redefining the company's core values. One of the first core values identified was "dedication to every client's success." From a sales perspective, this is achieved through consultative or solution selling, which brings all of IBM's resources and expertise together to solve customer problems. This requires that the sales force thoroughly understand their customers' business environments and deliver the correct answers to their questions. As Palmisano points out, the company's business model has changed. It used to be "invent, build, and sell." Today it is "craft, solve, and deliver the solution."

Not surprisingly, solution selling has brought new challenges to the sales force. IBM believes that salespeople are not born, but trained. The company puts its salespeople through an extensive five-month training program that encompasses three major areas of focus: IBM's commitment to its customers, techniques of collaborative selling, and techniques for gaining understanding of a company's resources and infrastructure. For large projects, salespeople often work in teams comprised of one sales leader and four to five sales specialists who have expertise relevant to the project.

For the most part, IBM salespeople use the Socratic method of selling. This involves asking open-ended questions to better understand their customers' problems, desires, and needs. As might be expected, solution (or pull) selling is more complex than product (or push) selling. The salesperson's role in solution selling is to gather information concerning the customer's business problem, provide a point of view, solve the problem (with the help of other team members), and determine the potential impact on the customer's business once the recommended solution is implemented.

The most accurate and important indicator of the success of the solutions service is customer reaction. An example of IBM achieving its sales objective of "insuring our clients are successful" is their Sales Connections Program. Actuate, an Independent Software Vendor (ISV) and IBM customer, used the Sales Connection website to express concerns about a customer dragging its feet on an applications deal. IBM discovered that the person Actuate was working with lacked the authority to close the deal. IBM provided Actuate with the correct contact person and the sale was quickly closed.

Another example is IBM's Software-as-a-Service program, which delivers software via the Internet. This eliminates the need for companies to buy, build, manage, and maintain applications that address areas such as accounting, human resources, customer relationship management, and enterprise resource planning. Companies benefit from this concept because they can reduce their operational costs and maintenance expenses, therefore increasing profits. In an effort to sell this service more broadly, an IBM sales team designed a sales incentive that awards a 10 percent referral fee and additional marketing incentives to IBM customers that submit leads resulting in business for IBM. The marketing incentives include direct mail, telemarketing, advertising, and technical resources to help businesses generate leads. This program enabled one of IBM's customers to generate 800 sales leads in one year.

With this kind of dedication, there is little doubt that IBM's solutions service will continue its success.

QUESTIONS FOR DISCUSSION

1. What are the advantages for IBM in selling solutions rather than goods?
2. Why is solution selling more complex than hardware and software selling? Identify the sales skills needed for each approach.
3. What are some ways that IBM can measure the effectiveness of its solutions or consultative selling?

"IBM Steps Up Efforts to Drive the Adoption of Software as a Service—Offers Broadest Range of Resources Enabling Business Partners to Transition to Rapid Delivery Model," Market Wire, Feb. 23, 2006, www.marketwire.com/mw/release_html_b1?release_id110803; Dan Neel, "IBM Connects the Partner Dots," Computer Reseller News, Nov. 7, 2005; IBM, www.ibm.com (accessed Feb. 22, 2008);
Video Interviews with IBM employees: Dan Pelino, Greg Pushalla, Karen Lowe, Monica Chambers (accessed Feb. 28, 2006).

Careers in Marketing

APPENDIX

Changes in the Workplace

Between one-fourth and one-third of the civilian workforce in the United States is employed in marketing-related jobs. Although the field offers a multitude of diverse career opportunities, the number of positions in each area varies. For example, millions of workers are employed in many facets of sales, but relatively few people work in public relations and marketing research.

Many nonbusiness organizations now recognize that they perform marketing activities. For that reason, the number of marketing positions in government agencies, hospitals, charitable and religious groups, educational institutions, and similar organizations is increasing. Today's nonprofit organizations are competitive and better managed, with job growth rates often matching those of private-sector firms. Another area ripe with opportunities is the World Wide Web. The federal government makes more sales to consumers online than even Amazon.com. With so many businesses setting up websites, demand will rise for people who have the skills to develop and design marketing strategies for the Web.

Many workers outplaced from large corporations are choosing an entrepreneurial path, creating still more new opportunities for first-time job seekers. Even some individuals with secure managerial positions are leaving corporations and heading to smaller companies, toward greater responsibility and autonomy. The traditional career path used to be graduation from college, then a job with a large corporation, and a climb up the ladder to management. This pattern has changed, however. Today people are more likely to experience a career path of sideways "gigs" rather than sequential steps up a corporate ladder.

Career Choices Are Major Life Choices

Many people think career planning begins with an up-to-date résumé and a job interview.[1] In reality, it begins long before you prepare your résumé. It starts with *you* and what you want to become. In some ways, you have been preparing for a career ever since you started school. Everything you have experienced during your lifetime you can use as a resource to help you define your career goals. Since you will likely spend more time at work than at any other single place during your lifetime, it makes sense to spend that time doing something you enjoy. Unfortunately, some people just work at a *job* because they need money to survive. Other people choose a *career* because of their interests and talents or a commitment to a particular profession. Whether you are looking for a job or a career, you should examine your priorities.

PERSONAL FACTORS INFLUENCING CAREER CHOICES

Before choosing a career, you need to consider what motivates you and what skills you can offer an employer. The following questions may help you define what you consider important in life:

1. *What types of activities do you enjoy?* Although most people know what they enjoy in a general way, a number of interest inventories exist. By helping you determine specific interests and activities, these inventories can help you land a job that will lead to a satisfying career. In some cases, it may be sufficient just to list the activities you enjoy, along with those you dislike. Watch for patterns that may influence your career choices.
2. *What do you do best?* All jobs and all careers require employees to be able to "do something." It is extremely important to assess what you do best. Be honest with yourself about your ability to succeed in a specific job. It may help to make a list of your strongest job-related skills. Also, try looking at your skills from an employer's perspective: What can you do that an employer would be willing to pay for?
3. *What kind of education will you need?* The amount of education you need is determined by the type of career you choose. In some careers, it is impossible to get an entry-level position without at least a college degree. Other careers may also require technical or hands-on skills. Generally, additional education increases your potential earning power.
4. *Where do you want to live?* Initially, some college graduates will want to move to a different part of the country before entering the job market, whereas others may prefer to reside close to home, friends, and relatives. In reality, successful job applicants must be willing to go where the jobs are. The location of an entry-level job may be influenced by the type of marketing career selected. For example, some of the largest advertising agencies are in New York, Chicago, and Los Angeles. Likewise, large marketing research organizations are based in metropolitan areas. On the other hand, sales positions and retail management jobs are available in medium-size as well as large cities.

Job Search Activities

When people begin to search for a job, they often first go online or turn to the classified ads in their local newspaper. Those ads are an important source of information about jobs in a particular area, but they are only one source. Many other sources can lead to employment and a satisfying career. Because there is a wealth of information about career planning, you should be selective in both the type and the amount of information you use to guide your job search.

In recent years the library, a traditional job-hunting tool, has been joined by the Internet. Both the library and the Internet are sources of everything from classified newspaper ads and government job listings to detailed information on individual companies and industries. You can use either resource to research an area of employment or a particular company that interests you. In addition, the Internet allows you to check electronic bulletin boards for current job information, exchange ideas with other job seekers through online discussion groups or e-mail, and get career advice from professional counselors. You can also create your own webpage to inform prospective employers about your qualifications. You may even have a job interview online. Many companies use their websites to post job openings, accept applications, and interview candidates.

As you start your job search, you may find the following websites helpful. (Addresses of additional career-related websites can be accessed through the Student Career Center at **www.cengage.com/international**)

CareerBuilder.com: **www.careerbuilder.com**

This site is one of the largest on the Internet, with more than 900,000 jobs to view. The site allows a job seeker to find jobs, post résumés, get advice and career resources, and obtain information on career fairs.

The Monster Board: **www.monster.com**

The Monster Board carries hundreds of job listings and offers links to related sites, such as company homepages and sites with information about job fairs.

Federal jobs: **http://usajobs.opm.gov**

If you are interested in working for a government agency, this site lists positions all across the country. You can limit your search to specific states or do a general cross-country search for job openings.

Other web addresses for job seekers include:

www.careers-in-marketing.com

www.marketingjobs.com

www.careermag.com

www.salary.com

In addition to the library and the Internet, the following sources can be of great help when trying to find the "perfect job":

1. *Campus placement offices.* Colleges and universities have placement offices staffed by trained personnel specialists. In most cases, these offices serve as clearinghouses for career information. The staff may also be able to guide you in creating a résumé and preparing for a job interview.
2. *Professional sources and networks.* A network is a group of people—friends, relatives, and professionals—who are in a position to exchange information, including information about job openings. According to many job applicants, networking is one of the best sources of career information and job leads. Start with as many people as you can think of to establish your network. (The Internet can be very useful in this regard.) Contact these people and ask specific questions about job opportunities they are aware of. Also, ask each individual to introduce or refer you to someone else who may be able to help you in your job search.
3. *Private employment agencies.* Private employment agencies charge a fee for helping people find jobs. Typical fees can be as high as 15 to 20 percent of an employee's first-year salary. The fee may be paid by the employer or the employee. Like campus placement offices, private employment agencies provide career counseling, help create résumés, and provide preparation for job interviews. Before you use a private employment agency, be sure you understand the terms of any contract or agreement you sign. Above all, make sure you know who is responsible for paying the agency's fee.
4. *State employment agencies.* The local office of your state employment agency is a valuable source of information about job openings in your immediate area. Some job applicants are reluctant to use state agencies because most jobs available through them are for semiskilled or unskilled workers. From a practical standpoint, though, it can't hurt to consult state employment agencies. They will have information about some professional and managerial positions available in your area, and you will not be charged a fee if you obtain a job through one of these agencies.

Many graduates want a job immediately and are discouraged at the thought that an occupational search can take months. But people seeking entry-level jobs should expect their job search to take considerable time. Of course, the state of the economy and whether employers generally are hiring can shorten or extend a job search.

During a job search, you should use the same work habits that effective employees use on the job. Resist the temptation to "take the day off" from job hunting. Instead, make a master list of the activities you want to accomplish each day. If necessary, force yourself to make contacts, do job research, or schedule interviews that might lead to job opportunities. (In fact, many job applicants look at the job hunt as their actual job and "work" full time at it until they find the job they want.) Above all, realize that an occupational search requires patience and perseverance. According to many successful applicants, perseverance may be the job hunter's most valuable trait.

Planning and Preparation

The key to landing the job you want is planning and preparation—and planning begins with goals. In particular, it is important to determine your *personal* goals, decide on the role your career will play in reaching those goals, and then develop your *career* goals. Once you know where you are going, you can devise a feasible plan for getting there.

The time to begin planning is as early as possible. You must, of course, satisfy the educational requirements for the occupational area you desire. Early planning will give you the opportunity to do so. However, some of the people who will compete with you for the better jobs will also be fully prepared. Can you do more? Company recruiters say the following factors give job candidates a definite advantage.

- *Work experience.* You can get valuable work experience in cooperative work/school programs, during summer vacations, or in part-time jobs during the school year. Experience in your chosen occupational area carries the most weight, but even unrelated work experience is useful.
- *The ability to communicate well.* Verbal and written communication skills are increasingly important in all aspects of business. Yours will be tested in your letters to recruiters, in your résumé, and in interviews. You will use these same communication skills throughout your career.
- *Clear and realistic job and career goals.* Recruiters feel most comfortable with candidates who know where they are headed and why they are applying for a specific job.

Again, starting early will allow you to establish well-defined goals, sharpen your communication skills (through elective courses, if necessary), and obtain solid work experience. To develop your own personal career plan, go to the **www.cengage.com/international** student site and access the Student Career Center. There you will find personal career plan worksheets.

The Résumé

An effective résumé is one of the keys to being considered for a good job. Because your résumé states your qualifications, experiences, education, and career goals, a potential employer can use it to assess your compatibility with the job requirements. The résumé should be accurate and current.

In preparing a résumé, it helps to think of it as an advertisement. Envision yourself as a product and the potential employers as your customer. To interest the customer in buying the product—hiring you—your résumé must communicate information about your qualities and indicate how you can satisfy the customer's needs—that is, how you can help the company achieve its objectives. The information in the résumé should persuade the organization to take a closer look at you by calling you in for an interview.

To be effective, the résumé should be targeted at a specific position, as Figure A.1 shows. This document is only one example of an acceptable résumé. The job target section is specific and leads directly to the applicant's qualifications for the job. The qualifications section details capabilities—what the applicant can do—and also shows that the applicant has an understanding of the job's requirements. Skills and strengths that relate to the specific job should be emphasized. The achievement section ("Experiences" in Figure A.1) indicates success at accomplishing tasks or goals on the job and at school. The work experience section in Figure A.1 includes an unusual listing, which might pique the interviewer's interest: "helped operate relative's blueberry farm in Michigan for three summers." It tends to inspire rather than satisfy curiosity, thus inviting further inquiry.

Another type of résumé is the chronological résumé, which lists work experience and educational history in order by date. This type of résumé is useful for those just entering the job market because it helps highlight education and work experience.

Common suggestions for improving résumés include deleting useless or outdated information, improving organization, using professional printing and typing, listing duties (not accomplishments), maintaining grammatical perfection, and avoiding an overly elaborate or fancy format.[2] Keep in mind that the person who will look at your résumé may have to sift through hundreds in the course of the day in addition to handling other duties. Consequently it is important to keep your résumé short (one page is best, never more than two), concise, and neat. Moreover, you want your résumé to be distinctive so it will stand out from all the others.

In addition to having the proper format and content, a résumé should be easy to read. It is best to use only one or two kinds of type and plain, white paper. When sending a résumé to a large company, several copies may be made and distributed. Textured, gray, or colored paper may make a good impression on the first person who sees the résumé, but it will not reproduce well for the others, who will see only a poor copy. You should also proofread your résumé with care. Typos and misspellings will grab attention—the wrong kind.

Along with the résumé itself, always submit a cover letter. In the letter, you can include somewhat more information than in your résumé and convey a message that expresses your interest and enthusiasm about the organization and the job.

THE JOB INTERVIEW

In essence, your résumé and cover letter are an introduction. The deciding factor in the hiring process is the interview (or several interviews) with representatives of the firm. It is through the interview that the firm gets to know you and your qualifications. At the same time, the interview gives you a chance to learn about the firm.

Here again, preparation is the key to success. Research the firm before your first interview. Learn all you can about its products, its subsidiaries, the markets in which it operates, its history, the locations of its facilities, and so on. If possible, obtain and read the firm's most recent annual report. Be prepared to ask questions about the firm and the opportunities it offers. Interviewers welcome such questions. They expect you to be interested enough to spend some time thinking about your potential relationship with their organization.

Also, prepare to respond to questions the interviewer may ask. Table A.1 lists typical interview questions that job applicants often find difficult to answer. But don't expect interviewers to stick to the list given in the table or to the items appearing in your résumé. They will be interested in anything that helps them decide what kind of person and worker you are.

Make sure you are on time for your interview and are dressed and groomed in a businesslike manner. Interviewers take note of punctuality and appearance just as they do of other

FIGURE A.1 A Résumé Targeted at a Specific Position

LORRAINE MILLER
2212 WEST WILLOW
PHOENIX, AZ 12345
(416) 862-9169

EDUCATION: B.A. Arizona State University, 2004, Marketing, achieved a 3.4 on a 4.0 scale throughout college

POSITION DESIRED: Product manager with an international firm providing future career development at the executive level

QUALIFICATIONS:

- Communicates well with individuals to achieve a common goal
- Handles tasks efficiently and in a timely manner
- Understands advertising sales, management, marketing research, packaging, pricing, distribution, and warehousing
- Coordinates many activities at one time
- Receives and carries out assigned tasks or directives
- Writes complete status or research reports

EXPERIENCES:

- Assistant Editor of college paper
- Treasurer of the American Marketing Association (student chapter)
- Internship with 3-Cs Advertising, Berkeley, CA
- Student Assistantship with Dr. Steve Green, Professor of Marketing, Arizona State University
- Solo cross-Canada canoe trek, summer 2003

WORK RECORD:

2003–Present	Blythe and Co., Inc. —Junior Advertising Account Executive
2001–2002	Student Assistant for Dr. Steve Green —Research Assistant
2000–2001	The Men —Retail sales and consumer relations
1998–2000	Farmer —Helped operate relative's blueberry farm in Michigan for three summers

In some cases, education is more important than unrelated work experience because it indicates the career direction you desire despite the work experience you have acquired thus far.

personal qualities. Bring a copy of your résumé, even if you already sent one to the firm. You may also want to bring a copy of your course transcript and letters of recommendation. If you plan to furnish interviewers with the names and addresses of references rather than with letters of recommendation, make sure you have your references' permission to do so.

Consider the interview itself as a two-way conversation rather than a question-and-answer session. Volunteer any information that is relevant to the interviewer's questions. If an important point is skipped in the discussion, don't hesitate to bring it up. Be yourself, but emphasize your strengths. Good eye contact and posture are also important; they should come naturally if

TABLE A.1 Interview Questions Job Applicants Often Find Difficult to Answer

1. Tell me about yourself.
2. What do you know about our organization?
3. What can you do for us? Why should we hire you?
4. What qualifications do you have that make you feel you will be successful in your field?
5. What have you learned from the jobs you've held?
6. What are your special skills, and where did you acquire them?
7. Have you had any special accomplishments in your lifetime that you are particularly proud of?
8. Why did you leave your most recent job?
9. How do you spend your spare time? What are your hobbies?
10. What are your strengths and weaknesses?
11. Discuss five major accomplishments.
12. What kind of boss would you like? Why?
13. If you could spend a day with someone you've known or know of, who would it be?
14. What personality characteristics seem to rub you the wrong way?
15. How do you show your anger? What types of things make you angry?
16. With what type of person do you spend the majority of your time?

Source: Adapted from *The Ultimate Job Hunter's Guidebook,* 4th ed., by Susan D. Greene and Melanie C. L. Martel. Copyright © 2004 by Houghton Mifflin Company.

you take an active part in the interview. At the conclusion of the interview, thank the recruiter for taking the time to see you.

In most cases, the first interview is used to *screen* applicants, that is, choose those who are best qualified. These applicants are then given a second interview and perhaps a third, usually with one or more department heads. If the job requires relocation to a different area, applicants may be invited there for these later interviews.

After the interviewing process is complete, applicants are told when to expect a hiring decision.

AFTER THE INTERVIEW

Attention to common courtesy is important as a follow-up to your interview. You should send a brief note of thanks to the interviewer and give it as much care as you did your résumé and cover letter. A short, typewritten letter is preferred to a handwritten note or card, or an e-mail. Avoid not only typos, but also overconfident statements such as "I look forward to helping you make Universal Industries successful over the next decade." Even in the thank-you letter, it is important to show team spirit and professionalism, as well as to convey proper enthusiasm. Everything you say and do reflects on you as a candidate.

AFTER THE HIRE

Clearly, performing well in a job has always been a crucial factor in keeping a position. In a tight economy and job market, however, a person's attitude, as well as his or her performance, counts greatly. People in their first jobs can commit costly political blunders by being insensitive

Source: Data from Robert Half Finance & Accounting survey. Margin of error: ±2

to their environments. Politics in the business world includes how you react to your boss, how you react to your coworkers, and your general demeanor. Here are a few rules to live by.

1. *Don't bypass your boss.* One major blunder an employee can make is to go over the boss's head to resolve a problem. This is especially hazardous in a bureaucratic organization. You should become aware of the generally accepted chain of command and, when problems occur, follow that protocol, beginning with your immediate superior. No boss likes to look incompetent, and making him or her appear so is sure to hamper or even crush your budding career. However, there may be exceptions to this rule in emergency situations. It is wise to discuss with your supervisor what to do in an emergency, before an emergency occurs.[3]
2. *Don't criticize your boss.* Adhering to the old adage "praise in public and criticize in private" will keep you out of the line of retaliatory fire. A more sensible and productive alternative is to present the critical commentary to your boss in a diplomatic way during a private session.
3. *Don't show disloyalty.* If dissatisfied with the position, a new employee may start a fresh job search, within or outside the organization. However, it is not advisable to begin a publicized search within the company for another position unless you have held your current job for some time. Careful attention to the political climate in the organization should help you determine how soon to start a new job campaign and how public to make it. In any case, it is not a good idea to publicize that you are looking outside the company for a new position.
4. *Don't be a naysayer.* Employees are expected to become part of the organizational team and to work together with others. Behaviors to avoid, especially if you are a new employee, include being critical of others; refusing to support others' projects; always playing devil's advocate; refusing to help others when a crisis occurs; and complaining all the time, even about such matters as the poor quality of the food in the cafeteria, the crowded parking lot, or the temperature in the office.
5. *Learn to correct mistakes appropriately.* No one likes to admit having made a mistake, but one of the most important political skills you can acquire is minimizing the impact of a blunder. It is usually advantageous to correct the damage as soon as possible to avoid further problems. Some suggestions: be the first to break the bad news to your boss, avoid being defensive, stay poised and don't panic, and have solutions ready for fixing the blunder.[4]

Types of Marketing Careers

In considering marketing as a career, the first step is to evaluate broad categories of career opportunities in the areas of marketing research, sales, industrial buying, public relations, distribution management, product management, advertising, retail management, and direct marketing. Keep in mind that the categories described here are not all-inclusive and that each encompasses hundreds of marketing jobs.

MARKETING RESEARCH

Clearly, marketing research and information systems are vital aspects of marketing decision making. Marketing researchers survey customers to determine their habits, preferences, and aspirations. The information about buyers and environmental forces that research and information systems provide improves a marketer's ability to understand the dynamics of the marketplace and therefore make effective decisions.

Marketing research firms are usually employed by a client organization such as a provider of goods or services, a nonbusiness organization, a research consulting firm, or an advertising agency. The activities performed include concept testing, product testing, package testing, advertising testing, test market research, and new-product research.

Marketing researchers gather and analyze data relating to specific problems. A researcher may be involved in one or several stages of research depending on the size of the project, the organization of the research unit, and the researcher's experience. Marketing research trainees in large organizations usually perform a considerable amount of clerical work, such as compiling secondary data from the firm's accounting and sales records and from periodicals, government publications, syndicated data services, the Internet, and unpublished sources. A junior analyst may edit and code questionnaires or tabulate survey results. Trainees may also participate in gathering primary data through mail and telephone surveys, personal interviews, and observation. As a marketing researcher gains experience, he or she may become involved in defining problems and developing research questions; designing research procedures; and analyzing, interpreting, and reporting findings. Exceptional personnel may assume responsibility for entire research projects.

Although most employers consider a bachelor's degree sufficient qualification for a marketing research trainee, many specialized positions require a graduate degree in business administration, statistics, or other related fields. Today trainees are more likely to have a marketing or statistics degree than a liberal arts degree. Courses in statistics, information technology, psychology, sociology, communications, economics, and technical writing are valuable preparation for a career in marketing research.

The Bureau of Labor Statistics indicates that marketing research provides abundant employment opportunities, especially for applicants with graduate training in marketing research, statistics, economics, and the social sciences. Generally, the value of information gathered by marketing information and research systems rises as competition increases, thus expanding opportunities for prospective marketing research personnel.

The major career paths in marketing research are with independent marketing research agencies/data suppliers and marketing research departments in advertising agencies and other businesses. In a company in which marketing research plays a key role, the researcher is often a member of the marketing strategy team. Surveying or interviewing customers is the heart of the marketing research firm's activities. A statistician selects the sample to be surveyed, analysts design the questionnaire and synthesize the gathered data into a final report, data processors tabulate the data, and the research director controls and coordinates all these activities so each project is completed to the client's satisfaction.

Salaries in marketing research depend on the type, size, and location of the firm, as well as the nature of the position. Overall, salaries of marketing researchers have increased slightly during the last few years. However, the specific position within the marketing research field determines the degree of fluctuation.[5] Generally, starting salaries are somewhat higher and promotions somewhat slower than in other occupations requiring similar training. The typical salary for a market analyst is $24,000 to $50,000; a marketing research director can earn $75,000 to $200,000.[6]

SALES

Millions of people earn a living through personal selling. Chapter 17 defines personal selling as paid personal communication that attempts to inform customers and persuade them to purchase products in an exchange situation. Although this definition describes the general nature of sales positions, individual selling jobs vary enormously with respect to the types of businesses and products involved, the educational background and skills required, and the specific activities sales personnel perform. Because the work is so varied, it offers numerous career opportunities for people with a wide range of qualifications, interests, and goals. The two types of career opportunities we discuss relate to business-to-business sales.

Sales Positions in Wholesaling

Wholesalers buy products intended for resale, for use in making other products, and for general business operations, and sell them directly to business markets. Wholesalers thus provide services to both retailers and producers. They can help match producers' products to retailers' needs and provide services that save producers time, money, and resources. Some activities a sales representative for a wholesaling firm is likely to perform include planning and negotiating transactions; assisting customers with sales, advertising, sales promotion, and publicity; facilitating transportation and storage; providing customers with inventory control and data processing assistance; establishing prices; and giving customers technical, managerial, and merchandising assistance.

The background needed by wholesale personnel depends on the nature of the product handled. A sales representative for a drug wholesaler, for example, needs extensive technical training and product knowledge, and may have a degree in chemistry, biology, or pharmacology. A wholesaler of standard office supplies, on the other hand, may find it more important that its sales staff be familiar with various brands, suppliers, and prices than have technical knowledge about the products. A person just entering the wholesaling field may begin as a sales trainee or hold a nonselling job that provides experience with inventory, prices, discounts, and the firm's customers. A college graduate usually enters a wholesaler's sales force directly. Competent salespeople also transfer from manufacturer and retail sales positions.

The number of sales positions in wholesaling is expected to grow about as rapidly as the average for all occupations. Earnings for wholesale personnel vary widely because commissions often make up a large proportion of their incomes.

Sales Positions in Manufacturing

A manufacturer's sales personnel sell the firm's products to wholesalers, retailers, and industrial buyers; they thus perform many of the same activities as a wholesaler's representatives. As in wholesaling, educational requirements for a sales position depend largely on the type and complexity of the products and markets. Manufacturers of nontechnical products usually hire college graduates who have a liberal arts or business degree and train them so they become knowledgeable about the firm's products, prices, and customers. Manufacturers of highly technical products generally prefer applicants who have degrees in fields associated with the particular industry and market.

Sales positions in manufacturing are expected to increase at an average rate. Manufacturers' sales personnel are well compensated and earn above-average salaries; most are paid a combination of salary and commission. Commissions vary according to the salesperson's efforts, abilities, and sales territory, as well as the type of products sold. Annual salary and/or commission for sales positions range from $63,511 to $78,348 for a sales manager and $30,000 to $52,000 for a field salesperson. A sales trainee would start at about $35,500 in business sales positions.[7]

INDUSTRIAL BUYING

Industrial buyers, or purchasing agents, are responsible for maintaining an adequate supply of the goods and services an organization requires for its operations. In general, industrial buyers purchase all items needed for direct use in producing other products and for use in day-to-day operations. Industrial buyers in large firms often specialize in purchasing a single, specific class of products—for example, all petroleum-based lubricants. In smaller organizations, buyers may be responsible for many different categories of purchases, including raw materials, component parts, office supplies, and operating services.

An industrial buyer's main job is to select suppliers that offer the best quality, service, and price. When the products to be purchased are standardized, buyers may base their purchasing decisions on suppliers' descriptions of their offerings in catalogs and trade journals. Buyers who purchase highly homogeneous products often meet with salespeople to examine samples and observe demonstrations. Sometimes buyers must inspect the actual product before purchasing it; in other cases, they invite suppliers to bid on large orders. Buyers who purchase equipment made to specifications often deal directly with manufacturers. After choosing a supplier and placing an order, an industrial buyer usually must trace the shipment to ensure ontime delivery. Sometimes the buyer is also responsible for receiving and inspecting an order and authorizing payment to the shipper.

Training requirements for a career in industrial buying relate to the needs of the firm and the types of products purchased. A manufacturer of heavy machinery may prefer an applicant who has a background in engineering. A service company, on the other hand, may recruit liberal arts majors. Although not generally required, a college degree is becoming increasingly important for industrial buyers who wish to advance to management positions.

Employment prospects for industrial buyers are expected to increase faster than average. Opportunities will be excellent for individuals with master's degrees in business administration or bachelor's degrees in engineering, science, or business administration. Companies that manufacture heavy equipment, computer equipment, and communications equipment will need buyers with technical backgrounds.

PUBLIC RELATIONS

Public relations encompasses a broad set of communication activities designed to create and maintain favorable relationships between an organization and its stakeholders—customers, employees, stockholders, government officials, and society in general. Public relations specialists help clients create the image, issue, or message they wish to present and communicate it to the appropriate audience. According to the Public Relations Society of America, about 120,000 people work in public relations in the United States. Half the billings of the nation's 4,000 public relations agencies and firms come from Chicago and New York. The highest starting salaries are also found there. Communication is basic to all public relations programs. To communicate effectively, public relations practitioners must first gather data about the firm's stakeholders to assess their needs, identify problems, formulate recommendations, implement new plans, and evaluate current activities.

Public relations personnel disseminate large amounts of information to the organization's stakeholders. Written communication is the most versatile tool of public relations; thus, good writing skills are essential. Public relations practitioners must be adept at writing for a variety of media and audiences. It is not unusual for a person in public relations to prepare reports, news releases, speeches, broadcast scripts, technical manuals, employee publications, shareholder reports, and other communications aimed at both organizational personnel and external groups. In addition, a public relations practitioner needs a thorough knowledge of the production techniques used in preparing various communications. Public relations personnel also establish distribution channels for the organization's publicity. They must have a thorough understanding of the various media, their areas of specialization, the characteristics of their target audiences, and their policies regarding publicity. Anyone who hopes to succeed in public relations must develop close working relationships with numerous media personnel to enlist their interest in disseminating clients' communications.

A college education combined with writing or media-related experience is the best preparation for a career in public relations. Most beginners have a college degree in journalism, communications, or public relations, but some employers prefer a business background. Courses in journalism, business administration, marketing, creative writing, psychology, sociology, political science, economics, advertising, English, and public speaking are recommended. Some employers ask applicants to present a portfolio of published articles, scripts written for television or radio programs, slide presentations, and other work samples. Other agencies require written tests that include such tasks as writing sample press releases. Manufacturing firms, public utilities, transportation and insurance companies, and trade and professional associations are the largest employers of public relations personnel. In addition, sizable numbers of public relations personnel work for health-related organizations, government agencies, educational institutions, museums, and religious and service groups.

Although some larger companies provide extensive formal training for new personnel, most new public relations employees learn on the job. Beginners usually perform routine tasks such as maintaining files about company activities and searching secondary data sources for information to be used in publicity materials. More experienced employees write press releases, speeches, and articles, and help plan public relations campaigns.

Employment opportunities in public relations are expected to increase faster than the average for all occupations. One caveat is in order, however: competition for beginning jobs is keen. The prospects are best for applicants who have solid academic preparation and some media experience. Abilities that differentiate candidates, such as an understanding of information technology, are becoming increasingly important. Public relations account executives earn $30,000 to $45,000. Public relations agency managers earn in the $51,460 to $62,874 range.[8]

DISTRIBUTION MANAGEMENT

A distribution manager arranges for transportation of goods within firms and through marketing channels. Transportation is an essential distribution activity that permits a firm to create time and place utility for its products. It is the distribution manager's job to analyze various transportation modes and select the combination that minimizes cost and transit time while providing acceptable levels of reliability, capability, accessibility, and security.

To accomplish this task, a distribution manager performs many activities. First, the individual must choose one or a combination of transportation modes from the five major modes available: railroads, trucks, waterways, airways, and pipelines. The distribution manager must then select the specific routes the goods will travel and the particular carriers to be used, weighing such factors as freight classifications and regulations, freight charges, time schedules, shipment sizes, and loss and damage ratios. In addition, this person may be responsible for preparing shipping documents, tracing shipments, handling loss and damage claims, keeping records of freight rates, and monitoring changes in government regulations and transportation technology.

Distribution management employs relatively few people and is expected to grow about as fast as the average for all occupations in the near future. Manufacturing firms are the largest employers of distribution managers, although some distribution managers work for wholesalers, retail stores, and consulting firms. Salaries of experienced distribution managers vary but generally are much higher than the average for all non-supervisory personnel. Entry-level positions are diverse, ranging from inventory control and traffic scheduling to operations or distribution management. Inventory management is an area of great opportunity because of increasing global competition. While salaries in the distribution field vary depending on the position and information technology skill requirements, entry salaries start at about $40,000.[9]

Most employers of distribution managers prefer to hire graduates of technical programs or people who have completed courses in transportation, logistics, distribution management, economics, statistics, computer science, management, marketing, and commercial law.

A successful distribution manager is adept at handling technical data and is able to interpret and communicate highly technical information.

PRODUCT MANAGEMENT

The product manager occupies a staff position and is responsible for the success or failure of a product line. Product managers coordinate most of the activities required to market a product. However, because they hold a staff position, they have relatively little actual authority over marketing personnel. Nevertheless, they take on a large amount of responsibility and typically are paid quite well relative to other marketing employees. Being a product manager can be rewarding both financially and psychologically, but it can also be frustrating because of the disparity between responsibility and authority.

A product manager should have a general knowledge of advertising, transportation modes, inventory control, selling and sales management, sales promotion, marketing research, packaging, pricing, and warehousing. The individual must be knowledgeable enough to communicate effectively with personnel in these functional areas and help assess alternatives when major decisions are being made.

Product managers usually need college training in an area of business administration. A master's degree is helpful, although a person usually does not become a product manager directly out of school. Frequently several years of selling and sales management experience are prerequisites for a product management position, which is often a major step in the career path of top-level marketing executives. Product managers can earn $60,000 to $120,000, while an assistant product manager starts at about $40,000.[10]

ADVERTISING

Advertising pervades our daily lives. Business and nonbusiness organizations use advertising in many ways and for many reasons. Advertising clearly needs individuals with diverse skills to fill a variety of jobs. Creativity, imagination, artistic talent, and expertise in expression and persuasion are important for copywriters, artists, and account executives. Sales and managerial abilities are vital to the success of advertising managers, media buyers, and production managers. Research directors must have a solid understanding of research techniques and human behavior. A related occupation is an advertising salesperson, who sells newspaper, television, radio, or magazine advertising to advertisers.

Advertising professionals disagree on the most beneficial educational background for a career in advertising. Most employers prefer college graduates. Some employers seek individuals with degrees in advertising, journalism, or business; others prefer graduates with broad liberal arts backgrounds. Still other employers rank relevant work experience above educational background.

"Advertisers look for generalists," says a staff executive of the American Association of Advertising Agencies. "Thus, there are just as many economics or general liberal arts majors as M.B.A.'s." Common entry-level positions in an advertising agency are found in the traffic department, account service (account coordinator), or the media department (media assistant). Starting salaries in these positions are often quite low, but to gain experience in the advertising industry, employees must work their way up in the system. Assistant account executives start at $25,000, while a typical account executive earns $30,000 to $50,000. Copywriters earn $30,000 to $50,000 a year.[11]

A variety of organizations employ advertising personnel. Although advertising agencies are perhaps the most visible and glamorous employers, many manufacturing firms, retail stores, banks, utility companies, and professional and trade associations maintain advertising departments. Advertising jobs are also available with television and radio stations, newspapers, and magazines. Other businesses that employ advertising personnel include printers, art studios, letter shops, and package design firms. Specific advertising jobs include advertising manager, account executive, research director, copywriter, media specialist, and production manager. About 59 percent of advertising employees are between 25 and 44 years of age compared to 51 percent of all workers in the U.S. economy.[12]

RETAIL MANAGEMENT

Although a career in retailing may begin in sales, there is more to retailing than simply selling. Many retail personnel occupy management positions. Besides managing the sales force, they focus on selecting and ordering merchandise, promotional activities, inventory control, customer credit operations, accounting, personnel, and store security.

Organization of retail stores varies. In many large department stores, retail management personnel rarely engage in actual selling to customers; these duties are performed by retail salespeople. Other types of retail organizations may require management personnel to perform selling activities from time to time.

Large retail stores offer a variety of management positions, including assistant buyers, buyers, department managers, section managers, store managers, division managers, regional managers, and vice president of merchandising. The following list describes the general duties of four of these positions; the precise nature of their duties may vary from one retail organization to another.

A section manager coordinates inventory and promotions and interacts with buyers, salespeople, and ultimate consumers. The manager performs merchandising, labor relations, and managerial activities, and usually works more than a 40-hour workweek.

The buyer's task is more focused. This fast-paced occupation involves much travel and pressure, and the need to be open-minded with respect to new, potentially successful items.

The regional manager coordinates the activities of several stores within a given area, usually monitoring and supporting sales, promotions, and general procedures.

The vice president of merchandising has a broad scope of managerial responsibility and reports to the organization's president.

Most retail organizations hire college graduates, put them through management training programs, and then place them directly in management positions. They frequently hire candidates with backgrounds in liberal arts or business administration. Sales positions and retail management positions offer the greatest employment opportunities for marketing students.

Retail management positions can be exciting and challenging. Competent, ambitious individuals often assume a great deal of responsibility very quickly and advance rapidly. However, a retail manager's job is physically demanding and sometimes entails long working hours. In addition, managers employed by large chain stores may be required to move frequently during their early years with the company. Nonetheless, positions in retail management often offer the chance to excel and gain promotion. Growth in retailing, which is expected to accompany the growth in population, is likely to create substantial opportunities during the next ten years. While a trainee may start in the $30,000 to $47,250 range, a store manager can earn from $50,000 to $200,000 depending on the size of the store.[13]

DIRECT MARKETING

One of the more dynamic areas in marketing is direct marketing, in which the seller uses one or more direct media (telephone, online, mail, print, or television) to solicit a response. The telephone is a major vehicle for selling many consumer products. Telemarketing is direct selling to customers using a variety of technological improvements in telecommunications. Direct-mail catalogs appeal to such market segments as working women and people who find going to retail stores difficult or inconvenient. Newspapers and magazines offer great opportunity, particularly in special market segments. *Golf Digest,* for example, is obviously a good medium for selling golfing equipment. Cable television provides many opportunities for selling directly to consumers. Home shopping channels, for instance, have been very successful. The Internet offers numerous direct marketing opportunities.

The most important asset in direct marketing is experience. Employers often look to other industries to locate experienced professionals. This preference means that if you can get an entry-level position in direct marketing, you will have an advantage in developing a career.

Jobs in direct marketing include buyers, such as department store buyers, who select goods for catalog, telephone, or direct-mail sales. Catalog managers develop marketing strategies for each new catalog that goes into the mail. Research/mail list management involves developing lists of products that will sell in direct marketing and lists of names of consumers who are likely to respond to a direct-mail effort. Order fulfillment managers direct the shipment of products once they are sold. The effectiveness of direct marketing is enhanced by periodic analysis of advertising and communications at all phases of contact with the consumer. Direct marketing involves all aspects of marketing decision making. Most positions in direct marketing involve planning and market analysis. Some direct marketing jobs involve the use of databases that include customer information, sales history, and other tracking data. A database manager might receive a salary of $53,750 to $88,750. A telemarketing director in business-to-business sales could receive a salary of about $35,000.[14]

E-MARKETING AND CUSTOMER RELATIONSHIP MANAGEMENT

Today only about 1.5 percent of all retail sales are conducted on the Internet.[15] Currently approximately one-half of all businesses order online. One characteristic of firms engaged in e-marketing is a renewed focus on relationship marketing by building customer loyalty and retaining customers—in other words, on customer relationship management (CRM). This focus on CRM is possible because of e-marketers' ability to target individual customers. This effort is enhanced over time as the customer invests more time and effort in "teaching" the firms what he or she wants.

Opportunities abound to combine information technology expertise with marketing knowledge. By providing an integrated communication system of websites, fax, telephone, and personal contacts, marketers can personalize customer relationships. Careers exist for individuals who can integrate the Internet as a touch point with customers as part of effective customer relationship management. Many Internet-only companies ("dot-coms") failed because they focused too heavily on brand awareness and did not understand the importance of an integrated marketing strategy.

The use of laptops, cellular phones, e-mail, voice mail, and other devices is necessary to maintain customer relationships and allow purchases on the Internet. A variety of jobs exist for marketers who have integrated technology into their work and job skills. Job titles include e-marketing manager, customer relationship manager, and e-services manager, as well as jobs in dot-coms.

Salaries in this rapidly growing area depend on technical expertise and experience. For example, a CRM customer service manager receives a salary in the $40,000 to $45,000 range. Database administrators earn salaries of approximately $70,500 to $90,000. With five years of experience in e-marketing, individuals responsible for online product offerings can earn from $50,000 to $85,000.

NAME INDEX

ORGANIZATION INDEX

SUBJECT INDEX

GLOSSARY

A

accessory equipment Equipment that does not become part of the final physical product but is used in production or office activities

advertising Paid nonpersonal communication about an organization and its products transmitted to a target audience through mass media

advertising appropriation Advertising budget for a specified period

advertising campaign Designing a series of advertisements and placing them in various advertising media to reach a particular target audience

advertising platform Basic issues or selling points to be included in the advertising campaign

advocacy advertising Promotes a company's position on a public issue

aesthetic modifications Changes to the sensory appeal of a product

agents Intermediaries that represent either buyers or sellers on a permanent basis

aided recall test A posttest that asks respondents to identify recent ads and provides clues to jog their memories

allowance A concession in price to achieve a desired goal

approach The manner in which a salesperson contacts a potential customer

arbitrary approach Budgeting for an advertising campaign as specified by a high-level executive in the firm

artwork An ad's illustrations and layout

Asia-Pacific Economic Cooperation (APEC) An alliance that promotes open trade and economic and technical cooperation among member nations throughout the world

atmospherics The physical elements in a store's design that appeal to consumers' emotions and encourage buying

attitude An individual's enduring evaluation of, feelings about, and behavioral tendencies toward an object or idea

attitude scale Means of measuring consumer attitudes by gauging the intensity of individuals' reactions to adjectives, phrases, or sentences about an object

average fixed cost The fixed cost per unit produced

average total cost The sum of the average fixed cost and the average variable cost

average variable cost The variable cost per unit produced

B

bait pricing Pricing an item in the product line low with the intention of selling a higher-priced item in the line

balance of trade The difference in value between a nation's exports and its imports

barter The trading of products

base-point pricing Geographic pricing combining factory price and freight charges from the base point nearest the buyer

benchmarking Comparing the quality of the firm's goods, services, or processes with that of the best-performing competitors

benefit segmentation The division of a market according to benefits that customers want from the product

Better Business Bureau A local, nongovernmental regulatory agency, supported by local businesses, that helps settle problems between customers and specific business firms

blogs Web-based journals in which people can editorialize and interact with other Internet users

brand A name, term, design, symbol, or any other feature that identifies one marketer's product as distinct from those of other marketers

brand competitors Firms that market products with similar features and benefits to the same customers at similar prices

brand equity The marketing and financial value associated with a brand's strength in a market

brand extension Using an existing brand to brand a new product in a different product category

brand insistence The degree of brand loyalty in which a customer strongly prefers a specific brand and will accept no substitute

brand licensing An agreement whereby a company permits another organization to use its brand on other products for a licensing fee

brand loyalty A customer's favorable attitude toward a specific brand

brand manager The person responsible for a single brand

brand mark The part of a brand not made up of words

brand name The part of a brand that can be spoken

brand preference The degree of brand loyalty in which a customer prefers one brand over competitive offerings

brand recognition A customer's awareness that the brand exists and is an alternative purchase

branded entertainment Branded content, which includes product placement, that is designed to combine electronic media with an advertiser to create an integrated, entertaining product

breakdown approach Measuring company sales potential based on a general economic forecast for a specific period and the market potential derived from it

breakeven point The point at which the costs of producing a product equal the revenue made from selling the product

brokers Intermediaries that bring buyers and sellers together temporarily

buildup approach Measuring company sales potential by estimating how much of a product a potential buyer in a specific geographic area will purchase in a given period, multiplying the estimate by the number of potential buyers, and adding the totals of all the geographic areas considered

bundle pricing Packaging together two or more complementary products and selling them for a single price

business analysis Evaluating the potential contribution of a product idea to the firm's sales, costs, and profits

business (organizational) buying behavior The purchase behavior of producers, government units, institutions, and resellers

business cycle A pattern of economic fluctuations that has four stages: prosperity, recession, depression, and recovery

business market Individuals or groups that purchase a specific kind of product for resale, direct use in producing other products, or use in general daily operations

business products Products bought to use in an organization's operations, to resell, or to make other products

business services The intangible products that many organizations use in their operations

buy-back allowance A sum of money given to a reseller for each unit bought after an initial promotion deal is over

buying allowance A temporary price reduction to resellers for purchasing specified quantities of a product

buying behavior The decision processes and acts of people involved in buying and using products

buying center The people within an organization, including users, influencers, buyers, deciders, and gatekeepers, who make business purchase decisions

buying power Resources, such as money, goods, and services, that can be traded in an exchange

buzz marketing An attempt to incite publicity and public excitement surrounding a product through a creative event

C

captioned photograph A photo with a brief description of its contents

captive pricing Pricing the basic product in a product line low while pricing related items at a higher level

cash discount Price reduction given to buyers for prompt payment or cash payment

cash-and-carry wholesalers Limited-service wholesalers whose customers pay cash and furnish transportation

catalog marketing A type of marketing in which an organization provides a catalog from which customers make selections and place orders by mail, telephone, or the Internet

category killer A very large specialty store concentrating on a major product category and competing on the basis of low prices and product availability

category management A retail strategy of managing groups of similar, often substitutable products produced by different manufacturers

cause-related marketing The practice of linking products to a particular social cause on an ongoing or short-term basis

centralized organization A structure in which top management delegates little authority to levels below it

cents-off offer A promotion that lets buyers pay less than the regular price to encourage purchase

channel capacity The limit on the volume of information a communication channel can handle effectively

channel captain The dominant member of a marketing channel or supply chain

channel power The ability of one channel member to influence another member's goal achievement

client-based relationships Interactions that result in satisfied customers who use a service repeatedly over time

closing The stage in the selling process when the salesperson asks the prospect to buy the product

co-branding Using two or more brands on one product

codes of conduct Formalized rules and standards that describe what the company expects of its employees

coding process Converting meaning into a series of signs or symbols

cognitive dissonance A buyer's doubts shortly after a purchase about whether the decision was the right one

combination compensation plan Paying salespeople a fixed salary plus a commission based on sales volume

commercialization Deciding on full-scale manufacturing and marketing plans and preparing budgets

commission merchants Agents that receive goods on consignment and negotiate sales in large, central markets

Common Market of the Southern Cone (MERCOSUR) An alliance that promotes the free circulation of goods, services, and production factors and has a common external tariff and commercial policy among member nations in South America

communication A sharing of meaning

communications channel The medium of transmission that carries the coded message from the source to the receiver or audience

community shopping centers Shopping centers with one or two department stores, some specialty stores, and convenience stores

company sales potential The maximum percentage of market potential that an individual firm can expect to obtain for a specific product

comparative advertising Compares the sponsored brand with one or more identified brands on the basis of one or more product characteristics

comparison discounting Setting a price at a specific level and comparing it with a higher price

competition Other firms that market products that are similar to or can be substituted for a firm's products in the same geographic area

competition-based pricing Pricing influenced primarily by competitors' prices

competition-matching approach Determining an advertising budget by trying to match competitors' ad outlays

competitive advantage The result of a company's matching a core competency to opportunities in the marketplace

competitive advertising Tries to stimulate demand for a specific brand by promoting its features, uses, and advantages

component parts Items that become part of the physical product and are either finished items ready for assembly or products that need little processing before assembly

concentrated targeting strategy A strategy in which an organization targets a single market segment using one marketing mix

concept testing Seeking potential buyers' responses to a product idea

conclusive research Research designed to verify insights through objective procedures and to help marketers in making decisions

consideration set A group of brands that a buyer views as alternatives for possible purchase

consistency of quality The degree to which a product has the same level of quality over time

consumer buying behavior Buying behavior of people who purchase products for personal or household use and not for business purposes

consumer buying decision process A five-stage purchase decision process that includes problem recognition, information search, evaluation of alternatives, purchase, and postpurchase evaluation

consumer contests Sales promotion methods in which individuals compete for prizes based on analytical or creative skills

consumer games Sales promotion method in which individuals compete for prizes based primarily on chance

consumer jury A panel of a product's actual or potential buyers who pretest ads

consumer market Purchasers and household members who intend to consume or benefit from the purchased products and do not buy products to make profits

consumer products Products purchased to satisfy personal and family needs

consumer sales promotion methods Ways of encouraging consumers to patronize specific stores or try particular products

consumer socialization The process through which a person acquires the knowledge and skills to function as a consumer

consumer sweepstakes Sales promotion in which entrants submit their names for inclusion in a drawing for prizes

consumerism Organized efforts by individuals, groups, and organizations to protect consumers' rights

contract manufacturing The practice of hiring a foreign firm to produce a designated volume of product to specification

convenience products Relatively inexpensive, frequently purchased items for which buyers exert minimal purchasing effort

convenience store A small self-service store that is open long hours and carries a narrow assortment of products, usually convenience items

cooperative advertising An arrangement in which a manufacturer agrees to pay a certain amount of a retailer's media costs for advertising the manufacturer's products

copy The verbal portion of advertisements

core competencies Things a firm does extremely well, which sometimes give it an advantage over its competition

corporate strategy A strategy that determines the means for using resources in the various functional areas to reach the organization's goals

cost comparison indicator A means of comparing the cost of vehicles in a specific medium in relation to the number of people reached

cost-based pricing Adding a dollar amount or percentage to the cost of the product

cost-plus pricing Adding a specified dollar amount or percentage to the seller's cost

coupons Written price reductions used to encourage consumers to buy a specific product

cultural relativism The concept that morality varies from one culture to another and that business practices are therefore differentially defined as right or wrong by particular cultures

culture The values, knowledge, beliefs, customs, objects, and concepts of a society

cumulative discounts Quantity discounts aggregated over a stated period

customary pricing Pricing on the basis of tradition

customer advisory boards Small groups of actual customers who serve as sounding boards for new-product ideas and offer insights into their feelings and attitudes toward a firm's products and other elements of marketing strategy

customer contact The level of interaction between provider and customer needed to deliver the service

customer forecasting survey A survey of customers regarding the types and quantities of products they intend to buy during a specific period

customer relationship management (CRM) Using information about customers to create marketing strategies that develop and sustain desirable customer relationships

customer services Human or mechanical efforts or activities that add value to a product

customers The purchasers of organizations' products; the focal point of all marketing activities

cycle analysis An analysis of sales figures for a period of three to five years to ascertain whether sales fluctuate in a consistent, periodic manner

cycle time The time needed to complete a process

D

dealer listings Advertisements that promote a product and identify the names of participating retailers that sell the product

dealer loader A gift, often part of a display, given to a retailer purchasing a specified quantity of merchandise

decentralized organization A structure in which decision-making authority is delegated as far down the chain of command as possible

decline stage The stage of a product's life cycle when sales fall rapidly

decoding process Converting signs or symbols into concepts and ideas

Delphi technique A procedure in which experts create initial forecasts, submit them to the company for averaging, and then refine the forecasts

demand curve A graph of the quantity of a product taken by buyers in the market at various prices, given that all other factors are held constant

demand-based pricing Pricing based on the level of demand for the product

demonstrations A sales promotion method manufacturers use temporarily to encourage trial use and purchase of a product or to show how a product works

department stores Large retail organizations characterized by wide product mixes and organized into separate departments to facilitate marketing and internal management

depth of product mix The average number of different product items offered in each product line

derived demand Demand for industrial products that stems from demand for consumer products

descriptive research Research conducted to clarify the characteristics of certain phenomena and thus solve a particular problem

differential pricing Charging different prices to different buyers for the same quality and quantity of product

differentiated targeting strategy A strategy in which an organization targets two or more segments by developing a marketing mix for each

direct marketing The use of telecommunications and nonpersonal media to introduce products to consumers, who then can purchase them via mail, telephone, or the Internet

direct ownership A situation in which a company owns subsidiaries or other facilities overseas

direct response marketing A type of marketing that occurs when a retailer advertises a product and makes it available through mail or telephone orders

direct selling The marketing of products to ultimate consumers through face-to-face sales presentations at home or in the workplace

discount stores Self-service, general merchandise stores offering brand name and private brand products at low prices

discretionary income Disposable income available for spending and saving after an individual has purchased the basic necessities of food, clothing, and shelter

disposable income After-tax income

distribution The decisions and activities that make products available to customers when and where they want to purchase them

distribution centers Large, centralized warehouses that focus on moving rather than storing goods

drop shippers Limited-service wholesalers that take title to products and negotiate sales but never take actual possession of products

dual distribution The use of two or more marketing channels to distribute the same products to the same target market

dumping Selling products at unfairly low prices

E

early adopters Careful choosers of new products

early majority Those adopting new products just before the average person

electronic data interchange (EDI) A computerized means of integrating order processing with production, inventory, accounting, and transportation

embargo A government's suspension of trade in a particular product or with a given country

empowerment Giving customer-contact employees authority and responsibility to make marketing decisions on their own

environmental analysis The process of assessing and interpreting the information gathered through environmental scanning

environmental scanning The process of collecting information about forces in the marketing environment

ethical issue An identifiable problem, situation, or opportunity requiring a choice among several actions that must be evaluated as right or wrong, ethical or unethical

European Union (EU) An alliance that promotes trade among its member countries in Europe

evaluative criteria Objective and subjective characteristics that are important to a buyer

everyday low prices (EDLP) Setting a low price for products on a consistent basis

exchange controls Government restrictions on the amount of a particular currency that can be bought or sold

exchanges The provision or transfer of goods, services, or ideas in return for something of value

exclusive dealing A situation in which a manufacturer forbids an intermediary to carry products of competing manufacturers

exclusive distribution Using a single outlet in a fairly large geographic area to distribute a product

executive judgment Sales forecasting based on the intuition of one or more executives

experimental research Research that allows marketers to make causal inferences about relationships

expert forecasting survey Sales forecasts prepared by experts such as economists, management consultants, advertising executives, college professors, or other persons outside the firm

exploratory research Research conducted to gather more information about a problem or to make a tentative hypothesis more specific

exporting The sale of products to foreign markets

extended problem solving A type of consumer problem-solving process employed when purchasing unfamiliar, expensive, or infrequently bought products

external customers Individuals who patronize a business

external reference price A comparison price provided by others

external search An information search in which buyers seek information from outside sources

F

family branding Branding all of a firm's products with the same name

family packaging Using similar packaging for all of a firm's products or packaging that has one common design element

feature article A manuscript of up to 3,000 words prepared for a specific publication

Federal Trade Commission (FTC) An agency that regulates a variety of business practices and curbs false advertising, misleading pricing, and deceptive packaging and labeling

feedback The receiver's response to a message

fixed costs Costs that do not vary with changes in the number of units produced or sold

F.O.B. destination A price indicating the producer is absorbing shipping costs

F.O.B. factory The price of the merchandise at the factory, before shipment

focus-group interview A research method involving observation of group interaction when members are exposed to an idea or a concept

franchising A form of licensing in which a franchiser, in exchange for a financial commitment, grants a franchisee the right to market its product in accordance with the franchiser's standards

free merchandise A manufacturer's reward given to resellers for purchasing a stated quantity of products

free samples Samples of a product given out to encourage trial and purchase

freight absorption pricing Absorption of all or part of actual freight costs by the seller

freight forwarders Organizations that consolidate shipments from several firms into efficient lot sizes

full-service wholesalers Merchant wholesalers that perform the widest range of wholesaling functions

functional modifications Changes affecting a product's versatility, effectiveness, convenience, or safety

G

General Agreement on Tariffs and Trade (GATT) An agreement among nations to reduce worldwide tariffs and increase international trade

general merchandise retailer A retail establishment that offers a variety of product lines that are stocked in considerable depth

general merchandise wholesalers Full-service wholesalers with a wide product mix but limited depth within product lines

general-line wholesalers Full-service wholesalers that carry only a few product lines but many products within those lines

generic brands Brands indicating only the product category

generic competitors Firms that provide very different products that solve the same problem or satisfy the same basic customer need

geodemographic segmentation Market segmentation that clusters people in zip code areas and smaller neighborhood units based on lifestyle and demographic information

geographic pricing Reductions for transportation and other costs related to the physical distance between buyer and seller

globalization The development of marketing strategies that treat the entire world (or its major regions) as a single entity

good A tangible physical entity

government markets Federal, state, county, and local governments that buy goods and services to support their internal operations and provide products to their constituencies

green marketing A strategic process involving stakeholder assessment to create meaningful long-term relationships with customers while maintaining, supporting, and enhancing the natural environment

gross domestic product (GDP) The market value of a nation's total output of goods and services for a given period; an overall measure of economic standing

growth stage The stage of a product's life cycle when sales rise rapidly and profits reach a peak and then start to decline

H

heterogeneity Variation in quality

heterogeneous markets Markets made up of individuals or organizations with diverse needs for products in a specific product class

homogeneous market A market in which a large proportion of customers have similar needs for a product

horizontal channel integration Combining organizations at the same level of operation under one management

hypermarkets Stores that combine supermarket and discount store shopping in one location

hypothesis An informed guess or assumption about a certain problem or set of circumstances

I

idea A concept, philosophy, image, or issue

idea generation Seeking product ideas to achieve objectives

illustrations Photos, drawings, graphs, charts, and tables used to spark audience interest

import tariff A duty levied by a nation on goods bought outside its borders and brought in

importing The purchase of products from a foreign source

impulse buying An unplanned buying behavior resulting from a powerful urge to buy something immediately

in-home (door-to-door) interview A personal interview that takes place in the respondent's home

individual branding A policy of naming each product differently

industrial distributor An independent business organization that takes title to industrial products and carries inventories

inelastic demand Demand that is not significantly altered by a price increase or decrease

information inputs Sensations received through the sense organs

innovators First adopters of new products

inseparability Being produced and consumed at the same time

installations Facilities and nonportable major equipment

institutional advertising Promotes organizational images, ideas, and political issues

institutional markets Organizations with charitable, educational, community, or other nonbusiness goals

intangibility A service that is not physical and cannot be touched

integrated marketing communications (IMC) Coordination of promotional efforts for maximum informational and persuasive impact

intended strategy The strategy the company decides on during the planning phase

intensive distribution Using all available outlets to distribute a product

intermodal transportation Two or more transportation modes used in combination

internal customers A company's employees

internal marketing Coordinating internal exchanges between the firm and its employees to achieve successful external exchanges between the firm and its customers

internal reference price A price developed in the buyer's mind through experience with the product

internal search An information search in which buyers search their memories for information about products that might solve their problem

international marketing Developing and performing marketing activities across national boundaries

introduction stage The initial stage of a product's life cycle—its first appearance in the marketplace—when sales start at zero and profits are negative

inventory management Developing and maintaining adequate assortments of products to meet customers' needs

J

joint demand Demand involving the use of two or more items in combination to produce a product

joint venture A partnership between a domestic firm and a foreign firm or government

just-in-time (JIT) An inventory-management approach in which supplies arrive just when needed for production or resale

K

kinesic communication Communicating through the movement of head, eyes, arms, hands, legs, or torso

L

labeling Providing identifying, promotional, or other information on package labels

laggards The last adopters, who distrust new products

late majority Skeptics who adopt new products when they feel it is necessary

layout The physical arrangement of an ad's illustration and copy

learning Changes in an individual's thought processes and behavior caused by information and experience

level of involvement An individual's degree of interest in a product and the importance of the product for that person

level of quality The amount of quality a product possesses

licensing An alternative to direct investment requiring a licensee to pay commissions or royalties on sales or supplies used in manufacturing

lifestyle An individual's pattern of living expressed through activities, interests, and opinions

lifestyle shopping centers A type of shopping center that is typically open air and features upscale specialty, dining, and entertainment stores

limited problem solving A type of consumer problem-solving process that buyers use when purchasing products occasionally or when they need information about an unfamiliar brand in a familiar product category

limited-service wholesalers Merchant wholesalers that provide some services and specialize in a few functions

line extension Development of a product that is closely related to existing products in the line but meets different customer needs

logistics management Planning, implementing, and controlling the efficient and effective flow and storage of products and information from the point of origin to consumption in order to meet customers' needs and wants

M

mail survey A research method in which respondents answer a questionnaire sent through the mail

mail-order wholesalers Limited-service wholesalers that sell products through catalogs

manufacturer brands Brands initiated by producers

manufacturers' agents Independent intermediaries that represent two or more sellers and offer complete product lines

marginal cost (MC) The extra cost a firm incurs by producing one more unit of a product

marginal revenue (MR) The change in total revenue resulting from the sale of an additional unit of a product

market A group of individuals and/or organizations that have needs for products in a product class and have the ability, willingness, and authority to purchase those products

market density The number of potential customers within a unit of land area

market manager The person responsible for managing the marketing activities that serve a particular group of customers

market opportunity A combination of circumstances and timing that permits an organization to take action to reach a target market

market potential The total amount of a product that customers will purchase within a specified period at a specific level of industrywide marketing activity

market segment Individuals, groups, or organizations with one or more similar characteristics that cause them to have similar product needs

market segmentation The process of dividing a total market into groups with relatively similar product needs to design a marketing mix that matches those needs

market share The percentage of a market that actually buys a specific product from a particular company

market test Making a product available to buyers in one or more test areas and measuring purchases and consumer responses

market-growth/market-share matrix A strategic planning tool based on the philosophy that a product's market growth rate and market share are important in determining marketing strategy

marketing The process of creating, distributing, promoting, and pricing goods, services, and ideas to facilitate satisfying exchange relationships with customers and to develop and maintain favorable relationships with stakeholders in a dynamic environment

marketing channel A group of individuals and organizations that direct the flow of products from producers to customers within the supply chain

marketing citizenship The adoption of a strategic focus for fulfilling the economic, legal, ethical, and philanthropic social responsibilities expected by stakeholders

marketing concept A managerial philosophy that an organization should try to satisfy customers' needs through a coordinated set of activities that also allows the organization to achieve its goals

marketing control process Establishing performance standards and trying to match actual performance to those standards

marketing decision support system (MDSS) Customized computer software that aids marketing managers in decision-making

marketing environment The competitive, economic, political, legal and regulatory, technological, and sociocultural forces that surround the customer and affect the marketing mix

marketing ethics Principles and standards that define acceptable marketing conduct as determined by various stakeholders

marketing implementation The process of putting marketing strategies into action

marketing information system (MIS) A framework for the management and structuring of information gathered regularly from sources inside and outside an organization

marketing intermediaries Middlemen that link producers to other intermediaries or ultimate consumers through contractual arrangements or through the purchase and resale of products

marketing management The process of planning, organizing, implementing, and controlling marketing activities to facilitate exchanges effectively and efficiently

marketing mix Four marketing activities—product, pricing, distribution, and promotion—that a firm can control to meet the needs of customers within its target market

marketing objective A statement of what is to be accomplished through marketing activities

marketing orientation An organizationwide commitment to researching and responding to customer needs

marketing plan A written document that specifies the activities to be performed to implement and control an organization's marketing activities

marketing planning The process of assessing opportunities and resources, determining objectives, defining strategies, and establishing guidelines for implementation and control of the marketing program

marketing research The systematic design, collection, interpretation, and reporting of information to help marketers solve specific marketing problems or take advantage of marketing opportunities

marketing strategy A plan of action for identifying and analyzing a target market and developing a marketing mix to meet the needs of that market

markup pricing Adding to the cost of the product a predetermined percentage of that cost

Maslow's hierarchy of needs The five levels of needs that humans seek to satisfy, from most to least important

materials handling Physical handling of tangible goods, supplies, and resources

maturity stage The stage of a product's life cycle when the sales curve peaks and starts to decline as profits continue to fall

media plan Specifies media vehicles and schedule for running the advertisements

megacarriers Freight transportation firms that provide several modes of shipment

merchandise allowance A manufacturer's agreement to pay resellers certain amounts of money for providing special promotional efforts

merchant wholesalers Independently owned businesses that take title to goods, assume ownership risks, and buy and resell products to other wholesalers, business customers, or retailers

micromarketing An approach to market segmentation in which organizations focus precise marketing efforts on very small geodemographic markets

mission statement A long-term view of what the organization wants to become

missionary salespeople Support salespersons who assist the producer's customers in selling to their own customers

modified-rebuy purchase A new-task purchase that is changed on subsequent orders or when the requirements of a straight-rebuy purchase are modified

money refunds A sales promotion technique offering consumers money when they mail in a proof of purchase, usually for multiple product purchases

monopolistic competition A competitive structure in which a firm has many potential competitors and tries to develop a marketing strategy to differentiate its product

monopoly A competitive structure in which an organization offers a product that has no close substitutes, making that organization the sole source of supply

motive An internal energizing force that directs a person's behavior toward satisfying needs or achieving goals

MRO supplies Maintenance, repair, and operating items that facilitate production and operations but do not become part of the finished product

multinational enterprise Firms that have operations or subsidiaries in many countries

multiple sourcing An organization's decision to use several suppliers

multiple-unit pricing Packaging together two or more identical products and selling them for a single price

N

National Advertising Review Board (NARB) A self-regulatory unit that considers challenges to issues raised by the National Advertising Division (an arm of the Council of Better Business Bureaus) about an advertisement

negotiated pricing Establishing a final price through bargaining

neighborhood shopping centers Shopping centers usually consisting of several small convenience and specialty stores

new-product development process A seven-phase process for introducing products

new-task purchase An initial purchase by an organization of an item to be used to perform a new job or solve a new problem

news release A short piece of copy publicizing an event or a product

noise Anything that reduces a communication's clarity and accuracy

noncumulative discounts One-time reductions in price based on specific factors

nonprice competition Emphasizing factors other than price to distinguish a product from competing brands

nonprobability sampling A sampling technique in which there is no way to calculate the likelihood that a specific element of the population being studied will be chosen

North American Free Trade Agreement (NAFTA) An alliance that merges Canada, Mexico, and the United States into a single market

North American Industry Classification System (NAICS) An industry classification system that will generate comparable statistics among the United States, Canada, and Mexico

O

objective-and-task approach Budgeting for an advertising campaign by first determining its objectives and then calculating the cost of all the tasks needed to attain them

odd-even pricing Ending the price with certain numbers to influence buyers' perceptions of the price or product

off-price retailers Stores that buy manufacturers' seconds, overruns, returns, and off-season merchandise for resale to consumers at deep discounts

oligopoly A competitive structure in which a few sellers control the supply of a large proportion of a product

online retailing Retailing that makes products available to buyers through computer connections

online survey A research method in which respondents answer a questionnaire via e-mail or on a website

operations management The total set of managerial activities used by an organization to transform resource inputs into products

opinion leader A reference group member who provide information about a specific sphere that interests reference group participants

order getter The salesperson who sells to new customers and increases sales to current ones

order processing The receipt and transmission of sales order information

order takers Salespersons who primarily seek repeat sales

outsourcing The contracting of physical distribution tasks to third parties who do not have managerial authority within the marketing channel

P

patronage motives Motives that influence where a person purchases products on a regular basis

penetration pricing Setting prices below those of competing brands to penetrate a market and gain a significant market share quickly

percent-of-sales approach Budgeting for an advertising campaign by multiplying the firm's past or expected sales by a standard percentage

perception The process of selecting, organizing, and interpreting information inputs to produce meaning

performance standard An expected level of performance

periodic discounting Temporary reduction of prices on a patterned or systematic basis

perishability The inability of unused service capacity to be stored for future use

personal selling Paid personal communication that attempts to inform customers and persuade them to buy products in an exchange situation

personal-interview survey A research method in which participants respond to survey questions face to face

personality A set of internal traits and distinct behavioral tendencies that result in consistent patterns of behavior

physical distribution Activities used to move products from producers to consumers and other end users

pioneer advertising Tries to stimulate demand for a product category (rather than a specific brand) by informing potential buyers about the product

pioneer promotion Promotion that informs consumers about a new product

point-of-purchase (P-O-P) materials Signs, window displays, display racks, and similar means used to attract customers

population All the elements, units, or individuals of interest to researchers for a specific study

posttest Evaluation of advertising effectiveness after the campaign

power shopping centers A type of shopping center that combines off-price stores with category killers

premium money (*or* push money) Extra compensation to salespeople for pushing a line of goods

premium pricing Pricing the highest-quality or most versatile products higher than other models in the product line

premiums Items offered free or at a minimal cost as a bonus for purchasing a product

press conference A meeting used to announce major news events

prestige pricing Setting prices at an artificially high level to convey prestige or a quality image

prestige-sensitive Drawn to products that signify prominence and status

pretest Evaluation of ads performed before a campaign begins

price Value exchanged for products in a marketing transaction

price competition Emphasizing price and matching or beating competitors' prices

price discrimination Providing price differentials that injure competition by giving one or more buyers a competitive advantage

price elasticity of demand A measure of the sensitivity of demand to changes in price

price leaders Product priced below the usual markup, near cost, or below cost

price lining Setting a limited number of prices for selected groups or lines of merchandise

price skimming Charging the highest possible price that buyers who most desire the product will pay

price-conscious Striving to pay low prices

pricing objectives Goals that describe what a firm wants to achieve through pricing

primary data Data observed and recorded or collected directly from respondents

primary demand Demand for a product category rather than for a specific brand

private distributor brands Brands initiated and owned by resellers

private warehouses Company-operated facilities for storing and shipping products

probability sampling A sampling technique in which every element in the population being studied has a known chance of being selected for study

process materials Materials that are used directly in the production of other products but are not readily identifiable

producer markets Individuals and business organizations that purchase products to make profits by using them to produce other products or using them in their operations

product A good, a service, or an idea

product adoption process The stages buyers go through in accepting a product

product advertising Promotes products' uses, features, and benefits

product competitors Firms that compete in the same product class but market products with different features, benefits, and prices

product deletion Eliminating a product from the product mix

product design How a product is conceived, planned, and produced

product development Determining if producing a product is technically feasible and cost effective

product differentiation Creating and designing products so that customers perceive them as different from competing products

product features Specific design characteristics that allow a product to perform certain tasks

product item A specific version of a product that can be designated as a distinct offering among a firm's products

product life cycle The progression of a product through four stages: introduction, growth, maturity, and decline

product line A group of closely related product items viewed as a unit because of marketing, technical, or end-use considerations

product manager The person within an organization responsible for a product, a product line, or several distinct products that make up a group

product mix The total group of products that an organization makes available to customers

product modification Change in one or more characteristics of a product

product placement The strategic location of products or product promotions within television program content to reach the product's target market

product positioning Creating and maintaining a certain concept of a product in customers' minds

product-line pricing Establishing and adjusting prices of multiple products within a product line

professional pricing Fees set by people with great skill or experience in a particular field

promotion Communication to build and maintain relationships by informing and persuading one or more audiences

promotion mix A combination of promotional methods used to promote a specific product

prospecting Developing a list of potential customers

proxemic communication Communicating by varying the physical distance in face-to-face interactions

psychological influences Factors that partly determine people's general behavior, thus influencing their behavior as consumers

psychological pricing Pricing that attempts to influence a customer's perception of price to make a product's price more attractive

public relations Communication efforts used to create and maintain favorable relations between an organization and its stakeholders

public warehouses Storage space and related physical distribution facilities that can be leased by companies

publicity A news story type of communication transmitted through a mass medium at no charge

pull policy Promoting a product directly to consumers to develop strong consumer demand that pulls products through the marketing channel

pure competition A market structure characterized by an extremely large number of sellers, none strong enough to significantly influence price or supply

push policy Promoting a product only to the next institution down the marketing channel

Q

quality Characteristics of a product that allow it to perform as expected in satisfying customer needs

quality modifications Changes relating to a product's dependability and durability

quantity discounts Deductions from list price for purchasing large quantities

quota A limit on the amount of goods an importing country will accept for certain product categories in a specific time period

quota sampling A nonprobability sampling technique in which researchers divide the population into groups and then arbitrarily choose participants from each group

R

rack jobbers Full-service, specialty-line wholesalers that own and maintain display racks in stores

random discounting Temporary reduction of prices on an unsystematic basis

random factor analysis An analysis attempting to attribute erratic sales variation to random, nonrecurrent events

random sampling A type of probability sampling in which all units in a population have an equal chance of appearing in a sample

raw materials Basic natural materials that become part of a physical product

realized strategy The strategy that actually takes place

rebates A sales promotion technique whereby a customer is sent a specific amount of money for purchasing a single product

receiver The individual, group, or organization that decodes a coded message

reciprocity An arrangement unique to business marketing in which two organizations agree to buy from each other

recognition test A posttest in which individuals are shown the actual ad and asked if they recognize it

reference group Any group that positively or negatively affects a person's values, attitudes, or behavior

reference pricing Pricing a product at a moderate level and displaying it next to a more expensive model or brand

regional issues Versions of a magazine that differ across geographic regions

regional shopping centers A type of shopping center with the largest department stores, the widest product mix, and the deepest product lines of all shopping centers

regression analysis A method of predicting sales based on finding a relationship between past sales and one or more variables, such as population or income

reinforcement advertising Assures users they chose the right brand and tells them how to get the most satisfaction from it

relationship marketing Establishing long-term, mutually satisfying buyer–seller relationships

relationship selling The building of mutually beneficial long-term associations with a customer through regular communications over prolonged periods of time

reliability A condition existing when a research technique produces almost identical results in repeated trials

reminder advertising Reminds consumers about an established brand's uses, characteristics, and benefits

research design An overall plan for obtaining the information needed to address a research problem or issue

reseller markets Intermediaries who buy finished goods and resell them for profit

retail positioning Identifying an unserved or underserved market segment and serving it through a strategy that distinguishes the retailer from others in the minds of consumers in that segment

retailer An organization that purchases products for the purpose of reselling them to ultimate consumers

retailing All transactions in which the buyer intends to consume the product through personal, family, or household use

role Actions and activities that a person in a particular position is supposed to perform based on expectations of the individual and surrounding persons

routinized response behavior A type of consumer problem-solving process used when buying frequently purchased, low-cost items that require very little search and decision effort

S

sales branches Manufacturer-owned intermediaries that sell products and provide support services to the manufacturer's sales force

sales contest A promotion method used to motivate distributors, retailers, and sales personnel through recognition of outstanding achievements

sales force forecasting survey A survey of a firm's sales force regarding anticipated sales in their territories for a specified period

sales forecast The amount of a product a company expects to sell during a specific period at a specified level of marketing activities

sales offices Manufacturer-owned operations that provide services normally associated with agents

sales promotion An activity and/or material meant to induce resellers or salespeople to sell a product or consumers to buy it

sample A limited number of units chosen to represent the characteristics of the population

sampling The process of selecting representative units from a total population

scan-back allowance A manufacturer's reward to retailers based on the number of pieces scanned

screening Choosing the most promising ideas for further review

seasonal analysis An analysis of daily, weekly, or monthly sales figures to evaluate the degree to which seasonal factors influence sales

seasonal discount A price reduction given to buyers for purchasing goods or services out of season

secondary data Data compiled both inside and outside the organization for some purpose other than the current investigation

secondary-market pricing Setting one price for the primary target market and a different price for another market

segmentation variables Characteristics of individuals, groups, or organizations used to divide a market into segments

selective demand Demand for a specific brand

selective distortion An individual's changing or twisting of information when it is inconsistent with personal feelings or beliefs

selective distribution Using only some available outlets to distribute a product

selective exposure The process of selecting inputs to be exposed to our awareness while ignoring others

selective retention Remembering information inputs that support personal feelings and beliefs and forgetting inputs that do not

self-concept Perception or view of oneself

selling agents Intermediaries that market a whole product line or a manufacturer's entire output

service An intangible result of the application of human and mechanical efforts to people or objects

shopping products Items for which buyers are willing to expend considerable effort in planning and making purchases

shopping-mall intercept interviews A research method that involves interviewing a percentage of persons passing by "intercept" points in a mall

single-source data Information provided by a single marketing research firm

situational influences Influences resulting from circumstances, time, and location that affect the consumer buying decision process

social class An open group of individuals with similar social rank

social influences The forces other people exert on one's buying behavior

social media Involves electronic technologies that link people to networks and allow the exchange of personal and professional information as well as common interests such as product and brand preferences

social networks Web-based services that allow members to share personal profiles that include blogs, pictures, audios, and videos

social responsibility An organization's obligation to maximize its positive impact and minimize its negative impact on society

sociocultural forces The influences in a society and its culture(s) that change people's attitudes, beliefs, norms, customs, and lifestyles

sole sourcing An organization's decision to use only one supplier

source A person, group, or organization with a meaning it tries to share

special-event pricing Advertised sales or price cutting linked to a holiday, season, or event

specialty products Items with unique characteristics that buyers are willing to expend considerable effort to obtain

specialty-line wholesalers Full-service wholesalers that carry only a single product line or a few items within a product line

stakeholders Constituents who have a "stake," or claim, in some aspect of a company's products, operations, markets, industry, and outcomes

statistical interpretation Analysis of what is typical or what deviates from the average

storyboard A mockup combining copy and visual material to show the sequence of major scenes in a commercial

straight commission compensation plan Paying salespeople according to the amount of their sales in a given time period

straight salary compensation plan Paying salespeople a specific amount per time period, regardless of selling effort

straight-rebuy purchase A routine purchase of the same products under approximately the same terms of sale by a business buyer

strategic alliances Partnerships formed to create a competitive advantage on a worldwide basis

strategic business unit (SBU) A division, product line, or other profit center within a parent company

strategic channel alliance An agreement whereby the products of one organization are distributed through the marketing channels of another

strategic philanthropy The synergistic use of organizational core competencies and resources to address key stakeholders' interests and achieve both organizational and social benefits

strategic planning The process of establishing an organizational mission and formulating goals, corporate strategy, marketing objectives, marketing strategy, and a marketing plan

strategic windows Temporary periods of optimal fit between the key requirements of a market and a firm's capabilities

stratified sampling A type of probability sampling in which the population is divided into groups according to a common attribute, and a random sample is then chosen within each group

styling The physical appearance of a product

subcultures Groups of individuals whose characteristic values and behavior patterns are similar to each other and differ from those of the surrounding culture

supermarkets Large, self-service stores that carry a complete line of food products, along with some nonfood products

superregional shopping centers A type of shopping center with the widest and deepest product mixes that attracts customers from many miles away

superstores Giant retail outlets that carry food and nonfood products found in supermarkets, as well as most routinely purchased consumer products

supply chain All the activities associated with the flow and transformation of products from raw materials through to the end customer

supply management In its broadest form, refers to the processes that enable the progress of value from raw material to final customer and back to redesign and final disposition

supply-chain management A set of approaches used to integrate the functions of operations management, logistics management, supply management, and marketing channel management so that products are produced and distributed in the right quantities, to the right locations, and at the right time

support personnel Sales staff members who facilitate selling but usually are not involved solely with making sales

sustainable competitive advantage An advantage that the competition cannot copy

SWOT analysis A tool that marketers use to assess an organization's strengths, weaknesses, opportunities, and threats

T

tactile communication Communicating through touching

target audience The group of people at whom advertisements are aimed

target market A specific group of customers on whom an organization focuses its marketing efforts

team selling The use of a team of experts from all functional areas of a firm, led by a salesperson, to conduct the personal selling process

technical salespeople Support salespersons who give technical assistance to a firm's current customers

technology The application of knowledge and tools to solve problems and perform tasks more efficiently

telemarketing The performance of marketing-related activities by telephone

telephone depth interview An interview that combines the traditional focus group's ability to probe with the confidentiality provided by telephone surveys

telephone survey A research method in which respondents' answers to a questionnaire are recorded by interviewers on the phone

television home shopping A form of selling in which products are presented to television viewers, who can buy them by calling a toll-free number and paying with a credit card

test marketing Introducing a product on a limited basis to measure the extent to which potential customers will actually buy it

time-series analysis A forecasting method that uses historical sales data to discover patterns in the firm's sales over time and generally involves trend, cycle, seasonal, and random factor analyses

total budget competitors Firms that compete for the limited financial resources of the same customers

total cost The sume of average fixed and average variable costs times the quantity produced

total quality management (TQM) A philosophy that uniform commitment to quality in all areas of the organization will promote a culture that meets customers' perceptions of quality

trade (functional) discount A reduction off the list price given by a producer to an intermediary for performing certain functions

trade name Full legal name of an organization

trade sales promotion methods Ways of persuading wholesalers and retailers to carry a producer's products and market them aggressively

trade salespeople Salespersons involved mainly in helping a producer's customers promote a product

trademark A legal designation of exclusive use of a brand

traditional specialty retailers Stores that carry a narrow product mix with deep product lines

transfer pricing Setting prices on products sold by one unit to another unit in the same company

transportation The movement of products from where they are made to intermediaries and end users

trend analysis An analysis that focuses on aggregate sales data over a period of many years to determine general trends in annual sales

truck wholesalers Limited-service wholesalers that transport products directly to customers for inspection and selection

tying agreement An agreement in which a supplier furnishes a product to a channel member with the stipulation that the channel member must purchase other products as well

U

unaided recall test A posttest in which respondents identify ads they have recently seen but are given no recall clues

undifferentiated targeting strategy A strategy in which an organization designs a single marketing mix and directs it at the entire market for a particular product

uniform geographic pricing Charging all customers the same price, regardless of geographic location

unsought products Products purchased to solve a sudden problem, products of which customers are unaware, and products that people do not necessarily think about buying

V

validity A condition existing when a research method measures what it is supposed to measure

value A customer's subjective assessment of benefits relative to costs in determining the worth of a product

value analysis An evaluation of each component of a potential purchase

value-conscious Concerned about price and quality of a product

variable costs Costs that vary directly with changes in the number of units produced or sold

vendor analysis A formal, systematic evaluation of current and potential vendors

venture team A cross-functional group that creates entirely new products that may be aimed at new markets

vertical channel integration Combining two or more stages of the marketing channel under one management

vertical marketing systems (VMSs) A marketing channel managed by a single channel member to achieve efficient, low-cost distribution aimed at satisfying target-market customers

viral marketing A strategy to get consumers to share a marketer's message, often through e-mail or online video, in a way that spreads dramatically and quickly

W

warehouse clubs Large-scale members-only establishments that combine features of cash-and-carry wholesaling with discount retailing

warehouse showrooms Retail facilities in large, low-cost buildings with large on-premises inventories and minimal services

warehousing The design and operation of facilities for storing and moving goods

wholesaler An individual or organization that sells products that are bought for resale, for making other products, or for general business operations

wholesaling Transactions in which products are bought for resale, for making other products, or for general business operations

width of product mix The number of product lines a company offers

wikis Software that creates an interface that enables users to add or edit the content of some types of websites (also called wikipages)

willingness to spend An inclination to buy because of expected satisfaction from a product, influenced by the ability to buy and numerous psychological and social forces

word-of-mouth communication Personal, informal exchanges of information that customers share with one another about products, brands, and companies

World Trade Organization (WTO) An entity that promotes free trade among member nations

zone pricing Pricing based on transportation costs within major geographic zones

END NOTES

Chapter 1

1. Michael Futterman, "Red Sox Marketers Make Call to Bullpen," *Wall Street Journal*, January 9, 2009, B6; Ben Klayman, "Bull Riding Taps Red Sox Marketers for Sponsors," *Reuters*, January 9, 2009, http://www.reuters.com/articlePrint?articleId=USN0914927620090109 (accessed Feb. 5, 2009); "Welcome to the PBR," *Professional Bull Riders*, http://www.pbrnow.com/about/welcome.cfm (accessed Feb. 5, 2009); "All About Bull Riding," *Professional Bull Riders*, http://www.pbrnow.com/about/sportinfo/ (accessed Feb. 5, 2009).
2. American Marketing Association, 2007.
3. Michael Lev-Ram, "A Smartphone's BFF: Teens and Tweens," *Money.CNN.com*, August 24, 2007, http://money.conn.com/2007/08/23/technology/personaltech/theirdscreeen/smartphones.biz2/index.htm (accessed February 27, 2009); "Nike Unveils Shoe for Native Americans," Powows.com, September 26, 2007, http://www.powwows.com/gathering/news/40873-nike unveils-shoe-native-americans.html (accessed January 27, 2009).
4. Laura Petrecca, "Launch Week Also Marks Debut of Cross Promo Ads," *USA Today*, September 24, 2007, http://www.usatoday.com/money/advertising/adtrack/2007-09-23-track_N.htm (accessed January 27, 2009).
5. Tom Lowry, "Wow! Yao!" *BusinessWeek* (October 25, 2004): 86–90.
6. Kelly K. Spors, "Beyond Flowers: New Funeral Options Proliferate," *The Wall Street Journal*, October 19, 2005, D2, http://online.wsj.com/.
7. Mark Jewell, "Dunkin' Donuts Eyes Turn Westward: Chain Evolves from No Frills," *The [Fort Collins] Coloradoan*, January 17, 2005, E1.
8. Coach Official Website, http://www.coach.com (accessed February 20, 2009).
9. "About Subway," http://www.subway.com/subwayroot/AboutSubway/timeline.aspx (accessed February 20, 2009).
10. Ethan Smith and Yukari Iwatani Kane, "Apple Changes Tune on Music Pricing," *The Wall Street Journal*, January 1, 2009, B1.
11. Kibbles n'Bits, http://www.smoochablepooch.com (accessed February 27, 2009).
12. Eric Bontrager, "U.S. to Consumers: Turn Down Heat," *The Wall Street Journal*, October 4, 2005, D2, http://online.wsj.com/; Mathhew L Wald, "Shifting Message, Energy Officials Announce Conservation Plan," *The New York Times*, October 4, 2005, http://www.nytimes.com.
13. Rory J. Thompson, "Burger King Joins Healthy Food Initiative," *Brandweek*, September 12, 2007, http://www.brandweek.com/bw/esearch/article_display.jsp?vnu_content_id=1003638745 (accessed February 27, 2009).
14. "Dunkin' Donuts Slimming Down," *Brandweek*, August 27, 2007, http://www.brandweek.com/bw/esearch/article_display.jsp?vnu_content_id=1003631385 (accessed February 27, 2009).
15. *Campbell's Soup*, http://www.campbellsoup.com (accessed February 24, 2009); Campbell's V8 Soups, http://www.campbellsv8soup.com (accessed February 24, 2009).
16. Jena McGregor, "When Service Means Survival," *BusinessWeek* (March 2, 2009): 26–31.
17. Ajay K. Kohli and Bernard J. Jaworski, "Market Orientation: The Construct, Research Propositions, and Managerial Implications," *Journal of Marketing* (April 1990): 1–18; O. C. Ferrell, "Business Ethics and Customer Stakeholders," *Academy of Management Executive* 18 (May 2004): 126–129.
18. Eugene W. Anderson, Claes Fornell, and Sanal K. Mazvancheryl, "Customer Satisfaction and Shareholder Value," *Journal of Marketing* (October 2004): 172–185.
19. Kohli and Jaworski, "Market Orientation: The Construct, Research Propositions, and Managerial Implications."
20. Kwaku Atuahene-Gima, "Resolving the Capability-Rigidity Paradox in New Product Innovation," *Journal of Marketing* 69 (October 2005): 61–83.
21. Maria Halkieas, "Penney's American Living Brand Getting a Redo," *The Dallas Morning News*, August 15, 2008, http://www.dallasnews.com/sharedcontent/dws/bus/industries/retail/stories/0815208dmbuspenney.4c11d996.html (accessed February 24, 2009).
22. Gary F. Gebhardt, Gregory S. Carpenter, and John F. Sherry, Jr., "Creating a Marketing Orientation," *Journal of Marketing* 70 (October 2006), http://www.marketingpower.com.
23. Sunil Gupta, Donald R. Lehmann, and Jennifer Ames Stuart, "Valuing Customers," *Journal of Marketing Research* (February 2004): 7–18.
24. Lynn Russo Whylly, "Market: What a Girl Wants," *OMMA Magazine*, February 1, 2009, http://www.mediapost.com/publications/?fa=Articles.showArticle&art_aid=98355 (accessed February 24, 2009).
25. Janet Adamy, "McDonald's Tests Changes in $1 Burger as Costs Rise," *The Wall Street Journal*, August 4, 2008, B1.
26. Jena McGregor, "When Service Means Survival," *BusinessWeek* (March 2, 2009): 26–31.
27. Jacquelyn S. Thomas, Robert C. Blattberg, and Edward J. Fox, "Recapturing Lost Customers," *Journal of Marketing Research* (February 2004): 31–45.
28. Alan Grant and Leonard Schlesinger, "Realize Your Customers' Full Profit Potential," *Harvard Business Review* (September/October 1995): 59.
29. Jagdish N. Sheth and Rajendras Sisodia, "More Than Ever Before, Marketing Is under Fire to Account for What It Spends," *Marketing Management* (Fall 1995): 13–14.
30. Lynette Ryals and Adrian Payne, "Customer Relationship Management in Financial Services: Towards Information-Enabled Relationship Marketing," *Journal of Strategic Marketing* (March 2001): 3.
31. Best Buy Reward Zone Overview, https://myrewardzone.bestbuy.com/programOverview.jspx (accessed February 24, 2009).
32. Janet Adamy, "Starbucks Shifts Focus to Value, Cost Cutting," *The Wall Street Journal* (December 5, 2008): B1.
33. Werner J. Reinartz and V. Kumar, "On the Profiability of Long-Life Customers in a Noncontractual Setting: An Empirical Investigation and Implications for Marketing," *Journal of Marketing* (October 2000): 17–35.
34. Roland T. Rust, Katherine N. Lemon, and Valarie A. Zeithaml, "Return on Marketing: Using Customer Equity to Focus Marketing Strategy," *Journal of Marketing* (January 2004): 109–127.
35. Rajkumar Venkatesan and V. Kumar, "A Customer Lifetime Value Framework for Customer Selection and Resource Allocation Strategy," *Journal of Marketing* (October 2004): 106–125.
36. Sunil Gupta and Carl F. Mela, "What Is a Free Customer Worth?" *Harvard Business Review* (November 2008): 104.
37. O. C. Ferrell and Michael Hartline, *Marketing Strategy* (Mason, OH: South-Western, 2005): 108.
38. Gavin O'Malley, "Study: Email Strengthens Brand Image, Generates Sales," *Media Post News*, February 23, 2009, http://www.mediapost.com/publications/?fa=Articles.showArticle&art_aid=100814 (accessed February 26, 2009).
39. Paul Davidson, "It's Lights Out for Traditional Light Bulbs," *USA Today*, December 16, 2007, http://www.usatoday.com/money/industries/energy/environment/2007-12-16-lightbulbs_N.htm (accessed February 27, 2009).
40. Sharon Terlep, "Hyundai Plans 'Giveback' Program on Cars," *The Wall Street Journal* (January 6, 2009): B2.
41. "Kids' Food Pyramid Launched," CNN, September 28, 2005, http://www.cnn.com.
42. "U.S. Charitable Giving Estimated to Be $306.39 billion in 2007," *Giving USA Foundation*, http://www.givinginstitue.org/press_releases/20080622.html (accessed February 19, 2009).
43. Kelly Geyskens, Mario Pandlelaere, Siegfried DeWitte, and Luk Warlop, "The Backdoor to Overconsumption: The Effect of Associating 'Low-Fat' Food with Health References," *Journal of Public Policy & Marketing* 26 (Spring 2007): 118–125.
44. Heather Green, "How Amazon Aims to Keep You Clicking," *BusinessWeek* (March 2, 2009): 34–40.
45. "Southwest Airlines Fact Sheet," Southwest Airlines, http://www.iflyswa.com/about_swa/press/factsheet.html (accessed February 27, 2009).
46. Enid Burns, "Online Retail Sales Grew in 2005," *ClickZ*, January 5, 2006, http://www.clickz.com/showPage.html?page=3575456.
47. Pete Engardo, Kerry Capell, John Carey, and Kenji Hall, "Beyond the Green Corporation," *BusinessWeek* (January 9, 2007): 50–64; James Poniewozik, "Green Screens," *Time* (August 27, 2007): 62.

Feature endnotes

a. Alex Taylor III, "Wheeler Dealer," *Fortune*, October 15, 2007, http://money.cnn.com/2007/10/04/autos/smartcar_penske.fortune/index.htm (accessed February 20, 2009); Kellen Schetter, "Smart Car Offers Drivers New High MPG Option," *Greencar.com*, 2008, http://www.greencar.com/features/smart-car (accessed February 20, 2009); Michelle Krebs, "Smart Moves: Microcar Goes for Big Splash," *Auto Observer*, July 3, 2007, http://www.autoobserver.com/2007/07/smart-moves-mic.html (accessed February 20, 2009); *Smart Car of America*, http://www.smartcarofamerica.com/ (accessed February 20, 2009); Leila Abboud, "Small European Cars Shine," *The Wall Street Journal*, December 2, 2008 (accessed February 20, 2009); John Murphy, "Toyota Launches New Tiny Car," *The Wall Street Journal* (October 16, 2008): B10.

b. *Leatherman*, http://www.leathermn.com (accessed February 19, 2009); Fawn Fitter, "Outdoing the Swiss Army Knife," *Fortune Small Business*, July 25, 2007, http://money.cnn.com/magazines/fsb/fs/_archive/2007/07/01/100123045/index.htm (accessed February 19, 2009); Shelly Strom, "Leatherman Learns Patent Lesson the Hard Way," *Portland Business Journal*, April 12, 2002, http://www.bizjournals.com/portland/stories/2002/04/15/focus4.html (accessed February 19, 2009).

c. L. Bingham, "Enviros and City of Portland Cultivate a Movement to Top Buildings with Plants," *Oregon Environmental News*, January 9, 2009, http://www.oregonlive.com/environment/index.ssf/2009/01/environmentalists_and_the_city.html (accessed February 24, 2009).

Chapter 2

1. "All About Us," "Did You Know?," http://corporate.homedepot.com/wps/portal/!ut/p/.cmd/cs/.ce7_0_A/.s/7_0_113/_s.7_0_A/7_0_113 (accessed March 10, 2009); "Home Depot, Lowe's Facing Up to Challenges," Jennifer Waters, *MarketWatch*, July 9, 2007, http://www.marketwatch.com/news/story/goldman-sees-buyingopportunity-rivals/story.aspx?guid={84525FAB- C31A-4368-86B9-1254A5BA7652} (accessed March 10, 2009); Sheldon Liber, "Battle of the Brands: Home Depot vs. Lowe's," BloggingStocks.com, May 8, 2008, http://www.bloggingstocks.com/2008/05/08/battle-of-the-brands-home- depot-vs-lowes/2 (accessed February 11, 2009); "Corporate and Financial Overview," homedepot.com, http://corporate.homedepot.com/en_US/Corporate/Public_Relations/Online_Press_Kit/Docs/Corp_Financial_Overview.pdf (accessed February 11, 2009); "Fortune 500 2008," *Fortune*, http://money.cmm.com/magazines/fortune/fortune500/2008/full_list/ (accessed February 11, 2009).
2. O. C. Ferrell and Michael Hartline, *Marketing Strategy* (Mason, OH: South-Western, 2008), 10.
3. Christian Homburg, Karley Krohmer, and John P. Workman, Jr., "A Strategy Implementation Perspective of Market Orientation," *Journal of Business Research 57* (2004): 1331–1340.
4. Ferrell and Hartline, *Marketing Strategy*, 10.
5. Abraham Lustgarten, "iPod," in "Breakaway Brands," *Fortune* (October 31, 2005): 154–156.
6. Ferrell and Hartline, *Marketing Strategy*, 51.
7. Graham J. Hooley, Gordon E. Greenley, John W. Cadogan, and John Fahy, "The Performance Impact of Marketing Resources," *Journal of Business Research* 58 (2005): 18–27.
8. Associated Press, "Wal-Mart Expands Program Providing Drug Discounts," *The New York Times*, May 5, 2008, http://www.nytimes.com/2008/05/06/business/06drug.html?ref=business (accessed February 27, 2009).
9. Emily Bryson York, "Nestle, Pepsi and Coke Face Their Waterloo," *Polaris Institute*, October 8, 2007, http://www.polarisinstitute.org/nestle_pepsi_and_coke_face_their_waterloo (accessed February 27, 2009).
10. Derek F. Abell, "Strategic Windows," *Journal of Marketing* (July 1978): 21.
11. Cecile Rohwedder, "Tesco Tries to Catch a U.S. Curveball," *The Wall Street Journal* (March 2, 2009): B1.
12. David Kesmodel, "Constellation Brands to Change Its Product Mix," *The Wall Street Journal* (January 13, 2009): B7.
13. Ibid.
14. Jack Ewing, "Music Phones Tackle the iPod," *BusinessWeek Online*, July 11, 2006, http://www.businessweek.com.
15. Ibid.
16. "Designed to Grow," Procter & Gamble Annual Report, 2007, 5, http://thomson.mobular.net/thomson/7/2481/2810/ (accessed February 27, 2009).
17. Douglas Bowman and Hubert Gatignon, "Determinants of Competitor Response Time to a New Product Introduction," *Journal of Marketing Research* (February 1995): 42–53.
18. "Our Mission," Celestial Seasonings, http://www.celestialseasonings.com/whoweare/corporatehistory/mission.php (accessed May 16, 2007).
19. Cláudia Simões, Sally Dibb, and Raymond P. Fisk, "Managing Corporate Identity," *Journal of the Academy of Marketing Science* 33 (April 2005): 154–168.
20. "Johnson Controls Launches New Brand to Support Focus on Comfort, Safety and Sustainability," Encyclopedia.com, September 30, 2007, http://www.encyclopedia.com/doc/1G1-169292693.html (accessed February 27, 2009).
21. Jefferson Graham, "Google Cues Up with YouTube," *USA Today* (October 10, 2006): 1A.
22. Thomas Ritter and Hans Georg Gemünden, "The Impact of a Company's Business Strategy on Its Technological Competence, Network Competence and Innovation Success," *Journal of Business Research* 57 (2004): 548–556.
23. Kevin J. O'Brien, "Nokia Buys Software Maker for $8.1 Billion," *The New York Times*, October 1, 2007, http://www.nytimes.com/2007/10/01/technology/01cnd-nokia.html?scp=1&sq=Nokia%20Buys%Software%20Maker%20for%20&st=cse (accessed February 27, 2009).
24. "Designed to Grow," Procter & Gamble Annual Report, 2007, 4–5, http://thomson.mobular.net/thomson/7/2481/2801 (accessed February 27, 2009).
25. Information Resources, Inc., reported in Stephanie Thompson, "Nestlé, Hershey Figure Sticks Will Be Big Sellers," *Advertising Age* (October 3, 2005): 3.
26. Robert D. Buzzell, "The PIMS Program of Strategy Research: A Retrospective Appraisal," *Journal of Business Research* 57 (2004): 478–483.
27. Joseph P. Guiltinan and Gordon W. Paul, *Marketing Management: Strategies and Programs* (New York: McGraw-Hill, 1991), 43.
28. George S. Day, "Diagnosing the Product Portfolio," *Journal of Marketing* (April 1977): 30–31.
29. Serena Ng, Paul Glader, and Lingling Wei, "A Crisis of Confidence over GE Intensifies," *The Wall Street Journal Asia* (March 6–8, 2009): M1.
30. Isabelle Maignan, O. C. Ferrell, and Linda Ferrell, "A Stakeholder Model for Implementing Social Responsibility in Marketing," *European Journal of Marketing* 39 (September/October 2005): 956–977.
31. Shawn Tully, "Divorce Bank of America Style," *Fortune* (February 16, 2009): 70–72.
32. Maignan, Ferrell, and Ferrell, "A Stakeholder Model for Implementing Social Responsibility in Marketing."
33. G. Tomas, M. Hult, David W. Cravens, and Jagdish Sheth, "Competitive Advantage in the Global Marketplace: A Focus on Marketing Strategy," *Journal of Business Research* (January 2001): 1–3.
34. Kwaku Atuahene-Gima and Janet Y. Murray, "Antecedents and Outcomes of Marketing Strategy Comprehensiveness," *Journal of Marketing* (October 2004): 33–46.
35. Nancy Einhart, "How the New T-Bird Went Off Course," *Business 2.0* (November 2003): 74–76.
36. ACNeilson Analytics, as reported in Joe Bucherer, Libbey Paul, and Laurie Demeritt, "The Future of Health and Wellness," *Consumer Insight* (Summer 2006): 9.
37. Christian Homburg, John P. Workman, and Ove Jensen, "Fundamental Changes in Marketing Organization: The Movement Toward a Customer-Focused Organizational Structure," *Journal of the Academy of Marketing Science* (Fall 2000): 459–478.
38. Jack Neff, "Tissues Fit for the Toilet," *Advertising Age* (November 27, 2006): 3+.
39. Rajdeep Grewal and Patriya Tansuhaj, "The Chain of Effects from Brand Trust and Brand Affect to Brand Performance: The Role of Brand Loyalty," *Journal of Marketing* (April 2001): 67–80.
40. Steve Watkins, "Marketing Basics: The Four P's Are as Relevant Today as Ever," *Investor's Business Daily*, February 4, 2002, A1.
41. Bent Dreyer and Kjell Grnhaug, "Uncertainty, Flexibility, and Sustained Competitive Advantage," *Journal of Business Research* 57 (2004): 484–494.
42. Tara Kalwarski, "The American Household: A Nasty Dip in Net Worth," *BusinessWeek* (March 9, 2009): 12.
43. Ferrell and Hartline, *Marketing Strategy*, 257.
44. Maki Shiraki and Kazue Somiya, "Yoshinoya to Add 100 Restaurants as Consumers Seek Budget Meals," *Bloomberg News*, January 15, 2009, http://www.bloomberg.com/apps/news?pid=email_en&refer=japan&sid=aZPhvBeGwJo0 (accessed February 27, 2009).
45. Robert W. Palmatier, Lisa K. Scheer, and Jan-Benedict E.M. Steenkamp, "Customer Loyalty to Whom? Managing the Benefits and Risks of Salesperson-Owned Loyalty," *Journal of Marketing Research* XLIV (May 2007), http://www.marketingpower.com.
46. V. Kumar, "Customer Relationship Management," custom module for William M. Pride and O. C. Ferrell, *Marketing*, 14th ed. (Boston: Houghton Mifflin, 2006), http://www.prideferrell.com.
47. Chezy Ofir and Itamar Simonson, "The Effect of Stating Expectations on Customer Satisfaction and Shopping Experience," *Journal of Marketing Research* XLIV (February 2007), http://www.marketingpower.com.
48. V. Kumar, J. Andrew Peterson, and Robert P. Leone, "The Power of Customer Advocacy," in Jean L. Johnson and John Hulland (eds.), *2006: AMA Winter Educators' Conference*, in *Marketing Theory and Applications* 17 (Winter 2006), 81–82.

49. John Wieseke, Michael Ahearne, Son K. Lam, and Rolf von Dick, "The Role of Leaders in Internal Marketing," *Journal of Marketing* 73 (March 2009): 123–145.
50. Ian N. Lings, "Internal Market Orientation: Construct and Consequences," *Journal of Business Research* 57 (2004): 405–413.
51. Sybil F. Stershic, "Internal Marketing Campaign Reinforces Service Goals," *Marketing News* (July 31, 1998): 11.
52. White paper, "What Makes a Sales Contest Successful?" Kudo Spire, http://www.kudospire.com/what_makes_a_sales_contest_successful.htm (accessed March 8, 2009).
53. Betsy Spethmann, "Internal Affairs," *Promo,* March 1, 2006, http://promotmagazine.com.
54. Kee-hung Lee and T. C. Edwin Cheng, "Effects of Quality Management and Marketing on Organizational Performance," *Journal of Business Research* 58 (2005): 446–456; Wuthichai Sittimalakorn and Susan Hart, "Market Orientation Versus Quality Orientation: Sources of Superior Business Performance," *Journal of Strategic Marketing* (December 2004): 243–253.
55. Philip B. Crosby, *Quality Is Free: The Art of Making Quality Certain* (New York: McGraw-Hill, 1979): 9–10.
56. Nigel F. Piercy, "Market-Led Strategic Change," *The Marketing Review*, 2002, 2, 383–404, http://www.westburnpublishers.com/media/190619/m7e_chapters21_to_25.pdf (accessed October 26, 2009).
57. Douglas W. Vorhies and Neil A. Morgan, "Benchmarking Marketing Capabilities for Sustainable Competitive Advantage," *Journal of Marketing* (January 2005): 80–94.
58. Kenneth W. Thomas and Betty A. Velthouse, "Cognitive Elements of Empowerment: An Interpretive' Model of Intrinsic Task Motivation," *Academy of Management Review* (October 1990): 666–681.
59. Ferrell and Hartline, *Marketing Strategy.*
60. Rohit Deshpande and Frederick E. Webster, Jr., "Organizational Culture and Marketing: Defining the Research Agenda," *Journal of Marketing* (January 1989): 3–15.
61. REI, http://www.rei.com (accessed January 18, 2007).
62. Kathleen Cholewka, "CRM: Lose the Hype and Strategize," *Sales & Marketing Management* (June 2001): 27–28.
63. Peter Verhoef and Peter S. H. Leeflang, "Understanding the Marketing Deaprtments' Influence within the Firm," *Journal of Marketing* 73 (March 2009): 14–37.
64. Bernard J. Jaworski, "Toward a Theory of Marketing Control: Environmental Context, Control Types, and Consequences," *Journal of Marketing* (July 1988): 23–39.
65. "Toyota Prius Waits for the Air to Clear," Easier.com, http://www.easier.com/view/News/Motoring/Toyota/article-226274.html, 13 January 2009 (accessed March 9, 2009).
66. "Quality Ratings by Brand," JD Power, http://www.jdpower.com/autos/ratings/quality-ratings-by-brand (accessed March 9, 2009).
67. Jack Neft, "U.S. Consumers Cut Down on Razor Use," *Advertising Age* (July 14, 2008): 4.

Feature endnotes

a. P. C. Beller, "Unlikely Hero," *Forbes* (February 2, 2009): 52–58; M. Shields, *Media Week*, July 7, 2008, http://libproxy.unm.edu/login?url=http://search.ebscohost.com/login.aspx?direct-true&db=ufh&AN=33277448&site=ehostlive&scope=site (accessed February 4, 2009).
b. "Spudware®," http://excellentpackaging.com/pages/1/SpudWare.pdf (accessed March 5, 2009); Ilana DeBare, "Ridding World of Plastic Forks," *San Francisco Chronicle,* January 7, 2007, http://www.sfgate.com/cgi-bin/article.cgi?f=/c/a/2007/01/07/BUG8KNE27Q1.DTL&hw=ridding=world+of+plastic+forks&sn=001&sc=1000 (accessed March 5, 2009).

Chapter 3

1. Susan Berfield, "There Will Be Water," *BusinessWeek* (June 23, 2008): 40–45; David Case, "A Mighty Wind," *Fast Company* (June 2008): 80–83; Neil King, Jr., "Pickens' Windmills Tilt Against Market Realities," *The Wall Street Journal* (January 13, 2009): A12; "T. Boone Pickens Stalls Wind Farm Project," *New Mexico Business Weekly,* November 12, 2008, http://www.bizjournals.com/albuquerque/stories/2008/11/10/daily23.html (accessed February 13, 2009).
2. Julie Halpert, "Efficiency vs. Economics," *Newsweek*, January 14, 2009, http://www.newsweek.com/id/179517 (accessed March 20, 2009); Tom Incantalupo, "In a Down Market, Hybrid Sales Holding Up," *Newsday,* March 19, 2009, http://www.newsday.com/business/ny-bzhybr196074577mar19,0,604642.story (accessed March 20, 2009).
3. P. Varadarajan, Terry Clark, and William M. Pride, "Controlling the Uncontrollable: Managing Your Market Environment," *Sloan Management Review* (Winter 1992): 39–47.
4. "Carbonated Soft-Drinks Suffer Setback in 2005, Beverage Marketing Corporation Reports," Beverage Marketing Corporation press release, April 2006, http://www.beveragemarketing.com/news2zz.htm.
5. O. C. Ferrell and Michael D. Hartline, *Marketing Strategy* (Mason, OH: South-Western, 2008), 58.
6. Ibid.
7. Ibid.
8. Michelle Norris, "Your Money: American Express' $300 Deal Shows Industry Trend," National Public Radio, March 12, 2009, http://www.npr.org/templates.story/story.php?storyId=101152431 (accessed March 12, 2009).
9. Rodolfo Vazquez, Maria Leticia Santos, and Luis Ignacio lvarez, "Market Orientation, Innovation and Competitive Strategies in Industrial Firms," *Journal of Strategic Marketing* (March 2001): 69–90.
10. "The American Household: A Nasty Dip in Net Worth," *Businessweek* (March 9, 2009): 13.
11. Susan Page, "Poll Finds That as the Economy Falls, Success Is Being Redefined, and Expectations Lowered," *USA Today* (March 10, 2009): A1.
12. Kathy Chu, "Consumers Hit by Sliding Credit Scores," *USA Today* (March 6–8, 2009): A1.
13. Ann Zimmerman, "Retail Shows Signs of Life," *The Wall Street Journal* (March 6, 2009): A1.
14. "Top All-Time Donors," Center for Responsive Politics, http://www.opensecrets.org/orgs/list.php (accessed March 20, 2009).
15. Lorrie Grant, "Scrimping to Splurge," *USA Today* (January 28, 2005): 1B.
16. Joseph Pereira, "Price-Fixing Makes Comeback After Supreme Court Ruling," *The Wall Street Journal* (August 18, 2008): A1.
17. "FTC Order Bars Firm from Failing to Provide Timely Rebates," Federal Trade Commission, March 11, 2009, http://www.ftc.gov/opa/2009/03/ats.shtm.
18. "National Restaurant Company Settles FTC Charges for Deceptive Gift Card Sales," Federal Trade Commission, press release, April 3, 2007, http://www.ftc.gov/opa/2007/04/darden.shtm.
19. Sarah Ellison, "Why Kraft Decided to Ban Some Food Ads to Children," *The Wall Street Journal,* Octboer 31, 2005, via http://www.commercialalert.org/news/archive/2005/10/small-bites-why-kraft-decided-to-ban-some-food-ads-to-children (accessed November 3, 2009).
20. David Tyler, "BBB Hangs Up On Cingular," *Rochester Democrat & Chronicle,* September 10, 2005, via http://notjust4techs.com/?p=25 (accessed Novermber 3, 2009).
21. "P&G Takes Issue with McNeil Ad Claims for Tylenol Cold Product," National Advertising Division, press release, August 1, 2007, http://www.nadreview.org (accessed March 12, 2009).
22. "NAD Refers BIE Health Products to the FTC and FDA," National Advertising Division press release, July17, 2006, http://www.nadreview.org.
23. "New Subscribers to Telecom Services Continues Growing in 2005," Cellular-News.com, October 5, 2005, http://www.cellular-news.com/story/12792.php.
24. Gwen Moran, "Top New Marketing Trends," MSNBC, August 7, 2006, http://www.msnbc.msn.com/id/14231013/.
25. Samantha Rose Hunt, "YouTube Viewers in U.S. Exceed 100 Million for First Time," *TG Daily*, March 6, 2009, http://www.tgdaily.com/content/view/41650/113/ (accessed March 20, 2009).
26. Thorne, Ferrell, and Ferrell, *Business and Society*, Third Edition, New York: Houghton Mifflin Co., 2008, 36.
27. Ibid.
28. Ibid.
29. U.S. Bureau of the Census, *Statistical Abstract of the United States, 2007* (Washington: U.S. Government Printing Office, 2006), 13.
30. Ibid., 50, 53.
31. Ibid., 12.
32. U.S. Bureau of the Census, "U.S. Interim Projections by Age, Sex, Race, and Hispanic Origin," March 18, 2004, http://www.census.gov/ipc/www/usinterimproj/natprojtab01a.pdf (accessed November 3, 2009).
33. Jeffrey M. Humphreys, "The Multicultural Economy 2007," *Georgia Business and Economic Conditions* 67 (Third Quarter 2007), 7.
34. Carlotta Mast, "Latino Liftoff," *Denver Post*, August 2007, via http://goliath.ecnext.com/coms2/gi_0199-6968970/Latino-liftoff-Colorado-companies-targeting.html (accessed November 3, 2009).
35. Isabelle Maignan and O. C. Ferrell, "Corporate Social Responsibility and Marketing: An Integrative Framework," *Journal of the Academy of Marketing Science,* (January 2004): 3–19.
36. Indra Nooyi, "The Responsible Company," *The Economist* (March 31, 2008): 132.
37. Peter Loftus, "Number of Vioxx-Related Lawsuits Tops 22,000 as Deadline Nears," *The Wall Street Journal,* September 29, 2006, http://online.wsj.com/article/SB115956023286178324.html?mod=home_law_more_news; "Report: Merck Aware of Vioxx Problems," *The Austin American-Statesman,* November 2, 2004, http://statesman.com.

38. Avon Breast Cancer Crusader Homepage, http://www.avoncompany.com/women/avoncrusade/ (accessed March 20, 2009).
39. Thorne, Ferrell, and Ferrell, *Business and Society*, 48–50.
40. O. C. Ferrell, "Business Ethics and Customer Stakeholders," *Academy of Management Executive* (May 2004): 126–129.
41. "2005 Corporate Citizenship Report," Pfizer, http://www.pfizer.com/pfizer/subsites/corporate_citizenship/ report/stakeholders_table.jsp (accessed January 19, 2007).
42. Archie Carroll, "The Pyramid of Corporate Social Responsibility: Toward the Moral Management of Organizational Stakeholders," *Business Horizons* (July/August 1991): 42.
43. William T. Neese, Linda Ferrell, and O. C. Ferrell, "An Analysis of Federal Mail and Wire Fraud Cases Related to Marketing," *Journal of Business Research* 58 (2005): 910–918.
44. Sundar Bharadwaj, "Do Firms Pay a Price for Deceptive Advertising?" Knowledge@Emory, October 15, 2009, http://knowledge.emory.edu/article.cfm?articleid=1275 (accessed November 3, 2009).
45. Jonathan King and David Acklin, "Creating Common Ground: A Lesson from the Past," *Journal of Business Ethics 14* (January 1995): 13.
46. Carl Bialik, "In Ads, 1 Out of 5 Stats Is Bogus," *The Wall Street Journal,* March 11, 2009, http://online.wsj.com/article/SB123672828150888771.html (accessed November 3, 2009).
47. "Consumer Cries Foul over Kraft Dip," *The Austin American-Statesman,* November 30, 2006, http://www.statesman.com.
48. Tim Barnett and Sean Valentine, "Issue Contingencies and Marketers' Recognition of Ethical Issues, Ethical Judgments and Behavioral Intentions," *Journal of Business Research* 57 (2004): 338–346.
49. "Charitable Giving Rises 6 Percent to More Than $160 Billion in 2005," Giving USA Foundation press release, June 7, 2006, http://www.aafrc.org/press_releases/trustreleases/0606_PR.pdf (accessed Novermber 3, 2009).
50. Jessica Stannard-Friel, "Corporate Giving Responds to Hurricane Katrina," *OnPhilanthropy,* August 30, 2005, http://www.onphilanthropy.com/onthescene/os2005-08-30.html.
51. Stacy Perman, "Scones and Social Responsibility," *BusinessWeek* (August 21/28, 2006): 38.
52. "Take Charge of Education," Target, http://sites.target.com/site/en/corporate/page.jsp?contentId=PRD03-001825 (accessed January 19, 2007).
53. Marianne Wilson, "Doing Good Is More Than a Feel-Good Option," *Chain Store Age* (October 2005): 771.
54. Jasmine Malik Chua, "Home Depot, Habitat for Humanity, Build Green Building Partnership," Treehugger, April 15, 2008, http://www.treehugger.com/files/2008/04/home-depot-habitat-for-humanity.php (accessed November 3, 2009).
55. "How Much Trash We Toss," Environmental Protection Agency, *USA Today Snapshot* (August 27, 2008): A1.
56. "Garbage Powers Windex Plant," *CNN*, March 11, 2009, http://money.cnn.com/video/technology/2009/03/11/fortune-bg-scjohnson.fortune/ (accessed March 1, 2009).
57. Peter Asmus, "17th Annual Business Ethics Awards," *Business Ethics* (Fall 2005): 18–20.
58. Isabelle Maignan and Debbie Thorne McAlister, "Socially Responsible Organizational Buying: How Can Stakeholders Dictate Purchasing Policies?" *Journal of Macromarketing* (December 2003): 78–89.
59. Stephanie Thompson, "Aveda Pressures Mags to Go Green," *Advertising Age* (November 29, 2004): 19.
60. Jill Gabrielle Klein, N. Craig Smith, and Andrew John, "Why We Boycott: Consumer Motivations for Boycott Participation," *Journal of Marketing* (July 2004): 92–109.
61. Bruce R. Gaumnitz and John C. Lere, "Contents of Codes of Ethics of Professional Business Organizations in the United States," *Journal of Business Ethics* 35 (2002): 35–49.
62. Jeff Leeds, "2 Are Fired at Clear Channel after a Misconduct Inquiry," *The New York Times,* October 12, 2005, http://www.nytimes.com.
63. Ferrell and Hartline, *Marketing Strategy*, Fourth Edition, Mason, OH: Cengage Learning, 2008, 76-79.
64. Marjorie Kelly, "Holy Grail Found: Absolute, Definitive Proof That Responsible Companies Perform Better Financially," *Business Ethics,* Winter 2005, http://www.business-ethics.com/current_issue/winter_2005_holy_grail_article.html; Xueming Luo and C. B. Bhattacharya, "Corporate Social Responsibility, Customer Satisfaction, and Market Value," *Journal of Marketing* 70 (October 2006), http://www.marketingpower.com; Isabelle Maignan, O. C. Ferrell, and Linda Ferrell, "A Stakeholder Model for Implementing Social Responsibility in Marketing," *European Journal of Marketing* 39 (September/October 2005): 956–977.
65. "Multi-Year Study Finds 21% Increase in Americans Who Say Corporate Support of Social Issues Is Important in Building Trust," Cone, Inc., press release, December 8, 2004, http://www.coneinc.com/Pages/pr_30.html.
66. Maignan, Ferrell, and Ferrell, "A Stakeholder Model for Implementing Social Responsibility in Marketing."

Feature endnotes

a. Jamin Brophy-Warren, "The New Examined Life," *Wall Street Journal* (December 6–7, 2008): W1, W11; Tom Hayes and Michael S. Malone, "Marketing in the World of the Web," *Wall Street Journal* (November 29–30, 2008): A13; Jessica E. Vascellaro, "Facebook Aims to Connect Its Users to Other Sites," *Wall Street Journal* (December 5, 2008): B4.
b. Anderson Cooper, " A Life Saver Called 'Plumpy'nut'," *60 Minutes*, CBS News, October 21, 2007, http://www.cbsnews.com/stories/2007/10/19/60minutes/main3386661.shtml (accessed March 2, 2009); "WHO Experts Raise Antiquated Nutrition Standards," Doctors without Borders, October 10, 2007, http://doctorswithoutborders.org/news/issue.cfm?id=2396 (accessed March 2, 2009); "Plumpy'nut in the Field," Nutriset, http://www.nutriset.fr/index.php?option=com_content&task=view&id=41&Itemid=33 (accessed March 2, 2009).
c. S. Elliot, "Trumpeting a Move to Put the Sun in SunChips," *The New York Times,* March 27, 2008, http://www.nytimes.com/2008/03/27/business/media/27adco.html?_r=2&scp=2&sq=&st=nyt&oref=slogin (accessed March 2, 2009);
Projects & Partners (2009), Solar Electric Light Fund, http://www.self.org/index.asp (accessed March 3, 2009); *Incentives,* DSIRE: Database of State Incentives for Renewables & Efficiencies, http://www.dsireusa.org/index.cfm?EE=0&RE=1 (accessed March 2, 2009).

Chapter 4

1. "Tell Us What You Really Think: Collecting Customer Feedback," *Inc. Magazine* (December 2008): 52–53; Noreen O'Leary, "Study: Customer Feedback Ignored," *Ad Week,* January 26, 2009, http://www.adweek.com/aw/-content_display/news/client/e3ic96aa80f511fb30f5635f219369f11aa (accessed February 10, 2009); Aphrodite Brinsmead, "Twitter and Google as Customer Service Tools," *TMC News,* February 9, 2009, http://www.tmcnet.com/usubmit/2009/02/09/3974434.htm (accessed February 10, 2009).
2. Anne L. Souchon, John W. Cadogan, David B. Procter, and Belinda Dewsnap, "Marketing Information Use and Organizational Performance: The Mediating Role of Responsiveness," *Journal of Strategic Marketing* (December 2004): 231–242; Bradley Johnson, "Understanding the Generation Wireless' Demographic," *Advertising Age* (March 20, 2006).
3. "A Wake-up Call for Coffee," *BusinessWeek* (October 22, 2007): 23.
4. Ellen Byron, "Marketers Target Men's Hair as Promising Frontier," *The Wall Street Journal,* December 1, 2008, B4.
5. Catherine Arnold, "Self-Examination: Researchers Reveal State of MR in Survey," *Marketing News* (February 1, 2005): 55, 56.
6. Kenneth Chang, "Enlisting Science's Lessons to Entice More Shoppers to Spend More," *The New York Times,* September 19, 2006, http://www.nytimes.com.
7. Bobby White, "Cisco Sets Its Sights on $34 Billion Market," *The Wall Street Journal,* September 24, 2008, B3.
8. A. Parasuraman, Dhruv Grewal, and R. Krishnan, *Marketing Research* (Boston: Houghton Mifflin, 2007), 63.
9. Ken Manning, O. C. Ferrell, and Linda Ferrell, "Consumer Expectations of Clearance vs. Sale Prices," University of Wyoming working paper, 2007.
10. Parasuraman, Grewal, and Krishnan, *Marketing Research,* 64.
11. Ibid., 73.
12. Vikas Mittal and Wagner A. Kamakura, "Satisfaction, Repurchase Intent, and Repurchase Behavior: Investigating the Moderating Effects of Customer Characteristics," *Journal of Marketing Research* (February 2001): 131–142.
13. Brian Steel, "Kellogg's Goes Virtual to Test Real Life Packaging," *Marketing News* (January 30, 2009): 13.
14. "BMW of North America," *Nielson Claritas,* http://www.claritas.com/target-marketing/ (accessed March 22, 2009).
15. Haya El Nasser, "Census Bureau No Longer Waiting 10 Years for Data," *The Coloradoan* (January 17, 2005): A2.
16. "Information Resources, Inc.," *Marketing News* (August 15, 2006): H22–24.
17. "External Secondary Market Research," *CCH Business Owner's Toolkit,* http://www.toolkit.cch.com/text/P03_3011.asp (accessed January 23, 2007).
18. Arnold, "Self-Examination."
19. Jack Neff, "Consumers Rebel Against Marketers' Endless Surveys," *Advertising Age,* October 2, 2006, http://www.adage.com.

20. Ibid.
21. Maria Grubbs Hoy and Avery M. Abernethy, "Nonresponse Assessment in Marketing Research: Current Practice and Suggested Improvements," in *Marketing Theory and Applications,* American Marketing Association Winter Educators' Conference Proceedings, 2002.
22. David Jobber, John Saunders, and Vince-Wayne Mitchell, "Prepaid Monetary Incentive Effects on Mail Survey Response," *Journal of Business Research* (January 2004): 347–350.
23. John Harwood and Shirley Leung, "Hang-Ups: Why Some Pollsters Got It So Wrong This Election Day," *The Wall Street Journal* (November 8, 2003): A1, A6.
24. Ibid.
25. Robert V. Kozinets, "The Field Behind the Screen: Using Netnography for Marketing Research in Online Communities," *Journal of Marketing Research* (February 2002): 61–72.
26. Glen L. Urban and John R. Hauser, "'Listening In' to Find and Explore New Combinations of Customer Needs," *Journal of Marketing* (April 2004): 72–87.
27. Alissa Quart, "Ol' College Pry," *Business 2.0,* April 3, 2001. "Where the Stars Design the Cars," *Business 2.0* (July 2005): 32.
28. Susanne Vranica, "Media Firms Team Up to Test Online Video Ad Formats," *The Wall Street Journal* (January 22, 2009): B4.
29. "Critics Say Obama's Focus-Group Approach More Style Than Substance," *Fox News,* March 5, 2009, http://www.foxnews.com/politics/first 100days/2009/03/05obamas-focus-group-approach-style-substance/ (accessed March 23, 2009).
30. Peter DePaulo, "Sample Size for Qualitative Research," *Quirk's Marketing Research Review,* December 2000, http://www.quirks.com.
31. Theodore T. Allen and Kristen M. Maybin, "Using Focus Group Data to Set New Product Prices," *Journal of Product and Brand Management* (January 2004): 15–24.
32. David Armano, "Rethinking the Focus Group: Tropicana Design Flops," *Logic + Emotion,* February 23, 2009, http://darmano.typepad.com/logic_emotion/2009/02/tropicana-html (accessed March 15, 2009).
33. Sean Geehan and Stacy Sheldon, "Connecting to Customers," *Marketing Management* (November/December 2005): 37–42.
34. Kenneth Hein, "KFC Cooks Up Moms Panel," *BrandWeek,* August 22, 2006, www.brandweek.com.
35. Barbara Allan, "The Benefits of Telephone Depth Sessions," *Quirk's Marketing Research Review,* December 2000, http://www.quirks.com.
36. Bruce Horovitz, "Marketers Take a Close Look at Your Daily Routines," *USA Today,* April 29, 2007, http://www.usatoday.com/money/advertising/2007-04-29-watching-marketing_N.htm (accessed March 23, 2009).
37. Judy Strauss and Donna J. Hill, "Consumer Complaints by E-mail: An Exploratory Investigation of Corporate Responses and Customer Reactions," *Journal of Interactive Marketing* (Winter 2001): 63–73.
38. Kevin Kelleher, "66,207,986 Bottles of Beer on the Wall," *Business 2.0,* CNN, February 25, 2004, http://www.cnn.com.
39. D. Aacker, V. Kumar, and G. Day, *Marketing Research,* 8th ed. (New York: Wiley & Sons, 2004).
40. Marlus Wübeen and Florian von Wangenheim, "Predicting Customer Lifetime Duration and Future Purchase Levels: Simple Heuristics vs. Complex Models," in Jean L. Johnson and John Hulland, eds., *2006 AMA Winter Educators' Conference: Marketing Theory and Applications* 17 (Winter 2006): 83–84.
41. Thomas Mucha, "The Builder of Boomtown," *Business 2.0,* September 2005, http://www.business2.com.
42. "Ace Hardware," Claritas Case Study, http://www.claritas.com/target-mearketing/resources/case-study/ace-hardware-02.jsp (accessed March 13, 2009).
43. "Group Warns of Grocery Grab for Data," *Marketing News* (April 15, 2002): 7.
44. Noah Rubin Brier, John McManus, David Myron, and Christopher Reynolds, "'Zero-In' Heroes," *American Demographics* (October 2004): 36–45.
45. Laurence N. Goal, "High Technology Data Collection for Measurement and Testing," *Marketing Research* (March 1992): 29–38.
46. Behrooz Noori and Mohammad Hossein Salimi, "A Decision-Support System for Business-to-Business Marketing," *Journal of Business & Industrial Marketing* 20 (2005): 226–236.
47. Carlos Denton, "Time Differentiates Latino Focus Groups," *Marketing News* (March 15, 2004): 52.
48. Lambeth Hochwald, "Are You Smart Enough to Sell Globally?" *Sales & Marketing Management* (July 1998): 52–56.
49. Ibid.

Feature endnotes

a. iModerate, http://imoderate.com (accessed March 23, 2009); Eric Peterson, "Tech Startup of the Month," *ColoradoBiz,* August 2007, http://www.imoderate.com/cms_images/file_9.pdf (accessed March 23, 2009); Deborah Vence, "10 Minutes with...," *Marketing News* (February 15, 2009): 26.

b. Piet Levy, "All Together Now." *Marketing News* (February 15, 2009): 24; "Marketing Through Online Communications," *Pronenet Advertising,* http://www.pronetadvertising.com/articles/marketing-through-online-communities.html (accessed March 2, 2009); Emily Steel, "Skittles Cozies Up to Social Media," *Media & Marketing* (March 3, 2009): B4.

c. Amy Galland, "Waste & Opportunity: U.S. Beverage Container Recycling Scorecard and Report, 2008," As You Sow, http://www.asyousow.org/sustainability/bev_survey.shtml (accessed March 23, 2009); *PepsiCo Packaging and Solid Waste,* http://www.pepsico.com/Purpose/Environment/Packaging-and-Solid-Waste .aspx (accessed March 2, 2009);"Coca-Cola, URRC Open World's Largest Plastic Bottle-to-Bottle Recycling Plant," *The New York Times,* January 14, 2009, http://markets.on.nytimes.com/research/stocks/news/press_release.asp?docKey=600-200901141200BIZWIRE_USPR_____BW5918-5D90ISCLLMB2M7U464FJFH6SET&provider=Businesswire&docDate=January %2014%2C%202009&press_symbol=US%3BKO (accessed March 23, 2009).

Chapter 5

1. "High School Musical 3: Senior Year (2008)," *The Numbers,* http://www.the-numbers.com/movies/2008/HSM3.php; Simon Dumenco, "Could 455 Million 'High School Musical' Viewers Be Wrong?" October 2008, http://www.adage.com/mediaworks/article?_id=131793; Steve Mason, "Friday Box Office: High School Musical 3 Hits Huge with $16.5M, $55M Weekend Likely," October 2008, http://www.slashfilm.com/2008/10/24/friday-box-office-high-school-musical-3-hits-huge-with-165m-55m-weekend-likely/; Mike Reynolds, "Cable's All-Time, Most-Watched Show: 'HSM2' Edges 'MNF,'" October 2008, http://www.multichannel.com/article/80659-Cable_s_All_Time_Most_Watched_Show_HSM2_Edges_MNF_.php (all accessed February 6, 2009).
2. Josh Quittner, "World of Fore!-craft," *Fortune,* (January 21, 2008): 32–34.
3. Montblanc—Writing Instruments, http://www.montblanc.com/products/26.php (accessed February 13, 2009).
4. Vanessa O'Connell, "Neiman Marcus's Cusp Tries for Younger Crowd," *The Wall Street Journal* (June 13, 2007): B1, http://online.wsj.com.
5. Aidan Malley, "Apple AT&T Neophytes to Define iPhone Audience," *Apple Insider,* http://www.appleinsider.comppleinsider.com (accessed February 4, 2009).
6. Service Corporation International, http://premium.hoovers.com/subscribe/co/factsheet.xhtml?ID=rrycrfchkhjkrh (accessed January 30, 2009).
7. Teens Turning Green, www.teensturninggreen.org (accessed February 6, 2009).
8. "Kids and Commercialism," Center for New American Dream, http://newdream.org/kids/facts.php (accessed February 18, 2009).
9. U.S. Bureau of the Census, *Statistical Abstract of the United States,* 2007 (Washington, DC: U.S. Government Printing Office).
10. "Dora the Explorer Leads Doll Revolution," CNN, August 13, 2007, http://www.cnn.com.
11. Jason Fields, "America's Families and Living Arrangements: 2003," *Current Population Reports* (Washington, DC: U.S. Census Bureau, November 2004): 1–20.
12. "Clients and Case Studies," MicroMarketing, Inc., http://www.micromarketing.com/clients/index.html (accessed January 24, 2007).
13. Jena McGregor, "At Best Buy, Marketing Goes Micro," *Business Week* (May 26, 2008): 52–54.
14. Emily Bryson York, "Taco Bell, Starbucks Trot Out 'Light' Offerings for New Year," *Advertising Age,* December 27, 2007, http://www.adage.com.
15. Joseph T. Plummer, "The Concept and Application of Life Style Segmentation," *Journal of Marketing* (January 1974): 33.
16. SRI Consulting Business Intelligence, http://www.sric-bi.com/VALS (accessed February 18, 2009).
17. "Energy Statistics," NationMaster, data from CIA June 14, 2007, www.nationmaster.com/graph/ene_ele_con_percap-energy-electricity-consumption-per-capita.
18. Susan Bergman, "U.S. Baby Boomer Attitude and Opportunity: At Home, at Work, and on the Road," *Package Facts,* June 1, 2008, http://www.packaged-facts.com/Baby-Boomer-Attitudes-1634923/ (accessed February 13, 2009).
19. Philip Kotler, *Marketing Management: Analysis, Planning, Implementation, and Control,* 7th ed. (Englewood Cliffs, NJ: Prentice Hall, 2003), 144.
20. Charles W. Chase, Jr., "Selecting the Appropriate Forecasting Method," *Journal of Business Forecasting* (Fall 1997): 2, 23, 28–29.
21. "ACNielsen Market Decisions: Controlled Market Testing," ACNielsen, http://us.acnielsen.com/products/rms_amd_controlledmktest.shtml (accessed February 5, 2009).
22. Constantine von Hoffman, "P&G Plans to Shrink Line of Detergents," *Brandweek,* (October 16, 2006): 6, http://www.brandweek.com.

Feature endnotes

a. Michael Learmonth, "Marketers Adapt as Social Networks Attract Older Users," *Advertising Age* (February 23, 2009): 14; Suzanne Kapner, "Facebook Tries to Sell Its Friends Again," *Fortune* (February 16, 2009): 24; Becky Ebenkamp, "Behavior Issues: Behavioral Targeting Is a Tricky Issue for Marketers," *Brandweek* (October 20, 2008): 21; Jeremy Kirk, "MySpace User Ad Targeting Will Be Optional," *Industry Standard*, April 29, 2008, http://www.thestandard.com/news/2008/04/29/myspace-user-ad-targeting-will-be-optional.

b. Andrew Scott, "Natural Eats, Tasty Profits," *Fairfield County Business Journal* (July 25, 2005): 1+; "Tasty Bite May Raise $12M to Fuel Growth," *The Economic Times* (July 8, 2006); Shivani Vora, "Curry in a Hurry," *Time*, (Feb. 12, 2007): G10; Tasty Bite, http://www.tastybite.com (accessed February 18, 2009).

c. Grant Ray, "The Clean, Green 2009 Zero X Machine," *Fast Company*, February 18, 2009, http://www.fastcompany.com/articles/2009/02/zero-x-electric-motorcycle.html; Phillip Hennessey, "Green Initiatives Are Hot," *Successful Meetings*, (July 2007): 11; Jim Hanas, "A World Gone Green," *Advertising Age*, (June 11, 2007): S-1; Dan Alaimo, "Green Housewares Growing: Mintel," *Supermarket News*, March 19, 2007, n.p.; Julie Gallagher, "Earth-Friendly Packaging May Have Grocers Seeing Green," *Supermarket News*, January 15, 2007, n.p.

Chapter 6

1. Jennifer Saranow, "Retailers Give It the Old College Try," *Wall Street Journal* (August 28, 2008): B8; Stuart Elliott, "Marketers Are Joining the Varsity," *New York Times*, June 11, 2007, C1, C4; Brian Steinberg, "Gimme an Ad! Brands Lure Cheerleaders," *Wall Street Journal* (April 19, 2007): B4.
2. Wayne D. Hoyer and Deborah J. MacInnis, *Consumer Behavior*, 4th ed. (Mason, OH: South-Western/Cengage Learning, 2010), 47–49.
3. Andrew D. Gershoff and Gita Venkataramani Johar, "Do You Know Me? Consumer Calibration of Friends' Knowledge," *Journal of Consumer Research* 32 (March 2006): 496+.
4. Barbara Kiviat, "Why We Buy," *Time* (August 27, 2007): 50–51.
5. Russell W. Belk, "Situational Variables and Consumer Behavior," *Journal of Consumer Research* (December 1975): 157–164.
6. Nathan Novemsky, Ravi Dhar, Norbert Schwarz, and Itamar Simonson, "Preference Fluency in Choice," *Journal of Marketing Research* 44 (August 2007): 347–356.
7. "Sorry Cupid, Santa's the One Handing Out Engagement Rings This Year—and He's Buying Them Online," *PR Newswire*, December 6, 2004.
8. Chien-Huang Lin, HsiuJu Rebecca Yen, and Shin-Chieh Chuang, "The Effects of Emotion and Need for Cognition on Consumer Choice Involving Risk," *Marketing Letters* 17 (January 2006): 47–60.
9. Ellen Byron, "Is the Smell of Moroccan Bazaar Too Edgy for American Homes?" *Wall Street Journal*, February 3, 2009.
10. "Scented Hotel Rooms? Hampton Says Nonsense!" Hampton Hotels, Press Release, October 2007, http://hospitality-1st.com/PressNews/Hampton-102307.html.
11. SRI Consulting Business Intelligence, http://www.sric-bi.com/VALS (accessed March 23, 2009).
12. David B. Wooten, "From Labeling Possessions to Possessing Labels: Ridicule and Socialization Among Adolescents," *Journal of Consumer Research* 33 (September 2006): 188+.
13. Christopher Hart and Pete Blackshaw, "Internet Inferno," *Marketing Management*, (January/February 2006): 21.
14. Donnel A. Briley and Jennifer L. Aaker, "When Does Culture Matter? Effects of Personal Knowledge on the Correction of Culture-Based Judgments," *Journal of Marketing Research* 33 (August 2006), http://marketingpower.com (accessed March 23, 2009).
15. "ACS Demographic and Housing Estimates: 2005–2007," U.S. Census Bureau, http://factfinder.census.gov (accessed March 23, 2009).
16. Jeffrey M Humphreys, "The Multicultural Economy 2008," *Georgia Business and Economic Conditions* 68 (Third Quarter 2008), http://www.selig.uga.edu/forecast/GBEC/GBEC0803q.pdf.
17. Marissa Miley, *Advertising Age* 80 (February 2, 2009): 3–26.
18. Ann Zimmerman, "To Boost Sales, Wal-Mart Drops One-Size-Fits-All Approach," *The Wall Street Journal* (September 7, 2006): A1, http://online.wsj.com.
19. "Target Dreams in Color for King Day and Beyond," Target Press Release, January 11, 2007, http://news.target.com/phoenix.xhtml?c=196187&p=irol-newsArticle&ID=949530.
20. "ACS Demographic and Housing Estimates: 2005–2007," U.S. Census Bureau, http://factfinder.census.gov (accessed March 23, 2009); Humphreys, "The Multicultural Economy 2008," *Georgia Business and Economic Conditions*.
21. "Ethnic Analysis," http://www.databankusa.com/Services/Ethnic.asp (accessed March 23, 2009).
22. Humphreys, "The Multicultural Economy 2008," *Georgia Business and Economic Conditions*.
23. Mindy Fetterman, "Stores Embrace Hispanic Tradition of 3 Kings Day," *USA Today*, January 1, 2008, http://www.usatoday.com/money/industries/retail/2008-01-01-three-kings-day_N.htm.
24. Della de la Fuente, "American Takes Latinos Home for the Holidays," *Brandweek*, November 19, 2007, http://www.brandweek.com/bw/news/leisuretrav/article_display.jsp?vnu_content_id=1003674048.
25. "ACS Demographic and Housing Estimates: 2005–2007," U.S. Census Bureau, http://factfinder.census.gov (accessed March 23, 2009).
26. Humphreys, "The Multicultural Economy 2008," *Georgia Business and Economic Conditions*.
27. Carol Angrisani, *Supermarket News* (November 10, 2008): 1–7.

Feature endnotes

a. Bruce Horovitz, "'Two Nobodies from Nowhere' Craft Winning Ad," *USA Today* (February 2, 2009): 4B; Stephanie Clifford, "Finding a Gold Mine in Digital Ditties," *New York Times* (October 28, 2008): A1+; Teresa F. Lindeman, "Ad Contest Has Heinz Seeking More from Public," *Pittsburgh Post-Gazette*, September 15, 2007, http://www.post-gazette.com.

b. Kathy Jackson, "Toyota Hopes New, Lighter Prius Will Give Sales a Lift," *Automotive News* (January 19, 2009): 16; John K. Teahen Jr., "Hybrids Aren't Taking Auto World by Storm," *Automotive News* (September 17, 2007): 20; Micheline Maynard, "Toyota Hybrid Makes a Statement, and That Sells," *New York Times* (July 4, 2007): A1, A11.

c. Facebook, http://www.facebook.com (Feb. 18, 2009); Steven Levy, "Facebook Grows Up," *Newsweek* (Aug. 20, 2007): 41–46; Ellen McGirt, "Hacker, Dropout, CEO," *Fast Company* (May 2007): 74–80; Brad Stone, "In Facebook, Investing in a Theory," *New York Times* (Oct. 4, 2007): C1, C2; iThink Online, http://www.targetx.com/ithink/?p=680#more-680, "The Aging of Facebook," February 6, 2009.

Chapter 7

1. Jacqueline Renerow, "Small Business Owners Get Intimate with Visa's New Network," *Response* (December 2008): 32; Charlotte Woolard, "Virtual Events Keep Down Costs," *B to B* (April 23, 2007): 31; Maggie Rauch, "Virtual Reality: How IBM Uses Web 2.0 to Grow Its Brand, from Wikis to Viral Video to Second Life," *Sales and Marketing Management* (January–February 2007): 18+.
2. *MRO + Distribution/Purchasing*, January 2009, Vol. 138, Issue 1, 29 (accessed February 20, 2009).
3. Bureau of the Census, *Statistical Abstract of the United States, 2009*, http://www.census.gov/compendia/statab/ (accessed March 6, 2009), Table 1007.
4. Ibid., Table 1007.
5. Ibid., Table 645.
6. Ibid., Table 410.
7. *Business Wire*, February 20, 2009 (accessed February 23, 2009).
8. "ZANA Network Members Get Access to Thousands of Government Contracts, *PR Newswire*, New York (December 5, 2007).
9. Hussey Seating, http://www.husseyseating.com (accessed February 9, 2009).
10. "Boeing, RyanAir Agree to Order for 32 Additional 737-800s," Boeing press release, September 29, 2006, http://www.boeing.com/news/releases/2006/q3/060929a_nr.html.
11. Das Narayandas and V. Kasturi Rangan, "Building and Sustaining Buyer-Seller Relationships in Mature Industrial Markets," *Journal of Marketing* (July 2004): 63.
12. Ellen Byron, "Aiming to Clean Up, P&G Courts Business Customers," *The Wall Street Journal*, January 26, 2007, B1, http://online.wsj.com.
13. Alex R. Zablah, Wesley J. Johnston, and Danny N. Bellenger, "Transforming Partner Relationships Through Technological Innovation," *Journal of Business & Industrial Marketing* 20 (August 2005): 355–363.
14. Cindy Claycomb and Gary L. Frankwick, "Dynamics of Buyers' Perceived Costs during a Relationship Development Process: An Empirical Assessment," *Journal of Business Research* 58 (2005): 1662–1671.
15. Leonidas C. Leonidou, "Industrial Buyers' Influence Strategies: Buying Situation Differences," *Journal of Business & Industrial Marketing* 20 (January 2005): 33–42.
16. Frederick E. Webster, Jr., and Yoram Wind, "A Generic Model for Understanding Organizational Buyer Behavior," *Marketing Management* (Winter/Spring 1996): 52–57.
17. George S. Day and Katrina J. Bens, "Capitalizing on the Internet Opportunity," *Journal of Business & Industrial Marketing* 20 (2005): 160–168.
18. Niklas Myhr and Robert E. Spekman, "Collaborative Supply-Chain Partnerships Built upon Trust and Electronically Mediated Exchange," *Journal of Business & Industrial Marketing* 20 (2005): 179–186.
19. "Development of NAICS," U.S. Census Bureau, http://www.census.gov/epcd/www/naicsdev.htm (accessed February 9, 2009).

Feature endnotes

a. "American Airlines Partners with EPA," *New Mexico Business Weekly*, February 25, 2009, http://www.bizjournals.com/Albuquerque/stories/2009/02/23/daily37.html; Ann Keeton, "American Air Sets Plan to Show Its Green Side," *Wall Street Journal*, July 18, 2007; Tom Chesshyre, "Paper Chase: Travel News," *The Times (London)*, March 31, 2007, 22; Daniel Michaels and Susan Carey, "Airlines Feel Pressure as Pollution Fight Takes Off," *Wall Street Journal* (December 12, 2006): A6.

b. Maha Atal, "Sustaining the Dream," *BusinessWeek* (Oct. 15, 2007): 60; Kristen Gerencher, "Treadmill Desks Let Employees Feel the Burn," *Boston Globe*, Mar. 26, 2006, n.p.; Reena Jana, "Exercise More Than Just Your Options," *BusinessWeek* (Oct. 29, 2007): 24; "Making the Tough Call," *Inc.* (Nov. 2007): 36+.

c. Jena McGregor, "Costco's Artful Discounts," *BusinessWeek,* (October 20, 2008): 58; Jim Wyss, "Local Vendors Audition for Retail Giant," *Miami Herald,* May 30, 2008, http://www.herald.com.

Chapter 8

1. Tom Wright, "Poorer Nations Go Online on Cellphones," *The Wall Street Journal*, December 5, 2008, B4; Shannon Shinn, "Dial M for Mobile," *BizEd* (January/February 2009): 32–39; Ashifi Gogo, "Ghanian Innovation on the Global Scene," *My Joy Online*, February 5, 2009, http://news.myjoyonline.com/technology/200902/25956.asp (accessed February 10, 2009); Irwin Greenstein, "5.3 Billion Reasons to Like Emerging Markets," *Contrarian Profits*, January 21, 2009, http://www.contrarianprofits.com/articles/53-billion-reasons-to-like-emerging-markets/11929 (accessed February 10, 2009).
2. "Visa Consolidates Global Image with New Ads, Marketing Campaign," *ISO & Agent* (March 5, 2009): 5.
3. "About Us," Wal-Mart Stores, Inc., http://walmartstores.com/AboutUs/ (accessed April 2, 2009); "2008 Annual Report," Starbucks.com, http://media.corporate-ir.net/media_files/irol/99/99518/AR2008.pdf (accessed April 1, 2009).
4. "The U.S. Commercial Service," Export.gov, http://www.export.gov/comm_svc/about_us/about_home.html (accessed January 5, 2007).
5. Gary A. Knight and S. Tamer Cavusgil, "Innovation, Organizational Capabilities, and the Born-Global Firm," *Journal of International Business Studies* (March 2004): 124–141.
6. "In Depth: Unilever," *BusinessWeek* (December 22, 2008): 47.
7. Gordon Fairclough and Janet Adamy, "Sex, Skin, Fireworks, Licked Fingers—It's a Quarter Pounder Ad in China," *The Wall Street Journal,* September 21, 2006, B1, http://online.wsj.com; "What Made McDonald's Click in India?" Hindustan Times.com, September 7, 2006, http://content.msn.co.in/Lifestyle/Work/LifeStyleHT_070906_1906.htm.
8. Matthew Futterman, "Football Tries a New Play to Score Overseas," *The Wall Street Journal* (October 9, 2008): B5.
9. Anton Piësch, "Speaking in Tongues," *Inc.* (June 2003): 50.
10. "Product Pitfalls Proliferate in Global Cultural Maze," *The Wall Street Journal* (May 14, 2001): B11.
11. George Balabanis and Adamantios Diamantopoulos, "Domestic Country Bias, Country-of-Origin Effects, and Consumer Ethnocentrism: A Multidimensional Unfolding Approach," *Journal of the Academy of Marketing Science* (January 2004): 80–95.
12. Ming-Huel Hsieh, Shan-Ling Pan, and Rudy Setiono, "Product-, Corporate-, and Country-Image Dimensions and Purchase Behavior: A Multicountry Analysis," *Journal of the Academy of Marketing Science* (July 2004): 251–270.
13. Janet Adamy, "Eyeing a Billion Tea Drinkers, Starbucks Pours It On in China," *The Wall Street Journal* (November 29, 2006): A1, http://online.wsj.com.
14. "Stumble or Fall?," *The Economist* (January 10, 2009): 63; Bob Davis, "U.S. to Push for Global Stimulus," *The Wall Street Journal* (March 9, 2009): A1.
15. Richard Wolf, "Obama, G-20 Unite on Recovery Package," *USA Today*, April 2, 2009, http://www.usatoday.com/news/world/2009-04-02-g20-summit_N.htm (accessed April 7, 2009).
16. Frederick Balfour, "Prying Open Asian Wallets," *BusinessWeek* (March 30, 2009): 77.
17. CIA, *World Factbook*, https://www.cia.gov/library/publications/the-world-factbook/ (accessed March 31, 2009).
18. Eric Bellman, "Rural India Snaps Up Mobile Phones," *The Wall Street Journal,* February 9, 2009, http://online.wsj.com/article/SB123413407376461353.html (accessed March 30, 2009).
19. "An $8 Billion Scandal Goes a Long Way," *The Economist* (February 28, 2009): 42; David Crawford, "Tax Havens Pledge to Yield on Secrecy," *The Wall Street Journal* (March 13, 2009): A1; L. Gordon Crovitz, "Swiss Banks and the End of Privacy," *The Wall Street Journal,* March 23, 2009, http://online.wsj.com/article/SB123776401389908783.html (accessed March 28, 2009).
20. Greg Hitt, Christopher Conkey, and José de Córdoba, "Mexico Strikes Back in Trade Dispute," *The Wall Street Journal* (March 17, 2009): A1.
21. "Will the New Congress Shift Gears on Free Trade?" *The Wall Street Journal* (November 18–19, 2006): A7.
22. Ibid.
23. Scott Lilly, "Should We Be Grateful to China for Buying U.S. Treasuries?" Center for American Progress, April 1, 2009, http://www.americanprogress.org/issues/2009/04/china_report.html (accessed April 2, 2009).
24. Charles R. Taylor, George R. Franke, and Michael L. Maynard, "Attitudes Toward Direct Marketing and Its Regulation: A Comparison of the United States and Japan," *Journal of Public Policy & Marketing* (Fall 2000): 228–237.
25. Adapted from O. C. Ferrell, John Fraedrich, and Linda Ferrell, *Business Ethics: Ethical Decision Making and Cases,* 6th ed. (Boston: Houghton Mifflin, 2005), 217–221.
26. "Counterfeiting and Piracy," Brand Protection Alliance, http://www.brandprotectionalliance.com/news/piracy.html (accessed April 2, 2009).
27. Frederik Balfour, "Fakes!," *BusinessWeek* (Feb. 7, 2005): 54–64.
28. Stefano Ponte, Lisa Ann Richey, and Mike Baab, "Bono's Project (RED) Initiative: Corporate Social Responsibility That Solves the Problems of 'Distant Others'," *Third World Quarterly* 30, Issue 2 (March 2009): 301–317.
29. Dave Izraeli and Mark S. Schwartz, "What We Can Learn from the Federal Sentencing Guidelines for Organizational Ethics," *Journal of Business Ethics* (July 1998): 9–10.
30. Tamara Monosoff, "New Regulations Impact Toy Makers," *MSNBC.com*, March 11, 2009, http://www.msnbc.msn.com/id/29635506/ (accessed March 30, 2009).
31. "Monsanto," *BusinessWeek* (December 22, 2008): 51.
32. "This Is Systembolaget," Systembolaget, http://www.systembolaget.se/Applikationer/Knappar/InEnglish/Swedish_alcohol_re.htm (accessed January 8, 2007).
33. Eric Belman, "Tata Will Sell Inexpensive Car by Lottery," *The Wall Street Journal* (March 24, 2009): B2.
34. "Internet Usage Statistics," http://www.internetworldstats.com/stats.htm (accessed March 31, 2009).
35. Source: CIA, *World Fact Book*, http://www.cia.gov/library/publications/the-world-factbook/ (accessed March 30, 2009).
36. Edward G. Thomas, "Internet Marketing in the International Arena: A Cross-Cultural Comparison," *Journal of International Business Strategy* 8, Issue 3 (October 11, 2008): 84–98.
37. Andreas B Eisingerich and Tobias Kretschmer, "In E-Commerce, More Is More," *Harvard Business Review* (March 2008): 20–21.
38. John Kao, "Tapping the World's Innovation Hot Spots," *Harvard Business Review* 87, Issue 3 (March 2009): 109–114.
39. "Report: Mobile Phone Users Double Since 2000," CNN, December 9, 2004, http://www.cnn.com.
40. Ting Shi, "A Gas Pump for 300 Million Phones," *Business 2.0* (June 2005): 78.
41. Steve Zahnniser and Jeremy Crago, *NAFTA at 15: Building on Free Trade,* United States Department of Agriculture, March 2009, http://www.ers.usda.gov/Publications/WRS0903/WRS0903.pdf (acccssed April 5, 2009).
42. Ryan Emmot, "Drug War Hits Mexican Economy in Crisis," *Reuters,* April 3, 2009, http://www.reuters.com/article/worldNews/idUSTRE5325PG20090403 (accessed April 6, 2009).
43. Elisabeth Malkin, "NAFTA's Promise, Unfulfilled," *The New York Times,* March 23, 2009, http://www.nytimes.com/2009/03/24/business/worldbusiness/24peso.html (accessed April 5, 2009).
44. Sam Youngman and Bob Cusack, "Some Obama Promises Get Punted," *The Hill,* April 2, 2009, http://thehill.com/leading-the-news/some-obama-promises-get-punted-2009-04-02.html (accessed April 5, 2009).
45. "NAFTA Has a Record Trade Decline," Outsourced Logistics, April 1, 2009, http://outsourced-logistics.com/global_markets/news/nafta-record-declin-0401/ (accessed April 5, 2009).
46. Dave Michaels and Todd Gilman, "Pelosi Sees Mexican Truck Program's Revival as Unlikely," *The Dallas Morning News,* April 5, 2009, http://www.dallasnews.com/sharedcontent/dws/news/washington/tgillman/stories/DN-mexicantrucks_04bus.State.Edition1.124468d.html (accessed April 5, 2009).
47. "The European Union at a Glance," Europa (European Union) online, http://europa.eu.int/abc/index_en.htm# (accessed January 8, 2007).
48. Ibid.
49. Stanley Reid, with Ariane Sains, David Fairlamb, and Carol Matlack, "The Euro: How Damaging a Hit?" *BusinessWeek* (September 29, 2003): 63; "The Single Currency," CNN, http://www.cnn.com/SPECIALS/2000/eurounion/story/currency/ (accessed September 27, 2006).
50. T. R. Reid, "The New Europe," *National Geographic* (January 2002): 32–47.
51. Portal Oficial MERCOSUL/MERCOSUR, http://www.mercosur.int/msweb/ (accessed March 30, 2009).
52. Asia-Pacific Economic Cooperation, http://www.apec.org/ (accessed March 30, 2009).
53. Mina Kimes, "China's Drive into U.S. Car Market Stalls," *Fortune*, October 31, 2008, http://www.marketavenue.cn/upload/articles/ARTICLES_2024

.htm (accessed April 2, 2009); Chris Oliver, "ABD Cuts China Growth Outlook to 7% for 2009," Market Watch, March 31, 2009, http://www.marketwatch.com/news/story/adb-cuts-its-china-growth/story.aspx?guid=%7B92AAB619-06DD-40B9-A91C-B76C9157F101%7D&dist=google (accessed April 2, 2009); Keith Bradsher, "China Vies to Be World's Leader in Electric Cars," *The New York Times,* April 1, 2009, http://www.nytimes.com/2009/04/02/business/global/02electric.html?ref=global (accessed April 2, 2009).

54. Janet Adamy, "One U.S. Chain's Unlikely Goal: Pitching Chinese Food in China," *The Wall Street Journal* (October 20, 2006): A1, http://online.wsj.com.
55. Gordon Fairclough, "Dairymen Routinely Spike Milk in China," *The Wall Street Journal* (November 3, 2008): A1.
56. Stephanie N. Mehta, "Study: Dairy Scandal Taints all Chinese Brands," *Fortune*, November 12, 2008, http://money.cnn.com/2008/11/11/news/international/mehta_china.fortune/index.htm (accessed March 31, 2009).
57. "China Plans to Challenge U.S. Ban on Its Poultry," *The New York Times*, March 11, 2009, http://www.nytimes.com/2009/03/12/business/worldbusiness/12trade.html?scp=3&sq=china%20poultry&st=cse (accessed March 31, 2009).
58. Joe McDonald, "China Tries to Boost Exports, Risking Backlash," *Forbes*, http://www.forbes.com/feeds/ap/2009/03/31/ap6233013.html (accessed March 31, 2009).
59. "What Is the WTO?" World Trade Organization, http://www.wto.org/ (accessed January 8, 2007).
60. Leigh Thomas, "E.U., U.S., Canada Haul China Before WTO over Auto Parts Dispute," *Yahoo! News,* September 15, 2006, http://news.yahoo.com/s/afp/20060915/bs_afp/euuscanadachinawto_060915221834.
61. Joseph Lazaro, "WTO Predicts Worst Trade Decline in More Than 60 Years," *Daily Finance,* March 31, 2009, http://www.dailyfinance.com/2009/03/31/wto–predicts -the-worst-trade-decline-in-more-than-60-years/ (accessed March 31, 2009).
62. George Chryssochoidis and Vasilis Theoharakis, "Attainment of Competitive Advantage by the Exporter-Importer Dyad: The Role of Export Offering and Import Objectives," *Journal of Business Research* (April 2004): 329–337.
63. Vanessa O'Connell and Cheryl Lu-Lien Tan, "Designers Seek Foreign Sales," *The Wall Street Journal* (September 5, 2008): B2.
64. Gerry Khermouch, "'Whoa, Cool Shirt.' 'Yeah, It's a Pepsi,'" *BusinessWeek* (September 10, 2001): 84.
65. Farok J. Contractor and Sumit K. Kundu, "Franchising versus Company-Run Operations: Model Choice in the Global Hotel Sector," *Journal of International Marketing* (November 1997): 28–53.
66. "Tribune Outsourcing Customer Service, Cutting 250 Jobs," *USA Today,* August 28, 2006, http://www.usatoday.com/money/media/2006-08-28-tribune-cuts_x.htm.
67. J. Lynn Lunsford, "Outsourcing at Crux of Boeing Strike," *The Wall Street Journal* (September 8, 2008): B1.
68. Pankaj Ghemawat and Thomas Hout, "Tomorrow's Global Giants? Not the Usual Suspects," *Harvard Business Review* 86, Issue 11 (November 2008): 80–88.
69. Kathryn Rudie Harrigan, "Joint Ventures and Competitive Advantage," *Strategic Management Journal* (May 1988): 141–158.
70. "What We're About," NUMMI, http://www.nummi.com/co_info.html (accessed January 8, 2007).
71. Quentin Fottrell and Justin Scheck, "Dell Moving Irish Operations to Poland," *The Wall Street Journal* (January 9, 2009): B4.
72. Ronald Paul Hill and Kanwalroop Kathy Dhanda, "Globalization and Technological Advancement: Implications for Macromarketing and the Digital Divide," *Journal of Macromarketing* (December 2004): 147–155.
73. Deborah Owens, Timothy Wilkinson, and Bruce Kellor, "A Comparison of Product Attributes in a Cross-Cultural/Cross-National Context," *Marketing Management Journal* (Fall/Winter 2000): 1–11.
74. William E. Kilbourne, "Globalization and Development: An Expanded Macromarketing View," *Journal of Macromarketing* (December 2004): 122–135.
75. Anil K. Gupta and Vijay Govindarajan, "Converting Global Presence into Global Competitive Advantage," *Academy of Management Executive* (May 2001): 45–58.

Feature endnotes

a. TIER (Technology and Infrastructure for Emerging Regions), University of California at Berkeley, http://tier.cs.berkeley.edu/wiki/Wireless (accessed March 2, 2009); *Community Outreach*, Aravind Eye Care System, http://www.aravind.org/community/index.asp (accessed March 2, 2009).
b. BraBaby, http://www.brababy.com/ (accessed March 30, 2009); Jonathan Cheng, "A Small Firm Takes On Chinese Pirates," *The Wall Street Journal,* July 5, 2007, http://online.wsj.com/article/SB118359376477257609.html?mod=djemITP# (accessed March 30, 2009).
c. "Study: Dairy Scandal Taints All Chinese Brands," Stephanie N. Mehta, CNNMoney.com, November 11, 2008, http:/money.cnn.com/2008/11/11/news/international/Mehta_china.fortune/index.htm?postversion=2008111111 (accessed February 16, 2009); "Chinese Brands and the Financial Crisis: A Golden Opportunity?," Tom Doctoroff, *The Huffington Post,* February 9, 2009, http://www.huffingtonpost.com/tom-doctoroff/chinese-brands-and-the-fi_b_165435.html (accessed February 16, 2009); "The State of China's Brand Landscape in 2009: FAQs," Tom Doctoroff, *The Huffington Post*, October 26, 2008, http://www.huffingtonpost.com/tom-doctoroff/the -state-of-chinas-brand_b_138021.html (accessed February 16, 2009); "Made in China 2008: The Challenge for Chinese Brands Going Global," Interbrand, http://www.interbrand.com/images/studies/Made_in_China_2008.pdf (accessed February 16, 2009); Haier, http://www.haier.com/abouthaier/corporateprofile/index.asp (accessed February 16, 2009).

Chapter 9

1. David Kushner, "The Webkinz Effect," *Wired* (November 2008): 38; "Move Over, Beanie Babies, Webkinz Are Coming to a Store—and Virtual World—Near You," *Knowledge@Wharton,* September 19, 2007, http://knowledge.wharton.upenn.edu/article.cf?articleid=1805#; Bob Tedeschi, "Fuzzy Critters with High Prices Offer Lessons in New Concepts," *New York Times* (March 26, 2007): C4.
2. "Netflix Stock Sinks, Blockbuster Booms," *BusinessWeek Online*, January 2007, http://www.businessweek.com.
3. Steve Hargreaves, "Calming Ethanol-Crazed Corn Prices," *CNNMoney*, January 30, 2007, http://money.cnn.com/.
4. Ellen Byron, "Aiming to Clean Up, P&G Courts Business Customers," *The Wall Street Journal*, January 26, 2007, http://online.wsj.com.
5. Barry Janoff, "Reebock Sees Dollars, Scents in New Kool-Aid Line," *Brandweek*, January 29, 2009, http://www.brandweek.com/bw/news/apparelretail/article_display.jsp?vnu_content_id=1003703357.
6. Michael D. Johnson, Andreas Herrmann, and Frank Huber, "Evolution of Loyalty Intentions," *Journal of Marketing* 70 (April 2006), http://www.marketingpower.com.
7. OC Ferrell and Michael Heartline, *Marketing Strategy* (Mason, OH: South-Western, 2008), 172–173.
8. Dennis K. Berman and Ellen Byron, "P&G Sells Sure Deodorant Label to Private Firm Innovative Brands," *The Wall Street Journal* (September 26, 2006): B2, http://online.wsj.com.
9. Adapted from Everett M. Rogers, *Diffusion of Innovations* (New York: Macmillan, 1962): 81–86.
10. Ibid., 247–250.
11. "Dictionary of Marketing Terms," American Marketing Association, http://www.marketingpower.com/_layouts/Dictionary.aspx (accessed February 10, 2009).
12. Warren Church, "Investment in Brand Pays Large Dividends," *Marketing News* (November 15, 2006): 21.
13. Bethany McLean, "Classic Rock," *Fortune* (November 12, 2007): 35–40.
14. U.S. Bureau of the Census, *Statistical Abstract of the United States, 2009* (Washington, DC: U.S. Government Printing Office, 2008): 748.
15. C. D. Simms and P. Trott, "The Perception of the BMW Mini Brand: The Importance of Historical Associations and the Development of a Model," *Journal of Product & Brand Management* 15 (2006): 228–238.
16. Douglas B. Holt, *How Brands Become Icons: The Principles of Cultural Branding* (Boston: Harvard Business School Press, 2004).
17. Nigel Hollis, "Branding Unmasked," *Marketing Research* (Fall 2005): 24–29.
18. David A. Aaker, *Managing Brand Equity: Capitalizing on the Value of a Brand Name* (New York: Free Press, 1991): 16–17.
19. Don E. Schultz, "The Loyalty Paradox," *Marketing Management* (September/October 2005): 10–11.
20. "Store Brands Achieving New Heights of Consumer Popularity and Growth," Private Label Manufacturer's Association, http://plma.com/storeBrands/sbt08.html (accessed March 27, 2009).
21. Chiranjeev S. Kohli, Katrin R. Harich, and Lance Leuthesser, "Creating Brand Identity: A Study of Evaluation of New Brand Names," *Journal of Business Research* 58 (2005): 1506–1515.
22. Allison Fass, "Animal House," *Forbes* (February 12, 2007): 72–75.
23. Dorothy Cohen, "Trademark Strategy," *Journal of Marketing* (January 1986): 63.
24. Chiranjeev Kohli and Rajheesh Suri, "Brand Names That Work: A Study of the Effectiveness of Different Brand Names," *Marketing Management Journal* (Fall/Winter 2000): 112–120.
25. U.S. Trademark Association, "Trademark Stylesheet," no. 1A, n.d.

26. Dan Weeks, "Bacardi to Defend 'Vigorously' in Havana Club Lawsuit," *Caribbean Net News*, August 17, 2006, http://www.caribbeannetnews.com/cgi-script/csArticles/articles/000028/002823.htm.
27. Dorothy Cohen, "Trademark Strategy Revisited," *Journal of Marketing* (July 1991): 46–59.
28. "Kohl's Inks Exclusive Deal for Tony Hawk Footwear," *Los Angeles Business*, January 29, 2007, http://losangeles.bizjournals.com/losangeles/stories/2007/01/29/daily38.html.
29. Thomas J. Madden, Kelly Hewett, and Martin S. Roth, "Managing Images in Different Cultures: A Cross-National Study of Color Meanings and Preferences," *Journal of International Marketing* (Winter 2000): 90.
30. "Will Healthy Options = Healthy Sales?" *Packaging Digest* (July 2007): 28–33.
31. Joel Dresang, "Making Bacon Pop," *Milwaukee Journal-Sentinel*, November 17, 2007, http://www.jsonline.com/story/index.aspx?id=687166.
32. Valerie Folkes and Shashi Matta, "The Effect of Package Shape on Consumers' Judgment of Product Volume: Attention as a Mental Contaminant," *Journal of Consumer Research* (September 2004): 390.
33. "Looking for That Label," *Prepared Foods* (September 2006): 38.
34. Federal Trade Commission, http://www.ftc.gov (accessed March 25, 2009).

Feature endnotes

a. Cirque du Soleil, http://www.cirquedusoleil.com (accessed February 27, 2009); Douglas Belkin, "Talent Scouts for Cirque du Soleil Walk a Tightrope," *The Wall Street Journal* (Sept. 8, 2007): A1; Forrest Glenn Spencer, "It's One Big Circus," *Information Outlook* (Oct. 2007): 22–23.
b. Sarah Fister Gale, "How to Get Green Goods Flying Off the Shelves," *Green Biz*, March 2, 2009, http://www.greenbiz.com/feature/2009/03/02/how-get-green-goods-flying-off-shelves; Clifford Krauss, "Can They Really Call the Chainsaw Eco-Friendly?" *New York Times* (June 25, 2007): A1; Bruce Geiselman, "Aisle 7 for Eco Options," *Waste News* (April 30, 2007): 35; "Home Depot Hammers Out Eco Options ID Program," *Brandweek* (April 23, 2007): 5; http://www.homedepot.com.
c. Maggie Galehouse, "Going Green: Guitar Makers Are Strumming a New Tune," *Houston Chronicle* (January 23, 2009): 1; Greg Reitz, "Hotels Look to LEED to Boost Green Cred," *Green Lodging News*, February 6, 2009, http://greenerbuildings.com/news/2009/02/06/hotels-leed; Melissa Korn, "Cleaning Companies Go Green," *Wall Street Journal*, October 15, 2008, http://www.wsj.com; Randy Hofbauer, "On-product Labels Detail Green Claims," *Food & Beverage Packaging* (November 2008): 36; "USPS Goes LEED with Processing and Distribution Centers," *Building Design & Construction* (January 1, 2009): 14.

Chapter 10

1. Emily Lambert, "Cheap Thrills," *Forbes* (February 16, 2009): 72; Merlin Shrugs Off Gloom with Magical Results," *Leisure Report* (August 2008): 4; Penni Crabtree, "Legoland to Grow Again," *San Diego Union-Tribune*, November 7, 2007, http://www.signonsandiego.com; "Roll Up, Roll Up," *The Economist* (July 7, 2007): 66; "Merlin Outlines Three Key Reasons Behind Its Gardaland Purchase," *Leisure Report* (December 2006): 10.
2. Vanessa L. Facenda, "In Search of More Growth, P&G's Febreze Hits the Road," *BrandWeek*, August 6, 2007, http://www.brandweek.com.
3. Maria Sääksjärvi and Minuttu Lampinen, "Consumer Perceived Risk in Successive Product Generations," *European Journal of Innovation Management* 8 (June 2005): 145–156.
4. "Continental Introduces Five New Truck Tires at Mid-America Trucking Show," *PR Newswire*, March 19, 2009.
5. Arik Hesseldahl, "The Paperless Map Is the Killer App," *BusinessWeek* (November 26, 2007): 71–72.
6. Kate Macarthur, "Coke, Nestlé Offer a Workout in a Can," *Advertising Age* (October 16, 2006): 8.
7. "Making Headway with Helmets," *BusinessWeek* (January 15, 2007): 75.
8. Lee G. Cooper, "Strategic Marketing Planning for Radically New Products," *Journal of Marketing* (January 2000): 1–16.
9. Janet Adamy, "For McDonald's It's a Wrap," *The Wall Street Journal*, January 30, 2007, B1, http://online.wsj.com.
10. A. G. Lafley, "Proctor and Gamble," *BusinessWeek* (December 19, 2005): 62.
11. Stephen J. Carson, "When to Give Up Control of Outsourced New Product Development," *Journal of Marketing* 71 (January 2007): 49–66.
12. Dennis A. Pitta and Danielle Fowler, "Online Consumer Communities and Their Value to New Product Developers," *Journal of Product & Brand Management* 14 (2005): 283–291.
13. Deborah Ball, "As Chocolate Sags, Cadbury Gambles on a Piece of Gum," *The Wall Street Journal*, January 12, 2006, A1, http://online.wsj.com.
14. Jack Neff, "P&G Begins Slow Test of Probiotic Supplements," *Advertising Age*, December 12, 2007, http://www.adage.com.
15. John Reid Blackwell, "Philip Morris Joins SNUS Venture," *McClatchy-Tribune Business News*, February 4, 2009.
16. Alexander E. Reppel, Isabelle Szmigin, and Thorsten Gruber, "The iPod Phenomenon: Identifying a Market Leaders's Secrets through Qualitative Marketing Research," *Journal of Product & Brand Management* 15 (2006): 239–249.
17. Adapted from Michael Levy and Barton A. Weitz, *Retailing Management* (Burr Ridge, IL: Irwin/McGraw-Hill, 2001), 585.
18. Sidra Durst, "Shoe In," *Business 2.0 Magazine*, January 15, 2007, http://money.cnn.com/magazines/business2/business2_archive/2006/12/01/8394993/index.htm.
19. Steve Miller, "Ford Rises to a (Driving) Challenge," *BrandWeek*, January 5, 2007, http://www.brandweek.com/bw/news/autos/article_display.jsp?vnu_content_id=1003528228.
20. Stephanie Kang and Suzanne Vranica, "Condé Nast to Shutter House & Garden Magazine," *The Wall Street Journal* (November 6, 2007): B1, B10.
21. "Nikon to Stop Making Most Film Cameras," *Associated Press*, via http://www.msnbc.msn.com/id/10835599/.
22. Michelle Conlin, "Call Centers in the Rec Room," *BusinessWeek*, January 23, 2006, http://www.businessweek.com.
23. The information in this section is based on K. Douglass Hoffman and John E. G. Bateson, *Essentials of Services Marketing* (Mason, OH: South-Western, 2001); and Valarie A. Zeithaml, A. Parasuraman, and Leonard L. Berry, *Delivering Quality Service: Balancing Customer Perceptions* (New York: Free Press, 1990).
24. Don E. Schultz, "Lost in Transition," *Marketing Management* (March/April 2007): 10–11.
25. Jeremy J. Sierra and Shaun McQuitty, "Service Providers and Customers: Social Exchange Theory and Service Loyalty," *Journal of Services Marketing* 19 (October 2005): 392–400.
26. J. Paul Peter and James H. Donnelly, *A Preface to Marketing Management* (Burr Ridge, IL: Irwin/McGraw-Hill, 2003), 212.
27. Sabin Im, Charlotte H. Mason, and Mark B. Houston, "Does Innate Consumer Innovativeness Relate to New Product/Service Adoption Behavior? The Intervening Role of Social Learning via Vicarious Innovativeness," *Journal of the Academy of Marketing Science* 35 (2007): 63–75.
28. Sarah Nassauer, "Eliminating the Human Element," *The Wall Street Journal*, November 14, 2006, D7, http://online.wsj.com.
29. Robert Moore, Melissa L. Moore, and Michael Capella, "The Impact of Customer-to-Customer Interaction in a High Personal Contact Service Setting," *Journal of Services Marketing* 19 (July 2005): 482–491.
30. Michael D. Hartline and O. C. Ferrell, "Service Quality Implementation: The Effects of Organization and Managerial Actions of Customer Contact Employee Behavior," *Marketing Science Institute Report*, no. 93–122 (Cambridge, MA: Marketing Science Institute, 1993).
31. Raymond P. Fisk, Stephen J. Grove, and Joby John, *Interactive Services Marketing* (Boston: Houghton Mifflin, 2003), 91.
32. Ahmed Taher and Hanan El Basha, "Hetergeneity of Consumer Demand: Opportunities for Pricing of Services," *Journal of Product & Brand Management* 15 (2006): 331–340.
33. Laura Petrecca, "More Marketers Target Baby Boomers' Eyes, Wallets," *USA Today*, February 25, 2007, http://www.usatoday.com.
34. International Smart Tan Network Educational Institute, http://saloncertification.com/ (accessed March 25, 2009).
35. Pavel Strach and André M. Everett, "Brand Corrosion: Mass-Marketing's Threat to Luxury Automobile Brands after Merger and Acquisition," *Journal of Product & Brand Management* 15 (2006): 106–120.

Feature endnotes

a. Spanx, http://www.spanx.com (accessed Feb. 18, 2009); Meredith Bryan, "Spanx Me, Baby!," *The New York Observer*, Dec. 4, 2007, http://www.observer.com/2007/spanx-me-baby?page=1.
b. Claire Atkinson, "Carol's Daughter: Steve Stoute," *Advertising Age* (November 17, 2008): S14; "2008 Social Capitalist Awards: Profits with Purpose: New Leaf Paper," *Fast Company*, January 2008, http://www.fastcompany.com; Kemi Osukoya, "Small Firms See Big Potential in Going Green," *Wall Street Journal*, June 12, 2007, B4; Vanessa L. Facenda, "A Guide to the Small Green Health and Beauty Brands: Marketers Once Considered Niche Are Getting Exposure, Distribution in Mainstream Venues," *Brandweek* (August 6, 2007): 16; Julie Naughton, "At Carol's Daughter, the Family Continues to Grow," *WWD* (July 27, 2007): 5.
c. Sean Ludwig, "10 Corporate Accounts Worth Following," PCMag.com, February 28, 2009, http://www.pcmag.com/article2/0,2817,2341886,00.asp; Sarah Halzack, "Marketing Moves to the Blogosphere," *Washington Post* (August 25, 2008): D1; "Corporate Blogging: Conversation Starter," *New Media Age* (July 17, 2008): 19; Beth Snyder Bulik, "Does Your Company Need a Chief Blogger?" *Advertising Age* (April 14, 2008): 24; "A Peek into Corporate Blogging," *Advertising Age* (April 15, 2008): 24.

Chapter 11

1. Rob Pegoraro, "Amazon's Sequel to a Best-Selling Thriller," *Washington Post*, February 10, 2009, D1; Brad Stone, "Profit Rises at Amazon as Shoppers Seek Deals," *New York Times* (January 30, 2009): B3; Mylene Mangalindan, "Amazon's Latest Thriller: Growth," *Wall Street Journal* (October 24, 2007): A3; Brad Stone, "Amazon Says Profit Jumped in Quarter," *New York Times* (October 24, 2007): C3; Bob Tedeschi, "Nothing Says 'Buy' Like 'Free Shipping,'" *New York Times* (October 8, 2007): C8.
2. Rajneesh Suri and Kent B. Monroe, "The Effects of Time Constraints on Consumers' Judgments of Prices and Products," *Journal of Consumer Research* (June 2003): 92+.
3. "Hewlett-Packard," Professional Pricing Society, case study, http://members.pricingsociety.com/articles/not_free.pdf (accessed April 1, 2009).
4. Janet Adamy, "Corporate News: Starbucks—Coffee Empire Seeks to Seem Less Expensive in Recession," *Wall Street Journal* (February 9, 2009): B3.
5. David Krechevsky, "Target Ups Ante in Drug War," *Republican American*, November 23, 2006; "Wal-Mart Tests in Florida its $4 Generic-Drug Plan," *The Wall Street Journal*, September 21, 2006, http://online.wsj.com.
6. Lauren Young, "Candy's Getting Dandy," *BusinessWeek* (February 13, 2006): 88–89.
7. Heather Caliendo, "Tulsa-Based Fine Airport Parking Upgrades with Technology," *The (Oklahoma City) Journal Record*, March 16, 2009, www.journalrecord.com.
8. "Dictionary of Marketing Terms," American Marketing Association, http://www.marketingpower.com/_layouts/Dictionary.aspx (accessed April 1, 2009).
9. Ibid.
10. Elwin Green, "Gas Prices Aren't Slowing U.S. Motorists," *Pittsburgh Post-Gazette*, November 25, 2007, http://www.post-gazette.com/pg/07329/836591-28.stm.
11. Nicole C. Wong, "Sun Turning Around to See Profits Ahead," *The Mercury News*, February 6, 2007, http://www.siliconvalley.com/sunmicrosystems/ci_5171593.
12. Linda Halstad-Acharya, "Stuck in a Sea of Surcharges: Fuel Prices Abate, But the Add-Ons Keep Coming On," *Billings Gazette*, January 27, 2007, http://www.billingsgazette.net/articles/2007/01/27/news/local/25-stuck.txt.
13. Cecilie Rohwedder, Aaron O. Patrick, and Timothy W. Martin, "Grocer Battles Unilever on Pricing," *Wall Street Journal*, (February 11, 2009): B1.
14. Russell S. Winer, *Pricing* (Cambridge, MA: Marketing Science Institute, 2005), 20.
15. Manoj Thomas and Geeta Menon, "Internal Reference Prices and Price Expectations," *Journal of Marketing Research* XLIV (August 2007).
16. Donald Lichtenstein, Nancy M. Ridgway, and Richard G. Netemeyer, "Price Perceptions and Consumer Shopping Behavior: A Field Study," *Journal of Marketing Research* (May 1993): 234–235.
17. Gerald E. Smith and Thomas T. Nagle, "A Question of Value," *Marketing Management* (July/August 2005): 39–40.
18. Lichtenstein, Ridgway, and Netemeyer, "Price Perceptions and Consumer Shopping Behavior: A Field Study."
19. "Where Have All the Tightwads Gone?" *BusinessWeek* (October 15, 2007): 16.
20. Lichtenstein, Ridgway, and Netemeyer, "Price Perceptions and Consumer Shopping Behavior: A Field Study."
21. "Coty Inc. and HSN Announce New Partnership," HSN, Press Release, April 4, 2008, www.hsni.com/releasedetail.cfm?ReleaseID=327241.
22. Marc Levy, "Europe Studies Candy Prices of Hershey, Mars," *USA Today*, February 19, 2008, http://www.usatoday.com/money/industries/food/2008-02-19-candy-price-fixing_N.htm.

Feature endnotes

a. Arik Hesseldahl, "The iPhone Eyes Blackberry's Turf," *BusinessWeek* (June 23, 2008): 38; Andrea Chalupa, "Extravagant Electronics," *Portfolio.com*, Dec. 14, 2007, http://www.portfolio.com; "Marketing Society Awards for Excellence: International Brand Development," *Marketing* (June 20, 2007): 12; "Samsung Accused of Heavy Cost-Cutting," *UPI NewsTrack* (June 5, 2007): n.p.; "Samsung and LG Hear the Call for Low-End Mobiles," *Financial Times* (Mar. 26, 2007): 21: "Vertu Rings Till for British-Made Luxury Goods," PC Magazine Online, July 16, 2007, http://www.pcmag.com; John Walko, "Q3 Cell Phone Stats," *Electronic Engineering Times* (Dec. 3, 2007): 8; Interview with salesman at Exquisite Timepieces, Naples, FL, March 12, 2009.

b. Kim Yeager, "The Trend: Green and Colorful," *Star Tribune (Minneapolis-St. Paul)*, February 24, 2009, http://www.startribune.com/lifestyle/homegarden/40222152.html?elr=KArks7PYDiaK7DUHPYDiaK7DUiD3aPc:_Yyc:aUUr; Theresa Sullivan Barger, "Paint Free of Fumes, Pollution," *Hartford Courant* (June 29, 2007): H1; Amanda Schupak, "An Inconvenient Paint," *Forbes* (March 26, 2007): 70; Jim Edwards, "Dowdy Paint Gets Polish—and the Price Doubles," *Brandweek* (January 29, 2007): 12.

c. Mary Hance, "Peruse These Sites and Never Again Pay Full Price," *Tennessean*, March 8, 2009, http://www.tennessean.com; Mary Cowlett, "Online: Compare and Contrast," *Marketing* (January 28, 2009): 28; "Back-to-School Spending Slows as Shoppers Seek Bargains Online," *InformationWeek*, August 28, 2008, http://www.informationweek.com.

Chapter 12

1. Philip Elmer-DeWitt, "iPhone Sales Grew 245% in 2008—Gartner," *Fortune*, March 12, 2009, http://apple20.blogs.fortune.cnn.com/2009/03/12/iphone-sales-grew-245-in-2008-gartner; Mary Ellen Lloyd and Ben Chamy, "Wal-Mart to Sell iPhone Near Full Price," *Wall Street Journal* (December 27, 2008): B5; Alice Z. Cuneo, "iPhone: Steve Jobs," *Advertising Age* (November 12, 2007): S13; Katie Hafner and Brad Stone, "iPhone Owners Crying Foul over Price Cut" (September 7, 2007): C1, C7; Josh Krist, "The Painful Cost of First-on-the-Block Bragging Rights," *PC World* (December 2007): 53; Alex Markels, "Apple's Mac Sales Are Surging," *U.S. News & World Report* (September 26, 2007): n.p.
2. Mara der Hovanesian and Christopher Palmeri, "That Sinking Feeling," *BusinessWeek* (October 15, 2007): 32–36.
3. William C. Symonds and Robert Bernes, "Gillette's New Edge," *BusinessWeek Online*, February 6, 2006.
4. "New Bentley Pricing," Automotive.com, http://www.automotive.com/new-cars/pricing/01/Bentley/index.html (accessed February 21, 2009).
5. Robert J. Frank, Jeffrey P. George, and Laxman Narasimhan, "When Your Competitor Delivers More for Less," *McKinsey Quarterly*, http://www.mckinseyquarterly.com.
6. George J. Avlonitis and Kostis A. Indounas, "Pricing Objectives and Pricing Methods in the Services Sector," *Journal of Services Marketing* 19 (January 2005): 45–47.
7. "Five Actions CPOs Should Take Now to Address an Economic Downturn," *Marketwire*, April 23, 2008, http://www.marketwire.com/press-release/Emptoris-847780.html.
8. Marla Royne Stafford and Thomas F. Stafford, "The Effectiveness of Tensile Pricing Tactics in the Advertising of Services," *The Journal of Advertising* (Summer 2000): 45–46.
9. Dan Gallagher, "iPhone Price Raises Issue for Apple," *The Seattle Times*, January 15, 2007, http://seattletimes.nwsource.com/html/businesstechnology/2003525467_btapplepricing15.html.
10. Lee Gomes, "A Peek under PlayStation 3's Hood Shows Sony Is Selling at a Loss," *The Wall Street Journal*, November 21, 2006, http://online.wsj.com.
11. Mark Phelan, "$100,000 Corvette Supercar Aims to Best Exotic Rivals," *USA Today*, December 20, 2007, http://usatoday.com/money/autos/2007-12-20-corvette-zr1_N.htm.
12. Kris Hudson, "Competing Retailers Dispute Wal-Mart Trademark Request," *The Wall Street Journal*, November 7, 2006, http://online.wsj.com.
13. Christine Harris and Jeffery Bray, "Price Endings and Consumer Segmentation," *Journal of Product & Brand Management* 16 (March 2007): 200–205.
14. Rita Rubin, "Placebo Tests 'Costlier is Better' Notion," *USA Today*, March 4, 2008, http://www.usatoday.com/news/health/2008-03-04-placebo- effect_N.htm.
15. "Best Ideas," *BusinessWeek* (December 19, 2005): 76–77.

Feature endnotes

a. Lisa Rein, "Maryland Couple Basks in Savings from a 19-Year-Old Solar System," *Washington Post* (March 12, 2009): B1; "Green as Houses: Environmentalism and Building," *The Economist* (September 15, 2007): 42; Christopher Palmeri, "Green Homes: The Price Still Isn't Right," *BusinessWeek* (February 12, 2007): 67.

b. Gwendolyn Bounds, "TerraCycle Fashions a New Life for Old Wrappers," *The Wall Street Journal* (July 1, 2008): B5; Arden Dale, "Green Products Gain from New Price Equation," *The Wall Street Journal* (June 24, 2008): B7; Christopher Shulgan, "The Worm Wrangler," *Maclean's* (June 4, 2007): 34+; http://www.terracycle.net (accessed Feb. 27, 2009).

c. Elliot Zweibach, "Supervalu Accelerates EDLP," *Supermarket News* (November 24, 2008): n.p.; Mark Hamstra, "Making EDLP Credible," *Supermarket News* (January 14, 2008): n.p.

Chapter 13

1. "Charles Weiss, Blue Bell Creameries," *Kansas City Star*, February 23, 2009, http://www.kansascity.com/771/story/1050032.html; "Blue Bell Creameries' Sweet Success: Ice Cream Manufacturer Improves Inventory Visibility & Lot Control with ClearOrbit," *Business Wire*, July 11, 2007, http://www.allbusiness.com/services/business-services/4520976-1.html; "Blue Bell Creameries L.P.," http://www.referenceforbusiness.com/history2/63/Blue-Bell-Creameries-L-P.html; Amanda Loudin, "Blue Bell Creameries Licks Its Storage Shortage," *Inbound Logistics* (October 2007): 77, 79.
2. Kenneth Karel Boyer, Markham T. Frolich, and G. Tomas, *Extending the Supply Chain* (New York: AMACOM, 2005).
3. Ricky W. Griffin, *Principles of Management* (Boston: Houghton Mifflin, 2007), 400.
4. Lisa Harrington, "Getting Service Parts Logistics Up to Speed," *Inbound Logistics*, November 2006, http://www.inboundlogistics.com/articles/features/1106_feature02.shtml.

5. *The Supply Chain Management Spending Report, 2007-2008* (AMR Research).
6. Soonhong Min, John Mentzer, and Robert T. Ladd, "A Market Orientation in Supply Chain Management," *Journal of the Academy of Marketing Science* 35 (2007): 507–522.
7. Anthony J. Dukes, Esther Gal-Or, and Kannan Srinivasan, "Channel Bargaining with Retailer Asymmetry," *Journal of Marketing Research* 43 (February 2006).
8. W.W. Grainger, http://www.hoovers.com (accessed January 28, 2009).
9. "Ocean Spray and PepsiCo Form Strategic Alliance," Ocean Spray, press release, July 13, 2006, http://www.oceanspray.com/news/pr/pressrelease104.aspx.
10. Leo Aspinwall, "The Marketing Characteristics of Goods," in *Four Marketing Theories* (Boulder, CO: University of Colorado Press, 1961), 27–32.
11. Wroe Alderson, *Dynamic Marketing Behavior* (Homewood, IL: Irwin, 1965), 239.
12. Andrew Martin, "The Package May Say Healthy, but This Grocer Begs to Differ," *The New York Times*, November 6, 2006, http://www.nytimes.com.
13. Scott Kilman, "Smithfield to Buy Hog Farmer Premium Standard," *The Wall Street Journal*, September 19, 2006, A12, http://online.wsj.com.
14. Hans Greimel, "Japan Tobacco Buying Gallaher for $14.7B," *BusinessWeek Online*, December 15, 2006, http://www.businessweek.com/; Andrew Morse and Jason Singer, "Japan Returns to Global Stage as an Acquirer," *The Wall Street Journal*, December 16, 2006, A1, http://online.wsj.com.
15. Pete Engardio, with Michael Arndt and Dean Foust, "The Future of Outsourcing," *BusinessWeek* (January 30, 2006): 50–58.
16. Vicki O'Meara, "Take a Deep Breath Before Diving into Global Outsourcing," *Inbound Logistics* (September 2007): 36.
17. Lee Pender, "The Basic Links of SCM," *CIO*, http://www.itworld.com/CIO010205basic (accessed February 25, 2009).
18. "RedTail Solutions Announces Three New Modules for Its Managed EDI Service for Microsoft Dynamics GP," *Business Wire*, March 9, 2009, via http://www.supplychainmarket.com/article.mvc/RedTail-Solutions-Announces-Three -New-Modules-0001?VNETCOOKIE=NO.
19. Claire Swedberg, "Daisy Brand Benefits from RFID Analytics," *RFIDJournal*, January 18, 2008, http://www.rfidjournal.com/article/articleview/3860/1/1/.
20. "RFID Eyeing Bright Future," *Inbound Logistics* (September 2007): 25–26.
21. Amanda Loudin, "Giving Voice to Warehouse Productivity," *Inbound Logistics* (November 2006): 81–83.
22. Anne T. Coughlan, Erin Anderson, Louis W. Stern, and Adel I. El-Ansary, *Marketing Channels* (Upper Saddle River, NJ: Prentice-Hall, 2006), 510.
23. Merrill Douglas, "Taking an Eagle's-Eye View," *Inbound Logistics* (July 2007): 20–22.
24. Accuship, http://www.accuship.com/ (accessed April 8, 2009).
25. Anne T. Coughlan, Erin Anderson, Louis W. Stern, and Adel I. El-Ansary, *Marketing Channels* (Upper Saddle River, NJ: Prentice-Hall, 2006).

Feature endnotes

a. Martin LaMonica, "Microwind Turbines a Tough Sell in Massachusetts," *Cnet News*, March 17, 2009, http://news.cnet.com/8301-11128_3-10196182-54 .html; Jennifer Alsever, "Wind Power the Home Edition," *Business 2.0* (January/February 2007); Southwest Windpower, http://www.windenergy.com/index_wind.htm, "Skystream 3.7," Southwest Windpower, http://www .skystreamenergy.com/skystream/product-info; Skystream 3.7 factsheet, Southwest Windpower, http://www.skystreamenergy.com/documents/datasheets/skystrea_%203.7t_datasheet.pdf.

b. "The World's Billionaires: #10 Amancio Ortega," *Forbes*, March 11, 2009, http://www.forbes.com/lists/2009/10/billionaires-2009-richest-people_Amancio-Ortega_9PLV.html; Kerry Capell, "Zara Thrives by Breaking All the Rules," *BusinessWeek* (October 20, 2008): 66; Christina Passariello, "Logistics Are in Vogue with Designers," *Wall Street Journal* (June 27, 2008): B1.

c. Lillian Kafka, "For Rail-Sent Fries, Supersized Benefits," MHW Group, white paper, Nov. 1, 2006, http://www.mhwgroup.com/Documentation/Manassas%20Rail%20Article.pdf; Amanda Loudin, "Freezing Transport Costs in Their Tracks," *Inbound Logistics*, Jan. 27, 2007, 251–254, http://www .inboundlogistics.com/articles/casebook/casebook0107.shtml; http://www .reyesholdings.com/martin_brower.html (accessed March 3, 2009).

Chapter 14

1. Mike Duff, "Target Luring Customers to Discount Stores with Meat, Produce, Bakery," Bnet Retail, February 24, 2009, http://industry.bnet.com/retail/1000699/target-luring-customers-to-discount-stores-with-meat -produce-bakery; "Target Will Slow Expansion," *MMR* (September 8, 2008): 1; "Target Adds 43 Units to Store Base," *MMR* (August 11, 2008): 2; Sharon Edelson, "On and Off the Mark: Wal-Mart Finding Way with Target in Sights," *WWD* (January 31, 2008): 1+; Sharon Clott, "Target to Showcase Diffusion Lines in Manhattan Pop-Up Shops," *New York Magazine*, August 20, 2008, http://www.nymag.com; http://target.com.
2. U.S. Bureau of the Census, *Statistical Abstract of the United States, 2009* (Washington, DC: U.S. Government Printing Office, 2008), Table 1008.
3. Wal-Mart Fact Sheet, Hoover's Online, http://www.hoovers.com/free (accessed April 6, 2009).
4. Georgia Lee, "Value-Oriented Chains Look to Seize Moment," *Women's Wear Daily*, December 9, 2008.
5. National Association of Convenience Stores, December 2007, http://www .naicsonline.com/NACS/News/FactSheet/Pages/IndustryStoreCount.aspx (accessed April 6, 2009).
6. Katy Bachman, "Suit Your Shelf," *Brandweek* (January 19, 2009): 10.
7. Sam's Club Fact Sheet, Costco Wholesale Corporation Fact Sheet, B.J.'s Wholesale Club Fact Sheet, Hoover's Online, http://www.hoovers.com/free (accessed April 6, 2009).
8. Rachel Brown, "Tiffany's Smaller Format Opens in California," *Women's Wear Daily* (October 27, 2008).
9. Janet Adamy, "For Subway, Every Nook and Cranny on the Planet Is Possible Site for a Franchise," *The Wall Street Journal*, September 1, 2006, A11, http://online.wsj.com.
10. Mall of America, http://www.mallofamerica.com/ (accessed April 6, 2009).
11. Debra Hazel, "Wide-Open Spaces," *Chain Store Age* (November 2005): 120; "ICSC Shopping Center Definitions," International Council of Shopping Centers, http://icsc.org/srch/lib/USDefinitions.pdf (accessed March 5, 2009).
12. Stephanie Kang, "After a Slump, Payless Tries on Fashion for Size," *The Wall Street Journal*, February 10, 2007, A1, http://online.wsj.com.
13. Amy Merrick, Jeffrey A. Trachtenberg, and Ann Zimmerman, "Department Stores Fight to Save a Model That May Be Outdated," *The Wall Street Journal*, March 12, 2002, http://online.wsj.com.
14. Steve Finlay, "RFID Offers Personal Touch," *Ward's Dealer Business* 43:4 (April 2009): 46.
15. Velitchka D. Kaltcheva and Barton A. Weitz, "When Should a Retailer Create an Exciting Store Environment?" *Journal of Marketing* 70 (January 2006), http://www.marketingpower.com.
16. Mindy Fetterman and Jayne O'Donnell, "Just Browsing at the Mall? That's What You Think," *USA Today*, September 1, 2006, http://usatoday.com.
17. Anick Bosmans, "Scents and Sensibility: When Do (In)Congruent Ambient Scents Influence Product Evaluations?" *Journal of Marketing* 70 (July 2006), http://www.marketingpower.com.
18. "Direct Marketing Expenditures Account for 50% of Total Advertising Expenditures, DMA's 2007 'Power of Direct Marketing' Report Reveals," Direct Marketing Association, press release, October 16, 2007, http://www.the-dma.org/cgi/disppressrelease?article=1015.
19. "Direct Marketing an $8 Billion Auto Industry Driver," *Brandweek*, January 28, 2008, http://www.brandweek.com/bw/news/recent/_display.jsp?vnu _content_id=1003702944.
20. "Current Do Not Call Registrations," Federal Trade Commission, http://www.ftc .gov/bcp/edu/microsites/donotcall/pdfs/DNC-Registrations-10-06-2008.pdf (accessed April 6, 2009).
21. "National Do-Not-Call Registry," Federal Trade Commission, http://www.ftc.gov/donotcall/ (accessed April 6, 2009).
22. "FTC Announces Law Enforcement Crackdown on Do Not Call Violators," Federal Trade Commission, press release, November 7, 2007, http://www.ftc.gov/opa/2007/11/dncpress.shtm.
23. Sucharita Mulpuru, "U.S. eCommerce Forecast: 2008 to 2012," Forrester Research, January 18, 2008, http://www.forrester.com/Research/Document/Excerpt/0,7211,41592,00.html.
24. "Fact Sheet: U.S. Direct Selling in 2005," *Direct Selling Association*, http://www .dsa.org/pubs/numbers/calendar05factsheet.pdf (accessed March 10, 2009).
25. "Impact on U.S. Economy," International Franchise Association, http://www .buildingopportunity.com/download/National%20Views.pdf (accessed April 6, 2009); "Franchise Industries," International Franchise Association, http://www .franchise.org/franchisecategories.aspx (accessed April 6, 2009).
26. Raymund Flandez, "New Franchise Idea: Fewer Rules, More Difference," *The Wall Street Journal*, September 18, 2007, http://online.wsj.com.
27. U.S. Bureau of the Census, *Statistical Abstract of the United States, 2009*, Table 1007.
28. "Genuine Parts Company," Hoover's Online, http://www.hoovers.com/free (accessed March 15, 2009).
29. "Universal Corporation," Hoover's Online, http://www.hoovers.com/free (accessed March 15, 2009).
30. "Red River Commodities, Inc.," Hoover's Online, http://www.hoovers.com/free (accessed March 15, 2009); Red River Commodities, Inc., http://www.redriv.com (accessed March 10, 2009).

Feature endnotes

a. Laura Paskus, "Owner Won't Melt Under Stress of Ice Cream Niche Business," *New Mexico Business Weekly* (July 27–August 2, 2007): 15; "Tara's Gets Organic in New Mexico," *Ice Cream Reporter,* Oct, 2005, www.allbusiness.com/manufacturing/food-manufacturing-dairy-product-ice-cream/592756-1.hrml; Tara's Organic Ice Cream, www.tarasorganic.com/ (accessed Feb. 26, 2009).
b. John Spears, "You May Have to Pay Tax on Plastic Bags," *Toronto Star,* March 11, 2009, http://www.thestar.com/News/GTA/article/600104; "Wal-Mart Sets Goal to Reduce Its Global Plastic Shopping Bag Waste by One-Third," *Biotech Week* (October 8, 2008): 3951; "IKEA Bags Use of Plastic Bags," *Atlanta Business Chronicle,* October 1, 2008, http://atlanta.bizjournals.com; Ellen Gamerman, "An Inconvenient Bag," *Wall Street Journal,* September 26, 2008, http://www.wsj.com; Elisabeth Rosenthal, "With Irish Tax, Plastic Bags Go the Way of Snakes," *New York Times* (February 2, 2008): A3.
c. Connie Robbins Gentry, "Green Means Go: Wal-Mart Raises Expectations for Transportation Sustainability," *Chain Store Age* (March 2009): 47+; "When It Comes to Sustainability, Wal-Mart Raises the Bar," *MMR* (December 15, 2008): 52; "Renewable Energy," Wal-Mart, http://walmartstores.com/GlobalWMStoresWeb/navigate.do?catg=347; Justin Thomas, "Wal-Mart Creates Its Own Electricity Company, Eyes Wind Power," *The Dallas Morning News,* January 29, 2007.

Chapter 15

1. Suzanne Vranica, "Fresh Palates for Burger King," *The Wall Street Journal* (December 4, 2008): B8; "Burger King Corp. Bets on World's Purest Taste Test," *Burger King News Release,* http://investor.bk.com/phoenix.zhtml?c=87140&p=irol-newsArticle_print&ID=1232415& (accessed March 25, 2009); Sharyn Alfonsi, Jim Bunn, and Imaeyen Ibanga, (Dec. 9, 2008). "Burger King Ads Flame-Broiled in Controversy," *ABC News,* December 9, 2008, http://abcnews.go.com/print?id=6423256 (accessed March 25, 2009).
2. Don Babwin, "IOC Takes Olympic Road Trip," *Victoria Advocate,* April 5, 2009, http://www.victoriaadvocate.com/news/2009/apr/05/bc-il-chicago-20164th-ld-writethru/?features (accessed April 5, 2009).
3. Bob Liodice, "Essentials for Integrated Marketing," *Advertising Age,* June 9, 2008, http://adage.com/print?article_id=127599 (accessed April 2, 2009).
4. Andrew Hampp, "How Branded Entertainment is Holding Up Amid Recession," *Advertising Age,* February 12, 2009, http://adage.com/print?articleid=134580 (accessed April 8, 2009); Michael Learmonth, "Got an Idea for Branded Content Play? Go to Google," *Advertising Age,* October 13, 2008, http://adage.com/print?articleid=131659 (accessed April 8, 2009).
5. Terence A. Shimp, *Advertising, Promotion, and Supplemented Aspects of Integrated Marketing Communications* (Fort Worth: Dryden Press, 2000), 117.
6. "Health Benefits," http://www.pomwonderful.com/health_benefits.html (accessed April 8, 2009).
7. Salvador Ruiz and María Sicilia, "The Impact of Cognitive and/or Affective Processing Styles on Consumer Response to Advertising Appeals," *Journal of Business Research* 57 (2004): 657–664.
8. John S. McClenahen, "How Can You Possibly Say That?" *Industry Week* (July 17, 1995): 17–19; Anton Piësch, "Speaking in Tongues," *Inc.* (June 2003): 50.
9. Samuel D. Bradley III and Robert Meeds, "The Effects of Sentence-Level Context, Prior Word Knowledge, and Need for Cognition on Information Processing of Technical Language in Print Ads," *Journal of Consumer Psychology* 14, no. 3 (2004): 291–302.
10. David M. Szymanski, "Modality and Offering Effects in Sales Presentations for a Good Versus a Service," *Journal of the Academy of Marketing Science* 29, no. 2 (2001): 179–189.
11. Rich Thomaselli, "How CBS Sports Can Use March Madness Success to Grow Online," March 11, 2009, http://adage.com/digital/article?article_id=135186 (accessed April 8, 2009).
12. Jim Downing, "Almond Industry May Go Way of Economy," *Sacramento Bee,* February 27, 2009, http://www.fresnobee.com/business/story/1229558.html (accessed April 10, 2009).
13. "Cause Related Marketing Campaign of the Year 2009," *PR Week,* March 5, 2009, http://www.prweekus.com/Cause-Related-Campaign-of-the-Year-2009/article/123791/ (accessed April 10, 2009).
14. "Monkey Magic," *The Independent,* January 11, 2007, http://news.independent.co.uk/media/article2144921.ece.
15. Emily Bryson York and Natalie Zmuda, "Top New Products of 2008: Gatorade G2 and Dunkin' Coffee," *Advertising Age,* March 25, 2009, http://adage.com/article?article_id=135523 (accessed April 10, 2009).
16. Emily Bryson York, "Looking for a Special Night Out? Try Hardees," *Advertising Age,* March 16, 2009, http://adage.com/article?article_id=135246 (accessed April 10, 2009).
17. Emily Bryson York and Natalie Zmuda, "Sampling: The New Mass Media." *Advertising Age,* May 12, 2008, http://adage.com/article?article_id=126983 (accessed April 10, 2009).
18. Time Media Kit, "2009 U.S. National Edition Rates," *Time,* http://www.time.com/time/mediakit/1/us/timemagazine/rates/national/index.html, (accessed April 10, 2009).
19. Joann Peck and Jennifer Wiggins, "It Just Feels Good: Customers' Affective Response to Touch and Its Influence in Persuasion," *Journal of Marketing* 70 (October 2006), http://www.marketingpower.com.
20. Charlie Moran, "Will Chris Brown Slow the Tempo of Artist Endorsements?" *Advertising Age,* February 11, 2009, http://adage.com/songsforsoap/post?article_id=134514 (accessed April 10, 2009).
21. "True North Nuts Help Homeless," *Cause Why Not?,* February 24, 2009, http://causewhynot.wordpress.com/2009/02/24/true-north-nuts-help-homeless/ (accessed April 2, 2009).
22. Mya Frazier, "Wal-Mart Looks to Refurbish Image with Political-Style Ads," *Advertising Age,* January 8, 2007, http://adage.com/article?article_id5114179.
23. John J. Burnett, *Promotion Management* (Boston: Houghton Mifflin, 1993): 7.
24. Andrew Hampp, "How 'Top Chef' Cooks Up Fresh Integrations," *Advertising Age,* October 30, 2008, http://adage.com/madisonandvine/article?article_id=132146 (accessed April 10, 2009).
25. Aaron Lewis, "US Ad Spending Fell 2.6% in 2008, Nielsen Reports," Nielsen Media Research, March 13, 2009, http://www.nielsenmedia.com/nc/portal/site/Public/menuitem.55dc65b4a7d5adff3f65936147a062a0/?vgnextoid=7df70529761ff110VgnVCM100000ac0a260aRCRD (accessed April 10, 2009).
26. Xueming Luo and Naveen Donthu, "Marketing's Credibility: A Longitudinal Investigation of Marketing Communications Productivity and Shareholder Value," *Journal of Marketing* 70 (October 2006), http://www.marketingpower.com.
27. "Most Memorable New Product Launch Nominee: Pepsi Tava," Launch PR, February 26, 2008, http://launchpr.typepad.com/schneiderassociates/2008/03/2007-most-memor.html (accessed April 10, 2009).
28. Geoffrey A. Fowler, "China Bans Nike's LeBron Ad as Offensive to Nation's Dignity," *The Wall Street Journal,* December 7, 2004, http://online.wsj.com.
29. John Eaton, "e-Word-of-Mouth Marketing," *Teaching Module* (Boston: Houghton Mifflin Company, 2006).
30. "The New Realities of a Low-Trust World," *Advertising Age,* February 13, 2006, http://www.adage.com.
31. Jack Neff, "Few CEOs Think They Are Effectively Tracking Social Media, Word-of-Mouth," *Advertising Age,* January 26, 2009, http://adage.com/cmostrategy/article?article_id=134085 (accessed April 10, 2009).
32. Jamin Warren and John Jurgensen, "The Wizards of Buzz," *The Wall Street Journal* (February 10–11, 2007): P1, P4.
33. Jon Fine, "OfficeMax's Wacky Marketing Strategy," *Business Week,* January 29, 2009, http://www.businessweek.com/magazine/content/09_06/b4118065841575.htm (accessed April 10, 2009).
34. Gerry Khermouch and Jeff Green, "Buzz Marketing," *BusinessWeek* (July 30, 2001): 50–51.
35. Andrew Hampp, "Turner Agrees to Pay Boston $2 Million," *Advertising Age,* February 5, 2007, http://adage.com/mediaworks/article?article_id=114825 (accessed April 10, 2009).
36. Allison Fass, "A Kingdom Seeks Magic," *Forbes* (October 16, 2006): 68–70.
37. Scott D. Lewis, "Fiona Apple vs. Sony," *The Oregonian* (April 15, 2005): D1.
38. Michael Bush, "DVR Households to Almost Double by 2014," *Advertising Age,* December 5, 2008, http://adage.com/mediaworks/article?article_id=133047 (accessed April 10, 2009).
39. Emma Hall, "Product Placement Faces Wary Welcome in Britain," *Advertising Age* (January 29, 2007): 4, 35.

Feature endnotes

a. Moira Lavelle, "Gold Medalist in Hot Water," *The Harriton Banner Online,* March 2009, http://www.hhbanner.com/2009/03/gold-medalist-in-hot-water/ (accessed April 14, 2009); Matthew Futterman, "How Phelps Became the Face of PureSport," *The Wall Street Journal* (December 3, 2008): B6; "USA Swimming Suspends Phelps for 3 Months," *WJZ TV,* February 6, 2009, http://wjz.com/local/Michael.Phelps.pot.2.928277.html?detectflash=false (accessed March 29, 2009).
b. "The PIVMAN System for Secure ID Checking," Core Street, http://www.corestreet.com/solutions/prod_tech/id/ (accessed April 14, 2009); *PIVMAN for First Response* comic, http://www.corestreet.com/about/library/other/pivman_comic-lores.pdf (accessed October 26, 2009).
c. Coleen Slevin, "Senate Committee Backs Ban on Plastic Bags," *Forbes,* February 12, 2009, http://www.forbes.com/feeds/ap/2009/02/12/ap6045313.html (accessed March 2, 2009); Lisa McLaughlin, "Paper, Plastic or Prada?" *Time,* August 2, 2007, http://www.time.com/time/magazine/article/0,9171,1649301,00.html (accessed March 3, 2009).

Chapter 16

1. Charisse Jones, "Winning Ad Made for Less Than $2,000." *USA Today* (February 3, 2009): B1; Stuart Elliott, "Amateur TV Ad Makers Are in the Chips," *The New York Times*, February 4, 2009, http://tvdecoder.blogs.nytimes.com/2009/02/04/amateur-tv-ad-makers-are-in-the-chips/?page (accessed February 5, 2009); Bruce Horovitz, "'Two Nobodies from Nowhere' Craft Winning Super Bowl Ad," *USA Today,* February 4, 2009, http://www.usatoday.com/money/advertising/admeter/2009admeter.htm?csp=34 (accessed February 7, 2009).
2. "Starbucks Revs Up Advertising with Taxi Rooftop Campaign," *Marketing News* (February 1, 2005): 12.
3. Aaron O. Patrick, "U.K. Spends Millions Nagging Its Citizens," *The Wall Street Journal,* January 24, 2006, B1, http://online.wsj.com.
4. "100 Leading National Advertisers," *Advertising Age,* December 29, 2008, http://adage.com/marketertrees08update/ (accessed April 22, 2009).
5. Emily Bryson York, "Quiznos Throws Subway Curve with 'Sexy' $4 Foot-Long," *Advertising Age,* March 23, 2009, http://adage.com/article?article_id=135435 (accessed April 11, 2009).
6. Christopher Palmeri, "Tesla's Electric Car for the (Well-Off) Masses," *Business Week,* March 27, 2009, http://www.businessweek.com/bwdaily/dnflash/content/mar2009/db20090326_679423.htm (accessed April 11, 2009).
7. Stewart Cockburn, "Netbooks—The New Breed of Ultra Portable Laptops," *Ezine @rticles,* March 28, 2009, http://ezinearticles.com/?Netbooks---The-New-Breed-of-Ultra-Portable-Laptops&id=2155901 (accessed April 11, 2009).
8. Joe Pereira, "New Balance Sneaker Ads Jab at Pro Athletes' Pretensions," *The Wall Street Journal* (March 10, 2005): B1.
9. Ibid.
10. Max Lakin, "Online Advertising Set to Contract," *Advertising Age,* February 26, 2009, http://adage.com/digital/article?article_id=134883, accessed April 11, 2009.
11. Mya Frazier, "Why a Texas Oilman Is Spending $58 Million to Promote Wind Power," *Advertising Age,* July 21, 2008, http://adage.com/article?article_id=129753 (accessed April 11, 2009).
12. Ilona A. Berney-Reddish and Charles S. Areni, "Sex Differences in Responses to Probability Markers in Advertising Claims," *Journal of Advertising* 35 (Summer 2006): 7–17.
13. Daniel J. Howard and Roger A. Kerin, "The Effects of Personalized Product Recommendations on Advertisement Response Rates: The 'Try This. It Works!' Technique," *Journal of Consumer Psychology* 14, no. 3 (2004): 271–279.
14. Suzanne Vranica, "Kodak Ads Get More Aggressive," *Wall Street Journal,* March 30, 2009, http://online.wsj.com/article/SB122383653307646 7327.html (accessed April 2, 2009).
15. Rik Pieters and Michel Wedel, "Attention Capture and Transfer in Advertising: Brand, Pictorial, and Text-Size Effects," *Journal of Marketing* (April 2004): 36–50.
16. William F. Arens, *Contemporary Advertising* (Burr Ridge, IL: Irwin/McGraw-Hill, 2007).
17. Jeremy Mullman, "Citibank Yanks Spots Starring Pair of Oddballs," *Advertising Age* (January 22, 2007): 25.
18. Natalie Zmuda, "Taking Stock of Successes and Stumbles," *Advertising Age,* February 23, 2009, http://adage.com/article?article_id=134742 (accessed April 11, 2009).
19. Brian Steinberg, "Bad Times Affect Ad Recall for Bowl Spots," *Advertising Age,* January 20, 2009, http://adage.com/mediaworks/article?article_id=133928 (accessed April 11, 2009).
20. "National Anti-Drug Strategy Youth Drug Prevention Campaign—Parent Component: 2007–2009," http://www.hc-sc.gc.ca/ahc-asc/activit/marketsoc/camp/nads-sna-eng.php#ce (accessed April 11, 2009).
21. Rupal Parekh, "Agency of the Year: Crispin, Porter & Bogusky," *Advertising Age,* January 19, 2009, http://adage.com/agencya-list08/article?article_id=133815 (accessed April 11, 2009).
22. George E. Belch and Michael A. Belch, *Advertising and Promotion* (Burr Ridge, IL: Irwin/McGraw-Hill, 2001), 576–577.
23. Shelly Banjo and Kelly K. Spors, "Musician Finds a Following Online," *The Wall Street Journal,* December 30, 2008, http://online.wsj.com/article/SB123060241431841475.html (accessed April 14, 2009).
24. Ben Klayman, "McDonald's Not Cutting' 09 Sponsorship Budget," *Reuters,* March 9, 2009, http://www.reuters.com/article/sportsNews/idUSTRE52864Q20090309 (accessed April 14, 2009).
25. Brent Bowen and Dean Headley, "2009 Airline Quality Ranking," April 2009, http://aqr.aero/aqrreports/2009aqr.pdf (accessed April 14, 2009).
26. Belch and Belch, *Advertising and Promotion*, 598.
27. Jeff Bailey, "JetBlue's CEO Is 'Mortified' After Fliers Are Stranded," *The New York Times,* February 19, 2007, http://www.nytimes.com/; Rich Thomaselli, "Management's Misjudgment Gives JetBlue a Black Eye," *Advertising Age,* February 19, 2007, http://www.adage.com.
28. Deborah L. Vence, "Stand Guard: In Bad Times, An Ongoing Strategy Keeps Image Intact," *Marketing News* (November 15, 2006): 15.
29. Bailey, "JetBlue's CEO Is 'Mortified' After Fliers Are Stranded"; Thomaselli, "Management's Misjudgment Gives JetBlue a Black Eye."

Feature endnotes

a. "The State of the News Media: An Annual Report on American Journalism," The Project for Excellence in Journalism, http://www.stateofthenewsmedia.com/2008 (accessed February 16, 2009); "New York Times Nov. Ad Revenue Drops 20.9 Percent," Associated Press, December 24, 2008, http://www.businessweek.com/ap/financialnews/D9595DCG4.htm (accessed January 20, 2009); David Folkenflik, "Imagining a City Without Its Daily Newspaper," National Public Radio, February 19, 2009, http://www.npr.org/templates/story/story.php?storyId=100256908&sc=emaf (accessed February 19, 2009).

b. Preserve, http://www.preserveproducts.com/ (accessed April 2, 2009); "Recycling: Sitting on Mainstream's Doorstep," Sustainable is Good, March 21, 2007, http://www.sustainableisgood.com/blog/2007/03/recycline_produ.html (accessed April 2, 2009); Nitasha Tiku, "Making the Most of a Brush with Fame," *Inc.* (August 2007): 19; Rob Walker, "Revalued," *The New York Times Magazine*, March 4, 2009, http://www.nytimes.com/2009/03/08/magazine/08wwln-consumed-t.html (accessed April 16, 2009).

c. Susan Gunelius, "Womenkind Uses Women to Create Ads," *Brand Curve,* November 21, 2007, http://www.brandcurve.com/womenkind-uses-women-to-create-ads/ (accessed April 2, 2009); Andrew McMains, "Womenkind Opens Doors," *AdWeek,* November 16, 2007, http://www.adweek.com/aw/national/article_display.jsp?vnu_content_id=1003673910 (accessed April 2, 2009); Susanne Vranica, "Ads Made for Women, by Women," *The Wall Street Journal,* November 21, 2007, B3.

Chapter 17

1. Jessi Hempel, "IBM's All-Star Salesman," CNNMoney.com, September 26, 2008, http://money.cnn.com/2008/09/23/technology/hempel_IBM.fortune/index2.htm (accessed January 27, 2009); "Challenges in OSS/BSS and Optimized Provisioning," *Sasken,* http://www.sasken.com/downloads/TGJ/issue3/challenges_in_oss_bss.htm (accessed Jan. 29, 2009); Rajesh Mahapatra, "IBM Wins Order from Vodafone's India Arm," *Washingtonpost.com,* December 10, 2007, http://www.washingtonpost.com/wp-dyn/content/article/2007/12/10/AR2007121000473.html (accessed Jan. 29, 2009).
2. "Advancing Patient Care Worldwide," Baxter International 2008 Annual Report, February 19, 2009, 15.
3. Jon M. Hawes, Anne K. Rich, and Scott M. Widmier, "Assessing the Development of the Sales Profession," *Journal of Personal Selling & Sales Management* (Winter 2004): 27–37.
4. "Research and Markets: The Cost of the Average Sales Call Today Is More Than 400 Dollars," *M2 Presswire* (February 28, 2006).
5. Eli Jones, Paul Busch, and Pater Dacin, "Firm Market Orientation and Salesperson Customer Orientation: Interpersonal and Intrapersonal Influence on Customer Service and Retention in Business-to-Business Buyer-Seller Relationships," *Journal of Business Research* 56 (2003): 323–340.
6. Sarah Lorge, "The Best Way to Prospect," *Sales & Marketing Management* (January 1998): 80.
7. Bob Donath, "Tap Sales 'Hot Buttons' to Stay Competitive," *Marketing News* (March 1, 2005): 8.
8. Ralph W. Giacobbe, Donald W. Jackson, Jr., Lawrence A. Crosby, and Claudia M. Bridges, "A Contingency Approach to Adaptive Selling Behavior and Sales Performance: Selling Situations and Salesperson Characteristics," *Journal of Personal Selling & Sales Management* 26 (Spring 2006): 115–142.
9. Richard G. McFarland, Goutam N. Challagalla, and Tasadduq A. Shervani, "Influence Tactics for Effective Adaptive Selling," *Journal of Marketing* 70 (October 2006), http://www.marketingpower.com. access date.
10. John Andy Wood, "NLP Revisted: Nonverbal Communications and Signals of Trustworthiness," *Journal of Personal Selling & Sales Management* 26 (Spring 2006): 198–204.
11. Stephen S. Porter, Joshua L. Wiener, and Gary L. Frankwick, "The Moderating Effect of Selling Situation on the Adaptive Selling Strategy—Selling Effectiveness Relationship," *Journal of Business Research* 56 (2003): 275–281.
12. Gary K. Hunter and William D. Perreault, Jr., "Making Sales Technology Effective," *Journal of Marketing* 71 (January 2007): 16–34.
13. Abbie Klaasesen, "Using Social Media to Listen to Consumers," *Advertising Age* (March 30, 2009): 32.
14. Fernando Jaramillo, Jay Prakash Mulki, and Paul Solomon, "The Role of Ethical Climate on Salesperson's Role Stress, Job Attitudes, Turnover Intention, and Job

Performance," *Journal of Personal Selling & Sales Management* 26 (Summer 2006): 272–282.

15. Eric G. Harris, John C. Mowen, and Tom J. Brown, "Re-examining Salesperson Goal Orientations: Personality, Influencers, Customer Orientation, and Work Satisfaction," *Journal of the Academy of Marketing Science* 33, no. 1 (2005): 19–35.
16. Michael A. Wiles and Rosann L. Spiro, "Research Notes: Attracting Graduates to Sales Positions and the Role of Recruiter Knowledge: A Reexamination," *Journal of Personal Selling & Sales Management* (Winter 2004): 39–48.
17. Jacqueline Durett, "Road Warriers: Making Honda a Fit for Gen-Y," *Sales & Marketing Management* (September 2006): 46–48.
18. Andrew B. Artis and Eric G. Harris, "Self-Directed Learning and Sales Force Performance: An Integrated Framework," *Journal of Personal Selling & Sales Management* 27 (Winter 2007), http://www.marketingpower.com.
19. Christine Galea, "Average Salary for Sales Staffers in 2005," *Sales & Marketing Management* (May 2006): 30.
20. Tara Burnthorne Lopez, Christopher D. Hopkins, and Mary Anne Raymond, "Reward Preferences of Salespeople: How Do Commissions Rate?" *Journal of Personal Selling & Sales Management* 26 (Fall 2006): 381–390.
21. Kirk Shinkle, "All of Your People Are Salesmen: Do They Know? Are They Ready?" *Investor's Business Daily* (February 6, 2002): A1.
22. "100 Best Companies to Work For 2009," *Fortune*, February 2, 2009, http://money.cnn.com/magazines/fortune/bestcompanies/2009/snapshots/32.html (accessed April 14, 2009).
23. Ibid.
24. John W. Barnes, Donald W. Jackson, Jr., Michael D. Hutt, and Ajith Kumar, "The Role of Culture Strength in Shaping Salesforce Outcomes," *Journal of Personal Selling & Sales Management* 26 (Summer 2006): 255–270.
25. Fernando Jaramillo, Jay Prakash Mulki, and Paul Solomon, "The Role of Ethical Climate on Salesperson's Role Stress, Job Attitudes, Turnover Intention, and Job Performance," *Journal of Personal Selling & Sales Management* 26 (Summer 2006): 272–282.
26. William H. Murphy, Peter A. Dacin, and Neil M. Ford, "Sales Contest Effectiveness: An Examination of Sales Contest Design Preferences of Field Sales Forces," *Journal of the Academy of Marketing Science* 32, no. 2 (2004): 127–143.
27. Patricia Odell, "Motivating the Masses," *Promo*, September 1, 2005, http://promomagazine.com.
28. Fernando Jaramillo, Jay Prakash Mulki, and Greg W. Marshall, "A Meta-Analysis of the Relationship Between Organizational Commitment and Salesperson Job Performance: 25 Years of Research," *Journal of Business Research* 58 (2005): 705–714.
29. Tracy Turner, "Wendy's Newest Pitch Aimed at Online Crowd," *The Columbus Dispatch*, April 3, 2009.
30. George E. Belch and Michael A. Belch, *Advertising and Promotion* (Burr Ridge, IL: Irwin/McGraw-Hill, 2001): 526–532.
31. Eric T. Anderson and Inseong Song, "Coordinating Price Reductions and Coupon Events," *Journal of Marketing Research* (November 2004): 411–422.
32. "All About Coupons," Coupon Council, http://www.couponmonth.com/pages/allabout.htm (accessed January 16, 2007); "Coupons Add Value: Education as Well," Coupon Council press release, August 23, 2006, http://www.couponmonth.com/pages/news.htm; Betsy Spethmann, "FSI Coupon Worth Reaches $300 Billion in 2006: MARX," *Promo*, January 4, 2007, http://promomagazine.com/othertactics/news/fsi_coupon_worth_300_billion_010407/.
33. Michel Laroche, Maria Kalamas, and Qinchao Huang, "Effects of Coupons on Brand Categorization and Choice of Fast Foods in China," *Journal of Business Research* (May 2005): 674–686.
34. Arthur L. Porter, "Direct Mail's Lessons for Electronic Couponers," *Marketing Management Journal* (Spring/Summer 2000): 107–115.
35. Rajneesh Suri, Srinivasan Swaminathan, and Kent B. Monroe, "Price Communications in Online and Print Coupons: An Empirical Investigation," *Journal of Interactive Marketing* (Autumn 2004): 74–86.
36. Karen Holt, "Coupon Crimes," *Promo*, April 1, 2004, http://promomagazine.com/mag/marketing_coupon_crimes/.
37. Brian Grow, "The Great Rebate Runaround," *BusinessWeek* (December 5, 2005): 34–37.
38. "For Our Members," Hallmark, https://www.hallmark.com/webapp/wcs/stores/servlet/ForOurMembersView?storeId=10001&cataloged=10051 (accessed April 14, 2009).
39. Mya Frazier, James Tenser, and Tricia Despres, "Retail Lesson: Small Programs Best," *Advertising Age* (March 20, 2006): S2–S3.
40. Amy Johanes, "Borders Launches Contests for Reward Members," *Promo*, February 7, 2007, http://promomagazine.com/contests/borders_contests_reward_members_020707/.
41. Amy Garber, "BK Franchisees File Class Action Suit Against McD," *Nation's Restaurant News* (August 29, 2005): 1.
42. Burt A. Lazar, "Agencies Held Liable for Client Ads, Promos," *Marketing News* (February 15, 2005): 6.

Feature endnotes

a. EarthCraft House, http://www.earthcrafthouse.com/ (April 14, 2009); Dawn Kent, "Green Home-Building Catching On in Birmingham during Slump," *The Birmingham News*, April 6, 2009, http://blog.al.com/businessnews/2009/04/green_homebuilding_catching_on.html (accessed April 14, 2009).

b. Sports Management Network, http://www.sportsmanagementnetwork.com/who .html (accessed April 2, 2009); Caponigro Public Relations, Inc., http://www.caponigro.com/html/strategicalliances.html (accessed April 2, 2009); "Individual Clients," Sports Management Network, http://www.sportsmanagementnetwork.com/clients_management.html (accessed April 2, 2009).

c. Nathalie Zmuda, "Coke: Buy 1 Rival, Get our Brand Free," *Advertising Age* (March 9 and 16, 2009): 1, 19; "Coke Promotion Gives Free Vault to Mountain Dew Customers," *Convenience Store News* (April 10, 2009): 1; "Coca Cola Brings Vault Drink Head to Head with Mtn Dew," yumsugar, March 11, 2009, http://www.yumsugar.com/2912146, (accessed April 11, 2009).

Appendix

1. This section is adapted from William M. Pride, Robert J. Hughes, and Jack R. Kapoor, Business (Boston: Houghton-Mifflin, 2002): A1-A9.
2. Sal Divita, "Résumé Writing Requires Proper Strategy," Marketing News (July 3, 1995): 6.
3. Andrew J. DuBrin, "Deadly Political Sins," Wall Street Journal's Managing Your Career (Fall 1993): 11–13.
4. Ibid.
5. Cyndee Miller, "Marketing Research Salaries Up a Bit, but Layoffs Take Toll," Marketing News (June 19, 1995): 1.
6. Careers in Marketing, "Market Research—Salaries," www.careers-in-marketing.com/mrsal.htm (accessed November 2, 2009).
7. Payscale, www.payscale.com (accessed November 2, 2009).
8. Ibid.
9. Ibid.
10. Careers in Marketing, "Product Management—Salaries," www.careers-in-marketing.com/pmsal.htm (accessed November 2, 2009).
11. Careers in Marketing, "Advertising and Public Relations—Salaries," www.careers-in-marketing.com/adsal.htm (accessed November 2, 2009).
12. Ibid.
13. Payscale, www.payscale.com (accessed November 2, 2009).
14. Ibid.
15. PCWorld.com, www.pcworld.com (accessed November 2, 2009).